D0983428

Aspects of
Samuel Johnson

Aspects of Samuel Johnson

Essays on His Arts, Mind, Afterlife, and Politics

Howard D. Weinbrot

DELAWARE

Newark: University of Delaware Press

© 2005 by Rosemont Publishing & Printing Corp.

Associated University Presses
2010 Eastpark Boulevard
Cranbury, NJ 08512

The author, the University of Delaware Press, and Associated University Presses gratefully thank the William Freeman Vilas Trust of the University of Wisconsin for a generous subvention to support publication of this book.

The paper used in this publication meets the requirements of the American National Standard for Permanence of Paper for Printed Library Materials Z39.48-1984.

Library of Congress Cataloging-in-Publication Data

Weinbrot, Howard D.
    Aspects of Samuel Johnson : essays on his arts, mind, afterlife, and politics / Howard D. Weinbrot.
        p.   cm.
    Includes bibliographical references and index.
    ISBN 0-87413-874-4 (alk. paper)
    1. Johnson, Samuel, 1709–1784—Criticism and interpretation.   2. Johnson, Samuel, 1709–1784—Political and social views.   3. Johnson, Samuel, 1709–1784—Knowledge and learning.   4. Johnson, Samuel, 1709–1784—Influence. I. Title.
PR3534.W45   2005
828'.609—dc22   2005003464

PRINTED IN THE UNITED STATES OF AMERICA

For
Paul Alkon
and
Eric Rothstein

Contents

Preface

Most of the essays within have appeared in several venues over several years. "Johnson and Genre" and "'Obstinate Contests of Disagreeing Virtues'" are new. "What Johnson's Illustrations Illustrate" and "Johnson Before Boswell in Eighteenth-Century France" also are new but may appear in other places within this year. "Johnson and the Arts of Narration" was a plenary address organized by the late David Fleeman and held in 1984 at the Pembroke College Oxford bicentennial anniversary of Johnson's death. It was published in Beirut, probably is known to as many readers as can fill a Lilliputian's thimble, and is essentially new to the Johnson community. I have reordered seven essays on Johnson and Jacobitism into the four with which the book concludes. To paraphrase Win Jenkins in *Humphry Clinker*, the words are the same but the language is different.

A long scholarly career incurs a long list of debts. These include the earlier generations of scholars on either side of the Atlantic, those whom I could only know by name and work. David Fleeman engineered my one brief meeting with the aged L. F. Powell, to whom respect was deservedly due and gladly given. Such admiration was due as well to Johnson's ultimate bibliographer himself and to the other ancestors who returned Johnson and his texts to intellectual and emotional prominence after Victorian condescension. The Yale Edition of Johnson's works and Bruce Redford's Hyde Edition of Johnson's letters are the final great tributes to that restorative tradition. Gwin J. Kolb was my first Johnsonian mentor, and in different ways Donald Greene and Walter Jackson Bate followed and taught me much about Johnson's inner and outer lives. The community of Johnsonians has always been welcome and welcoming.

It remains so today, both with institutions and with too many valued friends to list. I here cite a few. In looking at these essays and their notes, readers will see several references to the annual *Age of Johnson*. Its first number appeared in 1987, volume 15 now is in hand, and it shows every sign of continuing its demonstrable distinction. *The Age of Johnson* was founded by Paul J. Korshin at the University of Pennsylvania, now is co-edited by Professor Korshin and Jack Lynch and, like Kevin Cope's fine annual *1650–1850: Ideas, Aesthetics, and Inquiries*, is published by Gabe Hornstein at AMS Press. *The Age of Johnson* in particular has become the major scholarly outlet for mid and later eighteenth-century and Johnsonian studies and a sign of the ongoing strength of research and publication within our field. Such strength is well reflected in presses like Delaware and AMS who perform so handsomely on our behalf, and who make their books reasonably affordable for colleagues and students. I thus am glad to thank Donald Mell of the University of Delaware Press, and Christine Retz and Julien Yoseloff at Associated University Presses for helping to bring this book from its varied wombs. The acknowledgment page lists the places of publication of relevant essays, and I thank the editors of the journals and the presses for permission to reprint those works.

Since 1987 I have had the great privilege of being William Freeman Vilas Research Professor in the College of Letters and Science as well as Ricardo Quintana Professor of English at the University of Wisconsin, Madison. The Vilas Trust supports Vilas professors' research and seeks to make their findings available for readers. It has provided a generous subvention to help reduce the cost of this book, for which I am grateful. The university, the English Department, and my students also have provided enviable support and stimulation. I am especially pleased to acknowledge the help of my colleague Eric Rothstein, from whom I always learn, and whose friendship I long have valued. Helen Ashmore offered patience, learning, and warmly appreciated and reciprocated affection. Brian Williams was uncommonly helpful with computer work to prepare the typescript for the press. Over the years, several of my graduate students also have served as research assistants before starting their own professional lives. These students include Matthew Kinservik, Heather King, Stephen Karian, Amanda Kenny, and David Nunnery. I thank them all.

Whether readers offer comparable gratitude to this collection now is out of my hands. In compiling the book, I have left most of the annotation as it was in its original place, though adapted to recent press style. I nonetheless have changed the source of quotations if a superior edition has since appeared, and I have added a few further sources if superior scholarship appeared. Some of the notes will not be timely, but in most cases such annotation has been brought up to date by later essays. Authorial vanity fantasizes that readers will start on the first page and, like Sir Joshua Reynolds with Johnson's *Life of Savage*, be riveted to all subsequent pages—until colliding with the index. Authorial reality suggests otherwise. I thus have provided full and new citations for each essay and allowed necessary overlap in use of evidence and quotations. Like Johnson and his illustrative quotations, the same remark can be made to do double duty. Where possible and without ambiguity, I have either used internal citations of sources or bunched footnotes to help ease the reading process.

Along the way, I have corrected a few errors, polished some prose, and I hope reasonably organized the book. I could say that I have emulated the great Persian rug makers and allowed a few errors to suggest human weakness before the gods. I could say that, but it no doubt would offend both the rug makers and the gods. It also would diminish reviewers' pleasure in finding such bêtises as there are—for which I accept full responsibility, for which I apologize, and for which I know my dedicatees will forgive me. Paul Alkon has been an admired friend and distant colleague for some forty-four years. Eric Rothstein has been an admired friend and immediate colleague for some thirty-six years. These essays were variously conceived and written during the decades of such enduringly rewarding friendship. They are part of the exemplary audience whose standards I can only hope to meet. They also may join me in seconding Johnson's characteristically wise counsel in his fourteenth *Rambler* (1750): "having first set positive and absolute excellence before us, we may be pardoned though we sink down to humbler virtue, trying, however, to keep our point always in view, and struggling not to lose ground, though we cannot gain it."[1]

NOTE

1. Johnson, in The Yale Edition of the Works of Samuel Johnson, vol. 3, *The Rambler*, ed. W. J. Bate and Albrecht B. Strauss (New Haven: Yale University Press, 1969), p. 78.

Acknowledgments

IT IS A PLEASURE TO THANK THE FOLLOWING EDITORS, JOURNALS, AND presses for permission to reprint material previously published. I wish also to thank those scholarly societies and specific institutions that invited me to present papers that grew into several of the essays below. I specifically note that a shorter draft of "Johnson and the Domestic Metaphor" was read as part of the conference that opened the University of Birmingham's Johnson Centre in September of 1996. I thank Anne McDermott and Nigel Wood for the invitation. "Johnson Before Boswell in France" had two godmothers: Lance Wilcox invited it as a plenary session at the Midwest American Society for Eighteenth-Century Studies in November of 2003. Maximillian Novak invited a slightly different version in March of 2004 for the William Andrews Clark Memorial Library's series "An Age of Projects," whose proceedings will appear shortly. I again thank these and other colleagues for the opportunity to present my work before always stimulating and challenging audiences— certainly including those students in my classes at the University of Wisconsin, Madison.

"Samuel Johnson's *Plan* and Preface to the *Dictionary*: The Growth of a Lexicographer's Mind," in *New Aspects of Lexicography: Literary Criticism, Intellectual History, and Social Change*, ed. Howard D. Weinbrot (Carbondale: Southern Illinois University Press, 1972), pp. 73–94, 179–86.

"What Johnson's Illustrative Quotations Illustrate: Language and Viewpoint in the *Dictionary*," forthcoming in *Anniversary Essays on Johnson's Dictionary*, ed. Jack Lynch and Anne McDermott (Cambridge: Cambridge University Press, 2005).

"The Poetry of Samuel Johnson," in *The Cambridge Companion to Samuel Johnson*, ed. Greg Clingham (Cambridge: Cambridge University Press, 1997), pp. 34–50.

"Johnson's *London* and Juvenal's Third Satire: The Country as 'Ironic' Norm," *Modern Philology* 73 (1976): 56–65.

"No 'Mock Debate': Questions and Answers in *The Vanity of Human Wishes*," *Modern Language Quarterly* 41 (1980): 248–67.

"Johnson and the Arts of Narration: *The Life of Savage, The Vanity of Human Wishes*, and *Rasselas*," in *Samuel Johnson: Commemorative Lectures delivered at Pembroke College, Oxford*, ed. Magdi Wahba (Beirut: Librairie du Liban, The Egyptian International Publishing Company-Longman, 1986), pp. 13–38.

"Johnson and the Domestic Metaphor," *Age of Johnson* 10 (1999): 127–63.

"The Reader, the General, and the Particular: Johnson and Imlac in Chapter Ten of *Rasselas*," *Eighteenth-Century Studies* 5 (1971):80–96.

"Samuel Johnson, Percival Stockdale, and 'Brickbats from Grub-street': Some Later Response to the *Lives of the Poets*," *Huntington Library Quarterly* 56 (1993): 105–34.

"Johnson Before Boswell in Eighteenth-Century France: Notes Toward Reclaiming a Man of Letters," forthcoming in *The Age of Projects* (Toronto: University of Toronto Press).

All or portions of the final four essays of this volume have appeared in the following essays:

"Johnson, Jacobitism, and the Historiography of Nostalgia," *Age of Johnson* 7 (1996): 163–211;

"Who Said He Was a Jacobite Hero? The Political Genealogy of Johnson's Swedish Charles," *Philological Quarterly* 75 (1996): 411–50;

"Johnson and Jacobitism Redux: Evidence, Interpretation, and Intellectual History," *Age of Johnson* 8 (1997): 89–125;

"Johnson, Jacobitism, and Swedish Charles: Heroism, Scholarly Method, and *The Vanity of Human Wishes*," *ELH* 64 (1997): 945–81;

"Johnson and the Jacobite Truffles," *Age of Johnson* 12 (2001): 273–90;

"Jacobite Wars XLV: 'Certain Topics . . . Never are Exhausted,'" *Age of Johnson* 14 (2003): 307–40;

"The Politics of Samuel Johnson and the Johnson of Politics," *1650–1850: Ideas, Aesthetics, and Inquiries* 8 (2003): 3–26.

Introduction

LITERARY ANNIVERSARIES OFFER MOMENTS OF CELEBRATION AND, FOR the celebrators, often moments of reflection. The 250th anniversary of the publication of Samuel Johnson's *Dictionary of the English Language* (1755) is one of those times. It was the rare cultural document that soon became a national and international event. It has demonstrable weaknesses but is demonstrably enduring in its greatness, and it remains as much a source of study, pleasure, and challenge today as in 1755. The year 2005 should bring publication of the Gwin J. Kolb and Robert DeMaria, Jr., edition of the lexical works for the Yale Johnson. There also will be at least one important collection of essays regarding the *Dictionary*, together with numerous scholarly conferences, seminars and, in all likelihood, papers and presentations for the nonacademic audience. It is appropriate that the foremost prize for British nonfiction is the Samuel Johnson Prize sponsored by BBC Four. That honor awards the winner with £30,000, the short-listed authors with £1,000, and for all of them televised presentation of the awards ceremony at Johnson's House. He might again say, "It is rather wonderful that so much has been done for me."[1]

Johnson would have been pleased with such hard cash as well as popular recognition of his later colleagues. The *Dictionary* overwhelmingly was Johnson's achievement, but it was made possible by two factors external to him. One was an increasingly wealthy, literate, and leisured society with enough money to purchase his expensive books. The other factor was the courage and entrepreneurial spirit of the consortium of booksellers who financed the project; they took a chance on the odd, energetic, and no-longer young man then becoming known within the London publishing world. Like the commercial Parnassus of the later *Lives of the Poets* (1779–81), the *Dictionary* was in part a function of the complex world of trade's intermarriage with the different but equally complex world of reading. Johnson the bookseller's son and frank correspondent with Lord Chesterfield recognized a major implication of this relationship:

Now learning itself is a trade. A man goes to a bookseller, and gets what he can. We have done with patronage. In the infancy of learning, we find some great man praised for it. This diffused it among others. When it becomes general, an author leaves the great, and applies to the multitude. (*Life*, 5:59)

Eighteenth-century Britain had moved from intellectual and commercial infancy to "general" maturity. All this is to the good for a lexicon about which the Abbé Prevost said: "Cet Ouvrage est un des plus importans de la Langue Angloise; & c'est un des plus grands qui ait jamais été composé par un seul homme, dans aucune Langue; L'Auteur est M. *Samuel Johnson*." Better still, the Preface is a model for "ceux d'entre nous qui seroient tentés de rendre le même service à la Langue Françoise." To facilitate the effort to improve French lexicography, Prévost translates the entire Preface "avec quelqu' exactitude."[2]

By the early nineteenth century, of course, Johnson's eminence was recognized in other genres as well. Though literary judgment had begun to change, the *Monthly Review* was among those journals for whom Johnson's *Lives of the Poets* created a "code of national taste." Johnson has "forced a standard of public opinion, which, though contested on some points, acquires additional authority from its duration." Moreover, the *Lives* are so valuable as comments on "Man as well as on books, and they convey such a mass of information under an agreeable form, that they are justly intitled to the pre-eminence which they have acquired in our literature; and their dictates, if not always to be implicitly followed, ought surely to be questioned with calm and respectful consideration" (59 [1808]:138).[3] Across the Channel, Albin-Joseph Ulpien Hennet's three-volume *La Poétique anglaise* (1806) characterized Johnson as "l'oracle littéraire de son pays" (2:438). Hennet's Johnson is "l'écrivain le plus instruit, le plus fécond qu'ait produit l'Angleterre." Hence, "tout ce qu'il a fait méritait d'être conservé" (2:451).

Celebration of the *Dictionary*, in short, leads to celebration of the broader canon of this most instructive and fecund writer England has ever produced. Thanks to Donald Mell and his colleagues at the University of Delaware Press, I have been able to do that by assembling a series of earlier, recent, and new essays that range widely over Johnson's body of work. I have tried to order these essays into approximate categories of Arts, "mentalité" or Mind, Afterlife, and Politics. In the nature of things, these categories overlap. They are on a spectrum rather than cemented to a seat, and are guides to approximate areas rather than road maps to a specific location.

Contents of the Essays

Given the anniversary year, I give pride of place in the "Arts" section to essays on the *Dictionary*. One concerns the conceptual changes from Johnson's *Plan* of 1747 to the Preface of 1755. Johnson's empiricism long has been a sensible commonplace of criticism concerning his life and works. The practical experience actually of compiling the *Dictionary* taught him much about the nature of language, his own limitations, and the vanity of human wishes. The movement from disembodied theory to practice and then back to embodied theory suggests the "growth of a lexicographer's mind." The many thousands of illustrative quotations in the *Dictionary* long have been a source of delight and contention. Do they have an ideological and religious agenda, as some have argued, or are they the altered embodiments of meaning as used in the printed word? Johnson sometimes had an agenda, as in the exclusion of Hobbes, but his title page and practice make plain that the book concerns the English language, not Johnson's language.

Like other major eighteenth-century figures, Johnson often suffered from being characterized as part of an age of reason and prose: he wrote some poems, but he was not a poet. Johnson himself, however, hoped to be buried in Westminster Abbey—about which, Boswell reports, he "seemed to feel a satisfaction, very natural to a Poet" (*Life,* 4:419). That limited vision of Johnson's achievement began to enlarge upon the publication of two very different sorts of work. In 1941 David Nichol Smith and Edward L. McAdam, Jr., issued their Clarendon edition of *The Poems of Samuel Johnson*. Nichol Smith was part of the two remarkable generations of British and North American scholars who brought Johnson and other eighteenth-century authors back to prominence in the English-speaking world. Nichol Smith had begun his edition in 1913 shortly before World War I. That work obviously was delayed for many years, during which McAdam began his doctoral dissertation at Yale on an edition of Johnson's poems, the Boswell manuscripts were discovered, the Huntington Library acquired *Thraliana,* the Hyde Collection, now at the Houghton Library, was being formed, and Johnson was being redefined for new readers.

Johnson indeed soon would be recognized as among the small class of great poet-critics that include Dryden, Pope, Coleridge, Arnold, and T. S. Eliot. To Eliot belongs the brass ring of Johnson-as-poet prizes. His introduction to a reprint of *London* (1738) and *The Vanity of Human Wishes* (1749) brought popular aesthetic, rather than scholarly, notice to those poems. His "Johnson as Critic and Poet" in 1957 was slightly less sympathetic, but it nonetheless fed the modest but growing appetite for Johnson's poetry.[4] Eliot's often learned and self-annotated poetry also enhanced appreciation of Johnson's imitations—a term regarded as *infra-dig* for the Romantic/Victorian sensibility still prominent well into the twentieth century. Eliot said about his practice of referring to Dante in the notes to *The Waste Land* (1922): "I gave the references in my notes, in order to make the reader who recognizes the allusion, know that I meant him to recognize it, and know that he would have missed the point if he did not recognize it."[5] Johnson could have said the same about either of his own imitations. Two of the essays here included deal with those imitations, and a third offers a general overview of Johnson's achievement as a poet—about which, we might say, if Johnson be not a poet, where is poetry to be found?

Poetry need not always be found in rhythm or rhyme. Metaphor is among its essential defining traits, and there are few prose writers with a more metaphorical style than Johnson's. Too often, however, Johnson's style has been characterized as latinate, scientific, or generally elevated and distant from the normal concerns of normal readers. In "Johnson and the Domestic Metaphor" I suggest some of the different levels on which Johnson's prose functions, a key one of which is the resolutely grounded and homely images with which he is comfortable. These are likely to have been drawn in part from the Old Testament images and parallelisms that he regularly heard as a boy and adolescent. His domestic images may concern gardens, or families, or conflicts within families, or with servants, and they almost always bring abstract concepts into the immediacy of daily life. In the Preface to Shakespeare (1765) Johnson wants to show that the drama moves by means of our association with the actors' feigned situation. He takes us into unutterable grief: we "rather lament the possibility than suppose the presence of misery, as," he says in a startling and primal figure that evokes the human and Christian divine maternal situation, "a mother weeps over her babe, when she remembers that death may take it from her."[6]

Too often as well, Johnson's narrative style has been characterized as the one-note of an elegant and learned whale. I hope that "Johnson and the Arts of Narration" can modify that view. Johnson lacked the subtle modulation of genuine novelistic nuance within characters; but he well knew how and when to alter his tone to alter his narrative effect. That might include change of voice, as we move from Johnson as narrator in *The Life of Savage* (1744) to Savage himself or to the hanging Judge Page. Or it might mean shifting from the confident guiding voice of

Imlac in *Rasselas* (1759) to the anxious searching for confidence by Rasselas or Nekayah. Or it might mean shifting to a different social class and gender in giving Pekuah her own story and the chance to select her own fate. Or it might mean allowing the frantic reader to burst into *The Vanity of Human Wishes* and implore the narrator's help in a world he has convinced us is dark, dangerous, and treacherous. In all of those cases, Johnson sets the variation in voice against the hitherto stable voice and dramatically changes the reader's response.

These seven essays comprise the "Arts" section of *Aspects of Samuel Johnson*. With apologies for apparent and unintended hubris, there are three essays in the "Mind" section. These essays share some of their concerns with those in "Arts." We can not look at Johnson's theory of the general and particular or his theory of genre without looking at the practice of narrative or of genre in several of the examples above. Nonetheless, in "The Reader, the General, and the Particular" I focus on how Johnson uses those concepts. He enlarges the generalization so that we ourselves can become part of the creative process and make the general specific and concrete. "Johnson and Genre" concerns his attitude toward genre as it relates to the human situation as well as to the literary practice that records the human situation. Johnson insisted that art must imitate nature, but he mistrusted unaccommodated man and unpolished nature. Within limits, nature must be moralized and within appropriate constraints formed into recognizable literary kinds. Those limits did not extend to the French formalist theory that Johnson respected but saw as inadequate because too rigid in practitioners like le Bossu and Voltaire. He also insisted that whatever the admitted weaknesses of the best British practice in imitating nature, it was superior to the best French practice in imitating art.

It is equally true that the essay on Johnson and skepticism relates to his often typical variation among voices and alternatives—as in the final chapter of *Rasselas* in which nothing claims to be concluded. During the last few years the persistent small voice proclaiming Johnson as indecisive skeptic has become an ample chorus. We have been told that Johnson and Hume in fact share many basic thoughts and values, that gloomy Johnson well may have been suspicious of Revelation and the possibility of eternal reward, and that he reflected a century of indeterminate and wavering belief. Such putative skepticism, however, is alien to Johnson's deeply held belief that only religion can lead to happiness and that skepticism leads to secular and spiritual misery. When Johnson was "skeptical" in some way, it was likely to be on secular matters indifferent, for which legitimate options may be legitimately available. He also followed Dryden's sort of skepticism. One holds options in suspension, examines evidence, and then makes a decision based upon the most probable alternative in an uncertain world.

One premise of these essays is that Johnson is worth writing and reading about. However obvious that may be, it was not universally believed by all of Johnson's contemporaries or by some moderns—hence an investigation of his "Afterlife." Percival Stockdale was at the fringes of the Johnson circle and was an impoverished and often depressed author, clergyman, and at first an admirer of Johnson who unsuccessfully tried to help him. Stockdale thought that he was to have received the contract for the lives of the poets until bigotry and the power of name rather than talent moved that job into Johnson's unworthy hands. The result was what Stockdale called "a disgrace to English literature." Johnson appears often in Stockdale's sadly moving *Memoirs* (1809) and is the target of his *Lectures on the Truly Eminent English Poets* (1807). Those lectures, he thought, surely and finally would bring him deserved fame through hordes of adoring auditors, followed by as many purchasers of the printed books. Alas, public presentations was cancelled for lack of interest and the books themselves soon lined pie-pans, curlers, and dust bins. Stockdale partially succeeded in enlarging Johnson's afterlife, but did little for his own.

Readers will have noticed that I quoted eighteenth- and nineteenth-century French remarks in praise of Johnson. "Johnson Before Boswell in Eighteenth-Century France" includes many such quotations and makes plain that modern French willful ignorance of Johnson is radically uncharacteristic of eighteenth-century willful awareness of Johnson. That normally was positive, often enthusiastic, and roughly mirrored the positive and negative stages of British response. Until the later eighteenth century, the French almost always regarded Johnson as a major man of letters in a sister intellectual culture. After Boswell, and especially after Macaulay's review of Croker's Boswell in 1831, Johnson became Mr. Oddity, the freakish John Bull more appropriate for caricature or indeed oblivion than literary engagement. Thanks to Macaulay, French letters were bereft of Johnson as a man of letters. He had become something that a French Rébecca Tranchant could chuck out the window without regret.

Perhaps many readers today will want to chuck out the final section of this book, Johnson's politics. It embodies a controversy that has been alive in Johnson studies for some fifteen years. I must hope that it has educated both sides, perhaps especially so in the nature of literary scholarship, the relationship of that scholarship to modern political ideology, and the relationship of each to reasonably neutral historical inquiry. To those uninitiated in the exchange, the second edition of Donald J. Greene's *The Politics of Samuel Johnson* appeared in 1990, with a new introduction that savaged J. C. D. Clark and Howard Erskine-Hill. Either together or singly, they argued that Johnson was a nonjuring Tory Jacobite. He refused to sign the oaths of Allegiance or Abjuration, deprived himself of a university degree and virtually all public positions for which such oaths were required. He lived in a repressive Hanoverian state that threatened him and his beliefs in the divine right of kings and the legitimacy of the Stuart claim to the British throne. Virtually the complete body of his work has a Tory and Jacobite agenda that these critics and like-minded colleagues sought to make plain. The Charles of Sweden passage in *The Vanity of Human Wishes* thus reminds readers that Charles was a Tory and Jacobite hero. Johnson treats him sympathetically and uses him to recall the even more sympathetic Charles Edward whose failed '45 Johnson lamented and might have chosen to join.[7] Those who ignore the neo-Jacobite advice do so at their intellectual peril and practice inadequate historiography and literary criticism.

The controversy plainly has had its dark and often unpleasant side, perhaps in part because several of the neo-Jacobite scholars are themselves politically and emotionally involved with that cause. It also for the most part has set North American against British scholar-critics. I suspect that by now most of those who can change their minds already have, and so after an introduction in which I lay out the genesis of the conflict, I reduce seven of my essays on the subject to three main topics. Is Johnson likely to have taken or to have been able to take the relevant oaths at Oxford or elsewhere? Was Charles of Sweden a Tory and Jacobite hero? How should we read that passage in the *Vanity* and, thereafter, what further can we say about the politics of Samuel Johnson?

REREADING

In compiling this book I have avoided an omnibus and artificial explanation presumed to unlock the door to Johnsonian mysteries. The miscellaneous nature of the collection and my own intellectual bias reject such an approach. In rereading these essays written over about thirty-five years, though, I have noticed some common threads in my own work and in the development of Johnson studies. I had the good fortune of being trained at the University of Chicago between 1958 and 1963, especially with Gwin J. Kolb but also with some other senior professors still sympathetic to the intellectual sway of R. S. Crane. In spite of what was a family argument among formalists, Chicago neo-Aristotelianism was in scholarly quarrel with Yale New Criticism, much to the benefit and sharpening of each side's skills, even after the New Critical victory. Crane had retired by the time I arrived in Chicago, thus allowing me to benefit from his writings without having to take sides in the argument, or to confront the personality against which I probably would have rebelled.

One of the difficult but I think healthy tenets of the Crane legacy was the coupled insistence on evidence and on approaching a work with as much neutrality as possible—an approach recently made accessible to modern students in the theory and practice of Robert D. Hume. Crane regularly argued in favor of several critical principles: plural approaches to literary texts, awareness of one's critical assumptions, testing of one's hypotheses, trying not to impose one's personal agenda on a text, casting a wide intellectual net, avoiding deductive contexts into which one fits the particular work, and insisting that the author, so far from being "dead," is paramount in his or her text. Culture is filtered through the individual talent, who then shapes that aspect of culture for a specific literary work with its own idea of the whole.[8]

I have sought at least in part to adapt such reasonable scholarly restraint and practice. I thus have been sensitive to authorial "intention" so far as it can be verified, and especially to the danger of positing a literary or cultural theory that the author or text then is assumed to reflect. As I reread these essays, I could chronicle a series of such intellectual events through which the Anglo-American academic enterprise has passed, and to which I have tried to apply Crane's standards. For example, at one time we were told that irony was central to poetry: Johnson's *London* therefore reflected irony. Others told us that Johnson's prose always was elevated and scientific: his prose therefore reflected the elevated and scientific. Yet others knew that the eighteenth century was radically indeterminate in its judgments: Johnson's politics, poetry, and *Rasselas* therefore were radically indeterminate. Johnson never was read in France: therefore Johnson never was read in France. For many years we have been told as well that Johnson was a Jacobite. Here is the most recent exemplification of that deductive mode of proceeding: "Johnson is a figure who indeed allows us to interpret his age"—and since Johnson was a Tory-Jacobite-nonjuror, the age was Tory-Jacobite-nonjuring, which in turn allows us "to establish an authentic reading of his works," which are Tory-Jacobite-nonjuring.[9]

I have tried, instead, to avoid subtly or crudely prescriptive concepts like an "age" which often also is "Augustan," or "Christian Humanist," or "neoclassical," or "ancien" or some other construct to which the individual is subordinated, and through which he or the "age" should be read. Instead, as well, I have tried to follow Crane's admonition that the scholar have "a mind as free as possible from doctrinal prepossessions":

> The marks of the good scholar are many, but surely one of the most important is what I would call a habitual distrust of the a priori; that is to say, of all ways of arriving at particular conclusions which assume the relevance and authority, prior to the concrete evidence, of theoretical doctrines or other general propositions concerning the subject matter in question.[10]

Like any other sentient being, I cannot claim utter immunity from prejudice, though I can claim efforts to eradicate such prejudice in my approach to literary texts and contexts. I must therefore hope that such retreat from the a priori can help to illumine the varied aspects of Samuel Johnson's arts, mind, afterlife, and politics that I investigate in the collected essays below. I offer them in homage to the 250th anniversary of his *Dictionary of the English Language*, and to the larger world of Johnsonian studies that continues to flourish.

Notes

1. Johnson, in *Boswell's Life of Johnson Together with Boswell's Journal of a Tour to the Hebrides*, ed. George Birkbeck Hill and rev. L. F. Powell (Oxford: Clarendon Press, 1934–50), 4:172. Subsequent references are given in the text as *Life*.

2. *Journal étranger*, December 1756, pp. 111, 112. See the chapter on Johnson in France within for further relevant information.

3. Compare the *Edinburgh Review* 12 (1808): 62, 73–74, 80, 81.

4. For these, see Eliot's introduction to *London: A Poem, and The Vanity of Human Wishes* (London: Haslewood Books, 1930), reprinted in *English Critical Essays: Twentieth Century*, ed. Phylis M. Jones (London: Oxford University Press, 1947), pp. 301–10; Eliot, "Johnson as Critic and Poet," in *On Poetry and Poets* (London: Faber and Faber, 1957). Eliot there claims about *London* that "Johnson utters generalizations, and the generalizations are not true" (p. 157).

5. Eliot, "What Dante Means To Me," in *To Criticize the Critic and Other Writings* (New York: Farrar, Strauss, 1961), p. 128.

6. A mother weeps, The Yale Edition of the Works of Samuel Johnson, vol. 7, *Johnson on Shakespeare*, ed. Arthur Sherbo, with an introduction by Bertrand H. Bronson (1968), p. 78. Subsequent references to this edition are cited as YE with appropriate bibliographical information appended.

7. See, for example, Clark, *Samuel Johnson: Literature, religion and English cultural politics from the Restoration to Romanticism* (Cambridge: Cambridge University Press, 1994), p. 175: "It must be emphasised that there is no evidence that Johnson himself

participated in the rising of 1745. But given what is now known of the extent of Jacobite commitment, as well as the unexplained circumstances of Johnson's life, it is a realistic possibility rather than a romantic speculation that for a time in 1745–6 he held himself in readiness for dramatic events in circumstances which may have arisen but, as only hindsight makes evident, did not." See also pp. 7–8, 75, 121, 173.

8. For Hume, see *Reconstructing Contexts: The Aims and Principles of Archaeo-Historicism* (Oxford: Oxford University Press, 1999). I have outlined some ways in which Crane's theory and practice may be adapted for modern use, in "Historical Criticism, Hypotheses, and Eighteenth-Century Studies: The Case for Induction and Neutral Knowledge," in *Theory and Tradition in Eighteenth-Century Studies*, ed. Richard B. Schwartz (Carbondale: Southern Illinois University Press, 1990), pp. 66–92. Those interested in the Chicago criticism should see *Critics and Criticism Ancient and Modern*, ed. Crane (Chicago: University of Chicago Press, 1952). Several of Crane's important, and by now wrongly neglected, essays were collected in his *The Idea of the Humanities*, especially volume 2 (Chicago: University of Chicago Press, 1967). The most germane essays probably are "History versus Criticism in the Study of Literature" (1957), "Criticism as Inquiry: or, The Perils of the 'High Priori' Road" (1957), "Questions and Answers in the Teaching of Literary Texts" (1953), "Every Man His Own Critic" (1956), and "On Hypotheses in 'Historical Criticism': Apropos of Certain Contemporary Medievalists" (1961). Crane's valuable and again neglected Alexander Lectures for 1951–52 appeared as *Languages of Criticism and the Structure of Poetry* (Toronto: University of Toronto Press, 1953).

9. The joint preface to *Samuel Johnson in Historical Context*, ed. Jonathan Clark and Howard Erskine-Hill (Houndsmill, Basingstoke Hampshire, UK: Palgrave, 2002), p. x.

10. Crane, in "Criticism as Inquiry," in *The Idea of the Humanities*, 2:30 (mind free), 29 (good scholar). I again refer readers to Robert D. Hume's *Reconstructing Contexts* as a handsome adaptation of Crane.

Aspects of
Samuel Johnson

I
Arts

1

Samuel Johnson's *Plan* and
Preface to the *Dictionary*:
The Growth of a Lexicographer's Mind

THE RECEPTION OF JOHNSON'S *PLAN OF AN ENGLISH DICTIONARY* (1747) was largely favorable.[1] Dodsley's *Museum*, No. 36 (1747), observes that it "has excited great Expectation," and has given "universal Satisfaction" not only to the generality of readers, but to its generous and noble patron so elegantly complimented therein.[2] The Earl of Orrery tells Thomas Birch that he has just read the *Plan* "addressed to Lord Chesterfield" and was much pleased with it. He regards it as "one of the best that I have ever read," and observes that "the language . . . is good, and the arguments . . . properly and modestly expressed."[3] Boswell insists that "the 'Plan' has not only the substantial merit of comprehension, perspicuity, and precision, but that the language of it is unexceptionably excellent," that it is "altogether free from . . . inflation of style" and that, regarding the passages addressed to Chesterfield, "never was there a more dignified strain of compliment" (*Life*, 1:183–84).

Significantly, each of these commentators mentions both Johnson's language and the presence of Chesterfield in the *Plan*. Indeed, those with less happy feelings for it often mention language and Chesterfield as well. Thomas Birch labels its style "flatulent" and Daniel Wray, who wrote a critique of the *Plan*, alludes to its style as one of "high-scented Flowers."[4] Sir John Hawkins is harsher, insists that Chesterfield is "a smatterer in learning, and in manners a coxcomb," discusses his apparent influence on the *Plan*, observes that Johnson "was betrayed to celebrate [Chesterfield] as the Maecenas of the age," and adds that "the stile and language of that address which his plan includes are little less than adulatory."[5]

Hawkins's estimate of Johnson's prose and attitude toward Chesterfield seems to me accurate. I conjecture that Johnson was in fact betrayed, probably by his own pride and wishes for financial success and that, partially as a result of Chesterfield's presence, the *Plan* is less successful as a rhetorical and lexicographical document than Johnson hoped. I further conjecture that shortly after publishing the *Plan* Johnson realized his error, disliked Chesterfield, his own moral compromise, and some of the beliefs regarding language that were a function of his temperament and circumstances while writing the *Plan*. Consequently, in the later Preface, he disowned several of the concepts and much of the rhetoric of the *Plan* and certain aspects of his character that allowed the plea to Chesterfield in the first place. Much of this takes place between February of 1749 and February of 1755, when Johnson wrote his "Celebrated Letter" to Chesterfield.

1

In 1755 Chesterfield remarked that he was so used to flattery that he could no longer respond to it.[6] When one examines some of the dedications of works written to him, one can see why. The anonymous author of *The Triumph of Wisdom* (1745) tells Chesterfield that he is inspired and beloved by Wisdom and Poetry; as Lord Lieutenant of Ireland he will bring boundless virtue, harmony, and plenty to the country. Hence, if he should "raise the Poet's Genius to his Theme" the poem will necessarily be "Sacred to TRUTH, to PLATO'S, STANHOPE'S Praise!"[7] Samuel Madden's long panegyric, *Boulter's Monument* (1745), was not only known to Johnson but for the second edition, which never appeared, corrected and improved by him. There Johnson read that Chesterfield's arrival in Ireland was like an inscribed "*Tablet* from the *Sun*," that he is "the *Muses* mighty *Lord*, and *Friend*" who would save the country from death and be at once a ministering angel, a sweetly singing David, and a powerful Saint "indulg'd by Heav'n" and thus capable of removing ills and restoring health. All nature will conspire to bring the Earl to Ireland, and "*welcome* hither that *exalted Mind! / The Friend* of *Merit*, and of *Human-kind!*"[8]

Even this praise was modest when compared to that with which Madden graced Chesterfield in 1748, before the first canto of an as yet unidentified poem. "As to the Dedication," Chesterfield wrote to Madden upon receiving a copy, "I must tell you very sincerely, that I heartily wish you would lower it. . . . The few light, trifling things that I have accidentally scribbled in my youth . . . do by no means entitle me to the compliments which you make me."[9] The author of *The History of the Rise, Progress, and Tendency of Patriotism* (1747) is hardly less discreet than

Madden. This writer regards Chesterfield's sole fault as that of monopoly of all the good traits and virtues of "Learning and Politeness, all the talents natural and acquired." Chesterfield is thus a greater orator than Cicero or Demosthenes, and as a poet rivals Horace in his odes.[10] By 1750 this growing group addressing itself to Chesterfield included Teresia Constantia Phillips Muilman, the notorious "Con Phillips" mentioned in 1.vi of Fielding's *Amelia* (1751) as "not least" among courtesans and shrewish women of some repute. In 1721 she accused Chesterfield, in print, of having seduced, impregnated, and abandoned her; her popular *Apology* appeared between 1748 and 1750 and relumed this episode; and in 1750 she published her *Letter* to Chesterfield, a thinly veiled reiteration of her earlier charge regarding Chesterfield's paternity of her child.[11] This *Letter*, according to "a Lady" attempting to refute it, "is universally read."[12]

Not even William Warburton's relatively modest praise—which Chesterfield enjoyed but also rejected as too lavish—can alter the nature of this dedicating mob of largely inferior poets, politicians, and others.[13] Even in 1747, it is odd to find Johnson in such company; but it is odder to find that the speaker of the *Plan* sometimes sounds like Samuel Madden rather than Samuel Johnson, for Johnson is flattering a man whose literary merits he must at least have suspected, if not positively known, were overrated, whose politics he had probably come to mistrust, and whose serious interest in language was spurious.[14] For instance, considering his relationship with Dodsley in 1747, he may have known that several of Chesterfield's pleasant but flimsy occasional poems would be published in the second edition of Dodsley's *Collection* (1748), the volumes in which his own *London* (1738) and "Prologue Spoken by Mr. Garrick at the Opening of . . . Drury Lane" (1747) also reappeared.[15] Whether or not he had read these poems at the time, he would have realized that Chesterfield's literary efforts were both meager and trifling. Furthermore, considering Chesterfield's remarks on the manuscript of the *Plan*,[16] he would probably have been aware of what is clear on reading Chesterfield's relevant letters concerning language, and his subsequent numbers of the *World* puffing the *Dictionary*: namely, that the earl's interest in language was largely a social rather than intellectual matter.[17] Thomas Sheridan's plea to Chesterfield in 1756 to become an "establisher" of the language and the founder of an academy to "*correct, ascertain, and fix*" the language, was more congenial to Chesterfield's thought than to Johnson's.[18] Moreover, though Johnson probably would not have agreed with Horace Walpole's depreciation of Chesterfield as a debater, he probably would have agreed that Chesterfield's talents were overpraised. Samuel Johnson wrote all eight of the speeches attributed to Chesterfield between 1741 and February 1743. These appeared in the Parliamentary Debates of the *Gentleman's Magazine* between 1742 and 1744. Upon seeing Chesterfield's *Works* in 1778, Johnson was amused to find that two speeches ascribed to Chesterfield were actually by him: "and the best of it is, they have found out that one is like Demosthenes, and the other like Cicero."[19] Sledd and Kolb have shown that the "Ciceronian" Chesterfield made eight minor suggestions for revision of Johnson's *Plan*, and conclude that "Chesterfield's reputation as a man of wit and sense will not be enhanced" by them.[20] Johnson later told Boswell that these remarks were solicited only because of Dodsley's urging and his own laziness, and not because of Chesterfield's natural role as patron of those concerned with the English language.[21]

This evidence supports the following hypothesis: in the process of puffing the projected dictionary, Johnson's unwarranted praise of Chesterfield served as a source of compromise, humiliation, and anger against both Chesterfield and himself. Hawkins, for example, reports that "Johnson was so little pleased with his once supposed patron, that he forebore not ever after to speak of him in terms of the greatest contempt." Some of this contempt, Hawkins continues, resulted from their discussions "on the subject of literature, in which [Johnson] found [Chesterfield] so deficient as gave him occasion to repent the choice he had made, and to say, that the labour he had bestowed in his address to Lord Chesterfield resembled that of gilding a rotten post."[22] We can thus see several reasons for Johnson's break from Chesterfield: though Johnson was beginning to emerge from the class of literary hack, he nevertheless joined an undistinguished group seeking noble patronage; he was led to have great literary and financial expectations from a patron who soon emerged as meager of both intellectual and monetary reward; yet shortly after receiving inappropriate praise, the patron apparently refused to see his charge. To the compromise of a proud and scrupulous man, was added compromise for no reward or purpose.

Sledd and Kolb conjecture that by about early February of 1749 Johnson had decided not to wait upon Chesterfield any longer.[23] Perhaps as a result of this decision, the *Rambler*, No. 163 (1751), attacks patrons who encourage "expectations which are never to be gratified," and laments the consequent "elation and depression of the heart by needless vicissitudes of hope and disappointment."[24] In the final *Rambler*, No. 208 (1752), Johnson insists that he will not attempt "to overbear [the censures of criticism] by the influence of a patron," as he seemed to do in the *Plan*, and adds that "having laboured to maintain the dignity of virtue, I will not now degrade it by the meanness of dedication" (YE 5:317). Indeed, Johnson had already rejected another patron, since, sometime between late March and early May 1750, he refused Bubb Dodington's offer of friendship.[25] Furthermore, *The Vanity of Human Wishes* (1749) was to be reprinted in the fourth volume of Dodsley's *Collection* (1755), much of which was apparently gathered by September 29, 1753, when Dodsley wrote to Shenstone seeking his contribution and saying: "I am now thinking of putting my Fourth Volume of Poems to Press."[26] It may have been within a few months of this date that Johnson changed line 160 of the *Vanity*'s description of the scholar's ills from "Toil, envy, want, the garret, and the jail," to "the patron and the jail."[27] Johnson probably wrote his double-edged definition of "patron" in mid-May of 1753: "one who countenances, supports, or protects. Commonly a wretch who supports with insolence, and is paid with flattery." The animus here is directed at Johnson himself as well as at Chesterfield. This is suggested, among other ways, in the definition of "flattery" written sometime in late 1749: it is "False praise; artful obsequiousness; adulation."[28]

In the definition of "patron" I suggest, Johnson glances at Chesterfield's insolence and his own artful obsequiousness in the *Plan*. If Hawkins is correct, Johnson may also have felt himself obsequious at their private meeting which, given the "defensive pride" Johnson admitted to, was bound to trouble him (*Life*, 1:265). He confesses as much in the opening paragraphs of the *Plan*, when he characterizes his pre-Chesterfield conception of the *Dictionary* as a labor that would not "throw in my way any temptation to disturb the quiet of others by censure, or my own by flattery."[29] In the "Celebrated Letter" Johnson again admits his earlier pride in seeking Chesterfield's patronage: I "could not forbear to wish that I might boast myself Le Vainqueur du Vainqueur de la Terre, that I might obtain that regard for which I saw the world contending." He concludes with a contrasting thought: "I have been long awakened from that Dream of hope, in which I once boasted myself with so much exultation, My Lord, Your Lordship's Most humble, most obedient Servant."[30] The last time Johnson thus wrote to Chesterfield was in the *Plan* of the *Dictionary*, part of which included, Johnson makes clear to Chesterfield and himself, an ephemeral dream, an empty boast, and false exultation.[31]

When writing the *Plan*, then, Johnson was flattering in order to acquire the rewards due to the conqueror of the conqueror of the fashionable world. Republication and redistribution of the *Plan* in 1755 was commercially wise but, since Johnson long disowned it, personally em-

barrassing. Chesterfield's allusion to it in his papers in the *World* probably added further embarrassment, particularly since in the forthcoming
Preface to the *Dictionary* Johnson rejected much of the *Plan*.[32] For instance, he found that his initial notion that "every quotation should be
useful to some other end than the illustration of a word," might be morally enlightening, but would require several lifetimes and several tomes.
"Such is design, while it is yet at a distance from execution," and so in
the present volumes the reader will find only "Some passages" which
will instruct and please him (5:38). Shortly thereafter, he again portrays
the enthusiastic novice and the tones of the *Plan*: when he began this
work, he says, he hoped to examine words, things, and ideas, amass
huge treasures of learning, triumphantly display his acquisitions to mankind, and thereby cause his dictionary to replace all others. "But these
were the dreams of a poet, doomed at last to wake a lexicographer"
(5:43). Similarly, he admits that he had formerly "flattered" himself with
the possibility of fixing the language and stopping "those alterations
which time and change have" previously made in language. Now, however, he fears that he has "indulged expectation which neither reason
nor experience can justify" (5:45–46). Major parts of the *Plan* dedicated
to Chesterfield, Johnson thereby admits, were excessive in their demands
on the lexicographer and were the products of pride, self-flattery,
dreams, and indulgences of the irrational and naïve.

   Moreover, Chesterfield encouraged substantial parts of Johnson's audience to reread-the *Plan* and regard it as a definitive statement of the
Dictionary's guiding principles. In *The World*, No. 100 (1754), Chesterfield insists that Johnson's *Plan* is a proof of his ability to bring the work
"as near to perfection as any one man could do. Nothing," he continues,
"can be more rationally imagined, or more accurately and elegantly expressed. I therefore recommend the previous perusal of it to all those
who intend to buy the dictionary."[33] Matthew Maty, already Chesterfield's protégé, did apply the *Plan*'s theory to the *Dictionary*'s practice
as portrayed in the Preface and duly noted Johnson's overlapping yet
clearly different attitudes in the two works. In his *Journal britannique*
for July–August of 1755, he insists that Johnson should have reprinted
the *Plan* at the head of the *Dictionary*, and accuses him of attempting to
disparage his former patron. In 1747 one could have seen the *Plan* that
Johnson proposed in his pamphlet addressed to Lord Chesterfield.

> Les vues neuves & approfondies, que contenoit ce projet, prévinrent en fa-
> veur d'un travail entrepris sous de tels auspices & dirigé par de telles règles.
> On a lieu d'être surpris que cette pièce ne se trouve point à la tête du diction-

naire, dont elle contenoit l'annonce. Elle eût épargné à l'Auteur la composition d'une nouvelle préface, qui ne contient qu'en partie les mêmes choses, &
qu'on est tenté de regarder comme destineé a faire perdre de vue quelques
unes des obligations, que M. Johnson avoit contracteés, et le Mécène qu'ils'
s'étoit choisi.[34]

We are, then, justified in adapting Johnson's subdued and Maty's
overt device of comparison and contrast of the two documents, and de-
termining some of their essential differences, strengths, and weaknesses.
In so doing, Chesterfield's role and influence will be important.

2

According to the *Plan*'s own rhetoric, Chesterfield greatly influenced
its conception and practice. Though lexicography is a menial task, it
was, Johnson says, regarded as a "safe" and "useful" performance
which would keep life "innocent; . . . would awaken no passion, engage
[him] in no contention, nor throw in [his] way any temptation to disturb
the quiet of others by censure, or [his] own by flattery." Though "princes
and statesmen" of earlier ages were said to protect those who improved
the tongue, he could only regard "such acts of beneficence as prodigies"
(5:2). Johnson thus establishes two aspects of time past: his own innocent and safe occupation, and an earlier golden age of the nobles' interest in language. Both are changed when Johnson's time-present is altered
by Chesterfield, whose protection establishes him as a prodigy and Johnson as the possible center of controversy and concern; hence he becomes
anxious lest Chesterfield's patronage "should fix the attention of the
publick too much upon me; and as it once happened to an epick poet of
France" (5:2). The earlier lonely and lowly but useful toil is transmuted
into an epic task performed under public scrutiny. Near the end of the
Plan the lexicographer's efforts which once were "not splendid" but
"useful" now are discussed in terms of "the difficulty" and "importance
of philological studies" (5:17). This change is not the earned result of
Johnson's revaluation of the lexicographer's role: it is the result of the
scheme now being "prosecuted under your Lordship's influence" (5:2).
Consequently, Johnson is publishing this *Plan* in order to gain suggestions or approbation from those who will surely *now* regard it as important, since it is "a design that you, my Lord, have not thought unworthy
to share your attention with treaties and with wars" (5:3). One of Ches-

terfield's roles in the *Plan*, then, is significantly to heighten both the public's regard and the lexicographer's anxiety and fame.

Chesterfield appears again briefly when Johnson observes that the earl is aware of Britain's unsettled orthography. Since this is hardly an observation original to Chesterfield or particularly distinguished in its own right, we are surprised to find that in Chesterfield's next appearance he is likened to no less a figure than Caesar.

> Ausonius thought that modesty forbad him to plead inability for a task to which Caesar had judged him equal. . . . And I may hope, my Lord, that since you, whose authority in our language is so generally acknowledged, have commissioned me to declare my own opinion, I shall be considered as exercising a kind of vicarious jurisdiction, and that the power which might have been denied to my own claim, will be readily allowed me as the delegate of your Lordship. (5:19)

Chesterfield, once among princes and statesmen, is now exalted to the level of emperor who silences dissent against his powerful decrees and rewards the man of letters faithful to him. This example both overpraises Chesterfield and places Johnson among those who rise by the patronage of the great. Moreover, Johnson is not speaking with his own voice or authority, but merely as Chesterfield's mouthpiece. At first Chesterfield as Caesar was the emperor Gratian who aids Ausonius; he soon becomes the emperor Claudius invading England, and Johnson becomes one of "the soldiers of Caesar" looking on Britain "as a new world, which it is almost madness to invade," but during which invasion the process of civilization may at least begin. Whatever the outcome, even if the invasion should fail, Johnson "shall not easily regret" the attempt, which has procured him "the honour" of appearing publicly as his Lordship's most humble servant (5:21–22).

Johnson's subservient attitude toward Chesterfield cannot be dismissed merely as the conventional and irrelevant nod to power, since it shows Johnson sharing some of Chesterfield's values regarding language. In the rough draft of the *Plan*, called "A Short Scheme for compiling a new Dictionary of the English Language" (1746), Johnson observes that orthography is now "settled with . . . propriety."[35] In the *Plan* Johnson reverses his opinion—or at the very least substantially changes his emphasis—and says that "according to your Lordship's observation, there is still great uncertainty among the best criticks" (5:6). Chesterfield's concern with fixing the language also appears in Johnson's *Plan*. This difficult task is both desirable and largely achievable. Since "the first change" in language "will naturally begin by corruptions in the living speech," Johnson hopes to supply new "rules for . . . pronunciation" and thereby "to provide that the harmony of the moderns may be more permanent." This is consistent with one of the lexicographer's "great" ends, fixing the language. "A new pronunciation will make almost a new speech," and so Johnson will "determine the accentuation of all polysyllables by proper authorities" (5:8).

The need to stabilize language appears throughout the *Plan*. It is, for example, "necessary to fix the pronunciation of monosyllables" in order to avoid "the danger of . . . variation" (5:8). Moreover, by tracing every word to its etymon, "and not admitting, but with great caution, any of which no original can be found, we shall secure our language from being overrun with *cant*" (5:11). Johnson does tell Chesterfield that one cannot properly expect permanence in words, since "language is the work of man, of a being from whom permanence and stability cannot be derived"; but he also wonders who "can forbear to wish" that the "fundamental atoms of our speech might obtain the firmness and immutability of the primogenial and constituent particles of matter" (5:12). Hence it is not surprising to hear him insist that "barbarous or impure words and expressions . . . are carefully to be eradicated wherever they are found," and to liken his work "to the proposal made by Boileau to the [French] academicians" to review their best authors and expunge their impurities, lest they contribute "to the depravation of the language" (5:19). He begins his peroration by telling Chesterfield that in his "idea of an English Dictionary . . . the pronunciation of our language may be fixed, and its attainment facilitated; by which its purity may be preserved, its use ascertained, and its duration lengthened." Undertaking such a task may be an act of near-madness, but it surely will be undertaken and, with Chesterfield's patronage, will at least make it easier for another lexicographer "to reduce [the English, and hence their language] wholly to subjection, and settle them under laws" (5:20–21).

Much of the force of the invading soldiers comes from Caesar's authority—and in the *Plan* that authority is often alluded to and generally external to Johnson. It is, chiefly, Chesterfield's for Johnson insists that he is but "the delegate of your Lordship" (5:19). He will also find "proper authorities" (5:8) for pronunciation and will recognize that the different sounds of some words are "equally defensible by authority" (5:9). His use of etymology to determine how English words were deduced from foreign languages (5:9) will be facilitated by the excellent "writers of our glossaries" (5:10); Quintillian supports his notion that speech cannot be immutable (5:11); for aid in definitions he will "consult the best writers" (5:14); and he insists that "the credit of every part of this work must depend" upon "citing authorities" for illustrative quotations (5:19–20). Finally, he attempts to silence criticism by telling us on "what authority the authorities are selected." Again, the source often is external to Johnson's own efforts: "many of the writers whose testimonies will be alleged, were selected by Mr. Pope, of whom I may be justified in affirming, that were he still alive, solicitous as he was for the success of this work, he would not be displeased, that I have undertaken it" (5:20).

We might also notice the *Plan*'s conception of the *Dictionary*'s audience: it is composed largely of purchasers. The first paragraph, for instance, begins by mentioning Johnson's "prospect" of the "price of [his] labor" (5:1). Part of this price will come from the sale of the *Dictionary*, and Johnson is therefore careful to include what the reader hopes to find: some foreign words "seem necessary to be retained," because the purchaser who looks into his dictionary for such a word "will have reason to complain if he does not find it" (5:5). Similarly, "the terms of war and navigation should be inserted so far as they can be required by readers of travels, and of history" (5:5). A few pages later we hear that "common readers" should find the definitions sufficient for their use, "since without some attention to such demands the dictionary cannot become generally valuable" (5:14).

Of course the desire to increase the sale and approbation of his book is hardly unnatural; but the importance of Chesterfield and the combined attention to external authority and the needs of the purchaser suggest that in the *Plan* Johnson is "other-directed." There is nothing morally culpable about such a state; but in the case of Samuel Johnson it is out of character and affects the speaker's ability to convince us of the high level of lexicographical competence and emotional maturity necessary for his job. Indeed, as I have already suggested, this view of the speaker in the *Plan* probably would have been shared by Johnson as portrayed in the Preface to the *Dictionary*. I should now like to show how the later character of Johnson approaches the rhetorical aspects discussed above: the roles of patronage and authority; fixing of the language; the nature of the audience; and how, along the way, these suggest a speaker who is more convincing than he was in the *Plan*. By the end of the Preface, Johnson offers a frightening insight into the nature of his own and of humanity's achievements.

3

The attempt to acquire a patron is a social act, one in which, if successful, the gentleman and scholar combine efforts. Such patronage

probably appealed to Johnson's ego, purse, and sense of community between the intellectual and fashionable worlds. In spite of the Preface's
appearance at the head of the *Dictionary*, however, it is essentially a private essay and paradoxically portrays Johnson as the lexicographer
whose work will touch thousands but who is himself cut off from all
human contact. This is made clear in the first five paragraphs, which establish both the Preface's dominant tone and its place as one of the most
moving of English prose pieces. In the *Plan* it "appeared" that the province of lexicography was "the least delightful" and fruitful "of all the
regions of learning" (5:1); but, as we have seen, Johnson later reverses
that judgment and elevates lexicography, so that all "who desire the
praise of elegance or discernment must contend in the promotion" of
his dictionary (5:3). In the Preface Johnson implies that the *Plan*'s first
description was reality not appearance, and that he must look at his literary province through his own eyes rather than through those of a
noble lord's. The first paragraph thus portrays members of the class of
"those, who toil at the lower employments of life," as passive, driven
by fear and exposed to censure, disgrace, or punishment. Johnson then
introduces and repeats the word *without*: such a person is not only "exposed to censure," but exposed "without hope of praise," and is "punished for neglect, where success would have been without applause, and
diligence without reward" (5:23).

He then moves from general to particular, places the writer of dictionaries among the class of "unhappy mortals," and continues the paradoxical premise of the actively engaged passive scholar. He is the "slave of
science, the pioneer of literature, doomed only to remove rubbish and
clear obstructions from the paths through which Learning and Genius
press forward to conquest and glory, without bestowing a smile on the
humble drudge that facilitates their progress" (5:23). The lexicographer
is thus acted upon by cosmic forces of fate and doom, while he himself
acts on rubbish and obstruction; he is a slave who helps to make others
free, a mere pioneer who makes a path for the conqueror. The martial
image highlights an important difference from the *Plan*. There Johnson
was one of the soldiers of the invading Caesar and took pleasure and
pride in his modest share of the imperial, civilizing, role. In the Preface
he is merely a foot soldier, the pioneer "whose business is to level the
road, throw up works, or sink mines in military operations" (*Dictionary*). The first two paragraphs of the Preface thus reverse the dominant
tone of the *Plan*. The view of the lexicographer as drudge dealing with
rubbish was suggested in the *Plan* and then dismissed as clearly wrong,
since Chesterfield would not trouble himself with such unimportant and
gross matters. Reality now replaces appearance, and the image of a

lonely yet brave, heroic, and selfless man replaces what for Johnson is the inappropriate social pose of Chesterfield's client.

The concept of a heroic task to be performed and a pioneer drudge to do it is consistent with the paradox of the active lexicographer acted upon by fate, fear, censure, disgrace, and punishment. We are thus aware of the immensity of the task, the paucity of reward, and the necessarily inadequate abilities of the lexicographer. Hence in the third paragraph we respond positively to the speaker's honesty, courage, and selflessness, as he says: "I have, notwithstanding this discouragement, attempted a Dictionary of the English language." Once more we see a paradoxical inversion, as the gardener acquires the traits of an untended garden. The English language was "employed in the cultivation of every species of literature," but in the process "has itself been . . . neglected, suffered to spread, under the direction of chance, into wild exuberance; resigned to the tyranny of time and fashion; and exposed to the corruptions and ignorance, and caprices of innovation" (5:23). Both the extent of the task and the courage and isolation of the lexicographer are made clearer still upon repetition of the term *without* and the words or phrases it modifies:

> When I took the first survey of my undertaking, I found our speech copious without order, and energetic without rules: wherever I turned my view, there was perplexity to be disentangled, and confusion to be regulated; choice was to be made out of boundless variety, without any established principle of selection; adulterations were to be detected, without a settled test of purity; and modes of expression to be rejected or received, without the suffrages of any writers of classical reputation or acknowledged authority. (5:22–23)

While creating order from disorder, Johnson comments obliquely on his former patron and former attitude toward authority. He now has "no assistance but from general grammar," and so depends upon his own lights, examines writers, notes what might best illustrate a word and "accumulated in time the materials of a dictionary, which, by degrees, I reduced to method, establishing to myself, in the progress of the work, such rules as experience and analogy suggested to me" (5:24). He has begun to prune the unhealthy luxuriance of the garden; and he is doing so through his own efforts rather than through those of Chesterfield or Pope.

His earned independence impresses us favorably, as does his healthy respect both for the work of others and for the intelligence of his readers. He says of disputed areas like orthography: "I have left, in the examples, to every author his own practice unmolested, that the reader may balance suffrages, and judge between us" (5:26). Moreover, he will not change orthography to suit ephemeral pronunciation, mere fashion, or pedantic idiosyncrasies. Instead, he has proceeded "with a scholar's reverence for antiquity, and a grammarian's regard to the genius of our tongue" (5:27). As such a scholar he establishes his right to correct authorities if he believes them wrong. In matters of pronunciation, for instance, the reader will sometimes find that the author in the illustrative quotation has placed the emphasis differently from Johnson's: "it is then to be understood that custom has varied, or that the author has, in my opinion, pronounced wrong" (5:28). Similarly, when discussing the word list, Johnson mentions the "deficiency of [previous] dictionaries" and stresses the difficulty of finding new words in his "unguided excursions into books" or in "the boundless chaos of a living speech." Nevertheless, he adds, his search "has been either skilful or lucky; for I have much augmented the vocabulary" (5:31). The evidence for that augmentation is in front of the reader in two substantial folio volumes. Upon examining the evidence and finding the remark likely to be true, one believes all the more in the integrity of the speaker. Johnson's balanced evaluation of Skinner and Junius as etymologists, and Bailey, Ainsworth, and Philips as compilers of word lists, again enhances our confidence in him, as he clearly states their strengths and weaknesses, and insists that he alone is responsible for inclusion of specific words: other words not in dictionaries, he says, "which I considered as useful, or know to be proper, though I could not at present support them by authorities, I have suffered to stand upon my own attestation" (5:33–34). Authority is both respected and limited by the governing mind of Samuel Johnson.

Johnson, though, never forgets that he is still the drudge faced with giving order to chaos; and so, paradoxically again, he buttresses his character by admitting his weaknesses. Hostility will be directed to his definitions, he predicts, not only by the malign, but, because of the supreme difficulty of the task, by Johnson as well: "I have not always been able to satisfy myself" (5:35), he confesses, since many words do not admit of easy definition, and others, like particles, which "are not easily reducible under any regular scheme of explication," can only be defined with as much success "as can be expected in a task, which no man, however learned or sagacious, has yet been able to perform." He is bound by his own intelligence, and admits: "some words there are which I cannot explain, because I do not understand them." Significantly, Johnson inverts the use of authority in the *Plan*, by using the authority of ignorance not knowledge: Cicero and Aristotle confessed their ignorance, and so

"I may surely, without shame, leave some obscurities to happier industry, or future information" (5:35). Johnson's rhetorical stance, then includes both awareness of an impossible task and his knowledge of his own great abilities, authority, and intelligence: these operate in a selfless way for the glory of learning, genius, and the English language and nation rather than for his own pride or material gain. Johnson's depth of perception is made clear in the three passionate and beautiful concluding paragraphs of the essay. They include acceptance of the human situation, of the subservient but necessary role of lexicography and, finally, of his own personal and terrible isolation.

The *Dictionary* is devoted to "the honour of my country, that we may no longer yield the palm of philology, without a contest, to the nations of the continent." Since the "chief glory of every people arises from its authors," and since Johnson cannot yet know whether his own writings will enhance English literature, he will not regard his employment as either "useless or ignoble, if, by [his] assistance foreign nations, and distant ages, gain access to the propagators of knowledge, and understand the teachers of truth; if [his] labours afford light to the repositories of science, and add celebrity to Bacon, to Hooker, to Milton, and to Boyle" (5:49–50). This generous wish to propagate the work of greater men both animates and gives him pleasure—not the prideful pleasure of the *Plan*, but the pleasure of having endeavored well and achieved much, though imperfectly. He has learned "that no dictionary of a living tongue ever can be perfect," since words live and die while the book is being published (5:50), and that the weaknesses of the flesh, the intellect, and the spirit will prevail in many instances. He has, then, accepted the role of the pioneer of literature, and passed the fruits of his labors to an enriched science and posterity, rather than to the reputation of Samuel Johnson or the Earl of Chesterfield.

The Preface does more than discuss personal matters in abstract terminology; it discusses them in personal terminology as well. Hence Johnson again rejects the *Plan*'s plea for patronage and discusses his discomforts during the process of writing. We recall that in the *Plan* Chesterfield was characterized as a prodigy whose attentions would induce the emulation of "those who desire the praise of elegance or discernment." In contrast, the *Dictionary* "was written with little assistance of the learned, and without any patronage of the great; . . . amidst inconvenience and distraction, in sickness and in sorrow" (5:51). Moreover, Johnson concludes, even the praise which one normally and fairly seeks is irrelevant to him; the social act of praise is valuable only for one active in a social world, not for one so wholly alone. The final paragraph of the Preface thus takes many of the terms of the opening paragraphs and moves them from a broadly intellectual to a personally emotional level. *Fear, hope, censure,* and *praise* now reappear in a grim context; earlier Johnson is alone, ahead of the army, but still aware of his human reactions, since he is "driven by the fear of evil," and a few lines later, admits that he can "only hope to escape reproach" (5:23). One may read the *Plan* and Preface as signposts in the growth of the lexicographer's mind, as the records of intellectual and personal discovery. It is almost as if during the process of writing Johnson had reviewed the emotional trauma of his dictionary years, found himself now suffering not only an understandable postpartum depression, but found that depression heightened by the loss of many of those whom the completed *Dictionary* was designed to please. The *Dictionary* leaving his hands evokes memories of his wife leaving this world almost three years earlier. During the final summation of his seven years of work on the *Dictionary,* intellectual isolation is transmuted into personal isolation. Considering the difficulty of his task, Johnson says,

> I may surely be contented without the praise of perfection, which, if I could obtain, in this gloom of solitude, what would it avail me? I have protracted my work till most of those, whom I wished to please, have sunk into the grave, and success and miscarriage are empty sounds; I, therefore, dismiss it with frigid tranquility, having little to fear or hope from censure or from praise. (5:51)

All readers of Johnson know the frequency with which the terms *hope* and *fear* appear in his work; they are generally part of the usual passions of mankind which the moralist must direct toward proper concerns.[36] "Where then shall Hope and Fear their objects find?" (line 343) Johnson asks in *The Vanity of Human Wishes.* By the end of the Preface, though, he virtually divorces himself from hope and fear, associates himself with those who have already "sunk into the grave," and declares that some of the words that he has been defining for the last seven years are merely "empty sounds." The Preface concludes with rejection not only of public honor and Chesterfield, but of the ordinary pleasures of life. It is against these somber tones, against the ability to view the major achievement of his life as personally irrelevant, that the genteel obsequiousness of the *Plan* must be judged.

The changed attitude toward fixing the language is also a sign of Johnson's maturity. We recall the *Plan*'s brash confidence in the possibility of making at least a handsome start in that direction; and we will also see the Preface's embarrassed reaction toward and clear rejection of that earlier stance. Johnson now only hopes that he can slow down the speed with which the language changes, since a living language is "variable by the caprice of everyone that speaks it," and words are "hourly shifting their relations" (5:35). Hence he admits that though he has "laboured" at "settling the orthography," he has "not always executed [his] own scheme, or satisfied [his] own expectations" (5:41). We are, therefore, not surprised when we hear Johnson say what would have been impossible in the *Plan*; the overlapping meanings of words in some illustrative quotations are "not to be imputed to me, who do not form, but register the language; who do not teach men how they should think, but relate how they have hitherto expressed their thoughts" (5:44). Johnson then repeats some of the terminology of the *Plan*, alludes to it, and clearly rejects its concept of a potentially static language.

> Those who have been persuaded to think well of my design, will require that it should fix our language, and put a stop to those alterations which time and chance have hitherto been suffered to make in it without opposition. With this consequence I will confess that I flattered myself for a while; but now begin to fear that I have indulged expectation which neither reason nor experience can justify. (5:45–46)

Indeed, a lexicographer who wishes to separate language from the human condition of growth and decay uses foolish imagination, proudly overrates his own powers, and misunderstands the nature of language. The man who fancies "that his dictionary can embalm his language, and secure it from corruption and decay, that it is in his power to change sublunary nature, and clear the world at once from folly, vanity, and affectation" is both vain and morally dangerous: "sounds are too volatile and subtile for legal restraints; to enchain syllables, and to lash the wind, are equally the undertakings of pride, unwilling to measure its desires by its strength" (5:46). Johnson here telescopes two facts about Xerxes—the enchaining and lashing—which, in *The Vanity of Human Wishes*, he used to show the madness and pride which led to the death of thousands at Salamis:

> Attendant Flatt'ry counts his myriads o'er,
> Till counted myriads sooth his pride no more;
> Fresh praise is try'd till madness fires his mind,
> The waves he lashes, and enchains the wind.
>
> (lines 229–32)

"Causes of change," Johnson insists, ". . . are, perhaps, as much superi-our to human resistance, as the revolutions of the sky, or intumescence of the tide" (5:46). Attempting to enchain syllables thus also affronts the healthy processes of human thought.

> Those who have much leisure to think, will always be enlarging the stock of ideas; and every increase of knowledge, whether real or fancied, will produce new words, or combinations of words. When the mind is unchained from necessity, it will range after convenience; when it is left at large in the fields of speculation, it will shift opinions. (5:47)

On the *Plan*'s side of the ledger, then, we see self-flattery, irrationality, inexperience, concepts worthy of derision, vanity, false imagination, un-natural and impossible restraint, and pride. On the Preface's side, we see proper modesty, experience, freedom, thought, and growth. Johnson now hopes only "to acquiesce with silence, as in the other insurmount-able distresses of humanity"; he hopes to "retard what we cannot repel," and give longevity to the language which finally must decay (5:49). The nature of language and the nature of man are intimately related in their pattern of growth and decline.

Man and language are different in an important way as well, and here too we see an advance over the thinking of the *Plan*. One of the reasons Johnson no longer attempts to fix the language is that he realized the demands of civilization and its written language are at variance with the "wild and barbarous jargon" of oral speech (5:24). Thus the earliest at-tempts to record speech induce great diversity of spelling, and this "per-plexes or destroys analogy, and produces anomalous formations, that . . . can never be afterward dismissed or reformed" (5:25). Language is not only the purveyor of noble truths; as the martial image with which the Preface opens suggests, it also is the lexicographer's intransigent enemy. He hopes to normalize and make analogies, whereas language hopes to destroy analogy. It will baffle the finest lexicographer, since there are "spots of barbarity impressed so deep in the English language, that criticism can never wash them away" (5:25). Language is wanton and capricious; the lexicographer seeks uniformity and system. Lan-guage will borrow its words from other languages; the lexicographer warns against "the folly of naturalizing useless foreigners to the injury of the natives" (5:31). Language is "variable by the caprice of every one that speaks it"; the lexicographer hopes "to circumscribe . . . by . . . limitations" (5:35). "Words are seldom exactly synonymous"; yet "the rigour of interpretative lexicography requires that the *explanation, and the word explained, should be always reciprocal*" (5:36, 35). Language has an "exuberance of signification"; the lexicographer trying to record such exuberance finds it "scarcely possible to collect" words' many senses (5:37). Language's "sounds are too volatile and subtile for legal restraints" (5:46); yet the lexicographer puts sounds on paper and hopes they will be properly retranslated into the same sound. Language as an intransigent and ultimately triumphant enemy is thus quite different from language as discussed in the *Plan*. There Johnson believed that he could make "the harmony of the moderns . . . more permanent" than that of former ages (5:8), and that the adjustment of orthography and pronunciation is a long step toward "the attainment of our language" (5:9). The *Plan* emphasizes facility and attainment; the Preface insists on what criticism can never wash away.

Johnson's different attitude toward his present audience is consistent with his growth and change from the *Plan*. In that work, we recall, he discussed the purchaser and, though addressing himself to Chesterfield, could not escape an occasionally commercial remark. In the Preface the members of the audience are not regarded as an adjunct to Johnson's purse; instead, he hopes to help their minds and guide them toward improved understanding of their language. He has, for instance, sometimes inserted different spellings of the same word, so "that those, who search for them under either form, may not search in vain" (5:26). In order to aid the foreigner, he has clarified anomalies that "interrupt and embarrass the learners of our language" (5:28). Similarly, he has inserted many verbs with a particle subjoined, "as to *come off*" because foreigners have "the greatest difficulty" with these, and no longer need find this difficulty "insuperable" (5:33). Johnson admits that he will not regard his work as "useless or ignoble if by [his] assistance foreign nations, and distant ages, gain access to the propagators of knowledge, and understand the teachers of truth" (5:50).

We have seen several significant changes between the *Plan* and the Preface of Johnson's *Dictionary*. He has abjured Chesterfield and the notions of external authority and a clearly fixable language; he has reconsidered the role of the lexicographer and placed it in its proper necessary but subservient place; he has stopped regarding the audience as purchaser and turned, instead, to the audience as composed of those in need of a reasonably clear path through the boundless chaos of language, so that they may more easily arrive at truth; he convinces us of his wisdom, maturity, and skill necessary for the task; and he makes several allusions to the general puerility of the *Plan*. In sum, he overtly and covertly rejects the *Plan*, many of his own earlier notions regarding language, and much of the rhetorical stance of the brash young man flexing his muscles, convinced of his own omnipotence, but incapable of so convincing us. He becomes the mature and weary man, with a huge effort behind him, and a realization of the failings of the human situation within him. In the process of watching this change we see some of the steps in the making of a great mind and a great English dictionary, the growing intellectual and emotional sophistication of its maker, and his awareness of a central paradox regarding man's nature: the infinite importance and infinite irrelevance of human achievement.

NOTES

1. For extensive details concerning the composition, publication, and reception of the *Plan*, see James H. Sledd and Gwin J. Kolb, *Dr. Johnson's Dictionary: Essays in the Biography of a Book* (Chicago: University of Chicago Press, 1955), pp. 46–84. For reconsideration of some aspects of Sledd and Kolb's view of the writing of the *Plan*, see Jacob Leed's essay—originally presented to the Johnson Society of the Central Region, the University of Wisconsin, 1970—"Johnson and Chesterfield: 1746–47," in *Studies in Burke and His Time* 12 (1970): 1677–90. For an important recent study of the *Dictionary*, see Allen Reddick, *The Making of Johnson's Dictionary 1746–1773* (Cambridge: Cambridge University Press, 1990).

2. *The Museum: or, the Literary and Historical Register* (London, 1747), 3:385.

3. *Boswell's Life of Johnson Together with Boswell's Journal of a Tour to the Hebrides*, ed. George Birkbeck Hill and rev. L. F. Powell (Oxford: Clarendon Press, 1934–50), 1:185. Subsequent references to Boswell's *Life* are to this edition and are cited in the text.

4. Birch, in Hardwicke Papers, vol. 49. Correspondence of the 2nd Lord Hardwicke with Dr. T. Birch 1746–1750; letter dated August 8, 1747, in British Museum Add. Ms. 35,397. I am indebted to Sledd and Kolb pp. 99, 225n. 55, for this and the following reference; Wray, Hardwicke Papers, vol. 53. Correspondence of . . . Hardwicke and D. Wray 1740–67, letter dated August 8, 1747 in British Museum Add. Ms. 35,401.

5. Hawkins, *The Life of Samuel Johnson, LL. D.*, 2nd ed., rev. (London, 1787), pp. 188–89.

6. *The Letters of Philip Dormer Stanhope, 4th Earl of Chesterfield*, ed. Bonamy Dobrée (London: Eyre & Spottiswoode, 1932), 5:2169. Subsequent references to Chesterfield's *Letters* are to this edition. Chesterfield is referring to Sheridan's *British Education* (see n. 18, this chapter), which, he says, "upon the whole . . . is both a very useful and entertaining book."

7. *The Triumph of Wisdom, A Poem: Inscribed to His excellency The Earl of Chesterfield, Lord Lieutenant of Ireland* (Dublin, 1745), pp. 5–6.

8. *Boulter's Monument: A Panegyrical Poem, Sacred to the Memory of . . . the Most Rev. Dr. Hugh Boulter* (Dublin, 1745), pp. 65, 67. In "A Postscript To The Reader" Madden observes that "some Hundred Lines have been prun'd from [the poem] in order to lessen the Tediousness of the panegyrcial Part" (p. 92). These deletions, however, must have taken place for the first edition, and were not seen by Johnson, who read the printed copy, "blotted a great many lines, and might have blotted many more, without making

the poem worse" (*Life*, 1:318). See also Hawkins, *Life of Samuel Johnson*, p. 391, for a more precise account than Boswell offers. I am indebted to Donald J. Greene for advice on this matter.

9. Chesterfield, *Letters*, 4:1217.

10. *The History of the Rise, Progress, and Tendency of Patriotism . . . Dedicated to the Rt. Hon. The Earl of CHESTERFIELD*, 3rd ed. (London, 1747), pp. iv–vi.

11. See *A Letter Humbly Addressed to the Right Honourable, The Earl of Chesterfield* (London, 1750). For comment regarding Mrs. Muilman and Fielding, see F. Homes Dudden, *Henry Fielding: His Life Works, and Times* (Oxford: Clarendon Press, 1952), 2:799n. 2, and Martin C. and Ruthe R. Battestin, *Henry Fielding: A Life* (London: Routledge, 1989), pp. 439, 492.

12. *Remarks on Mrs. Muilman's Letter to the Right Honourable The Earl of Chesterfield. In a Letter to Mrs. Muilman, By a Lady* (London, 1750), p. 56.

13. Chesterfield, *Letters*, 3:1078. Warburton dedicated *The Alliance Between Church and State* (London, 1748) to Chesterfield. See *The Works of the Right Reverend William Warburton* (London, 1788), 4:8–10. Of course there were numerous other works dedicated to Chesterfield. For a few more of these see Willard Connely, *The True Chesterfield: Manners-Women-Education* (London: Cassell & Co., 1939), pp. 493–94. Matthew Maty, Chesterfield's first editor, observes that "it would be equally difficult to enumerate [the praises of Chesterfield while he was Lord Lieutenant], and to point out the best." The value of "common dedications," he suggests, ". . . is exactly in an inverse ratio to what the authors receive or expect for their panegyric": *Miscellaneous Works of the Late Philip Dormer Stanhope, Earl of Chesterfield* (London, 1777) 1:165–66.

14. In 1784 Johnson told Boswell that, though Chesterfield "had more knowledge than I expected . . . in the conversation which I had with him I had the best right to superiority, for it was upon philology and literature" (*Life*, 4:332–33). Paul J. Korshin argues that, as early as 1741, Johnson would have been opposed to Chesterfield's political positions: see "The Johnson-Chesterfield Relationship: A New Hypothesis," *PMLA* 85 (1970): 247–59. Leed, "Johnson and Chesterfield, 1746–47," takes a different view. These changes had solidified by the writing of the *Dictionary*. Maty, writing in the *Journal britannique* for July–August of 1755, criticizes Johnson's style, and adds:

Quand on voit sous les noms des *Torys* & des *Whigs*, & dans quelques autres articles également délicats, des descriptions, qui certainement ne sauraient plaire à ceux qui s'intéressent à l'Administration présente, n'est-on pas tenté de reprocher à l'Auteur, comme un second défaut, la foiblesse qu'il a eue de faire connoitre ses principes de politique et de religion? (17 [1755]:226–27)

See also A. De Morgan, "Dr. Johnson and Dr. Maty," *N&Q*, 2nd Series, 96 (1857): 341. See n. 34 this chapter, and "Johnson Before Boswell in Eighteenth-Century France," within, for further comment on Maty and Johnson.

15. Chesterfield's poems appeared both in "Volume IV" (1748) of the *Collection*, the volume containing poems added to the second edition, and in the first volume of the second edition which appeared in January, 1749. See 4:67–72, and 2nd ed. 1:334–39. The intricacies of Dodsley's *Collection* have been discussed by William Prideaux Courtney, *Dodsley's Collection of Poetry: Its Contents & Contributors* (London: Printed for Private Circulation, 1910 [rpt. New York: Burt Franklin, 1968]); Ralph Straus, *Robert Dodsley: Poet, Publisher & Playwright* (London: John Lane, 1910), pp. 101–52; R. W. Chapman, "Dodsley's *Collection of Poems* (Collations, Lists, and Indexes)," *Oxford Bibliographical Society, Proceedings and Papers* 3 (1933): 269–316; Donald D. Eddy, "Dodsley's *Col-*

lection of Poems by Several Hands (Six Volumes), 1758. Index of Authors," *Bibliographical Society of America. Papers* 60 (1966): 9–30.

16. See Sledd and Kolb, *Dr. Johnson's Dictionary*, pp. 90–93. Most of Chesterfield's remarks concern propriety: he often says, for example, "can one properly say . . . ?"; or "should it not be . . . ?"; or "is it not . . . ?"; or "This is no French expression"; or "is Davis a sufficient Authority"?; or Rowe's "bad Rhyme . . . should not be quoted as an authority."

17. For some of these letters, see Chesterfield, *Letters*, 2:535–36; 4:1390, 1620–21; 5:1860, and J. H. Neumann, "Chesterfield and the Standard of Usage in English," *Modern Language Quarterly* 7 (1946): 468–69. See also the *World*, No. 100, and No. 101 (1754). Both numbers stress the value of a dictionary for the fair sex and their suitors.

18. *British Education: or, The Source of the Disorders of Great Britain* (London, 1756), pp. xvii, vi. Compare Chesterfield, in the *World*, No. 100 (1754). Johnson's *Plan* and Preface, and their attitudes toward fixing the language, have been studied by Scott Elledge. "The Naked Science of Language, 1747–1786," in *Studies in Criticism and Aesthetics, 1660–1800: Essays in Honor of Samuel Holt Monk*, ed. Howard Andersen and John S. Shea (Minneapolis: University of Minnesota Press, 1967), pp. 266–95, especially pp. 266–79. More recently, Leo Braudy has returned to the view, unwarranted I believe, that even in the Preface Johnson wished to fix the language. See "Lexicography and Biography in the *Preface* to Johnson's *Dictionary*," *Studies in English Literature* 10 (1970): 552–56.

19. For Walpole's attack on Chesterfield as a debater, see *Horace Walpole's Marginal Notes, Written in Dr. Maty's Miscellaneous Works and Memoirs of the Earl of Chesterfield*, ed. R. S. Turner (London, 1868?), pp. 6–7; on March 28, 1772, Johnson called Chesterfield "the best speaker in the House of Lords" (*Life*, 2:161). For relevant information concerning Johnson and the Parliamentary Debates, see Benjamin Beard Hoover, *Samuel Johnson's Parliamentary Reporting: Debates in the Senate of Lilliput*, (Berkeley: University of California Press, 1953), pp. 43–44, and passim, Korshin, "Johnson-Chesterfield Relationship," and Thomas Kaminski, *The Early Career of Samuel Johnson* (New York: Oxford University Press, 1987), pp. 123–43. Johnson's remark regarding the erroneous attribution to Chesterfield is in Boswell's *Life*, 3:351.

20. Sledd and Kolb, *Dr. Johnson's Dictionary*, p. 93.

21. *Life*, 1:183. See also Sledd and Kolb: "Johnson went a long way in the composition of the 'Scheme' with no thought of dedication to Chesterfield. Very probably he did not entertain that thought until after he had signed his contract on June 18, 1746" (*Dr. Johnson's Dictionary*, p. 96).

22. Hawkins, *Life of Samuel Johnson*, p. 189. The remark regarding "gilding a rotten post" is also reported in the *Gentleman's Magazine* 64 (1794): 18, and Straus, *Dodsley*, pp. 91–92, but it is clearly a commonplace. See also Thomas Tyers, "A Biographical Sketch of Dr. Samuel Johnson," *Gentleman's Magazine* 56 (1784): 903; Tyers's expanded pamphlet of the *Biographical Sketch* (London, 1785), p. 8; Rebecca Warner, *Original Letters . . . with Biographical Illustrations* (Bath and London, 1817), p. 204. Miss Warner's amplificaton is an interesting example of (probable?) mythologizing:

> One morning, on Mr. [Joseph] Fowke's calling on Dr. Johnson, he found the Sage somewhat agitated. On enquiring the cause, "I have just dismissed Lord Chesterfield," said he; "if you had come a few moments sooner, I could have shewn you my letter to him." Then musing a little, he added, "However, I believe I can recollect it pretty well;" and immediately repeated a very long and very severe epistle; much longer, Mr. Fowke used to say, than that which is given by Boswell.

Mr. Fowke further remarked, that, upon this occasion, Johnson told him, Lord Chesterfield sent a present of 100£ to Johnson, to induce him to dedicate the Dictionary to him; "which I returned," said he, "to his Lordship with contempt:" and then added, "Sir, I found I must have gilded a rotten post! Lord Chesterfield Sir, is a wit among lords, but only a lord among wits."

23. Sledd and Kolb, *Dr. Johnson's Dictionary*, pp. 95–96.
24. The Yale Edition of the Works of Samuel Johnson, vol. 5, *The Rambler*, ed. W. J. Bate and Albrecht B. Strauss (New Haven: Yale University Press, 1969), p. 100. Hereafter referred to as YE with the appropriate citation and details.
25. The incident is reported by Hawkins, who says that he has seen the letter, in his *Life of Samuel Johnson*, p. 329, and Courtney, *Dodsley's Collection*, p. 97. The fullest description of the event is in Edward Cave's letter to Samuel Richardson, August 29, 1750. Cave tells Richardson that, as he suspected, "Mr. *Johnson* is the Great Rambler," and then says:

> When the Author was to be kept private (which was the first scheme) two gentlemen, belonging to the Prince's Court, came to me to enquire his name, in order to do him sevice; and also brought a list of seven gentlemen to be served with the Rambler. As I was not at liberty, an inference was drawn, that I was desirous to keep to myself so excellent a Writer. Soon after, Mr. Doddington sent a letter directed to the Rambler, inviting him to his house, when he should be disposed to enlarge his acquaintance. In a subsequent number a kind of excuse was made, with a hint that a good Writer might not appear to advantage in conversation.

See John Nichols, *Literary Anecdotes of the Eighteenth Century* (London, 1812–15), 5:38–39. The first *Rambler* appeared on March 20, 1750, and *Rambler* No. 14, to which Cave is apparently referring, above, appeared on May 5, 1750. Lloyd Sanders, *Patron and Place-Hunter: A Study of George Bubb Dodington, Lord Melcombe* (London: John Lane 1919), pp. 89–90, accepts Cave's version. It is thus unlikely that the editors of Dodington's *Political Journal*, are correct in their conjecture regarding Johnson and Dodington. On Sunday, January 7, 1750, Dodington records: "At Leicester Fields. Din'd at Lord Poulet's, with Messrs Breton, Mildmay, Johnson, Williams, Ellison." The editors believe that this is "Not improbably Samuel Johnson, then launching The Rambler," since Dodington was known to have made contact with him. It seem to me unlikely that, more than three months before the fact, Dodington would have known anything about the launching; indeed, we do not really know when the *Rambler*'s conception would have been public knowledge. Even if it were known, there is little reason to think that Johnson's achievement to date would have merited an invitation to such an exalted board. Johnson of course is common name. See *The Political Journal of George Bubb Dodington*, ed. John Carswell and Lewis Arnold Dralle (Oxford: Clarendon Press, 1965), p. 35, and 35 n. 2.
26. Straus, *Dodsley*, p. 118. One cannot determine exactly when Johnson made his corrections, particularly since the correspondence of Shenstone and Dodsley concerning Shenstone's contributions makes clear that poems were being sent to Dodsley as late as December of 1754 and January of 1755. See *Letters of William Shenstone*, ed. Duncan Mallam (Minneapolis: University of Minnesota Press, 1939), pp. 308–9. On January 22, 1755, Shenstone states that he expects proof "before the close of this week"; the volume was published in March 1755. Shenstone's packet of his own and his friends' poems was initially sent in December 1753 and January 1754 (Mallam, pp. 307–8; 309–10), though on January 10, 1755, he insists that "The Autumn Verses have been in Dodsley's hands this twelvemonth" (Mallam, pp. 309–10, 283). These works comprised the final section

(pp. 302–63) of the volume. If Dodsley or his printer John Hughes consistently set the works in the order received, the placement of Johnson's poems on pages 156–70 may suggest that Dodsley received Johnson's revised *Vanity of Human Wishes* before January of 1755. Sledd and Kolb suggest that Johnson made the corrections "at about the same time" as he wrote his letter to Chesterfield in February, 1755 (*Dr. Johnson's Dictionary* p. 225 n. 62). This probably is some months too late. Johnson might have changed one word at the last minute, but it seems just as likely that he wrote the definition of "patron" (May, 1753?) and changed "garret" to "patron" within a few months of one another. This last change then may have come late in the autumn or early in the winter of 1753–54.

27. YE 6 *Poems*, ed. E. L. McAdam, Jr., with George Milne (1964), p. 99. I quote Johnson's poetry from this edition.

28. Both definitions are taken from the first edition of the *Dictionary* (London, 1755). The definition of "A flatterer" is also interesting: "a fawner; a wheedler; one who endeavours to gain favour by pleasing falsities."

Again, one can only offer conjecture regarding the dates of composition of specific definitions. On Thomas Birch's authority, Sledd and Kolb report that "by August, 1748 . . . Johnson's amanuenses had almost finished transcribing his authorities; by September, 1749, some part of the *Dictionary* was 'almost ready for the press'; and by October 20, 1750, . . . the first three letters of the alphabet" had been printed (*Dr. Johnson's Dictionary*, p. 107). Johnson started volume 2 (L–Z) in April 1753 and finished most of it "by July or August, 1754" (ibid., pp. 108–9).

29. *The Works of Samuel Johnson, LL. D.* (Oxford, 1825), 5:2. All quotations from the *Plan* and Preface are from this edition, and subsequent page references are cited in the text.

30. *The Letters of Samuel Johnson*, ed. Bruce Redford (Princeton: Princeton University Press, 1992–94), 1:95, 97.

31. For a very different letter to a nobleman, see Johnson's letter of thanks to Bute on July 20, 1762, upon receiving notice of his pension. See Redford, *Letters of Samuel Johnson*, 1:207–8. Johnson also wrote the Dedication to Orrery for Charlotte Lennox's *Shakespear Illustrated* (1753).

32. See Sledd and Kolb, *Dr. Johnson's Dictionary*, pp. 100–104, for relevant comment. See also Maty's remark in *the Journal britannique* (n. 14, this chapter).

33. *The World . . . By Adam Fitz-Adam* (London, 1756), 1:600. Sledd and Kolb observe that Chesterfield's papers were widely reprinted, and in at least two instances writers assumed that Chesterfield was Johnson's active patron and guide (*Dr. Johnson's Dictionary*, p. 103). I have discussed Johnson's possible reactions to these papers in "Johnson's *Dictionary* and the *World*: The Papers of Lord Chesterfield and Richard Owen Cambridge," *Philological Quarterly* 50 (1971): 663–69.

34. *Journal britannique*, July–August 17 (1755): 220, and see A. De Morgan, "Dr. Johnson and Dr. Maty," p. 341. Maty knew Chesterfield well before writing this review, since he records having "a conversation . . . with his lordship, soon after his election into the French academy of *inscriptions and belles lettres*," and offered to write Chesterfield's life to celebrate the occasion (*Miscellaneous Works*, 1:265 n. 3). The academy's offer was made in June of 1755, "which he communicated to me in English, and for the translation of which he did me the honor to borrow my pen" (1:207).

35. Sledd and Kolb, *Dr. Johnson's Dictionary*, p. 89.

36. For "hope," see this example, among many: "Hope is itself a species of happiness,

and perhaps the chief happiness which this world affords" (Redford, *Letters of Samuel Johnson*, 1:203, June 8, 1762, to and unidentified woman). For "fear," see the *Rambler*, No. 110 (1751): "Sorrow, and fear, and anxiety, are properly not parts, but adjuncts of repentance" (YE 4:223). Some of the roles of hope and fear in Johnson's moral thought have been discussed by Paul K. Alkon, *Samuel Johnson and Moral Discipline* (Evanston, IL: Northwestern University Press, 1967), pp. 170–72. Chris Pearce discusses Johnson's own "striking vacillations between pride and humility in the Preface." See his "Johnson's Proud Folio: The Material and Rhetorical Context of Johnson's Preface to the *Dictionary*," *Age of Johnson* 15 (2004): 1–35, p. 23 quoted.

2

What Johnson's Illustrative Quotations Illustrate: Language and Viewpoint in the *Dictionary*

MUCH RECENT SCHOLARSHIP ON JOHNSON'S *DICTIONARY OF THE English Language* (1755) has included three at once overlapping and divergent points of view. The Right sees it as a principled Tory political and theological document. It urges a High Church and Jacobite concept of British culture, for which it should be praised. The Left comparably sees it as a Tory political and theological document that privileges written over spoken, gentleman's over plebeian's, and English over Scottish language and culture. It is an imperialist document for which it should be blamed. Some scholars presumably in the Center also regard the *Dictionary*, but especially its fourth edition in 1773, as a source of illustrative quotations that are politically and theologically agenda driven.[1]

There are two shared assumptions behind these views. One assumption is that in the Preface, definitions, and illustrations, the *Dictionary* is of Johnson's language not of the English language prominent on the title page. Johnson himself, however, says that he does "not form, but register the language"; he does "not teach men how they should think, but relate how they have hitherto expressed their thoughts."[2] The other, related, assumption is that Johnson's own words regarding his mode of proceeding are largely irrelevant to his mode of proceeding. In the 1747 *Plan of an English Dictionary* Johnson says that he will select his authorities for their "elegance of language, or some precept of prudence or piety" (5:20)—that is, generalized secular or spiritual counsel. The Preface itself makes plain that his illustrations came from "fortuitous and unguided excursions into books" and were subject to "industry . . . or chance" not design (5:31). When he was more focused, he sought "from divines striking exhortations" again presumably pious rather than polemical. Those exhortations are within "mutilated" quotations and "are no longer to be considered as conveying the sentiments or doctrine of their authors" (5:38–39). For many ideological critics of the Left, Right, and Center, then, Johnson must either have been uninformed regarding his own intention or said the Thing That Was Not. I propose to examine whether such proponents listen with credulity to the whispers of fancy.

The Case on Either Side

The ideological assumption indeed has eighteenth-century precedent. In 1755 Matthew Maty scolded Johnson for not inculcating virtues presumably exemplified in Maty's patron Lord Chesterfield. Johnson too feebly acquaints readers with proper "principes de politique & de religion." Thomas Edwards was scarcely so oblique. As "a vehicle for Jacobite and High-flying tenets" the *Dictionary* is filled with "many examples from the party pamphlets of Swift, from South's Sermons and other authors in that way of thinking."[3]

This approach is not wholly wrong. Johnson excluded the morally odious Hobbes, the theologically heterodox Samuel Clarke and, so far as I can tell and Milton obviously excepted, any friend to the civil wars and interregnum. Johnson also initially designed the illustrations as moral exemplars, however much his design when practiced wanted modification. Such a concept of language and its organizers also is consistent with a general and a particular Johnsonian given. He regularly regards the world as divinely made: "infinite goodness is the source of created existence."[4] As the agent of that goodness Johnson uses his talent, as recorded in the Matthew 25:14–30 biblical sense and in his elegy on Dr. Levett (1782), to teach religious and moral knowledge through letters. The particular example begins the Preface to the *Dictionary* in which Johnson images himself as the humble pioneer ahead of a civilizing army in a wilderness. Organization must proceed in some way, and Johnson's "pioneering" way of course is broadly moral, Anglican Christian, literary, and English. As he again says in the Preface, he hopes to make his own and other nations aware of the glories of Hooker, Bacon, Newton, and Boyle and certainly of the often cited Shakespeare, Milton, Dryden, and Pope (5:40, 50). Johnson enlivens these and many other ancestral voices for their conversations with posterity.

That much being said, however, it scarcely follows that from 1747 to 1755, or especially for the fourth edition revised from 1771 to 1773, Johnson ordered some 116,000 quotations or their supplements along polemically political or theological lines. He initially compiled his *Dictionary* during about eight years, with the help of his own and borrowed

books, and with the human help of one English and five Scottish amanuenses. Much of the illustrative venture surely was a function of random
accident perhaps aided by those amanuenses rather than coherent design. The consortium of booksellers who wanted Chesterfield as their
patron and who paid Johnson at least £1,575 for the job would not have
tolerated an audience-limiting venture. Johnson himself always was
sympathetic to booksellers' concerns. On July 20, 1763, he thus criticizes Edinburgh's Alexander Donaldson for undercutting the price of
English books. Johnson "uniformly professed much regard" for London
booksellers and lamented that they had too little profit.[5] It would be a
peculiar strategy to filter judgments into his lexicon that were anathema
to then dominant political concepts and to the deserved profit for booksellers' risk. His Preface often mentions the purchaser as an object of
his attention. That commercial sensitivity respected a politically broad
audience willing to spend a substantial £4/10 for a benign rather than
malign text. Apparently the Hanoverian government recognized his lexicon as politically acceptable and worth publicizing. On June 12, 1755,
the British chargé d'affaires presented a copy of the *Dictionary* to the
Académie Française. It gratefully acknowledged receipt, promised its
own dictionary in return, and recognized the international importance
of Johnson's national achievement.[6]

There were indeed genuine differences between religious sects and political groups, perhaps especially so during the years from the late 1670s
to 1714; but there also was essential overlap among them. Gordon Rupp
well argues that we should not "forget the coherent body of convictions
which for Church of England men cut across the labels 'Whig', 'Tory',
or even 'high church' and 'low church.'"[7] As Johnson told Boswell in
1781, "A wise Tory and a wise Whig . . . will agree. Their principles are
the same, though their modes of thinking are different" (*Life*, 4:117).
Johnson also thought Anglicans and Catholics more divided by political—that is national and international competition—than by religious
differences (*Life*, 1:405 and 2:150).[8] When in the *Rambler*, No. 185
(1751), Johnson asks us to exercise "a continual reference of every action to the divine will" (YE 5:209) he speaks of the general human need
for general adherence to a general Western European view of general
Christian theology. Some others indeed occasionally claimed to perceive
a putative ideological agenda in the illustrative quotations; but on commercially prudent and intellectually communal grounds, Johnson
avoided rather than courted such controversy.

We see some of this theological pacifism in his 1755 use of divines
together with, though very different from, Robert South in his often

quoted volume 2 of *Twelve Sermons Preached on Several Occasions* (1694). Here is Tory high-flying South as quoted in part under the adjective "Independent" (1): "creation must needs infer providence, and God's making the world irrefragably proves that he governs it too." Here is Richard Bentley, the Great Satan Modern Whig favorite enemy of Swift and the Christ Church Wits.[9] "Bentley's Sermons" illustrate the adverb "Accurately": "that all these distances, motions, and quantities of matter, should be so *accurately* and harmoniously adjusted in this great variety of our system, is above the fortuitous hits of blind material causes, and must certainly flow from that eternal fountain of wisdom." Here is John Tillotson, William III's Latitudinarian Archbishop of Canterbury on the noun "Frame" (1): "we see this vast *frame* of the world, and an innumerable multitude of creatures in it; all which we, who believe a God, attribute to him as the author." All three draw upon physico-theology confirmed by the divinely ordered Newtonian universe.

I offer one more group of easily multiplied instances of general Christian belief in the *Dictionary*: the further friendly yoking of apparent enemies, as in South and Tillotson. Johnson uses nearly the same number of quotations from each man—about 1,100 in each case. He can do so because of "the coherent body of convictions which for Church of England men cut across the labels 'Whig', 'Tory', or even 'high church' and 'low church' "—as on the afterlife. For the adjective "promiscuous," Tillotson says, "No man, that considers the *promiscuous* dispensations of God's providence in this world, can think it unreasonable to conclude, that after this life good men shall be rewarded, and sinners punished." South shares that view with the adjective "remorseless": "O the inexpressible horrour that will seize upon a sinner, when he stands arraigned at the bar of divine justice! when he shall see his accuser, his judge, the witnesses, all his *remorseless* adversaries." In each case, shared belief dominates differences of tone, nuance, and context. Johnson often thus includes apparent theological and political enemies in one illustrative mosaic. "To Advance" (v.a.) cites both Tillotson and South; "To Affect" (v.a.), "Atheist" (n.s.), and "Beyond" (prep.) cite both South and Bentley; and "Argument" (n.s.) cites both Tillotson and Atterbury.

If we examine South alone, we again see how Johnson moves toward consensus rather than confrontation. As Thomas Edwards's remark makes plain, even in 1755 South was known as a high-flying Tory. That judgment was consistent with aspects of South's 1694 *Twelve Sermons*, but not consistent with Johnson's use of them.

Angry South, Amiable Johnson

Johnson heavily annotated that second volume of abrasive sermons against Latitudinarians and various Dissenters. The Latitudinarians, for example, insisted that *"Little Things"* in worship and doctrine should be abandoned for the sake of Church unity.[10] For South the *Little* is merely the wedge with which the *"Innovating Spirit"* seeks to attack and destroy Anglican doctrine and discipline. South's sermons here are less exposition of faith than aggressive defenses against "the *Hand* which is lifted against us." Such an enemy is as dangerous "in *Ninety-three* . . . [as] in *Forty-one*" (2:sigs. A3^{r-v}) South thus writes against threats of "a Total Abolition" of religion by the same crew of earlier rebels, regicides, and enemies to episcopy. Those motives "in Religion and Religious Matters are generally fatal and pernicious" (2:sigs. A4^{r-v}).

South's sermons reflect the mingled fear and hostility of his Epistle Dedicatory. In his sermons upon Proverbs 10:9 he excoriates drunken wits "magisterially censuring the Wisdom of all Antiquity, scoffing at all Piety, and (as it were) new modelling the whole World" (2:48). "They are enough to make the Nation like *Sodom* and *Gommorha* in their Punishment, as they have already made it too like them in their Sins." In a remark that surely alludes to the Royal Society, South recognizes "a kind of *Diabolical society* for the finding out *new experiments* in Vice" (2:49–50). Dissenters and Latitudinarian churches, we hear about Ecclesiastes 5:2, are "Mints of Treason and Rebellion" at which congregants learn "a *Spirit* of Pride, Faction, and Sedition" (2:160).

The sermon on Romans 1:32 further exemplifies South's rhetoric consistent with other High Church pamphlets and sermons that savage perceived threats to Church and state. These enemies, we now hear, preach doctrines "to be lookt upon as the Devil's Prophets and Apostles." They induce sin in others and one day will be punished as if they "had actually and personally committed it themselves" (2:286). Such Modern casuists are "like the Devil's *Amanuenses*, and Secretaries to the Prince of Darkness." They have taken evil notions from the Devil's cabinet and propagated them through "Magazines and Store-houses of all Immorality and Baseness" (2:287). When the time comes, they will cut our throats, seize our estates, and let "the Rabble . . . loose upon the Government once again" (2:298). In South's tenuous world and fear of *again*, an "*Ocean of Vice* . . . now *swells*, and *roars*, and *lifts up it self* above all Banks and Bands of humane Laws" (2:319). That militant voice recalled 1641 and did everything it could to deny innovation that even hinted at challenges to Anglican episcopacy.

Johnson recognized South's severity. On April 7, 1778, he answers Sir John Pringle's question regarding "what were the best English sermons for style." South "is one of the best, if you except his peculiarities, and his violence, and sometimes coarseness of language" (*Life*, 3:248).[11] Johnson often quoted South in the *Dictionary*, but he also acted on those "exceptions." The quotations overwhelmingly expel South's violence and exclusionary tactics. Instead, they concentrate upon his shared Christian religious values. Many illustrative quotations from South in fact could serve as introductory mottos to the *Rambler*'s Christian moralism. Under the noun "Appellation" we see that "Good and evil commonly operate upon the mind of man, by respective names or *appellations*, by which they are notified and conveyed to the mind." Under the noun "Ardour" (2) we see that "Joy, like a ray of the sun, reflects with a greater *ardour* and quickness, when it rebounds upon a man from the breast of his friend." Under the noun "Avenue" (1) we see that "Truth is a strong-hold, and diligence is laying siege to it: so that it must observe all the *avenues* and passes to it." These are what Johnson meant by "striking exhortations."

We recall that Johnson often truncated and thereby changed the quotations' meaning. Here is one instance of how in 1755 he mingles his own temperament, concern with general truths, and accommodation for space through an illustration from South's sermon on John 3:21: "I am sure, no other *Alteration* will satisfie *Dissenting Consciences*; no, nor this neither, very long, without an utter Abolition of all that looks like Order or Government in the Church" (2:615–16). Johnson uses and abbreviates the sentence to illustrate "Alteration" (2): "no other *alteration* will satisfy; nor this neither, very long, without an utter abolition of all order." As printed, this lacks polemic and neutralizes South's take-no-prisoners anger. Johnson drops the attack upon Dissenters, the specific threat to the Anglican Church, and the consequent particularity. Instead, he moves the remark towards richly human rather than defensively English conduct. In the same sermon South scolds the Catholic Church as vain, proud, putrefied, and "a Church which allows *Salvation* to none without it, nor awards *Damnation* to almost any within it" (2:545–46, 1 John 3:21). Johnson's verb "To Award" (1) again mutes hostility by refusing to name a target: "a church which allows salvation to none without it, nor *awards* damnation to almost any within it."

Such irenic generalizing indeed characterizes Johnson's typical mode of proceeding in his illustrative quotations from South, which generally are not theologically oriented. As a sample by the Canon John E. Wallis long ago demonstrated, only 5.8 percent of the words Johnson quoted from South's sermons "are specifically theological."[12] Most of the quotations indeed also are based on broad Christian belief. Under the adjective "All-wise," for example, we see that "There is an infinite, eternal, *all-wise* Mind governing the affairs of the world." The adjective "Ascendant" (1) tells us that "Christ outdoes Moses, before he displaces him; and shews an *ascendant* spirit above him." This is the orthodox belief that the New Testament supersedes the Old Testament, as Mercy supersedes Justice.

The generalizing and softening mode of proceeding is extensive but not uniform; there surely are exceptions among the illustrations, as with those hostile to atheists, schismatics, and other apparent enemies to the Church. The illustration from South for the adjective "Atheistical" thus reads: "men are *atheistical*, because they are first vicious; and question the truth of christianity, because they hate the practice." Under the noun "Bane" (2) South says that "False religion is, in its nature, the greatest *bane* and destruction to government in the world." Even such occasional forays provide further evidence that Johnson sought agreement available in the received and commonplace dicta of Christian wisdom rather than polemic and confrontation. Robert De Maria, Jr., observes that the "overwhelming majority of theological material in the *Dictionary* is made up of unsophisticated reminders of religious fundamentals." Indeed, "an unwillingness to take sides in intramural religious disputes is characteristic of all of Johnson's religious pronouncements, but he seems to have taken special care to avoid such presumption in the *Dictionary*."[13]

The Revised Version

Thus far I have been dealing with illustrative quotations in the 1755 first edition of the *Dictionary*. One of the *Dictionary*'s most distinguished students also tells us that Johnson's 1773 fourth, revised, text is more polemical: Johnson adds quotations from Stuart, nonjuring, and sometimes Jacobite theologians and others who urge Anglican values against the skeptical tides as, for example, exemplified in the movement to eliminate subscription to the Thirty-nine Articles for university admission. Failure to recognize such change limits oneself to the first edition's less politically engaged approach.[14] Examination of that hypothesis, however, offers results comparable to those for the 1755 text. After all,

Johnson's respect for and gratitude to his booksellers was at least as strong in 1773 as it was in 1755. The vast number of illustrative quotations was but slightly enlarged in the revised version. Immigrants were both swamped by lexical natives and were not singled out as a coherent ideological body. Johnson would oddly overestimate the power of a harmless drudge to think that many readers might notice or be moved by his additions on a fleeting topic, about which even fewer were likely to consult a dictionary.

Moreover, when Johnson discusses agitation against the Thirty-nine Articles he is more dismissive than threatened. He was in the midst of revising the *Dictionary* when on March 21, 1772, Boswell mentioned "the petition to Parliament for removing the subscription to the Thirty-nine Articles." Johnson immediately says: "it was soon thrown out." With Edmund Burke among the leaders, on February 6, 1772, the petition was defeated by the wide margin of 217 to 71 and denied the right to be raised again (*Life*, 2:150–51, 150–51 n. 7). On March 4, 1773, Johnson wrote to the Reverend Dr. William White informing him about relevant political and theological matters: "opposition seems to despond; and the dissenters, though they have taken advantage of unsettled times, and a government much enfeebled, seem not likely to gain any immunities" (*Life*, 2:208).[15] As Johnson thus well knew, attempts to loosen Church authority were defeated and Dissenters thwarted. There is no reason for Johnson to add polemical quotations after the petition "was soon thrown out," and then to respond ideologically and "surreptitiously to the public and parliamentary debates" in order to buttress "symbols of orthodox belief . . . as a reaction to the topical debate."[16] So far as he could tell, even in unsettled times, those orthodoxies were well protected.

Johnson's Advertisement to the 1773 fourth edition alerts readers to the changes he made in the *Dictionary*. He discusses the difficulty and fatigue of his job, the inevitable errors that creep in and that he hopes at least partially to correct, and the nature and quantity of his revisions:

Many faults I have corrected, some superfluities I have taken away, and some deficiencies I have supplied. I have methodised some parts that were disordered, and illuminated some that were obscure. Yet the changes or additions bear a very small proportion to the whole. The critick will now have less to object, but the student who has bought any of the former copies needs not repent; he will not, without nice collation, perceive how they differ; and usefulness seldom depends upon little things. . . . I have left that inaccurate which never was made exact, and that imperfect which never was completed. (5:52)

According to Johnson, then, the new illustrative quotations essentially are imperceptible. The putatively polemical additions must also be a small proportion of a very small proportion. Whether Johnson was wrong about his own practice in 1774 remains now to be considered.

As the Advertisement suggests, focus on one group distorts the breadth of revision in the fourth edition. As some "nice collation" shows, Johnson or someone else corrected typographical errors and changed many etymologies.[17] Under "Yet" (conjunct.) a quotation from South that began with "Thou such men" becomes "Though such men" in 1773. Johnson continued to edit and often condense nonjudgmental quotations, as in the third meaning of the noun "Advantage," in "Superiority gained by stratagem, or unlawful means." I have italicized the words Johnson eliminates: "*it is a noble and a sure defiance of a* great malice, backed with a great interest; *which* yet can have no advantage of a man." He also slightly enhances some definitions or comments (To Baffle, 1; Gird, n.s.), adds other definitions (Arrest, n.s.3), adds illustrative quotations (Avocation, n.s.2; Accommodation, adj. from Tillotson; widely, adv.[2], from South), and drops some words (hence). When Johnson adds a quotation from South in the fourth edition he also is humanly general. Under "Aching" (n.s.) as "Pain; uneasiness," we see that "When old age comes to wait upon a great and worshipful sinner, it comes attended with many painful girds and *achings*, called the gout." For the most part, the other nominal High Church Tory additions are unrecognizable as such and, as Johnson makes plain, are too few to be noticed "without nice collation" that no common reader is likely to endure.

At least as important, though, is Johnson's concept of normally competing nuances within definitions. Johnson's mosaic of quotations is designed to show the several paths to truth that "diversities of signification" encourage (5:41).

This hypothesis gains support when we examine the illustrative quotations in the apparently key term "Unity." That concept long had been the cry of the higher Church of England men. Like South, they regularly accused Dissenters, Latitudinarians, and many Whigs of being agents of darkness. Schism is a sin; unity of Protestants is necessary for protection against the unholy trinity of the devil, Rome, and France. Nonetheless, the dominant example of actual schism was the Altitudinarian nonjurors who both alienated their colleagues and attempted to found their own line of nonjuring bishops.[18] Moreover, lower churchmen also regularly argued on unity. For them, the High Church wrongly excluded their brethren for small matters indifferent, like crossing, the priest's surplice, and genuflection, all of which should be abandoned in the cause of unity among Protestants who overwhelmingly shared belief. The plea for unity thus was not peculiar to one side and is not a necessary ideological marker. Low Church Benjamin Hoadly so spoke to Dissenters in 1704 in the cause of Protestant concord:

> There is no one thing, in which all *Protestants* amongst us, as well as *Dissenters* as *Conformists* do more agree, than in this plain Proposition, *That all causeless and unnecessary Divisions and Distinctions, are most carefully and conscientiously to be avoided by Christians.* In a deep sense of this Truth, the best *Writers* on all sides, have, with one Consent, and with one common Zeal and Concern, pressed upon the Consciences of Men, the Duty and Importance of *Peace* and *Concord*, and the Guilt and Mischief of *needless distinctions and Divisions.*[19]

A call for unity among Christians is demonstrably ecumenical, as indeed was much even of the earlier eighteenth-century Anglican Church. For example, the *Spectator*'s country Tory Sir Roger de Coverly installed an amiable clergyman, to whom he presented a collection of the best English sermons to be read on various Sunday services. Upon inquiring whose sermon he would read next, the clergyman answers that in the morning it is the Whig William Fleetwood, Bishop of St. Asaph, and in the afternoon Tory Robert South. The list of preachers for the year included Latitudinarian Tillotson, Tory Robert Sanderson, Latitudinarian Isaac Barrow, and, probably, the higher churchman Benjamin Calamy.[20] Here indeed is a benevolent theological and social *concordia discors* that increased rather than decreased later in the eighteenth century. In Fielding's *Amelia* (1752), for example, Captain Booth reforms when he reads Isaac Barrow's sermons; but South also was one of Fielding's favorite and admired divines, whom he often quoted and often complimented.[21]

The *Dictionary* quotations themselves under "Unity" generally follow the pattern of general Christian or secular knowledge generally received within general literate culture. As one example, definition 4 is "Principles of dramatick writing, by which the tenour of the story, and propriety of representation is preserved." Johnson there includes a presumably normative illustration from Dryden saying that *All for Love* exactly observes the unities. Immediately thereafter he provides a condensed version of lines from Addison's *Spectator,* No. 409 (1712): the unities should be "thoroughly understood, but there is still something more essential, that elevates and astonishes the fancy."[22] Whatever Johnson's own beliefs, he presents both sides because both sides have eminent authorities for a legitimate alternative regarding what men have thought.

The fourth edition's slightly enlarged discussion of "Unity" includes twelve illustrative quotations from twelve authors for five shades of meaning. There are three changes from the first edition. Johnson adds one quotation from Barten Holyday and one from John Pearson. Neither is recognizably polemic or ideological. Holyday (1593–1661) was Archdeacon of Oxford and indeed a supporter of the Stuart Church and dispensation. By 1773, however, his largely irenic sermons and his deservedly ignored poem *A Survey of the World in Ten Books* (Oxford, 1661) would almost surely have been forgotten.[23] Those who knew the name in 1773 probably would have recalled his posthumously published translation of Juvenal and Persius in 1673, to which Dryden referred and which was familiar to interested readers. Moreover, the illustrative quotation Johnson cites is based on commonplace physics and physico-theology: "take unity then out of the world, and it dissolves into chaos." True enough.

The citation from John Pearson (1613–1688), Bishop of Chester, is comparably pacific. Pearson's well-regarded *Exposition of the Creed* (1659) is a centrist church document that draws upon the Church fathers. It cites three variously mainstream targets of variously mainstream divines: atheists, Photinians—Arians and Socinians who denied the divinity of Christ—and Jews. Socinians, for example, were unprotected by William III's Toleration Act of 1689.[24] By the late 1760s Socinianism had indeed returned to theological argument, but the illustrative quotation from Pearson is innocent of such squabbles. Johnson quotes from "Article IX. The holy Catholick Church, the Communion of Saints." He omits the italics, the biblical citation, and the opening eight words up to "nature." These make plain that Pearson is speaking of Christian charity not dissent: "charity is of a fastning, and uniting nature, [Johnson begins here] nor can we call those many, who *endeavour to keep the unity of the Spirit in the bond of peace. By this*, said our Saviour, *shall all men know that ye are my disciples, if ye have love one to another*. And this is the Unity of charity."[25] Pearson's marginal note identifies the respective italicized sections as from Ephesians 4:3 and John 13:35. He goes outside of his book towards the ultimate religious authority and emphasizes Christian love not anger.

The passage is framed in positive rather than negative terms. In its context it exalts the unity of Christians worldwide as congregants of "one Church. And this under the name of *Church* expressed in this Article, I understand a body, or collection of humane persons professing faith in *Christ*, gathered together in several places of the world for the worship of the same God, and united into the same corporation" (p.

341). Johnson is not likely to have found or encouraged polemic regarding dissent in the Church of England if Pearson is talking about world wide rather than insular Christian unity.[26]

There is another sign of the essential coherence of the illustrative quotations regarding "Unity" from the first to the fourth edition. The third change is small: the removal of the identifying "*b. iv*" from "*Hooker*" (1554?–1613; n.s.3, "Agreement; uniformity"), whose words from *The Laws of Ecclesiastical Polity* (1594–1613) remain the same: "to the avoiding of dissension, it availeth much, that there be amongst them an *unity*, as well in ceremonies as in doctrine." That is from 4.13.2, in a book devoted to the reconciliation of the reformed Church of England with the Church of Rome. By the earlier eighteenth century Hooker had been adopted by at least some Latitudinarian divines as the paternal ecclesiastical voice of contract theory—as in the eighth book among other places: every society has "full dominion over it self. . . . God creating mankinde did indue it naturally with full power to guide it self in whatever kinds of societies soever it should choose to live."[27]

Benjamin Hoadly noticed such remarks and used them to support the concept of limited constitutional monarchy behind the Williamite anti-Stuart revolution. *The Original and Institution of Civil Government, Discuss'd* (1710) characterizes Hooker as overtly founding "*Civil Government* upon the *Voluntary Agreement, Composition,* or *Compact* of the Members of the *Govern'd Society;* from whom *originally* comes all the *Authority* of *Governours.*" The people have "a reserve of *Right* to change" a government they perceive to be intolerable and of which "they were not at first apprehensive."[28] Like "Unity," Hooker's presence in Johnson's quotations signals broad agreement rather than isolated polemic. The father of conservative Anglican order also advocated what would become Lockean theory of a revocable "*Voluntary Agreement*" of people and rulers.

Indeed, according to Hawkins, Johnson filtered Hooker on the obedience of subject to crown "as explained by Hoadly." Johnson thus "condemned the conduct of James the second" during his reign and embraced a position that "leads to whiggism."[29] In this respect, Johnson was the ancestral paradigm of Tory man and Whig measures. Accordingly, within the meaning of "Unity" Johnson encourages us to read illustrative quotations that combine Hooker, via Hoadly, and Milton, Dryden, and Addison, the secular and theological, Tory and Whig. As Carey McIntosh well observes, Johnson typically "implies that no one person or book has all the knowledge his reader needs even from a single field."[30]

JOHNSON AND BEATTIE

One of those fields, though, has been called part of polemic in the fourth edition. Namely, Johnson included quotations from James Beattie's *Essay on the Nature and Immutability of Truth, In Opposition to Sophistry and Scepticism* (Edinburgh, 1770) in his campaign to support "orthodox Anglicanism and its establishment."[31] Johnson's illustrations for "skeptic" and other words suggest otherwise.

For Johnson's culture, "skepticism" (n.s.) like the Pyrrhonism from which it stems, is "universal doubt." The skeptic (n.s.) is "One who doubts, or pretends to doubt of every thing." Under "skeptical" (adj.) Johnson includes words from Bentley in hopes that such painful doubt can be alleviated by divine certainties: "may the Father of mercies confirm the *sceptical* and wavering minds."[32] Under "skeptick" Johnson's citations include Anglican Whig Blackmore, Catholic Pope, and Non-Conformist Isaac Watts who, Johnson said, "every Christian Church would rejoice to have adopted" (*Lives*, 3:303). The illustration from Watts's *Logic*, for example, observes that "The dogmatist is sure of every thing, and the *sceptick* believes nothing." In all cases Johnson generalizes on to human conduct and to the peace that belief may bring. Johnson returns to the conflict between skepticism and mercy by means of the broadly popular *Essay* by that Scottish professor of moral theology.

Johnson and James Beattie were mutually admiring and sympathetic allies when they met at the end of July 1772. On August 3, 1772, Johnson wrote to Boswell saying that "Beattie's book is . . . every day more liked; at least I like it more as I look upon it" (*Letters*, 2:391). The chief skeptic Beattie's *Essay* lashes is David Hume. On the fourth of October 1771 Beattie gave Johnson the second edition of his book with its long postscript. Beattie there defends himself from charges of excess severity, a defense Johnson found convincing and that Burke called "one of the most masterful pieces of eloquence he has ever seen."[33] The Postscript includes a remark that becomes an illustrative quotation for the second definition of the verb to violate, "To infringe": "those reasonings which, by *violating* common sense, tend to subvert every principle of rational belief, to sap the foundations of truth and science, and to leave the mind exposed to all the horrors of scepticism."

Johnson of course rejects skepticism as an acceptable conclusion to rational thought. He just as clearly selects his illustration from an attack upon Hume, who deserves every condemnation appropriate for someone whose values, Beattie argued and Johnson agreed, "are totally subversive of science, morality, and religion both natural and revealed."[34] Beattie does not consider Church of England unity and grants the power of "natural" religion. The bigger fish he hopes to fry is David Hume's apparent attack upon revelation and Christianity. Johnson himself is concerned with human spiritual peace. Anglican theology is a smaller part of something on which all Christians should agree in the face of threats to belief.

CONCLUDING

Johnson indeed occasionally deviates from the straight and narrow of neutral illustration. He also regularly views his job as one of encouraging moral education through broadly Christian values consistent with his Protestant Anglicanism. When he deploys higher churchmen like South or Latitudinarian churchmen like Tillotson, he normally either quotes or modifies quotations so that they embody received and broadly acceptable Christian commonplaces. Though the fourth edition adds several putatively even more "conservative" Church of England men, they often are included with several other illustrations and they too generally utter commonplaces. Moreover, they are merely a part and not the whole of the *Dictionary*'s revisions that include many merely cosmetic corrections as well. The safest and most persuasive way to regard the illustrative quotations is to start by accepting Johnson's stated title. It is *A Dictionary of the English Language* in which he registers rather than forms the language. He does "not teach men how they should think, but relate how they have hitherto expressed their thoughts" (5:44), whether in 1755 or 1773. It is reasonable to assume that Johnson knew what Johnson had done.

NOTES

1. For a study on the Right (as for all of these citations, among others) see J. C. D. Clark, *Samuel Johnson: Literature, religion and English cultural politics from the Restoration to Romanticism* (Cambridge: Cambridge University Press, 1994), pp. 74–75, 125, 130–31, 134, 137, 184–87, 211–12, 237. For some studies on the Left see John Barrell, *English Literature in History 1730–80* (London: Hutchinson, 1983), pp. 144–61, and Tony Crowley, *Language in History: Theories and Texts* (London: Routledge, 1996), pp. 56–57, 60, 81–83. For the Center, see Allen Reddick, *The Making of Johnson's Dictionary 1746–1773* (Cambridge: Cambridge University Press, 1990), pp. 90–91, 94, 120–21, 140–44, 151–69, passim.

2. Preface to the *Dictionary* in *The Works of Samuel Johnson, LL. D.* (Oxford, 1825), 5:44. Johnson may be playing the role of "impartial" lexicographer. Consistency between the early *Plan* and the later Preface nonetheless suggests a link between intention and achievement. I will cite this edition and volume in the text as 5, with appropriate page numbers.

3. Maty, *Journal britannique* 17 (July–August 1755): 227; Edwards, in James H. Sledd and Gwin J. Kolb, *Dr. Johnson's Dictionary: Essays in the Biography of a Book* (Chicago: University of Chicago Press, 1955), p. 135. In contrast, others found the *Dictionary* vulgarly accommodating to inappropriately low speech. See [James Thomson Callender], *Deformities of Dr. Samuel Johnson. Selected From His Works*, 2nd ed. (London, 1782), pp. 53, 60, 68, 71, 74. On p. 74, for example, Callender reminds the reader of "what a profusion of low, and even blackguard expressions are to be met with in the Doctor's celebrated work." See also [Callender], *A Critical Review of the Works of Dr. Samuel Johnson*, 2nd ed. (London, 1783), p. v. Donald T. Siebert has discussed such words in "*Bubbled, Bamboozled,* and *Bit*: 'Low Bad' Words in Johnson's *Dictionary*," *Studies in English Literature* 26 (1986): 485–96. Jack Lynch has conveniently included relevant lists as well as "Ludicrous Words" in his "Index of Piquant Terms" in *Samuel Johnson's Dictionary: Selections from . . . 1755* (Delray Beach, FL: Levenger Press, 2002), p. 642. There are numerous "low" words scattered throughout other categories.

4. The Yale Edition of the Works of Samuel Johnson vol. 3, *The Rambler*, No. 44 (1750), ed. W. J. Bate and Albrecht Strauss (New Haven: Yale University Press, 1969), p. 239. Religion is the speaker. All further references to this edition will be cited in the text as YE with appropriate volume and page number.

5. *Boswell's Life of Johnson Together with Boswell's Journal of a Tour to the Hebrides*, ed. George Birkbeck Hill and rev. L. F. Powell. (Oxford: Clarendon Press, 1934–50), 1:438.

6. "Aujourd'hui Mr de Cosne, chargé des affaires du Roi de la Grand Bretagne, a remis à M^r le Secretaire, un Dictionnaire anglois en deux volumes in folio, dont Mr Johnson, auteur de cet ouvrage fait présent à l'Académie. M^r le Secretaire l'a prié d'assurer Mr Johnson que la Compagnie étoit fort sensible à cette marque d'attention qu' elle reçevoit de sa part, et qu' elle lui en donneroit un preuve en lui en voyant la nouvelle édition de son Dictionnaire, aussitôt qu' elle paroitiroit." See Institut de France, *Les Registres de l'Académie Françoise 1672–1793*, ed. Charles Camille Doucet (Paris, 1895), 3:67. The minutes record "Mrs Mirabaud, Dulivet, Alary, DeBernis, Duclos, Marivaux, De Bissy, Chateaubrun" present at the time. Presentation of the *Dictionary* by the British chargé d'affaires also suggests that the British government thought Johnson sufficiently loyal to act as his agent on an international matter of national pride. One supposes that these eminent men of letters at the Académie also discussed Johnson's *Dictionary* with others. Claude de Thyrad, Comte de Bissy, was admitted to the Académie on December 29, 1750, and was especially interested in British literature. He translated and commented on the first of Edward Young's *Night Thoughts* in Jean-Baptiste-Antoine Suard and François Arnaud's *Variétés littéraires* (Paris, 1768–69), 2:38–62. He also was the lover of Shakespeare Sterne met in 1762, and his surrogate Yorick meets in his *Sentimental Journey* (1768). See *Laurence Sterne. A Sentimental Journey Through France and Italy by Mr. Yorick*, ed. Gardner D. Stout, Jr. (Berkeley and Los Angeles: University of California Press, 1967), pp. 215–33.

7. The Oxford History of the Christian Church, ed. Henry and Owen Chadwick, Rupp, *Religion in England 1688–1791* (Oxford: Clarendon Press, 1986), p. 74. For argu-

ments on later accommodation within the Church of England, see William Gibson, *The Church of England 1688–1832: Unity and Accord* (London: Routledge, 2001).

8. On March 2, 1772, Johnson says that "all denominations of Christians have really little difference in point of doctrine." Forms of worship in Presbyterian and Italian Catholic churches are different, "yet the doctrine taught is essentially the same" (*Life*, 2:150). That clearly is even more true of lower and higher Church Anglicans. See also two other sources. One is the *Life of Boerhave* (1756): however much "Men may differ . . . in many religious opinions . . . all may retain the essentials of Christianity" (6:502), and in the photographic reproduction from the nominal second edition of Browne's *Christian Morals: Early Biographical Writings of Dr. Samuel Johnson*, intro. J. D. Fleeman (Weatherness, England: Gregg International, 1973), p. 470 with slight textual variants. The other source is Sir John Hawkins, *The Life of Samuel Johnson, LL. D.* (Dublin, 1787). Hawkins there quotes Johnson quoting Howells: the "complete Christian" should "have the works of a Papist, the words of a Puritan, and the faith of a Protestant" (p. 479).

9. For some of the bitter "orthodox" hostility to Bentley, see my " 'He Will Kill Me Over and Over Again': Intellectual Contexts of the Battle of the Books," in *Reading Swift: Papers from the Fourth Münster Symposium on Jonathan Swift*, ed. Hermann J. Real and Helgard Stöver (Munich: Wilhelm Fink Verlag, 2003), pp. 225–48.

10. South, Epistle Dedicatory, To the University of Oxford, in *Twelve Sermons*, 2: sig. A2[r], with italics reversed.

11. Compare the use of Smith here discussed and in Robert DeMaria, Jr., *Johnson's Dictionary and the Language of Learning* (Chapel Hill: University of North Carolina Press, 1986), pp. 155–56, 223, 239, with Thomas Edwards's remark, as in Sledd and Kolb, *Dr. Johnson's Dictionary* at n. 3, above.

12. Wallis, "Doctor Johnson and His English Dictionary," *The Johnson Society [of Lichfield] Addresses and Transactions* 4 (1939–53; reprint, 1969): 18. Cannon Wallace, however, does not define what he means by "specifically theological." If one includes references to God, Jesus, or the Church fathers the proportion is higher.

13. De Maria, Jr., *Johnson's Dictionary*, pp. 222, 223. It also seems possible that the addition of older authors was a function of books Johnson acquired from the leavings of his father's bookshop. These well may have included the sort of nonjuring texts that Michael found attractive, but for which the commercial market no longer was friendly. By the early 1770s Johnson's friends also were reluctant to lend him books they knew would be ravaged. He thus would have called on whatever was available from earlier slips and from other books on hand, perhaps including inherited stock. I am indebted to Anne McDermott for this suggestion.

14. Reddick, "Johnson Beyond Jacobitism," *ELH* 64 (1997): 985, 992–93. Reddick had considered and rejected the notion of ideological organization in the first edition: "critical emphasis on the content of the quotations rather than context reflects a misunderstanding of what the *Dictionary* represents and indeed how one encounters it. The vehicle of the text, as arranged by Johnson, is inadequate to the preservation of a consistent didactic programme." See Reddick, "Johnson's *Dictionary of the English Language* and its Texts: Quotation, Context, Anti-Thematics," *Yearbook of English Studies* 28 (1998): 67. As I shall argue, this seems to me accurate for the fourth edition as well.

15. See also the *Journal of a Tour*, in *Life*, 5:64–65, on the need for university students to subscribe the Thirty-nine Articles. For the letter in its modern edition, see, *The Letters of Samuel Johnson*, ed. Bruce Redford (Princeton: Princeton University Press, 1992–94), 2:12–14.

16. See Reddick, "Johnson beyond Jacobitism," *ELH* 64 (1997):988. Reddick offers an excellent brief summary of the petition and its parliamentary fate: pp. 986–88, and 1004 n. 10.

17. For changes in etymology, see Daisuke Nagashima, "Johnson's Revisions of His Etymologies," *Yearbook of English Studies* 28 (1998): 94–105. Robert De Maria, Jr., and Gwin J. Kolb speculate that many of the added illustrative quotations in 1773 were made by the amanuenses. See their "Johnson's *Dictionary* and Dictionary Johnson," ibid., pp. 33–35, based in part by a suggestion from Robert Burchfield, who edited the Supplement to the *OED*. This of course remains conjectural.

18. See Gibson, *The Church of England*, p. 54. Johnson himself said that he never knew a nonjuror who could reason, and described Elijah Fenton's "perverseness of integrity" in refusing the oaths. See, respectively, *Life*, 4:286; *Lives of the Poets*, ed. George Birkbeck Hill. (Oxford: Clarendon Press, 1905), 2:257. Johnson admired the rabid Charles Leslie's energetic reasoning and faith; but he must have disapproved of Leslie's self-alienation from the Church of England. This contrasts with Johnson's admiration for Fenton's refusal to accept such zealous enthusiasm.

19. Hoadly, *A Persuasive to Lay-Conformity: Or, the Reasonableness of Constant Communion with the Church of England; Represented to the Dissenting Laity* (Dublin, 1704), sig. A2ᵛ. Whig and Latitudinarian arguments on unity were especially powerful during the controversial attempt to repeal the Test Act. See David Nokes, *Jonathan Swift, A Hypocrite Reversed. A Critical Biography* (Oxford: Oxford University Press, 1985), pp. 76, 89, 103.

20. See *The Spectator*, No. 106 (1711), ed. Donald F. Bond (Oxford: Clarendon Press, 1965) 1:441–42. For further discussion of the breadth of unity in the eighteenth-century Anglican Church, see Gibson, *The Church of England 1688–32*, passim, and the introduction and several articles in *The Church of England, 1689–1833: From Toleration to Tractarianism*, ed. John Walsh, Colin Haydon, and Stephen Taylor (Cambridge: Cambridge University Press, 1994). Gibson makes plain that Sir Roger's clergyman was characteristic of country parishes that discouraged division and dispute (p. 56).

21. Fielding, The Wesleyan Edition of the Works of Henry Fielding, *Amelia*, ed. Martin C. Battestin (Oxford: Clarendon Press, 1983), book 12, chapter 5, p. 511 and 511 n. 1 for Booth. For South, see pp. 364 n. 1 and 391 n. 3. I owe this reference to Eric Rothstein.

22. Johnson in fact makes Dryden's remark more normative than did Dryden himself. See The California Edition of the Works of John Dryden, vol. 13, *Plays. All for Love . . .* , ed. Maximillian Novak (Berkeley and Los Angeles: University of California Press, 1984), p. 10: "the Unities of Time, Place and Action, [are] more exactly observed, than, perhaps, the *English* Theater requires." For Addison, see *The Spectator*, 3:530. I have italicized the lines Johnson alters or omits exclusive of capitalization and punctuation, at least as based upon the Bond edition. The passage begins with Addison's hopes that authors went beyond "the Mechanical Rules" and "would enter into the very Spirit and Soul of fine Writing." Shortly thereafter he says: "*Thus altho'*in Poetry it be absolutely necessary that the Unities of Time, Place and Action, *with other Points of the same Nature* should be thoroughly *explained and* understood; there is still something more essential, *to the Art, something* that elevates and astonishes the Fancy, *and gives a Greatness of Mind to the Reader, which few of the Criticks besides Longinus have consider'd.*"

23. Holyday's *Motives to a Good Life In Ten Sermons* (Oxford, 1657) are not likely to have offended anyone not looking to be offended by conventional trinitarian orthodoxies.

24. J. C. D. Clark, *English Society 1689–1832* (Cambridge: Cambridge University Press, 1985), p. 283, and Gibson, *Church of England*, p. 15.

25. Pearson, *An Exposition of the Creed. By John Pearson D. D. and Margaret Professor in Cambridge, And Chaplain to His Majestie*, 3rd ed., rev. (London, 1669), p. 341.

26. The career of Thomas Sprat (1635–1713) suggests the danger of labeling someone a "Tory" and then assigning both a political position and public awareness of it. By 1773, Sprat was better known as the historian of the Royal Society (1667) than as the Bishop of Rochester. Though a nominal High Church Tory, he also "assisted at the coronation of William and Mary. It was his hand that added to the service of 5 Nov. the sentences of the church's gratitude for her second great deliverance on that day" (*DNB*).

27. The Folger Library Edition of the Works of Richard Hooker, *Of the Laws of Ecclesiastical Polity*, ed. Georges Edelen (Cambridge, MA: Belknap Press of Harvard University Press, 1977), 1:328. For "full dominion," see *Laws* 8.2.5–10 (3:334). Mark Goldie notes the Whigs' post-Revolution use of Hooker on contract theory. See "The Revolution of 1689 and the Structure of Political Argument: An Essay and an Annotated Bibliography of Pamphlets on the Allegiance Controversy," *Bulletin of Research in the Humanities* 83 (1980): 486.

28. The full title is helpful: *The Original and Institution of Civil Government, Discuss'd. Viz. I. An Examination of the Patriarchal Scheme of Government. II. A Defense of Mr. Hooker's Judgment, &c. against the Objections of several late Writers. To which is added, A Large Answer to Dr. F. Atterbury's Charge of Rebellion: In which the Substance of his late Latin Sermon is produced, and fully examined. By Benjamin Hoadly, M. A. Rector of St. Peter's Poor* (London, 1710), pp. 137–38. Hoadly extensively discusses Hooker.

29. Hawkins, *Life of Samuel Johnson*, n. 8 above, pp. 446–47. If Hawkins was correct, Johnson was more Erastian as well as more Whiggish than is commonly assumed. For further discussion of these points, see "Reading Johnson's Politics" in the last chapter, within.

30. McIntosh, "English Dictionaries and the Enlightenment," *Yearbook of English Studies* 28 (1998): 16.

31. Reddick, *Making of Johnson's Dictionary*, p. 164.

32. Quotations are from *A Dictionary of the English Language* (London, 1755). I am pleased to acknowledge the help of Amanda Kenny with my use of Anne McDermott's splendid Cambridge CD-ROM of the first and fourth editions of the *Dictionary*. It helped me quickly to find the fourth edition's use of Beattie, below. For further such discussion, see also Reddick, *Making of Johnson's Dictionary*, pp. 122, 160, 165–66, and "Johnson Beyond Jacobitism," pp. 983–1005.

33. Burke said this when Beattie visited him on May 14, 1773. See *James Beattie's London Diary 1773*, ed. Ralph S. Walker (Aberdeen: The University Press, 1946), p. 33. The diary includes several instances of Beattie's pleasant and approving visits with Johnson and his friends. See also Everard H. King, *James Beattie* (Boston: Twayne, 1971), p. 22. Beattie's presentation copy, with Johnson's handwritten note on the inner flyleaf, is in the British Library. The conflict between Christian Johnson and skeptic Hume was well remembered. See William Agutter, *On the Difference between the Deaths of the Righteous and the Wicked, Illustrated in the Instance of Dr. Samuel Johnson, and David Hume, Esq. A Sermon. Preached Before the University of Oxford, at St. Mary's Church, On Sunday, July 23, 1786* (London, 1800). Each man, however, here embodies a point of view rather than an individual. For further discussion of Johnson and skepticism, see " 'Obstinate Contests of Disagreeing Virtues,' " within.

34. See the second edition, 1771, of Beattie's *Essay*, p. 539. See also *Life,* 3:11: "those only who believed in Revelation have been angry at having their faith called in question; because they only had something upon which they could rest as matter of fact." For brief discussion and an illustration of Sir Joshua Reynolds's portrait of Beattie and *The Triumph of Truth* (1774) see *Reynolds*, ed. Nicholas Penny (New York: Harry N. Abrams, 1986), pp. 257–59, and Richard Wendorf, *Sir Joshua Reynolds: The Painter in Society* (London: National Portrait Gallery, 1996), pp. 116–17. Frances Reynolds, Sir Joshua's sister, also painted Beattie's portrait. Johnson was part of a larger European movement against skepticism in general and Hume in particular. See John Christian Laursen, "Swiss Anti-Skeptics in Berlin," *Schweizer im Berlin des 18. Jahrhunderts*, ed. Martin Fontius and Helmut Holzhey (Berlin: Akademie Verlag, 1996), pp. 261–81. Laursen demonstrates that Hume was translated to be refuted.

3

The Poetry of Samuel Johnson

SAMUEL JOHNSON'S PREEMINENCE RESTS UPON THE EXTRAORDINARY intellectual and moral achievements within his prose. That truth universally acknowledged nonetheless admits a complementary truth—Johnson is a great prose writer in part because he is a great poet. Johnson wrote poetry throughout his life. Even after a stroke and, later, upon his deathbed he turned to prayer in Latin verse. He wrote a blank-verse tragedy, translations, adaptations of classical poems, satires, love poems, poems warning of the dangers of love, elegies, epitaphs, comic parodies, serious prayers, odes, sonnets, meditations on his inner psychological and spiritual being and, in the nature of things, poems that combined several of these genres. Johnson said that at Pembroke College Oxford his group of student-poets was a "nest of singing birds."[1] However naturally artful, Johnson's poetic production is small in comparison with other great poets, but several of his poems nonetheless are major and minor masterpieces. They include many devices that make his prose memorable, for his prose is memorable in part because it is so poetic. I begin by exploring some of his characteristic modes of proceeding.

1

Johnson's dramatically figurative prose reflects and creates insight. In the Preface to his edition of Shakespeare (1765), for example, Johnson repudiates the largely modern French neoclassical orthodoxies regarding the three unities. We require unity of action, but advocates of the unities of time and place wrongly assume that we think the actors real and the stage really Rome. Johnson reinforces his perception with a startling simile based on the realities of maternal love and fear: "If there be any fallacy, it is not that we fancy the players, but that we fancy ourselves unhappy for a moment; but we rather lament the possibility than suppose the presence of misery, as a mother weeps over her babe, when she remembers that death may take it from her." Johnson's more extensive metaphor characterizes the difference between Shakespeare's copious dramas and classicized French or Addisonian drama: theirs "is a garden accurately formed and diligently planted, varied with shades, and scented with flowers; the composition of Shakespeare is a forest in which oaks extend their branches, and pines tower in the air, interspersed sometimes with weeds and brambles, and sometimes giving shelter to myrtles and to roses; filling the eye with awful pomp, and gratifying the mind with endless diversity." Such images from Johnson's prose could appear in the best poetry. Each encapsulates a complex human activity or response, makes it comprehensible and attractive, and enhances perception or response.[2]

Response is indeed what Johnson seeks both from us and with us. As a benevolent guide he is a companion in enquiry. He knows that we follow our own paths to the place he wishes to guide us, and that he can best help us by offering general guidelines which we as readers particularize. In so proceeding, Johnson follows John Locke in the *Essay concerning Human Understanding* (1690), a portion of which appears in the *Dictionary*'s (1755) third illustrative quotation for the adjective "general": "A *general* idea is an idea in the mind, considered there as separated from time and place, and so capable to represent any particular being that is conformable to it." Such particularizing of the general was a principal of eighteenth-century psychological and aesthetic theory. In the *Spectator*, No. 512 (1712), Addison argues that the enjoyable fable allows the reader to apply "Characters and Circumstances, and is in this respect both a Reader and a Composer." In 1788 Sir Joshua Reynolds praises Gainsborough's "undetermined" portrait manner; his "general effect" reminds "the spectator of the original; the imagination supplies the rest, and perhaps more satisfactorily, if not more exactly, than the artist, with all his care, could possibly have done."[3]

The intimate relationship between the general and the particular, the author and the reader, informs much of Johnson's literary theory and poetic practice. He uses a rich image that suggests two of his *Dictionary* definitions of "conception"—both birth and knowledge—in order to criticize Cowley's excessively detailed description of the archangel Gabriel in *Davideis* (1656): a general idea allows us to "improve the idea in our different proportions of conception."[4] Hence in *The Vanity of Human Wishes* (1749) Johnson invokes History to "tell where rival kings command, / And dubious title shakes the madded land." In such a case, "statutes glean the refuse of the sword" and we learn "How much more safe the vassal than the lord" (lines 29–32). This general statement evokes readers' particular associations: it can apply to ancient Roman civil wars, numerous English dynastic conflicts, the English revolution of the 1640s, the Jacobite rebellions of 1715 and 1745–46, or other comparable situations that readers recognize as conformable to the general statement.

Johnson also uses questions pleasurably to involve us in his poems and in our own education—that is, as his *Dictionary* defines the term, in our nurture and instruction. In 1738 he argues that questions give "the reader the satisfaction of adding something that he may call his own, and thus engage his attention by flattering his vanity." Questions encourage personal involvement and one's "different faculties of memory, judgment, and imagination." In the *Dictionary* Johnson uses an illuminating quotation from Bacon's essay "Of Discourses" to illustrate the verb "To question": "He that *questioneth* much shall learn much, and content much; but especially if he apply questions to the skill of the persons whom he asketh." In a sentence Johnson does not quote, Bacon adds that "he shall give them occasion to please themselves in Speaking, and himself shall continually gather Knowledge."[5] Each side profits from the process of questioning and asking. To be sure, as poetic narrator Johnson normally is the superior questioner, but so long as we also learn, engage various intellectual faculties and are variously pleased, our dialogues with Johnson, with ourselves, and with our culture proceed generously—as we shall see in the Drury Lane "Prologue" (1747) and in *The Vanity of Human Wishes*.

Johnson ably uses two other poetic devices both in his prose and poetry. One device insists on empiricism that urges us to look around us, see reality as it is, gather a large sample from our observation, and draw the appropriate inferences that books and precepts cannot supply. Johnson's poems frequently exhort us to examine, look, mark, observe, remark, see, survey, and then apply the fruits of discovery to our actual lives. He thus often includes varied known tribulations, as in his satire *London* (1738), that includes images of danger familiar to the modern urban dweller, who also understands that "SLOW RISES WORTH BY POVERTY DEPRES'D" (line 177):

> Here malice, rapine, accident, conspire,
> And now a rabble rages, now a fire;
> Their ambush here relentless ruffians lay,
> And here the fell attorney prowls for prey.

(lines 13–16)

Such lines also make clear that Johnson figuratively embodies his empiricism. Personification turns things, abstractions, or emotions into persons. Internal concepts become allegorical actors when empiricism looks inward and through art becomes an observable part of human life. Johnson makes his well-populated poetry visual by means of externalized emotions as well as by "real" individuals in action. That is why in *London* malice, rapine, and accident "conspire" to attack the poor and innocent Londoner. That also is why the opening of *The Vanity of Human Wishes* includes both personification and empiricism. "Observation with extensive view" widely surveys the world's strife, remarks, watches, and can "Then say how hope and fear, desire and hate, / O'erspread with snares the clouded maze of fate" (lines 5–6).

One aspect of Johnson's inner and outer empirical world was its Christianity that so improved classical paganism. Johnson and the small, male, educated classes in the eighteenth century were grateful to have been instructed by Greek and especially Roman literature. Numerous students and their teachers nonetheless shared Milton's familiar assessment in *Paradise Lost* (1667, 1674): classical knowledge was "Vain wisdom all, and false Philosophie!" (2:565). Johnson's Preface to Dodsley's *Preceptor* (1748) provides an appropriate syllabus for young men. He warns his reader to avoid "vitiating his Habits, and depraving his *Sentiments*" and recommends three helpful texts, "two of which are of the highest Authority in the ancient *Pagan* World. But at this he is not to rest; for if he expects to be Wise and Happy, he must diligently study the SCRIPTURES of GOD."[6]

Samuel Johnson himself so studied and so refused to rest on ancient authority. Hence his striking "Upon the Feast of St. Simon and St. Jude" (1726) begins with a characteristic denigration of martial heroism and those who sing "fields with dead bestrew'd around, / And cities smoking on the ground" (lines 1–2). His own "nobler themes" and "nobler subjects" (lines 7–8) will concern the proselytizing martyr saints. They are motivated by heaven not by this world, by God's love not human hate, by God's concern for humanity not for individual acclaim at others' expense, by desire "To raise them from their fall" (line 30) not to push them into a grave. Johnson demonstrates the benevolence of divine victory:

> When Christ had conquer'd hell and fate
> And rais'd us from our wreched state,
>   O prodigy of love!
> Ascending to the skies he shone

Refulgent on his starry throne
Among the saints above.

(lines 19–24)

Johnson's poems, then, often include some of the best traits of his prose, as his prose includes some of the best traits of his poems. They can be at once figurative and realistic, general and particular, empirical and concrete, and personified and apparently abstract. They often engage readers in their own education and encourage response and partnership with a humane, experienced guide. He urges us toward a specific moral end while also recognizing variations in the path we may choose to take. That path, though often bordered with classical flowers, is British and Christian. A fuller examination of several of his poems suggests how well Johnson uses those poetic devices. I shall look first at some of his elegies, prologues, and a splendid poem advising "Stella" how to navigate in the shoals of sexual attraction.

2

Johnson wrote excellent poems honoring the dead. His "Epitaph on Claudy Phillips, a Musician" (1740) responds to David Garrick's reading of Richard Wilkes's roughly comparable six-line epitaph. Johnson said that he would do better and soon recited his own version:

Phillips! whose touch harmonious could remove
The pangs of guilty pow'r, and hapless love,
Rest here, distrest by poverty no more,
Find here that calm, thou gav'st so oft before;
Sleep undisturb'd, within this peaceful shrine,
Till angels wake thee, with a note like thine.

(YE 6:68–69)

Johnson names his subject, celebrates his skills as musician and musical psychologist, and contrasts his rewards in death with his poverty in life. Those rewards are functions both of Phillips's own and of divine goodness. His music removed personal misery; the angels' reciprocating music removes his misery. He gave calm and rest; he receives calm and rest in a temporary sleep before eternal harmony. Johnson's concrete six lines about an obscure musician affirm a profound and general religious system that we also can apply to our lives. One part of that application is awareness that ultimate worth depends more upon inner decency made overt than on grander accomplishments.

"On the Death of Dr. Robert Levet" includes several similar qualities but is longer, more moving, and more personal. Levet was one of the impoverished residents Johnson supported in his home. He especially admired Levet who, though not a licensed physician, had some medical training and walked long distances to help London's yet more indigent families. His peaceful death on January 17, 1782, evoked this poem published in August of 1783, when Johnson knew that his own end was slowly approaching. Johnson honors Levet, records his response to loss, and helps to make that response significant for others.

Hence as "Levet" begins Johnson writes that "we" are all condemned to a daily life in penal mines, and that as we age "Our social comforts drop away" (lines 2, 4). He particularizes the soon-named Levet as one of his social comforts. He is more. Levet medically comforts the poor and, we as readers know, like Johnson himself is "Of ev'ry friendless name the friend" (line 8). He worked "In misery's darkest caverns," among the lonely and hopeless whom he respected and aided (line 17). Though these virtues may be ignored by the powerful world, they are seen by the more powerful God. Johnson strikingly reverses the parable of the talents in Matthew 25:13–30. There the bad servant is eternally punished for burying rather than investing his absent master's gift of a single talent—a sum of money. Here Johnson knows that God will reward his friend who handsomely used God's humble but essential gift:

> His virtues walk'd their narrow round,
>   Nor made a pause, nor left a void;
> And sure th' Eternal Master found
>   The single talent well employed.
>
> (lines 25–28)

Levet's earthly rewards are awareness of a life well spent, a healthy age, a peaceful rapid death, and a consequent freedom from temporal prison. As the allusion to Matthew denotes, the Eternal Master also rewards Levet: "Death broke at once the vital chain, / And free'd his soul the nearest way" (lines 35–36)—nearer to God who welcomes Levet as a good and faithful servant who has entered the far country that is Heaven. Johnson's secular poem spiritually comforts the poet and the poet's readers. As Johnson says in his prologue to Oliver Goldsmith's *The Good Natured Man* (1768), "social sorrow loses half its pain" (line 4).

Johnson's insistence on exchange with readers, on sympathetic questioning that leads to education, extends to some of his five prologues as well. Both the prologues to the new performance of Milton's *Comus* (1750) and to the revival of Hugh Kelly's *A Word to the Wise* (1777), for example, are designed to win audience support for distressed surviving family members. The prologue to Goldsmith's *The Good Natured Man* has a comparable function, for Johnson there lends his authority to his nervous friend's first comedy. As we expect from a form that requires direct address, the prologues also share Johnson's insistence on the author's responsibility to engage the audience in moral or at least in wise aesthetic decisions. The prologue to *Comus* ends with "Yours is the charge, ye fair, ye wise, ye brave! / 'Tis yours to crown desert—beyond the grave" (lines 37–38). He tells the auditors at *The Good Natured Man* that "confident of praise, if praise be due, / [Goldsmith] Trusts without fear, to merit, and to you" (lines 29–30). The very title of Kelly's *A Word to the Wise* allows Johnson to compliment the audience and urge it to exercise "liberal pity" and "bounty" (lines 22, 24).

The best of Johnson's prologues illustrates his view of the reciprocal relationship between author and audience. The full title suggests how well Johnson adapted his poem to the occasion: "Prologue Spoken by Mr. Garrick at the Opening of the Theatre in Drury-Lane, 1747." As new partner and actor-manager Johnson's former student had begun to reform British acting, theatrical business, the stage, and its canon now friendlier to Shakespeare. Though illness kept Garrick from acting, on September 15, 1747, the redecorated Drury Lane theater opened to a performance of *The Merchant of Venice*. Johnson's prologue blends the presence of Shakespeare and of renewal with insistence upon the auditors' role in making a healthy stage. This sophisticated but comprehensible prologue and progress-poem also encapsulates English drama from the late sixteenth to the mid-eighteenth century, and does so with the dominant metaphors of warfare and the extent of a ruler's kingdom. Johnson knows that improvement is a battle. He also knows that the local stage suggests the world beyond its borders and influences and reflects the larger world of real action.

We hear about personified Learning who triumphs "o'er her barb'rous foes." The triumph allows peace, and the military event becomes an emblem of maternal nurture and national identity: when this triumph "First rear'd the stage, immortal SHAKESPEAR rose" (lines 1–2). Like other children he liked to draw imaginative pictures; but his were plays that ignored the unities of time and place:

> Each change of many-colour'd life he drew,
> Exhausted worlds, and then imagin'd new:
> Existence saw him spurn her bounded reign,
> And panting Time toil'd after him in vain.

(lines 3–6)

When Johnson returns to the martial image Shakespeare becomes the benevolent warrior who drafts—impresses—truth into his army and uses his play to conquer an audience: "His pow'rful strokes presiding truth impress'd, / And unresisted passion storm'd the breast" (lines 7–8). Immortal Shakespeare is subject neither to time nor space and lives now as he lived then, in our hearts energized by passion.

The next three stanzas reorient earlier devices and initiate the poem's "progress." The admired but laborious Ben Jonson is "instructed from the school" and associated with a neatly ordered, tentatively advancing European army. He "By regular approach essay'd the heart" and can only win the bays from "Cold approbation." Jonson's regnal image is the finite triangular tomb of an ancient nation: "A mortal born he met the general doom, / But left, like Egypt's kings, a lasting tomb" (lines 9–16). Thereafter, the intellectually and morally slothful Restoration wits look inward and find obscenity all too appropriate for their mirror images in the audience. "They pleas'd their age, and did not aim to mend," but they nonetheless "proudly hop'd to pimp in future days" (lines 22, 24). The grand martial and regnal images in the first two stanzas dwindle to a skirmish and a dynasty in which slavery to mean passions is overthrown by human decency: "shame regain'd the post that sense betray'd, / And Virtue call'd oblivion to her aid" (lines 27–28). The fourth stanza evokes a world of tired elders snoozing to drama crushed by rules, refined into weakness, frigidly cautious, loudly declamatory, and passionless. Though virtue and philosophy remained in this unnatural world, Tragedy was "forc'd at length her antient reign to quit" (line 35). Folly, pantomime, and raucous song replace her.

Johnson brings us to the immediate moment, freezes hitherto rapidly moving time, and requires a decision regarding the future. What will be the direction of Drury Lane, and of British theater in general? Will Lear and Hamlet be replaced by Behn and Durfey? Will boxers, stage farce, flashy machinery, and exotic rope-dancers entertain "distant times" (line 41)? Johnson's brilliant turn makes plain that the audience no longer merely may listen. It must act and decide what it wishes to see. Having already banished the pseudo-Aristotelian rules, Johnson announces the source of theatrical law—the boxes, pit, and gallery now listening to the call for renewal. Lawgivers must be just, wise, and responsible:

> Ah! let not censure term our fate our choice,
> The stage but echoes back the publick voice.
> The drama's laws the drama's patrons give,
> For we that live to please, must please to live.
>
> (lines 51–54)

Johnson's symbolic transfer of the audience to the stage allows him unthreatening incrimination and benevolent return to healthy origins: "Then prompt no more the follies you decry, / As tyrants doom their tools of guilt to die" (lines 55–56). With correct prompting on a corrected stage, Drury Lane can recreate the genius portrayed in the first stanza. We recall its use of Nature, Truth, and Learning's triumph over barbarism that immediately rears the stage and evokes Shakespeare. With Garrick's Shakespearean emphasis and the audience's reformed moral state, a new reign in the British theater can begin with an enlightened people's conscious decision:

> 'Tis yours this night to bid the reign commence
> Of rescu'd Nature, and reviving sense;
> To chase the charms of sound, the pomp of show,
> For useful mirth, and salutary woe;
> Bid scenic virtue form the rising age,
> And Truth diffuse her radiance from the stage.
>
> (lines 57–62)

The Drury Lane "Prologue" is a significant achievement. It harmonizes metaphors, theories of causation, chronological movement, narrative elegance, audience response, and trust in that audience's ultimate intelligence.

Johnson, then, characteristically intrudes upon his poems, making plain that as human beings adrift in a dangerous world we need the guide he is willing to be until revelation replaces reason. Being a moral guide, though, denotes good intentions but not necessarily good poetry. One test of whether the moral also is the poetic is whether the poem persuades and pleases, often in appropriately figurative language. Johnson's best-known poetry handsomely passes such a test. Another of his short poems does so as well and should be better known.

The poem's short action is based upon its long title: "To Miss—— On Her Playing Upon the Harpsichord in a Room Hung with some Flower-Pieces of Her Own Painting" (1738–39?). The woman is both artist and subject of art and is pleasingly threatened by an aggressively amorous but charming young man. In this hothouse environment, "Stella's" music imitates the sounds of Spring as her painting imitates the flowering sights of Spring. Johnson as guide, however, warns her that she is not art but nature, and as such is a tasty meal in a predatory sexual world:

> Ah! think not, in the dang'rous hour,
> The nymph fictitious, as the flow'r;
> But shun, rash youth, the gay alcove,
> Nor tempt the snares of wily love.
>
> (lines 7–10)

The charms of sense, the hopes of conquest, and the vanity of desire accompany her music as she fantasizes that her "unerring art" will enchain the approaching youth and ameliorate his hunt (line 17). Johnson sets his moral song against her amorous song, and his poet's voice of truth against her suitor's voice of hormones-as-love. If she listens, "*Instruction* with her flow'rs might spring, / And wisdom warble from her string" (lines 23–24). Johnson does not refrigerate warm love; he encourages the vulnerable woman to "Mark . . . Mark," properly to see the dangerous world (lines 25, 29, 26), and to balance passion with restraint. Whether in prose or in poetry Johnson hopes to guide us toward a problem's solution. Nature here is the normal passions of men and women in a sensuous, perhaps sensual, springtime environment that for human beings should include desire and limits. Johnson's paradigm for such amiable conflict is the ancient concept of *concordia discors*, of a benevolent God making a world from reconciled opposites. Johnson engages the art of music as a friendly check upon the art of love: notice "How passion's well-accorded strife / Gives all the harmony of life" (lines 31–32). Let energetic nature learn from the already taught lessons of Stella's music and art. Be sufficiently beautiful beautifully to attract; but be sufficiently artful artfully to restrain attraction and thus to restrain danger. Good courtship is like good art, at once free and controlled.

> Thy pictures shall thy conduct frame,
> Consistent still, though not the same;
> Thy musick teach the nobler art
> To tune the regulated heart.
>
> (lines 33–36)

We know that Johnson's own heart was not as regulated as he hoped Stella's would be and that his public and private personas do not always cohere. Johnson the public poet alerts us to the world's dangers and difficulties and helps us to cope with them while we prepare ourselves for a better place. He is a companionate guide who asks questions, urges us to ask improving questions, and continues to help us find answers and options rather than despair and death.

Johnson earned this public posture. He himself had at least three episodes of what psychiatrists call severe agitated depression. He understood the human potential for darkness and the physical and spiritual danger surrender to it entailed. Some of his private poems without a guiding benevolent narrator embody that danger. Johnson wrote and recited "An extempore Elegy" (1778?) with Mrs. Thrale and Frances Burney, and both the assignment of parts and of the stanzas' order are uncertain. The grimly realistic poem was not designed for publication; it nevertheless both skillfully explores some of modern life's dangers for an isolated poor woman and forces the reader to ponder apparent truths.

The poem begins with a flippant dismissal of a prostitute presumably known within her small area. She is "as dead as any nail!" and perhaps in an unmarked pauper's grave (line 2). Her natural and coltish youth colors the description of her body plump as a cherry, her cheeks rosy as a pear, and her "Rump" nubile and sexual: it "made the Neighbours stare" (lines 5–8). Her guilty success soon evokes its own failure and reorients the animal imagery. She does poorly "Till purse and carcase both were low" (line 12) and a country squire removes her from squalor to his rural seat. The final stanza forces us to rethink our response to the beginning of the tale:

> Black her eye with many a blow,
>   Hot her breath with many a dram,
> Now she lies exceeding low,
>   And as quiet as a lamb.

(lines 17–20)

The senseless piece of driven metal becomes a lamb led to slaughter—by her own vain youth, ignorance, and misplaced ambition; by the neighbors who saw and feared her animal attraction; by "her friends and sire" (line 15) who allowed her to be seduced away; and by the larger culture that ignores the brute who apparently beat her to death. Johnson and his admired female colleagues need not overtly homilize. The poem offers an intense inversion, a rapid movement from amused distant observation regarding a dead nail to a theory of causation that makes us potential accomplices. The woman's demonstrably guilty life is replaced by the squire's demonstrably guilty life. Only she pays. If we do not berate him and his context, the guilt is ours. No one else cares enough to mourn her and to mark her perhaps nonexistent stone. Do you?

Two other even darker poems also suggest the difference between Johnson the public and private poet. One is Johnson's Latin poem "Post Lexicon Anglicanum Auctum et Emendatum" (1772). Johnson often would write in Latin, a language that allowed him to hide sensitive thoughts from some others while exploring those thoughts himself. In "Post Lexicon Anglicanum" Johnson records his emotional exhaustion after revising the *Dictionary* for its fourth folio edition (1773).

The episode ignited firestorms of self-examination and self-recrimination. Johnson wonders whether he used his talents well, whether his intellectual and moral life has meaning, and whether he can indeed survive his postpartum depression. From 1755 on, he was known as "Dictionary Johnson," Britain's most distinguished man of letters, and a serious competitor to the best of continental Europe's best. Is that enough? Is it all? Is that what he is designed for? Is it true? Where does he go from here? Is there any where to go?

Johnson begins his sad meditation by likening himself to Joseph Justus Scaliger (1540–1609) who upon finishing his own dictionary regarded lexicography as a form of punishment. Yes, Johnson says no doubt thinking of himself, Scaliger was fit for more exalted tasks. Johnson laments that he cannot match Scaliger's achievements or his extensive and deserved applause. With the revisions finished, Johnson now sees nothing but gloomy idleness, sleeplessness, bouncing from late noisy dinners to solitude, from wanting the night to fearing the day, and perpetual seeking of the unachievable, a superior life. Whatever he does and wherever he is taken, his financial and intellectual limits arrest his efforts. Johnson finds solace neither in nature nor in super-nature, neither in his achievements nor in his potential. He sees only vast silent nocturnal expanses haunted by flitting ghostly shapes.

Like *The Vanity of Human Wishes* the rivetting "Post Lexicon Anglicanum" ends with a series of questions—but without answers. The first recalls a pitiful outburst that begins a work written in prison, John Bunyan's *Pilgrim's Progress* (1678). There Christian dreams of seeing a ragged man, "*a Book in his hand, and a great burden upon his Back.*" He opens the book, reads, weeps, trembles, "and not being able longer to contain, he brake out with a lamentable cry; saying, *what shall I do?*"[7] Johnson the public writer tries to answer that question; Johnson the private writer only raises it. Paradoxically, even in his isolation he asks what Bunyan's Christian and so many others seeking counsel ask—"Quid faciam?" What shall I do? The Latin below is Johnson's; the English is Arthur Murphy's translation for his *Essay on the Life and Genius of Samuel Johnson* (1792):

> Quid faciam? tenebrisne pigram damnare senectam
> Restat? an accingar studiis gravioribus audax?
> Aut, hoc si nimium est, tandem nova lexica poscam?
>
> (lines 52–54)

> What then remains? Must I in slow decline
> To mute inglorious ease old age resign?
> Or, bold ambition kindling in my breast,
> Attempt some arduous task? Or, were it best
> Brooding o'er lexicons to pass the day,
> And in that labour drudge my life away?
>
> (YE 6:274)

Johnson understands our concerns because they are his own.

He also knows that such concerns must be met by individual responsibility within a larger community. Failure to meet obligations, to use one's talent, endangers ourselves and those who depend upon us. Johnson's more overheated youthful political poems excepted, his public voice generally mutes anger. In private he lets us know how he feels—as in the manuscript poem he sent to Mrs. Thrale with a request that she not show it to others.

"Long-Expected One and Twenty" (1780) also is called "A Short Song of Congratulation" for the Thrales' profligate nephew Sir John Lade, who at twenty-one assumes the ancient family estate. The normally optimistic birthday poem regards the day as one among many such happy events. The poem to Sir John rejects that pattern because as a tragic Tony Lumpkin Sir John rejects his communal obligations in favor of sordid personal pleasures.

Sir John now eliminates the voice of parents, guardians, and ancestors, for whom he substitutes "the Bettys, Kates, and Jennys / Ev'ry name that laughs at Care" (lines 9–10)—that is, at guardianship. In so doing, Sir John transforms himself from responsible human male who helps others, to hunted animal on the food chain. Delighted gamblers, moneylenders, and assorted Bettys see their meal out of the covert: "All that prey on vice and folly / Joy to see their quarry fly" (lines 13–14). They so joy because Sir John fails to understand his true role—he is not owner but steward for what his ancestors have given to him and what he should give to his posterity. Sir John regards adulthood as pomp, pleasure, pride, profligacy, and transience. He is "Wild as wind, and light as feather"; he wastes his "grandsire's guineas"; and his wealth wanders (lines 7, 11, 17–18). The consequences are as grave for his inheritance as they are for him: "What are acres? What are houses?" Johnson asks, mimicking and then answering for Sir John: "Only dirt, or wet or dry" (lines 23–24). For Sir John, the busybody filial guides are too dim to recognize his brave new world. For Johnson, such a path leads to the grave: "Scorn their counsel and their pother, / You can hang or drown at last" (lines 27–28). Johnson reduces the cheery birthday poem to a potential deathday poem—for the celebrant, his chronologically extended family, and the estate he will reduce to dirt. Johnson denegrates this violation of duty and failure to carry a burden that is also a privilege. He expresses his anger in the private poem, whereas in a public poem, as indeed in public when he met and at first scolded Sir John, he is more likely to instruct than to blame.

3

London and *The Vanity of Human Wishes* are Johnson's longest nondramatic public poems. Each falls into that rich eighteenth-century genre called the "imitation." In this form, an earlier or even contemporary or foreign poem is adapted to modern British or other different circumstances. Often in the imitation the specific lines adapted are printed on the bottom of the page, on the facing page, or alluded to with their line references. In other cases an author may assume general knowledge of the poem imitated.

As Johnson's lives of Pope and of West make plain, he later disapproved of the genre of imitation because it required knowledge of the parent-poem fully to engage its audience. This is partially true since, as a form, imitation asks us to move between poets, poems, cultures, and centuries. A skillful poet, though, can make the modern work valuable in its own right, however much greater knowledge enhances our pleasure.

Johnson's *London* imitates Juvenal's (AD 60–140?) third satire, a poem in which Umbricius tells his friend that he must leave degenerate un-Roman Rome for the country, where he can find old Roman values. For Juvenal, Rome crumbles through the weight of voracious foreigners, corruption, and crowded urban life. Johnson's adaptation was part of his early, and thereafter repudiated, political opposition to the controversial administration of Sir Robert Walpole. It regards the collapse of London as an emblem of the larger collapse of the nation, laments

French influence and British political decay, and portrays its speaker Thales as having to vacate the morally un-British city. In so writing, Johnson well exploits Juvenal's reputation as the chronicler of Roman decline. Johnson's imitation implies that the government of King George II and of Sir Robert Walpole was doing to Britain what, say, Nero and Domitian had done to Rome.

In the process, Johnson's familiar opposition tactics praise Queen Elizabeth for defeating Spain and blame Walpole for allowing Spain to threaten British trade. The poem is vigorous, vibrant, and often urgent in its youthful anger and characterization of urban danger: "Some frolick drunkard, reeling from a feast, / Provokes a broil, and stabs you for a jest" (lines 228–29). Unlike Pope's imitations, however, *London* lacks a necessary part of successful satire—a speaker, unlike "injur'd Thales" and "Indignant Thales" (lines 2, 34) whom we like and whose judgment we trust. Johnson's rural "elegant Retreat" (line 212) is standard political opposition praise of the country at the expense of Walpole's commercial London; but it lacks the attractive specificity that Pope supplies for Twickenham's squirearchic alternative in *An Epistle to Dr. Arbuthnot* (1735). *London* is better at outrage than at providing a demonstrable political norm. After all, Johnson claims that Britons are too clumsy to be good liars and cheats, rather than that they refuse lying and cheating (lines 144–51).

London is well worth reading, but *The Vanity of Human Wishes* is one of the great poems in the English language. It follows the outline of Juvenal's tenth satire, embraces some of what Johnson thought as its "sublimity," but also uses it as a touchstone rather than an argument on authority.

The two opening paragraphs of *The Vanity of Human Wishes* depict a dark, misty, dangerous world in which Johnson asks us to observe, survey, remark, watch, and only "Then say" how ominous is the world before and within us (line 5). The first paragraph ends with "restless fire precipitates on death" (line 20). The second paragraph ends with "The dangers gather as the treasures rise" (line 28). This world and its actors need correction—if possible, for the poem's title tells us that we are dealing with inherent human nature.

Johnson, however, characteristically provides a theory of causation and, at the least, palliation. We see "wav'ring man, betrayed by vent'rous pride, / To tread the dreary paths without a guide" (lines 7–8), and we observe "How rarely reason guides the stubborn choice, / Rules the bold hand, or prompts the suppliant voice" (lines 11–12). Johnson as narrator hopes to become a guide we will trust and follow.

He takes several approaches within his poem. He unifies different portraits through a common denominator of vain human wishes and
through interlocking metaphors, like collapsing buildings and life as a
battle. The portraits include several classes of human activity, as with
the invading general who takes life and the birthing mother who gives
life. As this example suggests, Johnson contrasts those portraits, so that
the doting and dying old men Marlborough and Swift precede the preg-
nant and optimistic young mother, and the withdrawn scholar anxious
for acclaim in the enclosed academic world appears just before the public celebration for a general's foreign victory. Such breadth and contrast
suggest broad induction and a wide variety of human wishes. As guide,
Johnson uses a plural pronoun to suggest that he shares our human
weakness. The rejected statesman evokes our amused contempt: "now
no more we trace in ev'ry line / Heroic worth, benevolence divine" (lines
87–88). When Johnson invokes the laughing philosopher Democritus
(lines 49–72) to mock eternal folly in the human farce, he reminds us of
the importance of continuing our search before we draw inferences:
"How just that scorn ere yet thy voice declare, / Search every State, and
canvass ev'ry pray'r" (lines 71–72).

Johnson shows his skill in human and moral psychology in several of
the character portraits. Cardinal Wolsey rose so high that he seemed to
threaten his monarch. He is cast down, takes refuge in a monastery,
"And his last sighs reproach the faith of kings" (line 120)—not religious
but secular faith still so important to the prince of the Church. The ambitious Oxford scholar, surely like Johnson himself, must "pause awhile
from letters to be wise" (line 158). The old man "Hides from himself his
state, and shuns to know, / That life protracted is protracted woe" (lines
257–58).

The portrait of Charles XII of Sweden (1682–1718) is deservedly famous. He was the overreaching monarch and general whose bold but
finally fatal attacks terrorized much of Europe. The passage skillfully includes many of Johnson's familiar themes—repulsion with slaughter
that aggrandizes one man and kills and impoverishes thousands; understanding of the human need to glorify heroes; and subtle contrast with
the classical parent-poem and its inadequate moral vision. Characteristic
poetic devices include the metaphor of the insecure building, personifi-
cations that energize the poem with externalized emotions, questions
that further involve the reader, a shocking rapid reversal, and an inference drawn from what we have just seen.

Johnson knows that pompous martial glory and its rewards "With
force resistless o'er the brave prevail" (line 178) as it does for us as ad-

mirers of the apparent national success in which we safely share. Yet this is irrational, for nations may die to celebrate one man, grandchildren may be impoverished to pay for their ancestors' triumphs, and conquerors wreaths will "rust on medals, or on stones decay" (line 190). In that case, "On what foundation stands the warrior's pride?" (line 191)—let us look at Swedish Charles.

He is fearless, tireless, immune to female temptation, and defeats king after king. "Peace courts his hand, but spreads her charms in vain" (line 201), we hear, not surprised by Charles's indifference to feminized peace in favor of masculine, possessive war and the first-person singular that thinks nothing his until "all be mine beneath the polar sky" (line 204). He enjoys only advance and victory until, in a brilliant couplet that encapsulates the brevity of fame, "He comes, not want and cold his course delay;—/ Hide, blushing Glory, hide Pultowa's Day" (lines 209–10). Defeat by Peter the Great leads to collapse, exile, loss of royal authority, and dependence upon hitherto irrelevant women to help him. Johnson anticipates our response, a series of questions that show how we cherish our myths. Surely he could not die ignobly:

> But did not Chance at length her error mend?
> Did no subverted empire mark his end?
> Did rival monarchs give the fatal wound?
> Or hostile millions press him to the ground?
>
> (lines 215–18)

No. He died in obscurity, at an insignificant battle, and perhaps by his own soldiers' hands. The general who extended his power over thousands of miles and men requires only the space of a grave. He leaves "the name, at which the world grew pale, / To point a moral, or adorn a tale" (lines 221–22). The once terrible warrior now is contained in a homily.

Johnson's ultimate target and audience is the human situation—hence he includes Juvenal and his parochial treatment of the North African Hannibal, Juvenal's original of Swedish Charles. When reading the *Vanity* our response includes some kind of compassion for Charles, but pity for Europe and for ourselves. In contrast, Juvenal enjoys the barbarian lunatic's death and miniaturization into Roman schoolboys' declamation. The great empire perpetually triumphs over and torments the elephant driving one-eyed alien who humiliated republican Rome at Cannae (Satire 10:164–66). Johnson is cosmopolitan; Juvenal is local. Johnson is sympathetic; Juvenal is vengeful. Like Democritus, Juvenal is an inadequate guide for the Christian empiricist. The conclusion to the poem further illustrates its moral and poetic grandeur, and satisfies a key expectation of formal verse satire—praise of the virtue opposed to the vice attacked.

The final portrait before the *Vanity*'s conclusion exploits that most enduring and endearing emblem of human renewal—the birth of a child. After all, what parent does not wish to have an attractive child? That child, alas, becomes a prisoner of the dangerous, cloudy, snare-encrusted world of Johnson's first paragraph, but now with special reference to female fragility. He transfers the martial imagery of earlier passages to a siege image in the battle of and within the sexes: "Against your fame with fondness hate combines, / The rival batters, and the lover mines" (lines 331–32). The young woman "falls betray'd, despis'd, distress'd, / And hissing infamy proclaims the rest" (lines 341–42).

By now the reader has been with Johnson on a long journey. He began by urging us to look carefully at the world and "Then say how hope and fear, desire and hate" (line 5) confuse, disorient, and generally lead to failure or death. Enough, we now say. Human desire is indigenous to fallen humanity. If even the wish for a pretty daughter is vain and use-less, what are we to do? The reader virtually breaks into the poem, re-peats some of the earlier key words in this new context, proclaims several questions, and gives Johnson the opportunity to reorient our vi-sion:

> Where then shall Hope and Fear their objects find?
> Must dull Suspence corrupt the stagnant mind?
> Must helpless man, in ignorance sedate,
> Roll darkling down the torrent of his fate?
> Must no dislike alarm, no wishes rise,
> No cries attempt the mercies of the skies?
> Enquirer, cease, petitions yet remain,
> Which heav'n may hear, nor deem religion vain.
> Still raise for good the supplicating voice,
> But leave to heav'n the measure and the choice.
> Safe in his pow'r, whose eyes discern afar
> The secret ambush of a specious pray'r.

(lines 343–54)

The antidote for vain human wishes is non-vain spiritual wishes; the antidote for an unreliable monarch is a reliable God; the antidote for overreaching is trust in God's knowledge of what is best for us. For Juve-nal, god is anthropomorphic; since we create him, we also can create our own improvement. For Johnson, God is the creator to whom we turn to help us control our passions, restlessness, impatience, and anger. "Ill" in this world can never be eliminated; but it can be "transmuted" if we pray for God's "love, which scarce collective man can fill," and "For faith, that panting for a happier seat, / Counts death kind Nature's signal of retreat" (lines 361–64). The poem's final couplet returns us to one of Johnson's key images—the empiricist who looks at the world and draws appropriate inferences. Now, however, that empiricist no longer is the lonely human searcher. Personified "celestial wisdom" also searches and also sees our misery. She can look up, rather than look only to human beings, and so "calms the mind, / And makes the happiness she does not find" (lines 367–68). As Johnson says in his Sermon 12, on Ecclesiastes 1:14, earthly vanity does not infect "religious practices, or . . . any actions immediately commanded by God, or directly referred to him."[8] Revelation removes earthly vanity.

Here is Johnson's alternative to his first paragraph that ends with death and his penultimate paragraph that ends with infamy: find celestial wisdom and you make happiness. Look in the proper celestial direction and the restless mind can be calmed. *The Vanity Human Wishes* was published in 1749, but it includes many of the moral and poetic traits that permeate the best of Johnson's public poetry in English. It answers the darkness in his private poetry in English and Latin, and it does so with a narrator and guide who urges "love, which scarce collective man can fill." We can say of Johnson as a poet and as a man what Johnson said in his "Epitaph on William Hogarth":

> If genius warm thee, reader, stay,
>   If merit touch thee, shed a tear,
> Be vice and dulness far away
>   Great [Johnson's] honour'd dust is here.

(YE 6:268)

NOTES

1. *Boswell's Life of Johnson Together with Boswell's Journal of a Tour to the Hebrides,* ed. George Birkbeck Hill and rev. L. F. Powell (Oxford: Clarendon Press, 1934–50), 1:75.

2. For Shakespeare, see The Yale Edition of the Works of Samuel Johnson, vol. 7, *Johnson on Shakespeare,* ed. Arthur Sherbo (New Haven: Yale University Press, 1968), pp. 78 (mother), 84 (regular). I note other citations to this edition as YE. I quote the poetry from YE 6, ed. E. L. McAdam, Jr., with George Milne (1964). This also is the source of a modernized version of Arthur Murphy's translation of Johnson's "Post Lexicon Anglicanum." Readers seeking an excellent old-spelling edition should see *Samuel*

Johnson: The Complete English Poems, ed. J. D. Fleeman (Harmondsworth, UK: Penguin Books, 1971). Readers seeking a longer overview of Johnson's poetry should see David F. Venturo, *Johnson the Poet: The Poetic Career of Samuel Johnson* (Newark, DE: Univeristy of Delaware Press, 1999).

3. Addison, *The Spectator*, ed. Donald F. Bond (Oxford: Clarendon Press, 1965), 4:318; Reynolds, *Discourses on Art*, ed. Robert R. Wark (New Haven: Yale University Press for The Paul Mellon Centre, 1975), p. 259.

4. "Cowley" in Johnson's *Lives of the English Poets*, ed. George Birkbeck Hill (Oxford: Clarendon Press, 1905), 1:53.

5. Questions, "Examination of a Question Proposed in the [Gentleman's] Magazine of June, p. 310," in YE 10, *Political Writings*, ed. Donald J. Greene (1977), pp. 9, 10; Bacon, *The Essays of Francis Lo. Verulam* (London, 1625), p. 196.

6. *Preceptor*, in *Samuel Johnson's Prefaces and Dedications*, ed. Allen T. Hazen (New Haven: Yale University Press, 1937), p. 188.

7. Bunyan, *The Pilgrim's Progress from this World to That which is to Come*, 2nd ed., ed. James Blanton Wharey and Roger Sharrock (Oxford: Clarendon Press, 1967), p. 8.

8. YE 14, *Sermons*, ed. Jean Hagstsrum and James Gray (1978), p. 130.

4

Johnson's *London* and Juvenal's Third Satire: The Country as "Ironic" Norm

THE AFFIRMATION OF JOHNSON'S DISTINCTION AS A POET HAS RENEWED interest in *London* (1738), his first major poem and the first work that brought him literary reputation. The Juvenalian texts that he used have been meticulously traced; much of the poem's political background and satiric and rhetorical techniques have been discovered; and its successes and failures have become the object of lively, if not always enlightened, controversy.[1] This last issue has an importance beyond that of simple evaluation, for in the case of *London* that evaluation is linked to the larger question of how to read an imitation. We have learned that knowledge of the parent-poem is necessary for understanding of the imitation; but historical reclamation often surrenders to modern impressionism, the Loeb text replaces that of Heinsius or Casaubon, and we read Horace or Juvenal as if they were our rather than Pope's or Johnson's "contemporaries."[2] The reader of *London* needs to know both how Johnson is likely to have read Juvenal's Third Satire and how to acquire such information. The assumption that Johnson read Juvenal as we do leads to inappropriate methodology and mistaken literary criticism. Specifically, according to several recent critics, Johnson failed to see that in Juvenal's Third Satire the poet was ironic and not serious in praising the country, missed part of his point, some of his resonance and, it would seem, some of his greatness as well.

As far as I can tell, this view first reached print in 1959, when Mary Lascelles told the readers of her "Johnson and Juvenal" that Juvenal's

> real theme is not country pleasures but the mingled attraction and repulsion exercised by the great cosmopolitan city. . . . The two men [Umbritius and Juvenal] are represented as going together to the point of departure from Rome, the gate on the Appian Way. There, Umbritius urges his friend to follow his example; but in much of what he says ironic overtones can be heard: in his allusions, for example, to the insignificant, depopulated village where

he means to settle, or the even more desolate regions which Juvenal ought to prefer to Rome's tawdry splendour. These wry hints are surely but the echo of Juvenal's own thoughts: of his inmost certainty that, if life in Rome is disagreeable, dangerous, degrading, outside Rome there is nothing to be called life, at all.[3]

She illustrates Johnson's frail understanding of Juvenalian irony in his portrait of the country seat. When Umbritius describes the place of his retreat, he

> names little hill towns (romantic, perhaps, to us, but for him uncouth, cold, and dull); towns in which, for the price of a Roman garret, you can have the best house there is, with a little patch of kitchen-garden—a *very* little patch; there will be room enough merely to raise the vegetables on which you will have to subsist, with a lizard for livestock. . . . But Johnson turns *hortulus* into a country estate, and Juvenal's sour acceptance of a countryman's life into a little pastoral. . . . In such a mood, [of loneliness and anger in London, Johnson] might perhaps miss the irony in Juvenal's tale of country pleasures, yet find the denunciation of Rome (to which [the country scenes] had been a merely conventional foil) heartily congenial.[4]

Lascelles concludes that "Johnson's *London* has not the brilliance of its original, because it lacks the lightning flash of its irony."[5]

A few years later her view of Juvenal's irony was quoted, approved, and elaborated upon by John Hardy who, in turn, was praised by William Kupersmith.[6] Hardy, Kupersmith says, argues "rightly, that Juvenal's praise of the country is ironic," and he himself insists that it is certainly "wrong to take Juvenal's jokes in 229 and 231 [the one hundred Pythagoreans as guests and the single lizard as subject] as serious descriptions of rural pleasures." More recently still, Ian Donaldson has seconded Lascelles's "shrewdly observed" ironic interpretation.[7]

Such a view of Juvenal's poem, however, has little to recommend it. The statements above have no evidence, contemporary or otherwise, to support them. There is hardly much reference to Juvenal's poem. Instead, we merely have three critics who congenially borrow from and support one another on the strength of *ipsa* and *ipse dixit*. In spite of their arguments on authority, they have not considered the important reading of the Third Satire by William S. Anderson. He argues that Juvenal's poem is about the loss of Roman values in Rome and their preservation in the country. Aquinum has a variety of pleasant associations, like friendship, divinities, and closeness to the land, whereas Rome is stripped of all pleasant connotations and is filled with faults and degeneration from virtue. By the end of the satire, Rome's

> traditional values have abandoned it, and it remains an empty shell, a glittering facade which conceals its total rejection of the past, its complete subjection to foreign and debased practices. In Rome, men violate Nature; in Cumae she constitutes the only immediate attraction. . . . The natural state of things possesses a freshness, an innocence, that can exist only in the country; in Rome, innocence can only be violated, so that the cheap decoration of the fountain [of Egeria] symbolizes the whole scale of tawdry values of the city. As the Satire proceeds, the innocence of Nature comes to represent the original Roman character, and, in the charm of the country, Juvenal sets former Roman customs, Roman clothes, and Roman values now discarded in Rome itself. Since the country really constitutes the last stronghold of the Roman character, Umbricius must withdraw to Cumae, because there alone a true Roman will find satisfaction.[8]

The nonironic reading of the Third Satire's country scenes appears to be literal minded but in fact is profoundly symbolic. That Johnson might have been aware of this interpretation is suggested in his (unsuccessful) attempt to relate the attack on the city to praise of the old virtues of British strength, poverty, defiance of foes, and control of the sea.[9] The ironic interpretation and the implied criticism of Johnson's deafness in not hearing it are denied by one of the best classicists writing on the subject.

Since it is possible that even the best and the brightest can be wrong, however, we should establish criteria for a permitted ironic reading that exists independent of such authority. Let me, then, suggest four ways to determine whether Johnson could or should have read the Third Satire as being ironic: (1) what was Juvenal's characteristic attitude toward the presumed subject of irony in other poems? (2) Does the Third Satire itself demand or exclude an ironic reading of its apparent norms? (3) Is there a tradition of ironic interpretation of Juvenal which Johnson is likely to have accepted? (4) What was Johnson's attitude toward and use of irony in general at the time he wrote *London* and, in particular, did he discuss irony in Juvenal's poem?

1. Juvenal does not often write about the country, but when he does it is appreciative, lyrical, and wholly like the nonironic country of his Third Satire. William Congreve translated the Eleventh Satire for Dryden's 1693 version of Juvenal and Persius, and there tenderly communicated Juvenal's praise of rural life that provides wholesome, humble

food: suckling kid, asparagus, large eggs, rich grapes, and pears. The country farm represents the old Roman values,

> When the good *Curius* thought it no Disgrace,
> With his own Hands, a few small Herbs to Dress;
> And from his little Garden, cull'd a Feast,
> Which fetter'd Slaves wou'd now disdain to taste.[10]

John Dryden Junior's translation of the Fourteenth Satire again emphasizes that the country is the home of the true old Roman values:

> Give me, ye Gods, the Product of one Field,
> As large as that which the first *Romans* Till'd;
> That so I neither may be Rich nor Poor,
> And having just enough, not covet more.
>   'Twas then, Old souldiers cover'd o'er with Scars,
> (The Marks of *Pyrrhus*, or the *Punick* Wars,)
> Thought all past Services rewarded well,
> If to their share at last two Acres fell:
> . . . .
>   Yet, then, this little Spot of Earth well Till'd,
> A num'rous Family with Plenty fill'd;
> The good old Man and thrifty Housewife spent
> Their Days in Peace, and fatten'd with Content.
> Enjoy'd the Dregs of Life, and liv'd to see
> A long-descending Healthful Progeny.
> The Men were fashion'd in a larger Mold;
> The Women fit for Labour, Big and Bold,
> Gygantick Hinds, as soon as Work was done,
> To their huge Pots of boiling Pulse wou'd run:
> Fell too, with eager Joy, on homely Food;
> And their large Veins beat strong with wholesom Blood.
> Of old, two Acres were a bounteous Lot,
> Now, scarce they serve to make a Garden-Plott.

(pp. 299–300)

Juvenal's vision of the country in Satires Three, Eleven, and Fourteen is substantially the same: serious, nonironic, lyrical, and patriotically early Roman.[11]

2. Let us also look carefully at the poem itself, and especially at lines 229 and 231 which we are told are jokes. Since Dryden has eliminated a key word (the Circus becomes the playhouse), here is Madan's literal translation of 1789:

> Could you be plucked away from the Circenses, a most excellent house
At Sora, or Fabrateria, or Frusino, is gotten
At the price for which you now hire darkness for one year.
Here is a little garden, and a shallow well, not to be drawn by a rope,
It is poured with an easy draught on the small plants.
Live fond of the fork, and the farmer of a cultivated garden,
Whence you may give a feast to an hundred Pythagoreans,
It is something in any place, in any retirement,
To have made one's self master of one lizard.[12]

The presumed ironic jokes are the hundred Pythagoreans ("Unde epu-
lum possis centum dare Pythagoraeis")[13] and the single lizard ("Unius
sese dominum fecisse lacertae"). Throughout the poem, however, Umbritius pictures the formerly free Roman enslaved by his own poverty,
the heartless oppression of the rich and ambitious, the illicit triumph of
immoral foreigners, and the decay and dangers of life in Rome. At strate-
gic points he places the exiled Roman in a true Roman setting, where he
may attain humble poverty, hospitality, love of the land and its products
and, most important, control over his own life. It is pitiful that a Roman
must leave his city and define proper mastery as lord of a lizard; but it is
nonetheless preferable to non-Roman slavery in the Greek city still
called Rome.

Moreover, the poet behind Umbritius highlights the contrast between
city servitude and country sovereignty. In the country one can feast one
hundred vegetarian Pythagoreans from his garden, in which his sole subject is a lizard; in Rome we see one hundred humble clients and their
servants coming from a great man's elaborate dole ("Nonne vides
quanto celebretur sportula fumo? / Centum convivae; sequitur sua
quemque culina": lines 249–50).[14] Each servant has the food resting
upon a chafing dish heated by live coals; the dish, in turn, rests upon his
head as he marches to the master's home. The Roman, metaphorically
enslaved to the rich, also enslaves the "Servulus infelix" (line 253) whose
lot is even worse than his master's. There is thus no joke in being lord
of a single lizard and humble host of one hundred invited and equal Pythagoreans: it is, in fact, a position morally superior to the urban Roman
who is one of the one hundred faceless dependents of a rich man and
merely putative master of his own overworked slave. Insistence upon the
loss of real Roman liberty is again made clear late in the poem where the
drunken bully beats the poor Roman and gives him the "liberty" ("liber-
tas pauperis haec est": line 299) of begging to keep a few teeth in his
head. The poor man can only hope that the bully will not also bring him

before a magistrate and charge him with assault. As a free country resident Umbritius will be master of a lizard; as an enslaved city resident he will be tyranized by all. That may be black humor, but Juvenal surely means us to take seriously the emblematic sovereignty over a lizard and the projected invitation to one hundred guests.

3. There is, then, no warrant either in Juvenal's other discussions of the country or in the poem itself for concluding that the country in the Third Satire is presented as anything but a positive norm. Nor is there justification for such a reading in any Latin edition and commentary or English translation or imitation from the early seventeenth to the early nineteenth century or in the work of Boileau and his compatriots in France. I have not been able to examine every possible Latin commentary, but I have seen most of those that Johnson might have seen and will here report on those of Brittanicus and Curio (1627), Schrevelius (1648, 1671 ed. quoted), and Prateus (1684, 1736 ed. quoted). None of these, or any other commentator, sees ironic undercutting of the country anywhere in the poem. Though such scholars are not famous for their wit, they nonetheless were able to see and label irony when they thought it appeared. Prateus, for instance, reading Juvenal's praise of the divine poetry of Codrus (3.207), says: "this is ironic; in fact he called Codrus raucous in Satire I" ("Ironice, Raucum enim Codrum dixit Sat. I" [p. 55]). Brittanicus and Curio comment upon the opening of the poem and Umbritius's decision to go to Cumae. If they had noted irony, here would surely be a place to mention it. Instead, they tell us that Juvenal introduces Umbritius

> who is prepared to quit the city because of its moral depravity: he presents his own account of the city's most outstanding horrors: therefore the poet says: though I am not unmoved because my friend Umbritius is leaving the City, yet because it is all thought out in his mind, I praise his resolution since, leaving Rome behind, he has decided to go to Cumae.[15]

Schrevelius's discussion of the opening is substantially the same and also laments the loss of his dear friend to Cumae, the very ancient city in Campania and the home of the Sybil of Cumae ("Cujus dulci consuetidune & familiaritate mihi carendum").[16] Prateus similarly remarks that Umbritius attacks Rome and is leaving to go to Cumae, the home and shrine of the Sybil.[17] These commentators cannot find anything wrong with Cumae, or the towns Juvenal mentions later in the poem; nor can they see irony in the one hundred Pythagoreans or single lizard. Schrevelius, borrowing from Lubin, includes this gloss on the lizard:

"migrating from the city to whatever place may receive you, that is considered the best home, where you may have a house and garden so small that hardly a single lizard itself can run about."[18] However small the land and its home, it is nonetheless preferable to life in Rome and is "optimum putato domicilium."

The English translations, imitations, and commentaries were of course influenced by the Latin and would have reinforced Johnson's literal reading of the rural virtues. In 1682, for example, Oldham imitates the Third Satire, praises the country in the several expected places, and says that in Kent, or Surrey, or Essex

> Had I the smallest Spot of Ground, which scarce
> Would Summer half a dozen Grasshoppers,
> Not larger than my Grave, tho hence remote,
> Far as St. *Michael's Mount*, I would go to 't,
> Dwell there content, and thank the Fates to boot.[19]

Dryden, who has not often been accused of lacking an ear for irony, is no less explicit in his translation of 1693. He portrays Umbritius as going to "quiet *Cumae*"

> Where, far from noisie *Rome* secure he lives,
> And one more Citizen to *Sybil* gives.
> The Road to Bajae, and that soft Recess
> Which all the Gods with all their Bounty bless.
>
> (p. 31)

Dryden becomes more lyrical when he describes the "Sweet Country Seats" and their "Crystal Streams" that water "all the pretty Spot of Ground."

> There, love the Fork, thy Garden cultivate,
> And give thy frugal Friends a Pythagorean Treat.
> 'Tis somewhat to [be] the Lord of some small Ground
> In which a Lizard may, at least, turn round.
>
> (p. 48)

In 1763 Edward Burnaby Greene's loose imitation attacks the Scottish triumphs in England and shows their power in banishing the English to the barren hills of Scotland.[20] That is the only such negative use of the country within the more than two hundred years I have surveyed. It is the exception that proves the rule, since Burnaby Greene's inversion of country values can best be appreciated only when set against the received interpretation of a positive and revivifying country.

One later eighteenth-century comment upon the lizard will characterize what I think the attitude of the century's readers of Juvenal's Third Satire as a whole. In 1789 Madan says: "the poet means, that, wherever a man may be placed, or wherever retired from the rest of the world, it is no small privilege to be able to call one's self master of a little spot of ground of one's own, however small it may be, though it were no bigger than to contain one poor lizard. This seems a proverbial or figurative kind of expression." Madan's remark is supported both by a note in the Casaubon edition of 1695 and by Smith's more modern Latin *Dictionary*. There, under *lacerta* we see the line from Juvenal's Third Satire, see also that it is "Prov." and that it means "to get a place of one's own, however small."[21]

Furthermore, no less a satiric ironist than Boileau annotated and adapted Juvenal's Third Satire. Although he sees ironic lines in the poem, he fails to see them in the country scene and glosses "Cumae" by describing it as leading to an amiable retreat: "cumes est un passage pour aller à Baies, un rivage fort agréable, une solitude charmante."[22] In 1701 he read and corrected Pierre Le Verrier's commentaries upon hs work and thus provided a gloss upon his own First and Sixth Satires and Juvenal's Third Satire. With slight modifications, the commentary passed into the major editions by Brosette (1717) and Saint-Marc (1747) as the "Avis sur la I. Satire" of Boileau in which a wise philosophe wisely leaves the corrupt city for the country: "c'est une imitation de la troisième Satire de JUVÉNAL, dans laquelle est aussi décrite la retraite d'un Philosophe qui abandonne le séjour de Rome, à cause des vices affreux qui y regnoient. *Juvénal* y décrit encore les embarras de la même ville; & à son exemple, Mr. *Despréaux*, dans cette première Satire, avoit fait la description des embarras de Paris."[23]

This is a sample of the nearly unnimous view of the commentators, translators, and imitators of Juvenal's Third Satire on the Continent, in England, and in America from about 1600 to 1800:[24] they agree that the country as Juvenal presents it is the norm of a poem in which Rome is an antinorm. There is, in short, no tradition of reading which could have shown Johnson that Cumae or the other country retreats were unpleasant.

4. Nevertheless, when faced with so independent a reader as Samuel Johnson, especially the young Sam Johnson, the lack of such a tradition need not exclude the possibility that he could have found irony in the relevant scenes. The preponderance of evidence—so great that it virtu-

ally amounts to proof—is that he in fact did not hear Juvenal's irony because it is not to be heard. We should remember, after all, that Johnson's "Swiftian" political pieces *Marmor Norfolciense* and *A Compleat Vindication of the Licensers of the Stage* were published in 1739 and that *London* itself is filled with ironies—of those who "vote a patriot black, a courtier white,"[25] of Frenchmen who use industry to escape industry (line 113), and of a great man whose palace is destroyed by Heaven and restored in abundance by men (lines 194–209). At this point in Johnson's literary career his ear was as finely tuned to irony as it ever was.

Moreover, the opening of the poem makes clear that we are to see Thales' departure as intelligent and thoughtful. The first speaker echoes Juvenal and insists: "yet still my calmer thoughts his choice commend, / I praise the hermit, but regret the friend" (lines 3–4). Johnson revised the first edition's reading of the following two lines in order to stress Thales' wise decision. He changed the couplet which began "Who now resolves from vice and London far" to "Resolved at length, from vice and London far, / To breathe in distant fields a purer air."[26] As A. D. Moody has shown, Johnson also revised the country scenes in order to make them more attractive.[27]

Perhaps, it might be argued, Johnson really did find irony in the poem but chose to ignore it, since it did not suit his purposes. Though we cannot reclaim Johnson's exact attitude in 1738, we do have several of his subsequent remarks regarding Juvenal's Third Satire. On March 8, 1758, he wrote to Bennet Langton: "I am satisfied with your stay at home, as Juvenal with his friend's retirement to Cumae: I know that your absence is best, though it be not best for me." He then quotes the first three lines of Juvenal's Third Satire—Boswell's note to the *Life* adds the first eight of *London*—and adds: "*Langton* is a good *Cumae*, but who must be Sibylla? Mrs. Langton is as wise as Sibyl, and as good; and will live, if my wishes can prolong life, till she shall in time be as old."[28] Near the end of 1770 when the Reverend Dr. William Maxwell was to return to Ireland, Johnson, Maxwell reports, told him that "he knew, it was a point of *duty* that called me away.—'We shall all be sorry to lose you,' said he: '*laudo tamen*'" (*Life*, 2:133)—that is, from the second line of Juvenal's poem as Johnson rendered it, "Yet still my calmer thoughts his choice commend" (line 3). Finally, on April 9, 1778, Boswell, Johnson, and others discussed the erstwhile lizard without hinting at ironic meanings that no one else found as well:

> One of the company asked him the meaning of the expression in Juvenal, *unius lacertae*. JOHNSON. "I think it clear enough; as much ground as one may have a chance to find a lizard upon."

Commentators [Boswell adds] have differed as to the exact meaning of the expression by which the Poet intended to enforce the sentiment contained in the passage where these words occur. It is enough that they mean to denote even a very small possession, provided it be a man's own. (*Life*, 3:255)[29]

Let me now sum up the findings of the four points regarding irony in Juvenal and its perception, or lack of it, in Johnson: (1) in his other satires Juvenal is consistently favorable to the country and uses it as an emblem of the old Roman values; (2) the Third Satire itself insists that the one hundred Pythagoreans and mastery of a single lizard in the country be contrasted with the one hundred dinnertime dependents and metaphorical enslavement in Rome; (3) English, Latin, and French commentators, translators, and imitators—including some conspicuous ironists—for over two hundred years regard the country sections as serious norms that are not undercut; (4) Johnson was particularly sensitive to irony during 1738 and is not likely to have missed something that was in the poem. His own work on *London* and his subsequent comments as late as forty years thereafter indicate that, like other eighteenth-century readers and commentators, he regarded the praise of the country as clear, positive, and, in its opening at least, warm and touching.

Several obvious but neglected points emerge from this review. In general, an undefended modern interpretation should not be foisted upon an ancient poem; if that poem is the model for an eighteenth-century imitation the student should attempt to reclaim the contemporary reading. In particular, it is misleading to apply a hitherto unknown interpretation of Juvenal's Third Satire to show Johnson's benighted understanding of his parent-poem; and it is similarly misleading to suggest that Johnson's ignorance can explain the comparatively diminished brilliance of *London* or explain aspects of the poem that other hypotheses fail to do. There are many obstacles in the way of "proper" reading of an eighteenth-century imitation: perhaps the first is acceptance of the tautology that it is an eighteenth-century imitation.

NOTES

1. For some of the relevant works, see Edward A. and Lillian D. Bloom, "Johnson's *London* and Its Juvenalian Texts," *Huntington Library Quarterly* 34 (1970): 1–23; Bloom and Bloom, "Johnson's *London* and the Tools of Scholarship," ibid., 34 (1971): 115–39; and "Johnson's 'Mournful Narrative': The Rhetoric of *London*," in *Eighteenth-Century Studies in Honor of Donald F. Hyde*, ed. W. H. Bond (New York: Grolier Club, 1970), pp. 107–44; Howard D. Weinbrot, *The Formal Strain: Studies in Augustan Imita-*

tion and Satire (Chicago: University of Chicago Press, 1969), pp. 165–91; Donald J. Greene, *The Politics of Samuel Johnson* (New Haven: Yale University Press, 1960), pp. 81–111; D. V. Boyd, "Vanity and Vacuity: A Reading of Johnson's Verse Satires," *ELH* 39 (1972): 387–403.

2. For a useful discussion of several pitfalls in the way of reading imitations, see William Kupersmith, "Pope, Horace and the Critics: Some Reconsiderations," *Arion* 9 (1970): 205–19.

3. Mary Lascelles, "Johnson and Juvenal," in *New Light on Dr. Johnson*, ed. Frederick W. Hilles (New Haven: Yale University Press, 1959), pp. 41–42.

4. Ibid., pp. 42–44. Lascelles apparently assumes that Johnson read the Third Satire for the first time, or reread it with new spectacles, while in London during 1737–38. In fact he took "Dryden's Juvenal" with him to Oxford in 1728, and had it with him in 1735. See Allen Lyell Reade, *Johnsonian Gleanings* (London: privately printed, 1928) 5:225, 115; *The Letters of Samuel Johnson*, ed. Bruce Redford (Princeton: Princeton University Press, 1992–94), 1:7–8; James L. Clifford, *Young Sam Johnson* (New York: McGraw-Hill, 1955), pp. 156–57. The rest of this paper deals with the likelihood of Johnson's myopia. Moreover, Lascelles probably is wrong to regard Juvenal's towns as insignificant, cold, dull, and desolate. Aquinum, Baiae, Gabii, Cumae, Fabrateria, Frusino, Praeneste, Sora, Tivoli, and Volsinii were either towns of great beauty, of minor but real commercial, agricultural, or vinicultural distinction, or of religious or historical importance. This information has been gathered in William Smith's *Dictionary of Greek and Roman Geography* (London, 1854). Some of the same information would have been available to Johnson in Strabo, Stephanus's *Dictionarium historicum, geographicum, poeticum* (1561), and Louis Moréri's *Grand dictionnaire historique* (1674).

5. Lascelles, "Johnson and Juvenal," p. 46.

6. John Hardy, "Johnson's *London*: The Country versus the City," in *Studies in the Eighteenth Century: Papers Presented at the David Nichol Smith Memorial Seminar, Canberra 1966*, ed. R. F. Brissenden (Toronto: University of Toronto Press, 1968), pp. 253, 258.

7. William Kupersmith, "Declamatory Grandeur: Johnson and Juvenal," *Arion* 9 (1970): 58 n. 5. This is an otherwise valuable essay. Ian Donaldson, "The Satirists' London," *Essays in Criticism* 25 (1975): 106–22.

8. Anderson, "Studies in Book 1 of Juvenal," in *Yale Classical Studies*, ed. Harry M. Hubbel, 15 (1957): 57–63. Anderson also mentions the manuscript titles of the poem: "De urbis incommodis et de digressu Umbricii," and "Quare Umbricius urbem deserat" (p. 56 n. 29). For further useful discussion of Juvenal's satire along the nonironic lines suggested, see Anna Lydia Motto and John R. Clark, "*Per iter tenebriciosum*: The Mythos of Juvenal 3," *Transactions of the American Philological Association* 96 (1965): 365–76, and William S. Anderson, "*Lascivia* vs. *ira*: Martial and Juvenal," *California Studies in Classical Antiquity* 3 (1970): 1–34.

9. See *The Formal Strain*, pp. 181–89. This association is also suggested by Johnson's probable knowledge of Barten Holyday's "Argument" to his translation of the Third Satire. Since "No place for Honest men is left. . . . / *Umbritius* then from *Rome* departs, / Because he wants the *Roman* Arts" (*Decimus Junius Juvenalis and Aulus Persius Flaccus* [Oxford, 1673], p. 36). Of course Juvenal's poem itself also suggests the disappearance of native virtues, especially at line 119 where, according to Holyday, "No place / Is for a *Roman* left at *Rome*" (p. 39).

10. *The Satires of Decimus Junius Juvenalis*, 3rd ed. (London, 1702), pp. 238–39. Subsequent quotations are from this edition and are cited in the text.

11. Johnson uses lines 5–8, above, as the illustrative quotation for the noun "Mark" in the *Dictionary* (1755). Basil Kennett cites much of the final paragraph as an example of Roman "Panegyricks upon the honest People of the first Ages of the Commonwealth" (*Romae Antiquae Notitia* [London, 1696], p. 63).

12. Madan, *A New and Literal Translation of Juvenal and Persius* (London, 1789), 1:137–39. Samuel Derrick's *The Third Satire of Juvenal Translated into English Verse* (London, 1755), pp. 15–16, describes comparable "rural joys" (p. 15). Thomas Sheridan's prose translation of 1739 (reprinted 1745, 1769, 1777) also is faithful to a similar vision.

13. All Latin quotations from the Third Satire are from *D. Junii Juvenalis, et A. Persii Flacci Satirae*, ed. Ludovicus Prateus, 7th ed. (London, 1736). As the Blooms have shown in "Johnson's *London* and Its Juvenalian Texts" (see n. 1), this was the text (but not necessarily this reprint) which Johnson knew best, though the annotations of Schrevelius were more influential.

14. For a brief statement regarding "The Duties of a 'Client'" in Juvenal's Rome, see Jérôme Carcopino, *Daily Life in Ancient Rome: The People and the City at the Height of the Empire*, trans. E. O. Lorimer (London: George Routledge and Sons, 1946), pp. 171–73.

15. "Introducitque Umbritium haruspicem sui temporis amicum suum, parantem ob pravitatem morum ab Urbe discedere: cui ad notanda vitia dat partes suas. Ait ergo Poeta: quamvis non possim non commoveri, quod amicus meus Umbritius ab Urbe discedat, tamen habita discessus ratione laudo ejus consilium, quod relicta urbe Roma, statuat migrare Cumas," as quoted in *D. Junii Juvenalis . . . Satyrae*, ed. Henricius Christianus Henninius (Utrecht, 1685), p. 455.

16. *D. Junii Juvenalis et Auli Persii Flacci Satyrae*, ed. Cornelius Schrevelius (Leyden, 1671), p. 56.

17. Prateus's "Interpretatio," a prose gloss in simpler Latin, reinforces the meaning of the lines and of the commentary: see pp. 37–38 and 56–57.

18. "Ex urbe migrans quocunque te receperis, optimum putato domicilium, ubi tuam habeas domum & hortum tam exiguum, ut vix una ipsum discurrat lacerta. *Lubin*" (Schrevelius, p. 89).

19. Oldham, *The Works of Mr. John Oldham, Together with his Remains* (London, 1686; new pagination and title page for *Poems and Translations. By the Author of The Satyrs upon the Jesuits* [London, 1684], p. 199).

20. Burnaby Greene, *The Satires of Juvenal Paraphrastically Imitated, And Adapted to the Times* (London, 1763), pp. 33–34. On August 18, 1763, Gibbon records his initiation to the Third Satire, and praises it without mentioning irony. By September 16, he had read the Fourteenth Satire as well and was impressed with the simple country scene described above ("Extraits de mon journal," in *Miscellaneous Works*, ed. John Lord Sheffield [London, 1796], 2:95–96, 113).

21. Madan, 1:138; I. and M. Casaubon, with J. C. Scaliger and H. C. Henninius, *D. J. Juvenalis Satyrae . . . accedit Auli Persi Flacci* (Leyden, 1695), p. 908 n. 231; Sir William Smith, *A Smaller Latin-English Dictionary*, rev. J. F. Lockwood (London, 1962 [1st. Ed., London, 1855]). The illustrative or "iconographic" evidence also supports the conservative view of Cumae as a place for one's retreat. The illustration in Holyday's *Juvenal* facing p. 47 shows a pleasant coast, groves, roads, and different structures, including theaters, homes, and military camps, on the way to Cumae. Holyday tells us that this "Baian prospect and delight" is from "Bertellius in his Theater of the Italian Cities" (p. 44). The

illustration to Dryden's *Juvenal* is more eloquent, if less pleasant, facing p. 30 (3rd ed., 1702): the walls of Rome are in the background and Umbritius and Juvenal, at the edge of the Tiber, are in the foreground. Behind them is the once sacred grove of Numa in which, from left to right, we see a rape, the untended altar of the god overgrown with weeds, Jewish merchants plying their wares, and one of the sacred trees being chopped down. Behind Umbritius and Juvenal are the farmer's two horses being whipped forward by the servant and a cart which holds two children and a variety of personal effects, including what may be the household gods.

22. Boileau, *Satires de Perse et de Juvénal. Expliquées, traduites et commentées par Boileau, publiées d'après le manuscrit autographe, par L. Parrelle* (Paris, 1827), 1:169. See also *Les Satires de Boileau commentées par lui-même et publiées avec notes par Frédéric Lachèvre: reproduction du commentaire inédit de Pierre le Verrier avec les corrections autographes de Despréaux* (Courmenil: Le Vésinet, 1906), p. 55. Bossuet, among others, seconded Boileau's interpretation. In 1684 he commented upon the satires of Juvenal and Persius for the benefit of the Grand Dauphin of France. He glosses "vacuis" (line 2) in this way: "c'est a dire que Cumes est une ville vuide des desordres et des embarras de Rome; c'est une raison fort bonne qui oblige Unbritius d'y aller habiter." He says of the lizard (line 231): "être le maitre de quelque chose; on dit encore *unius vermiculi*" (see *Oeuvres inédites de J.-B. Bossuet. . . . Tome I: Le Cours royal complet sur Juvénal*, ed. Auguste-Louis Ménard [Paris, 1881], pp. 81, 100). The translations by Martignac (Paris, 1683), Tarteron (Paris, 1695), and Dusaulx (Paris, 1770; 2nd ed. 1782; 3rd ed. 1789) are silent regarding irony.

23. *Oeuvres de Boileau Despréaux*, ed. M. de Saint-Marc (Amsterdam, 1772), 1:14. Italics and Roman type are inverted in the text.

24. For a convenient gathering of further comments in Latin, see the Casaubon edition (n. 21 above) and its "Cento variorum." For other translations and comments in English see *Juvenal's Sixteen Satyrs,* trans. Sir Robert Stapylton (London, 1673); [Thomas Sheridan], *Satires of Juvenal . . . With . . . Notes, Relating to the Laws and Customs of the Greeks and Romans* (London, 1739); *The Satires of Decimus Junius Juvenalis,* trans. William Gifford (London, 1802); Gifford's Juvenal was reprinted in Philadelphia in 2 vols. In 1803; *Satires of Decimus Junius Juvenalis*, trans. Rev. William Heath Marsh (London, 1804); *A New Translation with Notes, of the Third Satire of Juvenal,* trans. John Duer (New York, 1806); *The Satires of Juvenal,* trans. Francis Hodgson (London, 1807). The relevant commentary concerns the opening of the poem and the main country passage, especially lines 229 and 231. Other translators like Edward Owen in 1785, for example, say nothing, presumably because they regard the lines as clear enough without their gloss. Hodgson (pp. 32, 376–77) believes that Juvenal himself wishes to stay in Rome; he does not attribute irony to Juvenal but sees tolerance for the needs of his less literary friend.

25. The Yale Edition of the Works of Samuel Johnson, vol. 6, *Poems,* ed. E. L. McAdam, Jr., with George Milne (New Haven: Yale University Press, 1964), p. 50, line 53. Subsequent quotations are from this text as YE 6.

26. YE 6:48 n. 5.

27. A. D. Moody, "The Creative Critic: Johnson's Revisions of *London* and *The Vanity of Human Wishes,*" *Review of English Studies,* n.s. 22 (1971): 140–41.

28. *Boswell's Life of Johnson Together with Boswell's Journal of a Tour of the Hebrides*, ed. George Birkbeck Hill and rev. L. F. Powell (Oxford: Clarendon Press, 1934–50), 1:324–25. Subsequent quotations are from this edition.

29. For some of these interpretive squabbles, see Casaubon, *Juvenalis Satyrae,* p. 908; Gifford, *Satires,* pp. 97–98; Hodgson, *Satires,* p. 380. Boswell's final remark is justified.

5

No "Mock Debate": Questions and Answers in *The Vanity of Human Wishes*

"THEY WHO ARE DEMANDED BY OTHERS, INSTANTLY ROUSE THEM-selves with eagerness to make a reply; so this Figure of question and answer leads the hearer into a persuasion, that what is the effect of study is conceived and uttered without any premeditation." So Longinus says when discussing Demosthenes' use of questions, and when summing up much of this aspect of rhetorical theory among the ancients. He adds that "the spirit and rapidity of the question and answer, and the Orator's replying upon himself, as if he was answering another, not only ennoble his oration, but give it an air of probability."[1] In *The Vanity of Human Wishes* (1749) Johnson's own questions also achieve this sense of imme-diacy and exchange, of vigorous involvement between narrator and reader; they also help to make his poem convincing and to engage us in our own schooling.

Johnson's poetic technique is as firmly rooted in contemporary psy-chology and pedagogy as in ancient rhetoric. Questions, Johnson says in July 1738, allow "the reader the satisfaction of adding something that he may call his own, and thus engage his attention by flattering his van-ity." They encourage us to respond with our own thoughts, and summon our "different faculties of memory, judgment, and imagination." In the Preface to Dodsley's *Preceptor* (1748) Johnson shows how graduated questions can lead to the student's expanded vision and understanding through dialogue with and guidance by his benevolent master. The stu-dent should not merely answer the question with its own words, since that may be a limited and limiting act of memory. Instead, "it is always proper to vary the Words of the Question, to place the Proposition in different Points of View, and to require of the learner an explanation in his own Terms, informing him however when they are improper. By this Method the Scholar will become cautious and attentive, and the Master will know with Certainty the Degree of his Proficiency." Exchange, education, and pleasure therefrom are also present in Johnson's definitions and illustrations of the verb "To question," and also suggest that these traits were associated with the concept of questioning. The word means "1. To enquire . . . 2. To debate by interrogatories." The illustration of "To enquire" is drawn from Bacon's essay "Of Discourse": "he that *questioneth* much shall learn much, and content much; but especially if he apply his questions to the skill of the persons whom he asketh. For," Bacon adds in a sentence not quoted, "he shall give them occasion, to please themselves in Speaking, and himselfe shall continually gather Knowledge."[2]

In such a process, both teacher and student, poet and reader, must be willing to seek and share knowledge. In 1759 Edmund Burke stated his procedure in the *Enquiry* into the sublime and beautiful, one related to Johnson's own practice:

> I am convinced that the method of teaching which approaches most nearly to the method of investigation, is incomparably the best; since not content with serving up a few barren and lifeless truths, it leads to the stock on which they grew; it tends to set the reader himself in the track of invention, and to direct him into those paths in which the author has made his own discoveries, if he should be so happy as to have made any that are valuable.[3]

Burke's "method" obliquely describes one of Johnson's important techniques in *The Vanity of Human Wishes*, one that is in the manuscript of the poem and thus is his own, and not a compositor's. Johnson's generous poetics of reciprocity uses questions to help his speaker enlarge both the dramatis personae and the historical and chronological sweep of his poem. He also directly questions the reader and engages him first in an assumed and then in a more vocal dialogue. As the poem progresses, he allows us to try on different psychological roles (the harsh, the sympathetic), as well as choices of life (the statesman, scholar, hero), to see the weaknesses in each, and to enter into the poem ourselves, either in our own voice or in a voice that could be ours and is spoken for us by the perceptive speaker who knows how we will reply. He leaves us with the most likely series of questions a proper co-investigator, or perhaps fellow student in a Socratic dialogue, would have arrived at, for he has come to "the stock on which" spiritual truths grow: "where then shall Hope and Fear their objects find?" (line 343).[4] The clear discrimination between kinds of questions, some of which are scarcely veiled imperatives, nonetheless has an obvious and necessary common denominator—interrogation itself, and its consequent dialogue, energy, probability, education, and pleasure.

A recent commentator on the poem has argued that the *Vanity* "derives its structure from a search for a point of view" through questions.[5] That useful remark needs modification: it is not the poem or its narrator that seeks a point of view, but the reader, the questioner, the very object of keen but good-humored satire who is seeking what the poem already has, and who must learn to dismiss his own pernicious wishes for earthly success.[6] As Edward Young said in 1719, "he that asks the guilty person a question, makes him, in effect, pass sentence upon himself."[7] As Young could not have known, however, "the guilty person" in the *Vanity* also finds the way to help redeem and reprieve himself, and thereby to "learn much, and content much," and he does so in part by means of the accusatory questions themselves. I shall examine, seriatim, the *Vanity*'s different questions in order to see how they help us to move from frantic worldly to calming celestial wisdom.

1

The *Vanity* opens with a massive overview by observation with extensive view, a personification that remarks and watches man's strivings for happiness, and then says how we make a difficult job worse by our folly and vain human wishes. History (line 29) soon joins observation and tells of the dangers to those in high places. The vassal, however, is appreciably safer than his lord; the simple farmer, with nothing worth having, is secure as "confiscation's vulturs hover round" (line 36) his betters and feast on the carrion that is their estate. "The needy traveller," the itinerant rather than stable poor man, is equally "secure and gay" (line 37) on his path across the dangerous and perhaps thief-infested heath.

That is the context of Johnson's first question and of the first role he chooses for us to investigate. Why, after all, should the ignorant and socially inferior hind be happier than his industrious and ambitious master? Why should those of us apparently blessed with the ability to serve the nation be victims of "anxious toil" and "eager strife" (line 3) while the useless underling "sings his toil away" (line 38)? Johnson gives his reader the unpleasant power to remove that happiness by allowing us to give the poor man wealth and by assuming that he would accept the offered prize. "Does envy seize thee? crush th' upbraiding joy, / Increase his riches and his peace destroy" (lines 39–40). Fears in dreadfully ranked order "invade" (line 41) his mind, and pain and alarm follow naturally. The "wild heath" (line 38), which previously reflected the serenity of the traveler's song, now reflects his anxiety as both "rustling brake . . . and quiv'ring shade" alarm him (line 42).

The vassal's joy may be crushed, but the human condition has not changed; we have, after all, learned nothing from this resentful aggression in a continuously restless world, for "gain and grandeur [still]load the tainted gales" (line 46). Perhaps, however, someone wiser than ourselves or the ignorant traveler, someone with a classical genealogy, can change the situation through the mockery it deserves. Johnson thus invokes Democritus (*ca.* 400 BC) as an enlargement of our own lack of sympathy for our fellows. Observation and history merely relate the facts; Democritus responds to those facts with the sardonic laughter that much of Juvenal's Tenth Satire has for its victims. Democritus scorned his own relatively innocent culture; he would do more in the face of modern "motly life" (line 51):

> How wouldst thou shake at Britain's modish tribe,
> Dart the quick taunt, and edge the piercing gibe?
> Attentive truth and nature to descry,
> And pierce each scene with philosophic eye.
> All aid the farce, and all thy mirth maintain,
> Whose joys are causeless, or whose griefs are vain.
>
> (lines 61–68)

This passage has often been taken as Johnson's own voice wrongly adopting an inappropriate Juvenalian tone.[8] I suggest, instead, that Johnson is offering the reader another vantage point—overtly by means of the sort of question he raises on Democritus's behalf, but covertly on the reader's behalf. Is man in fact the subject of a farce worthy of laughter? Are his joys causeless and griefs vain? Does this pagan with his savage arsenal of taunts, darts, and piercers offer a path to truth and nature that a modern Christian would find acceptable? Juvenal's Democritus was placed next to Heraclitus, the weeping philosopher, as alternate ways of coping with the world. Juvenal chooses to ignore tears in favor of harsh mockery, and adopts Democritean tones thereafter. Johnson was not likely to have been as favorably impressed with the Greek philosopher, or to have allowed his readers to think that Democritus was the stock of his own truths. He eliminates both Juvenal's praise of Democritus as evidence that a wise man could come from a land of dunces, and all references to Heraclitus. Johnson replaces the choice between mockery and tears with a choice between mockery and love; he moves from Democritus and Heraclitus to Democritus and Johnson with the benevolent God behind him.

Johnson's abnegation of Democritus is predictable enough. Though Democritus was often given high praise, he was associated with Epicurus' and Lucretius' atheistic theory that the universe was created by the accidental union of atoms; he denied that the soul was incorporeal and immortal, and insisted that it perished with the body; he preferred retreat and speculation to practical experience, may have blinded himself, and even shut himself up in a tomb the better to meditate and test the strength of his imagination; he allowed suicide for those frustrated in the world; he seemed to have starved himself to death in his weariness of old age; and he claimed that "All Man is from his very Birth a disease" without hope of cure.[9] Lest we forget or be ignorant of those facts, or lest we remain willing to destroy another's peace, Johnson as speaker adds an implied question of his own, a question that is without precedent in his parent-poem, and is not directly answered now because we must do so ourselves, and will have done so with a silent negative by the time the poem ends.[10]

> Such was the scorn that fill'd the sage's mind,
> Renew'd at ev'ry glance on humankind;
> How just that scorn ere yet thy voice declare,
> Search every state, and canvass ev'ry pray'r.
>
> (lines 69–72)

Democritus is a philosopher who detaches himself from humanity, whose scornful mind merely glances at the world as he confuses the part with the whole, and who assumes that incorrigible man must forever be a subject of jest and a character in a farce (lines 52, 67).[11] We are invited to join the Christian narrator, who also invites observation, its extensive view, and history to help us in our examination of the external, every state, and internal, every prayer, so that we can try to change and to earn a part in God's divine comedy. Johnson's questions and our response make us skeptical of Democritus's philosophy as a norm, for his harsh view is as useless as the envious one we ourselves have just abandoned.[12] The conclusion of the poem will make clear the inferiority of pagan isolation and severity. There, religion leads us to "love, which scarce collective man can fill" (line 361), and to celestial wisdom, which calms rather than agitates the mind (line 367). Indeed, it would be logically impossible for Johnson to regard Democritus's views as "just" if he is to begin his final paragraph with another question and a sign of the continuing search: "where then shall Hope and Fear their objects find?" (line 343). It also would be theologically inconsistent in the poem and in his larger thought to hold that philosophy or reason, and not religion, could give the comfort which the reader is seeking. In Sermon 25, for example, which Johnson wrote for the funeral of his wife (1752), he urges that in the face of death few could "solace their passage with the fallacious and uncertain glimmer of philosophy." Religion is "our only friend in the moment of distress, in the moment when the help of man is vain." The reflections of "the voice of truth" offer "that comfort which philosophy cannot supply, and that peace which the world cannot give."[13]

Moreover, even two apparently normative words regarding Democritus might have evoked a context foreign to Johnson's values. He is supposed to have "chearful wisdom and instructive mirth" (line 50), neither of which is in Juvenal. Granting his "chearful" quality in the face of human suffering, "instructive mirth" is nonetheless tainted praise, and offers instruction different from that Democritus intended. Johnson defined the adjective "instructive" simply as "Conveying knowledge"; he illustrated the word with a conflation of a slightly longer line in Addison's *Spectator*, No. 179 (1711): "I would not laugh but in order to instruct; or if my mirth ceases to be instructive, it shall never cease to be innocent." It seems reasonable to assume that Johnson reread or at least recalled the *Spectator* in the months immediately preceding the writing of the *Vanity* in the fall of 1748, and that Addison's "Mirth ceases to be Instructive," as the *Spectator* had it, was either the evocative source or clear analogue of Johnson's invention of a Democritean "instructive mirth." Mr. Spectator, certainly a friend to good humor, also insisted that his humor must be "Innocent," and suppress "Stroaks of Raillery" and "glances of Ill-nature."[14] Democritus's "instructive mirth" came trailing sentimental clouds uncongenial to a pagan's mind filled with scorn, the justice of which already is doubtful.

Questions have allowed us to test and discard or suspect different roles, and thus to "reply" to the speaker. Johnson continues this approach in his discussion of the fallen statesman, who is a microcosm of all those who "mount, . . . shine, evaporate, and fall" (line 76); but he also is a particular instance of our vain wish to rise and succeed in this world. Johnson thus poses a question on the statesman's behalf and phrases it so that it may come from the reader and represent a familiar defense mechanism—namely, is there not a mistake? Will the nation rectify the error? If it does not, the nation, alas, is utterly corrupt. Like most other modern students of the poem, I have considered this passage an expression of Johnson's own attitude toward British politics in 1749.[15] It now seems to me that he is presenting the dismissed statesman's own point of view and is showing that it is either hyperbolic or solipsistic.

Johnson also is showing the statesman's vanity both in being suppliant to Preferment and to Fortune and in blaming anyone but himself for the consequences.

> But will not Britain hear the last appeal,
> Sign her foes' doom, or guard her fav'rites' zeal?
> Through Freedom's sons no more remonstrance rings,
> Degrading nobles and controuling kings;
> Our supple tribes repress their patriot throats,
> And ask no questions but the price of votes;
> With weekly libels and septennial ale,
> Their wish is full to riot and to rail.
>
> (lines 91–98)

These intemperate remarks do not characterize the severe but generally sympathetic voice in *The Vanity of Human Wishes*. If the speaker's question is correct, his wish to be a highly placed statesman would not be vain, for he would then return to (say, Walpolean?) ministerial power at the head of a prudent nation, and that opposes Johnson's intention in the poem. If the declarative sentence is correct, the statesman was foolish to wish to lead such a people in the first place. Moreover, there is no evidence in the portrait to suggest that he was or deserved to be Britain's favorite; we know only that he hoped to rise, not that he deserved to rise. The glowing inference is the statesman's about the statesman, and we need not accept it. Of course the British, as we often hear in the poem, ask far more "questions but the price of votes." Finally, the speaker's separation of himself from those he satirizes is precisely what Johnson hopes we will learn to avoid. The words I italicize in "Our supple tribes repress *their* patriot throats" and "*Their* wish is full to riot and to rail" are un-Johnsonian satiric thrusts in a poem that finally insists upon our collective responsibility for vice and our collective potential for God's love.

Since the portrait of a fallen, unregenerate Wolsey exemplifies the transient power of the statesman, the corrected reader will dismiss such a choice of life; he has learned the danger of public exposure and public greatness. Johnson thus takes a new tack with the fourth set of questions. Hitherto we have temporarily tried the roles of powerful envier, of Democritus, and of statesman, and seen how each was inadequate. By now the questioning reader is ready to enlarge his share in the debate and perhaps reconsider the previous role of humble poor man, the role he envied and tried to destroy; but we are educated, perhaps are gentlemen, and so must raise our expectations. After the portrait of Wolsey, the reader is presumed to be more active than before, and is prepared for a new role and a new question, one that bears its own dangers.

> Speak thou, whose thoughts at humble peace repine,
> Shall Wolsey's wealth, with Wolsey's end be thine?
> Or liv'st thou now, with safer pride content,
> The wisest justice on the banks of Trent?
> For why did Wolsey near the steeps of fate,
> On weak foundations raise th' enormous weight?
> Why but to sink beneath misfortune's blow,
> With louder ruin to the gulphs below?
>   What gave great Villiers to th' assassin's knife,
> And fixed disease on Harley's closing life?
> What murder'd Wentworth, and what exil'd Hyde,
> By kings protected, and to kings ally'd?
> What but their wish indulg'd in courts to shine,
> And pow'r too great to keep, or to resign?
>
> (lines 121–34)

We are encouraged to say—no, Wolsey's wealth and end will not be mine; or we are not likely to say more than the answers above couched as questions in the final couplet of each paragraph. We may add that perhaps the pleasures of rural peace, safer pride, and wisest justice are what we should wish to have after all; let us retire to private life. Accordingly, Johnson moves us to the relative obscurity but intellectual brilliance of the academy, where the "fever of renown" (line 137) breaks out in the desire to publish learned tomes for a learned university. Yet here too he challenges us with a question: "Are these thy views?" (line 141). This instance of safer pride still tortures the unwary, who must "Deign on the passing world to turn thine eyes, / And pause awhile from letters, to be wise" (lines 157–58). Such wisdom shows us that the earlier views were radically myopic and led to poverty or, if successful as in Laud's case, precisely the dangers of eminence that the private life was to obviate. The human condition, in our present cast of mind, is such that we invariably so repine at humble peace, cannot have safe pride, and seek control of others and the world's superlatives of any sort ("wisest justice") at a high price.

This is nowhere more apparent than in the portrait of Charles of Sweden, the most magnetic and destructive military hero of his age and a man, Johnson told Boswell, more attractive than the civilized and cerebral Socrates.[16] The "universal charm" of such martial fame (line 184) evokes the reader's uncomprehending response to the decline of Charles from "Unconquer'd lord of pleasure and of pain" (line 196) to the "needy supplicant" who waits "While ladies interpose, and slaves debate" (lines 213–14) on his behalf. The reader has temporarily lost control of his own life and is drawn to Charles's "resistless" tale (line 178), just as Charles is drawn to the resistless charms of conquest.[17] As such readers we are astounded at his collapse, and either break into the poem or hear our probable questions raised by the narrator. A created or a nonce "we" ask the questions; Johnson, "replying upon himself," supplies the answers that already are part of our expectations.

> But did not Chance at length her error mend?
> Did no subverted empire mark his end?
> Did rival monarchs give the fatal wound?
> Or hostile millions press him to the ground?
> His fall was destin'd to a barren strand,
> A petty fortress, and a dubious hand;
> He left the name, at which the world grew pale,
> To point a moral, or adorn a tale.
>
>   (lines 215–22)

The rejection of the epic end for the epic hero further demonstrates the flimsy foundation of the warrior's pride. It also answers one of Johnson's own muted questions regarding Charles, and invites us to recollect a comparable question regarding Democritus. Then we heard: "how just that scorn ere yet thy voice declare, / Search every state, and canvass ev'ry pray'r" (lines 71–72). Now we hear: "on what foundation stands the warrior's pride, / How just his hopes let Swedish Charles decide" (lines 191–92). The two passages have implied and parallel questions and answers that reinforce one another: Democritus's unjust scorn and its contempt for mankind are all too like the unjust martial hopes of Charles and his contempt for mankind. The negative and prompt answer regarding Charles reinforces our sense of the inadequacy of Democritus as a norm. Johnson has offered us the heroic option, let us join other men trapped by it, shown us its vanity, and in the process invited us to recall and enlarge upon the less destructive but still hostile ("Dart . . . taunt . . . edge . . . piercing" [line 62]) and vain approach of the pagan philosopher.

The different questions allow us to see how the poem and its audience "grow," how we move from having the narrator question us, to the point at which we seem to or could raise our own questions, whose answers remind us of the vanity of human wishes. There is another change in the next question, the framing of which again suggests that we see the insufficiency of the Democritean option. In fact, our presumed compassion for Laud and the enthusiastic young scholar already leads us in this direction. Specifically, we abandon the destructive for the sympathetic, as we wish not enviously to crush a poor man's peace, much less that of a poor country, but lovingly to extend an innocent good man's life. He is "The gen'ral fav'rite as the gen'ral friend: / Such age there is, and who shall wish its end?" (lines 297–98).

Not I, each of us must say. The aggression of "Increase his riches and his peace destroy" has been discarded in favor of benevolence which, Johnson would say in Sermon 19, stems from God's dictates, is celebrated in all nations, and is "the most amiable disposition of the heart, and the foundation of all happiness" (YE 14:208). The world's act of destruction nonetheless is as powerful as ever, for even the wish to have a peaceful and healthy age may be pernicious. If we do not punish the happy man the human condition itself will, as "ev'n on this her load Misfortune flings" (line 299). The aging man sees his family and friends die, and feels his "joy" (line 306) drop from life ("crush th' upbraiding joy" [line 39], we were told when involved in a punitive role; laugh at those "Whose joys are causeless" [line 68], Democritus believed). He sees himself as superfluous and forgotten, and waits only "Till pitying Nature signs the last release" (line 309), just as the statesman, defeated by his briefly fulfilled wish, waited fruitlessly for Britain to "Sign her foes' doom, or guard her fav'rites' zeal" (line 92). The virtuous, lonely man is indeed among the lucky ones. Misfortune, unlike the reader, does not repent of its severe role and shows us that even the most exalted of men collapse in the face of the body's frailty.

> In life's last scene what prodigies surprise,
> Fears of the brave, and follies of the wise?
> From Marlb'rough's eyes the streams of dotage flow,
> And Swift expires a driv'ler and a show.
>
> (lines 315–18)

The reader's acceptance of sympathy is emphasized in the last question before the poem's concluding great paragraph. Johnson enlarges the range of his audience by adding female concerns and by showing how the daughter pays for the mother's pride. He juxtaposes the old man's death with the familiar wish of "The teeming mother, anxious for her race," who begs that her daughter be beautiful and prosper accordingly (lines 319–20). A similar offspring had been a threat to the scholar's success, for the narrator hoped that "Beauty [would] blunt on fops her fatal dart, / Nor claim the triumph of a letter'd heart" (lines 151–52). This is one of the several instances of the poem's interlocking portraits that expand the objects of the poem's satire and our concern for those, like ourselves, sharing dangers in life's treacherous mist. Indeed, for all the obvious differences between the scholar and the beauty, both are victims of fulfilled vain human wishes. The clever young man must "pause awhile from letters, to be wise" (line 158); the radiant young woman's pleasure "keeps [her] too busy to be wise" (line 324). We no longer wish unhappiness for such fragile joy, and so we ask an elegiac question on the young woman's behalf. We also see that the martial imagery that permeates the poem is as important and destructive for the dancing maiden as for the epic hero.

> What care, what rules your heedless charms shall save,
> Each nymph your rival, and each youth your slave?
> Against your fame with fondness hate combines,
> The rival batters, and the lover mines.
>
> (lines 329–32)

Soon "none the pass defend" (line 337) and "beauty falls betray'd, despis'd, distress'd, / And hissing Infamy" (lines 341–42) proclaims her social and moral ruin. What care can save her? None, for we have come closer to the narrator's own vision and now appreciate his earlier judgment: "fate wings with ev'ry wish th' afflictive dart, / Each gift of nature, and each grace of art" (lines 15–16). The beautiful young woman who can "smile with art" (line 327) is inviting her own seduction just as surely as, in the larger sphere, "nations sink, by darling schemes oppress'd" (line 13).

We started the poem as uncommitted recipients of knowledge; we soon become agents of our own nastiness; we then become active or at least comprehending questioners and saddened viewers of the world we have made and inhabit. The questions allow us to move from the role of malevolent to sympathetic actor and asker; from classical philosophic scorn to modern military achievement; from active participant in the nation's highest public offices of church and state to private scholar in the university; from surprise at the aged good man's senile end to sorrow at the fall of the young beauty. By now Johnson need not encourage us to inquire regarding many other classes. Presumably, we understand the point of this debate by interrogatories and see how each different role ends in unhappiness because it is a vain human wish. The response of the serious investigator is likely to be either despair or redefinition, either abandoning or rechanneling the earthly energy that motivates our "eager strife" (line 3). That is just what the reader indicates in the poem's four final questions. We have been set in Johnson's own track of invention and are on the verge of his own discoveries. The reader clearly wishes to resist the option of despair, to use his native energy to bring him closer to God. "Faith is opposed to infidelity, and *hope* to despair," Johnson reports in an illustrative quotation from Bishop Jeremy Taylor (*Dictionary*). The speaker thus becomes an intrusive and benevolent narrator who plays upon our potential for goodness, so well demonstrated by our refusal to persevere in aggression or Democritean severity. He builds upon our discoveries, human vitality, desire for free will, and need to ask questions and to receive answers. He also offers the one option hitherto unexamined, the one that responds to several of the questions raised earlier.

> Where then shall Hope and Fear their objects find?
> Must dull Suspence corrupt the stagnant mind?
> Must helpless man, in ignorance sedate,
> Roll darkling down the torrent of his fate?
> Must no dislike alarm, no wishes rise,
> No cries attempt the mercies of the skies?
> Enquirer, cease, petitions yet remain,
> Which heav'n may hear, nor deem religion vain.
>
> (lines 343–50)

The final couplet quoted makes clear that the reader is actively involved in the poem as a vocal inquirer and eagerly uses language on his own behalf. We no longer need to be urged to participate, as in "Speak thou" (line 121); but we do need the narrator's guidance—"nor deem religion vain"—and do need to know that religion is "Virtue, as founded upon reverence of God, and expectation of future rewards and punishments" (*Dictionary*).[18] Wolsey and Laud were nominally men of God, but actually men of this world and its power. To be sure, Wolsey's "last sighs reproach the faith of kings" (line 120); but that faith was secular, not religious, and was broken with Wolsey rather than with God. Genuine religious petitions bring us to a world of spiritual, not human, wishes, where questions disappear, for the debate has been resolved. Now the historical characters and indiscriminate masses everywhere else in the poem are replaced by our personal relationship with a timeless

God. Each of the following points refers to an earlier vain wish and rede-fines it. For example, "Unnumber'd suppliants" futilely appealed to and for preferment (line 73; see also lines 12, 112, 213, 256); with religion we "Still raise for good the supplicating voice, / But leave to heav'n the measure and the choice" (lines 351–52).

Earlier we were betrayed (line 7) and confused in the misty (line 9) and "clouded maze of fate" (line 6); we foolishly prayed for long life (line 255); we were tottering in a world where "wealth, nor truth nor safety buys" (line 27; see also lines 31–32); we ourselves were restless (lines 20, 105), and saw Wolsey denied his "refuge of monastic rest" (line 118). Similarly, the misguided mother "Begs" (line 320), a synonym for implores, her daughter's beauty; Xerxes' "pow'rs" (line 233) were unreliable and led to the death of thousands; and Wolsey's smile, it wrongly seemed, "alone security bestows" (line 104). Johnson alludes to all of these, as well as the earlier martial imagery, in his new evocation of *safety, power, perception, prayer, implore, rest*, and *security*. We are

> Safe in his pow'r, whose eyes discern afar
> The secret ambush of a specious pray'r.
> Implore his aid, in his decisions rest,
> Secure whate'er he gives, he gives the best.
>
> (lines 353–56)

The tack is quite the same when Johnson considers how best properly to channel man's energy, need to transcend his limitations, and wish to escape from solipsism. "Infinite wisdom . . . has not created minds with comprehensions never to be filled" (YE 14:135), we hear in Sermon 12, which also urges that revelation promises us the happiness we seek and does not leave us in the state of permanent disease in this world, and permanent soullessness in the next, as Democritus believed.[19] The healthful mind replaces the senile mind; "Obedient passions, and a will resign'd" (line 360) replace restless passions that alienate a father's will (line 282) and make our moral will alien to God's; God's love replaces love as attachment to a rising career (line 79), or as a trivial emotion the hero ignores (line 195), or as sexual love that destroys the beauty (lines 329–42); patience reigns over the ills that must come to all of us and, if viewed correctly, can prepare us for the next world; faith in God replaces Wolsey's reproach of the temporal "faith of kings" (line 120). The mate-rial possessions that we had so avidly sought have been changed from gold, mortgages, and buildings to spiritual coin one may keep. Laws that were unreliable and easily perverted by man are made immutable, and the wisdom that the scholar and beauty had to seek is transmuted from the secular to the celestial. The empiricism with which the poem began and by which it is guided reemerges, as a superior divine empiricist works to ease the unhappiness of those who try to find her.

> These goods for man the laws of heav'n ordain,
> These goods he grants, who grants the pow'r to gain;
> With these celestial wisdom calms the mind,
> And makes the happiness she does not find.
>
> (lines 365–68)

Such exalted answers are a direct result of the questions we have been urged to ask, of the roles we have been asked to evaluate by means of questions, of the inadequacies we have seen in those roles, and of the wisdom and generosity of the poem's narrator. He teaches us through serious debate and appears to investigate with us, though his own such job was long done. "What is the effect of study" seems to be "uttered without any premeditation."[20]

2

It may be useful briefly to contrast Johnson's with Juvenal's relevant poetic methods and moral assumptions. Johnson's characters do not speak to one another, as Juvenal's do in largely uncomplimentary ways (lines 67–72), so much as to the narrator himself and to other readers who are improved in the process. Juvenal, on the other hand, makes Democritus a consistent norm and adopts his hostility to his fellows throughout the poem: the people are the "turba" or mob, or derogatory "populus," the rabble (lines 73–74). Indeed, we are all basically hostile, since even those of us who do not want to kill are willing to have the power to do so: "et qui nolunt occidere quemquam, / Posse volunt" (lines 96–97). Aggression is a permanent part of human nature, is apparent in Juvenal's narrator himself, and is unmitigated by the religious comparison in Johnson's poem. Hannibal illustrates the vanity of human wishes; he also illustrates the folly of attempting to conquer Rome and Rome's ultimate vengeance for the disgrace of Cannae. For Juvenal, Hannibal is quite frankly "demens" (line 166) and encourages our pleasure at his humiliation rather than, as with Charles of Sweden, disbelief at a fall that might have been ours and that we briefly thought would be conventionally heroic. Dryden's translation captures Juvenal's mockery, without any of the grandeur that Johnson saw:

> Ask what a Face belong'd to this high Fame;
> His Picture scarcely wou'd deserve a Frame:
> A Sign-Post Dawber wou'd disdain to paint
> The one Ey'd Heroe on his Elephant.
> Now what's his End, O Charming Glory, say
> What rare fifth Act, to Crown this huffing Play?
> . . . .
> Poyson, drawn through a Rings hollow plate,
> Must finish him; a sucking Infant's Fate.
> Go, climb the rugged *Alps*, Ambitious Fool,
> To please the Boys, and be a Theme at School.[21]
>
> (lines 252–72)

When we near the end of the poem, we ask Juvenal's advice only once, in contrast to our fourfold request to Johnson: is there nothing we should pray for? ("Nil ergo optabunt homines?" [line 346]). This counsel is not that of a speaker with affection for the audience he has been respectfully debating and guiding for the last 348 lines; it is the counsel of someone who continues to be Democritean, to debunk our wishes and the notion of dependence upon something external to ourselves. We may ask for a wife and children; but the gods know better and will not give us those dubious blessings if we leave the choice to them. But if you must go through all the nonsense of sacrificing a little white pig's entrails and sausage meat, ask for all the happy ramifications of a sound mind in a sound body, which that man-made divinity Fortuna cannot give you in any case (lines 365–66). You can give those to yourself through a life of virtue (lines 363–64).

Juvenal, then, asks many questions of his readers and has them ask the wrong questions of one another and their gods; he assumes an audience and narrator perhaps morally static and certainly capable of less growth than their Johnsonian posterity. The Roman poem culminates not in a necessary looking upward towards celestial wisdom, but looking inward toward a stoic self-reliance that includes contempt for or detachment from other human beings and their wishes. The questions and answers between Johnson and his audience ultimately imply questions to and from a benevolent God. As we have seen, "nor deem religion vain" leads to an inversion of the insecurity, selfishness, crowded loneliness, and spiritual myopia of earlier vain human wishes. The questions and answers between Juvenal and his audience imply an earth-bound wisdom that Johnson would think atheistic, a contradiction in terms, and an insult to those capable of sympathy, not hostility, when led to virtue by the right guide. "Sympathy," he said in Sermon 11, is "the great source of social happiness" (YE 14:120).[22] Johnson's poem begins with Observation and History as the masters in our empirical quest; they show us, among other things, "How rarely reason guides the stubborn choice" (line 11), and so Johnson as severely corrective but good-humored and sympathetic narrator takes on that role. In the process, he becomes like the walking abstraction Reason in "The Vision of Theodore" (1748) who points the way to heaven but wisely surrenders to Religion thereafter. Reason says that

> there are asperities and pitfals, over which Religion only can conduct you. Look upwards, and you perceive a mist before you settled upon the highest visible part of the mountain, a mist by which my prospect is terminated, and which is pierced only by the eyes of Religion. Beyond it are the temples of Happiness, in which those who climb the precipice by her direction, after the toil of their pilgrimage repose for ever. I know not the way, and therefore can only conduct you to a better guide.[23]

Hence at the end of the *Vanity*, celestial wisdom replaces the personified secular Observation and Johnson's own reason, and thus more than any other force "calms the mind, / And makes the happiness she does not find." As James Grainger said in 1759, "The truth is, Virtue is the sole Parent of Happiness. See Mr. Johnson's admirable Poem, intitled the Vanity of Human Wishes."[24] As such a Parent, celestial wisdom can *make* where Observation merely could *see* and History merely *tell*; the capacity for change is directly related to Johnson's Christian, public, and religious as opposed to Juvenal's pagan, private, and stoical views. All this is rendered possible not by the chimerical Fortuna, but by Johnson's willingness to ask, attribute, encourage, and hear our questions.[25] These enable us to assume and to test a variety of roles, to see their weaknesses, and to see the strengths of the narrator who, in turn, like Adam at the end of *Paradise Lost*, finds his and our answers from above, and subjects himself to God at the right time, so that we will be encouraged to do so as well. As Johnson urges in Sermon 11, no "greater benefit [can] be conferred, than that of settling doubts, or comforting despair, and restoring a disquieted soul to hope and tranquillity" (YE 14:124). In the *Vanity* Johnson knows more profoundly than Bacon how "He that *questioneth* much shall learn much, and content much; but especially if he apply his questions to the skill of the persons whom he asketh."

NOTES

1. As quoted in Thomas Gibbons, *Rhetoric; or, A View of its Principal Tropes and Figures* (London, 1767), p. 187. Gibbons is considering the rhetorical figure erotesis, "by which we express the emotion of our minds, and infuse an ardor and energy into our discourses, by proposing questions" (p. 176).

2. For the 1738 remarks, see Samuel Johnson, "Examination of a Question Proposed in the [Gentleman's] Magazine of June, p. 310," The Yale Edition of the Works of Samuel Johnson, vol. 10, *Political Writings*, ed. Donald J. Greene (New Haven: Yale University Press, 1977), pp. 9–10. The essay is an attribution—but a generally accepted one. Unless otherwise specified, quotations from Johnson's works are from the Yale Edition, cited YE with the appropriate information appended. For the *Preceptor*, see *Samuel Johnson's Prefaces and Dedications*, ed. Allen T. Hazen (New Haven: Yale University Press, 1937), p. 181. The definition is quoted from Johnson's *Dictionary of the English Language* (London, 1755), as are subsequent citations. Bacon's other remark is in *The Essays . . . of Francis Lo. Vervlam* (London, 1625), p. 196.

3. *A Philosophical Enquiry into the Origin of our Ideas of the Sublime and Beautiful*, ed. J. T. Boulton (London: Routledge & Kegan Paul, 1958), pp. 12–13. Compare Johnson's remark in the Preface to *Shakespeare* (1765): "it is natural to delight more in what we find or make, than in what we receive": YE 7, *Johnson on Shakespeare*, ed. Arthur Sherbo (1968), p. 104. For further discussion of such reader-involvement in authorial invention, see "The Reader, the General, and the Particular: Johnson and Imlac in Chapter Ten of *Rasselas*," within; and Eric Rothstein, "'Ideal Presence' and the 'Non Finito' in Eighteenth-Century Aesthetics," *Eighteenth-Century Studies* 9 (1976): 307–32.

4. Quotations are from Samuel Johnson, YE 6, *Poems*, ed. E. L. McAdam, Jr., with George Milne (1964). I should add that the questions also appear, in varying quantity and quality, in all the other seventeenth- and eighteenth-century imitations and translations of Juvenal's Tenth Satire.

5. Lawrence Lipking," Learning to Read Johnson: *The Vision of Theodore* and *The Vanity of Human Wishes*," *ELH* 43 (1976): 532. There have been several useful discussions of the Vanity in recent years. For some of these, see Walter Jackson Bate, "Johnson and Satire Manqué," in *Eighteenth-Century Studies in Honor of Donald F. Hyde*, ed. W. H. Bond (New York: Grolier Club, 1970), pp. 145–60; Donald Greene, *Samuel Johnson* (New York: Twayne, 1970), pp. 56–63; William Kupersmith, "Declamatory Grandeur: Johnson and Juvenal," *Arion* 9 (1970): 52–72; Raman Selden, "Dr. Johnson and Juvenal: A Problem in Critical Method," *Comparative Literature* 22 (1970): 289–302; D. V. Boyd, "Vanity and Vacuity: A Reading of Johnson's Verse Satires," *ELH* 39 (1972): 387–403; William Kupersmith, "'More like an Orator than a Philosopher': Rhetorical Structure in *The Vanity of Human Wishes*," *Studies in Philology* 72 (1975): 454–72; and John E. Sitter, "To *The Vanity of Human Wishes* Through the 1740's" *Studies in Philology* 74 (1977): 445–64.

6. William Henry Hall observes that satire may be more effective in "the cause of religion and virtue than a sermon; since it gives pleasure, at the same time that it creates fear or indignation." To induce pleasure, "The satirist should always preserve good humour; and however keen he cuts, should cut with kindness" ("Satire," *The New Royal Encyclopaedia* [London, 1789]).

7. As quoted in Gibbons's *Rhetoric*, p. 188. For the full context, see "A Paraphrase on Part of the Book of Job," in *The Works of Dr. Edward Young* (London, 1783), 4:108,

where Young also observes that *"Longinus* has a chapter on interrogations"—that is section 18 in modern editions.

8. See, for example, Henry Gifford, *"The Vanity of Human Wishes," Review of English Studies* n.s. 6 (1955): 58; and Patrick O'Flaherty, "Johnson as Satirist: A New Look at *The Vanity of Human Wishes," ELH* 34 (1967): 83–84, 86–87. Bruce King, however, is more accurate in his "Late Augustan, Early Modern," *Sewanee Review* 76 (1968): 139–42. See also Weinbrot, *The Formal Strain: Studies in Augustan Imitation and Satire* (Chicago: University of Chicago Press, 1969), pp. 199–200.

9. D. E. Eichholz offers a helpful discussion of Democritus's scorn in "The Art of Juvenal and his Tenth *Satire," Greece and Rome,* 2nd ser., 3 (1956): 61–69. For Epicurus, see Thomas F. Mayo, *Epicurus in England, 1650–1725* (n.p.: Southwest Press, 1934). The common association of Democritus with Epicurus was made by Ludovicus Prateus in his *D. Junii Juvenalis et A. Persii Flacci Satirae,* 7th ed. (London, 1736), p. 200, note to line 34. Subsequent quotations are from this text, which Johnson knew well. Annotated editions of Juvenal and of Horace (*Epistles,* 1.22.12) offered glossed and relevant biographical information regarding Democritus. Standard reference works like Louis Moréri's *Grand Dictionnaire historique* (Lyons, 1674), Pierre Bayle's *Dictionnaire historique et critique* (Rotterdam, 1697), and Thomas Stanley's *History of Philosophy,* 2nd ed. (London, 1687) offered more abundant information. The quotation above, regarding man as diseased, is from Stanley, p. 760. Humphrey Prideaux discusses Democritus's "wholly . . . atheistical scheme" in *The Old and New Testament Connected,* 3rd ed. (London, 1717), 1:323. I am indebted to Joanne Murphy for some of these, and several other, contemporary references to Democritus.

10. Johnson uses this method of question and delayed answer by the reader with Swedish Charles as well in lines 191–92. The device was a familiar one, and also appears in Pope's *Epistle to Bathurst* (1733), lines 335–36, and its answer in the tale of Balaam. Randall Minshull (?) also uses questions to involve and to implicate the reader in *The Miser, A Poem: From the First Satire of the First Book of Horace* (London, 1735). Here the speaker asks the smug reader: "what—Why dost laugh? But only change the name, / The Fable [of Tantalus] proves thy self the very same" (p. 19). See also two remarks on Persius's use of questions in Edmund Burton, *The Satyrs of Persius* (London, 1752), p. 32; and Vicesimus Knox, *Essays Moral and Literary* (London, 1778), 2:151.

11. "Glance" here probably has the third meaning of the noun, "A snatch of sight; a quick view" (*Dictionary*). The illustrative quotation is favorable: "the ample mind takes a survey of several objects with one *glance. Watts's Improvement of the Mind"*; but the context of the poem and other definitions in the *Dictionary* suggest negative use here. The courtiers of Henry VIII, for example, "Mark the keen glance, and watch the sign to hate" Wolsey (line 110). The word there connotes the fourth or fifth definitions of the verb, from the noun, "To view with a quick cast of the eye; to play the eye," and "To censure by oblique hints." Bacon's illustration of the last meaning suggests the hostility of such glancing already seen in the language describing Democritus: "some men *glance* and dart at others, by justifying themselvs by negatives; as to say, this I do not." The lines also associate Democritus with the destructive qualities of hostile Fate, who "wings with ev'ry wish th' afflictive dart" (line 15).

12. Rejection of such mockery would have been familiar, as Edward Young's remarks in the Preface to *Love of Fame* suggest: "some Satyrical Wits, and Humorists, like their Father *Lucian,* laugh at every thing indiscriminately; which betrays such a poverty of wit, as cannot afford to part with any thing; and such a want of virtue, as to postpone it to a

jest. Such writers encourage Vice and Folly, which they pretend to combat, by setting them on an equal foot with better things: and while they labour to bring every thing into contempt, how can they expect their own parts should escape?" (2nd ed. [London, 1728], sig. a1ᵛ).

13. YE 14, *Sermons*, ed. Jean Hagstrum and James Gray (1978), pp. 262, 267, 268; subsequent references are cited as YE 14. For further discussion of Johnson's sermons and some of their major themes, see Paul K. Alkon, *Samuel Johnson and Moral Discipline* (Evanston, IL.: Northwestern University Press, 1967), pp. 51–53, 191–209; and James Gray, *Johnson's Sermons: A Study* (Oxford: Clarendon Press, 1972). The sermons and the *Vanity* are of course different works in different genres at different times; but Gray is correct in saying that in the sermons Johnson "stuck to his own beliefs and staunchly defended his own orthodoxy" (p. 185; see also p. 186). Many other remarks in the sermons are valuable as glosses to the *Vanity*; see, for example, Johnson's discussion of charity, pity, and courtesy in Sermon 11 (YE 14:123, 125). Furthermore, the distinction between inefficacious philosophy and friendly religion was so commonplace that even Fielding's misguided Man of the Hill could understand and use it: see The Wesleyan Edition of the Works of Henry Fielding, *The History of Tom Jones*, ed. Martin C. Battestin and Fredson Bowers (Middletown, CT: Wesleyan University Press, 1975), book 8, chap. 13 (pp. 470–71 and p. 470 n. 1).

14. See the *Spectator*, ed. Donald Bond (Oxford: Clarendon Press, 1965), 2:205–6. James H. Sledd and Gwin J. Kolb note Johnson's completed reading for the *Dictionary* in *Dr. Johnson's Dictionary: Essays in the Biography of a Book* (Chicago: University of Chicago Press, 1955), p. 107; for the time of the writing of the *Vanity*, see YE 6:90.

15. See *The Formal Strain*, p. 168 and p. 168 n. 10.

16. *Boswell's Life of Johnson Together with Boswell's Journal of a Tour to the Hebrides*, ed. George Birkbeck Hill and rev. L. F. Powell (Oxford: Clarendon Press, 1934–50), 3:265–66. For some of Johnson's comments on questions, and Boswell as annoying questioner, see 2:472; and 3:57, 268.

17. Charles, even more than the reader, has lost control in his narcissistic attraction to himself and his deadly way of life: "war sounds the trump, he rushes to the field" (line 198). Johnson also may be playing on the other, nonmusical meaning of trump: "a winning card; a card that has particular privileges in a game" (*Dictionary*).

18. See also Johnson's Preface to the *Preceptor* in 1748: "to counteract the Power of Temptations, Hope must be excited by the Prospect of Rewards, and Fear by the Expectation of Punishment; and Virtue may owe her Panegyricks to Morality, but must derive her Authority from Religion": Hazen, *Johnson's Prefaces*, p. 186.

19. Much of the rest of this sermon, on Ecclesiastes 1:14, provides a gloss on what Johnson means by the vanity of human wishes; see YE 14:129–30.

20. The narrator's changing but respectful, collaborative, if pedagogical, relationship with the reader is well illustrated in his use of *thee*, *thou*, and *thy* when addressing us. By 1749 *thou* had long passed out of common speech; it was indeed considered insulting "to thou" someone who was not an intimate. There were exceptions, and some more important than those for Quakers, pets, and abstractions. "Thou," Johnson said in his *Dictionary*, "is used only in very familiar or very solemn language. When we speak to equals or superiors we say you; but in solemn language, and in addresses of worship, we say *thou*." The tones of the *Vanity*'s "thou" change from the familiar, as in "Does envy seize thee?" (line 39), to the solemn, as in "Pour forth thy fervours for a healthful mind" (line 359).

21. The California Edition of the Works of John Dryden vol. 4, *Poems, 1693–1696*,

ed. A. B. Chambers, William Frost, and Vinton A. Dearing (Berkeley and Los Angeles: University of California Press, 1974), pp. 221–223. Johnson refers to Juvenal's "grandeur" in *Lives of the English Poets*, ed. George Birkbeck Hill (Oxford: Clarendon Press, 1905), 1:447.

22. Immediately thereafter, as if in contradiction to the Democritean spirit, he adds: "to gain affection, and to preserve concord, it is necessary not only to mourn with those that mourn, but to rejoice with them that rejoice."

23. YE 16, *Rasselas and Other Tales*, ed. Gwin J. Kolb (1990), p. 204. The passage embodies Johnson's own views on the relation of learning to religion and of even the best secular moral writing to gospel itself. "The Vision" was printed with Dodsley's *Preceptor* as one of three examples which caution the young student "against the Danger of indulging his Passions, of vitiating his Habits, and depraving his Sentiments . . . But at this he is not to rest, for if he expects to be Wise and Happy, he must diligently study the SCRIPTURES of GOD" (Hazen, *Johnson's Prefaces*, p. 188). This Preface, written in April 1748, also includes a reason over and above the Juvenalian parallels for the several historical characters in the *Vanity*, a reason based on the questioning nature of the human mind. There are "Enquiries which History alone can satisfy" (p. 182).

24. *A Poetical Translation of the Elegies of Tibullus; and of the Poems of Sulpicia* (London, 1759), 2:159.

25. For comments on Juvenal's ambiguous use of Fortuna, see "Extraits de mon Journal," *Miscellaneous Works of Edward Gibbon, Esquire*, ed. John, Lord Sheffield (London, 1796), 2:106–7. These comments were known and used by William Gifford in his *Satires of Decimus Junius Juvenalis* (London, 1802), p. 360.

6

Johnson and the Arts of Narration:
The Life of Savage, The Vanity of Human Wishes, and *Rasselas*

"There was," Johnson says of the conversation between Pope and Martha Blount, "an immediate coalition of congenial notions." For Johnson himself the coalitions need not have been congenial, so long as they were respectful and denoted the desired exchange of mind he found lacking with Goldsmith and others. When Johnson visited his old school fellow Charles Congreve he complained that "he is quite unsocial: his conversation is monosyllabical. . . . Don't," he cautions Edmund Hector, "grow like Congreve; nor let me grow like him, when you are near me."[1]

Vigorous and varied exchange seems to me the bedrock upon which Johnson's several works involving narrators are built, for there one finds the dialogue, community, shared response, and evoked faith in a speaker who is like us in ways, while also trying to guide us to his and our best selves. That guidance appears to have contradictory effects: Johnson seems at once to be at our side and leading. I cannot hope to resolve this benevolent paradox; I do hope to suggest some of the bases for Johnson's achievements as narrator in several works, but especially in *The Life of Savage* (1744), *The Vanity of Human Wishes* (1749), and above all *Rasselas* (1759).

1

One reason for Johnson's role as communicating teacher is his understanding of sympathetic literary response. As he says in the familiar *Rambler,* No. 60 (1750), we temporarily put ourselves in the subject's place, "so that we feel, while the deception lasts, whatever motions would be excited by the same good or evil happening to ourselves." Biography is especially valuable because it affords "parallel circumstances, and kindred images, to which we readily conform our minds."[2] On this hypothesis, we require and find bonding in the literature closest to our lives.

The ethical dimension of human response is even more important than the literary. Linking of the reader and life to literature is paralleled by the linking of man to man in a universe of willfully unalleviated loneliness. In the *Rambler*, No. 160 (1751), for example, "multitudes . . . swarm about" the isolated man who cannot "find some kindred mind with which he could unite in confidence and friendship," and instead is "straggling single about the world, unhappy for want of an associate, and pining with the necessity of confining" his sentiments to his own bosom. Such a world is like the one at the end of the Preface to the *Dictionary* (1755), in which the triumphant lexicographer laments that he has no one he "wished to please" and thus has neither hope nor fear for his book's reception. Some twenty years later Johnson visited the Palais Bourbon and noted that "as I entered, my wife was in my mind: she would have been pleased. Having now nobody to please, I am little pleased." The remedy for such self-imprisonment is made clear in the *Rambler*, No. 160: "To raise esteem we must benefit others, to procure love we must please them."[3]

For Johnson, the source of love far transcends human affection. To love one's neighbor is to love God; to use and not bury one's talent is to use God's gift. By sharing his own wisdom as the maker of didactic narratives, Johnson also is following the pattern of the ultimate teacher who wants us to join what Johnson's thirteenth sermon calls "the great community of relation to the universal Father."[4] This relation extends to those who have power in the state or in literature, and requires both exchange and proper authority properly used. In Sermon 1 Johnson says that since "knowledge is advanced by an intercourse of sentiments, and an exchange of observations," pleasures are imperfect "when they are enjoyed without participation" (YE 14:3). As a result of such human insufficiency, man "applies to others for assistance," and that person has "an opportunity of diffusing his satisfaction" and imitating God (YE 14:4). Whether we are humble or wise "Providence presents" relevant opportunities to help others that should be eagerly seized (YE 14:168–69) especially, we hear in Sermon 24, if one really has the power to rule. This is "to bestow upon [a man] the greatest benefit he is capable of receiving"—and the greatest of obligations to meet the legitimate expectations of the ruled and care for "the morals of the people" (YE 14:252). "No man," Johnson insists, "is born merely for his own sake," and those with the most honors have the most responsibilities (YE 14:251).

The moral and social obligations of power are clear: one connects one-self to God above by connecting oneself to man below. This "amicable reciprocation" (YE 14:126) is necessary because however much we have in this world, all gifts come from God, before whom we are as nothing, and to whom we owe the debt of bestowing on others what has been bestowed on us (YE 14:213). The authority we have, whether political, moral, or literary, is the authority that must be communicated.

That communication, of course, depends upon high art as well as high virtue, and so I shall suggest some of the ways in which Johnson adapted contemporary rhetorical and narrative devices for his own purposes.

2

Eighteenth-century rhetoric and aesthetics often urged that the reader join the author in the creative and moral process. Addison's *Spectator*, No. 512 (1712), regards the fable as the best genre for advice, because in it "we are made to believe we advise ourselves. We . . . consider the Precepts rather as our own Conclusions, than [the author's] Instruc-tions," and the reader thinks "he is directing himself, whilst he is follow-ing the Dictates of another." In these flattering works "the Reader comes in for half of the Performance; Every thing appears to him like a Discov-ery of his own" as he applies the work's characters and circumstances to his experience. "In this respect," Addison claims, one is "both a Reader and a Composer," and the mind, "pleased with it self, and . . . its own Discoveries," is equally pleased with the work, here *Absalom and Achitophel*, "which gave the Reader an Opportunity of exerting his own Talents" (4:318). Comparable remarks appear throughout the cen-tury. In the Preface to Shakespeare (1765) Johnson thus observes that "it is natural to delight more in what we find or make, than in what we receive"; and in 1781 he belabors Cowley for being so particularized in describing the archangel Gabriel that we cannot be "dismissed to im-prove the idea in our different proportions of conception."[5]

One way of inducing such collaboration between reader and author is through adapting the pedagogy of questions. This method of inducing response long had been noted, as Johnson shows in the *Dictionary*'s il-lustrative quotation from Bacon's "Of Discourse": "He that *questioneth* much shall learn much, and content much; but especially if he apply his questions to the skill of the persons whom he asketh. For he shall give them occasion, to please themselves in speaking, and himself shall con-tinually gather knowledge." In 1738 Johnson also urged the value of questions, which allow "the reader the satisfaction of adding something that he may call his own and thus engage his attention by flattering his vanity."[6] Such questioning of an involved reader, we know, is part of Johnson's narrative method in *The Vanity of Human Wishes*.

Such method also includes other devices of characterization, one of which is the skillful use of pronouns. Johnson's, and Boswell's, awareness of the power of such words is made clear on March 16, 1776, when they discuss Lord Mountstuart's proposal to pay for a Scots militia out of general funds, a plan Johnson opposes as a Scottish raid on the English treasury. "'Your scheme is to retain a part of your little land-tax, by making us pay and clothe your militia.' BOSWELL. 'You should not talk of *we* and *you*, Sir: there is now an *Union*. . . . A French invasion made in Scotland would soon penetrate into England.'"[7] That is, there is one national interest and therefore one national *we*.

Sensitivity to pronouns extended to the now moribund use of *thy* and *thine*, which indicated relationships among speakers. *Thou*, Johnson said in the *Dictionary*, "is used only in very familiar or very solemn language. When we speak to equals or superiors we say *you*; but in solemn language, and in addresses of worship, we say *thou*."[8] Such variation in the use and meaning of pronouns is well employed in *The Vanity of Human Wishes*. There the narrator establishes a personal relationship with the reader, whom he questions and thereby draws into the poem as we try several of the roles that our vain human wishes inflict upon us. The narrator's changing but finally respectful dialogue with the reader is well illustrated in the different tones of *thee*, *thou*, and *thy*, as his involving questions move us from familiar to solemn speech.

With the first questions in the poem we are the moral inferior of the narrator, who demands of our response to the poor, happy, secure man—"Does envy seize thee? crush th' upbraiding joy, / Increase his riches and his peace destroy."[9] We are compromised in this hostile exercise, as we are in another way when we see the fate of Wolsey, whose power we might have wanted; "Speak thou, whose thoughts at humble peace repine" (line 121): and we are sadly naïve and incompetent empiricists when we hear the fantasy life of the young scholar—"are these thy views?" (line 141). Yet this passage also marks a turning point, for we begin to associate with and admire the young man, rather than dissociate ourselves from an unjustly happy underling whom we briefly seem able to destroy. Hence, even "should thy soul indulge the gen'rous heat" (line 143) we still must learn to mark, see, and attend to reality (lines 159, 161, 163). We now adjust ourselves to the world, rather than try to adjust the world to ourselves. By the time we reach the conclusion of the poem, the narrator's tone in his use of *thou* has changed along with the further change in his enquirer, who begins to apprehend a different world entirely. "Pour forth thy fervours for a healthful mind" (line 359) is the last place we are specifically referred to, and that is when we seek to follow Johnson's advice, to become more like him, and are both solemn and addressing God in worship.

The *Vanity* also demonstrates another of Johnson's uses of the personal pronoun: it becomes a subdued metaphor of destructive self-gratification as embodied in the possessive *his* and *him* and its transformation into *mine*. Charles of Sweden exemplifies the expansionist martial hero. No dangers fright him, his empire extends over emotions, and nothing pacific brings him pleasure. By metonymy, he embodies all of his nation's men, as "War sounds the trump, he rushes to the field" with great success (line 98); his enemies capitulate and "Peace courts his hand, but spreads her charms in vain" (line 201). Nothing is gained till nothing remains except Swedish flags on Russian walls, "And all be mine beneath the polar sky" (line 204). His triumphs and threatened invasion force both allied and opposing nations to wait "on his eye suspended" (line 206). Against all odds of weather and numbers "He comes" (line 209), still embodying massive force and martial genius. As the portrait proceeds, though, it begins to redefine *his* and *him*, to suggest consequences and moral responsibility, and to show that the reality of death conflicts with the fantasy of power. After defeat at Pultowa, "The vanquish'd hero leaves his broken bands, / And shews his miseries in distant lands" (lines 211–12). Charles is alone, while those who followed him are annihilated; his miseries replace his triumphs, and women's intercession replaces rejected women's love and the charms of female peace. As if puzzled and wanting to resist this rapid decline, the uncomprehending reader tries to reestablish the myth of heroic Charles as destroyed only by monarchs and millions:

> But did not Chance at length her error mend?
> Did no subverted empire mark his end?
> Did rival monarchs give the fatal wound?
> Or hostile millions press him to the ground?
>
> (lines 215–18)

Instead, fate replaces chance, a skirmish replaces epic contest, and a bullet fired by an unidentified soldier or assassin replaces monarchs. The movement of the portrait is from Charles as *his*, meaning his nation's armies and the fruits of its conquests, to *his* as isolated and defeated general responsible for many thousands of deaths, to *he* as the occupant of six feet of earth, subjected to the preordained fate of irrational leaders and the insult of being a legacy of aphorisms. Now "His fall was destin'd to a barren strand" and "He left the name" used by moralists to demonstrate the vanity of human wishes (lines 219, 221). Johnson thus characterizes Charles as being isolated from mankind, which he seeks to subject or destroy and so must himself be destroyed as man and myth if civilization is to prosper.

Notice, however, Johnson's different approach when he seeks to bond himself and his reader. Instead of asserting authority he asserts fallibility and joins the reader he hopes to improve. The soaring statesman is revered, implored, and flattered as no doubt he should be for someone of such extraordinary worth—until he falls from office and then one must correct one's faulty perception:

> For now no more we trace in ev'ry line
> Heroic worth, benevolence divine;
> The form distorted justifies the fall,
> And detestation rids th'indignant wall.

(lines 87–90)

Johnson's "no more we trace" political greatness allows him to share our desire to correct our error. We more willingly follow an experienced guide who knows the pitfalls that he too must avoid.

3

This last example suggests another aspect of eighteenth-century and Johnsonian narrative art—creation of a fallible paragon who earns his authority both through virtue and the brotherhood of lesser, acceptable weakness. One source for this method is the rhetorical device of admitting weaknesses the better to induce belief in strengths. As Johnson tells Charles Burney, "We must confess the faults of our favourite, to gain credit to our praise of his excellencies. He that claims, either for himself or for another, the honours of perfection, will surely injure the reputation which he designs to assist." This remark glosses much of Johnson's literary criticism, in which he exposes flaws to help both reader and subject. "The defects and faults of *Paradise Lost*, for faults and defects every work of man must have, it is the business of impartial criticism to discover." After hearing these, we are even more confident of the work's virtues, the narrator's judgment, and the nation's literary greatness: "he who can put in balance [its faults] with its beauties must be considered not as nice but as dull, as less to be censured for want of candour than pitied for want of sensibility."[10]

Such characterization of narrator and subject also is at work in Johnson's Preface to his *Dictionary*, where he induces authority through demonstrable achievement and confessed insufficiency shared with other distinguished laborers. He says, for example that as to his definitions, "I have not always been able to satisfy myself" in this "task, which no man, however learned or sagacious, has yet been able to perform." Like others, he is limited by his intelligence, and thus "some words there are which I cannot explain, because I do not understand them." He shares the weaknesses of Cicero and Aristotle, who also were confounded by certain words in their language, and so "I may surely, without shame, leave some obscurities to happier industry, or future information." Error, like the spots of barbarity in our language, is part of the human situation; it can be reduced but not eradicated.[11]

The fallible paragon is appropriate in fiction as well as lexical or literary criticism. Novels, Johnson says in his fourth *Rambler* (1750), should show "virtue not angelical, nor above probability, for what we cannot credit we shall never imitate." The source for this aspect of his method is more important than secular rhetoric. Johnson told Edmund (or Edmond) Malone that if only the best side of characters were shown "we should sit down in despondency, and think it utterly impossible to imitate them in *any thing*." Accordingly, "the sacred writers . . . related the vicious as well as the virtuous actions of men," thereby kept mankind from despair, and supported them "by the recollection that others had offended like themselves, and by penitence and amendment of life had been restored to the favour of Heaven."[12]

In Johnson's didactic framework, then, narrator, character, and subject each must be within the imperfect limits of the best human achievement, as often guided by spiritual models. The narrator is especially important, for if he seems dictatorial he will alienate the reader and his response. "We favour the mirth of officiousness that solicits our regard," he says in the *Rambler*, No. 188 (1752), "but oppose the worth or spirit that enforces it" (YE 5:222). Johnson far prefers the amicable reciprocation exemplified in Sermon 11, in which a sympathetic auditor learns from a wise instructor who imparts "his knowledge, without fearing lest he should impair his own importance, by the improvement of his hearer" (YE 14:121). Johnson contributes to such reciprocation with a sophisticated device—variation of narrative voice that encourages readers to draw inferences based on those variations, and to engage ourselves in the education to which Johnson contributes.

4

The narrator's role as a guiding, benevolent, intrusive force is a major device of eighteenth-century authors. They seem also to have asked themselves and their readers what would happen if the narrator removed himself and left the fictive world to other forces and speakers, to, for example, the apparent control of questing unguided characters like young Wilson in *Joseph Andrews* (1742), or the Man of the Hill in *Tom Jones* (1749), who come to temporary or extended grief when cut loose from the family's and the narrator's moorings. Johnson also makes skillful use of this device, through both interpolated tales and their cousin, a temporary shift to other speakers.

The latter convention is well used in *The Life of Savage*, in which Johnson portrays the world as unreliable and often hostile to Savage, who normally does not respond in kind. We see this contrast when Johnson twice lets others speak for him, virtually juxtaposes their different tones, and thereby transcends simple verisimilitude through documentation. Here is Judge Page's exhortation to the jury about to decide Savage's fate.

> Gentlemen of the Jury, you are to consider, that Mr. *Savage* is a very great Man, a much greater Man than you or I, Gentlemen of the Jury; that he wears very fine Clothes, much finer Clothes than you or I, Gentlemen of the Jury; that he has abundance of Money in his Pocket, much more Money than you or I, Gentlemen of the Jury; but, Gentlemen of the Jury, is it not a very hard Case, Gentlemen of the Jury, that Mr. *Savage* should therefore kill you or me, Gentlemen of the Jury?[13]

Those gentlemen of course find Savage and Gregory guilty of murder and their unarmed friend Merchant guilty of manslaughter. The judge-become-prosecutor reinforces our confidence in the fair-minded narrator who allows us to become a judge of the judge. The outburst also evokes our sympathy for Savage, which Johnson allows him to enhance with a speech that in calendar time is four days after and in reading time a few seconds after that of Judge Page. It is polite, refuses to defend a sorry act, recognizes the court's intelligence and ability to make distinctions, and therefore appeals for mercy similar to that given to the instigator of the quarrel. Here are Savage's final words: "I hope, this will not be construed as if we meant to reflect upon that Gentleman, or remove any Thing from us upon him, or that we repine the more at our Fate, because he has no Participation of it: No, my Lord! For my Part, I declare nothing could more soften my Grief, than to be without any Companion in as great a Misfortune" (p. 36). We see justice set against mercy, brutality against compassion, and the powerful against the powerless. Johnson draws the reader into the evaluative process by allowing the protagonist and antagonist their own words; narrative becomes drama, and readers become spectators and auditors of a case which tries Savage, his judge, and his other tormentors. "Thus," the narrator says summing up Savage's enemies, "had [he] perished by the Evidence of a Bawd, a Strumpet, and his Mother" (p. 38).

Though Savage ultimately is pardoned, prison comes again to this unfortunate man, and now it is indeed fatal. By the end of the biography we must agree that Savage's death is his own not his mother's fault. Once he is jailed in Bristol for a small debt he undergoes a familiar prison enlargement; he is stable, tranquil, has time to write, and ingratiates himself with the warden who feeds him at his own table and at his own expense, so that Savage "suffered fewer Hardships in the Prison, than he had been accustomed to undergo in the greatest part of his Life" (p. 126). Once again, however, Johnson relinquishes the narrative with symbolic effect, for we see that Savage is his own jailer, is evidence against himself, and alienates most of those who would help him, whether the burghers of Bristol, numerous friends, or the reader.

Johnson provides four of Savage's sponging-house or prison letters. A short one is addressed to a friend in London, and shows him tranquil and emotionally collected while his mind ranges freely (p. 125). Another longer one is even more benevolent, and "remarkable" (p. 122). He praises the civility of the arresting officers; he urges the friend not to harbor resentment against his litigant or solicit money on his behalf; and he concludes with Christian resignation, aristocratic largesse suitable to his pretended rank, and thanks for his courteous treatment and alleviating circumstances.

> I murmur not, but am all Resignation to the *divine Will*. As to the World, I hope that I shall be endued by Heaven with that Presence of Mind, that serene Dignity in Misfortune, that constitutes the Character of a true Nobleman; a Dignity far beyond that of Coronets; a nobility arising from the just Principles of Philosophy, refined and exalted by those of Christianity. (p. 123)

Such equanimity cannot fail to endear—and end, for in Savage's two other letters he shows his familiar instability and disorientation. In one he complains that he is subjected to numerous foolish systems that have "quite made a Chaos of my Imagination, and nothing done—promised—disappointed—ordered to send every hour, from one part of the Town to the other" (p. 123). Chaos replaces collection, dependence replaces independence, and a supplicant's compliance replaces a nobleman's dignity. Since few of us could be benign in an eighteenth-century prison, vacillation of mood may be unavoidable. Even this excuse vanishes when Savage comes to oppose his own interests. The prisoner in Bristol, supported by Bristol charity, decides to write and sign a satire attacking Bristol's mean behavior. When the bookseller Edward Cave tries to dissuade him from so imprudent an act, he receives this bridge-burning reply:

> You understand not, why Secrecy is injoin'd, and yet I intend to set my Name to it. My Answer is—I have my private Reasons; which I am not obliged to explain to any One. You doubt, my Friend Mr. S[trong] would not approve of it—And what is it to me whether he does or not? Do you imagine that Mr. S[trong] is to dictate to me? If any Man, who calls himself my Friend, should assume such an Air, I would spurn at his Friendship with Contempt . . . You go on in saying, suppose, I should not put my Name to it. My Answer is, that I will not suppose any such Thing, being determined to the contrary; neither, Sir, would I have you suppose that I applied to you for want of another Press. (pp. 131–32)

The narrator confirms our own assessment of a rash act prevented only by Savage's death. He "disregarded all Considerations that opposed his present Passions, and . . . hazarded all future Advantages for any immediate Gratifications" (p. 132). Savage's instability here is an emblem of his instability in life—namely, we have admired his conduct as seen in his two warmly affectionate and noble letters, and as readers offer him our approbation, the reader's literary equivalent of help in life. Almost immediately thereafter we see his petulance, self-involvement, and inability to grow through help offered. We withdraw our approbation and understand those in life who do so as well. We also more than ever share the narrator's judgment—that mankind must be exonerated from being Savage's worst enemy (pp. 98–99), that he blamed everyone but himself for his misfortunes (p. 73), and that "he scarcely ever found a Stranger, whom he did not leave a Friend; but . . . he had not often a Friend long, without obliging him to become a stranger" (p. 69). Johnson as narrator makes these points by means of exposition in his own voice; he confirms the points by surrendering his voice to Savage's, so that the reader experiences the change from friend to stranger, understands Lord Tyrconnel who also felt obliged to dismiss so uncertain a guest, and reluctantly decides that the narrator's final sympathetic censure is correct. After giving Savage a share in the narrative, Johnson regains it with enhanced authority; his points are made the better for having Savage make them for him.

5

Rasselas is a more complex and mature work than *Savage*, and part of that complexity appears in its manifold variations of narrative, here characterized in part by the interpolated tale. Imlac's is the first.

The prince's aeronautic escape route collapses into the lake and his "imagination . . . was at a stand."[14] Rains and floods force him inside, where he listens to Imlac's poem on the several conditions of humanity, he is reinvigorated, and engages Imlac in five chapters of private conversation.

Imlac's history serves several functions. Its occasion in a flood anticipates subsequent uses of the Nile as a plot device, and as a metaphor of necessary movement in life and the impossibility of choosing incompatible options—like drinking from the source and the mouth of that river (YE 16:110). It also makes clear the analogical structure of the work and of life. Imlac's tale not only supports the preliminary findings and tone of the main narrator; it also is a tale of a young man rebelling against parentally defined good, who leaves his home, blunders about the world, becomes disillusioned, seeks a calm retirement in the Happy Valley, and then again seeks to escape to quotidian ambiguities. Shared human experiences bond the poet and prince, and suggest that Imlac will not allow Rasselas to enter the world without guidance.

Imlac's tale also introduces his own acceptable weaknesses, so that his later corrections by Pekuah are not wholly surprising. The dissertation on poetry in chapter 10, after all, includes a good deal of stuff that Johnson himself would reject—like the poet as "legislator of mankind" (YE 16:45)—and that even naïve Rasselas knows to be excessive (YE 16:46).[15] Imlac's choice of life as poet has deficiencies enough to recommend withdrawal both to and from the Happy Valley. Hence, by the end of chapter 13 and the long interview, Rasselas and the tale have direction and hope, each man confides that he wishes to escape from his gilded prison, and Rasselas anoints his friend as "the companion of my flight, the guide of my rambles, the partner of my fortune, and my sole director in the *choice of life*" (YE 16:56). One of the functions of the other interpolations or changes in narrative voice is to show what happens when Rasselas either shifts guides or attempts to become one himself. He later hears the eloquent stoic, for example, finds a new mentor, and wrongly proclaims: "This man shall be my future guide: I will learn his doctrines, and imitate his life" (YE 16:74). That Rasselas still needs a guide just had been made clear.

Once the royal fugitives are fit for the world, Imlac takes them to Cairo where Rasselas "associates with young men of spirit and gaiety" (YE 16:68), with sensualists who enjoy some of the Happy Valley's pleasures without its restraints. Rasselas soon finds that absence of mind is no more appealing without than within the valley and commences to lecture his well-gratified colleagues. His exuberant proselytism signals his distance from Imlac who briefly frees Rasselas from his tether. Happiness, the prince knows, "must be something solid and permanent, without fear and without uncertainty" (YE 16:69), and so he generously contributes his knowledge to his fellows, who should the more readily accept his wisdom. He thus speaks of *our* manners, prospects, and interests; he asks us to consider the brevity of youth and the proximity of age when we shall have only the comforts of the wise. "Let us," he concludes, "therefore, stop, while to stop is in our power: let us live as men who are sometime to grow old" and reform accordingly (YE 16:69–70). Good intentions and just sentiments evoke only laughter and the expulsion of the visitor who has not earned a share in *we* and *us*, and remains an outsider speaking to *them*. For the first time in his life, Prince Rasselas is subject to "the horrour of derision" (YE 16:70).

Imlac and Johnson have allowed this embarrassing lesson to make clear that Rasselas is not ready for successful independent inquiry; he is both mistaken regarding the certainty of happiness, and tactless in his preaching. In contrast, Imlac is like the work's general narrator who refuses to scold the chapter's soggy pilot as latter-day Icarus fallen from his own pride. Instead, he and Imlac normally allow the student to make his own errors and draw his own inferences. At the end of chapter 45 Imlac thus "forbore to force upon [Rasselas, Nekayah, and Pekuah] unwelcome knowledge, which time itself would too soon impress" (YE 16:157). Rasselas vocally scolds where Imlac silently teaches; Rasselas believes in certainty where Imlac believes in search; Rasselas is derided where Imlac is respected; and Rasselas separates where Imlac unites. Accordingly, even when Imlac's charges briefly leave him and fail, they return without damage or derision.

This happens upon Imlac's second major absence. By now, Rasselas has joined with Nekayah and against Imlac who, they convince themselves at the end of chapter 23, "favours not our search [for absolute happiness], lest we should in time find him mistaken" (YE 16:89). When Imlac again disappears, new voices control and report the narrative and divide into gender-specific roles. Rasselas investigates the larger world of power and politics, Nekayah the smaller world of family and marriage.[16]

Their interpolation thus begins with the harmony of optimistic brother and sister working in parallel areas. Hitherto, they had seen many failures but no fatalities in the choice of life. Now, however, Rasselas finds that in government ultimate power evokes ultimate risk. The Bassa was forever spied upon, soon was "carried in chains to Constantinople," and his name banished from memory. Shortly thereafter, "the second Bassa was deposed. The Sultan, that had advanced him, was murdered by the Janissaries, and his successor had other views and different favourites." Chains and murder enter the tale, and Rasselas, disillusioned with "the prerogatives of power" (YE 16:91), turns to his sister's inquiries into the domestic kingdom. Alas, its conflicts though less dangerous are not less intense, as parents and children, like sultan and bassa, torment each other. Having seen failure in both estates, Nekayah painfully asks, "where shall we look for tenderness and consolation?" (YE 16:97). The discord that Nekayah describes soon reappears when she and Rasselas squabble, and he accuses her of being no more than Imlac in skirts, for like him "she had surveyed life with prejudice, and supposed misery where she did not find it." Indeed, "your narrative . . . throws yet a darker gloom upon the prospects of futurity: the predictions of Imlac were but faint sketches of the evils painted by Nekayah" (YE 16:99). Without conciliating guidance Rasselas accuses her of harboring contradictory "wrong opinions," and Nekayah, stung by his unbrotherly insult, replies that "I did not expect . . . to hear that imputed to falsehood which is the consequence only of frailty." Happily, the poison of discord evokes its own antidote, as these good young persons exemplify the strength as well as the weakness of the family, which now heals rather than harms. The prince offers the lenitive of an apologetic brother, who asks that they "not add . . . to the other evils of life, the bitterness of controversy" or the subtleties of argument. "It is . . . fit that we assist each other" (YE 16:104–6). Yet again, though, good intentions lead only to confusion and self-deception, to Rasselas's charming dream that when he seeks a wife his first question shall be whether she is "willing to be led by reason" (YE 16:109), and to his consequent admission that the unhappiness of private life almost discourages him "from further search" (YE 16:110). His state now is even worse than when his imagination was at a stand before he met Imlac in the Happy Valley.

The episode that began with Rasselas and Nekayah excluding Imlac, working together, and searching for an expected answer, nearly ends with brother and sister patching together their tattered friendship, disillusioned with the unforeseen grim fruits of their inquiry, and recognizing that they have just suffered another choice of life—the bickering of the family that rejects paternal guidance. I said *nearly* so ends, because the nice symmetry of the interpolation returns Imlac to narration and to a protective role. The final paragraph of chapter 29 thus begins with Nekayah's reevocation of Imlac, for "Every hour," she says, "confirms my prejudice in favour of the position so often uttered by the mouth of Imlac, 'That nature sets her gifts on the right hand and on the left' " (YE 16:110). This wisdom is the cue for Imlac's own reappearance in chapter 30, as he corrects their insularity, unifies them in their search for the good, and convinces them that the past helps one judge the present, "for all judgement is comparative" (YE 16:112). With Imlac's restoration the relative replaces the absolute, movement replaces stagnation, and "they set out the next day" (YE 16:114) to visit the pyramids. The only voice hitherto unheard is that of Pekuah, whose abduction to the seraglio reopens narrative complexity and heightens the tale's limited character development.

In the *Rambler*, No. 60, Johnson insists that the reader is more likely to learn from biography if its main character is close to ordinary life. For most of us, "histories of the downfall of kingdoms, and revolutions of empires, are read with great tranquillity" and dismissed as useless (YE 3:319). Perhaps that is why Nekayah's tales of the family are so much longer than Rasselas's tales of sultans and bassas, and why Pekuah emerges as so attractive and sensible a character. Like much else in the structures of this work, Pekuah's tale is analogous to other tales. Upon her first appearance she is a nameless "single favourite, who did not know whither she was going" (YE 16:61). She is an ignorant secondary character subjected to the direction of the dominant restless male seeking his own happiness. Now, however, she becomes an aristocratic woman of beauty, authority, and intelligence. Along the way, she also shows that, unlike the royal Nekayah and Rasselas, she can absorb Imlac's lessons, avoid self-indulgent angst, and reject unacceptable choices of life without regret at the loss of mythology.

We at once see Pekuah assume command under stress. The other kidnapped servants look to her for help, and so in spite of her own fears she consoles and encourages them, preserves order, is treated with respect, and convinces the Arab's women that she is a princess worth a great price. Henceforth the "maid of common rank" quickly learns the value of appearance, influence, and control. She becomes "leader of the troop" who dictates the day's march and the night's rest, and transforms the abduction into a tour through the desert under the Arab's guidance (YE 16:131–36). Once they are in his fortress on an island of the Nile her power increases yet more, as she becomes an able student of astronomy, the focus of jealousy and adjudication for the native women, and their governess upon the Arab's frequent rambles (YE 16:138–41).

We thus learn about Pekuah's inner state, about her confidence and recognizable human vanities. She knows that "no sum would be thought too great for the release of Pekuah" (YE 16:135); she regards the denizens of the harem as merely having "that unaffecting and ignoble beauty which may subsist without spriteliness or sublimity, without energy of thought or dignity of virtue" (YE 16:139–40).[17] They are more like pretty birds, frisking lambs, or plucked flowers than the compelling presence Pekuah so well knows herself to be that she fears the Arab will fall in love with her and refuse her ransom. This fear is seconded when Imlac himself asks, "how could a mind, hungry for knowledge, be willing, in an intellectual famine, to lose such a banquet as Pekuah's conversation?" (YE 16:140).

Imlac's question, together with another regarding the Arab's pleasure in his seraglio, denotes his first change from informer to inquirer, and the first time that we see a failed choice countered by a successful one. The failure is of course the Arab's, who embodies the fantasies of absolute freedom, acquisition of power, and infinite sexual gratification with willing subjects. These sterile pleasures collapse in the face of one accidental meeting with an able woman to whom some of his authority gladly is relinquished; but only some, for this man is a prisoner of his own liberty and greed. Though he often delays sending for her ransom, once confronted with it his budding love for Pekuah surrenders to his full-bloom love of gold. "He hastened to prepare for our journey hither," Pekuah reports, "like a man delivered from the pain of an intestine conflict" (YE 16:141). On the other hand, Pekuah herself has no conflict. She might have been the mistress of many servants, the ruler of a fortress, and the consort of a reasonably learned man of courage, wealth, courtesy, and birth as one of the "natural and hereditary lords of this part of the continent" (YE 16:134). Instead, she chooses to return to subordination and love in her extended family, to the old order rather than creation of a new. Her interpolated tale thus serves as a further modification of the princess's inadequate vision of the family, for it supplies solace, support, and memory that translate into practical virtue. Pekuah returns to the distant, re-achievable, and fallible norm from which the intransigent nomad is self-exiled. Her growth suggests that the group at large now may be ready for its own mature decisions. The resolved dialogue between Rasselas and Nekayah leads to the pyramids; the resolved abduction of Pekuah leads back to Cairo, where an ancillary adventure begins, and Johnson again enhances his longer narrative by varying the lesser narratives within. Having let us hear Imlac, Rasselas, Nekayah, and Pekuah, he introduces a major new character and leads us towards a satisfactory conclusion.

Hitherto, we met several exemplars of a choice of life, saw their weaknesses, and left them enlightened or darkened as the case may be. The one exception within the Happy Valley is Imlac, who now is paralleled by the astronomer in Cairo, who becomes the only person to join the pilgrims. Such violation of pattern both requires and provides an explanation.

This astronomer immediately recalls the Arab rover, who also was an astronomer and taught the motions of the stars to Pekuah. These links with the Arab thus also are links with Pekuah, whose importance is reiterated. Imlac condescendingly tells her that she is incapable of understanding the astronomer's exalted teachings. Like the clever, slightly vain, and very attractive woman we know her to be, Pekuah responds with, "My knowledge is, perhaps, more than you imagine it, and by concurring always with his opinions I shall make him think it greater than it is" (YE 16:159). She is as good as her word. When she elegantly tells her tale to the astronomer "her conversation took possession of his heart," and "he looked upon her as a prodigy of genius" (YE 16:160). He also looked on her with love—not, I think, that of the Arab's hesitant, undesired, and ultimately sexual sort, but that of an aged parent for an uncommonly gifted child apparently in his own image. Hence his obsession with controlling the world's weather though merely "disentangled by the prince's conversation," is "instantaneously released at the entrance of Pekuah." The fallible paragon Imlac, finally accepting the power of the once obscure favorite, confirms the progress of the astronomer's cure and advises that when he is tempted back to the mastery of the stars, "fly to business or to Pekuah" (YE 16:162–63).

The astronomer's cure is possible because, unlike the Arab rover, he is benevolent, wishes to give not take, and is able to change through Pekuah's intervention. His illness is not that of an intestine conflict but, as Nekayah and Pekuah must be told, one of the mind that deserves our sympathy. Moreover, unlike the other wise old man who appears, is tired of the world, and casts his eyes upward only to think "with pain on the vicissitudes of life" (YE 16:155), the astronomer casts his eyes upward in order to determine how best to serve humanity.

The cure of the astronomer also is the cure of the group itself. For the first time we see them working together, not as Imlac's pupils but partners in an action that helps another decent man to escape from a bad choice of life; a mechanistic looking upward only for the sake of the design not the designer leads to frustration and madness. *Rasselas* nearly begins with improper indulgence of the senses; it nearly ends with improper indulgence of the mind.

The arrival of the astronomer leads to the work's final episode, the visit to the convent of Saint Anthony and its catacombs. This immediately recalls the visit to the Pyramid, an emblem of the vanity of human wishes and a free-standing elevated tomb into which Pekuah refuses to go and from which she is abducted. Now, however, she joins her friends in the catacombs and in hearing Imlac's dissertation on the immateriality of the soul. The astronomer's mechanism is answered by the poet's theology. Johnson moves as close as he dares to Christian solace in an oriental tale, as Rasselas, the young prince once so depressed about the apparent violence within the state and the family, sees that such darkness occurs only with limited vision, one made brighter by his experience underground: "How gloomy would be these mansions of the dead to him who did not know that he shall never die; that what now acts shall continue its agency, and what now thinks shall think on for ever." His sister and former disputant draws the logical inference: "the choice of life is become less important; I hope hereafter to think only on the choice of eternity" (YE 16:175). The last spoken word of dialogue in the tale is "eternity," as the enquiries both accept human unhappiness and see that it can be transmuted.

The narrative interludes and interpolations, then, serve several functions. Imlac establishes the voice of mature leadership that places the young inquirers in good hands as they repeat some of his adventures, and find that he is an acceptably flawed guide who also learns on their journeys. When Rasselas and Nekayah search on their own, they see how harsh life can be without a guide, and so Imlac must restore order, hope, and continuing investigation. Thereafter, the newly compelling Pekuah begins the upward movement of the work, and provides a character more like ourselves who can learn some of Imlac's lessons, reject an inadequate choice of life, and return to Nekayah and reasonable subordination. She also teaches Imlac about relationships between the sexes, as she and the royal siblings work with him actively to help the disturbed benevolent astronomer who is superior to her abductor, and inferior to the best self that the collective group helps him and themselves become. The interpolations thus vary the narrator's voices and experiences, allow the exchange of mind, comparisons and contrasts, and symbolic implications from literal events; they also complicate the plot while rendering it coherent and optimistic in the face of frequent failure frequently overcome.

These changes of voice, together with the significant personal pronoun and the fallible paragon, are among Johnson's most successful narrative devices. He asks us to be partners in creating the text and our own moral education. In so doing, he shares both eighteenth-century rhetoric and theology; he assumes our common father, the consequent reciprocity and brotherhood of man, and the obligation of those who have towards those who have not. Under such dispensation, the eternal master finds Johnson's talent both well employed and well distributed through arts of narration on behalf of an audience of colleagues.

NOTES

1. For Pope and Martha Blount, see the "Life of Pope" in *Lives of the English Poets*, ed. George Birkbeck Hill (Oxford: Clarendon Press, 1905), 3:190. For Congreve, see *Boswell's Life of Johnson Together with Boswell's Journal of a Tour of the Hebrides*, ed. George Birkbeck Hill and rev. L. F. Powell (Oxford: Clarendon Press, 1934–50), 2:460, on March 22, 1776; referred to hereafter as *Life*. See April 11, 1776, 3:37, for Goldsmith, who "never exchanged mind with you."

2. The Yale Edition of the Works of Samuel Johnson, vol. 3, *The Rambler*, ed. W. J. Bate and Albrecht B. Strauss (New Haven: Yale University Press, 1969), 3:319. Unless otherwise specified, all subsequent references to Johnson's works are from this edition and are cited as YE.

3. *Rambler*, No. 160, YE 5:86 ; Preface to *A Dictionary of the English Language*, in *The Works of Samuel Johnson, LL.D.* (Oxford, 1825), 5:51; Palais Bourbon, October 17, 1775, in *Life*, 2:393; *Rambler*, No. 160, YE 5:88. For the reference to the Palais Bourbon, see also YE 1, *Diaries, Prayers, and Annals*, ed. E. L. McAdam, Jr., with Donald and Mary Hyde (1958), p. 238.

4. YE 14, *Sermons*, ed. Jean Hagstrum and James Gray (1978), p. 146. Subsequent citations to this edition are given in the text. The sermons have been well discussed by James Gray in *Johnson's Sermons: A Study* (Oxford: Clarendon Press, 1972). Other aspects of Johnson's religious thought may be found in Paul K. Alkon's *Samuel Johnson and Moral Discipline* (Evanston, IL: Northwestern University Press, 1967), pp. 180–214; and Chester F. Chapin, *The Religious Thought of Samuel Johnson* (Ann Arbor, MI: University of Michigan Press, 1968). All of these, together with numerous other valuable studies, also cast light on Johnson as a moralist.

5. *The Spectator*, ed. Donald F. Bond (Oxford: Clarendon Press, 1965), 4:318; Preface to Shakespeare, YE 7, *Johnson on Shakespeare*, ed. Arthur Sherbo (1968), p. 104; "Life of Cowley," *Lives*, 1:53, regarding *Davideis*.

6. "To question, v.n. . . . 1. To enquire": Johnson's quotation ends with "asketh"; for the rest, see *The Essays . . . of Francis Lo. Vervlam* (London, 1625), p. 196; YE 10, *Political Writings*, ed. Donald J. Greene (1977), p. 9. This remark is from a work generally attributed to Johnson: "Examination of a Question Proposed in the [Gentleman's] Magazine of June, p. 310." For further discussion of ways in which eighteenth-century authors engage readers in their texts, see "The Reader, the General, and the Particular: Johnson and Imlac in Chapter Ten of *Rasselas*," and " 'No Mock Debate' " within; and Eric Rothstein, " 'Ideal Presence' and the 'Non Finito' in Eighteenth-Century Aesthetics," *Eighteenth-Century Studies* 9 (1976): 307–32.

7. *Life* 2:431–32.

8. Johnson also observes that the verb "To Thou" is "To treat with familiarity." For eighteenth-century examples of this, see Richardson's *Pamela* (1740), in the revised 14th edition (London, 1801), 1:116, after Mr. Andrews's receipt of Squire B's letter (this is heightened from the first edition), and Fielding's *Tom Jones* (1749), book 5, chapter 9. "Thou" also suggested the continental *tu-toi* of intimacy between equals, as in *Clarissa* (1747–48). Richardson adds a note to Lovelace's first letter to Belford: "These gentlemen affected what they called the Roman Style (to wit, the thee and the thou) in their letters: and it was an agreed rule with them, to take in good part whatever freedoms they treated each other with, if the passages were written in that style": *Clarissa*, intro. John Butt (London: Dent and Dutton 1967), 1:114 n.

9. YE 6, *Poems*, ed. E. L. McAdam, Jr., with George Milne (1964), p. 93, lines 39–40. Subsequent line numbers are given in the text. For some other studies, on varied aspects of the poem, see Weinbrot, *The Formal Strain: Studies in Augustan Imitation and Satire* (Chicago: University of Chicago Press, 1969), pp. 193–217; W. J. Bate, "Johnson and Satire Manqué," in *Eighteenth-Century Studies in Honor of Donald F. Hyde*, ed. W. H. Bond (New York: Grolier Club, 1970), pp. 145–60; Bate, *Samuel Johnson* (New York: Harcourt Brace Jovanovich, 1975), pp. 277–89; Donald J. Greene, *Samuel Johnson* (New York: Twayne, 1970), pp. 56–63; William Kupersmith, "Declamatory Grandeur: Johnson and Juvenal," *Arion* 9 (1970): 52–72; Raman Selden, "Dr. Johnson and Juvenal: A Problem in Critical Method," *Comparative Literature* 22 (1970):289–302; D.V. Boyd, "Vanity and Vacuity: A Reading of Johnson's Verse Satires," *ELH* 39 (1972): 387–403; Kupersmith, " 'More like an Orator than a Philosopher': Rhetorical Structure in *The Vanity of Human Wishes*," *Studies in Philology* 72 (1975): 454–72; Lawrence Lipking, "Learning to Read Johnson: *The Vision of Theodore* and *The Vanity of Human Wishes*," *ELH* 43 (1976): 517–37; and John E. Sitter, "To *The Vanity of Human Wishes* Through the 1740's" *Studies in Philology* 74 (1977): 445–64.

10. To Burney, *The Letters of Samuel Johnson*, ed. Bruce Redford (Princeton: Princeton University Press, 1992–94), 1:256, October 16, 1765. See also *Life*, 1:499–50, for the letter's context as part of the response to Johnson's Preface to Shakespeare. For the comments on *Paradise Lost*, see the "Life of Milton," *Lives*, 1:242, and 1:188, respectively.

11. *Works*, 1825, 5:34 (have not), 35 (task, some words, Cicero), 25 (barbarity).

12. *Rambler*, No. 4, YE, 3:24; *Life*, 4:53, March 15, 1782, in the context of including "an unpleasing account" of Addison's conduct towards Steele (4:52). Boswell regards this discussion as "of great importance" for his own biographical method (4:53).

13. Samuel Johnson, *Life of Savage*, ed. Clarence Tracy (Oxford: Clarendon Press, 1971), p. 34. Subsequent citations from this edition are given in the text. Tracy conjectures that this speech, unlike Savage's thereafter, "may be indebted considerably to [John-

son's] imagination" (p. 34 n); if so, the evidence for Johnson's shaping of his narrative by shaping those of others is stronger. Critical studies of *Savage* still profit from Tracy's *The Artificial Bastard: A Biography of Richard Savage* (Cambridge, MA: Harvard University Press, 1953). For more recent work, see William Vesterman, "Johnson and *The Life of Savage*," *ELH* 36 (1969): 659–78; John A. Dussinger, "Style and Intention in Johnson's *Life of Savage*," *ELH* 37 (1970): 564–80; Paul K. Alkon, "The Intention and Reception of Johnson's Life of Savage," *Modern Philology* 72 (1974): 139–50; Robert W. Uphaus, "The 'Equipoise' of Johnson's *Life of Savage*," *Studies in Burke and His Time* 17 (1976): 43–54; Virginia Spencer Davidson, "Johnson's *Life of Savage*: The Transformation of a Genre," *Studies in Biography*, ed. Daniel Aaron, Harvard Studies in English No. 8 (Cambridge, MA.: Harvard University Press, 1978), pp. 57–72; Robert Folkenflik, *Samuel Johnson, Biographer* (Ithaca, NY: Cornell University Press, 1978), pp. 195–213; and John J. Burke, Jr., "Excellence in Biography: *Rambler*, No. 60 and Johnsonian Early Biographies," *South Atlantic Bulletin* 44, No. 2 (1979): 14–34.

14. *Rasselas* is quoted from YE 16, *Rasselas and Other Tales*, ed. Gwin J. Kolb (1990), p. 29. Subsequent references are given in the text, as YE 16 and page number. Useful studies of *Rasselas* include Gwin J. Kolb, "The Structure of Rasselas," *PMLA* 66 (1951): 698–717; Frederick W. Hilles, "*Rasselas*, An 'Uninstructive Tale,'" in *Johnson, Boswell, and Their Circle: Essays Presented to Lawrence Fitzroy Powell* (Oxford: Clarendon Press, 1965), pp. 111–21; Emrys Jones, "The Artistic Form of *Rasselas*," *Review of English Studies* n.s. 18 (1967): 387–401; Mary Lascelles, "*Rasselas*: A Rejoinder," *Review of English Studies*, n.s. 21 (1970): 49–56; Carey MacIntosh, *The Choice of Life: Samuel Johnson and the World of Fiction* (New Haven: Yale University Press, 1973), pp. 93–102; Eric Rothstein, *Systems of Order and Inquiry in Later Eighteenth-Century Fiction* (Berkeley and Los Angeles: University of California Press, 1975), pp. 23–61; Earl S. Wasserman, "Johnson's *Rasselas*: Implicit Contexts," *Journal of English and Germanic Philology* 74 (1975): 1–25; and Irvin Ehrenpreis, "*Rasselas* and Some Meanings of 'Structure' in Literary Criticism," *Novel* 14 (1981): 101–17.

15. See "The Reader, the General, and the Particular," within, and for other doubts regarding Imlac's infallibility, see Alvin Whitley, "The Comedy of *Rasselas*," *ELH* 23 (1956): 48–70; Clarence Tracy, "Democritus Arise! A Study of Dr. Johnson's Humor," *Yale Review* 39 (1949): 294–310; William K. Wimsatt, Jr., "In Praise of *Rasselas*: Four Notes (Converging)," in *Imagined worlds: Essays . . . in Honour of John Butt*, ed. Maynard Mack and Ian Gregor (London: Methuen, 1968), p. 127, and Rothstein, *Systems of Order and Inquiry*, pp. 27–29. Imlac is, however, more than sufficient to the occasion. I refer to him as a "fallible paragon" and gratefully borrow the term from chapter 3 of Sheldon Sacks's *Fiction and the Shape of Belief* (Berkeley and Los Angeles: University of California Press, 1967).

16. Hilles, *"Rasselas,"* p. 113, and Rothstein, *Systems of Order and Inquiry,* pp. 41–42, observe the increase in dramatic action here. The greatest increase comes with the unified group's renovation of the astronomer. See also Bate, *Samuel Johnson,* p. 340, and T. F. Wharton, *Samuel Johnson and the Theme of Hope* (New York: St. Martin's Press, 1984), pp. 98, 111.

17. Johnson is softening the implications of life in the seraglio. In *Irene* (1749) Aspasia tells Irene:

> Soon shall the dire seraglio's horrid gates
> Close like th' eternal bars of death upon thee,

Immur'd, and buried in perpetual sloth,
That gloomy slumber of the stagnant soul.

(YE 6:165)

See also his definition of *Seraglio* in the *Dictionary* as "A house of women kept for debauchery," and the illustrative quotation from John Norris's *Collection of Miscellanies* (1687; final edition 1710): "There is a great deal more solid content to be found in a constant course of well living, than in the voluptuousness of a *seraglio*." Johnson must have approved of Pekuah's good judgment and, under the circumstances, temperate observations regarding the "debauched" harem women. On the other hand, he also could joke about a seraglio, including a fancied one of his own. See *Life*, 3:368, 5:216 and 5:538, the latter on the tour to the Hebrides.

7

Johnson and the Domestic Metaphor

THE CHORUS SINGING SAMUEL JOHNSON'S LITERARY STYLE HAS CHANTED the same notes for some 250 years. It ritually utters that he is abstract, abstruse, affected, alien, alliterative, allusive, Anglo-Latin, antiquated, antithetical, bombastic, cumbrous, extravagant, gigantic, Latinate, licentious, magnificent, metaphorical, parallel, pedantic, philosophical, pompous, rigid, scientific and, often, vicious.

Robert Burrowes epitomizes this multiverbal monotone. In 1787 he told the Royal Irish Academy in Dublin that wherever possible Johnson chose "the remote word of Latin derivation to the received English one, and has brought in the whole vocabulary of natural philosophy, to perplex and encumber familiar English writing." Burrowes uses a surely negative term in an Irish context. Johnson is like a colonial master "disdaining an association with the natives, and threatening the final destruction of our language." This is especially so in the *Rambler* with so many long foreign words and sounds that one needs "an interpreter." His allusions are "abstruse and scientific, and his expressions . . . studiously technical."[1]

Such remarks were and are commonplace—whether drawn from Archibald Campbell's Johnsonian Dr. Malaprop of 1767, or Arthur Murphy's "JUPITER TONANS" of 1792, or William K. Wimsatt, Jr.'s still dominantly influential generalizing Johnson of 1941. Even the sympathetic Murphy thinks that Johnson was unwilling "to descend to the familiar idiom and the variety of diction" it required.[2]

Some earlier and later commentators have tried to enliven this tired song. Robert Anderson accurately observes both that Johnson uses different styles for different works and that his poetry is less Latinate than his prose. Alexander Chalmers knows that Johnson's Latinate diction has been overstated and that he later revised and simplified his *Rambler*.[3] Donald Greene and Paul Fussell are among the few modern Johnsonians who have reiterated and expanded these insights while failing signifi-

146

cantly to change many minds and, certainly, not those still influenced by Wimsatt's important works.[4]

Exercise indeed has hardened and enlarged this ancient body of criticism. Wimsatt's admiring but politically neutral expositions have been supplemented by recent ideological judgments. The Right thinks it laudable that Johnson's Anglo-Latin style encodes his courageous and principled wise Tory Jacobitism. He was, the argument goes, part of a movement between about 1660 and 1750 in which "the classics were one means by which a social order, dynastic, gentlemanly, and episcopalian, came to conceive of itself and to resist what it defined as its enemies."[5] The Left thinks it lamentable that Johnson's Anglo-Latin style encodes his wicked and politically improper London-oriented hegemonic denigration of spoken or written English by other than the upper classes.[6]

In 1766 Johnson himself commented on comparably complacent intellectual homogeneity: "I wish there were some cure like the Lover's leap, for all heads of which some single Idea has obtained an unreasonable and irregular possession."[7] Scholars are even less willing than lovers to leap into voids to cure tunnel vision, but at least in our case the effort may be healthy rather than fatal.

If, after all, Johnson was as unrelentingly Latinate as Burrowes and others have claimed, he would not write sentences like these from his angry review of Soame Jenyns's *Free Enquiry* (1757): "life must be seen before it can be known." Jenyns's notion of gods who can toy with human beings evokes a largely monosyllabic reductive outburst: "as we drown whelps and kittens, they amuse themselves now and then with sinking a ship, and stand round the fields of *Blenheim* or the walls of *Prague*, as we encircle a cock-pit." Nor would he create Betty Broom in the *Idler*, No. 26 (1758): "I am a poor girl. I was bred in the country at a charity school." Nor would he allow Pekuah to describe the Arab's harem-girls in *Rasselas* (1759) as familiar creatures. "They ran from room to room as a bird hops from wire to wire in his cage. They danced for the sake of motion, as lambs frisk in a meadow." Nor in *A Journey to the Western Islands* (1775) would he complain that at Coriatachan in Sky the islanders "have milk, and eggs, and sugar, [but] few of them know how to compound them in a custard."[8]

If, after all, Johnson's prose reflected a classicist's Tory Jacobite gentleman's order he would not proclaim the irrelevance of classical history for modern culture. Talk of "*that* stuff," he said about the Punic War or Catiline's conspiracy, was "lost time . . . and carried one away from common life, leaving no ideas behind which could serve *living wight* as warning or direction." Nor in the Preface to *The Preceptor* (1748) would he tell young boys likely to be among the voting or perhaps even governing elite that they should study ungentlemanly Whiggish "Trade and Commerce . . . which it becomes every Man of this Nation to understand." Nor when he recommends books that "may qualify [the student] to act and judge as one of a Free People" would he offer a list that is a Whig, or worse, pantheon. It includes works by Sir John Fortescue, Nathaniel Bacon, Henry Neville, John Locke, Sir William Temple, Thomas Gordon, and William Blackstone. Bacon's Tacitean *Historical Discourse* (1647), for example, was drafted into parliamentary opposition to the Stuarts, who suppressed the 1672 edition. He glorified Britain's Saxon ancestors who "used their Kings in no other manner than as servants of state." Temple's *Introduction to the History of England* (1695) praises William of Normandy as a surrogate for his friend William of Orange.[9] Nor would Mrs. Piozzi rightly note Johnson's "prodigious" respect for "what we call low or coarse life" and his refusal to allow the upper classes to "be dignified with the name of *the world*."[10]

If, after all, Johnson was the willing tool of a class system, his dictionary would not sometimes be labeled too colloquial and slangy. Nor would he scold Sir Joshua Reynolds for defining fashion in terms of the swells who sat for him and ask Mrs. Piozzi that "if every man who wears a laced coat (that he can pay for) was extirpated, who would miss them?"[11] Nor in the *Adventurer*, No. 111 (1753) would he excoriate those who merely inherit rather than create wealth (YE 2:455). Nor would he be criticized for disrespect to his social betters and his style be attacked as wrongly teaching the "vulgar" to be uppity. That style was inappropriate for an eighteenth-century gentleman whose lordly lightness contrasts with Johnson's weighty words. Horace Walpole always treats Johnson's diction with contempt and berates its "masculine toughness that resists all ease and graceful movement." Walpole finds writers and authors "bad company. They are always in earnest, and think their professions serious, and dwell upon trifles, and reverence learning. I laugh at all those things," says the future fourth Earl of Orford in 1773.[12]

Perhaps we can return to a descriptive rather than prescriptive mode of proceeding. That method regards Johnson as valuable for his humane instruction and delight rather than for his role as a bearer of presumably more important political truths. I also suggest reconsideration of some conventional wisdom that confuses the part with the whole, the simple truth of Johnson's frequent Latinity with the complex fuller truth of his varied styles of which Latinity is one element.

I thus offer three possible and sometimes overlapping explanations for Johnson's colloquial style: the moral extension that his familiar language allows; the affective contrast between his homely metaphors in particular and his Latinate diction in general; and an alternative biblical moral source or explanatory reinforcing document for many of his stylistic devices, including presumed Latin parallelism. Johnson's homely diction thus allows an allusion to different ancient cultures and thereby enlarges his range of reference and affect. I conclude with an extended instance of Johnson's monosyllabic diction in verse.

THE DOMESTIC METAPHOR

Johnson's frequent use of homely language and metaphors insists upon basic human wants and human responses. Such language often focuses on the family, the home, its occupants, or activities associated with them. I call this device the domestic metaphor. By "domestic" I do not only mean those events that, as Johnson defines them, belong "to the house" and that are "Private; done at home; not open."[13] "Domestic" also may include the larger Latin sense of "domus," which sanctifies that privacy by extending it to a religious temple, and which adds pietas by extending it to lineage and nation. Domestic in this sense suggests how events at home imply rich inner values that epitomize the public nation's best hopes for itself or berate the nation for betraying those hopes. In the *Rambler*, No. 161 (1751), Johnson says, following Juvenal, "that a single house will show what is done or suffered in the world." Johnson may have alluded to this larger meaning in his *Journey to the Western Islands of Scotland*: "the true state of every nation is the state of common life. The manners of a people . . . are found in the streets, and the villages, in the shops and farms."[14]

Johnson is indeed part of a long tradition of using the familiar to suggest the solemn, the modest to suggest the grand, and the particular home to suggest the nation in general, often by contrast of one with the other. Here are three examples.

Dryden's *Essay of Dramatick Poesie* (1668) takes place on "a day wherein the two most mighty and best appointed Fleets which any age had ever seen, disputed the command of the greater half of the Globe, the commerce of Nations, and the riches of the Universe." The debaters on a Thames-barge listen to the air "break about them like the noise of distant Thunder, or of Swallows in a Chimney." Dryden uses the diminishing sound of the "horrour" of naval cannon to bring the English victory home to us.[15] The verbal and aural image of swallows in the chimney evokes the comforts of home for which the nation fights. Thereafter, Pope recognizes the power of contrast in book 6 of *The Iliad* (1716) and its exchange between Hector and Andromache that Johnson later translates (ca. 1728). Andromache urges her husband not to fight, risk his death, widow her, and orphan their frightened infant son Astyanax who shields his eyes from the glare of Hector's martial helmet. Pope agrees with Eustathius that Homer's "change of the scene" from savage warfare to domestic discourse allows a stunning opposition. The poem briefly abandons "*the fierceness and violence of battels, and . . . slaughter and blood, [and] becomes calm and smiling.*"[16] The domestic interlude is both metonymy for Troy bereft of its leader and a prediction of the human loss of innocent noncombatants who will be punished for others' errors. Finally, the concluding line of Christopher Smart's exalted *Song to David* (1763) is the Son's version of Longinus's paradigm of biblical sublimity. In "Let there be light and there was light" command and completion are simultaneous events by an omnipotent God. For Smart the matchless deed of voluntary sacrifice is "DETERMINED, DARED, and DONE" on humanity's behalf.[17] He thus periodically includes lines that humanize the heavens or cite human acts of protective love. Even heaven's angels appear as familiar domestic couples: there "dwells the seraph and his spouse, / The cherub and her mate" (lines 113–14). Amid the soaring song we hear: "sweet the young nurse with love intense, / Which smiles o'er sleeping innocence" (lines 433–34).

Johnson also normalizes the elevated and elevates the normal. The importance of common life is one of his enduring themes as a moralist and traits as a reader and writer of literature. "These little memorials sooth my mind," he says of maternal praise of his youthful Latin.[18] In the *Life of Savage* (1744) Johnson is outraged at the apparent desire of a mother to disown and even destroy her child. The act is yet worse because Lady Macclesfield represents the nation's corrupted aristocratic elite. He begins the Drury Lane "Prologue" (1747) with an image of youthful Shakespeare drawing and soon defining the nature of English drama. In 1750 Johnson persuades Garrick to present a benefit performance of *Comus* for Milton's surviving grandchild Elizabeth Foster. Johnson's prologue urges help and compassion for Milton's impoverished "offspring" and her "mild merits of domestic life." Both the audience and "Britannia's arms" should crown Milton through helping her.[19] Johnson's eastern and insular tales, like his allegories as in the *Rambler*, No. 33, commonly provide their characters' genealogy. In No. 190 Abouzaid is the son of Moran the son of Hanuth. Zosima in the *Rambler*, No. 12, is the distressed "daughter of a country gentleman." The shocking, original *Idler*, No. 22, uses a mother-vulture instructing her young on how vultures nourish themselves on human carnage. *Rasselas* concerns a small group of brother, sister, surrogate sister, and surrogate father seeking what we ourselves also seek. One compelling episode concerns Pekuah's abduction by the Arab rover. Her choice of life is whether to start her own version of a family with the attracted Arab or find her way back to Nekayah's circle—as she does while rejecting the degradation of a harem. Johnson concludes Goldsmith's *The Traveller* (1764), dedicated to his brother, with lines that observe how "With secret course, which no loud storms annoy, / Glides the smooth current of domestic joy." The *Journey to the Western Islands* regularly concerns itself with "the performance of daily duties"—with meals, houses, clothing, windows and local customs. On July 5, 1783, the melancholy, aged, and ill Johnson laments the loss of his created family. His companion and "old Friend Mr. Levett is dead . . . Mrs. Desmoulins is gone away, and Mrs. Williams is so much decayed, that she can add little to anothers gratifications."[20]

Johnson hopes to postpone social decay, and so condemns violation of family roles and applauds affirmation of them. His annotation for Othello's murder of Desdemona ends with this troubled remark: "I am glad that I have ended my revisal of this dreadful scene. It is not to be endured." He also later praises Rowe's *Jane Shore* (1714) for its "domestick scenes and private distress" that appeal to the heart: "the wife is forgiven because she repents, and the husband is honored because he forgives."[21]

Johnson had a morally and socially urgent reason for emphasizing the importance of the domestic in this life. As he knew from human experience and as he makes plain in his first sermon on marriage, domestic venues are the essential places of human activity and quotidian pain and pleasure. *The Rape of the Lock* (1712–17) deserves more "publick gratitude" than Boileau's *Le Lutrin* (1674–83) because troubles at home cause us more grief than squabbles by the clergy. The "commerce of mankind," Johnson says in the *Rambler*, No. 24, requires that a man not neglect "the endearments of his wife, and the caresses of his children." That is because "Society is the true sphere of human virtue," where we learn "a discipline of the human heart, useful to others, and improving to itself." As he says elsewhere, "To receive and to communicate assistance, constitutes the happiness of human life" and "we were born for the help of one another." Most of life is "composed of small incidents and petty occurrences." Hence "To be happy at home is the ultimate result of all ambition, the end to which every enterprise and labour tends, and of which every desire prompts the prosecution."[22]

Such happiness denotes variously fructifying human exchange. "Kindness is preserved by a constant reciprocation of benefits or interchange of pleasures," but the despised liar denies himself reciprocity and "has no domestic consolations, which he can oppose to the censure of mankind." That interchange transcends time and place. We live in a vast human republic in which others labor for us and oblige us "to repay" their labor with our own.[23]

Life is barren without such reciprocity, for we are insufficient unto ourselves and must join others to achieve "any great or extensive design"—or any humanly fulfilling emotional or sexual exchange. Johnson thus writes when he visits the Palais Bourbon: "as I entered my Wife was in my mind. She would have been pleased. Having now nobody to please, I am little pleased." There can be graver consequences. "The women of Rome threatened to put an end to conquest and domination, by supplying no children to the commonwealth."[24]

Not surprisingly, then, Johnson fairly punctuates his prose and poetry with domestic metaphors. These use homely language for a variety of homely relations based not upon "the schools of learning, or the palaces of greatness," but upon "The modest wants of ev'ry day."[25] Such "wants" required an answerable style that often drew upon daily events, the home in its ramifications of propagation, life, death, and the world of familiar commerce and of equally familiar external nature.

Johnson uses his domestic metaphors for a variety of purposes, as with the domestic circle as a basis for judging how well parents and children perform their respective roles. A wealthy young man in the *Rambler*, No. 35, for example, resents having "daughters . . . set out to show . . . in a state [not] much different from prostitution"—a complaint that angry Perdita also makes regarding her own father in the *Idler*, No. 42. Their parents may be "numbered with robbers and assassins." The useless Mr. Busy widows the useless Mrs. Busy who neglected "her children, whom she has taught nothing but the lowest household duties." A tradesman's wife in the *Idler*, No. 13, says that "boys are dirty things, and are always troublesome in a house." She raises her three daughters to be mindless household drudges as ignorant of the Bible as of "whether Ireland was in France" (YE 2:43, 45). The virtuous Tranquila, however, rejects marriage settlements "by which the children of a former marriage would have been injured."[26]

Johnson's most moving domestic metaphors in fact often concern children alone or in danger. In the fifteenth *Rambler* Johnson laments and exemplifies gambling's dangers to the individual and the nation. A mother ravaged by a gambling lust insists on her good family management: "the children are out at nurse in villages as cheap as any two little brats can be kept, nor have I ever seen them since; so [my husband] has no trouble about them" (YE 3:85). Johnson's Preface to Shakespeare (1765) rejects the theory of verisimilitude on which the three unities are based. How then, he asks, does the drama move? It moves us through our association with the actors' feigned problems: "we rather lament the possibility than suppose the presence of misery, as," he says in a startling and primal figure that evokes the human and Christian divine maternal situation, "a mother weeps over her babe, when she remembers that death may take it from her." The *Idler*, No. 38, deplores the British penal system that brutally incarcerates so many debtors. Johnson laments the punishment that extends from the debtor to his family, for "every man languishing in prison" causes "trouble of some kind to two others who love or need him." He then particularizes that need by visualizing the unnecessarily ruined family—"the wife bewailing her husband, or the children begging the bread which their father would have earned."[27]

As the evocative image of maternal tears makes plain, domestic concerns often lead Johnson to use strikingly basic language for strikingly basic activities. A coward "durst not enter a room if a rat was heard behind the wainscoat." The foolish young Mr. Frolick was "a tall boy, with lank hair, remarkable for stealing eggs, and sucking them." A suspicious man knows "the looks of a creditor, a borrower, a lover, and a pimp." Johnson also draws metaphors from humble manual labor or from simple comforts in a cold climate. "Sorrow is a kind of rust of the soul, which every new idea contributes in its passage to scour away." The English language includes "spots of barbarity impressed so deep . . . that criticism can never wash them away." Johnson likens a fire's varying warmth to varying literary pleasure. "If of Dryden's fire the blaze is brighter, of Pope's the heat is more regular and constant."[28]

Some of Johnson's domestic metaphors come from the language of trade, often in a negative context. Lazy critics who repeat others' remarks are "humble retailers of knowledge." When Shakespeare "found himself near the end of his work, and in view of his reward, he shortened the labour to snatch the profit." A conversationalist finds it difficult "to accumulate such a stock of materials as may support the expence of continual narration." Alternatively, Johnson may use the merchant's inappropriate house as an emblem of the vanity of human wishes. In the *Adventurer*, No. 102, "Mercator" bluntly says that "I have been for many years a trader in London. My beginning was narrow, and my stock small." Years of success allow him to purchase, improve, and be miserably idle in a large and temperamentally alien country estate.[29]

Johnson also may use the domestic to level both social and moral classes within the human situation. His *Idler*, No. 51, says that "We are all naked till we are dressed, and hungry till we are fed; and the general's triumph, and sage's disputation, end like the humble labours of the smith or plowman, in a dinner or in sleep" (YE 2:159–60). *The Idler*, No. 84, adds that "The prince feels the same pain when an invader seizes a province, as the farmer when a thief drives away his cow." Johnson can mock his own efforts as well as the gay Flirtilla's. In *Rambler*, No. 10, he laments that though he cannot "fly . . . over land and seas" and bring her fashions and intrigues from Paris and Madrid "I am yet not willing to incur her further displeasure, and would save my papers from her monkey on any reasonable terms."[30] A monkey-beshitted *Rambler* scarcely exemplifies sesquipedalian ponderosity.

The adult Londoner once had been a Lichfield country boy familiar with gardens, woods, and their various occupants. In the Preface to Shakespeare he likens the regular author to "a garden accurately formed and diligently planted"; Shakespeare is a forest of oaks, pines, weeds, brambles, myrtles, and roses, all "gratifying the mind with endless diversity." Like many other places, forests have bugs. One of Johnson's most basic sets of images enlarges in seriousness as it moves from annoyance to venom in the groves of academe. Warburton's edition of Shakespeare had two chief enemies, Thomas Edwards and Benjamin Heath: "the one stings like a fly, sucks a little blood, takes a gay flutter, and returns for more; the other bites like a viper and would be glad to leave inflammations and gangrene behind him." In the eleventh *Rambler* Johnson proposes to deal with the "troublesome" anger of "common life" which he ranks "rather with hornets and wasps, than with basilisks and lions."[31]

These homely and often terse examples are a small selection of Johnson's domestic diction and situations in which the family represents vital human activities and in some cases a paradigm of the national temper. His various uses include the language of love and concern, of anger at inadequate love and concern, or the language of the universal human situation that urges human kinship and the moral utility of the familiar. Such familiarity, even when sometimes masked behind Latinate diction, may require awareness of pimps, stinging flies, warm fires, weeping mothers, prostituting parents, scoured metal, and the washed garments that constitute and enrich our daily experiences as part of communal life.

I wish now further to explore some bases for these contrasts with Johnson's generally accepted verbal gigantism. Horace Walpole characterized Johnson's prose as a "heterogeneous" monster "composed of the limbs of clowns of different nations." Less malicious observers transformed the beast into a beauty. In 1787 an archdeacon speaking for William Hayley observed that Johnson's *Rambler* papers "exhibit a mental paradise, in which fancy and reason alternately entertain me with a succession of new delights, under the guidance and patronage of virtue and religion." Far later, Edmund Gosse perceptively remarks Johnson's productive clash of the colloquial with the more elevated Latinate style within which it often is embedded. Gosse notes Johnson's meticulously crafted sentences, antitheses, elegant rhythms and, he adds, "the contrast cunningly introduced between solemnity and familiarity" that partially characterizes his "individual manner of writing."[32]

CUNNING CONTRASTS

Several reasons have been suggested for Johnson's putative alien diction. It was natural to him; it stemmed from his scientific and philosophical reading for the *Dictionary*; it especially was influenced by Sir Thomas Browne's Anglo-Latin style; it was an overreaction to the fashionable French syntax he hoped to correct; it was a form of polishing the English language; and it was necessary because compendious thought needs compendious words.[33]

However true, these overlook one of Johnson's defining and linguistically relevant traits as a moralist and as a patron of the domestic metaphor—his insistence on human beings' shared pains, pleasures, and remedies for moral discomfort. His frequently invoked "observation" commonly sees what has been seen by numerous earlier observers. He speaks of every man's familiar perceptions, of repeated errors, of humanity's recurring experiences as we relate to one another, and of the insufficiency of our solutions to problems as we confront ourselves on the spectrum of human behavior—a *we* and an *our* that helps to bond Johnson to his reader. In the *Rambler*, No. 45, for example, he offers one reason for domestic discord: "we are always willing to fancy ourselves within a little of happiness, and when, with repeated efforts, we cannot reach it, persuade ourselves that it is intercepted by an ill-paired mate, since, if we could find any other obstacle, it would be our own fault that it was not removed."[34]

Johnson can remind us of universally shared experiences by anglicizing some of the rhythms and sounds of the oldest language most accessible to his audience by association, experience, or schooling. As John Courtenay puts it in his *Poetical Review* (1786) of Johnson the man and writer, he so rooted Latin in local "fost'ring soil" that it "grows a native of Britannia's plains." Latin still often was the language of international communication and of national events. "I would have at every coronation, and every death of a King, every *Gaudium*, and every *Luctus*," Johnson says in 1775.[35] Latin's associative moral weight extended more broadly. It was the language of education, of Cicero and, occasionally, of a dominantly English Anglican church service. Its allusive incorporation into Johnson's English buttresses his insistence on the shared human condition.

Johnson's style in particular works was a choice for a purpose, and he well knew that one choice could not satisfy all literary or moral needs. A stylistic allusion to Latin allows him to elevate the importance of recurring moral decisions and predicaments; but it also carries dangers of which Johnson was well aware. When discussing Milton's versification he hopes to avoid "that offence which is always given by unusual words." In the *Dictionary* he illustrates the noun "Latinism" with Addison on Milton's "antiquated words and phrases." He illustrates the verb "To Latinize" with perhaps self-mocking illustrations: "I am liable to be charged that I *latinize* too much. *Dryd*." and "He uses coarse and vulgar words, or terms and phrases that are *latinized*, scholastick, and hard to be understood. *Watts*." He illustrates the third meaning of language as "Stile; manner of expression" with Roscommon saying that "It must not be obscure and impudent." Johnson later could have been his own illustration for this definition. In the "Life of Dryden" (1779) he says that "words to which we are nearly strangers, whenever they occur, draw that attention on themselves which they should transmit to things."[36]

Johnson as moralist thus sought ways to preserve or even enhance his elevated mode while not losing his purpose and his audience in scholastic obscurity. He can do this by frequent excursions into simple language, by its engaging contrast with our expectation of his higher mode, and with our consequent pleasure in such verbal stratification. This method is consistent with Johnson's regard for "the mixed measure" in versification, without which long poems are "tiresome and disgusting."[37]

Simpler diction and homely images allow Johnson to extend his insights to a larger readership and reflect what Mrs. Piozzi called his "veneration for the voice of mankind." Use of simple language also is consistent both with Johnson's dialectical cast of mind and with his benevolent commitments in literary theory. His well-known respect and nurturing of the poor and unfortunate clearly filter into his work. Even Johnson's enemy Robert Potter observes that in the *Life of Savage* "Dr. Johnson has the feelings of humanity warm at his honest heart; he has therefore with a free and spirited indignation stigmatized the unnatural mother, and to her unrelenting cruelty ultimately refers the faults of the unhappy son."[38]

We may indeed usefully remind ourselves that Johnson often withdraws from the "great" like Savage's mother as models for normal human action or human speech. The *Rambler*, No. 60, insists upon the "parallel circumstances, and kindred images" that make biography the most "useful" of genres. Because nature is uniform we can learn more from private than from public acts, more from "domestick privacies" and "the minute details of daily life" than from "vulgar greatness." Johnson reiterates some of these points in the *Idler*, No. 84, that urges the associative power of narratives "which are levelled with the general surface of life, which tell not how any man became great, but how he was made happy." In 1765 he urges that Shakespeare "the poet of nature" supplies "practical axioms and domestic wisdom" drawn "from the living world" of men not of heroes or, as Dennis, Rymer, and Voltaire prefer, from literary decorum not from nature. Johnson also insists on the Shakespearean and English dramatic trait of tragicomedy that allows "an interchange of seriousness and merriment, by which the mind is softened at one time, and exhilarated at another." Such exhilaration exists in part because Shakespeare tapped permanently pleasing aspects of English as expressed in "the common intercourse of life."[39]

This remark suggests linguistic and psychological reasons for Johnson's mingled, often juxtaposed, complex and simple styles. The linguistic reason is the hybrid nature of the English language itself.[40] Johnson knows that its blending of Latin and Germanic roots allows the splendid flexibility of, say, this classic example from *Macbeth* (1606). The regicide recognizes a consequence of the crime whose blood he cannot wash away: "this my hand will . . . / The multitudinous seas incarnadine, / Making the green one red" (2.3.61–63). Johnson uses that memorable conflict of multisyllabic and monosyllabic words to illustrate his definition of "multitudinous." The illustration also exemplifies the complex impact possible upon the contrast of the elevated and the familiar, incarnadine and red, and the reality of Johnson's monosyllables or English against our expectation of his polysyllables or Latin.[41]

The psychological reason is Johnson's knowledge that contrast is a defining part of the restless human condition. As he says in his sixth

Rambler, whose style exemplifies its content, "such are the vicissitudes of the world, through all its parts, that day and night, labor and rest, hurry and retirement, endear each other; such are the changes that keep the mind in action; we desire, we pursue, we obtain, we are satiated; we desire something else, and begin a new persuit."[42]

AN ALTERNATIVE HYPOTHESIS AND CONTEXT

There is another possible basis for Johnson's use of the domestic metaphor. In 1711 Richard Steele observed, and Johnson surely would have agreed, that the Book of Common Prayer contained "the best Prayers that ever were Compos'd, and that in Terms most affecting, most humble, and most expressive of our Wants, and Dependance on the Object of our Worship . . . and void of all Confusion." Paul Fussell rightly says that Johnson "learned a style as well as a substance from" that book and its "irreducible simplicities" and "doublets." By 1712 Johnson as "a child in petticoats" was able almost immediately to read and memorize "the collect for the day." By 1766 he even thought of writing a basic primer "to teach the use of the Common Prayer."[43] For the Book of Common Prayer as for Johnson those uses and simplicities include the need to help the bereft family. The litany for Sunday, Wednesday, and Friday thus prays to God "That it may please thee to defend and provide for the fatherless children and widows, and all that are desolate and oppressed."[44]

These prayers, though, often were drawn from a more ancient and more holy book with more extensive affecting and humble language—of course the Bible and especially the language of the King James Version's Old Testament that, together with the Book of Common Prayer, had so deeply infused British thought and expression. In the *Spectator*, No. 405 (1712), Addison says that "the *Hebrew* Idioms run into the *English* Tongue with a particular Grace and Beauty. Our Language has received innumerable Elegancies and Improvements from that infusion of *Hebraisms*, which are derived to it out of the Poetical Passages in Holy Writ." The book of Psalms, he continues, demonstrates "how kindly the *Hebrew* Manners of Speech mix and incorporate with the *English* Language."[45] The Psalms of David were regularly printed with the prayer book and like the Old Testament in general were so regularly read in church that, John Ozell observes, they became "Part of the *English Liturgy*."[46]

Johnson himself knew the rudiments of Hebrew grammar and was concerned with Hebrew theology. He owned Adrian Reland's edition of the Rabbinical commentaries; he hoped that Benjamin Kennicott's Latin translation of the Hebrew Bible "would be quite faithful" for, he tells Boswell, "I know not any crime so great that a man could contrive to commit, as poisoning the sources of eternal truth." Johnson also understood at least one aspect of Hebrew poetry. He is unhappy regarding Elijah Fenton's "Paraphrase on Isaiah" because "the paraphrast has deserted his original by admitting images not Asiatick, at least not Judaical."[47]

Johnson also may have read a cogent and germane commentary upon such biblical domestic idioms. As he says, one should "not often assume the critick's privilege of being confident where certainty cannot be obtained."[48] I thus offer these remarks not to establish a source, but to suggest another allusive context and tradition. I refer to John Husbands's *A Miscellany of Poetry By several Hands* which in 1731 issued Johnson's first known publication, the Latin translation of Pope's "Messiah." I also refer to the familiar linguistic and moral values that book could have offered to Johnson.

Husbands says that "The Translation of Mr. *Pope's Messiah* was deliver'd to his Tutor [the Reverend William Jorden in 1728], as a College Exercise, by Mr. *Johnson*, a Commoner of *Pembroke-College* in *Oxford*, and 'tis hoped will be no Discredit to the excellent Original."[49] This must have been an exciting, intimidating, and troubling experience for young Johnson, whose poverty already had forced him from the Pembroke College in which Husbands was a Fellow. His list of 491 subscribers for 583 copies included eleven other Pembroke Fellows, its then Master Matthew Panting (six copies), representatives from nineteen other Oxford colleges, and an interloper from Peter House in Cambridge. There also were 130 Reverends, 57 M.A.'s, and eminent, potentially eminent, or at least known men of letters like Walter Harte, John Hughes, Benjamin Loveling, Uvedale Price, Oxford's Professor of Poetry Joseph Spence, a former such professor Joseph Trapp, and "Richard Savage, Esq" (sig. B4ᵛ) who, with a typically grand gesture, subscribed twenty copies. Moreover, the list boasted a duchess, two countesses, two earls, a viscount, a baron, and seven baronets or knights.

Johnson probably was in Lichfield when the long-delayed *Miscellany* appeared, but one may reasonably conjecture that at some point he read in the volume to which he was volunteered. He may even have corrected proof of his translation which he remembered well enough to quote a line of to Joseph Warton when they visited Pembroke College in 1754.[50] Husbands's errata lists eighteen corrections, six of which are from Johnson's seven pages. Some of the corrections are details an anxious young man might note: add a semicolon, delete a comma, add a comma; three others correct errors in transcription that affect sense.

Husbands's Preface is an important example of eighteenth-century British biblical literary criticism that culminates in Robert Lowth's brilliant Oxford lectures on the sacred poetry of the Hebrews (1741–50). Those praelections, Johnson said, had more learning than "all Scotland." Husbands himself offers impressive moral and anticlassical linguistic authority. It is based on biblical and hence divine resonance drawn from the perfect Hebrew language. As holy myth proclaimed, God spoke it, the prophets wrote it, and all other languages were inseminated by it.[51] Husbands also supports Johnson's developing or perhaps developed beliefs regarding language and its uses in moral teaching.

For example, Husbands provides an early version of Johnson's basic plot of "The Vision of Theodore" (1748) in which Reason surrenders to Revelation as a guide. He shares Johnson's dislike of outmoded classical mythology and history and his corresponding reverence for the truth of the Bible. He demonstrates both the Old Testament's frequent and compelling use of the abstract for the concrete—a man of blood, rather than a bloody man—and the Old Testament's numerous allegories, abrupt transitions, bold metaphors, and use of questions to engage the reader. He also agrees that "Men of Genius, and establish'd Character" should use the verbal arts in God's service as in the final *Rambler* Johnson overtly states he had done.[52]

Husbands discusses two further biblical devices that are especially relevant for Johnson's homely style and its hopping bird, biting fly, warm fire, and recipe for custard. Husbands uses Robert Boyle's remark to argue that since the scriptures were written "for all Ages, Nations, Sexes, Conditions, and Complexions, 'twas fit they shou'd be writ in such a way, as that none of All These might be quite excluded from the Advantages design'd in them." For Husbands, biblical language uses imagery taken from immediate surroundings, from sense perceptions, and "from sensible and familiar Objects, with which those, to whom the sacred Authors wrote, were daily conversant." These include dust, scales, hills, buckets, curtains, chambers, rivers, and the like that nonetheless are ennobled because of the sublime subject matter behind them.[53]

That immediacy also is endemic to basic Old Testament tales of human emotions and is an essential aspect of the domestic metaphor. It furthers what Husbands calls the mind's attachment to "what so deeply affects it, and . . . so entirely possess'd it." Even at the national level such emotions reflect primal responses of love, hate, family relations, grief, and need for solace in a painful world. We read about a father's love for his son and anguished decision regarding whether to sacrifice him to God; or a mother's grief as she watches and fears the outcome of that decision; or a boy's fear of abandonment and murder by his brothers, his consequent success, and forgiveness of his victimizers; or a servant's refusal to be seduced by his mistress and violate his master's confidence; or a father's recognition that he has blessed the wrong son; or a king's mourning cries when his rebel son dies; or a husband's enduring love for his wife and a wife's enduring love for her husband—as in the lines from Genesis 29:20 that Husbands quotes: "*and* Jacob *served seven Years for* Rachel, *and they seemed unto him but a few Days, for the Love He had unto her.*" Listen also to the painful emotions in the departure of Hagar and her son Ishmael: "behold the concern of a Father forced, yet unwilling, to part with a favourite Son! . . . Behold the Distress of the exiled Wanderers! . . . Behold the Grief and Tenderness of a fond afflicted Mother! . . . She cannot bear to see him die, and therefore sits down at a distance from him; yet She cannot bear to leave him, for, tho' at a distance, She sits down over against him."[54]

Here is a second major device useful for understanding Johnson's style—Husbands's recognition of biblical parallelism. Readers regularly observe this trait in Johnson and regularly ascribe it to his study of Latin. It seems to me equally true that Johnson learned such parallelism from the Bible before he learned it from the Lichfield Grammar School. Earlier commentators like Simon Patrick and the Abbé Fleury long had made parallelism a staple of biblical criticism. Robert Lowth contributed to an ongoing tradition when he characterized Hebrew poetry and its "equality, [or] resemblance . . . between the members of each period; so that in two lines (or members of the same period), things for the most part shall answer to things, and words to words, as if fitted to each other by a kind of rule or measure."[55]

Husbands is neither as precise nor as expansive as Lowth; but he well describes the multinamed trait he calls repetition, cites examples from Spenser and Milton, and, had he been prescient, could indeed have cited this further example from the devout but classically unlearned Samuel Richardson. In Clarissa's desperate pen-knife scene she says that she is "Delivered *for the present*; for the *present* delivered from myself."[56]

Husbands of course also cites Old Testament examples that heighten passion and beauty. In Deborah and Baruch we hear that "*The River* Kishon *swept them away, that ancient River, the River* Kishon." Heber's wife Jael shall be blessed because of her generosity: "*he asked Water, and she gave him Milk.*" When Sisera is killed, "*At her Feet He bowed,*

He fell, He lay down; at her feet He bowed, He fell." In the twenty-fourth psalm we read: "*lift up your Heads O ye gates, and be ye lift up, ye everlasting Doors, and the King of Glory shall come in.*"[57]

Hebrew biblical and Latin classical parallelisms of course differ. Latin emphasizes balanced clauses, phrases, terms, or even words within long and complex sentences; its order suggests a contained intellectual and political world. Hebrew emphasizes shorter sections of a shorter sentence in which part succinctly responds to part and variously modifies its predecessor. Pope's elegant parallelism of wit draws attention to art, to the secular balance and moral imbalance of stained honor or brocade. The moral order of Hebrew parallelism suggests the sublimity of a spiritualized world. For the nonspecialist, however, these modes may support or complement rather than contradict one another. The common denominator of Hebrew and Latin parallelism is paired corresponding words or concepts that comment, heighten, or in Lowth's term answer one another. Each form is sufficiently flexible to include antitheses within parallel structure—as, for example, in Proverbs 1:10: "a wise son maketh a glad father; but a foolish son is the heaviness of his mother."

Accordingly, "Latinate" Johnson can sound very biblical indeed. He describes his elderly bareheaded penance for not going to Uttoxeter market to sell his father's books some fifty years earlier: "I . . . stood on the spot where my father's stall used to stand. In contrition I stood." Look also at this line from *Rambler* 19: "they had both loved solitude and reflection, where there was nothing but solitude and reflection to be loved." Or this from *Rambler* 47: "though there is much kindness, there is little grief." Or this from *Rambler* 77: "his favourers are distant, but his enemies at hand." Or this from *Rambler* 111: "in youth we must learn to expect, and in age to enjoy." Johnson's prayers include comparable parallel sentences. He prays to God "by whose will I was created, and by whose Providence I have been sustained." He hopes to become pure in God's sight "so that I may live in thy fear, and dye in thy favour." In the sermon for Tetty's death (1752) we hear that "death no man has escaped, and therefore no man can hope to escape it." Such parallelism permeates Johnson's prose, whether in his famous February 7, 1755 letter to Chesterfield or the *Lives of the Poets* in 1779–81.[58]

Johnson's possible knowledge of Husbands's Preface and of Lowth's *Praelectiones* clearly were not his only sources of knowledge regarding biblical parallelism. As James Kugel says, "Parallelistic lines appear throughout the Bible" in poetic, narrative, legal, genealogical, and other sections.[59] Indeed, though parallelism is not as extensive in the New Tes-

tament, it appears there as well and the Book of Common Prayer includes Old Testament texts and all of the Psalter. In the Magnificat, for
example, we hear this from Luke 1:52: "he hath put down the mighty
from their seat; and hath exalted the humble and the meek" (p. [26]).
Shortly thereafter Psalm 98:9 says that "With righteousness shall he
judge the world; and the people with equity" (p. [27]). Whatever the
modern squabbles regarding the nature of biblical parallelism, no one
who from young childhood heard the repeated services or read the familiar texts needed to learn Latin in order to learn, at least emotively understand, and write in various parallel modes that had holy associations.
One of these associations was with the simple language appropriate for
the at once domestic and universal, the sensory and the spiritual.

Such language clearly had a lasting influence upon Johnson's moral,
psychological, and theological imperatives. He adapted Old Testament
texts for fifteen of his sermons and for 3,550 illustrative quotations in
the *Dictionary*. These include numerous examples of typical parallel
structures. Under the first definition of the preposition "against" we see
that "his hand will be *against* every man, and every man's hand *against*
him" (Gen. 16:12). Under the verb "to slay" we read that "Wrath killeth
the foolish man, and envy *slayeth* the silly one" (Job 5:2). Under the verb
"to sow" we read "*Sow* to yourselves in righteousness, and reap in
mercy" (Hosea 9:12). Under the first definition of the noun "tiller" we
see that "Abel was a keeper of sheep, but Cain was a *tiller* of the
ground" (Gen. 4:2). Under the second definition of the adjective "wise"
we read that "They are *wise* to do evil, but to do good they have no
knowledge" (Jer. 4:22).[60]

There is no evidence that Johnson read Husbands's Preface; but it
seems to me plausible that he read proof of his own poem, and that in
the process he would have sought out the book in which his first and
remembered publication appeared. Whether or not Johnson read that
Preface, it embodies commonplaces with which he was familiar. It also
embodies moral domestic language that includes the parallelism generally ascribed to Latin but that is at least equally at home in the Hebraism
that Addison knew so enriched the English language and that Johnson
knew so well. This Anglo-Hebraism supports neither praise nor blame
of Johnson for putative Tory diction and ideals. It is consistent with
Johnson as an author with stylistic relationships among home, local at-
tachments, respect for the importance of daily life, and uses of diction
that is as allusively biblical as allusively Latinate in the service of "all
Ages, Nations, Sexes, Conditions, and Complexions."

DESTROYING THE HOUSE

Thus far I have largely limited myself to Johnson's published prose, but his domestic metaphors are in fact widely distributed through his other kinds of spoken and written words. "We are a nest of singing birds," nostalgic Johnson recalls of his relatively protected Pembroke days. "Richardson had picked the kernal of life . . . while Fielding was contented with the husk," he says of two great novelists.[61] The domestic metaphors in his poetry also are continuous with those in his prose and speech. I thus wish now to focus on "A Short Song of Congratulation," a poem that both literally and figuratively concerns the family, houses, birth, and death.

Johnson regarded our life on earth as a stewardship of God's gift. In the *Rambler*, No. 108, he quotes Girolamo Cardana as likening time to an estate "which will produce nothing without cultivation, but will always abundantly repay the labours of industry." Life, we hear in the *Rambler*, No. 127, alluding to the parable of the talents, "is only deposited in [man's] hands to be employed in obedience to a Master who will regard his endeavours, not his success." It thus is everyone's "duty" to use "industry" and add "to the hereditary aggregate of knowledge and happiness." Johnson logically extends this duty to the literal hereditary estate and, like the master of Matthew 25, punishes the self-destructive steward. He will be eviscerated by vultures; or become "the scent of prey" by those who would feed off him; or be "torn to pieces by taylors and jockeys, vintners and attorneys, who at once rob and ridicule him." In lines that virtually gloss the "Short Song" Johnson berates the folly of those "who see their revenues hourly lessened, and the estates which they inherit from their ancestors mouldering away, . . . who persevere against all remonstrances, and go forward with full career, though they see before them the precipice of destruction."[62]

Johnson sent his later response to a comparable real situation to Mrs. Thrale on August 8, 1780, and asked her both to be indulgent and not to show it to others.[63] Though the "Short Song" often is regarded as rollicking fun, it records Johnson's troubled private response to those rushing themselves and their inheritance to the precipice of destruction. He avoids high seriousness, the usual instruction or reminder in his public efforts, and makes plainer than ever the consequences of ignoring the house as extended domus. The dark parody of optimistic birthday conventions tells the Thrale nephew Sir John Lade that death should signal his majority because he himself brings death to the living house.

The overwhelmingly monosyllabic and English poem begins with a celebration of the wrong kind of birthday acquisition—not the maturity and responsibility that should accompany Sir John's inheritance, but pomp, pleasure, pride, plenty, and consequently false freedom to destroy what had been long preserved. Sir John associates his ancestral home with slavery, the cadaver of controlling patriarchy, the pest of nurturing matriarchy, and unproductive shapeless dirt. He also associates his majority with physical and moral rambles, gambling, debt and, as consistent with other role reversals, being hunted instead of being the hunting squire, as "All that prey on vice and folly / Joy to see their quarry fly" (lines 13–14). The poem's nonmaternal women are plural Bettys, Kates, and Jennys—his social inferiors, or worse, rather than potential mates who suggest the stability and continuity that made his inheritance possible and toward which he is abusive. Sir John has symbolically squandered ancestral values, achievements, and the world they created, as he literally has squandered his "grandsire's guineas" (line 11). The home as emblem of generational bonding, familial nurturing, and repayment of obligation has been levelled: "what are acres? What are houses? / Only dirt, or wet or dry" (lines 23–24).

Johnson's final lines reflect his anger at Sir John whom he could well see "hang or drown at last" (line 28) as punishment for his crimes. The poem inverts much of the moral force behind the domestic metaphor in its positive, attractive, or acceptably diminished form, as with frisking lambs; but it also shows what happens when someone banishes the domus as a metaphor of protection, continuity, and reciprocity in both the family and the nation.

We can fruitfully contrast the poems that Johnson wrote about Sir John Lade and Dr. Robert Levet and fruitfully see how morally central Johnson thought the home. A destructive individualistic man violates trust and will go from ravaged home to, we assume, hell as he wastes his talents. A constructive social man reinforces trust and has gone from supported home to, we know, heaven as he uses his single talent and pleases God, his eternal master.[64] One man's desired death evokes private joy; the other man's lamented death evokes public grief.

In Which Something Is Concluded

I have suggested that Johnson's prose and poetry often record his domestic values in language that is simpler than normally recognized, that contrasts with its more elaborate Latinate foil, and may in part be drawn from a stylistic and moral tradition as superior to Marcus Tullius Cicero as Johnson was superior to Sir John Lade. We speak of the Anglo-Latin Johnson; perhaps we should also speak of the Anglo-Hebrew Johnson and speak less about the political Johnson in political prose. He spent much of his adult life attempting to create homes and support families—whether in Bolt Court, Streatham, or even with Boswell whom he tried to reconcile with his father and with Scotland. One such attempt was in the moral life and domestic metaphor vitally present in so much of his work.

NOTES

1. Burrowes, "Essay on the Stile of Doctor Samuel Johnson," in *Transactions of the Royal Irish Academy* (Dublin, 1787), 1:30–31, 49–50. Burrowes's perceptive and often severe essay nonetheless is designed as a tribute to Johnson. All his faults may be treated in an essay, "while volumes would not be sufficient for a treatise on his perfections" (p. 56). For a relevant fuller overview see W. Vaughan Reynolds, "The Reception of Johnson's Prose Style," *Review of English Studies* n.s. 11 (1935): 145–62. To be sure, Johnson's style was much praised. George Colman recreates a ghostly Johnson who complains about abuse by his biographers:

> I gave the Publick works of merit,
> Written with vigour, fraught with spirit;
> Applause crown'd all my labours.

See "A Posthumous Work of S. Johnson. An Ode. April 15, 1786," in George Colman, *Prose on Several Occasions; Accompanied with Some Pieces in Verse* (London, 1787), 3:165. There are other interesting comments in 1:185–86, 2:92–97, 2:97–100, 3:162, 3:59–76.

2. Campbell, *Lexiphanes, A Dialogue. Imitated from Lucian, and suited to the present Times. Being An Attempt to restore the English Tongue to its Ancient Purity*, 2nd ed. (London, 1767). Campbell tells his dedicatee Lord Lyttelton that he "ought not to suffer those *Lexiphanes*, those *Shiners*, those Dealers in *hard words*, and *absurd phrases*, those *fabricators* of *Triads* and *Quaternions*" (p. xvii). Murphy, *An Essay on the Life and Genius of Dr. Johnson*, in *The Works of Samuel Johnson, LL. D.* (London, 1792), 1:161, 159. For Murphy, Johnson as Jupiter "darts his lightning, and rolls his thunder in the cause of virtue and piety" (1:161). See also Wimsatt, *The Prose Style of Samuel Johnson* (New Haven: Yale University Press, 1941; reprint, 1963). His view is summarized in remarks insisting that Johnson relentlessly theorized and practiced generality. He used parallelism, antithesis, and philosophic pomp of diction that, in words his followers often quote, lent "to the abstract an emphasis, a particularity and thickness. He made a kind of poetry of abstraction" (p. 96). Wimsatt is uncomfortable with Johnson's lighter mode, which he thinks beneath the great man. See pp. 80–81 n. 34 and pp. 83–84. Johnson could not be properly "Johnsonian" in biographical portions of the *Lives of the Poets*. Several commentators confirm Wimsatt's continuing influence. See Leopold Damrosch, Jr., *The Uses of Johnson's Criticism* (Charlottesville: University Press of Virginia, 1976),

p. 58; Hoyt Trowbridge, "The Language of Reasoned Rhetoric in *The Rambler*," in *Greene Centennial Studies: Essays Presented to Donald Greene*, ed. Paul J. Korshin and Robert J. Allen (Charlottesville: University Press of Virginia, 1984), pp. 200–201; Frederick Bogel, *Literature and Insubstantiality in Later Eighteenth-Century England* (Princeton: Princeton University Press, 1984), pp. 44, 66–67; Alvin B. Kernan, *Samuel Johnson and the Impact of Print* (Princeton: Princeton University Press, 1987), p. 175; and *Modern Critical Views: Dr. Samuel Johnson and James Boswell*, ed. Harold Bloom (New York: Chelsea House, 1986), pp. 11–29, in which the only discussion of Johnson's relevant theory and practice is from Wimsatt's *Prose Style of Samuel Johnson*.

3. Anderson, *The Life of Samuel Johnson, LL. D. With Critical Observations on His Works* (London, 1795), 3rd ed. (Edinburgh, 1815), pp. 55–64. Chalmers, *The British Essayists, with Prefaces, Historical and Biographical* (London, 1808), 19:xxiii–xlii. Johnson's prose of course varies within the periodical essays, as made plain in putative numbers by young men and women in say, the *Rambler*, whose general style differs from most of the *Idler*s. His diaries and prayers also differ from his "official" public modes. Wimsatt finds many such variations lamentably un-Johnsonian—"frivolous" or "prattle and gossip" (*Prose Style*, pp. 80–81 n. 34. See also pp. 81–82 n. 36).

4. Greene, " 'Pictures to the Mind': Johnson and Imagery," in *Johnson, Boswell, and Their Circle: Essays Presented to Lawrence Fitzroy Powell* (Oxford: Clarendon Press, 1965), pp. 137–58. Greene observes "that Johnson drew far more on homely, everyday matters than on literature for his images" (p. 144 n. 1); Fussell, *Samuel Johnson and the Life of Writing* (New York: Harcourt, Brace, and Jovanovich, 1971), pp. 76–80. See also Herman W. Liebert, "Samuel Johnson & the Pendulum of Taste," *Transactions of the Johnson Society* (London, 1980), pp. 8–9, and Pat Rogers, "Johnson and the Diction of Common Life," *Transactions of the Johnson Society* (Lichfield, 1982), pp. 8–19. Caveats by Arthur Friedman in *Philological Quarterly* 21 (1942): 211–13 and R. W. Chapman in *Review of English Studies* n.s. 20 (1944): 84–86 only spurred Wimsatt to reiterate and expand his points in *Philosophic Words: A Study of Style and Meaning in the "Rambler" and "Dictionary"* (New Haven: Yale University Press, 1948). In 1980 Brian McCrea regretted that Wimsatt's view had not been seriously confronted: "Style or Styles: The Problem of Johnson's Prose," *Style* 14 (1980): 201–15. One of Chapman's remarks relates to a point I make below: "Wimsatt might have made more than I think he anywhere does of Johnson's use of very short words" (p. 85).

In providing secondary sources, I have largely excluded pre-Wimsatt twentieth-century academic studies of Johnson's prose. For some of the arguments on the "abstract" side, see the Wimsatt-influenced works cited in n. 2 above, and Alan T. McKenzie, "The Systematic Scrutiny of Passion in Johnson's *Rambler*," *Eighteenth-Century Studies* 20 (1987–88): 129–51. On the "particular" and imagistic side, see also relevant remarks in Ian Watt, "The Ironic Tradition in Augustan Prose from Swift to Johnson," in *Restoration and Augustan Prose* (Los Angeles: William Andrews Clark Memorial Library of the University of California, Los Angeles, 1956), pp. 19–46; John C. Riely, "The Pattern of Imagery in Samuel Johnson's Periodical Essays," *Eighteenth-Century Studies* 3 (1970): 384–97; Peter T. Koper, "Samuel Johnson's Rhetorical Stance in *The Rambler*," *Style* 12 (1978): 23–24. Mark E. Wildermuth ably tries to reconcile the two schools and suggest a basis for Johnson's blending of traits: "Johnson's Prose Style: Blending Energy and Elegance in *The Rambler*," *Age of Johnson* 6 (1994):205–35.

Paul K. Alkon makes useful distinctions between Johnson's style in his sermons and in other works. See chapter 6 of his *Samuel Johnson and Moral Discipline* (Evanston, IL:

Northwestern University Press, 1967), pp. 180–214. Louis T. Milic has skewered Macaulay's skewering of Johnson's written and formal words as inferior to his presumably more casual mode. See "Observations on Conversational Style," in *English Writers of the Eighteenth Century*, ed. John H. Middendorf (New York: Columbia University Press, 1971), pp. 276–81. Bruce Redford well analyzes Johnson's epistolary mode in *The Converse of the Pen: Acts of Intimacy in the Eighteenth-Century Familiar Letter* (Chicago: University of Chicago Press, 1986), pp. 206–43. Mark Pedreira also has contributed two full studies of Johnson's prose: "Johnson's Figures: *Copia* and Lockean Observation in Samuel Johnson's Critical Writings," in *1650–1850: Ideas, Aesthetics, and Inquiries* 1 (1994): 157–96, and "Johnson's Figures: A Cornucopia of Vanity, Idleness, and Death in Samuel Johnson's Prose Writings," *1650–1850: Ideas, Aesthetics, and Inquiries* 2 (1996): 241–73. See also n. 12 below.

5. These are the words of J. C. D. Clark in *Samuel Johnson: Literature, religion, and English cultural politics from the Restoration to Romanticism* (Cambridge: Cambridge University Press, 1994), p. 33. See the political essays below for further commentary on such views. John Wilkes also fancied a relationship between Johnson's "Tory" prose and "Tory" politics, but from a harshly negative point of view. See his *A Letter to Samuel Johnson, LL. D.* (London, 1770), as in Pedreira, "Johnson's figures," 1:171 n. 33.

6. See, for example, John Barrell, *English Literature in History, 1730–80: An Equal Wide Survey* (London: Hutchinson, 1983), pp. 144–61, especially pp. 144, 154–58. Note this, for example: the *Dictionary* is designed to justify "choosing the words to be represented . . . from the diction of the polite" (p. 155). By denigrating Scotticisms Johnson manipulates "the notion of the customary and the current . . . in such a way as to ensure that whatever is in London, is right for everywhere else" (p. 157). Barrell often bases his arguments on Johnson's *Plan*, much of whose fanciful notions regarding language's stability Johnson rejected in the Preface of 1755. Barrell also rarely looks at the *Dictionary* itself which, as some of Johnson's contemporary detractors and others recognized, is far more colloquial than Johnson's theory suggests. See the works cited in n. 12 below. Olivia Smith follows Barrell's lead in *The Politics of Language 1791–1819* (Oxford: Clarendon Press, 1984). She is concerned with ideas that "contributed to the hegemony of language, justifying and perpetuating class divisions" (p. 4). Johnson's Preface "disparages the language while it teaches it," supports class divisions by mocking those innocent of classical languages (p. 13) and, among other sins, produced "an authoritative dictionary and an authoritative style that was recognizably suited for gentlemen" (p. 20). See also pp. 14, 16–17, 19, 29. In *Language in History: Theories and Texts* (London: Routledge, 1996), pp. 81–83, Tony Crowley also regards Johnson as a hegemonist who seeks to exclude "words of a particular class" (p. 81), but here not for cohesion with gentlemen, but with "the bourgeois public sphere" (p. 82). This represents "symbolic violence" and "future programming" (p. 83). Such efforts rarely engage themselves with what Johnson actually did regarding language in the *Dictionary*, what he wrote and said about class divisions, and how his work was received.

7. *The Letters of Samuel Johnson*, ed. Bruce Redford (Princeton: Princeton University Press, 1992–94), 1:273, and referred to hereafter as *Letters*.

8. Jenyns, from Johnson's review of *A Free Enquiry into the Nature and Origin of Evil* in *The Literary Magazine Or Universal Review* 2 (1757): 174, 302, as reprinted in Richard B. Schwartz, *Samuel Johnson and the Problem of Evil* (Madison: University of Wisconsin Press, 1975), pp. 102, 108. Betty Broom, The Yale Edition of the Works of Samuel Johnson, vol. 2, *The Idler and the Adventurer*, ed. W. J. Bate, John M. Bullit, and

L. F. Powell (New Haven: Yale University Press, 1963), p. 80. Johnson uses this humble style for other correspondents as well. See the *Idler*, No. 53 (1759): "I have a wife that keeps good company" (2:164). Unless otherwise specified, subsequent references to Johnson's works are from this edition and after the first full citation as YE are given by volume number. Pekuah, YE 16, *Samuel Johnson: Rasselas and Other Tales*, ed. Gwin J. Kolb (New Haven: Yale University Press, 1990), p. 138. *Samuel Johnson: A Journey to the Western Islands* is edited by J. D. Fleeman (Oxford: Clarendon Press, 1985), p. 45; subsequent references are to this edition.

9. Punic War and Catiline, *William Shaw. Memoirs of the Life and Writings of the Late Dr. Samuel Johnson. Hesther Lynch Piozzi. Anecdotes of the Late Samuel Johnson, LL.D. During the Last Twenty Years of His Life*, ed. Arthur Sherbo (London: Oxford University Press, 1974), pp. 88–89 of Mrs. Piozzi's *Anecdotes*. Subsequent citations are to this edition, as *Anecdotes*. Preface to *The Preceptor*, in *Samuel Johnson's Prefaces & Dedications*, ed. Allen T. Hazen (New Haven: Yale University Press, 1937), pp. 187–88. See also Roger P. McCutcheon, "Johnson and Dodsley's *Preceptor*," *Tulane Studies in English* 3 (1952): 125–32. For Bacon see *An Historical Discourse of the Uniformity of the Government of England. The First Part. From the first Times till the Reigne of Edward the Third* (London, 1647), p. 49. For further discussion of the Tacitean contexts, see my "Politics, Taste, and National Identity: Some Uses of Tacitism in Eighteenth-Century Britain," in *Tacitus and the Tacitean Tradition*, ed. T. J. Luce and A. J. Woodman (Princeton: Princeton University Press, 1993), pp. 168–84. Johnson's list includes not only Neville's republican *Plato Redivivus* (1681), but also Sir John Fortescue's "Treatises"—that is, a work published as *The Difference Between an Absolute and Limited Monarchy; As it more particularly regards the English Constitution*, 3rd ed., ed. John Fortescue-Aland (London, 1724). This too is a Tacitean, "Saxon" document: see, for example, pp. xxx–xxxvii. Johnson's other authors and texts are Hooker's *Laws of Ecclesiastical Polity* (1593) and Richard Zouche's *Elementa Jurisprudentiae, definitionibus, regulis, et sententiis selectionibus Juris Civilis illustrata* (1629), which in the second edition replaced Harrington's *Oceana*, and Thornagh Gurdon, *The History of the High Court of Parliament* (London, 1731). Zouche's book largely sets forth the principles of legal science and, especially, Roman law, under the headings of "Jus" and "Judicium," of Rights and Remedies. Johnson apparently is recommending a legal treatise that codifies restraints upon authority. Gurdon's constitutional antiabsolute bias was comparable: "the farther I looked into our Constitution, the more I found Parliament to be the main Hinge upon which the Government moved regularly" (1:xvii–xviii); "*Caesar* and *Tacitus* both agree that the Laws and Customs of the *Germans, Gauls* and *Britons*, were much the same" (1:12, and see 1:15); James II's inability to understand English law, custom, and history forced the "abdicating his Crown and Country his only Safety" (2:301).

10. Piozzi, *Anecdotes*, p. 112.

11. Piozzi, *Anecdotes*, p. 112. Roy Porter quotes this remark, but instead of drawing the obvious inference, for which there is much supporting evidence, seems puzzled that it was spoken by "no less an idolator of rank than Dr Johnson." See Porter, *English Society in the Eighteenth Century* (Harmondsworth, Middlesex: Penguin Books, 1982), p. 79.

12. For masculine, see Walpole, "General Criticism of Dr. Johnson's Writings," in *The Works of Horatio Walpole Earl of Orford* (London, 1798), 4:362; for bad company, see *Horace Walpole's Correspondence with The Rev. William Cole*, ed. W. S. Lewis and A. Dayle Wallace (New Haven: Yale University Press, 1937), 1:310, 309. Walpole's several comments on Johnson's prose are implicit condemnations of the cumbersome scholar in-

capable of a gentleman's graceful prose. The effort immediately prior to Walpole's "Criticism" is "The New Whole Duty of Woman, In series of Letters from a Mother to a Daughter Being A Counter-Part to The Earl of Chesterfield's 'System of Education'." It embodies aristocratic superficiality and disdain for Johnsonian weight and learning: "the Muses have three mountains, two fountains, and one horse, which compose a territory about as large as that of a German prince" (4:360).

For other comments denigrating Johnson's ungentlemanly written or social behavior, and especially his impolite *Dictionary*, see Archibald Campbell, *Lexiphanes*, p. 24 n; the letter in *Lloyd's Evening Post [No. 2608]. To the Author of Lexiphanes* 34 (1774)—Johnson's elaborate expressions are adapted by the exalted "from whom they descend to the vulgar, who are always ambitious of aping their superiors"; [James Thomson Callender], *Deformities of Dr Samuel Johnson. Selected from His Works*, 2nd ed. (London, 1782), pp. 13, 18–19, 42, 53–54, 60, 74, 79, 88; [Callender], *A Critical Review of the Works of Dr. Samuel Johnson, Containing A particular Vindication of Several eminent Characters*, 2nd ed. (London, 1783), pp. v, 18–19, 47–48; [William Hayley], *Two Dialogues; Containing A Comparative View of the Lives, Characters, and Writings, of Philip, The Late Earl of Chesterfield, and Dr. Samuel Johnson* (London, 1787), pp. 8, 50, 161, 228.

See also Donald T. Siebert, "*Bubbled, Bamboozled*, and Bit: 'Low Bad' Words in Johnson's *Dictionary*," *Studies in English Literature* 26 (1986): 485–96. Siebert concludes that "a comprehensive inspection of the *Dictionary* reveals that 'Dictionary Johnson' was usually quite hospitable to neologisms and the colloquial language of his day" (pp. 485–86). Such evidence makes plain "that he was receptive to semantic change and delighted in the colloquial idiom of his day" (p. 491). For other relevant essays concerning Johnson's *Dictionary* and its putative conservative hegemonic aims, see Robert DeMaria, Jr., "The Politics of Johnson's *Dictionary*," *PMLA* 104 (1989): 64–74, and Nicholas Hudson, "Johnson's *Dictionary* and, the Politics of 'Standard English,'" *Yearbook of English Studies* 28 (1997): 77–93.

13. Johnson, *A Dictionary of the English Language* (London, 1755). Subsequent quotations are from this edition. Two other recent essays in *The Cambridge Companion to Samuel Johnson*, ed. Greg Clingham (Cambridge: Cambridge University Press, 1997) have noted some "domestic" aspects of Johnson's prose and thought. See Paul J. Korshin, "Johnson, the Essay, and *The Rambler*," pp. 54–56, 59–63; and Eithne Henson, "Johnson and the Condition of Women," pp. 67–84.

14. YE 5, *The Rambler*, ed. W. J. Bate and Albrecht B. Strauss (1978), p. 94, from Juvenal *Satires* 13.159–60; *Journey*, p. 16. Most readers prudently and regularly avoid footnotes as mere citations. Given necessarily abundant quotations from the periodical essays and other works, henceforth I will clutter the notes rather than the text the better to maintain narrative flow. Accordingly, I bunch footnote references with identifying tags for each quotation, but without citing the date for each periodical essay. The respective cumulative dates are: *Rambler*, Nos. 1–82, 1750; Nos. 83–187, 1751; Nos. 188–208, 1752; *Adventurer*, Nos. 34–120, 1753; Nos. 126–38, 1754; *Idler*, Nos. 1–37, 1758, including the original *Idler*, No. 22; Nos. 38–89, 1759; and Nos. 90–103, 1760.

15. The California Edition of the Works of John Dryden, vol. 17, *Prose 1668–1691. An Essay of Dramatick Poesie and Shorter Works*, ed. Samuel Holt Monk, A. E. Wallace Maurer, and Vinton A. Dearing (Berkeley and Los Angeles: University of California Press, 1971), pp. 8, 9.

16. *The Iliad of Homer Translated by Alexander Pope*, ed. Steven Shankman (London: Penguin Books, 1996), p. 319.

17. Smart, *The Poetical Works of Christopher Smart. II. Religious Poetry 1763–1771*, ed. Marcus Walsh and Karina Williamson (Oxford: Clarendon Press, 1983), p. 147, line 516. Subsequent references are cited in the text. For Longinus's well-known use of the biblical caveat, see *The Works of Mons*ʳ *Boileau Despreaux. . . . Containing I. Longinus's Treatise of the Sublime*, ed. John Ozell (London, 1711), 2:27–28, chap. 7.

18. YE 1, *Diaries, Prayers, and Annals*, ed. E. L. McAdam, Jr., with Donald and Mary Hyde (1958), p. 14, regarding words spoken in 1718 and recalled perhaps ca. 1768.

19. YE 6, *Poems*, ed. E. L. McAdam, Jr., with George Milne (1964), p. 241, lines 25, 31, 34.

20. Zosima, *Rambler*, No. 12, YE 3:62; Goldsmith, *Collected Works of Oliver Goldsmith*, ed. Arthur Friedman (Oxford: Clarendon Press, 1966), 4:269, lines 433–34; *Journey*, p. 22; Levet and Desmoulins, *Letters*, 4:167–68.

21. *Lives of the English Poets*, ed. George Birkbeck Hill (Oxford: Clarendon Press, 1905), 2:68–69; subsequently referred to as *Lives*.

22. Sermon 1, YE 14, *Sermons*, ed. Jean Hagstrum and James Gray (1978), on Genesis 2:24, pp. 3–15; Boileau, *Lives*, 3:234; commerce of mankind, *Rambler*, No. 24, YE 3:133; society, *Rambler*, No. 44, YE 3:241 and see also *Idler*, No. 80, YE 2:251; small incidents, *Rambler*, No. 68, 1750, YE 3:359–60 and see also *Idler*, No. 87, YE 2:272.

23. Kindness preserved, *Rambler*, No. 137, YE 4:364; the liar, *Adventurer*, No. 50, YE 2:362; human republic, *Idler*, No. 19, YE 2:2:59. Johnson uses the need for exchange among generations as a theory of causation for portraiture: "whoever is delighted with his own picture must derive his pleasure from the pleasure of another." He seeks a portrait "but for the sake of those whom he loves, and by whom he hopes to be remembered. This use of the art is a natural and reasonable consequence of affection" (*Idler*, No. 45, YE 2:140). Johnson also extends the metaphor of reciprocity to the future. Christian revelation is superior to pagan opportunistic benevolence which "will never settle into a principle of action, or extend relief to calamities unseen, in generations not yet in being" (*Idler*, No. 4, YE 2:13).

24. Great design, *Rambler*, No. 104, YE 4:190; Palais Bourbon, October 17, 1775, in *The French Journals of Mrs. Thrale and Dr. Johnson*, ed. Moses Tyson (Manchester: University of Manchester Press, 1932), p. 175, and see also *Diaries, Prayers, and Annals*, YE 1:238; women of Rome, *Rambler*, No. 146, YE 5:13.

25. Schools of learning, *Journey*, p. 16; modest wants, from "On the Death of Dr. Robert Levet," YE 6:315, line 23.

26. Daughters set to show, *Rambler*, No. 35, YE 3:192; Perdita, *Idler*, No. 42, YE 2:133; parents as robbers, *Rambler*, No. 39, YE 3:213; Mrs. Busy, *Rambler*, No. 138, YE 4:369; dirty boys and ignorant girls, *Rambler*, No. 13, YE 2:43,45; Tranquila, *Rambler*, No. 120, YE 4:274.

27. Brats, *Rambler*, No. 15, YE 3:85; a mother weeps, YE 7, *Johnson on Shakespeare*, ed. Arthur Sherbo, with an introduction by Bertrand H. Bronson (1968), p. 78; languishing in prison, bewailing wife, *Idler*, No. 38, YE 2:118, 121.

28. Coward, *Rambler*, No. 119, YE 4:272; Mr. Frolick, *Rambler*, No. 61, YE 3:326; creditor, *Rambler*, No. 103, YE 4:189; sorrow as rust, *Rambler*, No. 47, YE 3:258; spots of barbarity, *Dictionary*, sig. a1ᵛ; Pope, in *Lives*, YE 3:323. See also the *Idler*, No. 4, in which Johnson fears that because hospitals lack a "solid fund of support, there is danger lest the blaze of charity, which now burns with so much heat and splendor, should die away for want of lasting fuel" (YE 2:15).

29. Humble retailers, *Rambler*, No. 121, YE 4:281; Shakespeare, Preface, YE 7:72;

conversationalist, *Rambler*, No. 188, YE 5:222; Mercator, *Adventurer*, No. 102, YE 2:435.

30. Naked, *Idler*, No. 51, YE 2:159–60; prince's province, *Idler*, No. 84, YE 2:263; fly over lands, *Rambler*, No. 10, YE 3:55.

31. Shakespeare, garden, in Preface YE 7:84; Warburton's enemies, YE 7:100; anger of common life, *Rambler*, No. 11, YE 3:57.

32. Walpole, *Correspondence*, 28 (1955): 243; Hayley, *Two Dialogues*, p. 84, spoken by an Archdeacon; Gosse, *Leaves and Fruit* (London: Wm. Heinemann, 1927), p. 361.

33. For an early example of such speculation, see Burrowes's "Essay on the Stile of . . . Johnson," n. 1 above, pp. 37–39.

34. *Rambler*, No. 45, YE 3:245.

35. Courtenay, *A Poetical review of the Literary and Moral Character of the Late Samuel Johnson, LL.D. With Notes*, 2nd ed. (London, 1786), p. 19; luctus, *Boswell's Life of Johnson Together with Boswell's Journal of a Tour to the Hebrides*, ed. George Birkbeck Hill and rev. L. F. Powell (Oxford: Clarendon Press, 1934–50), 2:371. Subsequent references to this edition are cited as *Life*.

36. Milton and offence, *Rambler*, No. 86, YE 4:89; Dryden, *Lives*, YE 1:420. Johnson's characteristic complexity of thought, however, nonetheless allows him to defend "hard words" and concepts. See the *Idler*, No. 70: "they who can form parallels, discover consequences, and multiply conclusions, are best pleased with involution of argument and compression of thought" (YE 2:218).

37. *Rambler*, No. 86, YE 4:90.

38. Piozzi, veneration, *Anecdotes*, p. 143; Potter, *An Inquiry Into Some Passages in Dr. Johnson's Lives of the Poets: Particularly His Observations on Lyric Poetry, and The Odes of Gray* (London, 1783), p. 2.

39. Parallel circumstances and vulgar greatness, *Rambler*, No. 60, YE 3:319, 321; narratives' associative power, *Idler*, No. 84, YE 2:262; Shakespeare poet of nature, Dennis and Rymer, YE 7:63, 65–66; Shakespeare and tragicomedy, YE 7:68, 70. There were, though, limits to the degree of contrast Johnson would accept in drama or in his own or others' prose. See the *Rambler*, No. 125, on the dangers of inept tragicomedy, and the *Rambler*, No. 107. Johnson thinks it "an useless attempt to disturb merriment by solemnity, or interrupt seriousness by drollery" (YE 4:205).

40. In the *Journey* Johnson observes that Scottish Highland and Welsh Gaelic was the original British language, "while the other parts have received first the Saxon, in some degree afterwards the French, and then formed a third language between them" (p. 34).

41. As one example of Johnson's own use of this *concordia discors* in prose, see the conclusion to the *Rambler*, No. 166: "when we find worth faintly shooting in the shades of obscurity, we may let in light and sunshine upon it, and ripen barren volition into efficacy and power" (YE 5:120).

42. *Rambler*, No. 6, YE 3:34–35.

43. Steele, *The Spectator*, No. 147, ed. Donald Bond (Oxford: Clarendon Press, 1965), 2:80; Fussell, *Johnson and the Life of Writing*, pp. 79, 215; memorize, *Life*, 1:40; primer, *Diaries, Prayers, and Annals*, 1:103, and also in Sir John Hawkins, *The Life of Samuel Johnson, LL. D.* (London, 1787) from Johnson's own catalogue of projected works, as "A Dictionary to the Common Prayer in imitation of Calmet's Dictionary of the Bible. March—52." See Hawkins's *Life*, p. 83 n. Robert Anderson and Wimsatt also note the similarity between Johnson's private prayers and the collects in the Book of Common Prayer: *The Life of Samuel Johnson*, n. 3 above, pp. 548–49, and Wimsatt,

Prose Style, pp. 157–58. In 1759 the *Idler*, No. 89, alludes to the prayer book's triple exhortation to goodness through "soberness, righteousness, and godliness" (YE 2:276 and 276 n). See also the recent observation by Michael Suarez S.J. regarding Johnson's use of the rhythms and language of the Book of Common Prayer when he offered condolences: he "almost invariably turned to the Book of Common Prayer and composed a kind of liturgical collect informed by the rhythms and language of the prayer book." See "Johnson's Christian Thought" in Clingham, *The Cambridge Companion*, p. 198.

44. *The Book of Common Prayer as revised and Settled at the Savoy Conference Anno 1662. 14 Charles II. Reprinted from the Sealed Book in the Tower of London* (London, 1814), p. [39]. Subsequent references to the Book of Common Prayer are from this edition and are cited in the text. These passages in pre-1662 versions are essentially the same as those quoted. As I have pointed out above, Johnson was especially sensitive to the plight of orphans and widows—as in the *Idler*, No. 22. In the *Adventurer*, No. 81, he apparently absolves the Admirable Crichton from killing a brutal prize-fighter: "he divided the prize he had won among the widows whose husbands had been killed" (YE 2:405).

45. *Spectator*, 3:514–15. Voltaire shared this opinion but regarded Anglo-Hebrew similarities as barbaric. See his *An Essay upon the Civil Wars of France. . . . And also upon the Epick Poetry of the European Nations, From Homer down to Milton* (1727), 4th ed. (London, 1731), p. 84, *Letters Concerning the English* (London, 1733), pp. 177–78, and *Précis de L'Ecclésiaste, et du Cantique des Cantiques* (Geneva, 1759), pp. [iv], 8. The influence of the King James Version is widely accepted. Witness Gerald Hammond, with whom Northrop Frye would agree: "it is not easy to overestimate the effect upon English prose, and through it upon English culture, of the Renaissance translators' close adherence to the word order of their original texts." We need "to take into account how far our deepest structures of expression were formed by these more developed biblical texts." See Hammond, "English Translations of the Bible," in *The Literary Guide to the Bible*, ed. Robert Alter and Frank Kermode (Cambridge, MA: Belknap Press of Harvard University Press, 1987), p. 657.

46. Ozell, *Common-Prayer Not Common Sense, In Several Places of the Portuguese, Spanish, Italian, French, Latin, and Greek Translations of the English Liturgy* (London, 1722), p. 46. Ozell adds that the Common Prayer's translation, from the Great English Bible of Henry VIII and Edward VI, was superior to the King James Version. William Nicholls had made a similar point and offered a relevant theory of causation: the King James version is too literal, "which makes it *Hebrew* still, tho' in *English* Words." The translators "brought in as much *Hebrew* as ever they could." See Nicholls's *A Comment on the Book of Common-Prayer, and Administration of the Sacraments, &c. Together with the Psalter or Psalms of David* (London, 1710), sig. a2ʳ. Whichever text one read, biblical language was heard and inculcated early in a child's life. As Lockean Johnson says in the *Idler*, No. 89, "In childhood, while our minds are yet unoccupied, religion is impressed upon them, and the first years of almost all who have been well educated are passed in a regular discharge of the duties of piety" (YE 2:277).

47. For Reland, or Reeland, or Hadrianus Relandus, see Donald Greene, *Samuel Johnson's Library. An Annotated Guide* (Victoria, British Columbia: English Literary Studies University of Victoria, 1975), p. 96. The comment regarding Kennicott is in Boswell's *Journal of a Tour to the Hebrides*, in *Life*, 5:42, August 16, 1773. I am indebted to Mr. Gavin Murdoch of Toronto, Ontario, for bringing these references to my attention and for valuable discussions of Johnson's Hebraism.

48. *Observations on Macbeth*, 1745, YE 8:775.

49. *A Miscellany of Poems By several Hands. Publish'd by J. Husbands, A. M. Fellow of Pembroke-College, Oxon.* (Oxford, 1731), sig. a4ᵛ. Subsequent citations are to this, the scarce and only, edition.

50. *Life*, 1:272 and 272 n. 2.

51. For Johnson on Lowth, see *Dr. Campbell's Diary of a Visit to England in 1775*, ed. James L. Clifford (Cambridge: Cambridge University Press, 1947), p. 74. See also *Letters*, 3:286–87 and his reverence for Lowth's learning and authority. In 1772 "Johnson observed that Leibnitz had made some progress in a work tracing all languages up to the Hebrew" (*Life*, 2:156). Johnson may have tried to read the Hebrew of the Polyglot Bible (1654–57): *Diaries, Prayers, and Annals*, YE 1:154–55. In the *Adventurer*, No. 92 he also notes pastoral's pre-Virgilian heritage: "that it has long subsisted in the east, the Sacred Writings sufficiently inform us" (YE 2:417). The *Idler*, No. 108, also refers to the antiquity of "the Inspired Poets of the Hebrews" (YE 2:447). Donald Greene identifies Johnson's several different versions of the complete Bible and the Old and New testaments. See Greene, *Samuel Johnson's Library*, pp. 36–38.

52. Husbands, revelations, sig. b2ʳ; outmoded classical mythology, sigs. b3ʳ–4ʳ, i3ᵛ–4ᵛ; Piozzi, *Anecdotes*, p. 106; abstract for the concrete and other poetic devices, sigs. e4ʳ–ᵛ, e2ʳ–4ᵛ, h4ᵛ–g4ᵛ, h2ᵛ, n3ʳ; men of genius and verbal arts, sig. p3ʳ; *Rambler*, YE 5:319, 320.

53. Husbands, all ages, sig. e1ʳ; sensible objects, sig. f3ᵛ; dust, scales, hills, sigs. n1ʳ–3ʳ.

54. Husbands, the mind's attachment, sig. h3ʳ; Jacob and Rachel, sigs. h3ʳ–ᵛ; Hagar and Ishmael, sig. h2ʳ. Johnson approved of such simple diction as a way to appeal to "the common people." See his praise of Methodist preaching in Boswell's *Life*, 1:458–59 and 2:123.

55. For Patrick, see *The Book of Psalms paraphrased; with Arguments To each Psalm*, 3rd ed. (London, 1700), e.g., p. 581. For Fleury, see "A Discourse concerning Poetry in General, And concerning that of the Hebrews in Particular," in Augustin Calmet, *Antiquities Sacred and Profane: Or, A Collection of Curious and Critical Dissertations on the Old and New Testament*, trans. Nicholas Tindal (London, 1727), e.g., "Discourse," p. 5. For Lowth, *Lectures on the Sacred Poetry of the Hebrews* (1741–50; 1753, Latin; 1787 English), trans. George Gregory, 3rd ed. (London, 1835), p. 205. Robert Burrowes's good observations on Johnson's parallelisms do not mention a possible biblical Hebrew context. See his "Essay" on Johnson's style, n. 1 above, pp. 50–52. I have discussed various aspects of eighteenth-century Hebraic contexts and aspects of Hebrew poetry, Lowth, and parallelism in *Britannia's Issue: The Rise of British Literature from Dryden to Ossian* (Cambridge: Cambridge University Press, 1993), pp. 408–45, 455–63.

56. Letter 281 in *Samuel Richardson: Clarissa Or the History of a Young Lady*, ed. Angus Ross (Harmondsworth, Middlesex: Penguin Books, 1985), p. 951.

57. Husbands, the River Kishon, Sisera, sigs. f2ʳ–ᵛ, f4ᵛ.

58. Uttoxeter, *Life*, 4:373; solitude, *Rambler* 19, YE 3:102; kindness, *Rambler*, No. 47, YE 3:257; distant favourers, *Rambler*, No. 77, YE 4:42; youth expects, *Rambler*, No. 111, YE 4:228; prayers, YE 1:42, January 1, 1749/50; sermon for Tetty, YE 14:263; *The Letters of Philip Dormer Stanhope 4th Earl of Chesterfield*, ed. Bonamy Dobrée (London: Eyre and Spottiswoode, 1932), 1:94–97.

59. Kugel, *The Idea of Biblical Poetry: Parallelism and Its History* (New Haven: Yale University Press, 1981), p. 3, see also p. 286. Wimsatt rightly notes that the Book of Common Prayer exhibits "the formality of parallels" and that Johnson's *Rambler* essays also include "parallel and antithesis" (*Prose Style*, p. 158). Wimsatt helpfully discusses

these traits in his first two chapters. For other useful discussions of biblical parallelism, see Robert Alter, *The Art of Biblical Poetry* (New York: Basic Books, 1986); Alter, "The Characteristics of Ancient Hebrew Poetry," in *The Literary Guide to the Bible*, pp. 612–18; Adele Berlin, *The Dynamics of Biblical Parallelism* (Bloomington: Indiana University Press, 1985); Stephen Prickett, *Words and the Word: Language, Poetics, and Biblical Interpretation* (Cambridge: Cambridge University Press, 1986); S. E. Gillingham, *The Poems and Psalms of the Hebrew Bible* (Oxford: Oxford University Press, 1994); and the introductions by David A. Reibel to Lowth's *De Sacra poesi Hebraeorum* and *Isaiah: A New Translation* (London: Routledge/Thoemmes Press, 1995). None of these authors refers to Husbands's valuable pre-Lowth Preface. They also include bibliographies or helpful notes as guides to a difficult, and sometimes testy, area of biblical scholarship. Berlin and Alter, for example, reject Kugel's view that one cannot distinguish between biblical prose and poetry. I am pleased to be an innocent bystander in this argument.

60. I have been able painlessly to acquire this information through use of the CD-Rom of Johnson's Dictionary Project, The University of Birmingham: *Samuel Johnson. A Dictionary of the English Language: The First and Fourth Editions*, ed. Anne McDermott (Cambridge: Cambridge University Press, 1996)—an invaluable research tool for which a combination of admiration and envy seems appropriate. Many of the 1,460 illustrative quotations from the New Testament also include parallelism. I have limited myself to the *Dictionary*'s first edition and arrived at these numbers by adding the citations from each book of the Old and New Testaments.

61. Nest, *Life*, 1:75; Richardson and Fielding, Piozzi, *Anecdotes*, p. 127.

62. Girolamo Cardana, *Rambler* No. 108, YE 4:214; obedience to a master, *Rambler*, No. 127, YE 4:315; use industry, *Rambler*, No. 29, YE 4:325; vultures, *Rambler*, No. 38, YE 3:209; scent of prey, *Rambler*, No. 175, YE 5:161; revenues lessened, *Rambler*, No. 53, YE 3:287.

For comparable remarks, see the *Adventurer*, No. 34, YE 2:340–41, 343–44; *Adventurer*, No. 54, YE 2:367–68, 370; *Adventurer*, No. 62, YE 2:380; *Adventurer*, No. 111, YE 2:453–54; and *Idler*, No. 73, YE 2:229. Sir John Lade in 1780 clearly violated one of Johnson's long-standing bases for moral, financial, and generational responsibility.

63. See *Letters*, 3:296–97. The letter and the manuscript of the poem are at the Huntington Library in San Marino, California.

64. "Levet," lines 27–28, 6:315; Matthew 25.24–30.

II
Mind

8

The Reader, the General, and the Particular: Johnson and Imlac in Chapter Ten of *Rasselas*

FOR MANY YEARS THE LAMENTABLY FAMOUS TENTH CHAPTER OF *RAS-selas* has been regarded as virtually a seven-paragraph microcosm of the Drury Lane "Prologue" (1747), several reviews, numerous literary essays in the *Rambler* (1750–1752), *Adventurer* (1753–1754), and *Idler* (1758–1760), Preface and Notes to Shakespeare (1765), the *Lives of the Poets* (1779–81), and critical remarks scattered throughout the *Dictionary* (1755) as well as Boswell's *Life of Johnson* (1791). Imlac's attitudes toward general nature and the poet explain Johnson's attitudes since presumably they are both consistent with and emblematic of them. F. R. Leavis, for example, argues that Imlac's generality is part of the essence of "Johnsonian Augustanism." According to Leavis, Johnson as surrogate Imlac, rejects "all concrete specificity in the rendering of experience." James Sutherland tells us that "Johnson's fullest pronouncement of the necessary predominance of the general over the particular occurs in the tenth chapter of *Rasselas*," which also includes "Johnson's settled opinion about the business of the poet," and helps to explain "why originality was lightly stressed in the age of Pope and Johnson." H. W. Donner adds that "attentive readers" have surely noticed that Johnson "anticipates . . . Shelley" in his view of the poet as legislator for mankind.[1]

.

1

The equation of Johnson and Imlac and their common focus on the "general" thus has long prevailed in modern criticism; but it has been undergoing serious reconsideration. W. R. Keast stresses that much of Johnson's praise of the general appears when the poet discussed is excessively particular. Jean Hagstrum convincingly shows that Johnson's notion of the general is "arrived at inductively and empirically," and suggests that for Johnson the general is based upon the particular and is intended to recall it.[2] Partially as a result of such revisionism, Walter Jackson Bate generously retracted his earlier view that Imlac on generality is "a key to Johnson's critical thought." He further adds that Johnson merely "permits Imlac . . . to say that the poet should 'divest himself of the prejudices of his age and country'."[3]

One thus hopes that an attempt to distinguish between Imlac, Johnson, and their respective critical systems is unnecessary, and that to do so one would be guilty of flogging a seriously ill, if not dead, horse. This is hardly the case. Martin Kallich is confident that Imlac's dissertation upon poetry "neatly and systematically . . . summarizes Johnson's critical theory," and that "Imlac's little essay on literature is a distillation of all those principles which Johnson cherished and by means of which he formulated his critical credo." Kallich then attempts to demonstrate that each of Imlac's points in fact is part of "Samuel Johnson's Principles of Criticism." Geoffrey Tillotson also remarks that "Imlac's conception of the poet—a conception that he could not himself fulfill—is in all essentials that of Johnson himself. It represents the beau ideal of the poet as Johnson sees it."[4]

Several of Johnson's and Imlac's critical observations do overlap; but such commentators surely confuse the part for the whole.[5] Indeed, Johnson's theory of the persona encourages something of the sort. In the final *Rambler*, No. 208 (1752), he excuses "the seeming vanity" with which he has hitherto spoken of himself through the precedent of previous occasional essayists. He claims "the privilege which every nameless writer has been hitherto allowed. 'A mask,' says Castiglione, 'confers a right of acting and speaking with less restraint, even when the wearer happens to be known.' He that is discovered without his consent, may claim some indulgence, and cannot be rigorously called to justify those sallies or frolicks which his disguise must prove him desirous to conceal." Johnson then adds an interesting reservation regarding this distinction of man and mask: "I have been cautious lest this offence should be frequently or grossly committed; for, as one of the philosophers directs us to live with a friend, as with one that is sometimes to become an enemy, I have always thought it the duty of an anonymous author to write, as if he expected to be hereafter known."[6] Johnson's concept of the persona clearly allowed him to create a character whose remarks are different from but related to his own.

We thus should not be surprised to have Imlac and Johnson agree on certain points of critical theory. Both believe that the ancients have writ-

ten much of the best literature and possess nature, while later generations have elegance and art; that no man is great by imitation; that
poetry enforces or decorates moral or religious truth; and that one
should examine the species not the individual. Several of Imlac's views
also but partially overlap with Johnson's. Specifically, Johnson probably
would not wholly approve of those who regard poetry "with a veneration somewhat approaching to the angelick nature," that when a poet is
exercising his poetic craft no kind of knowledge should be overlooked,
and that all appearances of nature are to be utilized so that the reader
will be gratified with "remote allusions and unexpected instruction."[7]
Similarly, Johnson would also mistrust Imlac's notion that the poet must
"divest himself of the prejudices of his age or country" (YE 16:44;
"Time and place will always enforce regard," he says several years later,
and so "Pope wrote for his own age and his own nation" [Lives, 3:238]),
and that the poet must be so learned that he can acquire "every delicacy
of speech and grace of harmony" (YE 16:45). In the "Life of Milton"
Johnson indeed says that the ideal epic poet must be properly informed
by history, morality, life, physiology, and imagination, and that he is not
"yet a poet till he has attained the whole extension of his language, distinguished all the delicacies of phrase, and all the colours of words, and
learned to adjust their different sounds to all the varieties of metrical
modulation." The epic, after all, is the noblest genre and "requires an
assemblage of all the powers which are singly sufficient for other compositions" (Lives, 1:170–71). Imlac, however, is describing not the conventions and poetic temperament suitable for such sublime poetry, but "the
poet" generally, without the distinctions among literary kinds that Johnson often makes.

Moreover, there are at least two points at which Johnson and Imlac
almost certainly disagree. Discussion of these makes clear that Johnson
has created a dramatic scene in which the character Imlac expresses not
consistently acceptable principles of criticism, but an ultimately unreal-
istic and self-centered view which Rasselas and the reader reject. Johnson would deny that the poet is wise to condemn the applause of his
own time and seek that of posterity, and that the poet is an interpreter
of nature and legislator of mankind who presides "over the thoughts and
manners of future generations" (YE 16:45).

In the Preface to Shakespeare Johnson observes that Shakespeare neither demanded "any ideal tribute upon future times" nor "had any further prospect than of present popularity and present profit."[8] Though
this attitude is not necessarily the ideal for Johnson, he clearly shares
Shakespeare's emphasis upon the need to please the audience before one.

Apparent abandonment of present fame, Johnson says, is merely among the "consolatory expedients" of those who "are willing to hope from posterity what the present age refuses, and flatter themselves that the regard which is yet denied by envy, will be at last bestowed by time" (YE 7:59). Like Shakespeare, and unlike Imlac, Johnson earned his living through letters, and no man so engaged could scorn his audience or the money which came therefrom. On October 27, 1757, Johnson wrote to Thomas Warton regarding "some literary business for an inhabitant of Oxford." After outlining several projects, he adds: "I impart these designs to you in confidence that what you do not make use of yourself shall revert to me, uncommunicated to any other. The schemes of a writer are his property and his revenue, and therefore they must not be made common."[9]

Johnson also dislikes the exaggerated notion that the poet is a lawmaker who legislates for or presides over man's thoughts. He regarded poetry as one human activity among many, to which, as he states in the "Life of Cowley" (1779), a mind of great general powers turns by accident rather than divine preselection (*Lives*, 1:2). The poet at his best gives literary pleasure, helps man to live morally, vindicates God's ways, and attempts to teach us how to cope with the grim world within and without us. This does not imply either Imlac's or Shelley's notion of the poet as lawgiver. On the contrary, Johnson's *Dictionary* defines both "poet" and "poetry" in pedestrian terms. A poet is "An inventor; an author of fiction; a writer of poems; one who writes in measure." Poetry is "Metrical composition; the art or practice of writing poems. . . . Poems; poetical pieces."[10] The poet learns from life and nature which he shapes and communicates to us; he need not "interpret," for nature speaks a language which each man may understand.[11] He cannot legislate for man, since the poet's function is to instruct by pleasing not by fiat.

This last point recalls one of Johnson's major critical preconceptions and Imlac's apparent ignorance of it. Since "the purpose of a writer is to be read" (*Lives*, 3:240), the power of pleasing is essential; but Imlac approaches that end only once—when he hopes to gratify the "reader with remote allusions and unexpected instruction" (YE 16:43). These allusions may not be as gratifying to Johnson's reader as Imlac expects: "words to which we are nearly strangers, whenever they occur, draw that attention on themselves which they should transmit to things" (*Lives*, 1:420). Poor Rasselas is virtually frightened away from Imlac, who is so earnest in his desire to have the poet know everything that one of his students is likely to die before he can communicate anything.

Awareness of the larger function of chapter 10 in Johnson's scheme in *Rasselas* also indicates that Imlac is an actor in a scene which Johnson directs, and thus portrays the poet's occupation as a possible choice of life. "Enough! Thou hast convinced me, that no human being can ever be a poet," Rasselas cries out to his teacher, and reiterates that he "will at present hear no more of his labours" (YE 16:46). Poetry has many of the limitations of other human pursuits, among them the unhappy tendency to puff one's profession and values at the expense of others and, as a corollary danger, to be seduced by a lesser form of the dangerous prevalence of imagination. "Imlac," the narrator says, "now felt the enthusiastic fit, and was proceeding to aggrandize his own profession" (YE 16:46). He has temporarily withdrawn into his own world and, like Rasselas chasing villains, like the scientist who delivers "A dissertation on the art of flying" (YE 16:22), and like the astronomer who fancies he can control the weather, Imlac's perceptions and judgments are unreliable. His grandiose "dissertation upon poetry," whose title parallels and echoes the dotty scientist on flying, contradicts his own more sober remarks regarding the different but substantially overlapping life of the scholar. Hence shortly after Imlac recites a poem "upon the various conditions of humanity," Rasselas asks him to tell the story of his life. The poet responds with a history that associates the poetic and scholarly lives, both of which are "devoted to knowledge":

> Sir, said Imlac, my history will not be long: the life that is devoted to knowledge passes silently away, and is very little diversified by events. To talk in publick, to think in solitude, to read and to hear, to inquire, and answer inquiries, is the business of a scholar. He wanders about the world without pomp or terrour, and is neither known nor valued but by men like himself. (YE 16:31)

In Imlac's calmer moments, he rejects his own enthusiasm regarding poets—or at the very least that aspect of the poetic life devoted to the necessary acquisition of learning. We should not be surprised that Johnson rejects such enthusiasm as well. Given his design of showing the multiplicity of unacceptable choices of life, that should also be the reader's reaction.

2

Though many of Imlac's and Johnson's views are either the same or related, many also are too different to justify the frequent assumption of congruence. Moreover, one point of congruence has been misunderstood. Johnson's conception of poetic generality and particularity is not as broad as it has been represented. In chapter 10 of *Rasselas*, in his practical criticism, and in his practice as an artist, normative generality is based upon careful, detailed, and laudable close observation. It is intended to evoke not an "ideal" image, but the original and its sublunary specifics.

Let us examine two of the key words in the following line: "the business of a poet . . . is to examine not the individual, but the species; to remark general properties, and large appearances" (YE 16:43). Dictionary Johnson of course knew the conventional definition of definitions: the genus equals the species plus differentiae. His definition of the noun *species* is instructive: "1. A sort; a subdivision of a general term." His illustrative quotation from Isaac Watts's *Logic* (1725) indicates the particularity associated with and evoked by a species: "a special idea is called by the schools a *species*; it is one common nature that agrees to several singular individual beings: so horse is a special idea or *species* as it agrees to Bucephalus, Trot, and Snowball," three specific horses with specific traits.[12] The second definition also insists that the class and the individual are compatible, though here the illustrative quotations stress the individual. "2. Class of nature; single order of beings." His important third definition emphasizes the qualities of sensation and observation: "3. Appearance to the senses; any visible or sensible representation." The fourth definition is "Representation to the mind," whose illustration from Dryden conflates parts of a long sentence in the "Account" prefaced to *Annus Mirabilis* (1667).[13] The remark suggests that the term *species* was associated with the imaginative, poetic, faculty: "wit in the poet, or wit-writing, is no other than the faculty of imagination in the writer, which searches over all the memory for the *species* or ideas of those things which it designs to represent." Communication of the species thus relates to the image-making powers of the poet, a power in part enhanced by his ability to view nature and record its impressions in his memory. The relationship between species and perception also was suggested, among other places, in Ephraim Chambers's *Cyclopaedia* (1728). Species is "an idea, which relates to some other more general one; or is comprized under a more universal division of a genus." He then adds that "the word is Latin, formed from the ancient verb, *specio*, I see; as if a *species* of things were a collection of all the things seen at one view."[14]

The species, then, is a subdivision, and though larger than the "specifick" ("that which makes a thing of the species of which it is") is demonstrably and necessarily smaller than the genus, which no one can possibly see "at one view." The poet records the large idea of a perceivable group, the species, but he does not record the idea of the genus, which comprehends "under it many species; as *quadruped* is a *genus* comprehending under it almost all terrestrial beasts." To deal with the genus without evoking its species brings Johnson's censure. The speaker in *Marmor Norfolciense* (1739), for example, discusses a learned gentleman's translation of the inscription engraved on the buried Norfolk tablet. The writer "has succeeded better as a scholar than a poet," he says, and later offers an interesting illustration of poetical lapse: "*rubri colubri*" should be rendered "Red serpents" rather than "scarlet reptiles," for the latter is a licentious use of "a general term for a particular."[15] In 1746 Johnson states that "the praise [in epitaphs] ought not to be general, because the mind is lost in the extent of any indefinite idea, and cannot be affected with what it cannot comprehend. When we hear only of a good or great man, we know not in what class to place him, nor have any notion of his character, distinct from that of a thousand others."[16] In the "Life of Dryden" (1779), Johnson criticizes Dryden's elegy to *Eleonora*: "the praise being inevitably general fixes no impression upon the reader" (*Lives*, 1:441–42). In the same year, in the "Life of Rowe," Johnson observes: "I know not that there can be found in his plays any deep search into nature, any accurate discriminations of kindred qualities, or nice display of passion in its progress; all is general and undefined" (*Lives*, 2:76). Both poet and lexicographer should break the general into its particular species.

This negative use of the general is paralleled by several of Johnson's positive uses of the particular or related concepts and helps us to understand in what sense the "general properties" are good for poets to remark. Shakespeare, Johnson says, "was an exact surveyor of the inanimate world; his descriptions have always some peculiarities, gathered by contemplating things as they really exist" (YE 7:89). Similarly, Shakespeare has "a vigilance of observation and accuracy of distinction which books and precepts cannot confer" (YE 7:88). Pope's *Essay on Criticism* (1711) exhibits an admirable "nicety of distinction" (*Lives*, 3:94); whereas in the *Progress of Poetry* (1757) Gray's "'car' of Dryden, with his 'two coursers,' has nothing in it peculiar, it is a car in which any other rider may be placed" (*Lives*, 3:438). Thomson has "a mind that at once comprehends the vast, and attends to the minute"; he exhibits both "wide expansion of general views, and . . . circumstantial varieties" (*Lives*, 3:229).

Several definitions of "general" and similar words in the *Dictionary* enforce a view of the term as tied to sensational or empirically observed but not idiosyncratic details. The third definition of the adjective "general," for example, "not restrained by narrow or distinctive limitations," offers this important illustration from Locke: "a *general* idea is an idea in the mind, considered there as separated from time and place, and so capable to represent any particular being that is conformable to it."[17] The seventh definition is: "extensive, though not universal"; the noun "generality" is: "the state of being general; the quality of including species or particulars." The second definition of the adverb "generally" is: "extensively, though not universally"; of the noun "generalness," "wide extent, though short of universality; frequency, commonness." One cannot determine frequency or commonness without seeing many of the objects so regarded. Hence in 1769 Johnson criticized Samuel Foote's "talent of exhibiting character," because "his is not a talent; it is a vice, it is what others abstain from. It is not comedy, which exhibits the character of a species, as that of a miser gathered from many misers: it is a farce, which exhibits individuals" (*Life*, 2:95). Foote's miser, drawn from an inadequate sample of relevant characters seen, cannot include the species and thus belongs to an inferior, excessively individualized, and temporary art form.

There is nothing that suggests the "ideal" at all in any of Johnson's discussions of the general. Nor could there be, since he regarded the ideal as "Mental; intellectual; not perceived by the senses" and often, as in the "Life of Addison," disparages the "merely ideal" (*Lives,* 2:95). The immediate context of Imlac's remarks also shows the sensational, nonideal, basis of the general. He knows that he "could never describe what [he] had not seen" (YE 16:41). Since "no kind of knowledge was to be overlooked," he engages in highly particular searches of "mountains and deserts for images and resemblances, and pictured upon [his] mind every tree of the forest and flower of the valley." The attainment of an artistic mind Imlac insists, and Johnson would agree, demands careful study and consistent survey of the nature before and within one. *Seeing, observing, watching, studying, surveying*, and the objects to be so viewed, "store [the poet's] mind with inexhaustible variety" that is a reflection of the external worlds of nature, learning, and art. He combines observation of "all that is awfully vast or elegantly little," with "remote allusions and unexpected instruction" (YE 16:42–43). His imagination "strongly impresses on the writer's mind and enables him to convey to the reader the various forms of nature, incidents of life, and energies of passion" *(Lives*, 3:247). Imagination also collects the results of these observations of disparate aspects of nature, takes their variety with all their change and difference, and blends them into a general portrait that includes essentials and, where possible, dismisses accidentals. By so doing, however, Imlac's poet is helping the reader to "recall the original" object to his mind, an original that is not the ideal of tulipness, but the species tulip, with its relevant and necessary differentiae.

The original as so recalled surely is tinged with one's own notion of particularity. The nature of the human mind requires us to distinguish among tulips—whether red, yellow, or white, for instance—and some will have been more impressive than others. Several particular tulips are unified in the poet's mind and poem, make a "general" tulip that recalls an original and particular tulip in the reader's mind. The quotation from Locke concerning a general idea is worth hearing again: "a general idea is an idea in the mind, considered as separated from time and place, and so capable to represent any particular being that is conformable to it." The essential difference between Johnson's and Locke's "good" general, and the "bad" general of vague epitaphs or Gray's chariot, is that these are so undefined that they exclude the species, puzzle us because "we know not in what class to place" the person or thing discussed, and so cannot evoke a conformable particular.

This relationship between the general and particular was an essential aspect of Johnson's aesthetics and psychology throughout his literary career. We have seen that *Marmor Norfolciense* of 1739 embodies this view; it is also in the Preface to Dodsley's *Preceptor* (1748) nine years later. Here Johnson outlines *The Preceptor*'s aims and assumptions and adds several observations of his own regarding educational psychology. The basic methods of "teaching to *Read*, and *Speak*, and write *Letters*," he says, are given in "Rules, which are the most general" because they "admit a great Number of subordinate Observations, which must be particularly adapted to every Scholar." Johnson's understanding that the general evokes the particular reappears in his discussion of the teaching of rhetoric and poetry. Dodsley's book attempts only "to teach the Mind some general Heads of Observations, to which the beautiful Passages of the best Writers may commonly be reduced." The teacher, Johnson warns, should not "confine himself to the Examples before him, for by that Method he will never enable his Pupils to make just Applications of the Rules; but, having once inculcated the true Meaning of each Figure, he should require them to exemplify it by their own Observations, pointing to them the Poem, or, in longer Works, the Book or Canto in which an Example may be found, and leaving them to discover the particular Passage by the Light of the Rules which they have lately learned."[18]

In the *Rambler,* No. 60 (1750), Johnson discusses the empathy made possible by particularized biography which draws upon the many "par-

allel circumstances, and kindred images, to which we readily conform
our minds": "all joy or sorrow for the happiness or calamities of others
is produced by an act of the imagination, that realizes the event however
fictitious, or approximates it however remote, by placing us, for a time,
in the condition of him whose fortune we contemplate; so that we feel,
while the deception lasts, whatever motions would be excited by the
same good or evil happening to ourselves" (YE 3:318–319). Johnson admires Shakespeare because he is "above all [modern] writers" the poet
of general nature; but he also adds that "it is from this wide extension
of design that so much instruction is derived," since it offers "practical
axioms and domestick wisdom," as well as "a system of civil and œcon-
omical prudence" for the audience of the moment (YE 7:62). In the "Life
of Thomson" Johnson not only praises *The Seasons'* combination of
"wide expansion of general views and . . . enumeration of circumstantial
varieties," but insists that "the naturalist" shares in the common readers' pleasure: "he is assisted to recollect and to combine, to arrange his
discoveries, and to amplify the sphere of his contemplation" (*Lives*,
3:299). That is, Thomson's extended scenes and general effects evoke
particular images compatible with them. On the other hand, Johnson
criticizes Cowley because he is so particular that he deprives his reader
of the ability to bring the work into his own experience. "That Gabriel
was invested with the softest or brightest colours of the sky we might
have been told, and have been dismissed to improve the idea in our different proportions of conception; but Cowley could not let us go till he
had related where Gabriel got first his skin, and then his mantle, then
his lace, and then his scarfe, and related it in the terms of the mercer and
taylor" (*Lives*, 1:53). Excessive particularity by the poet is an impertinence, since it demands that we wholly accept the author's conception
however banal it might be; we are excluded from the artistic process,
and cannot "improve the idea in our different proportions of conception."

The process of recollection of the original is well illustrated in *Rasselas* itself. The narrator describes the sides of the mountains and says:
"all animals that bite the grass, or brouse the shrub, whether wild or
tame, wandered in this extensive circuit, secured from beasts of prey by
the mountains which confined them" (YE 16:9). Shortly thereafter, Rasselas "cast his eyes upon the pastures and mountains filled with animals,
of which some were biting the herbage, and some sleeping among the
bushes" (YE 16:12). No rational reader will hear of animals biting grass
without also recalling specific original cows, goats, or other conformable species. Nor can we think of the species "beasts of prey" without

also recalling cougars, lions, tigers, or similar creatures. In both cases Johnson supplies the essential generic traits, and the reader supplies the essential differentiae of conformable animals. On such a scheme it is impossible to separate the general from the particular; it is a scheme in which the reader is inextricably drawn into the act of creation.

The power of a general proposition to evoke the reader's own conclusions and artistic complicity was frequently discussed in theory and seen in contemporary practice. Addison's *Spectator,* No. 512 (1712), for example, argues that the fable is the finest and most universally pleasing form of giving advice, because in it "we are made to believe we advise our selves. We . . . consider the Precepts rather as our own Conclusions, than [the author's] Instructions." Such a method is successful because it flatters the mind's conception of its abilities:

> In Writings of this kind, the Reader comes in for half of the Performance; Every thing appears to him like a Discovery of his own; he is busied all the while in applying Characters and Circumstances, and is in this respect both a Reader and a Composer. It is no wonder therefore than on such Occasions when the Mind is thus pleased with it self, and amused with its own Discoveries, that it is highly delighted with the Writing which is the Occasion of it. For this Reason the *Absalom and Achitophel* was one of the most popular Poems that ever appeared in *English*. The Poetry is indeed very fine, but had it been much finer it would not have so much pleased, without a Plan which gave the Reader an Opportunity of exerting his own Talents.[19]

Readers of eighteenth-century novels were also expected to exert their own talents. Fielding's description of Sophia in *Tom Jones* (1749), for instance, provides us with a generalized portrait of a female beauty. She is of middle size but inclining to tall, has an exact and delicate shape, beautifully proportioned arms that suggest equally attractive legs, long, curling, black hair, a slightly low forehead, full, arched eyebrows above black eyes, a regular nose, luscious red lips with brilliant white teeth, and so on. None of this is really "particularized," yet Sophia is obviously personalized by each reader. The reason is made clear in Fielding's amiable excuse for not telling us about her inner, spiritual, charms. "But as there are no Perfections of the Mind which do not discover themselves, in that perfect Intimacy, to which we intend to introduce our Reader, with this charming young Creature so it is needless to mention them here: nay, it is a Kind of tacit Affront to our Reader's Understanding, and may also rob him of that Pleasure which he will receive in forming his own Judgment of her Character."[20]

Supplying general traits so that the readers may contribute their own particulars is parodied and reduced to comic absurdity in Sterne's description of the Widow Wadman: "never did thy eyes behold, or thy concupiscence covet any thing in this world, more concupiscible than Widow *Wadman.* . . . To conceive this right,—call for pen and ink— here's paper ready to your hand.—Sit down, Sir, paint her to your own mind—as like your mistress as you can—as unlike your wife as your conscience will let you—'tis all one to me—please but your own fancy in it." An empty page and one-half follow, thus allowing the reader so to "improve" the author's conception that his book will have at least that much which can not be attacked.[21] Somewhat later, probably in 1798, Jane Austen uses the same theory as part of a mildly comic description of Eleanor Tilney's noble husband. This lucky fellow, she says near the end of *Northanger Abbey* (pub. 1818), "was really deserving" of Eleanor: "independent of his peerage, his wealth, and his attachment, being to a precision the most charming young man in the world. Any further definition of his merits must be unnecessary: the most charming young man in the world is instantly before the imagination of us all.[22]

This aesthetic theory was not limited to the literary arts. Sir Joshua Reynolds also urges the relationship between the general and particular and the role of the reader's cooperating imagination. In Discourse 14 (1788) Reynolds exemplifies the way in which the general evokes, recalls, or represents the particular in portrait painting:

> The likeness of a portrait . . . consists more in preserving the general effect of the countenance, than in the most minute finishing of the features, or any of the particular parts. Now Gainsborough's portraits were often little more, in regard to finishing, or determining the form of the features, than what generally attends a dead colour; but as he was always attentive to the general effect, or whole together, I have often imagined that this unfinished manner contributed even to that striking resemblance for which his portraits are so remarkable. Though this opinion may be considered as fanciful, yet I think a plausible reason may be given, why such a mode of painting should have such an effect. It is presupposed that in this undetermined manner there is the general effect; enough to remind the spectator of the original; the imagination supplies the rest, and perhaps more satisfactorily to himself, if not more exactly, than the artist, with all his care, could possibly have done.[23]

The minutely detailed portrait cannot bring the original to mind as thoroughly as the general portrait which evokes it in the viewer's mind. This concept of generality demands audience participation in the artistic process.

We may say, then, that a minority of Imlac's critical principles in chapter 10 of *Rasselas* are wholly Johnson's, he would have misgivings about several others, and clearly disagree with two. Johnson does use Imlac to epitomize his own views of normative generality: this is based upon the empirical, particular, and sensational, embodies the species, which is a large class but hardly universal or ideal, and is intended to evoke the original "conformable to it." During his journey to the Hebrides Johnson carried a calibrated walking stick in order to measure the height and breadth of objects, and avoid a mere "gross and general idea."[24] Such an idea can neither help the reader to recall the original, nor make him a partner in the creative process. In his desire for such an aesthetic, Imlac fulfills at least one aspect of the beau ideal of the poet as Johnson saw it.

NOTES

1. Leavis, "Johnson as Critic," in *Samuel Johnson: A Collection of Critical Essays*, ed. Donald J. Greene (Englewood Cliffs, NJ: McGraw-Hill, 1965), p. 79; Sutherland, *A Preface to Eighteenth-Century Poetry* (Oxford: Clarendon Press, 1948), p. 3; Donner, "Dr. Johnson as a Literary Critic," in Greene, *Collection*, p. 106.

2. Keast, Review of Scott Elledge, n. 5 below in *Philological Quarterly* 22 (1948): 131–32; Hagstrum, *Samuel Johnson's Literary Criticism* (Minneapolis: University of Minnesota Press, 1952), p. 88.

3. Bate, *The Achievement of Samuel Johnson* (New York: Oxford University Press, 1955), p. 199; see also p. 240 n. 30. Bate's earlier remark is in *From Classic to Romantic* (1946; rpt. New York: Harper, 1961), p. 61, where he also refers to "the classical conception of ideal or general nature" in which Dryden, Swift, Pope, and Johnson believed. Bate's subsequent observation in *The Achievement* is more to the point: "the 'general nature' desired is . . . a species of symbolic value; it proceeds through the concrete detail, but the test is still how applicable it is beyond" (p. 199).

4. Kallich, "Samuel Johnson's Principles of Criticism and Imlac's 'Dissertation upon Poetry'," in *Journal of Aesthetics and Art Criticism* 25 (1966): 71, 78; Tillotson, "Imlac and the Business of a Poet," in *Studies in Criticism and Aesthetics, 1660–1800: Essays in Honor of Samuel Holt Monk*, ed. Howard Anderson and John S. Shea (Minneapolis: University of Minnesota Press, 1967), p. 298.

5. There are many other secondary works of interest regarding both the general and particular, and the relationship between Johnson and Imlac. Among the most important are Scott Elledge, "The Background and Development in English Criticism of the Theories of Generality and Particularity," *PMLA* 62 (1947): 147–82; W. K. Wimsatt, Jr., "The Structure of the 'Concrete Universal' in Literature," ibid., 262–80; Arthur Sherbo, *Samuel Johnson, Editor of Shakespeare*, Illinois Studies in Language and Literature, vol. 42 (Urbana: University of Illinois Press, 1956), pp. 53–56; William Youngren, "Generality in Augustan Satire," in *In Defense of Reading*, ed. Reuben A. Brower and Richard Poirier (New York: Dutton, 1962), pp. 206–34; Donald J. Greene, " 'Pictures to the Mind': Johnson and Imagery," in *Johnson, Boswell and Their Circle: Essays Presented to Lawrence Fitzroy Powell* (Oxford: Clarendon Press, 1965), pp. 137–58; Paul K. Alkon, *Samuel*

Johnson and Moral Discipline (Evanston, IL: Northwestern University Press, 1967), pp. 3–43; pp. 67–89; Youngren, "Science and Poetic Language in the Restoration," *ELH* 35 (1968): 158–87; Greene, *Samuel Johnson* (New York: Twayne, 1970), pp. 200–205.

6. The Yale Edition of the Works of Samuel Johnson, vols. 3–5, *The Rambler*, ed. W. J. Bate and Albrecht B. Strauss (New Haven: Yale University Press, 1969), 5:317–18. Subsequent citations to the Yale Edition will be cited as YE with editor and date of publication. For other remarks regarding Johnson's attitude toward the persona, see Johnson's *Lives of the English Poets*, ed. George Birkbeck Hill (Oxford: Clarendon Press 1905), 3:207, 211, 228. Subsequent references to the *Lives* are from this edition and are cited in the text. For further discussion of the persona, see my "Masked Men and Satire and Pope: Towards an Historical Basis for the Eighteenth-Century Persona," in Weinbrot, *Eighteenth-Century Satire: Essays on Texts and Contexts from Dryden to Peter Pindar* (Cambridge: Cambridge University Press, 1988), pp. 34–49, 214–17.

7. *Rasselas*, YE 16, *Rasselas and Other Tales*, ed. Gwin J. Kolb (1990), pp. 38–39 (veneration), 43 (remote). Subsequent citations are given in the text as YE. Imlac makes the following points in Chapter 10:

   i. Poetry is considered the highest learning, and is accorded "a veneration approaching to that which man would pay to the angelick nature" (YE 16:39).

   ii. Ancient poets are regarded as the best, and possess nature while later poets possess art.

   iii. No man is great by imitation of art alone, and so one must regard nature and life as well.

   iv. No kind of knowledge is to be overlooked; all appearances of nature are to be utilized for . . .

   v. "the inforcement or decoration of moral or religious truth" (YE 16:43) and . . .

   vi. the purpose of gratifying his "reader with remote allusions and unexpected instruction" (YE 16:43).

   vii. The poet examines the species, not the individual; general properties, large appearances, the "prominent and striking features as recall the original to every mind." He accordingly neglects "the minuter discriminations" (YE 16:42–43).

   viii. He must also know "all the modes of life, . . . all the passions in all their combinations, and trace the changes of the human mind as they are modified by various institutions and accidental influences of climate or custom" (YE 16:44).

   ix. "He must divest himself of the prejudices of his age or country" and work towards the "general and transcendental truths which will always be the same" (YE 16:44).

   x. He thus will "contemn the applause of his own time, and commit his claims [to fame] to the justice of posterity" (YE 16:45).

   xi. He is "the interpreter of nature, and the legislator of mankind," and presides "over the thoughts and manners of future generations" (YE 16:45).

   xii. He must know many languages and sciences, and must practice his craft in order to acquire "every delicacy of speech and grace of harmony" (YE 16:45).

8. YE 7, *Johnson on Shakespeare*, ed. Arthur Sherbo (1968), pp. 91–92. Subsequent references are cited in the text.

9. *The Letters of Samuel Johnson*, ed. Bruce Redford (Princeton: Princeton University Press, 1992–94), 1:156. Warton as recipient is a probable conjecture.

10. *A Dictionary of the English Language* (London, 1755). All quotations are from this edition.

11. In the *Dictionary* Johnson declares that the noun "nature" means: "10. Sentiments or images adapted to nature, or conformable to truth and reality." In the *Rambler*, No. 5 (1750), he portrays the restorative quality of the spring's external nature and uses its variety as an emblem of promise and "the inexhaustible stock of materials upon which [one] can employ himself." He also praises the spring as a source of "a certain prospect

of discovering new reasons for adoring the sovereign author of the universe" (YE 3:29). Vernal nature here implies "Sentiments conformable to truth and reality" and does not need the poet to mediate. Addisonian Johnson urges that the lessons of nature are available to anyone who opens his eyes. Similarly, in the *Rambler*, No. 36 (1750), he observes that "the works of nature, from which [pastorals] are drawn, have always the same thoughts, being at once obvious to the most careless regard, and more than adequate to the strongest reason, and severest contemplation" (YE 3:196). Of course this is only one of the many meanings of "nature" for Johnson and his readers. A. O. Lovejoy's "Nature as an Aesthetic Norm," *Modern Language Notes* 42 (1927): 444–50 remains a useful guide to such variety.

12. Arthur Sherbo notes that the quotation comes from Watts's chapter 3, section 3, "Of universal and particular ideas, real and imaginary." See *Samuel Johnson, Editor of Shakespeare*, p. 54.

13. *Of Dramatic Poesy and Other Critical Essays*, ed. George Watson (London: Everyman, 1962), 1:98.

14. *Cyclopaedia: or, An Universal Dictionary of Arts and Sciences*, 6th ed. (London, 1750). See also Nathan Bailey's definition of "species" in his *Universal Etymological Dictionary*, 4th ed. (London, 1728): "a kind or sort; . . . also Images or Representations of Objects." Johnson's definitions 3 and 4, cited above, as well as 5, "Show; visible exhibition," continue the association of "species" with visual perception.

15. YE 10, *Marmor*, in *Political Writings*, ed. Donald J. Greene (1977), pp. 36 (succeeded), 35 (general).

16. "Essay on Epitaphs," in *The Works of Samuel Johnson, LL. D.* (Oxford, 1825), 5:264.

17. This is similar to and may be drawn from Locke's *Essay* 3.3.6, though there are comparable observations in other places in book 3. That also is Chambers's source for much of his discussion of the term "general." By 1726 Locke's notion of the general idea and the conformable species had been too narrowly applied in literary criticism, or so Lewis Crusius believed. In his "Life of Lucretius" he complains: "*Aristotle* having laid it down as a maxim, that all Poetry should be an imitation of some action, (meaning the Epick and Dramatick) some have absurdly taken this in so strict and comprehensive a sense, as to take in all kinds under this rule, and exclude those, whose Writings are not conformable to it, from the class of Poets. Were it to hold good, *Hesiod* and *Virgil's Georgicks*, not to mention many more of the best compositions of the Ancients, must be rejected and condemned with LUCRETIUS." See Crusius, *Lives of the Roman Poets*, 3rd ed. (London, 1735), 1:5–6.

18. Johnson, Preface to *The Preceptor*, in *Samuel Johnson's Prefaces & Dedications*, ed. Allen T. Hazen (New Haven: Yale University Press, 1937), pp. 180, 183–84 respectively. The theory that I here suggest is the opposite of that often discussed as typical of the later eighteenth century: namely, that the particular evokes the general. For full discussion of the more traditional view, see Elledge, "The Background and Development . . . of the Theories of Generality and Particularity," n. 5 above, and Gordon McKenzie, *Critical Responsiveness: A Study of the Psychological Current in Later Eighteenth-Century Criticism* (Berkeley and Los Angeles: University of California Press, 1949).

19. Addison, *The Spectator*, ed. Donald F. Bond (Oxford: Clarendon Press, 1965), 4:318. Addison makes a similar point—here regarding identification of allusions—in *A Discourse on Antient and Modern Learning* (London, 1734), pp. 9–10. For further use of the reader's ability to "complete" the work as a norm of criticism, see The Twicken-

ham Edition of the Poems of Alexander Pope, vol. 10, *The Odyssey of Homer, Books XIII–XXIV*, ed. Maynard Mack (London and New Haven: Methuen and Yale University Press, 1967), p. 192, and Joseph Spence, *Remarks and Dissertations on Virgil; With some other Classical Observations: By the late Mr. Holdsworth* (London, 1768), p. 38. Holdsworth and Spence report Pope's observation that Homer "is like those painters of whom Apelles used to complain, that they left nothing to be imagined by the spectator."

20. Fielding, The Wesleyan Edition of the Works of Henry Fielding, *The History of Tom Jones A Foundling*, ed. Martin C. Battestin and Fredson Bowers (Middletown, CT: Wesleyan University Press, 1975), p. 157, book 4, chapter 2.

21. The Florida Edition of the Works of Laurence Sterne, *The Life and Opinions of Tristram Shandy, Gentleman*, ed. Melvyn New and Joan New (Gainesville: University Press of Florida, 1997), 2:565–66, book 6, chapters 37–38.

22. Austen, *Northanger Abbey*, in *The Novels of Jane Austen*, ed. R. W. Chapman (Oxford: Clarendon Press, 1923), 5:251.

23. Reynolds, *Discourses on Art*, ed. Robert R. Wark (San Marino, CA: Huntington Library Press, 1959), p. 259. For relevant remarks in Discourse 11, see pp. 192–99 and passim. For further discussion of Reynolds on the general and particular, see Harvey D. Goldstein, "*Ut Poesis Pictura*: Reynolds on Imitation and Imagination," *Eighteenth-Century Studies* 1 (1968): 213–35. See also Reynolds's "Notes on the Art of Painting" of Du Fresnoy (1783), "Note L. Verse 703," in *The Works of Sir Joshua Reynolds*, ed. Edmund (or Edmond) Malone (London, 1797), 2:260, for another statement regarding the dual talents of the painter and poet: "they must both possess a comprehensive mind that takes in the whole at one view, and at the same time an accuracy of eye or mind that distinguishes between two things that, to an ordinary spectator, appear the same, whether this consists in tints or words, or the nice discrimination on which expression and elegance depend."

24. YE 9, *A Journey to the Western Islands of Scotland*, ed. Mary Lascelles (1971), pp. 146–47. Note the remark's context: "he who . . . is not accustomed to require rigorous accuracy from himself [in recording what he sees while traveling], will scarcely believe how much a few hours take from certainty of knowledge, and distinctness of imagery; how the succession of objects will be broken, how separate parts will be confused, and how many particular features and discriminations will be compressed into one gross and general idea." Normative generality, like the normative particularity mentioned in n. 18 above, may be related to the rhetorical figure synechdoche, in which "the part is taken for the whole or the whole for [the] part" (*Dictionary*).

9

Johnson and Genre

Few studies of Samuel Johnson have been as powerful as W. R. Keast's "The Theoretical Foundations of Johnson's Criticism." That seminal article of 1952 has been called "crucial," "important and deservedly influential," undiminished in power, and one of the "shaping and identifying marks" of Johnson scholarship.[1] Keast's Johnson is a critic of commodious literary principles based upon nature not art. He knows that art should evoke pleasure for real readers who live in the real world and who share general human traits based on general human nature. Consequently, this empiricist Johnson eschews the rationalist demands of genre critics with narrower principles. His theoretical foundation, we hear, "regularly leads him to forsake the view of art as manifesting itself in distinct species . . . for the ampler domain of nature, in which . . . distinctions and definitions hitherto thought inviolable and 'natural' can be shown to be rigidities, arbitrary constrictions, or, at best, ideal manifestoes."[2] Keast's view of Johnson on genre has spawned a critical monolith. A recent commentator observed, "there is no evidence that [Johnson] took the least interest in different systems of generic classification as a theoretical issue."[3]

Keast thus often and properly begins much discussion of Johnson's criticism. He often and improperly also concludes much discussion. Perhaps we can see ways in which over a half-century's further study of Johnson might modify and even enrich this distinguished and persuasive ancestral effort, especially so in relation to Johnson on genres and the "rules" regarding them. For example, Johnson's criticism in general and in the Preface to Shakespeare (1765) in particular, not only are less hostile to genre than often is believed; they are in fact often friendly or at the least respectful to genre as a useful if sometimes secondary tool for literary judgment and analysis.

I add at once, however, that Johnson's sense of genre was more elastic than that of the French formalists or their English followers who built firewalls between the literary kinds. For these critics confounding of genres violates nature and verisimilitude and mimics the joining of incompatibles that begins Horace's *Ars poetica*. René Rapin thus regards blending of the serious and the comic as an unfortunate violation of decorum. André Dacier knows that Horace's satire is properly comic and familiar, whereas Persius and Juvenal who include the tragic and heroic are "fort méchant," and inferior to generically correct Horace. René le Bossu urges that the epic must exclude tragedy, comedy, or "any Piece of *Morality* writ in Verse."[4] Joseph Trapp's *Praelectiones poeticae* (1711–19) also stress that each form has a specific pleasure appropriate for it.

These critics largely limited themselves to the received modes and their "just degrees" of difference. In the *Praelectiones* Trapp "thought it proper to begin with the lowest [epigram], and so gradually proceed to others of a higher kind, till at last I come to the Epic or Heroic Poem." This approach denotes genres with enduring traits drawn from art. Such genre critics of course refer to "nature," but they are generally art based, as in le Bossu's definition that the "epic poem is a discourse invented by art to form the manners."[5]

In contrast, Johnson normally but not uniformly thinks of genres as in flux and as capable of absorbing traits of their cousin-forms. Genres live, change, die, or are created and enhance literary achievement. Skillful blending of genres thus is natural, not indecorous and capricious. Unlike le Bossu's epic poet who needs to be formed by art, Johnson's epic poet needs "an imagination capable of painting nature and realizing fiction." As that phrase denotes, Johnson's criticism necessarily includes both imitation of art and of nature. He even may use each approach in a shared discourse. The *Rambler*, No. 36 (1750), considers the pastoral as based on nature. It is "generally pleasing, because it entertains the mind with representations of scenes familiar to almost every imagination." The next *Rambler*, No. 37, then observes that these scenes are recorded in art, and are "easily found in the pastorals of Virgil, from whose opinion it will not appear very safe to depart."[6]

Johnson's broad-based theory indeed generally avoids both the judicial language of "just degrees" and of rigid definitions as inconsistent with human and British bloody-mindedness. He dismisses Swift's notion that an academy can fix the English language. That is "contrary to all experience" and would establish dictates "of which every man would have been willing, and many would have been proud to disobey."[7] As *Rambler*, No. 37, makes plain, though, Johnson recognized, used, and admired the practices of art that well codified an accurate vision of nature in its pastoral form.

Keast's admirable pioneering effort, then, simplifies Johnson's complex critical theory and practice regarding genre. It overstates the power of nature in Johnson's criticism and thus ignores one underlying basis for his concept of genre. Accordingly, I hope to show: 1) Johnson's reservations regarding nature and the consequent need for an author to improve upon it—that is, the moral basis for some genre theory; 2) a few of the practical literary uses of genre in his criticism; and 3) an extended example of how he uses and limits genre criticism both to characterize and patriotically to affirm British poetic art. In the process, I will suggest ways in which Johnson's conception of the human mind, the author's role in the world, and the place of the "rules" relate to his genre theory.[8]

1

Johnson combined generosity and reality of vision regarding human nature and the natural. He probably would have rejected the violence but approved the spirit of this remark by Henry Secheverell:

> Nature, by it self, is a meere State of Anarchy and Confusion, of Ruine, Rapine and War; and tho' it be Regulated, Restrain'd, and Tyed up by *Political Laws*, yet These Reach not to the *Intellectual* Part, the most Dangerous, Active, Busy, and Destructive part of Man. These take Cognizance only of *Evil in Act*, when it is Brought forth and Produc'd: it must be Religion alone that can Stifle it in the Birth, and Destroy the Seeds and Original Causes of Impiety and Injustice.[9]

For Johnson, as well, the "*Intellectual* Part . . . of Man" is a place of perpetual ferment. He observes in the "Essay on the . . . Importance of Small Tracts and Fugitive Pieces" (1743): "the mind once let loose to inquiry, and suffered to operate without restraint, necessarily deviates into peculiar opinions, and wanders in new tracks, where she is, indeed, sometimes lost in a labyrinth, from which . . . she cannot return, and scarce knows how to proceed." As Johnson says in the *Rambler*, No. 125 (1751), this restlessness is encouraged by imagination, "a licentious and vagrant faculty, unsusceptible of limitations, and impatient of restraint." It "has always endeavored to baffle the logician, to perplex the confines of distinction, and burst the enclosures of regularity."[10]

Wild energy requires containment. Johnson's *Rambler*, No. 8 (1750), urges us to "consider how we may govern our thoughts, restrain them from irregular motions, or confine them from boundless dissipation." He calls that government "the moral discipline of the mind" that extends to social, literary, and lexical worlds (YE 3:42). He asks a courted young woman playing on a harpsichord to restrain her natural passion: let "Thy Musick teach the nobler Art, / To tune the regulated Heart." In the *Rambler*, No. 92 (1751), Johnson's metaphor from conquest and colonizing suggests how readers and writers seek to bind the boundless: "Criticism reduces those regions of literature under the dominion of science, which have hitherto known only the anarchy of ignorance, the caprices of fancy, and the tyranny of prescription" (YE 4:122). Religion is the best aid for those who wish to "subdue passion, and regulate desire, . . . a task for which natural reason . . . has been found insufficient."[11] Johnson's map of the paths between anarchy and tyranny requires a formal construct like criticism, science, government, or religion, to "reduce" and limit nature.

The human bias toward the ungovernable also includes verbal "dissipations" and also requires sturdy pacification. Hence in the *Plan* (1747) of the *Dictionary* (1755) Johnson likens his lexical effort to Caesar's attempted conquest of the barbaric new world England. He knows that he cannot succeed, but hopes at least to "civilize part of the inhabitants" so that someone else may "reduce them wholly to subjection, and settle them under laws." He himself will have "retired without a triumph." The later Preface again characterizes his more mature and partially successful confrontation with the English language. The word "without" there characterizes a world of tangled disorder in need of roads, rules, and settlements:

> When I took the first survey of my undertaking, I found our speech copious without order, and energetick without rules: where ever I turned my view, there was perplexity to be disentangled, and confusion to be regulated; choice was to be made out of boundless variety, without any established principle of selection; adulterations were to be detected, without a settled test of purity; and modes of expression to be rejected, or received, without the suffrages of any writers of classical reputation or acknowledged authority.[12]

Literary texts long had been thought comparably endangered by unreduced energy. René Rapin's 1674 *Reflections* on Aristotle observed that a poet should not merely imitate "*Nature* which in certain Places is *rude* and *unpleasant*; he must choose in *her* what is *beautiful*, from what is *not*" (p. 54). Nature needs the constraint and shape that is civilization's response to disorder within the human mind and external culture. This view remained influential. Abbé Charles Batteux's *Les Beaux-Arts réduit à un même principe* (1746) was well known in Britain and appears in his omnibus *Principes de littérature* (1753). The artist selects only "the most striking and beautiful parts of nature." He selects from these to "form one exquisite whole which should be more perfect than mere nature" which is "always in some measure imperfect."[13]

Johnson is in this tradition but characteristically raises it to a higher ethical level. He laments that the senses "naturally gain" upon us and wrongly but understandably compete with conscience and religion (YE 3:39). Since raw nature is not an adequate norm, the author and audience should join to give it moral shape. The unregulated human mind "naturally" produces disorderly or often immoral acts that art should not reproduce. Johnson's Drury Lane "Prologue" (1747), for example, excoriates Restoration comedy's sexual naturalism as a destructive object of imitation. Dramatists studied themselves and their audience's intrigue and obscenity. Hence "Vice always found a sympathetick friend; / They pleas'd their age, and did not aim to mend" (YE 6:88; lines 20–21). Because "The drama's laws the drama's patrons give," the audience has the power "this night to bid the reign commence / Of rescu'd Nature and reviving sense" (6:89–90; lines 53, 57–58). Rescuing nature in art means moralizing, mending, and purging natural vice in art and in life.

Mending of nature also was an issue for the new genre of the novel. The *Rambler*, No. 4 (1750), analyzes modes of prose fiction and makes plain how imitation of nature can lead to bad art. The heroic romance of the previous generation drew upon knights, fairy tales, and mythic events largely drawn from other books. The "kind of writing" that pleases the present generation is the comic romance whose recognizable modern life infuses the form we call the novel (YE 3:19). By blending vice and virtue, by making a wicked character pleasing, the "kind" abdicates responsibility to its young audience. The morally superior novel should prepare that audience for life with "mock encounters" that teach how threatened virtue suffers but triumphs. The world should not "be promiscuously described" but made useful enough to "be seen hereafter with less hazard" (3:22). Hence, "in narratives where historical veracity has no place, I cannot discover why there should not be exhibited the most perfect idea of virtue: of virtue not angelical nor above probability, . . . but the highest that humanity can reach" (3:24).

Johnson as literary theorist in this *Rambler* characterizes four species of the genre "fiction" and gauges the nature or value of each. He makes plain that imitation of art, as in the romance, is as inadequate as the imitation of nature in the modern novel. The author not bound by historical fact should be bound by moral fact and obligation: it is "not a sufficient vindication of a character, that it is drawn as it appears, for many characters ought never to be drawn; nor of a narrative, that the train of events is agreeable to observation and experience" (3:22). Such nature is not adequately moral, as the new narrative kind should be when properly shaped for its impressionable audience.

Johnson extends the concept of nature moralized to other kinds of practical criticism. He adversely judges even major authors who either allow vice to find sympathetic friends, or fail to allow virtue to prosper. Shakespeare's "first defect" is his lack of "moral purpose": "he makes no just distribution of good or evil," for which he cannot claim contemporary manners as an excuse. "It is always the writer's duty to make the world better, and justice is a virtue independent on time or place" (YE 7:71).

Part of that duty includes limits on how tragic a tragedy can be. Johnson agrees that *Hamlet* wrongly lacks poetic justice and laments "the untimely death of Ophelia, the young, the beautiful, the harmless, and the pious" (YE 8:1011). *King Lear* is comparably offensive because Shakespeare "suffered the virtue of Cordelia to perish in a just cause, contrary to the natural idea of justice, to the hope of the reader, and, what is yet more strange, to the faith of chronicles" (8:704). Similarly, Swift's *Tale of a Tub* (1704) was a "wild work" and of "dangerous example" in its mockery of religion (*Lives*, 3:10). Pope's "Elegy to the Memory of an Unfortunate Lady" (1717) has "the illaudable singularity of treating suicide with respect" (*Lives*, 3:226). In *Paradise Lost*, on the other hand, "every line breathes sanctity of thought and purity of manners" and even the rebel angels "are compelled to acknowledge their subjection to God in such a manner as excites reverence and confirms piety" (*Lives*, 1:179–80).

Art, whether as a system of justice, a chronicle source, or religion, should trump nature, in which the good indeed perish unfairly. Johnson asks the artist not only to imitate nature by means of art, but to infuse nature with the values of supernature. This basis for reconsideration allows us to look at Johnson's more neutral practice as a critic and at his comments on the genres and theory of genre that he recognized and respected as "rules" of high if not the highest literary value.

2

Johnson the scholar, lexicographer, and editor accepted argument by groups as a necessary aspect of intellectual life. He says that the books in the Harleian catalogue "shall be distributed into their distinct classes, and every class ranged with some regard to the age of the writers." His Preface to *The Preceptor* recommends instructional texts for students: "the Art of Poetry will be best learned from *Bossu* and *Bouhours* in *French*, together with *Dryden*'s Essays and Prefaces, the critical Papers of *Addison*, *Spence* on *Pope*'s *Odyssey*, and *Trapp*'s *Praelectiones Poeticae*"—texts that either are prescriptive or descriptive of what is right and fitting in recognizable literary kinds. Le Bossu knows that Aristotle, Horace, Homer, and Virgil have become "a Just and Supreme Authority . . . to prescribe Laws and Rules to any Art." Rapin's *Reflections* argue that poetics is "nothing else, but *Nature* put in method, and *Good Sense* reduc'd to Principles." There is "no arriving at Perfection but by these Rules." Johnson called Dryden "the father of English criticism [and] . . . the writer who first taught us to determine upon principles the merit of composition" (*Lives*, 1:410). According to that paternal voice, heroic drama uses rhyme because it imitates "nature wrought up to a higher pitch" than in comedy. Moreover, the arts of rhetoric and of poetics also stem from imitation of nature: the tropes and figures they advance were observed to "have such and such effects upon the audience" that they regularly delighted.[14]

Johnson of course wrote in several different genres, adapted their appropriate devices, and assumed that they would affect audiences in specific ways. For example, he probably reread or certainly recalled Dryden's "Discourse" before Juvenal (1693) while preparing to write *The Vanity of Human Wishes* (1749) and the *Dictionary*. He quotes from the paragraph in which Dryden defines the genre of formal verse satire as an attack upon one vice and praise of its opposite virtue. This concept surely helped to formulate his approach in his own satire in progress. He seems as well to adapt that generic conception when in Sermon 6 he says that "every argument against any vice is equally an argument in favour of the contrary virtue; and whoever proves the folly of being proud, shews, at the same time, 'that with the lowly there is wisdom'."[15]

Johnson also analyzed several literary kinds consistent with generic distinctions: the new genre of the novel, the older genres of pastoral and epic, biography, tragicomedy, and the epistle among other forms. He says that Lord Hailes's *Annals of Scotland* is "in our language, I think, a new mode of history." In one paragraph of remarks in 1780 he encapsulates the genres of farce, epic, classical tragedy, and romance.[16] Various lives of the poets acknowledge various efforts in various genres—some of which no longer are useful: Cowley's evocation of the "Theban Strain" is "not worthy of revival," and Milton's pagan-Christian funeral pastoral is outmoded and puerile ("Cowley," *Lives,* 1:47; "Milton," *Lives,* 1:163–65).

Though Johnson indeed would always worry "arbitrary constrictions," he knew that not all constrictions were arbitrary, that some were necessary, and that distinct species both properly existed and were newly created. "Shakespeare's plays," he writes, "are not in the rigorous and critical sense either tragedies or comedies, but compositions of a distinct kind"—as based on the mingling of good and evil in life (YE 7:66). His capsule analyses of those plays often acknowledge their genre, variations within genres, and the plays' sense of literary order, including adherence to the three unities. The *Tempest* is laudably regular (YE 7:135). Though *Measure for Measure* is "indefinite" in its use of time, Johnson is pleased that "the unities of action and place are sufficiently preserved" (YE 7:216). He is troubled that the events in *Antony and Cleopatra* "are produced without any art of connection or care of disposition" (YE 8:731). If *Othello* had "opened in Cyprus, and the preceding incidents been occasionally related, there had been little wanting to a drama of the most exact and scrupulous regularity" (YE 8:1048). Within the genre of tragedy, he characterizes *Timon of Athens* by its domestic setting (YE 8:745) and *Hamlet* by its variety (YE 8:1011). Johnson recognizes that in history plays the author merely exhibits "a succession of events by action and dialogue" fit for the multitude (YE 8:658), and he thus regards the *Henry VI* cycle "merely as narratives in verse" (YE 8:611).

The *Lives of the Poets* also often note the ways in which authors organize life into literary kinds. Cowley "was the first who imparted to English numbers the enthusiasm of the greater ode, and the gaiety of the less" (*Lives,* 1:64). Prior's works "may be distinctly considered as comprising Tales, Love-verses, Occasional Poems, *Alma,* and *Solomon*" (*Lives,* 2:201). Shenstone's "poems consist of elegies, odes, and ballads, humorous sallies, and moral pieces" (*Lives,* 3:355). The "Life of Milton" defines the epic, characterizes its elements, distinguishes the Christian from the classical form, and observes that part of its greatness and weakness is its refusal to imitate quotidian nature (*Lives,* 1:177, 181). Johnson concludes "Milton" with a statement on genre, chronology, and quality: *Paradise Lost* "is not the greatest of heroick poems, only because it is not the first" (*Lives,* 1:194).

The discussion of *Paradise Lost* also includes a splendid passage that adapts Aristotle, le Bossu, and neoclassical standards and language of the epic: the moral, fable, characters, probable, marvelous, machinery, episodes, integrity of design, and sentiments (*Lives,* 1:171–79). He probably adds that passage for at least two prime reasons: whether one judges Milton on British or on Continental genre standards, on nominally modern or on ancient criteria, it succeeds as a transcendent epic poem. Evocation of Aristotle and le Bossu thus serves as national poetic affirmation. It also allows Johnson a way to evaluate those Greek and French criteria.

Johnson paraphrases le Bossu as saying that the epic poet's "first work is to find a *moral*, which his fable is afterwards to illustrate and establish" but "this seems to have been the process only of Milton" (*Lives*, 1:171).[17] Similarly, in the epic as in drama "Aristotle requires" the unified design of poetic integrity, and Milton exceeds Homer in this respect. The biographical incursions at the beginnings of books 3, 7, and 9 indeed can be spared: "But superfluities so beautiful who would take away? . . . since the end of poetry is pleasure, that cannot be unpoetical with which all are pleased" (*Lives*, 1:195). Johnson regards the story of the fall as religious historical narrative that requires veracity. He thus criticizes Dryden for imposing merely artificial literary standards upon *Paradise Lost*. He "petulantly and indecently, denies the heroism of Adam because he was overcome; but there is no reason why the hero should not be unfortunate except established practice, since success and virtue do not go necessarily together." If success is necessary, in the long run Adam nevertheless succeeds (*Lives*, 1:176). Johnson's criticism of the epic genre emphasizes Milton's ability to meet alien but limited standards. These stress either the art or criticism prior to art, instead of poetic pleasure produced sometimes by adhering to and sometimes by violating received critical wisdom. The passage indeed also suggests how Johnson uses his genre criticism to characterize and affirm British poetic arts.

3

I said earlier that civilizing barbarians, regulating the licentious, and moralizing nature were aspects of Johnson's genre theory. I said as well, that the presumed march of civilization included certain dangers, one made clear in Johnson's objection to "the tyranny of prescription," as with Dryden on *Paradise Lost*. Johnson is among those critics who respond to a competing foreign force that confuses civilization with artificial constraints or carries those restraints too far. That force of course is France.

As Laurence Sterne observed in a different context, they order these things better in France. As Sterne also made clear, some French ordering was done with a musket by a sentinel who forced a large German to allow a dwarf to stand in front of him at the theater. "This is noble! said I, clapping my hands together—And yet you would not permit this, said the old [helpful French] officer, in England.—In England, dear Sir, said I, *we sit all at our ease.*" The clash between French order and English ease, praise of noble force and fear of ignoble prescription, was a familiar Franco-English event. Pope's *Essay on Criticism* (1711) well expresses this view in remarks long thought to characterize the two peoples.[18] After the Renaissance,

> *Critic Learning* flourish'd most in *France.*
> The *Rules*, a Nation born to serve, obeys,
> And *Boileau* still in Right of *Horace* sways.
> But *we*, brave *Britons, Foreign Laws* despis'd,
> And kept *unconquer'd*, and *unciviliz'd*,
> Fierce for the *Liberties of Wit*, and bold,
> We still defy'd the *Romans*, as *of old.*

The poem then praises Sheffield, Roscommon, and Walsh as among "the *sounder Few*" who asserted "the *juster Ancient Cause*, / And here *restor'd* Wit's *Fundamental Laws*" as practiced in Britain.[19] Pope respects and denigrates the French political and critical temperament; he also respects and partially denigrates the British political and critical temperament while making clear that its freedom opens the possibility of reform based upon superior naturalized literary "*Laws.*"

Johnson admired the *Essay on Criticism* for its "knowledge both of ancient and modern learning as are not often attained by the maturest age and longest experience." Part of that admiration perhaps includes Pope's epitome of British national history and identity. In the "Account of the Harleian Library" (1743), for example, Johnson adapts the commonplace that the British constitution stemmed from the forests of Germany. He praises the holdings from "the Germanick empire," for these "are the works of those heroes by whom the Roman empire was destroyed; and which may plead, at least in this nation, that they ought not to be neglected by those that owe to the men whose memories they preserve, their constitution, their properties, and their liberties."[20]

Those liberties included the artistic freedom or license uncongenial to French or any criticism that seemed to impose artificial standards. This presumed lack of civilization caused little problem so long as British literature was terra incognita to readers *d'outre manche* and most of the balance of literary trade was on the French side. It became a matter of national injury when Letter 18 of Voltaire's *Letters concerning the English Nation* (London, 1733) included a public insult to the English language and its national dramatist. Voltaire insisted that tasteless Shakespeare ruined the English stage with his incoherent plots, barbaric characters, and linguistic excess. Shakespeare violates decorum and the unities, and turns his plays into "monstrous Farces to which the Name of Tragedy is given." Addison's *Cato* is the first regular, elegant, harmonious English tragedy and a "Master-piece" (p. 167).

The gravity of insult is clear when we read the *Dictionary*'s definition of "farce." It is "A dramatick representation written without regularity, and stuffed with wild and ludicrous conceits." "*Dryden's Dufresnoy*" gives Johnson the first and longest illustrative quotation. Farce is

> yet a lower sort of poetry . . . which is out of nature; for a *farce* is that in poetry which grotesque is in a picture; the persons and the actors of a *farce* are all unnatural, and the manners false; that is, inconsistent with the character of mankind; grotesque painting is the just resemblance of this.

Voltaire would replace Shakespeare with Addison, *Hamlet* with *Cato*, and if he could, the British with the French national temper, which mocks such unnatural, false, inconsistent, and grotesque drama. Here was a deeply resented Gallic reprise of the Roman imperium that both heroic ancestral Celtic Britain and Anglo-Saxon Germany defeated. Johnson regarded such civilizing invasions as no longer necessary; the age of British barbarism long was over, and he could not permit Voltaire and other French men of letters to confuse critic learning with British imitation of nature in general and by Shakespeare in particular. He would take up that challenge in the Preface to his edition of Shakespeare and its examen of the three unities. Voltaire then takes such a whipping that relevant attacks upon him were partially censored in France, but nonetheless so offended the unrepentant Voltaire that he called Johnson a drunken practical joker.[21]

Discussion of Shakespeare's apparent abuse of the unities exemplifies four of Johnson's purposes in the Preface: Shakespeare's role as the poet of nature; the inadequacy of French and Francophile criticism that is based upon art and authority; the human mind's response to drama; and Johnson's own role as a critic able to see Shakespeare's strengths and weaknesses while he also defends the English stage from French values. Johnson does not claim to be impartial; he does claim to make balanced judgments.

The passage begins after Johnson ends his section on Shakespeare's faults. Johnson affirms his critical bona fides by recognizing Shake-speare's insufficient morality, careless plotting, anachronisms, verbal grossness, and destructive petty punning. "It will be thought strange," however, that he has not included Shakespeare's "neglect of the unities, his violation of those laws which have been instituted and established by the joint authority of poets and critics" (YE 7:75). This introduction already colors the argument and establishes one basis for Johnson's re-jection of rules criticism and genre criticism that labels Shakespeare's tragedies as farce: such criticism comes from law, institution, and au-thority but not from nature.

There is, though, one objection to Johnson's reservations regarding authority—Shakespeare's "plan has commonly what Aristotle requires, a beginning, a middle, and an end." The unity of action is based on na-ture at least as much as upon authority, but as in Pope's *Essay on Criti-cism*, the authority is from the juster ancient not the French modern cause.[22] Like Shakespeare, Aristotle understands the human need for clo-sure. Shakespeare's drama itself, then, "makes gradual advances, and the end of the play is the end of expectation" (YE 7:75). Aristotle clearly has the virtue of not being French.

The case is altered with the unnatural unities of time and place that have been venerated only "from the time of Corneille," from 1660, and not coincidentally from the time at which Francophile Charles II was restored to the English throne. Johnson thus provides "a nearer view of the principles on which" those unities are based and immediately makes plain that they violate one of the chief ends of art: "they have given more trouble to the poet than pleasure to the auditor" (YE 7:75–76). They also are based upon a radical misreading of that auditor's response. Johnson proceeds to examine not what authority says *should* happen, but what actually happens in "the mind of man," where all action be-gins.

For the rules critics, the drama can only be made credible by constrict-ing the apparent passage through time which also constricts the appar-ent passage through space. A theatrical action cannot significantly transcend the approximate amount of time it takes for the real action that also cannot take place in, say, Alexandria and then Rome. The audi-tor "knows with certainty that he has not changed his place; and he knows that place cannot change itself" (YE 7:76). The mind will not accept such dramatic abuse of the obvious limits on time and space.

Johnson alters the terms of the debate. He rejects the authority of crit-ics who reject the authority of nature and of actual human response. Since Shakespeare is the poet of nature, Johnson answers such critics "by the authority of Shakespeare." The notion that a credible drama is based upon the stage's actual "materiality"—is false (YE 7:76). The reader or auditor always is in command of his senses, knows that he is watching a play, knows the difference between appearance and reality, and knows that he is in a theater in London. Hence "Delusion, if delusion be admitted, has no certain limitation" (YE 7:77). If the auditor thinks that he is in Alexandria, he is mad and need not worry about chronological or physical limits. Actually, however, he always knows where he is, recognizes his own complicity in theatrical illusion, and regards time and space as malleable and manageable: "Time is, of all modes of existence, most obsequious to the imagination." We do not fret about the passage of time as we see a play any more than when we read a play. In each case we easily accommodate deviations from compact "space or duration." We associate with the actors, fear for our possible harm, and allow the imitated action to bring a frightening reality to mind—"as a mother weeps over her babe when she remembers that death may take it from her" (YE 7:78–79). Tragedy pleases in part because we are both frightened, safe, and certainly not in the world of monsters and untragic farce "stuffed with wild and ludicrous conceits."

Shakespeare knew that only Aristotle's unity of action was essential, and whether through instinct or education dismissed the unities of time and place as irrelevant and based on "false assumptions." Yet more, he knew that such limitations hindered the drama's ability to evoke pleasure by limiting its variety. Shakespeare, like Johnson, rejects "rules merely positive." For Johnson such stuff is "suitable to the minute and slender criticism of Voltaire" (YE 7:79–80).

The reintroduction of a French critic brings this section to its own closure and unity of action. Johnson earlier had invoked the French Corneille and his "time" of 1660. Now he invokes French Voltaire and his more immediate "time" of contemporary writing and attacks upon Shakespeare and upon English drama. Johnson thus shifts the ground of his earlier discussion. He transforms himself from the balanced English critic who sees and demonstrates Shakespeare's faults, to the English defender of Shakespeare who sees and demonstrates Shakespeare's and his nation's dramatic strengths as imitators of nature. That can be uneven, rough, inadequately designed and perhaps need moralizing by an educated dramatist; but it is better than the artificial intrigues of French drama, the false assumptions of art, and dramatic laws that are nuisances to author and auditor alike. Here, Johnson says as an empiricist, a moralist, and an English critic-psychologist, is the way to "recall the principles of the drama to a new examination" (YE 7:80)—namely, through English nature. As for Voltaire, "Let him be answered" by Shakespeare. He is like a vast forest that has "weeds and brambles" but fills "the eye with awful pomp" and gratifies "the mind with endless diversity" (YE 7:84). That forest is a poor venue for the French fleur de lys and formal garden, or for Addison's Gallic Roman; but it is a good venue for thorny English roses and branching oaks.

This locus classicus of antigenre theory seems to support Keast's argument that Johnson rejected the concept of art as divided into distinct species. Johnson, though, certainly knew the difference between farce and tragedy and knew that his endorsement of violated unities was not unassailable. He thus adds a key paragraph of reservation. Though the question cannot be settled by mere authority, Johnson recognizes "how much wit and learning may be produced against me; before such authorities I am afraid to stand." Moreover, "it is to be suspected that these precepts have not been so easily received but for better reasons than I have yet been able to find." He himself is not persuaded, but in the face of such broad arguments against him, "I am ready to sink down in reverential silence; as Aeneas withdrew from the defense of Troy when he saw Neptune shaking the wall and Juno heading the besiegers" (YE 7:80–81). Johnson and British drama are under siege by powerful forces of classical and neoclassical culture that question the very basis of Shakespeare's tragic mode.[23]

Johnson's remark has been called humorous, but it is consistent with his dislike of singularity, respect for the opinion of mankind and for what in the Preface he already had called "due reverence to that learning which I must oppose" (YE 7:75).[24] He was well aware that the public could be misled, and that "A few, a very few, commonly constitute the taste of the time."[25] Nonetheless, he accepted the public's judgment as necessary and generally correct. The *Rambler*, No. 23 (1750), for example, anticipates the Preface to Shakespeare. Johnson argues on the appeal from criticism to the higher judge of "the publick, which is never corrupted, nor often deceived" as it passes "the last sentence upon literary claims" (YE 3:128). If so much wit and learning are marshalled against him, the concepts have been carefully examined and require the respect that Johnson urges in the third paragraph of his Preface: "What mankind have long possessed they have often examined and compared; and if they persist to value the possession, it is because frequent comparisons have confirmed opinion in its favour" (YE 7:60). Johnson was aware that such frequent comparisons also were made by many of his own countrymen and by even more across the channel in France, whose public demanded and was pleased by regular drama. René Rapin thus will "tell what we ought to judge of all those who have writ in verse for more than these two thousand years." He knows that by following Aristotle he follows the best model for the best regular poetry and is glad to "rely on the Publick, for the opinion we ought to have of their merit."[26]

We recall that Johnson's deference before "rules" and the genres they include also is consistent with his practical criticism, as in the *Rambler*, No. 139 (1751). He there analyzes Milton's *Samson Agonistes* "according to the indispensable laws of Aristotelian criticism" and finds that it lacks a necessary middle (YE 4:372, 376). In the *Rambler*, No. 156 (1751), he praises Shakespeare's ability to transcend rules and use the "natural" quality of tragicomedy; but he adds that it is not "safe to judge of works of genius merely by the event. . . . Perhaps the effects even of Shakespeare's poetry might have been yet greater, had he not counter-acted himself; and we might have been more interested in the distresses of his heroes had we not been so frequently diverted by the jokes of his buffoons" (YE 5:69). We also recall his largely positive use of the unities as a critical tool in the brief discussions of Shakespeare's plays. Johnson not only alluded to Juno shaking the walls of Troy as a sign of the unities' and of genre's power; he recognized and used that power.

Johnson obviously believes his standards for examining the drama, but he typically accepts reasonable variation within human activity and critical belief among colleagues. One of those colleagues was Joseph Warton, whose *Adventurer*, No. 127 (1753), supports Addison's view that the moderns are inferior to the ancients in poetry. For Warton, only Shakespeare, Corneille, and Racine can compete with Aeschylus, Sophocles, and Euripides. "The first is an author so uncommon and excentric, that we can scarcely try him by dramatic rules." Though he equals the Greeks in "strokes of nature and character . . . in all other circumstances that constitute the excellence of the drama, he is vastly inferior." The unities are among those excellences because they help to focus the plot and the audience's relevant emotion. The Greeks used a simple fable and made every act, scene, speech, and sentiment "concur to accelerate the intended event." In contrast, "the mazes and intricacies of modern plots" necessarily defeat "the ends of the drama" and dissipate attention.[27] This was not the only time that Johnson disagreed with Warton, but he could not be dismissed as a petty caviller with a petty mind.

Indeed, fluidity of thought and willingness to engage in the "but clause" of exception to received wisdom characterize Johnson's dialectical mode of proceeding and its acceptance of contradiction. Imlac thus tells Prince Rasselas, "Inconsistencies . . . cannot both be right, but, imputed to man, they may both be true."[28] As one example of dual truths, the *Dictionary*'s definition 4 of "Unity" is "Principles of dramatick writing, by which the tenour of the story, and propriety of representation is preserved." Johnson there includes a normative illustration from Dryden saying that *All for Love* exactly observes the unities. Immediately thereafter he provides a condensed version of lines from Addison's *Spectator*, No. 409 (1712): the unities should be "thoroughly understood, but there is still something more essential, that elevates and astonishes the fancy."[29] Whatever Johnson's own beliefs, he presents both sides because both sides have eminent authorities for a legitimate alternative regarding what men have thought. In such a case, the "rules" are necessary to be known but are only part of the appropriate response of the critic and the reader.

Johnson clearly uses "rules" and the generic categories implicit in them to categorize those who use generic categories. On January 11, 1779, he told Fanny Burney: "There are 3 distinct kind of Judges upon all new Authors or productions;—the first, are those who know no rules, but pronounce entirely from their natural Taste & feelings; The 2d are those who *know, & judge* by *rules*; and the 3d are those who *know*, but are *above* the rules. These last are those you should wish to satisfy: *next* to them, rate the *natural* judges,—but ever despise those opinions that are formed by the *rules*."[30] Johnson here supports his illustrative quotation from Addison: it is necessary to know but to transcend rules like those regarding the unities and distinctions among genres; nature and the unguided response are not enough. Works that best imitate "reduced" or "*rude*" nature and the morality of supernature are superior to works that only imitate nature. The unregulated human mind is one in which vice finds a sympathetic friend, and nature alone "is a . . . State of Anarchy and Confusion." When regulation proceeds subtly and without shackles, it can acknowledge rules and genre limits and produce a work like *Othello*. Its beauties "impress themselves so strongly upon the attention of the reader, that they can draw no aid from critical illustration" (YE 8:1047). Those beauties impress in part because we recognize them as appropriate for a tragedy rather than a comedy. Shakespeare has "not counter-acted himself" or his genre.

Johnson accepted, recognized, and used genre as a descriptive and sometimes prescriptive term. It included "art as manifesting itself in distinct species" and insisted that "the ampler domain of nature" alone was not an adequate model for imitation. Johnson suggests the moral basis of genre in texts that rescue nature by adding civilized art, as in the best novels or plays. He suggests genre's use as a tool to help analyze form and audience response, as in discussion of several of Shakespeare's plays. He uses the language of genre theory to show that Milton's great native epic meets and transcends French formalist standards. However useful, such standards should not be imposed upon Shakespeare, who had the good sense to have written his tragedies on the proper side of the English Channel. The theoretical foundation of Johnson's criticism supports a complex and grand building whose entryways we should continue to explore.

NOTES

1. For these, see R. D. Stock, *Samuel Johnson and Neoclassical Dramatic Theory: The Intellectual Context of the Preface to Shakespeare* (Lincoln: University of Nebraska Press, 1973), p. 19 (crucial); Leopold Damrosch, Jr., *The Uses of Johnson's Criticism* (Charlottesville: University Press of Virginia, 1976), p. 7 (important); James L. Battersby, *Rational Praise and Natural Lamentation: Johnson, Lycidas, and Principles of Criticism* (Rutherford, NJ: Fairleigh Dickinson University Press, 1980), p. 15, and "nothing has appeared since its publication to diminish confidence in its explanatory power or cognitive adequacy" (p. 152); Greg Clingham, "Resisting Johnson," in *Johnson Re-Visioned: Looking Before and After*, ed. Philip Smallwood (Lewisburg, PA: Bucknell University Press, 2001), pp. 22–23 (shaping). The late Oliver Sigworth read a paper at an American Society for Eighteenth-Century Studies meeting in, I believe, 1977, titled "A Critique of Critiques: The Fate of Johnson's Criticism, 1952–1976," a mimeographed copy of which he circulated. Here is its first sentence: "If there is something wrong with the criticism of Johnson's criticism during the last quarter century it may be attributed to a dangerous prevalence of Hagstrum and Keast." I do not think their work dangerous, though its prevalence has limited benevolent advances upon it.

2. Keast, "The Theoretical foundations of Johnson's Criticism," in *Critics and Criticism Ancient and Modern*, ed. R. S. Crane (Chicago: University of Chicago Press, 1952), p. 395.

3. Charles H. Hinnant, *"Steel for the Mind": Samuel Johnson and Critical Discourse* (Newark: University of Delaware Press, 1994), p. 152. Hinnant's valuable study is influenced by Keast, especially in its chapter 7, "Redefining Genre," from which this remark comes. Jean H. Hagstrum's *Samuel Johnson's Literary Criticism* (Minneapolis: University of Minnesota Press, 1952) is another distinguished ancestral voice. He expertly shows that "Traces of the generic method appear everywhere in Johnson's criticism," but concludes that "Johnson's heart was not in them" (p. 133).

4. Rapin, *Reflections on Aristotle's Treatise of Poesy*, trans. Thomas Rymer (London, 1674), pp. 15–16 (blending); Dacier, *Oeuvres d'Horace en latin et en français avec des remarques critiques et historiques* (1681–89), 3rd ed. (Paris, 1709), 6:607–8 (méchant); le Bossu, *Monsieur Bossu's Treatise of the Epick Poem*, trans. [W. J.] (London, 1695), pp. 6–7 (morality); Trapp, *Praelectiones* (1711–19), as *Lectures on Poetry Read in the Schools of Natural Philosophy at Oxford* (London, 1742), pp. 9–10.

5. Trapp, *Praelectiones*, as *Lectures*, pp. 153 (thought), 328 (just); le Bossu, *Monsieur Bossu's Treatise*, p. 7, book 1, section 3.

6. Johnson, "Life of Milton," in *Lives of the English Poets*, ed. George Birkbeck Hill (Oxford: Clarendon Press, 1905), 1:171 (imagination); Johnson, The Yale Edition of the Works of Samuel Johnson, vol. 3, *The Rambler*, ed. W. J. Bate and Albrecht B. Strauss (New Haven: Yale University Press, 1969), pp. 195 (pleasing), 200 (easily found). Johnson often thought of art and nature as cooperative cousins. See the *Rambler*, No. 124 (1751): "Novelty is indeed necessary to preserve eagerness and alacrity; but art and nature have stores inexhaustible by human intellects": YE 4:299. Subsequent citations will be cited in the text or notes as *Lives*, and YE, with the volume number as above, plus title, editor, and date of publication where necessary.

7. Johnson, "Life of Swift," *Lives*, 3:16.

8. James Engell rightly notes: "The so-called rules, or any principles of criticsm, would mean little unless applied to specific kinds of literature. The rules rely on an initial naming of kinds." See Engell, *Forming the Critical Mind: Dryden to Coleridge* (Cambridge, MA: Harvard University Press, 1989), p. 152. There are several useful remarks regarding Johnson and genre in Engell's seventh chapter. Alastair Fowler's earlier book remains an excellent study of the concept: *Kinds of Literature: An Introduction to the Theory of Genres and Modes* (Cambridge, MA: Harvard University Press, 1982).

9. Secheverell, *The Political Union. A Discourse Shewing the Dependence of Government on Religion* (Oxford, 1702), p. 23. There is a Hobbesian quality to the remark, though Hobbes would regard the state and its sovereign as the properly stifling power.

10. Johnson, "Essay on . . . Small Tracts," in *The Works of Samuel Johnson, LL. D.* (Oxford, 1825), 5:191, cited hereafter only by volume number and page; Johnson, *The Rambler*, YE 4:200.

11. Johnson, "To Miss——On Her Playing upon the Harpsichord in a Room Hung with Some Flower-Pieces of Her own Painting" (1746), in YE 6, *Samuel Johnson: Poems*, ed. E. L. McAdam, Jr., with George Milne (1964), p. 78, lines 35–36. In contrast, Sir John Lade in the "Short Song of Congratulation" casts off governing discipline and ruins his ancient estate and himself. See YE 6:307–8. For the remark regarding religion, see Sermon 18 in YE 14, *Sermons*, ed. Jean Hagstrum and James Gray (1978), p. 193.

12. Johnson, *Plan*, 5:21, and Preface, 5:24.

13. Batteux, *A Course of the Belles Lettres: Or the Principles of Literature*, trans. [?] Miller (London, 1761) 1:7 (striking), 8 (more perfect), 9 (always).

14. Johnson, Harleian catalogue, in 5:180; Preface to the *Preceptor, Samuel Johnson's Prefaces and Dedications*, ed. Allen T. Hazen (New Haven: Yale University Press. 1937), p. 184; le Bossu, *Monsieur Bossu's Treatise*, p. 2; Dryden, "Of Dramatic Poesy" (1668) in *Of Dramatic Poesy and Other Critical Essays*, ed. George Watson (London: Dent and Dutton; New York: Everyman's Library, 1962), 1:87 (rhyme), and "The Author's Apology for Heroic Poetry" as Preface to *The State of Innocence* (1677), 1:200 (rhetoric). There are similar arguments regarding exalted nature in "Of Heroic Plays" prefixed to *The Conquest of Granada* (1672). I say in passing that Dryden's "Examen of the *Silent Woman*" in *Dramatic Poesy* serves the same purpose as Johnson's use of le Bossu's terminology in the "Life of Milton."

15. See Weinbrot *The Formal Strain: Studies in Augustan Imitation and Satire* (Chicago: University of Chicago Press, 1969), pp. 70–71, and *Sermons*, YE 14:72–73.

16. Johnson on Hailes, to Boswell August 27, 1775, *The Letters of Samuel Johnson*, ed. Bruce Redford (Princeton: Princeton University Press, 1992), 2:266; genre distinctions as recorded by Bennet Langton in *Boswell's Life of Johnson Together with Boswell's Journal of a Tour to the Hebrides*, ed. George Birkbeck Hill and rev. L. F. Powell (Oxford: Clarendon Press, 1934–50), 4:16–17.

17. "The first thing we are to begin with for Composing a *Fable*, is to chuse the Instruction, and the point of Morality, which is to serve as its Foundation, according to the Design and End we propose to our selves": *Monsieur Bossu's Treatise*, p. 15, book 1, chapter 7.

18. Sterne, *A Sentimental Journey through France and Italy by Mr. Yorick*, ed. Gardner D. Stout, Jr. (Berkeley and Los Angeles: University of California Press, 1967), pp. 65 (ordering), 179 (noble). For the enduring character of the nations, see Albert-Joseph-Ulpien Hennet, *La Poétique Anglaise* (Paris, 1806): "les poésies des deux peuples sont assez bien charactérisées par ces vers" (1:15).

19. Pope, The Twickenham Edition of the Poems of Alexander Pope, *Pastoral Poetry and An Essay on Criticism*, ed. E. Audra and Aubrey Williams (London: Methuen; New Haven: Yale University Press, 1961), p. 323 (critic, lines 712–18), and (sounder, lines 719–22).

20. Johnson on Pope, *Lives*, 3:94; Harleian 5:185.

21. For British triumph over a crude past, see my *Britannia's Issue: The Rise of British Literature from Dryden to Ossian* (Cambridge: Cambridge University Press, 1993), and Nicholas Hudson, *Samuel Johnson and the Making of Modern England* (Cambridge: Cambridge University Press, 2003). For Johnson's Preface in France and Voltaire's response, see Weinbrot, "Censoring Johnson in France: Johnson and Suard on Voltaire. A New Document," *Review of English Studies* n.s. 45 (1994): 220–23.

22. Aristotle also expresses the power not merely of Greece but of a perceptive philosopher. In the Preface to the *Preceptor* Johnson praises Roman, French, and British critics, but adds that national learning soon will be augmented by "a more accurate and Philosophical Account . . . from a Commentary upon *Aristotle*'s Art of Poetry." See Johnson's Preface to the *Preceptor*, ed. Hazen, p. 184.

23. Johnson knew and mocked the British myth of foundation from Geoffrey of Monmouth: the nation was settled by Brutus the grandson of Aeneas. He refers to this as "a ridiculous fiction" (*Lives*, 3:188–89). For brief discussion of Pope's aborted attempt to write an epic poem about Brutus, see Maynard Mack, *Alexander Pope: A Life* (New York: W.W. Norton; New Haven: Yale University Press, 1985), pp. 771–74, and for the myth *Britannia's Issue*, pp. 559–60.

24. See Donald Greene, *Samuel Johnson* (New York: Twayne Publishers, 1970), p. 188: this is "one of the best examples of Johnson's occasional talent for boisterous humor."

25. Johnson, *The Adventurer*, No. 138 (1754) in YE 2, *The Idler and the Adventurer*, ed. W. J. Bate, John M. Bullitt, and L. F. Powell (1963), p. 496.

26. Rapin, *Reflections*, sig. C4$^\mathrm{v}$, in italics.

27. Warton, in *The Adventurer* (London, 1753), 2:338. In this respect, Warton could not object to René Rapin's 1674 treatise on poetry. He knows that for art to induce verisimilitude, it must reduce nature to method: "unless there be the *unity* of *Place*, of *time*, and of the *Action* in the great Poems, there can be no *verisimility*" (p. 18). Nature proceeds by artistic regulation.

28. Johnson, YE 16, *Rasselas and Other Tales*, ed. Gwin J. Kolb (1990), p. 33.

29. Johnson in fact makes Dryden's remark more normative than did Dryden himself. See The California Edition of The Works of John Dryden vol. 13, *All for Love. . . .*, ed. Maximillian Novak (Berkeley and Los Angeles: Univeresity of California Press, 1984), p. 10: "the Unities of Time, Place and Action, [are] more exactly observed, than, perhaps, the *English* Theater requires." For Addison, see *The Spectator*, ed Donald F. Bond (Ox-

ford: Clarendon Press, 1965), 3:530. I have italicized the lines Johnson alters or omits exclusive of capitalization and punctuation, at least as based upon the Bond edition. The passage begins with Addison's hopes that authors went beyond "the Mechanical Rules" and "would enter into the very Spirit and Soul of fine Writing." Shortly thereafter he says: "*Thus altho'* in Poetry it be absolutely necessary that the Unities of Time, Place and Action, *with other Points of the same Nature* should be thoroughly *explained and* understood; there is still something more essential, *to the Art, something* that elevates and astonishes the Fancy, *and gives a Greatness of Mind to the Reader, which few of the Criticks besides Longinus have consider'd.*"

30. Burney, *The Early Journals and Letters of Fanny Burney. Volume III. The Streatham Years. Part I: 1778–1779*, ed. Lars E. Troide and Stewart J. Cooke (Montreal and Kingston: McGill-Queen's University Press, 1994), p. 222.

10

"Obstinate Contests of Disagreeing Virtues": Johnson, Skepticism, the But Clause, and the Dialectical Imperative

WE ALL KNOW THE IMAGE OF JOHNSON THE DOGMATIC ABSOLUTIST, the dictator of values who kicks a rock to prove reliable solidity. Boswell fosters this notion of an epic hero as powerful monarch of literature at home in the royal library. The image is excessive, but it often seems present in Johnson's varied remarks and writings and their apparent foundation upon the rock-solid stability of truth. Three students of Johnson recently have inverted this view. They have enlarged the small but persistent group of readers who align Johnson with skepticism in general and with Hume in particular. I will examine both the strength of such claims and, thereafter, the nature of Johnson's investigative procedures. In the process, I follow Jonathan Swift's remark in "The Sentiments of a Church of England Man" (1708; pub. 1711): "surely no Man whatsoever ought in Justice or good Manners to be charged with Principles he actually disowns, unless his Practices do openly and without the least Room for Doubt, contradict his Profession: Not upon small Surmises, or because he has the Misfortune to have ill Men sometimes agree with him in a few general Sentiments."[1]

1

Perhaps the most venerable modern statement of the case comes from the distinguished Hume scholar Ernest Campbell Mossner. Johnson, we hear, never conquered his "religious skepticism" or "repressed religious skepticism." He "hated Hume because he recognized in him a kindred spirit," and feared "that Hume might conceivably be right." We also are told that because Johnson admittedly considered Hume's objections, he therefore was secretly sympathetic to them. Mossner's Johnson as closet-

Hume now regularly reappears and indeed has become a presumed truism. One commentator thus instructs us that Johnson's "antagonism toward Hume" appears only in Boswell's *Life* and not in Johnson's writings. The substantial overlap in Hume's and Johnson's moral positions is clear in their "largely compatible visions of human happiness." Johnson "was somewhat despite himself a religious skeptic." Another commentator concurs. This Johnson "dared not avow to himself how strong his own scepticism was—and dared not feed his own scepticism by reading Hume." Johnson indeed "refrained from attacking Hume in print because he found it too disturbing to grapple with the questions that Hume addressed."[2]

Johnson as intellectual coward is as unpersuasive as the mock-Freudian method and the theory of overlapping compatible visions. The overlapping, for example, is accidental, incidental, or misstated. It also violates Swift's decree that one should not be accused of practicing principles one actively disowns merely because "ill Men sometimes agree with him in a few general Sentiments." Moreover, Johnson need not overtly have confronted Hume. Surrogates like James Beattie did that; Johnson himself normally considers general propositions rather than specific examples; and one general proposition is the inadequacy of skepticism, within which Hume clearly is a target. If one secretly desires what one calls undesirable, Karl Marx was a closet capitalist and Margaret Thatcher a repressed Marxist. Johnson's *Rambler*, No. 8 (1750), in fact postulates the way in which to deal with dangerous and morally alien thoughts. Since "all action has its origin in the mind, . . . to suffer the thoughts to be vitiated, is to poison the fountains of morality: Irregular desires will produce licentious practices." One therefore must keep "reason a constant guard over imagination."[3] Such potential human darkness suggests the possibility of diabolical influences. Johnson evokes Milton's Adam to make plain that illicit thought is harmless so long as it remains only thought, and so long as reason indeed properly guards:

> I cannot forbear, under this head, to caution pious and tender minds, that are disturbed by the irruptions of wicked imaginations, against too great dejection, and too anxious alarms; for thoughts are only criminal, when they are first chosen, and then voluntarily continued.

> > Evil into the mind of god or man
> > May come and go, so unapprov'd, and leave
> > No spot or stain behind.
> > PARADISE LOST, V.117–119 (YE 3:45)

The evidence suggests that Johnson considered skepticism, exercised his reason upon it, and rejected it because unlike David Hume he regarded skepticism as uncongenial to human happiness. Johnson never takes skeptical "action." The astronomer in *Rasselas* (1759) has a similar if delayed intellectual response. Imlac advises him that the benevolent fantasy of controlling the weather is unreasonable: "'All this,' said the astronomer, 'I have thought, but my reason has been so long subjugated by an uncontrollable and overwhelming idea, that it durst not confide in its own decisions. I can now see how fatally I betrayed my quiet, by suffering chimeras to prey upon me in secret.'"[4] Johnson's public examination of destructive ideas banishes subjection to chimeras.

The view of Johnson as skeptic substitutes a new myth for an old reality. Specifically, Mossner and his modern inheritors clearly counter the well-documented history of Johnson's religious character. That indeed begins to take definitive shape with his early months at Oxford. Johnson tells Boswell that from about the ages of nine to fourteen he was both shy regarding his poor eyesight and unable to use a broken seat in the family pew at its Lichfield church; he thus would "go and read in the fields on Sunday." He also then "became a sort of lax *talker* against religion, . . . and this lasted till I went to Oxford [at age nineteen], when it would not be *suffered*." In addition,

> at Oxford, I took up "Law's Serious Call to a Holy Life," expecting to find it a dull book (as such books generally are,) and perhaps to laugh at it. But I found Law quite an overmatch for me; and this was the first occasion of my thinking in earnest of religion, after I became capable of rational inquiry.

From then on, Boswell continues, "religion was the predominant object of his thoughts."[5]

Contrast this experience with Hume's as he relayed it to Gilbert Elliot on March 10, 1751. Hume chronicles his youthful initiation into skepticism "before I was twenty." He then experienced an "anxious Search after Arguments, to confirm the common Opinion" regarding religious faith, but "Doubts stole in, dissipated, return'd, were again dissipated, return'd again; and it was a perpetual Struggle of a restless Imagination against inclination, perhaps against Reason."[6] Hume relies on his own restless mind and imagination, and accepts permanent doubt regarding religious truth. Johnson relies upon an external religious source, institutional obligation, and his own willingness to recognize an intellectual and moral argument superior to his own. He thus accepts religious certainty.

That certainty is manifest in some twenty-eight sermons, a lifetime of recorded prayers, *Rambler* essays written "exactly conformable to the precepts of Christianity" (YE 5:320) and, among numerous other examples in his written and personal life, *The Vanity of Human Wishes* (1749). Its conclusion urges us to seek nonvain religious wishes: "Celestial wisdom calms the mind, / And makes the happiness she does not find."[7] A brief look at Johnson's religious thought suggests an important reason for his anger at skeptics and the incompatibility of his view and Hume's view of human happiness.

As Johnson's pre-Oxford behavior suggests, he well knew the temptations of religious laxity and its consequences. On October 31, 1784, he records eleven causes of skepticism, points on which he probably would have enlarged for a contemplated book concerning devotions.[8] Johnson concludes the list with the term "Against Despair" (YE 1:414). Rejection of despair is consistent with an ethical concern virtually from the first to the last of Johnson's recorded prayers. On September 7, 1738, he prays to God as the "Father of all mercies," thanks him for his love, and asks that his own sins be forgiven "for the merits and through the mediation of our most holy and blessed Saviour Jesus Christ" (YE 1:38). In October of 1765 he will "consider the act of prayer as a reposal of myself upon God and a resignation of all into his holy hand" (YE 1:97). On December 5, 1784, shortly before his death, he again prays to the "Most merciful Father." He seeks forgiveness through Jesus and says that "my whole hope and confidence may be in his merits and in thy mercy." Johnson's final words of his final prayers are a request that the Holy Spirit "receive me at my death, to everlasting happiness, for the sake of Jesus Christ. Amen" (YE 1:418).

Words like hope, happiness, mercy, and love fairly punctuate Johnson's prayers and contrast with his deep sense of personal and human error. Remove the hope that religion supplies and, for Johnson, there is no nonvain answer to the reader's troubled questions near the end of the *Vanity*. Where shall human hope and fear find their true source? Must the mind stagnate with doubt? Must we be helpless, ignorant, and darkly roll to our death? Must we not be concerned for our fate and decisions? Must we not pray? (lines 343–48). Johnson's narrator rejects such fatalism and answers on our behalf: "Enquirer, cease, petitions yet remain, / Which heaven may hear, nor deem religion vain" (YE 6:108, lines 349–50). The following lines include words like good, aid, rest, secure, best, sacred, strong, devotion, healthful, love, patience, faith, kind, heaven, gain, celestial wisdom, and happiness. One need not resort to hidden and denied Humean affinities to account for Johnson's anger against skeptics. In his judgment, they remove the chief source of happiness in this world and the next. Johnson writes "Against Despair." So far as he could tell, the skeptic writes "For Despair" and threatens what in 1809 Thomas Moore called the "happiness of a Christian." That "depends so much upon his belief, that it is natural he should feel alarm at the progress of doubt, lest it steal by degrees into the region, from which he is most interested in excluding it, and poison at last the very spring of his consolation and hope."[9]

Johnson's hostility to such assaults upon happiness breaks through in his Sermon 20 against scoffers, a term that connotes skepticism. It is perhaps his harshest sermon and perhaps also the only one that includes more overt blame than overt spiritual counsel. The sermon's first two paragraphs catalogue evil terms and acts: wrong, guilt, crime, fault, passions, vice, artifice, dissimulation, effrontery, hypocrisy, deceit, impudence, immorality, wickedness, fury, and despair. The scoffer who has "arrived at the summit of impiety" has learned "not only to neglect, but to insult religion, not only to be vicious, but to scoff at virtue."[10] Johnson is astonished "that any man can forbear enquiring seriously whether there is a God, whether God is just." These and other aspects of religion are among those "which every reasonable being ought undoubtedly to consider with an attention suitable to their importance" (YE 14:222). Scoffers are criminal toward God and man. They seek "to corrupt the heart of their companion by perverting his opinions . . . and by destroying his reverence for religion . . . and all the means of reformation!" (YE 14:225). Those unhappy scoffers at the means of grace are the more in need of the mercy they denigrate. They make themselves and others miserable here and hereafter.

Johnson, then, was hostile to skepticism because skepticism seemed hostile to happiness. It was false, and especially as relates to religion, a danger to spiritual comfort. It also was intellectually facile and based on the seventh cause of skepticism Johnson listed in his prayers: "Absurd method of learning objection first" (YE 1:414). At one point Johnson accordingly produced an exercise in glib skeptical debunking based on such absurdity. "It is always easy," he tells Boswell, "to be on the negative side," even on so basic a matter as whether there was salt upon the table. He then plays this intellectual game with an invented dialogue. Johnson denies that the British have taken Canada. The more populous French would rebuff the British attempts. "But the ministry have assured us . . . that it is taken." Yes, but the ministry lies in order to justify the vast expense of the American war. "But the fact is confirmed by thousands of men who were at the taking of it." Yes, but they too deceive us in order to hide their disgrace. If you travel to Canada and determine that it is taken, we will believe that you have been bribed. Johnson of course dismisses the absurdity by means of confidence in testimony. "Yet, Sir, notwithstanding all these plausible objections, we have no doubt that Canada is really ours. Such is the weight of common testimony. How much stronger are the evidences of the Christian religion" (*Life*, 1:428).

Johnson was almost equally annoyed by the softer skepticism in Shaftesbury's often reprinted *Characteristics* (1711). His lordship argues that anyone who "is not *conscious* of Revelation, nor has *certain Knowledge* of any Miracle or Sign, can be no more than SCEPTICK in the Case." Since even the warmest Christian therefore depends on history, tradition, and distant reports, he is in fact "at best but *a Sceptick-Christian.*" One's faith is not in revelation, which we have not personally experienced, but in those *modern* Men, or *Societys of Men*" who preserve "*sacred Writ*, and *genuine* Story."[11] We were not present at revelation and must not be dogmatic regarding its validity.

John Brown was among those who worried this mode of reasoning. His *Essay on the Characteristics* (1751) observes that by logical extension we should be skeptical of everything "except only of what falls within the narrow circle of our own proper *Observation*" (p. 257). Does lunch really exist if I cannot see it? Brown knows that Shaftesbury uses such devices to offer "Insinuations and virulent Remarks, in Order to disgrace *revealed*" religion (p. 256). Johnson enhances such derision. His harsh Sermon 20 against scoffers confronts Shaftesbury's theory that ridicule is the test of truth. Ridicule of "whatever is . . . venerable or sacred" is imprudent, idle, ignorant, and raises horror and contempt (YE 14:220). Yet worse, those who employ that test "hazard their highest interest, without even the low recompense of present applause" (YE 14:221).

Certain *Dictionary* (1755) illustrations further denigrate Shaftesbury. Johnson borrows germane remarks from Isaac Watts for the verb "scourge," the verb "survive," and the noun "pertness." All mock Shaftesbury by name or obvious allusion. We see that "There is in Shaftesbury's works a lively *pertness* and a parade of literature; but it is hard that we should be bound to admire the reveries." Johnson denigrates Shaftesbury as well in the *Lives of the Poets* (1779–81). He blames Akenside for adopting Shaftesbury's "foolish assertion of the efficacy of ridicule for the discovery of truth." He also introduces a long quotation from Gray regarding Shaftesbury's fading vogue. Gray's "contempt . . .

is often employed where I hope it will be approved, upon scepticism and infidelity."[12]

In affirming both testimony and inherent belief, Johnson also affirms the ongoing Restoration insistence that science resists skepticism. In 1670, for example, Joseph Glanvill writes *Against Infidelity, Scepticism, and Fanaticism of all sorts*. He joins those who urge that reason is necessary for "the *Being* of a GOD under the *Authority* of *Scripture*." Reason "is *Divine* and *Sacred*" and an ally of Faith. A few years later, Glanvill labels skeptics "desperate Renegado's, whose Intellects are debauch'd by Vice." The undebauched trust their senses and testimony and enjoy "firmness of assurance" from their faculties: "It is enough for us, that we have such Principles, lodged in our minds, that we cannot but assent to; and we find nothing to give us occasion to doubt of the truth of them."[13] The clergyman Glanvill was demonstrably allied with Anglican rationalism's many pious believers in reason as a path to religious commitment.[14] Johnson allegorizes this belief in his "Vision of Theodore, the Hermit of Teneriffe" (1748).

Theodore tires himself while attempting to climb the mountain, falls asleep, and dreams of personified moral precepts regarding life's trials and pleasures. In the vision, he meets Reason who describes herself as "of all subordinate beings the noblest and the greatest; who, if thou wilt receive my laws, will reward thee . . . by conducting thee to Religion" (YE 16:202–3). Reason also advises other students "to inlist themselves among the votaries of Religion" (YE 16:203), but makes plain that she is only a means to an end. Existence has "asperities and pitfals over which Religion only can conduct you." She also only can conduct Theodore to the edge of the mist on the highest part of the mountain, "a mist by which my prospect is terminated, and which is pierced only by the eyes of Religion. Beyond it are the temples of Happiness, in which those who climb the precipice by her direction, after the toil of their pilgrimage repose for ever" (YE 16:204). The excellent secular guide Reason leads to the better divine guide Religion and the eternal happiness she offers. When those with good habits pierced the mists, "Reason . . . discerned that they were safe, but Religion saw that they were happy" (YE 16:209). In Johnson's "Theodore," as in his *Vanity of Human Wishes*, his sermons, and his prayers, religion provides the happiness for which we long and of which we too often are bereft.

Glanvill's remark that we have certain principles "lodged in our minds" also anticipates another of Johnson's assumptions. According to the later Scottish commonsense school, shared human knowledge offers shared truths that are prior to reason. Those truths are part of our natural and instinctive created spiritual and mental inheritance. As James Beattie put it in *An Essay on the Nature and Immutability of Truth* (1770), "truth is something fixed and terminate, depending not upon man, but upon the Author of nature." Any doctrine that attempts to denigrate "the evidence of our senses, external or internal, and to subvert the original instinctive principles of human belief," is dangerous and can lead "to universal scepticism." That philosophy may "overturn all truth, and pervert every human faculty," and certainly the inherent recognition of a benevolent God. Beattie knows that "when a sceptic attacks one principle of common sense, he doth in effect attack all" by inducing a chain of doubt. "The fatal fermentation, once begun, spreads wider and wider" and turns all "into rottenness and poison." Skeptics seek finally to show "that God, and religion, and immortality, are empty sounds."[15]

Since Beattie's main target was David Hume, we may usefully examine Johnson's opinion of this *Essay on . . . Truth*. One way to determine whether Johnson is in any valid way a skeptic, is cautiously to examine his definitions. These concern the English language, not Johnson's language, but they are guides to his meaning and are joined by variously enlightening illustrative quotations. For Johnson "skepticism," like the Pyrronhism from which it stems, is "universal doubt." The skeptic is "One who doubts, or pretends to doubt of every thing." Johnson adds words from Bentley in hopes that such painful doubt can be alleviated by divine truth: "May the Father of mercies confirm the *sceptical* and wavering minds."[16] Johnson returns to the conflict between skepticism and mercy by means of Beattie's attack on David Hume.

On October 4, 1771, Beattie gave Johnson the second edition of his book with its long new Postscript. Beattie there defends himself from charges of excessive severity, a defense Johnson found convincing and that Burke called "one of the most masterful pieces of eloquence he has ever seen."[17] Johnson and Beattie thus already were mutually admiring and sympathetic allies when they met at the end of July 1772. On August 3, Johnson wrote to Boswell saying that "Beattie's book is . . . every day more liked; at least I like it more as I look upon it."[18] The Postscript includes a remark that becomes an illustrative quotation for the revised *Dictionary*'s (1773) second definition of the verb to violate, "To infringe": "Those reasonings which, by *violating* common sense, tend to subvert every principle of rational belief, to sap the foundations of truth and science, and to leave the mind exposed to all the horrors of scepticism." Johnson clearly rejects skepticism as an acceptable conclusion to rational thought, and especially as it concerns religion. He just as clearly selects his illustration from an attack upon Hume, who deserves every condemnation appropriate for someone whose values, Beattie argued and Johnson agreed, "are totally subversive of science, morality, and religion both natural and revealed."[19]

The evidence is overwhelming that Johnson was not a religious skeptic in any philosophical sense of the word. He berates Shaftesbury and Hume not because he is secretly like them and fears that they are right, but because he is unlike them and believes that they are dangerously wrong. He regularly excoriates skepticism as an attack upon religious and secular certainties, and he approves of what he thought of Beattie's successful attack upon Hume. Johnson based that approval upon his long-standing belief that religion promised the hope of happiness and that skepticism promised horrible doubt. For Johnson, revelation supports religion and resists skepticism.

Nonetheless, readers and those in Johnson's living company regularly note that he often debunks received notions and easily argues on either side of an issue. Indeed, he comfortably falls into that debunking method in the little exercise that mockingly demonstrates Britain's inability to have taken Canada from the French. If Johnson is not a skeptic, how do we account for such apparent open-endedness, acceptance of competing and often contradictory responses, and apparent questioning of received opinion? One critic in the recent triad of books argues that Johnson so argued because he indeed was a skeptic, as was much of the eighteenth century.

2

Far from being stable, we hear, the eighteenth century from about Locke's philosophy to Johnson's *Lives of the Poets* was one of "flux and irresolution," of "variousness . . . plurality and indeterminacy." Though there were decisive "strong perceptions," normative skepticism "involves . . . a certain doubleness of stance. It is a practice or a process, not an intellectual position, and where it advances positions it does so with a certain playfulness or irony, with a consciousness of their necessary provisionality or contingency: as if opening a dialogue." *Rasselas* well exemplifies such skepticism in "the open-endedness of the narrative, with its 'conclusion, in which nothing is concluded'. This openness, however, is not just a matter of the ending, but pervasive."[20]

The blessedly defunct view of the eighteenth century as "the peace of the Augustans" has been replaced by a blend of the old New Criticism and its cousin deconstruction. This marriage of irony and tension with contingency and indeterminacy becomes a deductive standard that forces reluctant works into its syllogistic web. Proper skepticism is tentative and ironic; *The Vanity of Human Wishes* is properly skeptical; therefore the *Vanity* is tentative and ironic. The poem's apparent confidence thus "confesses itself as inextricably implicated in its own satire" (p. 241). The poem in fact seems to have failed to communicate an answer to its title's concerns. The *Vanity*'s apparent emphasis on hope, calm, love, and reliability cannot counter its vision of the world's snares, deceit, decay, and death. The Christian alternative of nonvain religious wishes that Johnson sets against vain human wishes is "muffled and uncertain in its articulation of any positive object for the will" (p. 242), and "as a whole will not bear any great weight" (p. 243).[21]

This Johnson-as-skeptic hypothesis has several significant weaknesses other than its false major and minor premises. Two weaknesses certainly are its deductive syllogistic stance, and its consequent refusal to recognize the power of religion for Johnson. As I have suggested, dismissing the *Vanity*'s conclusion as "muffled" and self-satiric misreads the text and ignores Johnson's confidence in his religion's stable truth in an unstable secular world: "In moral and religious questions only," he says, "a wise man will hold no consultations with fashion, because these duties are constant and immutable, and depend not on the notions of men, but the commands of Heaven."[22]

Misreading also is overt regarding the blunt old saw that nothing is concluded in *Rasselas*. Its putative open-endedness applies only to the continuing search for happiness in this world in general, and for Johnson's main characters in particular. Each "well knew that none [of their wishes] could be obtained" (YE 16:176). Such a remark is among the many conclusions that one draws from Prince Rasselas's search: a happy valley that gratifies the senses evokes boredom and unhappiness; human happiness does not consist in a mere choice of life whether high or low, urban or rural, married or single; all choices of life have strengths and weaknesses; permanence is a fantasy in our world of flux; women can be the intellectual equals of men; a life of cerebral isolation leads to madness; there are questions beyond human ability to answer; one needs a reliable guide through the difficult world in order to learn such lessons. Johnson here offers demonstrable statements of demonstrable and conclusive truth.

The Johnson-as-skeptic hypothesis also confuses variation based on varied situations with contingency and indeterminacy. Johnson cites two illustrative quotations from Watts that suggest such discrimination. An illustration for the noun "colour" is from his "Logick" (1725). Under "The appearance of Bodies to the eye only; hue; die," we read:

> It is a vulgar idea of the *colours* of solid bodies, when we perceive them to be a red, or blue, or green tincture of the surface; but a philosophical idea, when we consider the various *colours* to be different sensations, excited in us by the refracted rays of light, reflected on our eyes in a different manner, according to the different size, or shape, or situation of the particles of which the surfaces of those bodies are composed.

The vulgar and the philosophical ideas of color yield different perception. For everyday purposes, red is what we see. For more exalted thought, red is how light is refracted and reflected into our perception.

Similarly, under the verb "To complicate," "To entangle one with another; to join" we read: "There are a multitude of human actions, which have so many *complicated* circumstances, aspects, and situations, with regard to time and place, persons and things, that it is impossible for any one to pass a right judgment concerning them, without entering into most of these circumstances."[23] Johnson indeed often considers these "aspects, and situations" in his moral and literary judgments.

Boswell relates this familiar episode. "He loved to display his ingenuity in argument; and therefore would sometimes in conversation maintain opinions which he was sensible were wrong, but in supporting which his reasoning and wit would be most conspicuous. He would begin thus 'Why, Sir, as to the good or evil of card-playing—' 'Now (said Garrick) he is thinking which side he shall take'" (*Life*, 1:317). In assuming that Johnson knowingly takes the wrong side, Boswell is less perceptive than Garrick, who nonetheless also misses the point. Johnson considers a topic that includes at least two defensible sides whose circumstances require "entering into." He thinks because the complex topic requires thought, not because he planned to show his ingenuity. Both in the *Life of Johnson* itself and with Boswell on the *Tour to the Hebrides* (1785) Johnson laments that he had not learned to play the civilizing and socializing activity of cards (*Life*, 1:317, 5:404). In the *Rambler*, No. 80 (1750), among other places, he characterizes cardplaying as a waste of time and often money by the empty-headed.[24] Each characterization is correct from a particular "right judgment." Each also suggests Johnson's second unfortunate cause of skepticism: "Supposition that things disputed are disputable" (YE 1:414). Different views may be accurate in different circumstances. Thus, as in the *Adventurer*, No. 107 (1753), one man regards celibacy "as a state of gloomy solitude." Another man regards it "as a state free of encumbrances." That is not a matter of broad indeterminacy, but of different views "of an object." Hence, he concludes, "it is possible that each is right, but that each is right only for himself" (YE 2:445).

Johnson also understands situational ethics. He often considers the moral and theological bases for charity, and in the process makes clear that one must be judged by motive as well as action: "as the guilt, so the virtue, of every action arises from design," he says in Sermon 4 (YE 14:42). Selfless charity is essential and fulfills divine decrees; selfish charity to boost one's ego "is not acting upon the proper motives" (YE 14:43). Boswell records Johnson's conversational support for such a view in 1763:

> The morality of an action depends on the motive from which we act. If I fling half a crown to a beggar with intention to break his head, and he picks it up and buys victuals with it, the physical effect is good; but with respect to me, the action is very wrong. So, religious exercises, if not performed with an intention to please God, avail us nothing. (*Life*, 1:397–98)

Johnson acts promptly if deliberately in deciding the positive and negative aspects of a human activity like cardplaying or almsgiving as based in a specific human context. His conversation often is like his *Rambler*s in their weighty and consistent contemplation. It also is like his *Rambler*s in their thinking to the moment under the pressures of time and circumstance. We find thought processes played out before us, though I think those pressures enhance rather than determine Johnson's favored mode of proceeding.[25] Accordingly, we see him at work during individual episodes or texts. We also can view his works synthetically and see how such a secular dialectic of competing circumstances appears among different works, or even in consecutive works like the *Rambler* Nos. 82 (1750) and 83 (1751), in which Johnson sets out the virtuoso's weaknesses and strengths. In quotidian matters one assesses various alternatives' various aspects and makes a decision. In some cases the decision is yes and yes, and Johnson does what he calls for at the end of *Rambler* No. 158 (1751)—he irritates the intellectual appetite, as with his discussions of rules-criticism.

Johnson defends or employs the rules in the *Rambler* Nos. 139 and 140 (1751). He there analyzes *Samson Agonistes* "according to the indispensable laws of Aristotelian criticism" and with the regulatory precision of a French neoclassicist. His "Life of Milton" (1779) later performs a comparable task on *Paradise Lost*, where le Bossu helps to provide the official language by which an epic should be judged. In the *Rambler*, No. 156 (1751), Johnson argues that "perhaps" even Shakespeare might have yet more moved his audience "had he not counteracted himself; and we might have been more interested in the distresses of his heroes had we not been so frequently diverted by the jokes of his buffoons."[26] Nonetheless, in the Preface to Shakespeare (1765) Johnson robustly dismantles the Gallic three unities and praises Shakespeare's tragicomic counter-acting because it imitates nature.

Such presumed inconsistency is not "contingent." In each of these instances the situation guides the judgment. Johnson applies only Aristotle's conception of "a beginning, a middle, and an end," a requirement on which virtually all critics and authors agree (YE 4:370). He seeks to determine whether *Samson Agonistes* can properly be "opposed with all the confidence of triumph to the dramatick performances of other nations" (YE 4:371). For Johnson, the answer is No, because *Samson* lacks a requisite middle: "yet this is the tragedy, which ignorance has admired, and bigotry applauded" (YE 4:376).

In "Milton," the formalist rules serve another purpose. Johnson shows that even if judged on these standards *Paradise Lost* is a transcendent English epic poem. He also shows that those non-Aristotelian rules are indeed artificial. "Bossu is of opinion that the poet's first work is to find a *moral*, which his fable is afterwards to illustrate and establish. This seems to have been the process only of Milton" (*Lives*, 1:171). In the *Rambler*, No. 156, Johnson seeks both to determine the authority of rules and limit the authority of nature. Tragicomedy indeed imitates nature, but that potentially chaotic force diminishes design. Shakespeare's genius can overcome such faults; since other dramatists are less talented, Johnson's implicit message in this case is that one should imitate nature but impose design, as he also argues in *Rambler*, No. 4 (1750), regarding the novel. Johnson's illustrative quotation from the verb "To Perform" is from Isaac Watts's *Logick* (p. 300, 1725, with changes): "when a poet has *performed* admirably in several illustrious places, we sometimes also admire his very errors." Accordingly, these disparate responses to imitation of art, the rules, and imitation of nature are coherent and not indeterminate: Aristotle's unity of action is essential; the rules created by authoritarian critics are valuable but limit the artist and the audience, and one may break them without "needless fear" (YE 5:70); nature is the best but not infallible guide and needs to have reasonable moral and literary design imposed upon it.

Johnson's method of inquiry in secular matters, then, encourages readers and auditors to combine the situation with the appropriate judgment. That compartmentalization rarely extends to religious concerns, about which Johnson normally is definitive within the normal variations in Christian theology. He clearly was not willing to replace substance with vacuity.

3

Much of the supporting evidence for the nature of Johnson's presumed skeptical method actually is subsumed under what I call his secular dialectical imperative. He had an intellectual and temperamental need to examine those parts of secular life that allow for genuine difference of opinion or that require adjustment based on circumstance. One aspect of the evidence for Johnson as mediator between conflicting views often represents itself in a small word like "yet," "though," "however," or "but" that, as Paul Fussell observes, is the "very substance" of some *Rambler* essays.[27] It also contributes to the "very substance" of several other works and is one reason why we allow Johnson to assume his characteristically mingled roles as guide and companion. That guide, however, generally neither is contingent nor provisional, though he may indeed imply discrete truths for competing or discrete circumstances.

Johnson's "perhaps" and repeated "might have been" suggest both the intellectual context he evokes and the respect with which he treats his readers and bonds them to him. These words also guide us toward the kind of empirical method that Johnson accepted as part of his secular intellectual mode of proceeding, that characterizes his capacious mind, but that does not extend beyond the secular. Frances Reynolds records this remark as he was "Talking on the Subject of Scepticism": "The eyes of the mind are like the eyes of the Body. They can see but at such a distance. But because we cannot see beyond this point, is there nothing beyond it?"[28]

This acceptance of alternatives as a quotidian step within quotidian method also is clear in an illustration that Johnson uses and slightly varies from Dryden's modest, scientific, and process-skepticism. His Preface to *Sylvae* (1685) provides Johnson's words both for "dogmatical" and for "scepticism": "*accordingly I lay'd by my natural Diffidence and Scepticism for a while, to take up that Dogmatical way of his.*" Dryden describes Lucretius's ethics and persona, which is "*absolute command*" over both his patron and readers, whom he treats with schoolmaster-like threats and "*scorn and indignation.*" Lucretius's authorial "*perpetual Dictatorship,*" Dryden says, resembles the politics of Thomas

Hobbes. As if such contempt and Hobbesianism were not enough, Dryden reiterates what Johnson already knew: Lucretius was an atheist and a materialist. "*As for his Opinions concerning the mortality of the Soul, they are so absurd, that I cannot if I wou'd believe them.*"[29] Dryden adds that in order to be faithful to his poet, he had to abandon his natural skepticism and assume Lucretian dogmatism. Such skepticism clearly is not classical Pyrrohnist universal doubt. It is a mode of reasoning in secular matters that allows fluid thought, examination of alternatives, and a suspended decision until relative certainty can be determined. Isaac Watts's *Logick* states the case that Johnson shared. When propositions are doubtful, "the Mind which is searching for Truth ought to remain in a State of *Doubt* and *Suspence*, until superior Evidence on one Side or the other incline the Balance of the Judgment, and determine the *Probability* or *Certainty* to one Side" (pp. 277–78).

Johnson's periodical essays twice discuss abuse of that method, in which the skepticism as universal doubt or questioning replaces a movement toward truth. The *Rambler*, No. 95 (1751), is a letter from Pertinax. That child of a dysfunctional family describes his moral and intellectual illness that at first brought him success at university and in the law. He indeed becomes so polemically skeptical that he argues against the existence of Alexander the Great and the pyramids. Having once violated his reason, he alas spreads his illness to "weaken the obligations of moral duty, and efface the distinctions of good and evil." As a man with neither moral anchor nor compass, he loses "peace of conscience . . . principles of reason . . . motives of action" (YE 4:147). He finally realizes that only the wicked can be his friends, reeducates himself, and returns to spiritual health: "I rejoice in the new possession of evidence and reality, and step on from truth to truth with confidence and quiet" (YE 4:148). Skepticism flounders one into despair; Johnson's "intellectual position" marches one towards truths and peace. Thereafter, in the *Idler*, No. 87 (1759), Johnson distinguishes between the little mind that denies and the stronger mind that inquires. The lazy skeptic functions by "withdrawing attention from evidence and declining the fatigue of comparing probabilities" (YE 2:270). Sometimes that comparative probability means accepting the balance between different situations—as, perhaps, in a weighing of the good and evil of cardplaying in different times and places. Johnson extends this balanced thought to more urgent matters and does so both in the synthetic and focused manner I have discussed. I cite three topics: government, international warfare, and the human condition.

Johnson both relates and distinguishes concepts in the paragraph that

Boswell calls "Of Tory and Whig." It begins: "A wise Tory and a wise Whig, I believe, will agree. Their principles are the same, though their modes of thinking are different." Johnson is neither uncertain nor indeterminate and certainly not ironic. Wisdom evokes agreement between competing sides. Johnson thus assumes benign principles that accommodate apparently different political concepts. He so proceeds in part, I suspect, because he knows that "governments [are] formed by chance," and that these "fabricks of dissimilar materials, [are] raised by different architects upon different plans." Accordingly, he says elsewhere, "I would not give half a guinea to live under one form of government rather than another." Any reasonable government reasonably practiced over reasonable people is likely to work, whether it is run by wise Whig or wise Tory. If it does not, the people will rise up and slay their masters.[30]

They also may slay one another and define winners or losers from a national perspective. The *Idler*, No. 20 (1758), begins with this stern observation: "There is no crime more infamous than the violation of truth." Johnson at once modifies his decree with a dose of reality and a but-clause: "Yet the law of truth, thus sacred and necessary, is broken without punishment, without censure, in compliance with inveterate prejudice and prevailing passions" (YE 2:62). The essay then describes two views of the battle of Louisbourg on Cape Breton Island in Canada in 1758. For a nonce British historian, his nation exercised its natural right of victory over the inferior French "and terrified the garrison to an immediate capitulation" (YE 2:64). For a nonce French historian, the humane and brave French leave the garrison "with the admiration of their enemies, who durst hardly think themselves masters of the place" (YE 2:65). Johnson's point is not that sacred truth is unreachable, but that it has been abused by national prejudice and passion. Each side lies.

Johnson's contrast of theoretical purity and actual behavior indeed typifies his dialectical thought that is based upon his empirical approach to the secular world and its data. The *Life of Richard Savage* (1744) thus begins with the "rational . . . hope that intellectual greatness" should make men happy. "But this expectation, however plausible, has been very frequently disappointed." Thereafter, in the *Idler*, No. 4 (1758), Johnson says that any good institution based on charity ought to be made permanent: "But man is a transitory being, and his designs must partake of the imperfections of their authour. To confer duration is not always in our power." Instead, benevolently seize the moment "and employ it well, without too much solicitude for the future." Johnson also extends such actual behavior to the world of literary response. He knows that in *King Lear* as in life the "virtuous miscarry. . . . but since all reasonable beings naturally love justice," poetical justice is even more pleasing.[31]

We find this complex vision that leads to focus in several of Johnson's other works, for he accepts us as "finite beings" with different finite perspectives—some of which are contradictory because situations can be contradictory. We not only differ from one another, but "very often differ from ourselves" and, as Nekayah puts it, recognize "the obstinate contests of disagreeing virtues"—the key word of which is *virtue*, the normative end of the contest. Imlac sees an even larger psychological reference and characterizes human decision making: "Inconsistencies . . . cannot both be right, but imputed to man, they may both be true. Yet diversity is not inconsistency." As Johnson himself makes plain in the *Rambler*, No. 196 (1752), such disagreement not only is a necessary condition of life; it also is a preservative against unendurable monotony. It is a comforting not discomforting method; it makes plain that alternative and determinate virtues are available to us.[32]

I wish, however, to illustrate Johnson's secular contest-practice in a specific periodical essay that offers three aspects of Johnson's dialectical imperative: his fluidity of thought, his use of such fluidity to carry the reader with him as both colleague and student, and his consequent ability to use fluidity and companionship to arrive at a shared and approved goal of demonstrable virtue and responsibility within a specific circumstance—here the reading and writing of novels.

The necessary curse of the academic anthology makes Johnson's well-known fourth *Rambler* (1750) seem an isolated discourse on the novel.[33] His contemporaries were likely to have approached it in one of two other ways—as part of the series of essays published on Saturdays and Tuesdays, or in the collected editions that began in Edinburgh in 1750 and in London in 1752. Whatever Johnson's own immediate time pressures for individual essays, the first four numbers suggest a coherent design.

The introductory *Rambler* mingles confidence and modesty as it attempts to create a willing audience. He recognizes both the "dangers which the desire of pleasing is certain to produce" (YE 3:4), and the "captivating . . . spirit and intrepidity, to which we often yield, as to a resistless power; nor can he reasonably expect the confidence of others, who too apparently distrusts himself." He adds that "unless his judges are inclined to favour him, they will hardly be persuaded to hear the cause" (YE 3:5). Johnson overtly states the balance between these two acceptable and "so nearly equiponderant" approaches (YE 3:7). The second number, however, seeks audience approbation by stressing authorial vulnerability. Johnson accepts the judgment of a busy and fickle world as a condition of authorship, and he enhances the inclination to favor by not demanding too much. In the third number, though, Johnson actively limits the nature of his vulnerability. He accepts the voice of general humanity; he rejects the voice of self-created censors who "distinguish themselves by the appellation of Criticks," but have only "fragments of authority" without earned power (YE 3:19). Johnson himself knows that for an author to be effective, "men must not only be persuaded of their errors, but reconciled to their guide" whom they recognize as "more knowing than themselves" (YE 3:15).

The *Rambler*, No. 4, follows and exemplifies several traits laid out in its predecessors. It proceeds with confidence that engages the reader with Johnson as authority. It at once modifies and supports that authority by reconsideration of apparent truths as seen from a specific situation and by appealing to the audience's fine instinct to protect the young. Along the way, it also exemplifies criticism at its benevolent best, as a form of writing that is historically aware, respects alternatives, and establishes a coherent framework for the moral basis of art. Some of this works by means of Johnson's but clause.

Readers aware of Johnson's initial triad of *Rambler*s knew his acceptance of the world in which they lived. They thus would have been pleased to see the first paragraph of his fourth *Rambler*: it characterizes their world and its attractive fiction based on words like life, true, daily, world, really, converse, mankind, and natural. Johnson praises "our present writers" whose books "arise from general converse and accurate observation of the living world." He even cites ancient Horace and a sound judge of the real, an ancient shoemaker, to praise imitation of nature (YE 3:19–20). Here is both reasoned contemporary and historical approval.

Johnson now adds his familiar and respectful reservation based on redefining the moral circumstance: "But the fear of not being approved as just copiers of human manners is not the most important concern that an author of this sort ought to have before him" (YE 3:20–21). Modern concerns are important; the more important enduring one is based upon an author's general obligation to recognize his particular audience's needs. For novels it is "the young, the ignorant, and the idle, to whom they serve as lectures of conduct and introductions into life" (YE 3:21). Johnson's but clause makes plain why the situational *ought* modifies the situational *is*: "The highest degree of reverence should be paid to youth." Prior romance tales had no relationship to life and thus had no source of application. "But," Johnson again says, "when an adventurer is leveled with the rest of the world, and acts in such scenes of the universal drama, as may be the lot of any other man," one must select only the best examples for the best kind of imitation. He effectively summarizes his mingled ethical and literary ideals in this remark and its but clause: "It is justly considered as the greatest excellency of art, to imitate nature; but it is necessary to distinguish those parts of nature, which are most proper for imitation" (YE 3:21–22).

In the fourth *Rambler*, then, Johnson continues the devices he laid out in the first three numbers: mingled confidence and modesty, respect for the audience he corrects and that accepts correction, and his own willingness to accept the public's but not putative critics' judgments. He uses these heterogeneous devices in a splendidly homogeneous way while also setting the model for a new circumstance or situation. This is ethically based criticism concerned with "the proper" part of nature to imitate for the proper kind of audience that adults should protect through art. Johnson became the great critic we know him to be in part because he was able to think on either side of an issue that had legitimate sides. He may make clear which side is better, that each side is equally good from a specific perspective, or that each has advantages and disadvantages. He shows us how he thinks as he thinks and revises while respecting the idea revised and the revised situation; he performs that important act with so small a word as "but."

That is not contingency or irony or skeptical doubt. Nor is it "Indifference about opinions," for Johnson the first cause of skepticism (YE 1:414). It embodies the reasoning mind reasonably examining reasonable alternatives for reasonable circumstances. That mind then reasonably points out exceptions and reasonably decides which is best for the finite, inconsistent, human beings we remain until faced with divine truth, about which skepticism or alternative realities should be impossible. "But" and "Yet" each appear five times in *The Vanity of Human Wishes* to begin lines that alert us to grim aspects of life we have not yet considered. Each word appears only once in the final paragraph in which religion also appears as our unvain option and agreeable virtue. Unlike the earlier portions, those words point to positive not negative examples, as in this couplet's illuminating parallel: "Still raise for good the supplicating voice, / But leave to heav'n the measure and the choice" (YE 6:108, lines 351–52).

Such views cannot be reconciled with skepticism as universal doubt or as the moral violations to which Beattie, Johnson, and so many other eighteenth-century moralists, believed skepticism leads: "Those reasonings which, by *violating* common sense, tend to subvert every principle of rational belief, to sap the foundations of truth and science, and to leave the mind exposed to all the horrors of scepticism." Conrad's Kurtz well knew the danger of the horror the horror. Johnson's faith- and reason-based religion hoped to avoid that option. His dialectics hoped in turn to alert us to the varieties of secular truth and the best ways to find it for different circumstances, but he never doubted that there was a best way, if only for a specific person in a specific circumstance. In each case Johnson hoped to write "Against Despair." In each case, as well, Johnson should not be "charged with Principles he actually disowns," much less with the fear to confront them.

NOTES

1. Swift, "Sentiments of a Church-of-England Man with Respect to Religion and Government," in The Prose Works of Jonathan Swift vol. 2, *Bickerstaff Papers and Pamphlets on the Church*, ed. Herbert Davis (Oxford: Basil Blackwell, 1966), p. 4. Swift also asked: "why should any Party be accused of a Principle which they solemnly disown and protest against?" (p. 3).

2. Ernest Campbell Mossner, *The Forgotten Hume: Le bon David* (New York: Columbia University Press, 1943), pp. 206–7; Adam Potkay, *The Passion for Happiness: Samuel Johnson and David Hume* (Ithaca: Cornell University Press), pp. 203 (considers Hume's views), 1 (antagonism), 5 (compatible), 203 (somewhat); Stephen Miller, *Three Deaths and Enlightenment Thought: Hume, Johnson, Marat* (Lewisburg, PA: Bucknell University Press, 2001), pp. 97 (dared not), 95 (refrained). Miller also agrees with Potkay that the intellectual gap between Hume and Johnson regarding religion "seems very narrow" (p. 97). Hume of course had so many articulate enemies that Johnson need not have taken him on in print. See Isabel Rivers, *Reason, Grace, and Sentiment: A Study of the Language of Religion and Ethics in England, 1660–1780. Volume II. Shaftesbury to Hume* (Cambridge: Cambridge University Press, 2000), pp. 238–329.

3. The Yale Edition of the Works of Samuel Johnson, vol. 3, *The Rambler*, ed. W. J. Bate and Albrecht B. Strauss (New Haven: Yale University Press, 1969), pp. 42, 43. Subsequent references to Johnson are from this edition and are cited as YE with the volume, editor, date of publication, and page number.

4. YE 16, *Rasselas and Other Tales*, ed. Gwin J. Kolb (1990), p. 163.

5. *Boswell's Life of Johnson Together with Boswell's Journal of a Tour to the Hebrides*, ed. George Birkbeck Hill and rev. L. F. Powell (Oxford: Clarendon Press, 1934–50), 1:68; referred to hereafter as *Life*.

6. *Letters of David Hume*, ed. J. Y. T. Grieg (Oxford: Clarendon Press, 1932), 1:154.

7. YE 6, *Poems*, ed. E. L. McAdam, Jr., with George Milne (1964), p. 109, lines 367–68.

8. See *Life* 4:293, and YE 1, *Diaries, Prayers, and Annals*, ed. E. L. McAdam, Jr., with Donald and Mary Hyde (1958), pp. 414–15 n.

9. Moore, *The Sceptic: A Philosophical Satire. By the Author of Corruption and In-*

tolerance (London, 1809), p. 6. Moore goes on to argue that mild and rational skepticism limited only to "the pretensions of human knowledge" is acceptable (p. 7). Johnson would have agreed.

10. YE 14, *Sermons*, ed. Jean Hagstrum and James Gray (1978), pp. 217–18. Note also that when Rasselas is in the catacombs, he observes: "How gloomy would be these mansions of the dead to him who did not know that he shall never die; that what now acts shall continue its agency, and what now thinks shall think on for ever" (YE 16:175).

11. Shaftesbury, *Characteristicks of Men, Manners, Opinions, and Times*, 4th ed. (London, 1727), 3:72–73.

12. Johnson, *Lives of the English Poets*, ed. George Birkbeck Hill (Oxford: Clarendon Press, 1905), "Akenside," 3:413, "Gray," 3:432.

13. Glanvill, *[Logo Opthekeia]* . . . *Or, A Seasonable Recommendation, and Defence of Reason, In the Affairs of Religion; Against Infidelity, Scepticism, and Fanaticisms of all sorts* (London, 1670), pp. 1 (Being), 26 (Divine); Glanvill, "Philosophia Pia," in *Essays on Several Important Subjects in Philosophy and Religion* (London, 1676), pp. 45 (desperate), 50 (enough). Glanvill and his colleagues in the Royal Society needed to answer charges that their antischolastic empiricism encouraged skepticism, atheism, and Catholicism. See, for example, Henry Stubbe, *Legends no Histories: Or, A Specimen Of some Animadversions Upon the History of the Royal Society. . . . Together with the Plus Ultra of Mr. Joseph Glanvill* (London, 1670).

14. This term was coined by Phillip Harth in *Swift and Anglican Rationalism: The Religious Background of "A Tale of a Tub"* (Chicago: University of Chicago Press, 1961). Harth and four other Swift scholars return to the topic in *Swift Studies 1999: The Annual of the Ehrenpreis Center* (Munich: Wilhelm Fink Verlag, 1999), pp. 5–36. For Glanvill, see Jackson Cope, *Joseph Glanvill, Anglican Apologist* (St. Louis: Washington University Studies, 1956).

15. Beattie, *An Essay on the Nature and Immutability of Truth, In Opposition to Sophistry and Scepticism*, 2nd ed. (Edinburgh and London, 1771), pp. 146 (truth), 524 (evidence, *ff*). This was the edition that Johnson read and from which he quoted for the revised *Dictionary* of 1773. Potkay think that James Beattie "caricatures" Hume's positions (pp. 2, 57). Johnson clearly thought Beattie's refutation both admirable and convincing. See the discussion of Beattie within.

Johnson the anguished doubter permeates Walter Jackson Bate's essential *The Achievement of Samuel Johnson* (New York: Oxford University Press, 1955), especially pp. 167–70 regarding religion. James L. Clifford notes that there "was a basic skepticism which pervaded all his thought," but only discusses political and other secular subjects. See Clifford's *Young Sam Johnson* (New York: McGraw-Hill, 1955), pp. 105–6. See also what I think more accurate in this regard, Robert Voitle, *Samuel Johnson the Moralist* (Cambridge, MA: Harvard University Press, 1961), pp. 168–80. For further discussion of Johnson's putative skepticism, see Paul Fussell, *Johnson and the Life of Writing* (New York: Harcourt Brace Jovanovich, 1971), pp. 164, 171, 174, 175, and Raman Selden, "Deconstructing the *Ramblers*," in Prem Nath, *Fresh Reflections on Samuel Johnson: Essays in Criticism* (Troy: Whitston, 1987), and Leo Damrosch *Fictions of Reality in the Age of Hume and Johnson* (Madison: University of Wisconsin Press, 1989).

16. Quotations are from *A Dictionary of the English Language* (London, 1755). I am pleased to acknowledge my use of Anne McDermott's splendid Cambridge CD-ROM of the first and fourth editions of the *Dictionary*. It helped me quickly to find the fourth edition's use of Beattie, below. For further such discussion, see also Allen Reddick, *The*

Making of Johnson's Dictionary (Cambridge: Cambridge University Press, 1990), pp. 122, 160, 165–66.

17. Burke said this when Beattie visited him on May 14, 1773. See *James Beattie's London Diary 1773*, ed. Ralph S. Walker (Aberdeen: University Press, 1946), p. 33. The diary includes several instances of Beattie's pleasant and approving visits with Johnson and his friends. See also Everard H. King, *James Beattie* (Boston: Twayne Publishers, 1971), p. 22. The conflict between Christian Johnson and skeptic Hume was well remembered. See William Agutter, *On the Difference between the Deaths of the Righteous and the Wicked, Illustrated in the Instance of Dr. Samuel Johnson, and David Hume, Esq. A Sermon. Preached Before the University of Oxford, at St. Mary's Church, On Sunday, July 23, 1786* (London, 1800). Each man, however, here embodies a point of view rather than an individual.

18. *The Letters of Samuel Johnson*, ed. Bruce Redford (Princeton: Princeton University Press, 1992–94), 2:391.

19. See the *Essay's* second edition, 1771, p. 539. Beattie's presentation copy, with Johnson's handwritten note on the inner flyleaf, is in the British Library. See also *Life*, 3:11: "Those only who believed in Revelation have been angry at having their faith called in question; because they only had something upon which they could rest as matter of fact." On October 10, 1773, Johnson answered Boswell's question, whether Hume " 'is . . . the worse for Beattie's attack?'—Johnson: "He is, because Beattie has confuted him" (*Life*, 5:273–74). For brief discussion and an illustration of Sir Joshua Reynolds's portrait of Beattie and *The Triumph of Truth* (1774) see *Reynolds*, ed. Nicholas Penny (New York: Harry N. Abrams, Inc., 1986), pp. 257–59, and Richard Wendorf, *Sir Joshua Reynolds: The Painter in Society* (London: National Portrait Gallery, 1996), pp. 116–17. Frances Reynolds, Sir Joshua's sister, also painted Beattie's portrait.

20. Fred Parker, *Scepticism and Literature: An Essay on Pope, Hume, Sterne, and Johnson* (Oxford: Oxford University Press, 2003), pp. viii (variousness), pp. 2–3 (strong perceptions); *Rasselas*, p. 255. Subsequent references to this book are cited parenthetically in the text. Parker also cites presumed similarities between Johnson and Hume—as for example, on pp. 16, 23, 244. See also Parker's "The Skepticism of Johnson's *Rasselas*" in *The Cambridge Companion to Samuel Johnson*, ed. Greg Clingham (Cambridge: Cambridge University Press, 1997), pp. 127–42. Skeptical *Rasselas* is another commonplace of recent Johnson criticism, as in Potkay regarding *Rasselas's* "arch inconclusiveness" (p. 198, and see p. 200).

21. Such remarks are in the tradition of Sir John Hawkins's uncomprehending description of Johnson on Scottish culture: "he frequently raises an edifice which appears founded and supported to resist any attack; and then with the next stroke annihilates it, and leaves the vacuity he found." See *The Life of Samuel Johnson LL. D.* (Dublin, 1787), p. 428

22. YE 2, *The Idler and Adventurer*, ed. W. J. Bate, John M. Bullitt, and L. F. Powell (1963), p. 486.

23. The illustration for "colour" is from Watts's *Logick*, pp. 60–61, 1725, though I do not know whether Johnson used that edition. I have not identified the source of "complicate." As usual, Johnson condenses and sometimes changes words from their original citation.

24. For *Rambler*, No. 80, see YE 4:59. See also *Rambler*, No. 191 (1752).

25. See two useful recent germane essays: Paul J. Korshin, "Johnson's Conversation in Boswell's *Life of Johnson*," in *New Light on Boswell*, ed. Greg Clingham (Cambridge:

Cambridge University Press, 1991), pp. 174–93, and Bruce Redford, "Talk into Text: The Shaping of Conversation in Boswell's *Life of Johnson*," in *Eighteenth-Century Contexts: Historical Inquiries in Honor of Phillip Harth*, ed. Howard D. Weinbrot, Peter J. Schakel, and Stephen E. Karian (Madison: University of Wisconsin Press, 2001), pp. 247–64. Redford, for example, well observes: "As a moralist, Johnson was keenly aware of the gap between ideal code and actual conduct; as a practicing critic, he constantly violated, complicated, or undercut his own theoretical pronouncements" (p. 253). See also Isobel Grundy, "Samuel Johnson: Man of Maxims?" in *Samuel Johnson: New Critical Essays*, ed. Isobel Grundy (London: Vision; Totowa, NJ: Barnes and Noble, 1984), pp. 13–30, especially pp. 17–18, 28–29. Johnson's mode of proceeding in the *Rambler* indeed shares conversational flux and complication in part because of its mode of writing. Johnson's conversation with himself proceeds as he completed the second half of the essay while the just-finished first half was being printed. See remarks in *Life*, 1:203 and 3:42, and the *Rambler*, No. 134 (1751). These specific examples, I suggest, nonetheless are typical of Johnson's larger mode of thought.

26. For these references, see YE 4:372; *Lives*, 1:171–79; and YE 5:69.

27. Fussell, *Johnson and the Life of Writing*, p. 163. See also Potkay, *Passion for Happiness*, pp. 212–13.

28. Reynolds, "Recollections of Dr. Johnson by Miss Reynolds," in *Johnsonian Miscellanies*, ed. George Birkbeck Hill (Oxford: Clarendon Press, 1897), 2:287.

29. *The Poems of John Dryden*, ed. James Kinsley (Oxford: Clarendon Press, 1958), 1:395. For Dryden's method of skepticism, see Phillip Harth, *Contexts of Dryden's Thought* (Chicago: University of Chicago Press, 1968), pp. 1–31.

30. For these references, see *Life*, 4:117; YE 10, *The False Alarm* (1770), in *Political Writings*, ed. Donald J. Greene (1977), pp. 327–28 and see also *Idler*, No. 10 (1758); *Life*, 2:170. For further discussion of Johnson's license for political violence, see James G. Basker, " 'The Next Insurrection': Johnson, Race, and Rebellion," in the *Age of Johnson* 11 (2000): 37–51.

31. See *The Life of Richard Savage*, in *Lives*, 2:321; *Idler*, YE 2:15; *Lear*, YE 8, *Johnson on Shakespeare*, ed. Arthur Sherbo (1968), p. 704.

32. We differ from ourselves in *Adventurer*, No. 107 (1753), YE 2:441, 442; *Rasselas*, YE 16:104 (Nekayah), 33 (Imlac). See also Johnson's remark in *The False Alarm*: "Every diffuse and complicated question may be examined by different methods, upon different principles; and that truth, which is easily found by one investigator, may be missed by another, equally honest and equally diligent" (YE 10:325). Parker refers to "the potential discomfort of scepticism" in this *Adventurer* essay (p. 237). Compare Watts's *Logick*:

> When two different Propositions have each a *very strong and cogent Evidence*, and do not plainly appear inconsistent, we may believe both of them, tho' we cannot at present see the Way to reconcile them. *Reason*, as well as our own *Consciousness*, assures us that the *Will of Man is free*, and that *Multitudes of human Actions are in that Respect contingent*; and yet *Reason* and *Scripture* assure us that *God foreknows them all*, and this implies a *necessary Futurity*. Now tho' learned Men have not to this Day hit on any clear and happy Method to reconcile these Propositions, yet since we do not see a *plain Inconsistency* in them, we justly believe them both, because their Evidence is great. (p. 399)

33. For discussion of the *Rambler*, No. 4, as an isolated essay on the novel, see Mark Kinkead-Weekes, "Johnson on 'The Rise of the Novel,'" in Grundy, *Samuel Johnson*, pp. 70, 74, 77–78, 83, and Robert D. Spector, *Samuel Johnson and the Essay* (Westport, CT:

Greenwood Press, 1997), pp. 159–60. Steven Lynn has addressed some of the distortions and violations of sequence that anthologies of Johnson produce. See Lynn, *Samuel Johnson After Deconstruction: Rhetoric and the Rambler* (Carbondale: Southern Illinois University Press, 1992), pp. 4–19. Lynn also summarizes some other arguments on Johnson's apparent skepticism: see pp. 95–96. Students of Johnson should also consult the interesting chapter on Johnson's *Rambler*—as well as others on Swift and Burke—in James Boyd White, *When Words Lose Their Meaning: Constitutions and Reconstructions of Language, Character, and Community* (Chicago: University of Chicago Press, 1984).

III
Afterlife

11

Samuel Johnson, Percival Stockdale, and "Brickbats from Grubstreet": Some Later Response to the *Lives of the Poets*

WHO NOW READS STOCKDALE? WHO THEN READ STOCKDALE? EVEN when associated with Samuel Johnson his name hardly makes the heart leap with happy anticipation. This self-tortured and self-destructive man of letters exemplified the insecurities of the eighteenth-century literary and ecclesiastical marketplace. He also touched the fringes of much exalted intellectual life and was known, among others, to Boswell, Burke, Charles Burney and Fanny Burney, Richard Cumberland, Fox, Garrick, Gibbon, Goldsmith, Hawksworth, Bishop Lowth, Lyttelton, Pitt, Jane Porter, Wilkes and, perhaps most importantly, to Samuel Johnson. Nonetheless, Stockdale dwells in what Ralph Cohen elegantly calls "the realm of silent, or . . . the unhonoured dead."[1] Stockdale's *Lectures on the Truly Eminent English Poets* (1807), his *Memoirs* (1809), and extensive unpublished correspondence are largely untapped sources for the literary historian and historian of reception.[2] They illumine much of Stockdale's varied kinds of anguish and suggest an unwritten chapter in the reputation of Johnson's *Lives of the Poets* (1779–81). A modern student of Johnson rightly says: "almost everyone agrees that the *Lives* represent the permanent value, the *ponere totum*, of eighteenth-century criticism."[3] We need to stress that "almost," for Stockdale and many of his reviewers used the *Lectures* as an opportunity to assess Johnson's *Lives* in his and their own age. That contemporary reaction offers useful lessons in how Johnson and the British poetic canon were perceived from about 1779 to 1809. First, however, we need a brief overview of the life and career of a man unfamiliar even to students of the eighteenth century.

1

Stockdale was born on October 26, 1736, at Brampton in the Northumberland he later would hate. He was the only child of Dorothy Collingwood and Thomas Stockdale, Vicar of Brampton and perpetual Curate of Cornhill. He spent six years in the grammar school at Alnwick and in 1751 moved to the grammar school at Berwick-upon-Tweed. By then Stockdale was proficient in Greek, Latin, and French, had the rudiments of Hebrew, and knew that he could prosper at Oxford or Cambridge—an education, he claimed, denied him by stingy relatives. Instead, in 1754 he was awarded a bursary at the United Colleges of St. Leonard and St. Salvator at St. Andrews, where he engaged in frequent squabbles regarding discipline and religion. His modest resources were further reduced on April 7, 1755, when his father died. Though Stockdale returned to St. Andrews in October his strained finances and psyche competed with his zeal to serve in the Seven Years' War against France: "the vain, and timid CICERO; and the coward HORACE. . . . were quickly overset" by Xenophon and Caesar (*M*, 1:231)—as supplemented by Peter the Great and Charles the XII of Sweden (*M*, 1:241). In February of 1756 he left university and then his home at Berwick to become a second lieutenant in the Royal Welsh Fusiliers, during 1756–57 served on HMS *Revenge*, and was present when the unfortunate Admiral Byng failed to relieve the British garrison in Minorca.

Army life disagreed with Stockdale's generally poor health. After a stint as a recruiting officer in Bigglesworth, Bedfordshire, "I was in so weak a state, that I was hardly able to walk over the floor in my apartment" (*M*, 1:460). In mid-November of 1757 he resigned his commission and, virtually destitute, set out for his mother's home in Berwick. Along the way, he stopped at Durham and accepted the hospitality of Dr. Thomas Sharp, Archdeacon of Northumberland, and his son. He further improved his Greek, Hebrew, and theology, and with the Sharps' urging was ordained deacon on Michaelmas (September 29) 1759. Shortly thereafter he went to London as young Thomas Sharp's substitute in Duke's Place, Aldgate, and promptly threw himself into more literary than theological matters.

From 1762 to 1767 he was a curate in Berwick, again spending more time with books than with parishioners. When this position ended in the summer of 1767 he was without church employment, sailed for Italy, and stayed in Villafranca, two miles east of Nice. He lived there for two years, learning Italian, and Spanish, enjoying the mild Mediterranean climate, and perhaps the favors of his British inamorata, whom he later would marry, abandon, and despise. Upon returning to London in 1769 he lacked church prospects and again continued his zeal for letters. He learned, and disliked, German; he translated Tasso's *Amyntas* (1770); he met Johnson (1770); he edited the *Universal Magazine* (1771); he wrote a life of Waller (1772); he translated Lambert Bos's Latin *Antiquities of Greece* (1772); he published three *Discourses*, his best-known poem *The Poet*, and met Garrick (all in 1773). He refused an offer to instruct the Russian nobility in St. Petersburg (*M*, 2:98), but he accepted the chaplaincy of HMS *Resolution* for three years while living in Portsmouth, the Isle of Wight, and London. He was unhappy with naval life and with those like Mr. Fitzmaurice of the Isle of Wight who "made to me some specious, and important promises which were never fulfilled" (*M*, 2:104).

Whatever Stockdale's diaconal status he remained devoted to the religion of literature and worshipped in Garrick's splendid library of ancient and modern masters. One fruit of his visits was a translation of Sabbathier's *The Institutions of the Ancient Nations* (1776). He also wrote several poems and in a fit of gloom destroyed several manuscripts. As he explains what sounds like clinical depression, "when I have been particularly anxious to write well; I have hardly had any power to go on; I have found it inexpressibly difficult to please myself; and hence I have suffered a kind of mental torture. This was among the principal causes which repeatedly impelled me to abjure all intellectual exertion" (*M*, 2:112).

He nonetheless was happy with another effort that stemmed from reading in Garrick's library. *An Inquiry into the Nature and Genuine Laws of Poetry* (1778) attempted to demolish Joseph Warton's *Essay on the Writing and Genius of Pope* (1756). This brought him some fame, some both friendly and uncertain praise from Johnson (*M*, 2:120–21), and the patronage of Lord George Germain, whose willingness to find Stockdale a place in Jamaica may have had more than one motive.

When in London, Stockdale continued to write and preach against the American war, to seek literary positions and projects, preferment, a warmer climate, and the approbation of great men: "It drives us on, irresistibly, in our progress to glory" (*M*, 2:133). While being so driven he claims nearly to have received the contract for what became Johnson's *Lives of the Poets*, was Reader at Grosvenor Chapel (1778–79), tutor to Lord Craven's son (1779–80), and was awarded the curacy of Hinxworth in Hertfordshire (1780–81).

Stockdale there wrote several sermons and, at the age of forty-five, and twenty–three years after admission to the diaconate, was ordained priest on Trinity Sunday (the eighth Sunday after Easter) in 1781. He was examined by an entrapping chaplain, "one of the most vulgar, conceited, unmannerly pedants, with whom I ever conversed. . . . However,

I sprung out of all his traps; and eluded all his toils; very much, apparently, to his disappointment, and mortification" (M, 2:222).

By the autumn of 1781 Stockdale had returned to London for further literary adventures, some results of which were a treatise on the value of private education (1782) and an *Essay on Misanthropy* (1783). Near the end of November of 1784, he again retreated to Northumberland, when he was awarded the vicarage of Lesbury and the vicarage of Long Houghton, plural livings that required an M.A. The Archbishop of Canterbury consented to this "in a very austere, and repulsive manner" (M, 2:233).

Northumberland was exile for Stockdale, and so with his bishop's permission he engaged curates and returned to the magnetic but unappreciative literary and personal marketplaces of the metropolis and the larger world. His tragedy *Ximines* (1788) was printed but not produced, and Stockdale again faced the disappointment to which he both always and never became accustomed. In the autumn of 1788 he sailed to Gibraltar prior to his anticipated voyage to Tangier to join a friend Mr. Matra, the British consul. Here, Stockdale knew, would be a restorative psychological and secular climate, but when Matra arrived in Gibraltar his "vile, and disgusting" behavior nullified any shared journey (M, 2:252).

Thereafter Stockdale was chaplain to HMS *Leander* in Gibraltar, was offended by the vulgarity of naval life, and agreed to join one Major Grey on a visit to Mr. Logi, the British consul in Algiers. This enterprise also soon ended when they displayed unacceptable "licentiousness, absurdity, and nonsense" (M, 2:260) and mocked Stockdale's virtue. An English widow helped him to better lodgings, where he was visited by several European consuls and learned Portuguese. He sailed for Marseilles in February of 1790, and arrived in London at the end of March.

Between May of 1791 and the summer of 1799 he alternated between London, his principal residence, and Windsor Forest, Surrey, Durham, Monmouth (Wales), and Durham again—ever reading, writing, and ineffectually controlling nervous ailments. He also ever sought the contentment he could briefly find and quickly lose. "The illiberal, and baneful effects of . . . my unbiassed principles, and ingenuous language, [I] now experienced at DURHAM." He leaves there for Lesbury and his vicarage "after an absence from it, of almost twelve years" (M, 2:315).

During these long peregrinations he published *Thirteen Sermons to Seamen*, a *Letter to Granville Sharp* (both 1791) opposing slavery, notes to Thomson's *Seasons* (1793), and numerous other personal, poetical, polemical, and political pieces in praise of animals, his environs, himself, and his nation. He also began the *Lectures on the Truly Eminent English Poets* and wrote numerous letters in search of a better living in glorious Northumberland or an escape from miserable Northumberland. By then, however, he must have known, or feared, that Lesbury would be his final home. His *Lectures* of 1807, his *Memoirs* of 1809, and his *Poetical Works* of 1810 were written and organized from Lesbury and published at his own expense. He died at Lesbury on September 14, 1811—a man of many languages, many professions, many publications, and many disappointments. He nonetheless ended his *Memoirs* by urging young readers to remain studious and virtuous whatever their misfortunes: "In this excellent merit . . . I think that I may without arrogance, or presumption, propose my own conduct as an example for your persevering, and invincible emulation" (*M*, 2:332).

2

This at once painfully varied and consistent life was based as much on Stockdale's overly generous estimate of his needs and talents as on the world's impatience with him. Boswell's friend William Johnson Temple well describes the person Samuel Johnson called "Poor Stockdale."[4] On July 19, 1785, Temple writes to Edward Jerningham and adds some information, or gossip, that Stockdale does not include regarding his visit to Villafranca:

> As to Mr. Stockdale, I have known him long. He is a strange eccentrick character & has been guilty of great indiscretions, & it surprises me how he has fallen in your way. I find he attempts to make atonement for something disrespectful he had rhymed of you in some poem of his. He was first in the army,—then in the Church—engaged to a young Lady, married an old one— The young one prosecuted & recovered damages, which he paid. They then ran away together—to Nice, leaving the woman behind, who went mad & died. The lovers then returned & married & then seperated. For some time he was tutor to Lord Cravens children, but left them in disdain, because her Ladyship would not admit him of her private parties. Mr. Pitt it seems has given him a living which he might have bestowed on as good a man. It seems, he sets a high value on his praise, though he acknowledges it has often been thrown away on unworthy objects. If you offend his sensibility in any respect, & it is very easily offended, he will be as ready to make his retribution respecting yourself. I believe he can hardly mention a friend or benefactor with whom he has not quarrelled for imaginary slights, Dr Thorpe, Dr Johnson & c. He has not yet been able to quarrel with me & I have assisted him

out of some humanity when he was in great distress. But enough of this unhappy man.[5]

Unhappy Stockdale also made his actual and potential patrons unhappy. In 1792, for example, he asks Barrington Shute, Bishop of Durham, to award him yet a third living—Hartburn—in the Northumberland
from which Stockdale fled whenever possible. Bishop Shute says that the
position was filled; Stockdale calls him a liar, insults him and his "clerical *Blifils*," and again insists on the living as atonement for the world's
malice towards him.[6] When such moral suasion fails Stockdale makes
plain that Shute is a poor Christian and bishop who surrendered to the
bad influence of the selfish and despicable advisors around him (p. 42).
Stockdale threatens to publish all this correspondence with appropriate
prefatory matter unless he is immediately granted the living. He concludes by alluding to Shute as Darius at the head of a vast army of Persian slaves, soon to be defeated by Stockdale as Alexander at the head
of a plucky band of heroes (p. 55). Bishop Shute was not moved. The
unsavory event, Temple's letter, and the abstract of Stockdale's life embody certain common denominators in an emotionally painful career.

3

One is Stockdale's complaint of an unspecified "nervous disorder"
that saps his ability to work, to perform apparently nonsexual "manly"
deeds, and to reach his full potential. These ongoing bouts of depression
and perhaps psychosis may partially explain why Johnson sympathized
with him.

A second common trait is a regular but unfulfilled search for advancement and consequent denigration of those above him and those to whom
he was in some way committed. He wished to be a greater man of letters
than the narrow-minded Johnson and a greater bishop than the un-
Christian Bishop of Durham. In 1792 he proudly tells that dignitary: "if
I was a bishop, I should be the most extraordinary phoenomenon that
the world ever saw; I should be, all humility" (p. 42). In his *Memoirs*
he claims that with proper tutelage he "would have been secured, and
worshipped, under the awful protection of a mitre" (*M*, 1:42). Yet he
rarely acknowledges his clerical calling, frequently denigrates the church
and its servants, and on July 13, 1807, tells Jane Porter that he hopes to
live the rest of his life "agreeably to the practice of Jesus Christ (the slav-

ish humility of his doctrine excepted)."[7] The grandeur of expectation extended beyond the grave. His will creates about £2,150 in bequests but, his executor John Palfrey Burrell tells Jane Porter, "there will not be, by a great deal, sufficient to discharge the legacies."[8]

As these remarks suggest, a third strain was his sense of perpetual victimization by an uncomprehending, ever more decadent and malign world. He complains in his *Observations on . . . Our Present . . . Reformers* (1792) that "the annals of literature cannot produce an instance, in which more injustice has been done to the honest interest, and to the honest fame of any authour than to my own."[9] Here too, such negative energy remained vocal in death. He leaves £300 to William Beville "for the elegant publication of my works. . . . though I have been unfortunate and unpopular." He permits expunging but prohibits "substituting any other matter or in any respect adding to the same."[10]

Stockdale had a fourth trait of temperament that no doubt exacerbated his conflict with an ungrateful world: his high sensibility and emotional responses. More particularly, he stresses "the ingenuous nature, and independent habits of my own mind" (*M*, 1:[v]), the "freedom with which I always wish to write" (*M*, 1:[ix]), the "absolute independence of my mind . . . my constitutional, and habitual assertion of all important truth, without any unmanly fear of consequences;—a noble state of the soul" (*M*, 1:x). That independent nobility conflicted with his dependence on others for patronage; it also accounted for his perhaps idiosyncratic mode of address. His *Inquiry into the Nature, and Genuine Laws of Poetry* (1778), for example, is dedicated to Lord George Germain, as he then was, third and youngest son of the Duke of Dorset. In spite of earlier military disgrace Germain in 1778 was both Lord Commissioner of trade and plantations, and Secretary of State for the colonies in the North administration that so vigorously prosecuted the American war. The un-Horatian Stockdale dedicates his *Inquiry* to Lord George only because he admired his father and Germain's own literary talents. His part in Britain's "unconstitutional, sanguinary and destructive continental war, over which *you* preside," however, ruins "your political reputation.—I pay this homage to the polite scholar, and to the orator:—not a particle of my respect is intended for the Minister" (pp. v–vi).

Whether that is dedication or damnation may be left for casuists; but it is consistent with Stockdale's seriatim praise and blame of his sponsor or victim. The unknown, nasty but accurate, perpetrator of *An Humble. . . . Address . . . to P—— S—d—e* (1792) says this regarding Stockdale's violent exchange with the Bishop of Durham:

A bishop thou canst make a God,
Then decompose him to a clod
He yesterday who shone like gold,
To-day's too filthy to behold.[11]

Stockdale was zany but no fool. He was a man of uncommon intellectual diligence and modest but genuine literary talent; but he also combined John Dennis's destructive hostility to others with Richard Savage's destructive hostility to himself. As we recall, like each man, he also knew and was known to many eminent public and private figures. In the *Memoirs*, for example, Stockdale says that he still owns and cherishes letters from Garrick, Lyttelton, Johnson, Lord Thurlow, Burke, and Fox (*M*, 1:xix). Jane Porter sent him the manuscript preface of what becomes her enormously popular *Thaddeus of Warsaw* (1803) to correct.[12] In 1805 she also went from Surrey to Lesbury in Northumberland, prepared his *Memoirs* for the press, and was rewarded by the grateful and amazed old man by having the volumes dedicated to her (*M*, 1:[v]–viii).

Part of this activity and response was the fruit of Stockdale's endless search for allies and patrons in an unreliable world. Part also was genuine or grudging respect for a troubled and troubling but intelligent critic whose diffuse style too often obscured solid perceptions—as in his sympathetic discussion of Swift. The first paragraph below splendidly epitomizes the "hard school" view of *Gulliver's Travels* (1726) during a time when readers were beginning to condemn Swift's apparently insane harshness. The second paragraph splendidly epitomizes Swift's concept of imagination and its relationship to language. Each is from Stockdale's *Essay on Misanthropy* (1783) and each is excellent criticism:

I think the pictures [of the Yahoo's filth] . . . are extremely natural, and have a great moral use. I am, myself, warmly attached to delicate imagination, and taste; but if homely, and coarse representations tend to moderate our inordinate self-love; to humble that monstrous, and ridiculous arrogance which was not made for man; I shall always be ready, not only to bear, but to applaud them. Truth, and virtue, are of infinitely more consequence than false politeness, and refinement. Our Creator hath wisely contrasted our sublime capacities, and endowments, with very opposite, with mean, and miserable qualities, and appendages. Man is, in his animal nature, one of the *filthiest* of beings. And while he is far more odious, by his pride, and insolence, it is the duty of a great moral writer, to exert all the force of genius, to make him, in his own eyes, a mortifying spectacle. (p. 32)

His genius acts with more rapidity and energy [than Addison's]. *His* province is, the exertion, and display, of the more powerful and inventive imagination.

To ridicule folly, or to stigmatize vice, he introduces characters, and machinery of his own creation; characters, however, that are easily applied to those which they are intended to expose; and machinery which plays with a quick, and decisive effect on the human mind. And often, to our most agreeable surprize, and lively pleasure, he unexpectedly, and suddenly, gives a laconic, but high encomium; or he darts a concise, and poignant satire, by a new use, and association of signs, and things; by raising, or sinking a word, from its established rank, and, consequently, by giving it a new import; and by approximating, and uniting ideas, which, before, had always been kept remote from each other. (pp. 33–34)

4

There is another shared trait in Stockdale's ample writings: his mingled reverence and irreverence toward Samuel Johnson, who in ways represented much that Stockdale admired, needed, and feared. In Johnson he found a learned, pious, and powerful man whom he could compliment, to whom he could turn for help, and whose reflected light could nurture his own tender plants. Accordingly, in May of 1771 he publishes a mock funeral elegy on Johnson's cat Hodge.[13] In *The Poet* he quotes lines from the *Life of Savage* (1744) that well illustrate the poet's sad state, "though, I fear, the energy and harmony of their prose, will eclipse the poetry which they are cited to illustrate" (p. 10 n). About a year later he responds to Goldsmith's *Retaliation* (1774) and characterizes literary figures with "some drink":

> To *Johnson*, philosophic sage,
> The Moral *Mentor* of the age,
> Religion's friend, with soul sincere,
> With melting heart, but look austere,
> Give liquor of an honest sort,
> And crown his cup with priestly *Port*![14]

Thereafter, his *Enquiry into . . . the Laws of Poetry* refutes Joseph Warton's strictures on Pope. Stockdale borrows passages from Johnson's *Rambler*, No. 156 (1751), by "my admired, and respected friend . . . who, like a rational, and free Being, 'always thinks for himself,' . . . and whose extensive, and masterly learning" includes ". . . a most acute, and comprehensive judgement" (pp. 39–40). These are "noble strains of original sense, and manly eloquence" (p. 45). He even turned to Johnson for counsel regarding the excesses of wine—which, he tells young

Charles Burney on June 13, 1780, "at D^r. Johnson's advice, I have left
. . . quite off."[15]

So Stockdale could write when Johnson seemed his ally, argument on
authority, and possible patron. Stockdale did not always understand
that protection, as often resented needing it and finding it unsuccessful,
and ended his career giving Johnson and himself grief. Walter Scott records this reaction to Stockdale's *Memoirs*:

> This extraordinary effusion of egotism and vanity should be read by all who
> are visited by the folly of thinking highly of their own productions. I saw Mr.
> Percival Stockdale in London in 1809 or 1810, a thin, vivacious, emaciated
> spectre, fluttering about booksellers' shops, eager to attract attention and be-
> stow praise on the terms on which the Natives of Madagascar give presents:
> "I Salamanca you, you Salamanca me," the word Salamanca . . . signifying
> to bestow a gift. The judgments which this conceited cock-brained fidgetty
> man passes upon the motives and conduct of Bishop Moir [and] Dr. Johnson
> serve to shew that there is no wound festers and rankles so deeply as what is
> inflicted on personal vanity.[16]

The festering wound to which Scott refers probably is Stockdale's presumed role in the genesis of the *Lives of the Poets*. As Stockdale records
in his *Memoirs*, misremembering by two years, in 1779 several of the
major London booksellers decided "to publish a new edition of the english poets" together with "a previous very short account, or epitome of
the life of each poet; and a few general, and comprehensive critical remarks on his writings" (*M*, 2:193). In spite of many enemies and the
friends they preferred, Stockdale's talents and able life of Waller earned
him the consortium's recommendation.[17] Nathaniel Conant and
Thomas Evans offered him the position "in their united names," and
added "that they had very warmly recommended me to that employment" (*M*, 2:194–95). When Stockdale called upon Conant, however,
he was informed that "the preponderating, and imperious weight of
JOHNSON's name" had banished his. Stockdale's protests evoked Conant's insulting proposal that he "make an index to the new edition"
(*M*, 2:195–96). When Stockdale later related this tale to Johnson "The
man who used to be so open, and declamatory; and often so warm, and
violent, in his defence, or censure, even of actions of inferiour consequences, when they were related to him; on *this* occasion, made me no
reply; he was perfectly silent" (*M*, 2:197). Isaac D'Israeli's review of the
Memoirs in the *Quarterly* may explain Johnson's silence on this matter:
"To the needy author he would readily listen; to the importunate mendi-
cant for undeserved fame, he never failed to turn a deaf ear."[18]

Stockdale never forgot this episode. The success of Johnson's *Lives* must have seemed like theft of the fame that Stockdale regarded as his long-delayed birthright. Johnson's "Life of Waller" merely gave "a very transient, and anonymous notice" (*M*, 2:123) of Stockdale's own earlier life of that poet. In spite of Stockdale's "long and rather pathetick letter" (*M*, 2:124) asking Johnson to mention his *Enquiry into . . . the Laws of Poetry*, the "Life of Pope" ignored it entirely.[19] Many of Johnson's judgments and the included poets themselves also were anathema to Stockdale.

Moreover, Johnson's last great effort made him even more popular as a biographical subject, one which treated Stockdale himself as the smallest of bit players. Stockdale may have recognized himself in this remark Boswell records in 1784: "An author of most anxious and restless vanity being mentioned, 'Sir, (said he,) there is not a young sapling upon Parnassus more severely blown about by every wind of criticism than that poor fellow.' "[20] Johnson, Boswell also says, "was, upon many occasions, a kind protector" of Stockdale (*Life*, 2:113). Rubbish, Stockdale complains regarding one who was not the "kind and powerful protector" he could and should have been: "I never received from him any better offices than those of common civility."[21] For Stockdale there seemed to be little reason to honor the memory of so indifferent a friend, whose death, he insists in at least four different places, was un-Christian and unworthy.[22]

Stockdale reserved the bulk of his fire for the *Lives of the Poets*, for him perhaps the ultimate sign of triumphant bigotry. Stockdale's engraving as frontispiece to the *Lectures* uses the words "per fluctus" as a motto. It might as well have been a version of a line from *London* (1738): SLOW RISES WORTH, BY JOHNSON DEPRESS'D.

5

Stockdale's mingled praise and increasing blame of Johnson appears upon his death. On January 22, 1785, Stockdale writes to his attorney Thomas Loggen: "Dr Johnson is no more. As I was a friend to his glory, I wish he had died ten years ago, before he wrote his *Lives of the Poets*, and his political pamphlets. But he was a great and good man; and his death has made a large, melancholy, and irreperable chasm in society. This my generosity, if not my equity, says of him, for he acted very meanly as *my* friend."[23]

Stockdale publishes his grievances toward Johnson at least as early as

1792 in his *Observations on the Writings and Conduct of Our Present Political, and Religious Reformers*. By then Johnson already is Stockdale's inadequately Christian, polite, and moral demon as well as misguided and misguiding literary critic. Stockdale knows that "it will be in my power, hereafter, to convince ENGLAND, that Dr. JOHNSON was one of the most absurd, and injurious of criticks" (p. 19). His judgments of Gray and Fielding were "pompous and imperious" (p. 20n), and though his *Life of Savage* is immortal, his *Lives of the Poets* are the product of "the great man . . . magnified into a literary Giant, by the servile extravagance of capricious, and superficial fancy" (p. 23). As always with Stockdale, the fault is as much the world's as it is Johnson's.

Stockdale suggests that his *Lectures on the Truly Eminent English Poets* already were psychologically in process. More immediately, he probably was referring to his notes in a new edition of Thomson's *Seasons* in 1793.[24] Stockdale there calls Johnson's comments on Thomson absolute nonsense, absurd, arbitrary, dogmatic, futile, rude, ungenerous, and vulgar. He knows that he must suffer for his candor: "through the infatuation of prescription, I foresee the strictures with which I am to be assailed, by the stupidity of prejudice, and by the servility of fashion, and imitation." He will respond "with a calm, and consequently, with a proper contempt" (p. [235]). He concludes his tirade against Johnson by leaguing himself with the maligned dead and by including a phrase to which he would return: "When the present busy, and paltry machinations of interest shall act no more; when the talents of the Departed, and of the Living shall be justly appreciated by posterity; it will be found that *those lives* are a Disgrace to English Literature" (p. [246]).

In March of 1793 Edward Jerningham and George Cumberland, perhaps among others, express their irritation with so severe a remark, which Stockdale also may have repeated in public. On March 30, he writes to Jerningham wondering why he thinks the *Lives of the Poets* include a "profusion of bright, and eminent passages," a "Depth of Inquiry," and an unspecified "mode of critical investigation . . . perfectly new and original." In contrast, Stockdale again characterizes the *Lives* in a phrase he repeats four times, as "a *Disgrace to English Literature*." He hopes that Johnson's unprecedented methods, objections, and preferences "will ever be without adoption, and Imitation."[25]

Nonetheless, Stockdale apparently does not start this effort of wound cleansing until early in 1795, when he begins to chronicle its progress to Jane Porter and others. On January 21st of that year he tells her that he has not yet begun; on March 8th he still lacks "strength of mind enough to proceed in a very important work." By May 13th he complains about the arduous task and his mind's "terrible breaks," but has finished his introductory lecture "and my view of *Spenser*." He makes little progress that summer, but by December 4th completes Shakespeare and much of Milton, whose sublimity inspires him: "My literary ambition is, again, all alive," and he hopes that his lectures will allow him "to defeat . . . Time, Malice, & Persecution."[26] By December 14th he has finished Spenser, Shakespeare, and Milton and, in preparing for his anticipated public performance, comically mislead his servant Molly: "She has lately heard me in my soliloquies, often recite the names of *Johnson*, and *Milton*; she asked me if they were the men who near London not very long ago, fought a great Boxing-match." By February 20, 1796, he has almost finished reading Dryden, and is almost half finished with the lectures, which "will evidently produce me both Emolument, and Fame." By August 12, 1796, he has finished Dryden; by December 27, 1796, an unusual combination of "Serenity and Strength of mind" allows him to finish Pope and look forward to Young, Thomson, and Chatterton; and by August 27, 1797, he has finished Thomson.[27]

By then, however, he abandons his plans for public recitation. As he tells Edward Jerningham on June 22, 1801, "the world is not prepared generously to receive my lectures." Nonetheless, by February 2, 1802, he finally has finished Chatterton, and by July 1st of that year he is working on Gray and is ever more angry at Johnson's treatment of Gray, of Milton, and by implication of Stockdale. On July 1, 1802, the Reverend Mr. Stockdale uses theological language regarding this matter. He complains to Jane Porter that Johnson was consciously profane, depraved, sinful, and criminal regarding Milton. Worse, all this has been applauded, while his own defenses of Milton have been calumniated. Clearly, Dame Fashion "smiled on Johnson, with all his repulsive qualities:—I was, unfortunately always the object of her frowns." He wrote "independently, and in defence of political and religious freedom; [Johnson] has always been a champion for enormous power regal and ecclesiastical."[28] Stockdale makes comparable complaints regarding mistreatment of Gray to George Cumberland on August 10th, to Jane Porter on August 11th regarding Milton, and again on October 25th regarding Gray. He soon has finished his lecture and "vindication of Gray from Dr. Johnson's illiberal and absurd" criticism.[29]

Stockdale gradually completes all the lectures. By February 24, 1807, his friend William Beville takes charge of them and helps to see them through what Stockdale thought maliciously long delays in publication. By September 9th Beville assures Stockdale that the lectures will bring him fame. Their Preface is dated February 3, 1807, and the title page is dated 1807. The two octavo volumes, though, apparently do not appear until early in 1808, at an expensive one guinea for the two volumes in boards.[30]

Their 1,284 pages consist of lectures on Milton (2), Dryden (3), Pope (2), Young (2), Thomson, Chatterton (6), and Gray (2). The *Lectures* include interesting and sometimes important insights regarding eighteenth-century literary history. Here, for example, is a small part of a lecture on Milton when Stockdale is cogent, perceptive, energetic, and sympathetic to a subject that deeply moves him. He emphasizes divinity, morality, nature, and perhaps above all the reader's reaction to the poet's own mind that becomes an end in itself.

"No book, of human composition," he says, "is so well calculated as the Paradise Lost, to strengthen, refine, and elevate the mind; to raise it beyond the view of inferiour, and sordid objects. Religion and nature co-operate, while we read this authour, to make us spurn every selfish, and low passion; to make us assert the divine origin of the soul." Moreover, by communing with Milton "our mental powers, and affections are purified, and exalted, to their highest degree of sentiment, by . . . their communication, and contract with a great mind." Accordingly, "the productions of his genius dilate, and sublimate our souls with collateral ideas." We "leave all earthly dross behind us" as we survey his elevated natural and supernatural characters (1:156–57). Travelling with him enlarges our sentiments. "Our morality, and religion expand, with our excursions; we deem nothing so diminutive as human pride; indeed, this 'great globe itself, and all who inhabit it,' seem but specks on the creation. If such effects are produced by a great poet, in the mind of the reader, I will not, with other criticks, elaborately endeavour to find a moral in Milton" (1:158).

Stockdale also uses the reader's response to distinguish between Dryden and Pope. One reason that he prefers Pope is his greater ability to use poetic technique to move the reader: "He takes our hearts with a charming ambush; . . . he assails us with sentiments; with images; in firm, and splendid array" (1:412). These and comparable remarks are worth knowing for themselves and for one explanation of Stockdale's hostility to Johnson—namely, his prejudices seemed to inhibit his response to great poetry.

The *Lectures*, indeed, immediately announce their protagonist and antagonist. Stockdale places these lines on the title page of each volume:

> Johnson, with admiration oft I see
> The Critick and the Bard conjoined in thee;

> But prejudices, too, as oft I find,
> Corrupt, debase, mislead thy noble mind.
> Hence, against thee, I seize the cause of truth;
> A cause that I adored, from early youth.
> Oh! may her voice inspire my latest breath!
> And soothe reflexion in the hour death!

Stockdale's Preface continues the confrontation and the reasons for Johnson's critical inadequacy. These long-delayed lectures ignore the genesis of Johnson's *Lives* as the booksellers' commercial project. Hence, Stockdale deals with the *truly* eminent because "amongst the Poets of Dr. Johnson, there are names which have not the least pretensions to eminence" (1:ix, in italics). Others who should be there are not—like Chatterton. As Stockdale so often makes plain, Johnson mauls even those authors he considers. Such tyranny is to be expected from "our great literary dictator" (1:101), and "our great cavalier" (1:164). Stockdale demonizes Johnson's life and his *Lives of the Poets*—a work Britain has oddly glorified. Given Johnson's brutal treatment of Milton and others, Stockdale is surprised "that even the heavy tyranny of prejudice, combined with the coquettish tyranny of fashion, could have raised this biographer to the rank of a poetical law-giver, in a free and enlightened country" (1:164). As for Johnson the man, he "lived, in some respects, in a total moral ignorance of himself: and such a person is, on several occasions, merely a grown child; spoiled by himself, and by the flattery of others; and, therefore, very apt to lose all sight of temper, and justice, to those who, unfortunately, will not submit to *his* prejudices and humours" (1:226–27).

Such a man's influence must be resisted and reversed. Stockdale anoints himself as guardian of the British poetic tradition in general, and of its maligned heroes Milton and Gray in particular. One of Stockdale's normal modes of proceeding regarding the poets Johnson treated is to quote part of Johnson's commentary, analyze and attack each concept, and sing the poet's virtues. Here, briefly, is Stockdale on Johnson on Gray on Dryden in "The Progress of Poesy": "We are . . . told that 'the car of Dryden has nothing peculiar; it is a car, in which any other rider may be placed.'—This is, again, an instance of unjust, and impotent cavil; of unmeaning petulance. The car of Dryden moved with an accurate succeeding propriety, after 'the seraph wing of ecstasy' on which *Milton* 'rode'" (2:588).

Stockdale clearly preferred Juvenalian rage to Horatian ridicule. Merely in "Gray" alone, he often repeated words like these to characterize Johnson the man or critic: absurd, arbitrary, captious, cavilling, contemptible, desperate, despicable, dictatorial, disingenuous, distorting, dogmatic, envious, flimsy, imbecilic, incoherent, insolent, mutilating, nauseous, nonsensical, oppressive, precipitate, preposterous, ridiculous, rude, sacrilegious, sophistical, superficial, tainted, trifling, unjust, unreflecting, unworthy, and wanton. The list is selective. The last word in the book is "contempt" (2:656).

I have suggested some reasons for this parade of anger: Stockdale's own unstable psyche, his nervous ailments that induce paranoia, and his severe reaction to Johnson's apparent complicity or acquiescence in the theft of Stockdale's own projected lives of his own poets. As a man and as a man of letters on the fringe, Stockdale also sympathizes with others, like Milton and Gray, unfairly maligned by the dictator trying to impose his wrongheaded view and harm injured virtue. So wicked an activity is un-Williamite revolutionary, un-British, and un-Hanoverian. Stockdale resurrects the myth of Johnson's Jacobitism to argue that he is not a fit critical model for a free nation. Johnson hated Gray and other great men and freedom-loving poets and designed their destruction:

> He might hate them for their manly enthusiasm for William, and the revolution, while he sighed over the ruins of the Stuart race, or, with a feverish, and wild ambition, he might aspire to a perfect originality in criticism; he might aspire to give new laws for poetical composition, which were totally of his own invention; laws, which were at war with the essence, and genuine ornaments of poetry; and which, therefore, could only be adopted by the extreme weakness of passive obedience to a despotick master. The *new* poetical reign commenced with the sacrifice of a splendid victim selected from the *old*, and *Gray* was immolated at the inauguration of *Johnson*.
>
> I should impartially, and sincerely suppose that nothing less than the combined force of all the sinister, and baleful causes which I have now mentioned, could have impelled our celebrated, but most illiberal critick to such a fastidious, and irrational contempt of the long-established constituents of a divine art, as they were founded in nature. (2:549–50)

As this and earlier quotations suggest, Stockdale and Johnson were committed to different approaches to literary criticism. Like too many critics of too many generations, Stockdale did not see that asking different questions of a work means receiving different answers. He and Johnson work in parallel not competing planes. For Stockdale, Johnson's destructive standards nonetheless are politically and morally inferior and debase the main reason one reads. Aggressive response to emotionally aggressive poetry is all: "The poet, at once, attacks the source of our generous affections; he seizes your heart; he ravishes you into virtue; and from time to time; by the repetition of his enchanting strains, he keeps up your sublime emotions. Noble, and pathetick poems, like those of Gray, evidently written to meliorate, and refine our nature; are the heavenly panaceas of the soul" (2:637–38).

Much to Stockdale's dismay, his reviewers were willing to accept plural questions and answers, but generally were unwilling to regard Johnson as an incompetent wretch, Jacobite scourge, and Grand Inquisitor. They therefore also were unwilling to accept Stockdale's urgent hopes that this last great original effort would bring him the "literary immortality" and "rays of . . . orient lustre [to] warm, and animate my languid frame before it descends to the tomb" (1:x, in italics). Oblivion is a cold and friendless place.

6

Publication merely energizes anxiety. Stockdale was characteristically optimistic and pessimistic when the *Lectures* appeared. He received a ringing endorsement from Edward Jernigham, whose reaction to the Chatterton lectures overwhelmed him with delight. He tells Stockdale that he has been "moulded, heated, and purified in the focus of your own genius."[31] On February 24, 1808, he thanks George Cumberland for his "high approbation of my *Lectures*." He paid over £400, later amended to over £500, to print one thousand copies and has "written ardently to all my London-friends to push the circulation . . . as much as possible. . . . but I fear that the sale is as yet inconsiderable." On April 1st he again writes from Lesbury asking Cumberland in Bristol about sales there, in Clifton, and in Bath: "pray inform me in what manner they converse about it."[32] On April 27th he drafts a letter, to remain unpublished, asking Bristol's admirers of Chatterton to buy "the remaining copies" of his *Lectures*. Few purchasers were willing to pay a guinea to flatter Chatterton's shade. Perhaps in June Stockdale in London tells Cumberland that "Only 110 of my Lectures are sold" and that "I never will again publish at my own expense."[33]

By then reviews had not been heartening. On April 1, 1808, he complains to Cumberland that "The Critical review is contemptible; equally so is the *eclectick* published on March 11th:—it is written as I apprehend, by some little vindictive priest; & . . . abounds with such low, vulgar, ridicule, and servility that I think it will rather befriend than hurt me" by exciting "curiosity to buy my book." His own curiosity remains high regarding the imminent appearance of the *Monthly Review* and the *British Critic*: "Tell me the substance of what they say of me, if I am in them.—I expect from the Edinburgh review, ignorance, impertinence, and insolence." All such folk are "a set of superficial, presumptuous coxcombs."[34] On June 6th he tells Edward Jerningham that the *Edinburgh* reviewers indeed "treated me in their usually infamous manner," and that most of the booksellers "conspire against me." On July 20th he complains bitterly to Jane Porter that the June *Universal Magazine* had "abused and misquoted" his lectures, and that the reviewer "may be prosecuted for a libel, as he endeavoured to stab my moral character, with regard to my treatment of Dr. Johnson."[35] That treatment indeed was educational for poor Stockdale and, in a different way, for modern readers.

Johnson's active presence in the *Lectures* predicts his active presence in its reviews. Collectively, these offer a small index of Johnson's early nineteenth-century reputation as a critic. They are especially valuable since they ignore Boswell's conversational Johnson and focus on the literary criticism itself.

One response was to praise Stockdale for bravely scolding an over-rated absolute monarch in the kingdom of letters. John Foster in the *Eclectic Review*, for example, "often wished to see the great literary tyrant deposed" (4 [1808]:221). The *Critical*'s review is kind to Stockdale largely because he champions "traduced character . . . against the great dictator in English poesy, wherever his severity preponderates over his justice," as it does too often in the bigoted and partial *Lives of the Poets* (3rd series, 13 [1808]:143). Johnson's dismissal of the young woman's suicide in Pope's *Elegy to the Memory of an Unfortunate Lady* is a sign of barbarous, cruel, disgraceful, imbecile, and hard-hearted criticism that disgraces human nature (13:146). The sympathetic *Gentleman's Magazine*, praises the *Lectures*' "Energy, acuteness, sagacity, and . . . CANDOUR, . . . especially in opposition to our always great, but occasionally UNcandid Dr. Johnson." Stockdale is "the knight errant and champion of insulted Genius" who rescues poets "from the shackling hypercriticism of great and imposing names" (78, part 1 [1808]:324, 325).

Some recognized Johnson's fallibility but quarreled with Stockdale's abuse of one who deserved better. The *Monthly*'s reviewers lamented Stockdale's hanging-judge "furious accusations" against Johnson. His "code of national taste" may indeed be reconsidered, "but to direct against it a series of coarse attacks, distinguished both by violence and levity," harms literary interests and "the reverence . . . we owe to the manes of the illustrious dead."[36] As the *Eclectic*'s reviewer accurately puts it, "the name of Johnson . . . is sure to send him off in a violent invective against the bigotry, the spleen, the prejudice, the want of taste, and the illiberality of the great critic" (4 [1808]: 222–23). The *Universal Magazine* was harshest of all. Its reviewer neither had heard of Stockdale nor wished to hear of him again: "There is more literary coxcombry in these volumes than in any work we ever read" (n.s. 9 [1808]: 511). The *Universal* recognizes that Johnson probably is wrong in certain judgments (9:511, 513), but resents Stockdale's violation of Johnson's early friendship for him, and malicious pestering of a "lion" (9:511) who stands on a "proud eminence" (9:513). The *Universal* is blunt regarding Stockdale's misrepresentation of Johnson on book 6 of *Paradise Lost*: "We were absolutely shocked . . . and even now turn from it with abhorrence" (9:513).

In ways, Stockdale's attack on Johnson was self-defeating, for as the reviewers demonstrate, the *Lectures* helped to keep the *Lives of the Poets* before the public. The extremely kind *Annual Review* transmutes Stockdale's vitriol into nationalist balm: "to scatter through a wide circle the charms of [the *Lives*'] eloquence and the discriminations of their criticism, was to serve the cause of taste, of patriotism, and of fame" (6 [1808]:654). This apparently nonironic line is balanced by the *Edinburgh Review*'s observation, by Thomas Campbell, regarding the juxtaposition of Johnson's criticism and Stockdale's attack in the lecture on Pope. Stockdale is "entitled to the same sort of gratitude which we feel to a dull landlord who has invited us to dine with an interesting visitor. In fact, after the one has bewildered us, the other puts us right."[37]

Like others, the *Monthly* recognizes changing literary tastes and critical methods. Johnson's mingled formal and moral standards were well sprinkled with severe judgments. The *Monthly*'s Farrier knows that "every reader of poetical feeling has . . . defended [Gray] as often as he has perused 'The Lives of the Poets'" (59:147–48). Johnson was "rather sagacious than delicate; his criticisms demonstrate more good sense than feeling; and his preference of Blackmore is scarcely consistent with true poetic taste" (59:138). The *British Critic* puts the case bluntly: "The name of Johnson retains the just and high veneration which belongs to it, and which Mr. Stockdale himself supports, while his literary and other prejudices are known, acknowledged, and given up" (33 [1809]: 514). Sagacity and judgment surrender to delicacy and taste. Stockdale was not generously endowed with either set of norms; he did tap the wells of feeling, sensibility, and response to sublime poets rather than to formal wholes. As the perplexed *Eclectic Review* observes of Stockdale's style that mirrors his taste, "For epithets and enthusiasm, Longinus was a Scotch metaphysician in comparison" (4:224).

The *Eclectic* joins the *Monthly* in another important reaction to the *Lectures*, one implied by several remarks already quoted. Johnson is a virtual revered Ancient who has established and analyzed a national canon. However limited and of course in flux that canon was, Johnson set a standard his successors must consider and respect before emending. The *Eclectic* is sternly aware of "the wrongs which we all acknowledge to have been done by our celebrated biographer." Several of the lives offend as "a perpetual warning against the perversion of criticism and private history by political and religious bigotry and personal spleen." Nonetheless, the force of Johnson's mind and prose have so imposed themselves on literary history that "it is always Johnson's moral picture of Milton, and Johnson's estimate of the poetry of Gray, that are the first to recur to our minds when the names are introduced." Even after reading Stockdale, "Each of the poets will hold exactly the same place in the public, and in each reader's estimation as before" (4:221–22). The *Monthly*, with similar remarks from the *Edinburgh* (12:76), reinforces the view of Johnson's *Lives of the Poets* as, to repeat its term, a "code of national taste." Johnson has "forced a standard of public opinion, which, though contested on some points, acquires additional authority from its duration." Moreover, the *Lives* are so valuable as comments on "Man as well as on books, and they convey such a mass of information under an agreeable form, that they are justly intitled to the pre-eminence which they have acquired in our literature; and their dictates, if not always to be implicitly followed, ought surely to be questioned with calm and respectful consideration" (59:138).[38]

As these last remarks suggest, the *Lectures* and their reviews also allow some excellent early nineteenth-century commentators to review the national poetic canon, and in the case of the *Edinburgh*'s Thomas Campbell, reviewed by one who also was a poet familiar with the immediate literary landscape. Specifically, the *Edinburgh* believes that Stockdale is correct to include Spenser, for Johnson's view of the British canon is faulty. The metaphysical poets "were unworthy to stand in Johnson's list as the only surviving predecessors of Milton" (12:63). Other remarks are not consistent with the "Romantic" mythology dear to advocates of periodization and others keen to simplify the complexities of literary history. By 1808 *Lyrical Ballads* had been familiar for a decade; Wordsworth's first collected *Poems* had been out for a year; Coleridge's *Poems on Various Subjects* had seen three editions; between 1806 and 1808 Byron also issued four individual or collected poems. Yet none of

Stockdale's reviewers mentions "Romantic" poets as in any way changing the canon. In contrast, the *Edinburgh* is so persuaded by Dryden's
varied greatness that it is willing to "perhaps rank him in merit the
fourth after Spencer, Shakespeare and Milton, of English poets" (12:71).
Whatever the rankings, reviewers of the *Lectures* agree that no one can
either infallibly canonize one's contemporaries or predict the future.
Stockdale properly reclaims Gray but, the *Annual* says, the "no less popular names of Goldsmith and of Cowper were not yet the heirs of immortality," and Young's "rank in literature is still unsettled" (6:657,
655). As for estimations of the recent canon itself, the *Edinburgh* adds,
"the merits of poets are to be debated on their own grounds, not *merely*
on the critical authorities for or against them" (12:68). By 1808, Stockdale's setting of his authority against Johnson's authority was not an acceptable mode of proceeding. We should hardly be surprised that young
Wordsworth had even less authority in such a contest.

7

Many of these reviews were hard blows to Stockdale's lingering hopes
for immortality, hopes again bruised when his *Memoirs* appeared with
less than universal approbation some two years later.[39] Nonetheless,
these and of course the *Lectures on the Truly Eminent English Poets*
offer helpful and perhaps valuable lessons regarding modern study of
later eighteenth- and earlier nineteenth-century literary history.

For example, Stockdale's *Lectures* explicitly and violently engage the
eighteenth-century's best literary critic and historian. They are unattrac-
tive, and given Stockdale's own psychological pain, often unpleasant to
read; but these are not reasons enough to exile them from fruitful discussion of literary standards and of Johnson's posthumous reputation. The
Lectures also are supported by numerous manuscript letters that characterize their progress and the difficult internal, literary, and human life
of this angry reluctant supplicant. Indeed, reading Stockdale's letters to
Edward Jerningham at the Huntington Library, and his letters to Jane
Porter at the Houghton Library offer fascinating differences: in one a
man deals with a well-connected middle-aged man; in the other he deals
with a well-connected younger woman. The contrast, and Jane Porter's
moving and patient dealings with Stockdale, say much about the relations between the sexes in the eighteenth century. Any notion that scholarly work regarding a major figure like Johnson need go over the same
materials wants reconsideration. One also hopes at least for the begin-

nings of study of Jane Porter, an immensely popular and internationally acclaimed novelist in her time, and at least as important as many other women of letters now being so well studied.

Stockdale's *Lectures* and response to them also say much about Johnson as distinct from Boswell's Johnson. If the *Life of Johnson* had never appeared, the *Lives of the Poets* of course still would have been a major document in the history of canon formation, the history of national taste, and the development of serious literary standards for judgment, analysis, and biographical criticism. By some sixteen years after Johnson's death, he remained a critical icon and national treasure. Given the characteristic independence of contemporary British thought, that meant neither idolatry nor iconoclasm; it did mean a license for enlightened disagreement about enlightened issues in which, metaphorically, each side regarded the other with respect in a debate concerning the nation's interest.

Nonetheless, literary standards changed literary judgments. Stockdale's emotional response, sensibility, and sublimity are excessive; but these gradually were evolving into norms that demanded equal consideration with aesthetic, formal, and moral standards. Johnson helped to establish a canon that his heirs could borrow, build on, and sell; but his critical standards were becoming options rather than requirements.

Reading the reviews also immerses one in a golden age of serious literary reviewing. Each is the product of a thoughtful consideration of Stockdale, of Johnson, and of a richly complex literary inheritance. In some cases one also is rewarded with gems that encapsulate a poet's traits, as Thomas Campbell does in the *Edinburgh*: "When Thomson sacrifices a thought to false taste, he only dresses the victim in flowers, and leads it on procession. Young butchers it outright, and dissects it on the altar" (12:81).

Reading about Stockdale and Johnson also teaches us about the perceptive within the dim. As the *Edinburgh* puts it, "there is much matter in these lectures of a general and imperishable interest" (12:63). Finally, such reading teaches us about humanity—Johnson's in trying to help so difficult a man, and our own in trying to read and understand so difficult a man. He was, after all, suffering enormously in body, ego, and mind. His amiable correspondent Jane Porter moved to distant Lesbury to help organize his *Memoirs* and, temporarily, comfort his final years. She also wrote his affectionate and elegant biographical eulogy for the *Gentleman's Magazine*, urged understanding of his "constitutional nervous irritation" and the unintended insults that consequently produced. She concludes with a useful lesson for our consideration of Johnson as well as Stockdale in each man's frequently troubling conduct: "hard, and cold must be the heart, by whom it will ever be remembered, but with pity, regret, and the spirit of reconciliation."[40]

APPENDIX: SAMUEL JOHNSON AS
"A DISGRACE TO ENGLISH LITERATURE"
PERCIVAL STOCKDALE TO EDWARD JERNINGHAM,
MARCH 30, 1793: HEH JE 832

Saturday—Morning:
March 30th 1793

Dear Sir,

I am much obliged to you for your Letter of yesterday. If the weather is tolerable, on Tuesday, I shall, on *that* day, breakfast with you: if *not*, I hope to breakfast with you on Wednesday.

You always favour me by giving me *your* observations on my productions: your Criticisms seem to me always just when they are unmingled, and unbiassed with the unthinking sentiments of others;—and notwithstanding the hue, and cry that is against me, from *the great vulgar, and the small*, you are always ready generously to give to my Talents far more Consequence than they deserve. I shall submit a few Propositions to your Consideration ere we meet.

I have publicly asserted that Johnson's Lives of the English Poets would, by Posterity, be deemed "a Disgrace to English Literature."—I shall expect that award from the Impartiality and Justice of Posterity. No unprejudiced, and liberal mind will be *irritated*, or *indignant* at the Language of my assertion; for no *such mind* will find fault with a Man for differing from him, on literary Subjects, in mere Matter of opinion: for that the obnoxious Expression proceeds only from an ingenuous Explicitness, not from spleen and malignity, is evident, to demonstration, from the warm, and high praises which I am always ready to give to Merit of which I am convinced, and from all that I have written concerning D[r]. Johnson, in the notes in Question. I repeat it; his mind was extremely defective in Taste; when he wrote the Lives of the Poets, his Faculties were extremely on the Decline; his arrogance had arisen to an insufferable pitch; his high-church and rank Tory-Principles and Prejudices contaminated most of his Criticisms; what, then, were we to expect from him but such Lives as would, in fact be a *Disgrace to English Literature*? To Milton, both as a Man, and a Poet, he is often grossly unjust;—he treats Pope's Essay on Man with unqualified, and sovereign Contempt, though its *Poetry* is beautiful;—he insults the memory of Hammond, of Swift, of Akenside, of Gray;—and I have said that his Lives of the English Poets would, in proper Time, be found to be a *Disgrace to English Literature.*—

All the world know that both in his Conversation and in his writings, he promulged his observations, his opinions, and his Censures, in the most magisterial, and overbearing manner; all the world know that he had the audacity to pronounce Gray a heavy Fellow, and Fielding a Blockhead;—therefore, instead of irritating, or exciting Indignation, I should, at least have been candidly forgiven for expressing myself with some Severity against this most ungentlemanlike Dogmatist, if I had not, myself, been unfortunate and unpopular.

I am far from asserting, or thinking, that Johnson's Lives of the Poets are without eminent Merit, otherwise I should not have said that, on the whole, *they were a Disgrace to English Literature*; for if they had not had the features, though weakened, and mutilated, of a great Master, they would not have met the Eye of our remoter Posterity. As to "the Profusion of bright, and eminent Passages," which, in those Lives *you* have met with; as to the "Depth of Inquiry," which you have found there, I must attribute it to my want of Perspicacity, that they have not come under *my* observation. I quite agree with you that his "mode of critical Investigation is perfectly new, and original:"—for the Preferences which he gives, and the Causes of those Preferences; the Sources of his praises, and of the absurdity of his objections, and Condemnations, are without Example; and I hope, they will ever be without adoption, and Imitation.

I know that the Booksellers did not limit him in his Choice or classing of our English Poets; I never thought that Churchill deserved half of the Praise which was lavished on him by the fever of the Times—Smart was careless, unfortunate, poor;—but he was intimately acquainted with Johnson; and what is of more Consequence, he was a true poet; so, unquestionably, was Churchill: —therefore, with a shameful partiality, and with an unfeeling negligence, to exclude *these* two men from our Parnassus, and to drag up either a Yalden, a Pomfret, and a Watts, was a *Disgrace to English Literature.*

I do not think that I shall ever alter the word *Disgrace*; for two Reasons; because I think it properly applied; —and because, from the Publick, I should not, for my Condescension, meet with any analogous Return. They are already, I hope, in my Debt; and I do not feel myself disposed (I should be a mean wretch if I *did*) to increase the Score against

Them. As to the Number of my Literary Adversaries; a reasonable re-sentment, in a mind of any Generosity, may, by proper Expiations, be appeased: groundless, and acrimonious Prejudices are immoveable and implacable.—As I calmly wish, both as an Author, and a Man, for the approbation, and, the Esteem of the Ingenuous, and the Good, it is di-rectly in the Province of a Gentleman who professes a Regard for me, to show to *such* persons this artless, and unpremeditated Defence of an Expression which I have applied, and I think with most unequivocal Jus-tice, to one who brutally misapplied still heavier Language to characters, undoubtedly the most illustrious. I pray, keep this Letter for me; I have no Copy of it.—The War-hoop is not raised from any Zeal for the Mem-ory of *Samuel Johnson*, but from a charming Quality in our Species, to whom it is a Luxury *to oppress the oppressed. à la Lanterne* is the Senti-ment, if not the Parole; because the object is your sincere, and most obe-dient Servant,

Percival Stockdale

N. B. I do not wonder that Mr. C——is particularly irritated; I am sorry to know that we totally differ on many material Subjects: he owes *me* however more tenderness than he owes the memory of Johnson.

NOTES

I performed the manuscript research for this essay at the Huntington Library, the Houghton Library, the British Library, the Osborn Collection of the Beinecke Library, the Hyde Collection of Four Oaks Farm as made available by the Viscountess Eccles on microfilm at Princeton University's department of Special Collections, and the Bodleian Library. I express continuing gratitude to all those generous libraries and individuals for permission to use and to quote from their manuscripts. In so quoting, as with Stockdale's sometimes unusual capitalization and punctuation, I have avoided *sic* and allowed him his eccentricities. I also thank my then Research Assistant Mr. Matthew Kinservik for his help. Part of the essay's title is borrowed from Stockdale's letter of February 20, 1796, to Jane Porter: "I have been too often pelted with Brick-bats, from Grubstreet, to be morti-fied with its Hostilities": (Houghton, bMS Eng. 1250 [19]).

1. Cohen, *The Art of Discrimination: Thomson's "The Seasons" and the Language of Criticism* (Berkeley and Los Angeles: University of California Press, 1964), p. 9.

2. *Memoirs of the Life and Writings of Percival Stockdale; Containing Many Inter-esting Anecdotes of the Illustrious Men with Whom He was Connected. Written by Him-self* (London, 1809). Quotations from this two-volume work will be cited parenthetically in the text, preceded by *M*.

The *Lectures* and the *Memoirs* also should interest the historian of the canon. As one example of the importance of the apparently minor, see Robert W. Uphaus, "Vicesimus

Knox and the Canon of Eighteenth-Century Literature," *Age of Johnson* 4 (1991): 345–61. Thomas F. Bonnell is completing a long study, parts of which have appeared as "Bookselling and Canon-Making: The Trade Rivalry over the English Poets, 1776–1783," *Studies in Eighteenth-Century Culture* 19 (1989): 53–69, and "John Bell's *Poets of Great Britain*: The 'Little Trifling Edition' Revisited," *Modern Philology* 85 (1987): 128–52.

3. Lawrence Lipking, *The Ordering of the Arts in Eighteenth-Century England* (Princeton: Princeton University Press, 1970), p. 405. Lipking discusses Stockdale on pp. 465–70. Stockdale has had few students other than Cohen and Lipking. Pride of place goes to the excellent pioneering work of the late Philip Daghlian, "Percival Stockdale (1736–1811): A Biographical and Critical Study," unpublished doctoral dissertation, Yale University 1941. Professor Daghlian, however, did not have benefit of the Huntington, Houghton, or Osborn manuscript collections. I gratefully acknowledge his dissertation as the source of some of the obscure printed sources regarding Stockdale. See also John Hardy, "Stockdale's Defense of Pope," *Review of English Studies* n.s. 18 (1967): 49–54, and Thomas F. Bonnell, "The Historical Context of Johnson's *Lives of the Poets*: Rival Collections of English Poetry 1777–1810," unpublished doctoral dissertation, University of Chicago, 1983, pp. 19–26.

4. *The Letters of Samuel Johnson*, ed. Bruce Redford (Princeton: Princeton University Press, 1992), 3:291, to Hester Thrale. This concerns Stockdale's resignation from Lord Craven's patronage and inability to accept Lord George Germain's patronage for an ecclesiastical position in Jamaica.

5. Henry E. Huntington Library manuscript JE 931; cited hereafter as HEH. Temple's brief discussion of Stockdale's tortured relationship with his wife can be supplemented by two other HEH letters to Jernigham, JE 807, November 7, 1785, and JE 811, January 19, 1786. See also other Stockdale letters: October 16, 1773, to John Wilkes, British Library Additional Manuscript 30,871, f. 199, cited hereafter as BL, Add. MS; August 12, 1796, to Jane Porter, Houghton Library bMS Eng. 1250 (22), cited hereafter as HL; January 31, 1780 to Charles Burney, Beinecke Library, Osborn Shelves C6 H240[1]. For relevant printed sources, see John Cranford Hodgson, ed., *Publication of the Surtees Society* 118 (1910): 266–67; Hodgson, "Percival Stockdale, Sometime Vicar of Lesbury," *History of the Berwickshire Naturalist's Club* 24 (1923): 391, 397–99. Stockdale was happiest when he thought his wife dead and was shocked when she reappeared and invaded his "asylum." He bought her exclusion from his home with a £50 per year allowance. His letters to Jane Porter are paternal and pedagogical, sometimes mingled with the incipiently erotic. Perhaps, though, his true attitude towards women, and his religious role, is expressed in a letter to Edward Jerningham on May 31, 1790: "I want only ten Thousand Pounds, and a fine woman, to be far happier than any Prelate, or Prince in Europe": HEH, JE 822.

6. *Letters Between the Honourable, and Right Reverend Father in God, [Barrington] Shute . . . and Percival Stockdale: A Correspondence Interesting to Every Lover of Literature, Freedom, and Religion* (London, 1792), p. 24. Subsequent references are cited in the text.

7. HL, bMS Eng. 1250 (87). Stockdale approves of Christianity, but generally disapproves of its institutions and its priests when they limit his ambitions.

8. HL, bMS Eng. 1250 (106), with a manuscript copy of Stockdale's will, dated from Lesbury, May 5, 1807.

9. *Observations on the Writings and Conduct of Our Present Political, and Religious*

Reformers. . . . To which is Added, An Appendix, on the Literary . . . Character of the Critical Review (London, 1792), pp. 17–18. Subsequent references will be cited in the text.

10. HL, bMS Eng. 1250 (106).

11. *An Humble, Introductory, Prefatory, Adulatory, Consolatory, Admonitory, Epistolary, Address Indeed! To P——S—d—e, A Very Pious and Meek Divine Truly!!!* (London, 1792), p. 10. The author scolds Stockdale for being ungrateful, indiscriminately growling at friends or foe, doing anything for advancement, and defiling the innocent: "And heedless as a madden'd hound, / He spits his venom'd slaver round" (p. 20). Stockdale also is severely berated in the unsigned *A Letter to the Reverend Mr. Percival Stockdale, On the Publication of his Pretended Correspondence With the Lord Bishop of Durham* (London, 1792).

12. HL, bMS Eng. 1250 (53), October 25, 1802.

13. *"An Elegy written by* Mr. Stockdale *on the Death of a Friend's favourite Cat"* originally appeared in the May *Universal Magazine of Knowledge and Pleasure* 18 (1771): 261–62 and thereafter, misdated 1764, in Stockdale's *Poetical Works* (London, 1810), 2:255–57. That version was reprinted in the scarce pamphlet edited by Herman W. Liebert, *An Elegy on the Death of Dr. Johnson's Favourite Cat. . . . By Percival Stockdale. With a Note on Dr. Johnson's Cats* (New Haven: Yale University Press, 1949). Stockdale wrongly claimed that Hodge was Johnson's favorite. Stockdale's mock elegy is as good as Gray's "Ode on the Death of a Favourite Cat, Drowned in a Tub of Gold Fishes" (1748). Whether this elevates Stockdale as a poet or denigrates the genre may be debated by wiser heads than mine.

14. "A Poetical Epistle To Dr. Goldsmith, Or Supplement to his Retaliation, a Poem," ca. 1774 after *Retaliation* but presumably before Goldsmith's death. I have not yet found the poem's original home. This is quoted from a volume in the Harvard Theater Collection, TS 9373. 3, *The Life of David Garrick, and His Private Correspondence with the Most Celebrated Persons of His Time: Now First Published From the Originals, Illustrated with Portraits, Views, Autographs, Etc.* (London, 1831), 3: No. 69. Adam Rounce has photographically reproduced Stockdale's *An Inquiry into the Nature and Genuine Laws of Poetry*, in *Alexander Pope and His Critics* (London: Routledge, 2004), vol. 2.

15. Beinecke, Osborn Shelves C6 240[2#].

16. London *Times Literary Supplement*, Saturday, October 5, 1940: W. M. Parker, "Bibliography. Scott's Book Marginalia—III."

17. One possible reason for considering Stockdale might have been the frequently Johnsonian tones of *The Life of Edmund Waller* (London, 1772). Here are its opening lines:

It has been lamented by biographers, and echoed by their readers, that the life of a poet affords but few materials for a narrative; and that the time of his birth and death, with the intermediate dates of his publications, are the chief anecdotes of him which we can communicate to the world.

This opinion, like many others, is not controverted, because it hath been long received. It appears, upon a superficial view, to have substance; but it will vanish upon examination. (p. [i])

18. *Quarterly Review* 2 (1809): 384. The attribution is in Hill Shine and Helen Chadwick Shine, *The Quarterly Review Under Gifford. Identification of Contributors 1809–1824* (Chapel Hill: University of North Carolina Press, 1949), p. 6; it is partially rewritten by William Gifford. This review provided the impetus for the section on Stockdale in D'Israeli's *Calamities of Authors* (London, 1812), 2:313–33, several sentences of

which come from the *Quarterly*. Benjamin Disraeli outlines his father's affection for Johnson, immersion in literature, and anonymous reviewing, though Benjamin apparently is unaware that his father wrote four reviews for the *Quarterly* in 1809–10. See *Curiosities of Literature. By Isaac Disraeli. With a View of the Life and Writings of the Author. By His Son, The right Hon. B. Disraeli* (New York, 1881), 1:13, 30.

19. Stockdale also complains and comments on this request in his *Lectures* 1:424–25, 533–35.

20. *Boswell's Life of Johnson Together with Boswell's Journal of a Tour to the Hebrides*, ed. George Birkbeck Hill and rev. L. F. Powell (Oxford: Clarendon Press, 1934–50), 4:319; cited hereafter in the text as *Life*. The editors conjecture that this is Cumberland, but see *The Life of Samuel Johnson, LL. D.*, extra illustrated edition, ed. John Wilson Croker (London, 1874), 15:215—"Probably" Stockdale. In either case, so sensitive a soul as Stockdale could have seen his shadow where he never trod. Stockdale quickly and harshly judged Boswell as Johnson's "undistinguishing, and servile encomiast." See *Observations on The Writings*, p. 20 n.

21. *Observations on the Writings*, pp. 24–25. For a good example of how Johnson tried to help Stockdale, while embarrassing himself, see his letter to Robert Lowth, Bishop of London, asking his lordship to ordain Stockdale so that he could accept a position in Jamaica (Redford, *Letters*, 3:286–87). Bishop Lowth replies sternly regarding such "improper applications" by Stockdale and by extension by Johnson. See the *Bodleian Library Record* 1 (1940): 200–201. Stockdale discusses the episode in *Memoirs* 2:210–15, with warm thanks to Johnson, the better to contrast him with Lowth's "episcopal meanness" (*M*, 2:215).

22. *Observations on the Writings*, pp. 21–22; *Two Familiar Letters . . . To an Critical Reviewer . . . To the Monthly Reviewers* (London, 1792), pp. 8–9; letter to Jane Porter, July 13, 1807, HL, bMS Eng. 1250 (87); *Lectures*, on Young, 2:42–43. The *Critical* approvingly quotes the lines from "Young" in its review of the *Lectures*: 3rd series, 13 (1808): 148.

23. Hodgson, "Percival Stockdale," n. 5, above, p. 394.

24. *The Seasons, By James Thomson; With his Life, an Index, and Glossary. . . . and Notes to the Season, By Percival Stockdale* (London, 1793). I have continued the text's numbering in citing the unpaginated quotations below.

25. HEH, JE 832.

26. January 21, 1795, HL, bMS Eng. 1250 (8); March 8, 1795, ibid. (9); May 13, 1795, ibid. (10); December 4, 1795, ibid. (16).

27. December 14, 1795, HL, bMS Eng. 1250 (17); February 20, 1796, ibid. (19); August 12, 1796, ibid. (22); December 27, 1796, ibid. (26); August 27, 1797, ibid. (31).

28. June 22,1801, HEH, JE 839; February 2, 1802, HL, bMS Eng. 1250 (48); July 1, 1802, ibid. (51).

29. August 10, 1802, BL, Add. MS 36, 499, f. 127; August 11, 1802, HL, bMS Eng. 1250 (52); October 25, 1802, ibid. (53)—words largely repeated in Stockdale's *Memoirs* 2:322.

30. February 24, 1807, HL, bMS Eng. 1250 (85); September 9, 1807, ibid. (88). For discussion of the delay, see Stockdale's letter to George Cumberland, February 24, 1806, BL, Add. MS, 36, 501 f. 178. In *Memoirs* 2:322 Stockdale says that the *Lectures* "were published about a year ago"; his Appendix is dated January 24, 1809 (2:343).

31. *Memoirs*, 2:323, and reprinted in Jane Porter's elegiac celebration of Stockdale in the *Gentleman's Magazine* 81, part 2, (1811): 388–89.

32. February 24, 1808, BL Add. MS, 36, 501, f. 178, approbation, £400, and ardently; April 1, 1808, ibid., f. 196 (ff. 178 and 196 for the printing run), Bristol sales and converse.

33. April 27, 1808, letter to Bristol, BL, Add. MS 36, 501, f. 217; conjectural date regarding sales, ibid., f. 260.

34. April 1, 1808, BL, Add. MS, 36, 501, f. 196. The *Eclectic*'s review was written by John Foster, a Baptist minister. See *Life and Correspondence of John Foster*, ed. J. E. Ryland (London, 1846), 2:581.

35. June 6, 1808, HEH, JE 843; July 20, 1808, HL, bMS Eng. 1250 (90).

36. *Monthly* 59 (1809): 142 (furious), 130 (code). The review is by John Ferriar. See Benjamin Christie Nangle, *The Monthly Review Second Series 1790–1813. Indexes of Contributors and Articles* (Oxford: Clarendon Press, 1955), p. 208.

37. *Edinburgh* 12 (1808): 77. The attribution is in W. A. Copinger, *On the Authorship of the First Hundred Numbers of the "Edinburgh Review"* (Manchester, 1895), p. 16.

38. Compare the *Edinburgh Review* 12:62, 73–74, 80, 81.

39. See, for example, Isaac D'Israeli in the *Quarterly Review* and in his *Calamaties of Authors* at n. 18 above, and Sir Walter Scott at n. 16 above.

40. *GM* 81, part 2 (1811): 389. Stockdale's funeral obsequies include the contributions of Jane Porter's brothers: Robert's—R. P.—generous Latin epitaph, ibid., p. 528, and William's—W. P.—translation of it, ibid., p. 667. Stockdale was "ad eruditionem promovendam ardens," or "zealous in the promotion of learning," among other positive traits. The identifications are probable conjectures: initials other than J[ane] P[orter] are not identified in James M. Kuist's *The Nichols File of the Gentleman's Magazine: Attributions and Authorship* (Madison: University of Wisconsin Press, 1982).

12

Johnson Before Boswell in Eighteenth-Century France: Notes Toward Reclaiming a Man of Letters

RECORDED EIGHTEENTH-CENTURY FRENCH TRANSLATIONS OF JOHN-son's *Life of Savage* one; portions of the *Rambler* five; of the *Idler* one; of the *Adventurer* two; of *Rasselas*, ten; of the Preface to *Shakespeare* one; of the *Journey to the Western Islands* two.[1] Studies of these twenty-one works, their implications, their many possible cousins, or their possible influence—none. Samuel Johnson as perceived in eighteenth-century France and Francophone culture remains terra incognita.

The dissuasive force is not a mythical cartographic monster, but the real Dragon Preconception. Since Johnson was unknown or irrelevant in eighteenth-century France, we do not investigate whether Johnson was known or relevant in eighteenth-century France. The distinguished French anglicist Michel Baridon puts it this way while debunking the notion of an Age of Johnson: "Seen from the other side of the Channel, Johnson's intellectual stature has never assumed the size described by Anglo-Saxon literary historians." That aberration is "bien anglais," and seems to Frenchmen "very typical of their neighbours' endearing taste for oddities." It is among those British things "to be wondered at, humored and never understood, like cricket or savouries at the end of an Oxford dinner." Johnson's importance thus "has been exaggerated by an amiable perversion of national feeling."[2]

The analogy of Johnson and bad British cuisine surely is bien français. More importantly, its "never assumed" imposes lamentable twentieth-century French neglect of Johnson upon laudable eighteenth-century French attraction to Johnson. If we consider the breadth of Johnson's achievement it would be strange for him not to be valued in an often shared French literary culture. Periodical essays, lexicography, biography, canon formation, critical theory and practice, travel narratives, moral tales, voyages and, increasingly if grudgingly, the reading and performing of Shakespeare were familiar parts of cross-channel intellectual life. Exploration of Johnson as perceived in France thus has much to teach us: about the shape of Johnson's career and authority; about his role for continental Europe's most powerful arbiter of taste; about cross-cultural modes of adaptation; and about new documents for the bibliography of Johnson's works.

Moreover, Johnson long has been paired with Boswell, who so memorably recorded Johnson's heard brilliance and viewed oddities. Whether then or now in the anglophone world, literary, verbal, and physical Johnson are part of his biographical portrait.[3] What would happen if another culture knew Johnson only as a man of letters, if it knew neither his golden speech nor tarnished body? I hope at least in part to determine how Johnson the man of letters was received in Francophone Europe. I hope thereafter to suggest how the biographical impulse changed these literary perceptions.

Johnson's own symbolic and real visits to France generally reinforced his image as a man of letters. The symbolic visit was on June 12, 1755, when Ruvigny de Cosnes, the British chargé d'affaires in Paris, presented a copy of the *Dictionary* to the Académie Française. It gratefully acknowledged receipt, promised its own pending dictionary in return, and recognized the international importance of Johnson's national achievement. Members then in attendance included Marivaux and the anglophile Shakesepeare-loving Comte de Bissy, who later gave Sterne's Yorick a passport for travel in France. Johnson's two ample folio volumes probably attracted the attention of academicians still revising their own lexicon, with which Johnson's was to compare favorably. About 1769 Louise Flint in France translated Johnson's post-annotation judgments on Shakespeare's plays. These are likely to have circulated among small groups, but they were not published and apparently are lost. Johnson's real and generally less pleasant visit to France was in October and November of 1775. He there met Elie-Catherine Fréron, to whom he denigrated Voltaire and whose wish to translate Johnson's works was sadly denied by his death in 1776. In Paris on September 25, 1775, Johnson met the Abbé Roffette who leapt out of his chair to embrace Johnson for his "sublime" Latin celebration of *Paradise Lost*.[4] Johnson obviously spoke in France, but he normally spoke Latin with other men of letters and thus reinforced his image as a learned visitor—as also was made plain by most of Johnson's first Gallic readers.

Indeed, the evidence for Johnson's pre-Boswellian literary presence in eighteenth-century France is so substantial that I can only focus on representative responses to his major works. There is more to be said, found, and done—including study of Johnson as translated.[5] So far as I now can tell, though, his French reputation from about 1750 to 1825 had five sometimes overlapping phases that are roughly similar to his reputation in Britain. The first is response to Johnson the moralist, to Mr. Rambler.

Johnson the Man of Letters and Moral Writer

The early 1750s were uncharacteristically "peaceful" years between Britain and France. The 1748 treaty of Aix-la-Chapelle had concluded the War of the Austrian Succession; the North American and Indian imperial conflicts that emerged in 1751 often were fought with surrogates; the Seven Years' War itself concluded in distant continents through Clive's victory in India (1757) and Wolfe's in Canada (1759). Relations between the two countries nonetheless were strained on literary as on political matters. In spite of growing interest in British letters, much French attitude remained ambivalent and suspicious. Britain was capable of great things, especially in the ode that required imaginative leaps and in tragedy that required blood; but it was undisciplined, crude, and a threat to literary as to political order. In 1747 Edmé Mallet granted British literature's distinction but also thought it morally noxious, poetically licentious, and politically and religiously odious. Don't bother to learn English, he tells his readers.[6] "Correct" Addison and Pope slightly altered that image; Fielding and Richardson demonstrated English achievement in "sentiment"; Shakespeare began to appeal, if only as an exotic alternative within a relatively small circle.[7] Even in 1775, however, the *Journal anglais* knew that "A l'égard des Auteurs Anglais, la plus grande partie n'ent pas connue en France."[8] Johnson's impression upon France thus signals generous openness that begins during a rare moment of relative peace that literary journals enriched for the common good.

The Protestant refugee Matthew (or Matthieu) Maty lived and wrote in England but published his *Journal britannique* in Holland.[9] He begins the *Journal* in 1750 with optimistic words. Peace unifies nations, aids the exchange of knowledge, scholarly emulation, flourishing arts and artists, and most immediately French knowledge of British letters. Maty hopes to animate "tous les hommes à l'amour de la vérité & de la vertu" (1:I–ii), and to consider "les seules idées que la Raison donne d'un bon Journal" (1:iv). Accordingly, "les règles de la bienséance & de la politesse seront de sacrés & d'inviolables devoirs" (1:xi). Virtually by definition, then, anything Maty selects for inclusion and discussion is important. By 1754 the virtual becomes the announced in the *Journal étranger* initiated by the Abbé Antoine Prévost d'Exiles and François Arnaud.[10] They translate the best of neighboring modern culture into Europe's most familiar language to spread reason, philosophy, and the virtues of the exalted human spirit. "Nous n'en sçaurions placer aucun dans notre journal, sans lui donner tacitement un témoinage d'approbation." They also assemble "les chefs-d'oeuvres de tous les artistes, de tous les sçavans du monde en tout genre, & dans toutes les langues vivantes" (April, 1754; p. xxxiv). Pre-selection makes plain that Johnson's presence is a sign of respect, one that probably begins with Maty's *Journal britannique* as the first extensive French discussion of Johnson.[11]

Maty's February 1751 (4:235) *Journal britannique* announces publication of the *Rambler*, to which it soon returns. In April, Maty uses twenty-five pages to discuss individual *Rambler*s (4:363–87). In July and August of 1752 he adds thirty-two pages regarding its complete reprint. Along the way, Maty considers or mentions some ninety-two different *Rambler*s and provides numerous extended and translated extracts (8:243–74). Pierre Clément's *Nouvelles littéraires de France et d'Angleterre* briefly twice mentions the *Rambler* in October of 1751 and again in October of 1752.[12] Thereafter, the *Journal étranger*'s first volume and second month in 1754 analyzes the first three *Rambler*s (May, 1:183–92). In June it adds the next three, and thus provides nineteen pages of extracts and intelligent evaluation of a periodical elevated by association with the respected *Spectator* (1:227–35). Between 1754 and 1756 Urbain Roger's *Le Traducteur* in Copenhagen translates at least twenty four *Rambler*s and six *Adventurer*s.[13]

When these journals comment they generally agree that Johnson's style is demonstrably un-French, scholastic, and more elevated than entertaining or lively. It lacks fashionable lightness, and could have "un peu plus de vivacité, de variété & d'enjouement" (*JB*, 4:371). There also is broad agreement regarding Johnson's admirable breadth of topics (*JB*, 4:364, 381; 8:259–60), sustained elegance and quality of mind, confidence in the reader, and what Maty calls "un grand fond d'humanité" in the sometimes misanthropic author (8:[1752]:254). The *Journal étranger* is especially keen on those numbers concerning morality, criticism, and philosophy (1 [May 1754]: 183).

That *Journal* also exemplifies early French engagement with Johnson's intellectual positions, what he called exchange of mind.[14] It sometimes laments Johnson's puzzling remarks (1 [May 1754]: 187), but its mixed tone changes when it responds to his already important fourth

Rambler on the moral basis of the novel. The "raisonnable" exclusion of machines and romance fiction raises some problems, for the novel borrows these devices from successful epic practice. More importantly, Johnson rightly urges that the novel should inspire "l'amour de la vertu & l'horreur du vice. J'approuve celle ci de toute mon ame, & j'exhorte les Romanciers de mon siecle à ne s'en jamais écarter." The *Journal* then praises Johnson's rejection of the overlapping of vice and virtue in a character: "L'auteur a bien raison de combattre ce systéme" (1 [June 1754]:228–29, 230). Johnson soon has select essays filched without acknowledgment by, among others, Arnaud Berquin and Lewis Sebastien Mercier, and with some acknowledgment in the *Journal helvetique*, the *Censeur universel anglois*, and the *Bibliothèque universelle des romans*.[15] Extended versions of the *Rambler* appeared as *Morceaux choisis du Rambler, ou du Rodeur* in Paris in 1785, and as *Le Rodeur* in Maestricht in 1786. The Paris translator A. M. H. Boulard reminds us that Johnson was an "Ecrivain très distingué," a judgment probably shared by Aubin Louis Millin who soon borrowed four of Boulard's translated *Rambler*s for his own *Mélanges de littérature étrangère* (1785–86). In 1826 C. G. Lambert, Baron de Chamerolles, used five volumes for a complete translation of the *Rambler* and its author's "immortel écrits."[16]

Reviewers further spread Johnson's fame. *L'Année littéraire* warmly seconded Boulard's judgment and thanked him for rendering "un vrai service aux lettres en nous donnant la traduction d'un ouvrage dont la morale est aussi saine que le goût" (6 [1785]:232). The *Journal encyclopédique* was kinder still: "On trouve dans les morceaux ici traduits un observateur profond, & un écrivain agréable."[17] Johnson's reputation as Mr. *Rambler* was so substantial that when the *Dictionary* appeared in 1755 the *Bibliothèque des sciences et des beaux arts* called him "Le savant & ingénieux Mr. *Samuel Johnson*, qui dans l'incomparable feuille périodique intitulée le *Rambler*, apprenoit à ses compatriotes à penser avec justesse sur les matières les plus intéressantes" (2:482; see also 36 [1771]: 348).

Such relative popularity extended to the moralism of *Rasselas* (1759) as well. In 1760 Octavie Guichard Belot provides the first French translation of *Rasselas*. Her title page identifies Johnson as "*Auteur du Rambler.*" Madame Belot admires this "Roman philosophique" because, like Voltaire, Johnson knows that "le bonheur est une chimere" (pp. iij–iv).[18] As with Johnson's other major early works, French knowledge of *Rasselas* was spread through reviews. Fréron's *L'Année littéraire* finds that it sometimes languishes; but he admires Imlac's "très belle dissertation sur la poësie que je conseille à nos jeunes Poëtes de lire," but whose excellent rules nonetheless are unreachable (3 [1760]: 150–51).[19] Fréron contrasts *Rasselas* with his enemy Voltaire's *Candide* and distinguishes between kinds of response to human depravity. Voltaire leads to despair with the world and within ourselves. Johnson makes us the object of our own compassion and seeks to make us better (pp. 165–66). When in 1798 the Comte de Fouchecour adds his translation and commentary, he acknowledges "la célébrité de l'immortel auteur de Rasselas" whose beauties place it "à la tête des romans anglois." By the end of the eighteenth century *Rasselas* would be used to teach English to French readers, as early in the nineteenth century that "joli petit roman . . . par le célebre Samuel Johnson" would entertain them.[20]

Dictionary Johnson

Much of the distinction of the "savant et ingénieux" M. Rodeur nonetheless stemmed from his achievement as the recording voice of the English language. He indeed soon becomes Dictionary Johnson in France as in England. In 1747, for example, the *Bibliothèque raisonée des ouvrages des savans de l'Europe* praised Chesterfield's role as patron and encourager of "l'Auteur qui se nomme *Johnson*." In his *Plan* of the *Dictionary*, we hear, Johnson used a pure and elegant style to write brilliantly about language. If the completed work is as good, the English finally will have their standard lexicon. In 1751 both Maty and Clément describe Johnson as an admired author whose dictionary is expected, desired, and encouraged.[21] The *Journal des sçavans* for September–October lists the *Dictionary* among new English publications. By its January–March 1756 number, the books had arrived "à la Veuve Cavelier & fils, Libraires, rue S. Jacques." The same issue cited the *Dictionary*'s full title, its hefty price of 150 livres, and its role for the English language as that which "le Dictionnaire de l'Académie Française est pour notre langue."[22]

That refrain would be familiar among French commentators, but the primacy of Johnson's lexicon was not instantaneous. It had to leap the same hurdle in France that it did in Britain—namely, replacing the competition. Until well into midcentury, the best known English dictionary was Thomas Dyche's *The New General English Dictionary*, probably in the revised version by William Pardon in 1740 and thereafter. A new edition of the Abbé Prévost's *Manuel lexique ou dictionnaire portatif* appeared in Paris in 1755; Esprit Pezenos issued his *Nouveau diction-*

naire universel des arts et sciences, français, latin, et anglois in Avignon in 1756 and in Amsterdam in 1758. Each makes overt its debt to Dyche, who is at once a source and an argument on authority. Johnson's appearance on the French lexical scene, then, both parallels the Académie's efforts and replaces Dyche's as the norm of British lexicography. As we will see, it was at first a rocky and then a definitive incursion. By midsummer of 1755, indeed, the *Dictionary* begins a second phase of Johnson's literary reputation in France and evokes major and contradictory reviews in Maty's *Journal britannique* and the Abbé Prévost's *Journal étranger.*

Given the *Dictionary*'s presence in the Académie Française, there must already have been at least some modest stir when Maty published his long, occasionally admiring but generally hostile, discussion in the *Journal britannique* for July and August of 1755. The fiction that he will proceed "avec réserve mais avec impartialité" (17:221) soon evaporates. Maty's first loyalty was to his patron Chesterfield, as indeed he thinks Johnson's should have been. Maty's review thus only is sandwiched by high praise. Johnson's earlier work, he says, shows him as a "Philosophe profond, Littérateur solide, Ecrivain harmonieux." His dictionary will immortalize him as the dictionaries of the French and Italian academies immortalized them—except that Johnson wrote his alone, and thus is "en quelque sorte une Académie pour son Isle" (17:219). The review ends with Maty's praise of Johnson's erudition, and his confidence that Johnson offers England's "première idée d'un veritable Dictionaire" (17:244). That rich if thinly sliced bread, however, scarcely holds the rotten meat within. Maty scolds Johnson for not reprinting the fine 1747 *Plan* dedicated to Chesterfield, for adding the presumably redundant Preface, and thus for hiding an obligation to his aristocratic Maecenas. Maty will not seek the reasons for such conduct but will consider whether the *Dictionary* is worth its price and whether it fulfills the *Plan*'s promise (17: 220–21).

In addition to other matters—like the too symmetrical, rhythmic, obscure, and self-pitying Preface (17:222–23)—Maty finds six serious faults in the *Dictionary*. 1) Its principle of selection for words is too broad; 2) it is too impartial in recording politics and religion; 3) it is too reverent toward rough seventeenth-century English prose at the expense of superior and elegant modern prose; 4) it lacks dates for illustrative quotations; 5) its orthography, pronunciation, etymology, and accents are helpful, but neither its definitions nor illustrations adequately explain a word's different shades of meaning; 6) and its often useful illustrations should have been chronologically ordered.

I amplify the third point. Maty's review in part defends Chesterfield by berating Johnson; but it also defends the French language. Maty objects to Johnson's preference for seventeenth-century English as an excessive "amour pour l'antique" (17:232). Modern writers have added "plus d'harmonie, de précision & d'élegance dans leurs écrits" (17:231), whereas the early Stuart prose style Johnson praises is hard and obscure—that is, less like French. One's suspicion that Maty is defending French style is supported when he paraphrases Johnson's view that English has degenerated since 1660, "& s'être peu à peu approchée du François, dont il craint qu' elle ne devienne à la longue un barbare dialecte." The consequent decision to return to Hooker, Bacon, and Shakespeare is "hasardée" (17:230).

Maty largely is negative for reasons extrinsic to the *Dictionary*'s achievement but intrinsic to his alliance with Chesterfield and his own inability to accommodate Johnson's style in the *Rambler*. When discussing those essays, Maty scolds Johnson's apparently unsuccessful efforts to be light. Fair enough, but in an unfortunate couplet Maty crudely aligns Johnson with Colley Cibber: "Jamais C-bb-r ne sera sage, / Ni J-hns-n ne sera plaisant" (4:370). Whether or not Johnson knew that mischievous analogy, he surely knew Maty's article in the *Journal britannique* and its crude defense of Chesterfield. When Johnson awaited publication of the *Dictionary*, he wanted to begin a periodical that would "give my countrymen a view of what is doing in literature upon the continent." Dr. William Adams informs Johnson that Maty had just terminated his *Journal britannique* and might serve as Johnson's assistant. "*He*, (said Johnson), the little black dog! I'd throw him into the Thames."[23]

Johnson had no reason to throw the Abbé Prévost into the Seine. His *Journal étranger* twice exposes French readers to the *Dictionary* and perhaps also negatively alludes to Maty's points.

The July 1755 *Journal étranger* includes the *Dictionary* in its section on "Grammaire," but considers far more and refutes Maty in all ways. Prévost, for example, thinks that the Preface expresses "beaucoup de sçavoir" (p. 132). He acknowledges that Johnson is solicitous "en faveur des Etrangers" and believes that the "solidité de son jugement" (p. 141) makes the *Dictionary* useful for those who want to learn English (p. 148). Prévost thinks that Johnson has revived several obsolete words that contribute "à l'beauté du langage" (p. 140) and that by looking back to the relatively near Renaissance, Johnson "a mieux aimé remonter à la source de la vraie diction" (pp. 147–48). Prévost also admires the research and work behind the illustrative quotations that "doivent être agréables à ceux qui ont du goût pour la Littérature Anglo- ise" (p. 148). Unlike Maty again, Prévost admires Johnson's definitions and thinks "qu'il est parvenu à connoître par quels degrés un mot a pris differentes significations" (p. 147). Both men, however, agree that the remarkable *Dictionary* is a surprising achievement for "un seul homme" (p. 144).

The *Journal étranger* was so impressed with the *Dictionary* that in De- cember of 1756 it returns to it in the section on "Angleterre" and bluntly begins: "Cet Ouvrage est un des plus importans de la Langue Anglo- ise; & c'est un des plus grands qui ait jamais été composé par un seul homme, dans aucune Langue; L'Auteur est M. *Samuel Johnson*" (p. 111). Better still, the Preface is a model for "ceux d'entre nous qui ser- oient tentés de rendre le même service à la Langue Françoise." To facili- tate that effort, Prévost translates the entire Preface "avec quelqu' exactitude" (p. 112).[24] He thus overcomes Maty's grousing and further enhances Johnson's reputation among French readers.

For example, in 1765 Jean-Baptiste-Antoine Suard's *Gazette littéraire de l'Europe* elevates the *Dictionary* to a wrongly perceived unique role: Johnson gave the world "le premier Dictionnaire & le seul qui existe," presumably of the English language. In 1786 *Le Censeur universel an- glois* reports that Johnson the "grand génie du siècle" refused to gratify the proud and ungenerous Chesterfield by dedicating the *Dictionary* to him.[25] Comparable friendly judgments of the *Dictionary* and its maker begin the nineteenth century. In 1804 *La Decade philosophique, littér- aire et politique* reports that the English regard "le célèbre" Johnson as "*le colosse de la littérature.*" His works include "un Dictionnaire de leur langue que beaucoup de gens regardent comme l'ouvrage le plus parfait qu' existe en ce genre" (40:222–23). In that same year, the *Revue philo- sophique, littéraire et politique* describes the *Dictionary* as "si supérieur à notre Dictionnaire de l'Académie française" (42 [1804]: 40).[26]

SHAKESPEARE

By 1765, however, Johnson was not always thought so collosal in France. He then encountered an audience beginning to acknowledge Shakespeare's virtues but still impressed by his vices. Many such readers probably judged Shakespeare through Voltaire's dark spectacles. His *Letters concerning the English Nation* (1733) savaged Shakespeare as the tasteless unorthodox genius who both created and destroyed the English theater. Addison's regular *Cato* should have been England's proper dramatic model.[27]

Johnson's *Shakespeare* thus initiates a third phase of his reception in eighteenth-century France. It indeed becomes contentious when the Preface engages French criticism in general and Voltaire in particular.[28] France's great polemic man of letters even uses the term "un crime de haute trahison" when in 1776 he angrily responds to the growing popularity of Shakespeare in France.[29] Adaptations by Jean-François Ducis and the royally patronized translation by Pierre le Tourneur (1776–82) opened French gates to English barbarians. Jean-Baptiste-Antoine Suard trys at least partially to protect France in general and Voltaire in particular from the English invader.

Late in 1765 Suard's *Gazette littéraire* introduces its discussion with a harsh judgment of Shakespeare's form, moral structure, language, editors, and Johnson himself. His edition and its Preface have not been as successful as one might expect, and he said much good but also much bad about his author: "Les éloges paroîtront vraisemblament aux Etrangers un peu exagérés, & les critiques ont révoltés la plûpart des Anglois" (7:171–72). Suard nonetheless prints extracts from the Preface that extend from the beginning to the end of the critical sections and include softened versions of Johnson's skirmish with Voltaire.

The translation thus properly includes Voltaire among those who blame Shakespeare for indecorously showing a drunken king (7:176) and allows him to be called one of the "petits esprits" (7:177). That, though, is as far as Suard will go, and he even modifies certain insults. Here is Johnson's doublet regarding Dennis, Voltaire, and others who judge Shakespeare with uncongenial artificial rules: "These are the petty cavils of petty minds."[30] For Suard, that is "des chicanes de petits esprits"—a translation that eliminates half of the diminutives. More significantly, Suard eliminates Johnson's blunt attack upon Voltaire's insistence on the unities and his likening of Voltaire to Rymer and Dennis. Appropriate violations, Johnson said, "become the comprehensive genius of Shakespeare, and such censures are suitable to the minute and slender criticism of Voltaire." Johnson then quotes Lucan's *Pharsalia*, in which the petty laws of conquered lands gladly surrender to triumphant Caesar (YE 7:79–80). Suard deletes both the insult and the quotation.

Suard soon reprinted his translation in *Variétés littéraires* (1768–69). That text also is the basis for the *Journal helvetique*'s July 1769 partial reprint of the translated Preface, so Voltaire was triply leagued among the "petits esprits" (4:71).[31] He retaliated in *Questions sur l'encyclopéd-*

ie's discussion of the English theater. He there characterizes Johnson as a drunken practical joker who talked nonsense about Shakespeare.[32]

By the third quarter of the eighteenth century, however, Voltaire's judgments were often questioned and Shakespeare's genius often exalted. Pierre le Tourneur's preface to his own Shakespeare translation scolds Voltaire without naming him. No doubt to the noise of Voltaire spinning in his grave, it also regularly cites Johnson's edition. As le Tourneur says in 1776 regarding his text, "le plus communément nous suivons celle de Johnson." Such an accolade drew more attention to Johnson's Preface. The *Journal anglais* often praises and cites le Tourneur's edition and at one point confronts the unnamed Johnson on the unities (1776, 3:199–200).[33] By the early nineteenth century Johnson's Preface appears on both sides of the Shakespeare debate. In 1813 the *Mercure etranger* claims him as one of the sane English critics who recognize Shakespeare's faults (1:206). A decade later, Stendhal's *Racine et Shakespeare* (1823, 1825) uses Johnson's "célèbre préface" to argue against the classical unities and in favor of romanticism, whose patrimony he traces to Johnson.[34]

The fourth phase of French response provides further light on Johnson who already was an imported English voice in the French literary chorus.

BIOGRAPHER, TRAVELER, AND CRITIC

The January 1765 *British Magazine or Monthly Repository* (6:1–66) reprinted large portions of Johnson's *Life of Savage* (1744). By May, this in turn was further abridged in Pierre Rousseau's *Journal encyclopédique* (1 [1765]: 81–95). When Johnson's Shakespeare appeared in October of that year, French readers thus had been alerted to his biographical as well as critical acumen. One of those readers was the Shakespearean Pierre le Tourneur, who in 1771 published *Histoires de Richard Savage et de J. Thompson, Traduites de l'anglois* (Paris). Given Savage's obscurity, le Tourneur fears that his *Life* in France will not repeat its British success; but he knows that the biography "présente quelquefois au Sage des réflexions aussi intèressantes & non moins utiles" (p. ij, in italics).

Perhaps the most interesting aspect of le Tourneur's Avertissement, however, is its discussion of Savage as a mixed character appropriate both for biography and for tragedy (pp. ij–iv). Le Tourneur seems to have learned from and approved Johnson's Preface to *Shakespeare* and its theory of complex human rather than monolithic theatrical character.

Perhaps as well so attractive, if bizarre, a biographical character is why in 1771 le Tourneur's translation of *Savage* was praised and abstracted both in the *Bibliothèque des sciences et des beaux arts* (36 [1771]: 348–67) and in in *L'Année littéraire*. It was further abridged in 1774 in the *Journal des sçavans*.[35] In the *Bibliothèque* we read that *Savage* is by "l'ingénieux auteur du *Rambler*," and that the elegant translation indeed is likely to fare as well in France as the original did in Britain with its "succès le plus brillant & le plus soutenu" (2 [1771]: 337). That success is confirmed in 1776 when the *Journal anglais* prints another unattributed and abbreviated version of *Savage*, whom it regards as one of the victimized heroes of literary history (2:449; text 2:449–73). That judgment may also have been behind another reprinting in 1806.[36]

Johnson's later works would be equally sustaining. France's long political concern with Scotland blends with increasing European Celtomania and affection for Macpherson's Ossian poems. In 1775 the *Journal encyclopédique* thus reviews Johnson's *Journey to the Western Islands* (1775) with special emphasis on English colonial and punitive response to Scotland. The *Journal* does not fully understand Johnson's complex attitude toward Anglo-Scots relations, but it nonetheless recognizes that whatever the Highlanders' barbarism, their civilized occupiers are worse: "nous croyons voir dans son récit une horde d'Indiens détruite par une horde plus sauvage & plus nombreuse" (6, no. 1 [1775]: 251).[37]

Johnson's *Journey* also was recognized as a valuable guide to the still romantic Scottish Islands. In 1785 an abridged *Journey* appeared in Pierre-Henri Mallet's *Nouveau recueil de voyages au nord de l'Europe et de l'Asie* (Geneva and Paris). The *Journey* is both among "*les plus estimées*" of such narratives and by an author the English regard as "entre leurs meilleurs Ecrivains & leurs plus profonds moralistes." Mallet himself knows that the *Journey* embodies "L'esprit philosophique" (2:1).[38] Thereafter, it guides B. Faujas-Saint-Fond's *Voyages en Angleterre, en Ecosse et aux îles Hébrides* (1797), again is separately issued by Henri-Noël-François Huchet, Comte de la Bédoyère, in 1804 and is duly praised in *La Decade philosophique* (40 [1804]: 222–23). The reviewer shares Huchet's belief that among modern visits, the *Journey* "mérite le premier rang par l'etendue et la justesse de ses observations."[39]

The major publishing event of Johnson's final years of course was the *Lives of the Poets* (1779–81), and we again see active interest, translation, and hopes for further translation. In 1779 the *Journal encyclopédique* reviews the first two of the four volumes. It pays special attention to Johnson on Milton and concludes that his equitable remarks are "aussi justes, aussi vraies que délicates & neuves" (6, no. 1 [1779]: 277–78). It returns to the *Lives* and concludes that the two other volumes of the "belle collection . . . ne méritent pas moins d'éloges par la saine critique qui y regne" (6, no. 3 [1779]: 458). By the later eighteenth century Johnson's relevant lives are cited in numerous comments on English poets.

In 1785, for example, the *Journal des sçavans* reviews the first volume of *Mélanges de littérature étrangère*, abstracts key parts of "Cowley," urges that it merits being read, and notes that the "savant" Johnson himself was "aussi distingué par son érudition que par son esprit & son goût" (Dec. p. 771). In the same year the *Censeur universel anglois* urges that a full and good French version of the *Lives* would contribute "également à la réputation et à la fortune" of the translator. To help that process, the *Censeur* itself provides "Gray" in 1785, and "Prior" and "Otway" in 1786. Much of "Pope" appears in Aubin Louis Millin's *Magazin encyclopédique* in 1796 as borrowed from Boulard's translation. At the end of the long extract Boulard adds a note advising readers where to find the French versions of "Cowley," "Savage," and "Gray," and concludes with a puff for the still unpublished complete French *Lives* by "Le citoyen Sinson" (4:124 n).[40] No wonder that Johnson's Necrologie in the *Nouvelles de la république des lettres* observes that the *Lives* enjoyed "le plus grand succès" and that Johnson was "un Ecrivain supérieur & digne de l'admiration des étrangers" (29 [1785]: 228). No wonder also that the *Censeur universel*'s laudatory epitaph on Johnson praised "l'universalité de sa science" and "son talent critique & biographique" (1:83). That admiration no doubt was enhanced by the publication of Boulard's version of the life of Milton in 1797, of an English abridgment of the *Lives* sold in Paris in 1805, of Boulard's "Milton" and "Addison" in 1805, "Butler" twice in 1813, and the first volume of the larger *Vies des poètes anglais* in 1823.

HENNET'S POÉTIQUE ANGLAISE

By the mid-1780s, then, Johnson in France was a literary icon whom his contemporaries engaged and respected for his manifold contributions to European intellectual life. Such respect was made clear in a work that clarifies Johnson's fifth phase as a man of letters in France. Albin-Joseph Ulpien Hennet's three-volume *La Poétique anglaise* in 1806 characterizes Johnson as "l'oracle littéraire de son pays" (2:438), and one who helps him to understand the strange British poetry and people. When he began to read that poetry he thought himself "transporté dans un monde nouveau. La poésie anglaise, en effet, diffère entièrement de celle des autres peuples" (1:12). The English are "plus hardie, plus fière, plus libre" (1:13) than the French or other nations. He nonetheless attempts to make those alien works understood even to those who do not know the language (1:15). Hennet's second volume includes sometimes perfunctory and sometimes extensive and perceptive discussions of 122 English major and minor poets. Johnson clearly is Hennet's guide to the poets included in his *Lives of the Poets*, which probably were open before him as he wrote.[41] Though they sometimes were partial and judged from the heart, they have "une narration rapide, attachante, développée avec ordre et clarté, une critique sage et judiceuse sur leurs ouvrages" (2:456). Johnson the wise critic had several functions for Hennet.

The first was as collaborator, guide, and argument on authority. Hennet's pages are fairly punctuated with remarks like "ici un passage de Johnson" (1:118), "observe Johnson" (1:128), "dit Johnson" (1:156, 248; 2:21, and many others), "Johnson l'accuse" (1:248), "Johnson s'élève" (2:68), "Johnson appelle" (2:148), "Johnson ajoute" (2:248), and "Johnson a retrouvé" (2:297). Johnson also appears in extended quotations designed to support Hennet's points, to clarify aspects of the poet's achievement, to provide context, and along the way to show Johnson's own acuity (e.g., 2:243). At one place, he quotes a long passage in which Johnson praises Pope's achievement in the *Iliad* translation (2:302) that proves so much superior to a French translation that Hennet exclaims, "en anglais, quel rhythme enchaneur! quelle harmonie imitative" (1:103).

Johnson's overt appearance in the *Poétique anglaise*, however, is dwarfed by Hennet's unacknowledged but recognizable use of the *Lives of the Poets*. This is clear in several of his discussions, including those of Addison, Milton, and Pope. The most striking example is Hennet's thirty-four page section on Savage that epitomizes Johnson's longer biography added to the *Lives*. He eliminates some of Johnson's moral instruction as well as comments on Savage's poetry, and includes only one "dit Johnson" to suggest proper authorship (2:361). Hennet is not plagiarizing so much as popularizing—on behalf of English poetry and of Johnson as biographer. Hennet also uses Johnson to encourage debate and alternative viewpoints.

Johnson's strong opinions set Hennet thinking about significant aspects of English versification and critical evaluation. He rejects Johnson's severity toward Collins's oriental ecloques (1:256), and he thinks that "Johnson, si judicieux d'ailleurs, me paraît, en général, trop partisan de la rime" (2:189). He later characterizes the difference of opinion regarding Johnson and Mason on Gray's poetry and concludes: "C'est au lecteur à decider entre le critique et le panégyriste" (2:419). Hennet also extracts Johnson's "Parallèle de Dryden et de Pope" and its final bias toward Dryden. In so doing, Hennet invokes history and European judgment, which demonstrate that Pope regularly is reprinted and translated as Dryden was not. "Pour moi," he concludes, "je suis tenté de dire que Dryden est un grand poëte; mais que Pope est le dieu même de la poésie" (2:319).

By early in the nineteenth century the *Censeur universel anglois* had published Johnson's "The Winter's Tale" in English and in French (1785, 1:82), the English *Lives of the Poets* (1805) sold in France reminded readers that Johnson was a poet (p. 2), and Jean-Baptiste-Nelson Cottreau had published his translation of *London* (1808). Hennet thus was part of a small but genuine movement to acknowledge the poetic part of Johnson's achievement, as he does at the end of his second volume. Hennet candidly believes that Johnson holds a higher rank "parmi les littérateurs, que parmi les poëtes" (2:450), but he knows enough of Johnson's poetry to emphasize its distinction and its high place in the British canon (2:126). He is among the "redoutables adversaires" to the very best, like Shakespeare, Milton, and Dryden (2:184). Goldsmith and Johnson are "deux poëtes célèbres" who have simplicity and elegance (2:194). Hennet praises individual poems as well. The "Drury Lane Prologue" is "parfaitement écrit. . . . On le lira avec plaisir dans ses oeuvres" (1:320). *Irene* was "écrite d'un style nerveux, brillant de sentiment et de poésie" (2:455), and the satire *London* is "peut être le plus parfait" of its kind (1:205). While praising that poem, Hennet recognizes a Johnsonian trait especially congenial to a survivor of France's bloody revolution.

Hennet ascribes the origin of *La Poétique anglaise* to the therapeutic and liberating functions of art during the Terror. On those desolate evenings he would distract himself by translating Pope and Thomson. When enclosed due to danger in the streets, his free ideas could take him to happier lands and "le charme de la poésie soutenait mon âme abattue" (1:7). Such fear of violence also affected Hennet's judgment of Pope's and of Churchill's personal and violent satires. Who, he says of Churchill, "en sortant d'un revolution aussi terrible que celle de la France, aimer des poëmes dictés par le plus violente démogogie?" (2:87). In contrast, though Johnson's *London* was an Opposition party piece, its attacks were general not brutally personal. As a satire, *London*'s style est noble et vigoreux, sa versification est sage et généreuse; point d'injures grossières à de plats auteurs, point de personnalités jalouses contre des rivaux ou des ennemis: son pinceau fidèle, quoiqu'un peu rembruni, trace hardiment une peinture générale des moeurs et des caractères: jamais la satire n'eut un but plus noble, une exécution plus brillante. (1:205–6)

Such judgments clearly were neither parochial nor unexpected. Hennet's volumes in 1806 culminate almost sixty years of French judgment and broad if not universal enjoyment of Johnson as a critic, moralist, biographer, travel writer, lexicographer, and poet whose humanity permeates his work. Hennet's Johnson is "l'écrivain le plus instruit, le plus fécond qu'ait produit l'Angleterre." Hence, "tout ce qu'il a fait méritait d'être conservé" (2:451). Such admiration reflects the many years in which Johnson's periodical essays were regularly translated and discussed, the *Dictionary* became the envy of French linguistic theorists, *Rasselas* even gained Voltaire's approbation, the Preface to Shakespeare sparked admiration and debate, the *Journey to the Western Islands* became a controversial but philosophe document, and the *Lives of the Poets* and its criticism became guides to British letters.

We note that Hennet's role in this sequence lacks three major words or concepts: "Boswell," "conversation," and "idiosyncrasy." Hennet acknowledges but dismisses Johnson's quirks, and mentions only Hawkins's unsatisfactory *Life* of Johnson (2:450–51, 456–57). Others' responses, though, already had begun to change after Johnson's death, when the outpouring of biographies blends with, begins to supplement, and then replaces knowledge of Johnson's work. For example, the compiler of the *Detail authentiques des malheurs et de la fuite de prince Charles Edouard dans les Hébrides* (Paris, 1786) translates the relevant section from Boswell's *Journal of a Tour* and records "beaucoup de Pensées recueillies des conversations du Docteur Johnson" (on pp. 30–38). He also translates "plusiers autres que j'ai choisies dans ses différens Ouvrages" (p. [1]), many of which are from *Rambler*s, and all of which assume an epigrammatic voice of wisdom (pp. 30–38).

At about the same time, though, French response to Boswell's *Journal of a Tour* to the Hebrides with Johnson and biographies of him begin to turn the literary man into the talker and personality. Amplifying his powerful voice diminishes the power of his written works and thus begins the double tradition of Johnson studies. Knowledge of the later *Life of Johnson* then becomes even more dominant. The earlier modest imbalance changes dramatically upon the canonization of Boswell's *Life of Johnson* and its interpreter Macaulay. They often become nineteenth-century France's portals to Johnson, and make clear that his reclamation as a man of letters is scarcely more than a project.

Johnson in France after Boswell and Macaulay

In 1785 the *Censeur universel* used six articles to reprint portions of Thomas Tyers's biographical sketch of Johnson. Shortly thereafter, the *Journal encyclopédique* and their five double-column pages abstract Mrs. Piozzi's *Anecdotes . . . of Johnson* (1786, 2:429–33). Its review notes that the talents and moral character of the justly celebrated writer are the principal subjects of these interesting and instructive anecdotes (5, no. 1 [1786]: 231). Unfortunately, aspects of the instruction include Johnson's rudeness in conversation, severe manners, and probable exclusion from polite company if not for his purity of morals and useful precepts. The *Journal encyclopédique* concludes: "Il faut convenir avec Mistriss P., que tout ce qu'il disoit étoit dur, & tout ce qu'il faisoit estimable" (p. 235).

That judgment was similar to the one Guillaume Dubois de Rochefort reached in the *Journal des sçavans* for August of 1786. He warmly acknowledges Johnson's achievement as author of the *Rambler, Lives of the Poets* and, among other works, the "fameux Dictionnaire qui porte son nom." That very name excites curiosity, and few men of letters would not be interested in his life and thought. Mrs. Piozzi includes too many trivial details, but she also makes plain that Johnson was singular, morose, bizarre, and severe (pp. 536–37). The *Journal* indeed acknowledges some of Johnson's intellectual and literary achievement, but "le caractere impérieuse & dur que M. Johnson montroit dans la societé" dominates the review (p. 541).[42]

This personalizing process already had advanced substantially with two antagonistic reviews of Boswell's *Journal of a Tour* that set much of the tone for later discussion of Johnson. In March of 1786 the *Censeur universel anglois* severely scolds Boswell for revealing Johnson's many prejudices, follies, caprices, weaknesses, animosity, superstition, intolerance, and puerile pronouncements. Boswell has prostituted his homage to Johnson's follies (1:268, 267). In April, the *Journal encyclopédique*'s reviewer cannot easily distinguish the diverse sensations that reading Boswell's book induced. It grants that there are occasional judicious remarks and clever conversations, but in general it finds successive severe sarcasms, childish vanity, and "des choses si plates, que plus d'une fois on jette le livre de dépit. . . . Une chose qui étonne encore plus, c'est l'attention des personnages pour Johnson. Ils lui témoignent un respect qui va presque jusqu'à l'adoration" (3, no. 1 [1786]: 223).[43] We then see a translated portrait of Boswell's "aristarque anglois" that emphasizes his character, politics, manners, religion, and conversation and only briefly touches on some of the literary works that evoked such respect (pp. 224–25). By August of 1788 the review of *Two Dialogues containing a Comparative View . . . of Chesterfield and . . . Johnson* observed that the dragon of virtue Johnson has been widely written upon. "Malheureusement, aucun de ses biographes n'est parvenu à le faire aimer, à justifier la dureté de son humeur." Here indeed is "le philosophe sauvage" (6, no. 1 [1788]: 56, 59, but with mangled printing). Intensifying Anglo-French warfare limited subsequent reviewing journals' efforts, for I have not yet found reviews of Boswell's 1791 *Life of Johnson*.[44] When these surface, it seems reasonable to assume that they too will emphasize Johnson's character, rudeness, talk, and public incivility, as in fact he later was characterized. Anecdote after anecdote regularly appear regarding verbal exchanges, his hostility to the Scots, and his harsh and bizarre character.

Hermile Reynald, for example, published his doctoral dissertation on Johnson in 1856. He discusses and admires Johnson's work, but he is especially taken by Johnson the odd man and brilliant talker as shown by the "fameux Boswell." Indeed Johnson's conversation, "avec plus de force peut-être et plus d'éclat" than his books, disciplines in order to ameliorate both letters and manners. Reynald later adds that like Macaulay he too wonders how someone so indifferent to the form of government could be so angry against the partisans of "liberté."[45]

The union of Boswell and Macaulay as movers of judgment is even clearer in Hippolyte Taine's influential *Histoire de la littérature anglaise* in 1863. His book orients itself around national differences and national race. Taine admired English politics, economics, and education, but like many of his predecessors he regarded the English as splendidly vital but violent rude aliens who should be approached with caution.[46] At one point Taine tries an anthropological experiment: what if one of the brutes found himself in a civilized country with civilized manners? What if we transported Johnson, "this ruler of mind, . . . into France, among the pretty drawing-rooms, full of elegant philosophers and epicurean manners; the violence of the contrast will mark better than all argument, the bent and predilections of the English mind."[47]

We can predict the consequences when Taine describes the blunt, brown suited, oddly shaped, tick-besieged, facially scarred, half blind, politically rabid, dogmatic, religious zealot inflicted upon Taine's Gallic epicureans: "Frenchmen of the present time, the admirers of the *Contrat Social*, soon feel, on reading or hearing all this, that they are no longer in France" (2:187). Upon further exposure, "the astonishment of a Frenchman redoubles. . . . we yawn" (2:189). Johnson's periodic essays are blandly wholesome "national food. It is because they are insipid and dull for us that they suit the taste of an Englishman" (2:190). Taine knows why Johnson behaved as he did: his "eyes were English, and the senses are barbarous. Let us leave our repugnance behind us, and look at things as Englishmen do" (2:191). Accordingly, "Frenchmen will say that such lessons are good for barbarians" but will barely like such lay preaching by Johnson and others. "I reply that moralists are useful, and that these have changed a state of barbarism into one of civilisation" (2:192).

Taine in the nineteenth century anticipates Professor Baridon in the twentieth century: for each, Johnson is strange English food for the strange English nation. Each commentator includes a covert theory of causation overt in Reynald: influence by Boswell probably through and with Macaulay and their emphasis on conversation and peculiar personality rather than on literary achievement. Emphasis on such texts changes to an approximate balance between talk and text, and then to the idiosyncratic aristarque. After about 1786 for many across the channel Johnson becomes a learned version of the English eccentric, a quirky and diminished John Bull rather than the widely admired extraordinary man of letters able to instruct the Académie Française in the art of lexicography. Post-Boswellian commentators reject and redefine the earlier French history of literary response. Johnson the author then had been called England's most instructive and fecund writer, all of whose works deserved preservation. Once the verbal and visual replace the intellectual Johnson, once those parts replace or distort the whole, he is merely the repugnant if well-meaning alien barbarian, respect for whom is an "amiable perversion of national feeling." In such a case, the project of recovering Johnson as a man of letters indeed becomes impossible. Tant pis à nous.[48]

NOTES

1. I draw this partial list from David Fleeman's indispensable *Bibliography of the Works of Samuel Johnson* (Oxford: Clarendon Press, 2000). The terminal date for the count is 1800, though I go somewhat further in my own discussion. This essay will have added several items to Fleeman's lists. Francophone culture includes relevant publication

and commentary in the low countries and often culturally French Germany and Scandinavia.

2. Michel Baridon, "On the Relation of Ideology to Form in Johnson's Style," in *Fresh Reflections on Samuel Johnson: Essays in Criticism*, ed. Prem Nath (Troy, NY: Whitston Publishing Company, 1987), p. 85. See also René Wellek, *A History of Modern Criticism: 1750–1950. The Later Eighteenth Century* (New Haven: Yale University Press, 1955), p. 84: Johnson "has been dismissed—especially on the Continent—as a 'British superstition.'" Miriam Bridenne more recently asserts that without Boswell's *Life of Johnson* "le nome de Johnson n'aurait peut-être pas atteint les rives de la posterité." This is in *Samuel Johnson. Le Paresseux. Traduit de l'anglais par M. Varney* (Paris: Editions ALLIA, 2000), p. [119].

3. For aspects of physical and parodic Johnson, see Morris Brownell, *Samuel Johnson and the Arts* (Oxford: Clarendon Press, 1989), pp. 91–104, and Philip Smallwood, "The Johnsonian Monster and the *Lives of the Poets*: James Gillray, Critical History, and the Eighteenth-Century Satirical Cartoon," *British Journal for Eighteenth-Century Studies* 25 (2002): 217–45. The world aware of Johnson as talker also knew that Johnson himself distinguished between the dialectics of speech and of writing. As Boswell properly said in the *Journal of a Tour to the Hebrides* (1785), though Johnson "owned he sometimes talked for victory; he was too conscientious to make errour permanent and pernicious, by deliberately writing it." See *Boswell's Life of Johnson Together with Boswell's Journal of a Tour to the Hebrides*, ed. George Birkbeck Hill and rev. L. F. Powell (Oxford: Clarendon Press, 1934–50), 5:17. Subsequent references to the *Life* are from this edition.

4. I am indebted to Dr. James Caudle of the Yale Boswell edition for information regarding de Cosne. For the Académie, see Institut de France, *Les Registres de l'Académie Françoise 1672–1793*, ed. Charles Camille Doucet (Paris, 1895), 3:67. See Johnson's French letter to Miss Flint, dated March 31, 1769, in *The Letters of Samuel Johnson*, ed. Bruce Redford (Princeton: Princeton University Press, 1992), 1:321–22, and 1:321 n. 1; see also n. 32 below. I refer to this work hereafter as Johnson, *Letters*. For the visit to Fréron, see *The French Journals of Mrs. Thrale and Doctor Johnson*, ed. Moses Tyson and Henry Guppy (Manchester: Manchester University Press, 1932), p. 173, and Boswell, *Life*, 2:406, where Johnson thus labels Voltaire: "*Vir est acerrimi ingenii et paucarum literarum.*" Subsequent references to the *Life* are from this edition. Mrs. Thrale (Piozzi) offers two sometimes differing accounts of the meeting: *French Journals*, pp. 85–86, and her *Anecdotes of the Late Samuel Johnson* (1786), as recorded in *French Journals*, pp. 85–86 n. 1.

5. See, for example, the translation by Antoine-Marie Henri Boulard in *Morceaux choisis du Rambler, ou du Rodeur; ouvrage dans le genre du Spectateur, traduit de l'anglois de Johnson* (Paris, 1785; but see n. 16, below). Boulard significantly rearranges Johnson's order of publication. He follows Johnson's meaning with reasonable, but not consistent, fidelity but often changes his style along the following lines: fewer passive-voice sentences; simpler diction and sentence structure especially for Johnson's periodic sentences and doublets; changing of words to French concepts when the English word does not have a French equivalent; and eradication of many colloquialisms that seemed gross to French taste. We badly need a full study of the Johnson translations in France.

6. [Mallet], *Essai sur l'étude des belles-lettres* (Paris, 1747), pp. 11–13. Relevant passages are abstracted in the *Bibliothèque raisonée des ouvrages des savans de l'Europe* 42 (1749): 37–38. The *Bibliothèque* thinks Mallet excessive. Johnson's own attitude toward

France was generally hostile as well. See *French Journals of Mrs. Thrale*, pp. 169–88. She records Johnson's distaste for six French towns during their 1775 visit, when he already was an acknowledged eminence. He is more impressed with the splendors of Paris, which he nonetheless often thinks mean and slovenly. In assessing his tone, however, we need to accept his physical, linguistic, and emotional discomfort. As he enters the Palais Bourbon "my Wife was in my mind. She would have been pleased. Having now nobody to please, I am little pleased" (p. 175). For fuller discussion of Johnson and his knowledge of France and French, see James Gray, "Arras/Hélas! A Fresh Look at Samuel Johnson's French," in *Johnson After Two Hundred Years*, ed. Paul J. Korshin (Philadelphia: University of Pennsylvania Press, 1986), pp. 79–96.

7. See n. 27, below, for further remarks regarding the "incomprehensible" British taste for Shakespeare.

8. *Journal anglais. Contenant les découvertes dans les sciènces, les arts liberaux & méchaniques . . . des trois royaumes & des colonies qui en dépendent* (Paris, 1775), 1:10.

9. Uta Janssens, *Matthieu Maty and the Journal Britannique 1750–1755* (Amsterdam: Holland University Press, 1975), p. 4. See especially pp. 108–12 on Maty's discussion of Johnson.

10. The *Journal* was eagerly anticipated. See the remark in Fréron's *Lettres sur quelques écrits de ce temps* 13 (1754): 344: "Cet ouvrage qui étoit attendu depuis long-temps, vient enfin de paroître. . . . Quelques gens de Lettres connus & estimés on formé cette grand entreprise. . . . Avec de pareilles dispositions & des talens, on ne peut manquer de réussir."

11. One must be wary of Maty's motives. By 1751 Chesterfield was in effect Maty's patron, his occasional patient, and the aristocrat to whom Johnson dedicated the *Plan* of his *Dictionary* in 1747. It is at the least plausible that Maty's reviews of the *Rambler* are surrogate nods to Chesterfield. Maty's later often stern response to the *Dictionary* and its Preface support this hypothesis.

For the commercial importance of a patron, see The Wesleyan Edition of the Works of Henry Fielding, *The True Patriot and Related Writings*, ed. W. B. Coley (Middletown, CT: Wesleyan University Press, 1987), *The True Patriot*, No. 22 (1746). Fielding mockingly says that one way to judge the excellence of a book is "by observing whom it is dedicated to: And it can hardly be imagined what an Effect a Dedication to his Grace of—, my Lord C——, or Dr. M——, &c. has sometimes had, in filling the Bookseller's *Pocket*, and inhancing the *Reputation* of the Author" (pp. 254–55). Macaulay later would make a similar observation. On August 2, 1833, he wrote to his sister Hannah: "If you wish for a proof of the kind of influence which Chesterfield had over his contemporaries, look at the prospectus of Johnson's dictionary [i.e., the *Plan*]. Look even at Johnson's angry letter. It contains the strongest admission of the boundless influence which Chesterfield exercised over society": *The Letters of Thomas Babington Macaulay*, ed. Thomas Pinney (Cambridge: Cambridge University Press, 1974), 2:289. Johnson's overt rejection of Chesterfield in the famous letter, and his covert rejection in the Preface to the *Dictionary* seek to nullify such "exercise," at least over Johnson himself.

12. Pierre Clément's *Nouvelles littéraires* were reprinted as *Les Cinq années littéraires. . . . 1748–52* (Berlin, 1755); see Lettre 86, dated Londres October 15, 1751, 2:157. For association with the *Spectator*, see 2:157. These volumes were further reprinted as *Lettres critiques sur divers sujets de littérature* (Amsterdam, 1767), 2:157. See also Aubin Louis Millin in *Melanges de littérature étrangère* (Paris, 1785–86), 1:211, and the *Revue philosophique, littéraire et politique* 42 (1804): 40.

13. For these, see Roger, *La Traducteur. Ou Traduction de divers feuilles choisies tir-ées des papiers periodiques anglais*. I have been able to see only volumes 2 (1754–55) and 4 (1756) of these at the Bibliothèque Nationale de France. I assume that volumes 1 and 3 have several other *Rambler*s and perhaps *Idler*s. The *Rambler*s translated are numbers 8, 28, 29, 44, 33, 34, 45, 42, 46, 40, 54, 41, 43, 47, 49, 50, 57, 71, 74, 75, 176, 77, 58, 55.

14. Johnson complained that Goldsmith "never exchanged mind with you": Boswell, *Life*, 3:37. For the desirable nature of such exchange, see "Johnson and the Arts of Nar-ration: *The Life of Savage, The Vanity of Human Wishes*, and *Rasselas*" within.

15. We recall Arthur Murphy's fortunate fall. One day when in the country with Sam-uel Foote, he found it necessary to return to London to find a subject for his next *Gray's Inn Journal*. Foote suggests that he merely translate a nice little essay in a handy French magazine that, alas, turns out to be a French version of Johnson's *Rambler*, No. 190 (1752). Later discovery of the error allows red-faced Murphy to apologize to Johnson and become his lifelong friend and admirer: Boswell, *Life*, 1:356 and 1:356 n. 2. I have not yet been able to identify the "French magazine." The retranslated *Gray's Inn Journal* was No. 38, second series, June 15, 1754. It is omitted in contemporary reprints. For Berquin, see *Choix de tableaux tirés de diverses galeries*, with the *Idler*, No. 21 (1759), as praised in *L'Année littéraire* 2 (1775): 74–80. Mercier elaborates on *Rambler*, Nos. 204, 205 (1752), in *Eloges et discours philosophiques* (Amsterdam, 1776), pp. 165–79, and again in *Fictions morales* (Paris, 1792), pp. 1–28, with slight changes, as "Ou est le bonheur?" I am indebted for Mercier to Paul K. Alkon, who alerted me to Riikka Forss-tröm, Bibliotheca Historica 75, *Possible Worlds: The Idea of Happiness in the Utopian Vision of Louis Sébastien Mercier* (Helsinki: Suomalaisen Kirjallisuuden Seura, 2002), pp. 138, and 138 n. 236. The *Bibliothèque universelle des romans* also reprints these as "Histoire du roi Seged" with the *Rambler* but not Johnson acknowledged: 2 (1777): 26–32, and 1 (1783): 181–98. The *Journal helvetique* reprints the *Rambler*, No. 91 (1751), as "L'Esprit et La Science, Allegoire Angloise tirée Du *Rembler*" [*sic*], pp. 168–70, also without mentioning Johnson. The *Censeur universel* prints Boulard's version of this as "Histoire allégorique de Patronage" in its review of the *Morceaux choisis du Rambler* (3:291–93).

16. The *Morceaux chosis* with which I have worked is dated 1789, but it is reviewed by the *Journal encyclopèdique* in 1785, the *Journal des sçavans* in 1786, and in the *Censeur universel* in 1786 (3:291–93), and obviously is borrowed and acknowledged by Millin in 1785–86. The *Censeur* also notes publication of the 1786 Maestricht text (3:78), and observes that "cet Auteur justement célebre" is more difficult to translate even than most English poets: "& son *Rambler* est de tous ses écrits, celui où il a le plus tra-vaillé à caracteriser sa diction par l'énergie des termes q'il a souvent crées, & la hardiesse des inversions que l'Anglois autorisé" (3:73). I have not seen the 1785 edition, but as-sume that it is the same as 1789. See *Melanges*, 2:143–95. Millin follows Boulard in call-ing the *Rambler*s "Discours": Millin's "Discours I" also is Boulard's "Discours I" and Johnson's *Rambler*, No. 22; Millin's "Discours II" is Boulard's "Discours VIII" and *Rambler*, No. 19; Millin's "Discours III" is Boulard's "Discours XXI" and *Rambler*, No. 82; Millin's "Discours IV" is Boulard's "Discours XVII" and *Rambler*, No. 24. All of Johnson's essays were from 1750. The *Censeur* observes that "Tous les Journaux ont déja fait l'éloge de discernement qui l'a guidé dans ce Recueil, de l'exactitude de sa traduc-tion & de la sagesse, ainsi que de la pureté de son style" (3:291).

17. [Boulard], *Morceaux choisis du Rambler*, p. [v]. See also notes 5 and 16, above.

Boulard is most interested in the moral and domestic rather than the literary numbers, and is especially attracted to the English genre of the periodical essay. He translates the *Rambler* in his own rather than in Johnson's chronological order; but he gives Johnson's numbers in the left margin of his "Table des discours." His copy text is *"la huietième Edition du* Rambler, *faite à Londres en* 1771" (p. 500). *L'Année littéraire* reviews the *Morceaux choisis* in 6 (1785): 217–32, 6:232 quoted, as does Pierre Rousseau in the *Journal encyclopédique*, 8 (Nov. 1785): 70–74, p. 71 quoted. See 7:74 in which the editors cite enough to show "avec quel agrément l'auteur anglois traitoit les sujets les plus sérieux, & avec quelle pureté son traducteur écrit dans sa langue."

The fame carried over to the *Idler* later was enhanced by the *Dictionary*. The *Gazette littéraire* 8 (Dec.–March [1766]): 285–89 translates No. 37 (1758) as "L'Or et le Fer." It is *"Discours Moral traduit de l'OISIF*, (The Idler) *Ouvrage anglois dans le goût du* Spectateur, *& composé par M.* Johnson, *Auteur du* Dictionnaire de la Langue angloise, *du* Rambler *& de plusieurs autres ouvrages estimés."* The *Idler* was translated in two volumes by Jean-Baptiste Varney as *Le Paresseux, par le Docteur Johnson* (Paris, 1790). Given the fame and distinction of its author and the multiple editions in English, Varney says, he cannot understand why it has so long been neglected in France. Johnson's own name recommends it "si puissamment" (1:vij).

18. Even Voltaire was either polite or persuaded by Madame Belot's version, to whom on May 16, 1760, he responded with thanks for her gift: *Rasselas* "m'a paru d'une philosophie aimable, et très bien écrit": *The Complete Works of Voltaire, Correspondence and related documents*, ed. Theodore Besterman (Banbury, Oxfordshire: Voltaire Foundation, 1971), 21:309, D8913. Johnson knew and was pleased by such rapid translation of his philosophic tale. In 1766 he presented a copy of the French *Rasselas* to Mrs. Thrale, which she in turn presented to William Conway in 1820. Her marked copy includes marginal annotation at the end of chapter 46, when Imlac reminds the astronomer of his human insignificance before divine vastness: "Souvenez-vous surtout que vous êtes seulement un atome dans la masse de l'humanité, & que vous n'avez ni telle vertu, ni telle vice qui puisse vous attiroir exclusivement des faveurs ou des afflictions si surnaturelles." A marginal forearm and hand with a long index finger points to these words. The wrist area also is pierced by two intersecting but almost parallel lines, as if also to suggest marking an important passage. See Yale University Beinecke shelfmark, 1979.55, *Histoire de Rasselas, prince d'Abissinie. Par M. Jhonnson [sic], Auteur du Rambler, & traduite de l'anglois par Madame B***** (Amsterdam, 1760), p. 214; there are markings on p. 19 as well. Handwritten notes on the verso of a front marbled page indicate the respective gifts to Mrs. Thrale and to William Conway. "N.F.M." later purchased the book "at the sale of Mr. Conway's effects, May 24, 1828." I do not know whether the annotation is Mrs. Thrale's or another reader's. Johnson's gift to Mrs. Thrale, however, suggests that he wanted her to know about his relative French fame.

Johnson was pleased by all the several translations of *Rasselas*. On March 4, 1773, he tells William White: "The little Book has been well received, and is translated into Italian, French, German, and Dutch. It has now one honour more by an American edition." See Johnson, *Letters*, 2:13.

19. Fréron, *L'Année littéraire . . . par M. Fréron, des Académies d'Angers, de Montaubon & de Nancy* (Amsterdam, 1760), 3:160, 163, 164 (various longueurs), 3:150–51 (on Imlac's dissertation). As with several other French journals, the volume number represents the volume for the year only, not for the entire *Année littéraire*.

20. *Rasselas. Prince d'Abissinie. Roman. Traduit de l'anglais de Dr. Johnson, par le*

Comte de Fouchecour. Enrichie de taille douce (Londres, 1798), p. [iii]. Jean-François-Louis-Marie-Marguerile de Salivet de Fouchécourt (sic) was married in England on December 26, 1793, to Charlotte-Agathe Grant de Vaux. As an emigré in England to save his neck, he gratefully observes: "Heureux mes efforts me méritent l'approbation de mes lecteurs, et si la nation loyale et hospitalière à la quelle je fais hommage de ma traduction l'accueille avec indulgence" (p. [iii]). By "roman" Fouchecour probably means conte philosophique. *Rasselas*'s sense of the futility of search for a perfect world must have resonated among the French Revolution's enemies.

In 1787 the May *Journal des sçavans* optimistically reports that English now is so widespread in France "qu'elle est devenue aujourd'hui une partie de l'education de la jeunesse" (p. 312). This was included in a review of a prospectus of a series of English books that included "Johnson's Lives of the English Poets" (p. 313). For Johnson as an agent in that language-learning, see, for example, *La Vraie maniere d'apprendre une langue quelconque, vivante ou morte, par le moyen de la langue françoise; suite de la grammaire angloise, ou Traducteur littérale d'un ouvrage anglois, intitulé The Prince of Abissinia, Histoire de Rasselas, Prince d'Abyssinie* (Paris, 1787)—with facing French and English translations. There were comparable pedagogic versions. In 1818 "Johnson est reconnu pour l'autuer le plus classique de l'Angleterre." *Rasselas* is written "avec autant de force que de correction et d'élegance": *Nouveau cours de langue anglaise, contenant l'histoire de Rasselas, du Docteur Johnson, et le poëme du Village Abandonnée, de Goldsmith* (Paris, 1818), 1:iij. For "joli petit roman" see *La Vallon fortuné, ou Rasselas et Dinarbas*, trans. [?] McCarthy (Paris, 1817), p. [3]. The 1819 bilingual edition of *Rasselas* referred to "Le Docteur Samuel Johnson qui fut à juste titre considéré comme le plus brillant ornament du 18e siècle": *Rasselas, Prince of Abyssinia; A tale by Dr. Johnson. With the Life of the Author. Both in English and French* (Paris, 1819), pp. [2–3]. The honorific "Dr. Johnson" in such titles suggests further knowledge of the English literary scene. Diderot was not among *Rasselas*'s friends. He says of Madame Belot's translation and its prefatory linking of *Rasselas* and Voltaire's *Candide*: "tout le monde a trouvé le Candide français très-gai et très original, et le prétendu Candide anglais, ennuyeux et détestable." See *Correspondance littéraire, philosophique et critique par Grimm, Diderot, Raynal, Meister*, ed. Maurice Tourneux (Paris, 1878), 4:231, Diderot to Grimm April 15, 1760. "Tout le monde" was larger than Diderot thought.

21. *Bibliothèque raisonnée* in Article 14, "Nouvelles Literaires de Londres" in its July–August–September number: 39 (1747): 233–34. I am indebted to James Sledd and Gwin J. Kolb for bringing this to my attention: *Dr. Johnson's Dictionary: Essays in the Biography of a Book* (Chicago: University of Chicago Press, 1955), pp. 82–83, 98–99, and p. 219 n. 132. Given the warm praise of Chesterfield, one may reasonably suspect that Maty in London wrote or encouraged the *Bibliothèque*'s praise of Johnson's *Plan*. The *Bibliothèque* says that "pour être bon Critique il faut être bon Philosophe" (39:233–34). In the *Journal britannique* Maty himself praises what he expects will be rare in dictionaries, Johnson's philosophical and critical approach (4:236). Given Maty's consequent stern review of the *Dictionary*, one must again suspect that puffing Johnson was surrogate stroking of Chesterfield. For Clément, see *Les Cinq années littéraires*, 2:157 n. (i). I have not yet found the relevant original issue of October 1751 to determine whether the note was consistent with Maty's 1751 notice, or whether it was added for the 1755 edition, when publication of Johnson's *Dictionary* seemed imminent and the booksellers renewed their advertisements.

22. *Le Journal des sçavans*, Sept.–Oct., 1755, Octobre in "Nouvelles litteraires. Angle-

terre. De Londres," p. 2081; and listed in the annual *Bibliographie*, p. 2682; arrived in the book shop, Jan.-Mars, 1756, "Mars. Nouvelles litteraires. De Paris," p. 571.

23. See Boswell, *Life of Johnson*, 1:284. Maty ends his *Journal britannique* in December of 1755. In the *Life* Adams, or Boswell, mislabels it the *Bibliothèque britannique*. See also the Hill-Powell note, *Life*, 1:284 n. 3.

24. Maty gave several extracts, as did Prévost in the first *Journal étranger*'s discussion of the *Dictionary*. The translation in December of 1756 is complete. Boswell thought that Diderot translated this, or perhaps another, version, but does not cite his evidence and I can find none. See Boswell to Temple, November 6, 1775, in The Yale Edition of the Private Papers of James Boswell, Research Edition, vol. 6, *The Correspondence of James Boswell and William Johnson Temple 1756–1795*, ed. Thomas Crawford (Edinburgh: Edinburgh University Press; New Haven: Yale University Press, 1997), pp. 403 and 404 n. 5, in which Crawford and C. B. Tinker also "have been unable to trace this translation."

25. *Gazette littéraire* 7 (Sept.–Nov. 1765): 171. See below for further information regarding the *Gazette* on Johnson's Preface. Thereafter, the *Journal géneral de la littérature étrangère* notes the appearance of John Ebers's five-volume *Englisch deutsches, und deutsch englisches woertebuch* (Leipsig, 1799): Ebers "a pris pour guide le grand Dictionnaire de Johnson, édition de 1785": 4, no. 1(1801): 27. This *Journal* also announces Herbert Croft's attempted revision and correction of Johnson's *Dictionary*: see 4, no. 3 (1801): 137–38. The *Journal des sçavans* notes the appearance of the revised fourth edition (1773) of the *Dictionary*: July 1773, "Nouvelles littéraires. Angleterre de Londres" (p. 502). The *Censeur universel* for October 21, 1786, reported that the imprudent Chesterfield lacked the generosity of soul to be a proper literary patron. Johnson "dédaigna de satisfaire sa vanité" and wrote the memorable letter: it "vivra éternellement dans la mémoire de ceux qui ont eu le bonheur de l'entendre" (3:382). The article from which this remark comes, like many others in the *Censeur universel*, may translate an English source.

26. See also Hennet's *La Poètique anglaise* (Paris, 1806) discussed within. Hennet calls the *Dictionary* "ce grand ouvrage, le meilleur qui ait jamais existé dans ce genre, aussi vaste dans sa conception, aussi riche dans son exécution que le dictionnaire de l'académie française est faible et imparfait" (2:454).

27. See Letter 18, "On Tragedy," in Voltaire's *Letters concerning the English Nation*. Voltaire's attitude toward the English is summed up in this remark in a different context: "It is inadvertently affirm'd in the Christian Countries of *Europe*, that the *English* are Fools and Madmen" (p. 73). In literature, such men are best suited for the wildness of the ode and the terror of tragedy. I have further considered aspects of relevant problems in "Enlightenment Canon Wars: Anglo-French Views of Literary Greatness," *ELH* 60 (1993): 79–100, and "Censoring Johnson in France: Johnson and Suard on Voltaire: A New Document," *Review of English Studies* n.s. 45 (1994): 230–33.

French attitudes toward Shakespeare remained at the least uncertain for much of the eighteenth century. In 1765, for example, the Parisian *Gazette littéraire de l'Europe* says that British enthusiasm for Shakespeare is "une chose incompréhensible pour les Etrangers" (5:174). That incomprehension was encouraged by regular bowdlerizing of Shakespeare for performance or translation. Their response to Shakespeare in English performance in English theaters often was consternation at the drama, audience, and actors. See Simon Nicolas Henri, *Annales politiques, civiles, et littéraires du dix-huitieme siecle: ouvrage périodique, par M. Linguet* (Paris, 1777), 1:171–80, a Frenchman's visit to Covent Garden with his sister, where they sit in the upper gallery, are puzzled and intimidated by the rowdy behavior, and clearly dislike the brutality in *Othello*. See also 2:51–52, in which Pope's and Hume's praise of Shakespeare seems like nonsense, and 3:264 (also in 1:180) where the ironically labeled "divin *Shakespear*" is played in a vulgar, rowdy, plebeian theater peculiar to English taste. Linguet even writes a decidedly mixed estimate of David Garrick and is puzzled by the virtual state funeral more appropriate for a national hero: 5 (1779): 229–56. The French visitor, above, could not understand English. Nor did Shakespeare's nominal French translator (1783), Jean-François Ducis. See Joseph H. McMahon, "Ducis: Unkindest Cutter?" *Yale French Studies* 33 (1964): 14–25. One can see Ducis's work in *Oeuvres de J. F. Ducis* (Paris, 1813). For other discussion of Shakespeare in France, see J. J. Jusserand, *Shakespeare en France sous l'ancien régime* (Paris, 1880); Thomas R. Lounsbury, *Shakespeare and Voltaire* (New York: Charles Scribner's Sons, 1902); C. M. Haines, *Shakespeare in France: Criticism Voltaire to Victor Hugo*, Shakespeare Survey (London: Shakespeare Association, 1925); Theodore Besterman, Studies on Voltaire and the Eighteenth Century, vol. 54 *Voltaire on Shakespeare* (Geneva: Institute et Musée Voltaire, 1967).

28. For some aspects of this conflict, see Studies on Voltaire and the Eighteenth Century, vol. 179, *Voltaire and the English* (Oxford: Voltaire Foundation, At the Taylor Institution, 1979), and especially David Williams, "Voltaire's war with England: the appeal to Europe 1760–1764," pp. 79–100. Josephine Grieder has studied larger aspects of anglomania and anglophobia, in Histoire des idées et critique littéraire, no. 230, *Anglomania in France, 1740–1789: fact, fiction, and political discourse* (Geneva: Librairie Droz, 1985).

29. "Lettre de M. de Voltaire à l'Académie Française," August 25, 1776, as in *Oeuvres complètes de Voltaire, Mélanges*, vol. 9 (Paris, 1880), p. 352. Such Shakespearean corruption threatens "immoler la France" (p. 358) and "humilier sa patrie" (p. 359). Grace à dieu, French letters survived the sauvage, bas, absurde, barbarian onslaught.

30. The Yale Edition of the Works of Samuel Johnson, vol. 7, *Johnson on Shakespeare*, ed. Arthur Sherbo, with an intro. by Bertrand H. Bronson (New Haven: Yale University Press, 1968), p. 66. Subsequent citations from this edition are cited in the text as YE with the volume and page.

31. See "*OBSERVATIONS sur Shakespeare, tirées de la Préface que M. S. Johnson a mise à la tête d'une nouvelle édition des oeuvres de ce Poëte*" (4:65–94). There are several nuances, corrections, grammatical changes, and printer's variations (like et for &) in the *Variétés littéraires*' version; but the extracts and translations essentially are the same as those in the *Gazette littéraire*. See the *Journal helvetique* for July 1769, pp. 3–29, for its observations on Shakespeare "tirées de la Préface" of Johnson: p. 9 for Voltaire's remarks as among "des chicanes de petits esprits." Some scholars see more similarity between Johnson and Voltaire than is usually thought. See Donald Greene, "Voltaire and Johnson," in *Enlightenment Studies in Honour of Lester G. Crocker*, ed. Virgil Topazio (Oxford: Voltaire Foundation, 1979), pp. 111–31, and Mark J. Temmer, *Samuel Johnson and Three Infidels: Rousseau, Voltaire, Diderot* (Athens: University of Georgia Press, 1988).

32. Voltaire, *Questions sur l'encyclopédie*, 2nd ed. ([London], 1771), 2:171. Voltaire petulantly refers to Suard's term "*petits esprits*," which is scarcely an inevitable abbreviation of Johnson's "petty cavils of petty minds" (YE 7:66): "Je ne veux point soupçonner le sieur *Johnson* d'être un mauvais plaisant, & d'aimer trop le vin." Voltaire subtly enlarges his revenge in 1776, when he tells the Académie Française that Rymer correctly criticized irregular Shakespeare. See "Lettre d M. Voltaire à l'Académie Française," August 25, 1776, in *Oeuvres complètes de Voltaire*, 30:363. See also Johnson's letter to

young Louise Flint (*Letters*, 1:321), who would become the unfortunate wife of the counterrevolutionary student of language, Antoine Rivarol. He abandoned her shortly after their marriage and left her and their son in France during the Revolution. Madame Rivarol supported herself in part with translations from English into French. These included: Edmund Burke, *Appel des Whigs modernes aux Whigs anciens* (1791) and Robert Dodsley, *Encyclopédie morale, contenant les devoirs de l'homme en société, ou économie de la vie civile* (1803; 2nd ed., 1821). She began this process of translation as the companion to Frances Reynolds in Paris, from whence she sent Johnson her versions of his individual comments on Shakespeare's plays. Johnson replied to her in French on March 31, 1769, and mentioned "des traductions les plus belles" (*Letters*, 1:322).

33. The *Journal anglais*, No. 13, for April 15, 1776, included a long synopsis of *Othello* (2:257–81), as from le Tourneur's *Shakespeare*. It later offers synopses of *The Tempest*, No. 15, May 1776 (2:385–404), *Julius Caesar*, No. 20, July 30, 1776 (3:193–203), and *Henry IV*, January 1, 1778 (3:437–43). The discussion of *Julius Caesar* attacks Shakespeare's violation of the unities and asks about the bases for the unnamed Johnson and others' support for their own systems: "sont-elles solides?" (3:199). Long synopses suggest French lack of familiarity with the plays. The *Journal des sçavans* notes the 1773 appearance of the Johnson-Stevens Shakespeare, on which le Tourneur's French versions are based: "Nouvelles littéraires. Angleterre de Londres," January 1774, p. 51.

34. For le Tourneur, see *Shakespeare traduit de l'anglois, dédié au roi* (Paris, 1776) 1:4 n. 1. Le Tourneur's *Shakespeare* soon was joined by major continental commentaries and translations, including those by Johann Joachim Eschenburg (1771, 1778, 1787) for whom Johnson, often through the Stevens-Johnson revision, also is a regular source of notes and guidance. For Stendhal, *Stendhal. Oeuvres complètes. Racine et Shakespeare*, nouvelle édition, ed. Pierre Martino and Victor Del Litto (Geneva: Cercle du Bibliophile; Paris: Librairie Ancienne Honoré Champion, 1970), pp. 59, 61, and the notes on p. 337, where we learn that in 1819 Stendhal called Johnson's Preface "Le pére du romanticisme." Such interest in Shakespeare and English literature was joined by comparable interest in German literature. For many, these nations' letters were thought more "romantic," liberating, and appropriate for modern France than its more "classical" literary ancestors.

35. The *Journal des sçavans*'s belated October 1774 notice of le Tourneur's *Savage et . . . Thompson* (pp. 653–66) does not acknowledge Johnson's authorship. The review probably was designed to help publicize le Tourneur's pending Shakespeare translation, whose Prospectus it reprints in June of 1775 (pp. 429–32).

36. Diderot was not persuaded and was ambivalent regarding *Savage*: "Cet ouvrage eût été délicieux, et d'une finesse à comparer aux *Mémoires du Comte de Grammont*, si l'auteur anglais se fût proposé de faire la satire de son héros; mais malheureusement il est de bonne foi": *Denis Diderot: Oeuvres complètes*, ed. Jules Assézat and Maurice Tourneaux (Paris, 1875–77), 9:451.

37. The reviewer quotes Johnson at length on the lack of a written Erse language, and therefore the impossibility of Ossianic Erse manuscripts. It is hard to tell whether its concluding remark is ridicule or reverence: "Ainsi cette langue, qui a fait du bruit dans le monde littéraire, est reléguée par l'auteur dans le pays des chimeres, plus vaste encore que l'on ne pense. La voilà rangée parmi ces problèmes d'antiquités dont tant de sçavans ont cherché la solution, qui ont enfanté une multitude de volumes, & pas un rayon de lumiere" (p. 256). The *Journey*'s discussion of Ossian remained known and contested. See *Bibliothèque britannique . . . littérature et sciences et arts* (48 [1811]: 111). This is part

of its review of Henry Mackenzie's 1805 *Report of the Committee of the Highland Society of Scotland* concerning the authenticity of the Ossian poems.

38. The *Journal des sçavans* reviews the *Nouveau recueil* in its March 1786 number and briefly discusses the "Voyage en Ecosse . . . par le Docteur Johnson" (pp. 131–36, p. 132 quoted).

39. For Huchet, see *Voyages dans les Hébrides, ou iles occidentales d'Écosse, par le D*ʳ*. Johnson. Traduite de l'anglais* (Paris, An. XII), p. [i]. Huchet goes on to say that "rien n'a échappé à . . . son attention" regarding the Hebrideans' government, prejudices, superstitions, and the like. Johnson also offers "réflxions ingénieuses et profondes" in powerful style: "Son style extraordinairement travaillé, est plein de nerf et ne manque pas d'une certaine grâce; mais l'art s'y fait trop sentir" (p. [i]). Huchet praises his valued friend the Abbé Ricard for urging him to do the translation. Johnson's *Western Islands* clearly were familiar to the French literati.

40. See *Magazin encyclopédique* 4 (1796): 94–124 for its printing of Boulard's *"Jugement de Samuel Jonhson [sic] sur les ouvrages de Pope"* (4:94). Millin translated "Cowley" in the first volume of his *Melanges de littérature étrangère*, le Tourneur translated *Savage*, and *Gray* appears in Couret-de-Velleneuve's *Matinées d'été*, and *L'Esprit des journaux*, January 1780, reviewed the first four volumes (p. 124 n). The *Bibliothèque britannique . . . littérature et sciences et arts* offers "Remarques" on the "Life of Milton": 32 (1806): 314–337, and further "Remarques" on Johnson's view of English versification: pp. 470–93. Johnson "ce grand critique" (p. 473) clearly remained an engaging and fertilizing force in French criticism as in French knowledge of English (p. 489 n. 1). Boulard's "Citoyen" Sinson apparently is the M. Sinson who translated Shaftesbury's *Les Soliloques, ou entretiens avec soi-même* (London and Paris, 1771). I have not attempted to determine whether the putative manuscript has survived in private or in pubic hands.

41. Hennet must also have been using one of the other compendia of English poets, probably Chalmers or Bell. See Thomas F. Bonnell, "John Bell's *Poets of Great Britain*: The 'Little Trifling Edition' Revisited," *Modern Philology* 85 (1987): 128–52, and Bonnell, "Bookselling and Canon-Making: The Trade Rivalry over the English Poets, 1776–1783," *Studies in Eighteenth-Century Culture* 19 (1989): 53–69.

42. De Rochfort's review was thoughtful, but his familiarity with Johnson's canon was general rather than specific. Discussion of Johnson's poetry, for example, takes only one paragraph and is limited to a few "des vers latins" (p. 542). He seems to think that the Preface to Shakespeare is part of the *Lives of the Poets*, though this may only be careless writing (p. 543). He also thinks that Johnson's and Britain's denigration of Corneille by means of Shakespeare is strange and misguided (p. 543).

43. Contrast the tone and substance of these reviews with the warmly positive review of Boulard's *Morceaux choisis du Rambler* (81 [1785]: 70–74) cited in nn. 5 and 16 above. Perhaps thanks to Boulard and the Maestricht *Le Rodeur*, the *Journal encyclopédique* also prints what it calls "De la retraite," a translation of Johnson's *Rambler*, No. 6 (1750).

44. For example, in 1797 Boulard includes this remark in his translation of Johnson's *Vie de Milton et jugement sur ses écrits*. He had read in a German journal that Hayley is going to publish a new life of Milton: "Je suis fâché que la guerre ne m'ait pas permis de me le procurer" (p. 140). The *Journal des sçavans* ceased publication for almost five years, from December 1792, when it might have reviewed Boswell's *Life of Johnson*.

45. Reynald, *Samuel Johnson: étude sur sa vie et sur ses principaux ouvrages. Thèse de doctorat* (Paris, 1856), pp. ix (Boswell), x (conversation), 197–98 (Macaulay and liberté).

Reynald often quotes Johnson's apparent harsh language towards others: "Ces violences nous étonnent" (p. 199). Johnson makes limited appearances in other French nineteenth-century literary history. For Philarète Chasles he is part of the army of English eccentrics and a pedantic bear: *Le Dix-huitième siècle en Angleterre* (Paris, 1846), 2:28. At one point Abel-François Villemain lists Johnson as one of Macpherson's stern enemies: *Cours de littérature Française: table de la littérature au xviiie siècle*, new edition (Paris, 1868), 3:7–8. In other places Johnson appears briefly as a commentator, as in Villemain's *Vies des principaux poètes anglais* (Münster, 1870?), pp. 56 (vs. Voltaire on Shakespeare), 115 (on Milton), 133 (on Young), 156–57 (on Pope's Homer), 169–70 (vs. Macpherson).

46. Parochial views of course are not limited to French literary historians. For many on the other side of the channel, the worst of sins is not being British. Johnson himself was scarcely immune to that infection. For a full study of Taine's relations with England, see Bibliothèque de la revue de Littérature Comparée, Tome 6, F. C. Roe, *Taine et l'Anglettere* (Paris: Edouard Champion, 1923). Taine thought that Carlyle overrated Samuel Johnson (p. 68); Taine himself admired Macaulay, see pp. 76–78, who almost certainly influenced his view of Johnson.

47. Taine, *History of English Literature*, trans. H. van Laun (New York, 1871), 2:185. Subsequent citations are given parenthetically in the text. By then Mrs. Piozzi's *Anecdotes* long were eclipsed by Boswell's mingled fame and notoriety. See, for example, *Biographie universelle ancienne et moderne* (Paris, 1843–65). After noting the errors of Hawkins and Murphy, we read that the best life of Johnson is that of the Scottish Boswell, "son admirateur et son ami: . . . et, malgré son extrême prolixité, elle a été rémprimée un très grande nombre de fois. . . . On recherche encore les *Anecdotes sur le docteur Johnson*, par Madame Piozzi" (21:108). Her work may have moved on slightly away from the nineteenth-century back benches when included as part of George Birkbeck Hill's *Johnsonian Miscellanies* in 1897.

48. I end this essay with a plea for further research in the areas of Anglo-French relations in the eighteenth century. At least two generations of largely French, French-trained, or French influenced comparatists made remarkable contributions to our understanding of the various contacts between Europe's then two greatest cultural powers. In the process of turning over about a thousand French literary volumes, I discovered numerous references to British authors and texts, including new translations. It is time to rewrite earlier narratives of Anglo-French relations. This essay may be a start, and perhaps a guide to future colleagues who wish to work on Johnson as translated in France. There surely are more texts to be discovered, and more insights to be gained about cultural transmission and cross-cultural literary judgment.

IV
Johnson and Politics

13

The Genesis of a Controversy: The Politics of Samuel Johnson and the Johnson of Politics

Recent generations of Johnsonians have been graced by gifted biographers, critics, editors, and other scholars often concerned with healthy revisionism. Numerous writers have worked to free Johnson from Boswell's occasional distortions and from the potentially negative rather than complementary power of his great book—the substitution of Johnson's spoken for written word. They also have worked to free Johnson from the related Macaulayan and lingering legacy of Johnson as Mr. Oddity, Mr. Regressive Tory, and Mr. John Bull: Great Britain's Great Cham resisted the progressives' attempts to diminish hierarchy and royal authoritarianism and insure Parliament's control of the crown. Johnson became a muscular monument to be contained and labelled before being safely studied.

The revisionists drew a livelier perspective. Their Johnson produced some of the eighteenth-century's great poems. He was an empiricist with fluid principles well adapted to respect for particular authors' particular achievements. He also was an avid student of the arts, history, and science; he was hostile to the brutalities of imperialism and racism; and he was a pioneer encourager of the first wave of women writing for a commercial market. This list is easily expanded, but I shall briefly discuss one scholar-critic who is among the most prominent progenitors of such revisionism.

JOHNSON AND THE GREENE PARTY

Donald Greene's *The Politics of Samuel Johnson* (1960, 1990), *Samuel Johnson* (1970, 1989), *Age of Exuberance* (1977), and Yale Edition of *Samuel Johnson: Political Writings* (1977), among other works, have been central documents in the mingled efforts to review Johnson and his contribution to the intellectual and moral life of the eighteenth century and its posterity. Perhaps none of the late Donald Greene's many works, however, has been as influential as the two editions of his *Politics of Samuel Johnson*.

There as elsewhere Greene sought to rescue Johnson both from Boswell and from Macaulay. The biographer reflected his own romantic Toryism onto Johnson; the historian denigrated that apparent Toryism for his own political purposes. In each case Johnson emerges as a "conservative" monarchist committed to an unacceptable authoritarian government. Greene replaces Macaulay with Sir Lewis Namier as a guide. After 1714 all those in power during the eighteenth century were Whigs, and all squabbles essentially were among Whig factions. Disgruntled Whigs insulted one another with the label of Tory but shared common beliefs and politics. Those whom Johnson actually regarded as Tories consisted of about 20–25 percent of Commons, were country gentlemen who opposed the central government on behalf of their squirearchic constituency and, fruitlessly, resisted Whiggish commercial expansion. They also voted with the country Whig Walpole when necessary. Eighteenth-century politics overwhelmingly consisted of Whigs positioning themselves, their families, and their allies for professional and national aggrandizement. For Greene, Macaulay's battle between Whig progressive forces of light, and Tory regressive forces of darkness is self-serving fantasy.

Johnson's real pragmatic politics abandoned ideology for the art of effective practical governance. He is empirical, skeptical, and eclectic. What is the most effective way for government wisely to exercise power? How should the wise governed behave? Johnson's answers include each side's recognition of the other's rights. He accepts Locke's ideas regarding the sanctity of individual property and freedom; but he also accepts Hobbes's ideas regarding the necessity of a powerful functioning central authority; and he knows that human beings on each side are likely to disturb this balance and must be reminded of their obligations. Johnson as Christian practical moralist is very like Johnson as practical Christian political theorist: examine each case; improve the person and you will improve the politics; make changes slowly to accommodate human weakness; be flexible in the face of human complexity; remember that human behavior ultimately must be judged by a divine standard.

Donald Greene's Johnson, then, is a politically independent practical moralist most concerned with effective governance and preservation of a fluid order within a fluid hierarchic society of mutual obligation between governor and governed. Whatever the political facade, human beings will surrender to self-aggrandizement and want watching.

One can both share and disagree with aspects of this view of Johnson's politics. Eighteenth-century political arguments among those with power were largely among Hanoverian Whigs who adopted the policies of those they ousted. As Richard Newton says in 1735, "if the Government *Itself* be not of any Party, that I am not can be no Mark of Disaffection in me to it." Henry Brooke puts it even more bluntly in 1750:

> The real essential Difference between a Church of England Academick *Tory* and a Church of England Academick *Whig* is, I confess, a Secret to my Understanding; both these having subscribed the same Articles of *Religious* Faith; Both having given to the same Government the same Solemn Security for their *Civil* Obedience: Surely then there can be no Absurdity in an Assertion that a Distinction made between Members of the same Communion, *sworn* Subjects to the same Prince, is a Distinction without a *Difference*, an Opposition in *Name* only, destitute of any Foundation in *Fact*.[1]

On the other hand, Johnson often was sympathetic to the Stuarts and their claim of monarchic legitimacy. His mature sense of loss and gain taught him that blank verse was inappropriate for the English language but necessary for *Paradise Lost*. It also allowed him to recognize that thanks to James II's incompetence the undesirable Williamite revolution was necessary: it fractured the constitution but preserved the national Church and liberty. That mixed blessing was the sort of "innovation" Johnson found personally and politically troubling. One also can legitimately argue that there was more to eighteenth-century politics than parliamentary maneuvering and self promotion, and that political thinkers with different ideas concerning the power of the crown and Commons, land and money, commercial expansion and agricultural self-sufficiency, organized themselves loosely around an early form of "party." Johnson was indeed eclectic in selecting from different political systems; but he needed something from which to select. Other countries are free to invent a system congenial for them; Britain has chosen a constitutional monarchy in which the crown at its best holds significant power through duration and the respect of a willing nation it governs well. For Johnson, the monarch represents all of the people and not just, say, the small number of voting landholders in the West Riding or merchants in Bristol for whom, Edmund Burke found, self-interest transcended national interest. The crown also protects the middle ranks against the rich or powerful aristocrats—as Dr. Primrose argues in chapter 19 of *The Vicar of Wakefield* (1766).

I thus have no objection to ideological alternatives to Namierian historiography or to Greene's adherence to Namierian historiography. Each approach can illuminate aspects of Johnson's political philosophy and its contexts, and each asks different questions that require different answers. Discovering variant paths is part of the normal process of re-reading and reevaluating literary and historical texts. Such expansion may even encourage combining approaches and enriching response by, for example, demonstrating both personal and ideological motivation in Jonathan Swift or Edmund Burke.

During about the last two decades, however, some literary and intellectual historians sought not to offer alternatives but replacements in what could be a laudable effort to revise the revisors. Consequent renewed interest in Jacobitism is among the many fruits of contemporary eighteenth-century studies and its healthy awareness of the political complexity of the years from about 1688 to 1760. The Whig interpreters of history long had buried the abdicated, Tory, tyrannical, Catholic Stuart regime under its own rubble and the great edifice of Protestant parliamentary government gloriously begun by the Glorious Revolution. Nothing could have been clearer. Action now has had its reaction, and the Whig interpretation of history has been challenged by the Tory interpretation of history. That interpretation of the past has been championed, often polemically, by J. C. D. Clark, and has attached itself to modern British politics. According to Clark, Jacobite studies are in "harmony with the political and intellectual currents of 1980s Britain" that sought to banish socialism from the British landscape as Clark hoped to banish Marxism from British historiography.[2] Along the way, Samuel Johnson found himself in these ideological crosshairs and a proper dust-up began.

THE GENESIS OF A CONTROVERSY AND THE LAW OF UNINTENDED CONSEQUENCES

Donald Greene had retired from the University of Southern California by 1988, and he was keen both to continue and to enlarge his lively correspondence with friends and colleagues. Some time late in 1988 or early in 1989 I wrote and, among other matters, asked whether he had read Clark's *English Society 1688–1832*.[3] Like most students of the period, I thought it essentially wrong in its view of the eighteenth-century as an ancien regime devoted to the divine right of kings.[4] I also thought it learned and helpful when it urged the importance of religion and the Anglican Church for English subjects during the eighteenth century. This was a topic on which Greene long had been interested, and on which he had published with characteristic distinction. Greene promptly wrote back with a blast whose echoes would reverberate for the next fifteen years. The controversy engendered several exchanges in *The Age of Johnson*, a conference on eighteenth-century Jacobitism at the University of Pennsylvania (1997), publication of its proceedings, and most recently the Clark and Howard Erskine-Hill edited volume called *Samuel Johnson in Historical Context* (2001), in which all of the contexts are Jacobitical.

In 1989, though, I did not know that Greene was preparing a new preface for the University of Georgia Press reprint of his Namierian *Politics of Samuel Johnson*. Upon receipt of my letter, Greene must promptly have looked in Clark's index, found "Johnson, Dr. Samuel . . . Nonjuror" with appropriate pages cited. Thereafter he added Howard Erskine-Hill's interpretively comparable essay on Johnson's politics.[5] These became immediate ammunition for the cannon blast that the new Preface included.

Greene there did not so much refute as shred Clark and Erskine-Hill, and especially Clark's discussion of Johnson in *English Society*. Their notions that Johnson was a Jacobite nonjuror still loyal to the Stuart dynasty seemed to Greene variously astounding, absurd, nonsense, startling, incredible, and a fantasy (pp. xxix–xxx). Neither scholar knows much about Johnson or research regarding him (pp. xxxii, xxxvii); Erskine-Hill is naive regarding Boswell as a reliable source for Johnson's politics (pp. xl–xlvii); and each mistakenly denigrates Namier's central importance for understanding eighteenth-century politics (pp. xlvii–lvii). A new edition of a then thirty-year-old book was likely to have modest circulation. Instead of leaving the matter to respectable obscurity the shredees counterattacked, with Clark as chief combatant. He began in the October 14, 1994, *TLS*. "The Heartfelt Toryism of Dr. Johnson" (pp. 17–18) is a précis and an extended puff for *Samuel Johnson: Literature, religion and English cultural politics from the Restoration to Romanticism* (1994). Both the puff and the book ask us to cast aside antiquated orthodoxies and to accept an historically verifiable version of Johnson's "cultural politics."

Throughout, Clark characterizes himself as at the vanguard of the historians' brave new world. He banishes the positivist, anticlerical historiography of Sir Lewis Namier, whom Clark elsewhere has called, "that fine though overrated historian" whose "conversion to Anglicanism [from Judaism] late in life was not reflected in his work."[6]

The broom that sweeps away Namier also sweeps away the "all too

influential" Donald Greene who "fundamentally" misinterpreted Johnson. "Scholarship does not stand still," and now has demonstrated the
ideological differences between Whig and Tory that existed well into the
eighteenth century. Literary scholars need to catch up to historians. Boswell misrepresented Johnson's politics but, contrary to Greene's view,
Johnson was more not less of a Tory than Boswell thought. Literary
scholars also need to recognize that though Macaulay wrongly saw
Whig and Tory as synonyms for progressive and regressive, the new historiography can "give equal esteem to the ideologies of all the protago-
nists." That being done, we can respect Johnson for what he really
was—a Tory, a High Churchman, and a nonjuror: "Johnson refused the
oaths because he acknowledged . . . an unextinguished title to the throne
still remaining in the exiled dynasty" (*TLS*, p. 17).

Consequently, he could never accept opportunities that required his
oath to the new regime: he refused to take his Oxford degree or a later
Oxford chair, an ecclesiastical position, or a role in the Trained Bands.
Much of his literature reflects the Tory view, one that is influenced by
the Anglo-Latin humanist tradition cognate with Toryism and Jacobitism: the anti-Hanoverian *London* is an imitation of a classical poem;
his prose political pieces are uniformly anti-Hanoverian; the *Dictionary*
inculcates High Church religion and Tory politics; the *Lives of the Poets*
"contains an eloquent historical subtext in which Johnson's partisanship
in the public drama of the century is plainly described" (*TLS*, p. 18).

Johnson's transfer of loyalty to George III was typical of Tory politics
after 1760 and fooled no one. Johnson was consistently vilified as a Tory
Jacobite. By the early nineteenth century he was marginalized because
the "royalist, humanist, patrician, High Anglican and sometimes Catholic" 140-year project from Dryden to Pope to Johnson was played out
and made redundant by the debates of the 1830s and the Reform bill:
"literary critics who misread the history do so at their peril" (*TLS*, p.
18).[7]

Having scolded Greene in October, Clark ignored him in November
for the academic readers of his *Johnson* book. Clark's Preface alludes
to Greene's *Politics of Samuel Johnson* but, as if naming implied illicit
acknowledgment, merely calls it "the publication in 1990 of a second
edition of a monograph of 1960 which reasserted a Namierite interpretation" (p. xii). He cites the thing itself in his list of Abbreviations (p.
xiii), but then consigns it wholly to footnotes designed to characterize
Greene as an outmoded benighted adversary, the author of "a Columbia
University doctoral dissertation of 1954" (p. 4 n. 14). Clark even refuses
to quote from Greene's definitive edition of Johnson's *Political Writings*,

thus denying himself the opportunity to examine Johnson's extant corrections to the proof copy of *Taxation No Tyranny* (1775).

As an American republican, I have no political or emotional stake in whether Samuel Johnson was a Jacobite. Nor can I see much relationship between his putative Jacobitism and his literary or intellectual achievement. Like most American schoolchildren of my generation, indeed, I was taught that the virtual Beelzebub-clone Hanoverian George III hired German mercenaries to kill my freedom-loving national ancestors. I also was a partisan of the romantic underdog Scots treated badly by the Redcoats who were equally glad to repeat their shame at Bunker Hill. Nonetheless, I am not politically or emotionally engaged with whether a Stuart or Hanoverian dynasty would have been better for Britain and the world, or whether one such dynasty was legally or illegally removed from the English throne. I can have no stake in whether a positivist Namierian or an ideological Clarkian view is the key that unlocks the doors to Johnson's and eighteenth-century Britain's political world. One may ignore, use, or mingle each approach as the situation requires, and as I will do in the present section in hopes of contributing to the literary and historical debate. Nor do I feel obliged to defend or attack any other school or individual. I do, however, feel obliged to defend the canons of scholarly method, the nature of evidence, and the sorts of inferences that such evidence allows one legitimately to draw. The question to consider, after all, is not whether Donald Greene is wrong, but whether J. C. D. Clark is right. As Sir Lewis Namier said in an epigraph Clark quotes before his *English Society 1688–1832*, "The foremost task of honest history is to discredit and drive out its futile or dishonest varieties."

The neo-Jacobite variety of history and literary history shares certain assumptions and modes of proceeding by its several advocates.[8] Collectively they seek to redefine both our view of the eighteenth century, and eighteenth-century historiography. For several such scholars, the eighteenth century is a period of profound political conservatism that is unlike the apparent world of progress and political liberalism apparently dear to the academic left. It was characterized by persistent if repressed and underground Jacobitism that often burst out in riots or proceeded by codes known to the cognoscenti. It had consequent animosity to the illicit and alien Hanoverians on the British throne and regular repression by them. Clark long has argued that the Hanoverians' predecessor in a nominal Glorious Revolution really produced a "Glorious Reaction," with special emphasis on the second word. According to his nightmare scenario, the "practical consequences of the Revolution" included "civil war, massive bloodshed, military repression, religious schism, the repudiation of legal authority, continental entanglements." The Revolution's advocates essentially should prove a negative, create a verifiable new history, and plead guilty to affection for sanguinary disorder: "Anyone is entitled to celebrate such an episode who can demonstrate, not speculate, that the alternative would have been even worse."[9] Howard Erskine-Hill starkly characterizes the quasi-martial assault upon the received historiography: "The eighteenth century of Jonathan Clark and that of Paul Langford still confront one another."[10]

I choose here, however, to consider not all of the "eighteenth century," but Samuel Johnson as the center of the neo-Jacobite literary-historical enterprise. Erskine-Hill thus insists that "Johnson is a figure who indeed allows us to interpret his age" (*SJ Hist.*, p. x)—and since Johnson was a Tory-Jacobite-nonjuror, the "age" was Tory-Jacobite-nonjuring. Clark knows that Johnson's "peculiar authority as a moral critic derives from an austere position of internal exile which is no less acute for being, from one perspective, self-imposed" (*SJ Hist.*, p. 79). Johnson, it seems, lived in a Hanoverian gulag.

To help liberate Johnson and his readers, the neo-Jacobites reinterpret the Johnson canon to reflect the Jacobite agenda. Since, on this hypothesis, use of the classical past denotes Jacobite-Toryism, both *London* and the *Vanity of Human Wishes* are Jacobite virtually by definition. As we recall from the *TLS* article, the *Dictionary* is a High Church and Tory document and the *Lives of the Poets* subtly but plainly characterize Johnson's partisan Jacobitism. According to Paul Monod, Johnson's translation of Father Lobo's *Voyage into Abyssinia* (1735) was a trial run for *Rasselas*: "We may wonder . . . whether its translator was already thinking of remote Ethiopia as a metaphor for Staffordshire, the 'Happy Valley' free of moral challenges, from which Prince Rasselas would later escape" (*SJ Hist.*, p. 24). *Rasselas* itself is but another token of Johnson's Jacobitism: "The Prince of Abyssinia's voyage into the moral maelstrom of Cairo. . . . has similarities to Charles Edward Stuart's visit to London in 1750. Like Rasselas, Charles was a young prince searching for knowledge, who found that it did not increase his happiness" (*SJ Hist.*, pp. 34–35). Johnson's allegorical *Irene* began as so obvious a Jacobite drama that George II refused to attend: Irene "might have been seen as Britannia herself," and Aspasia "could be interpreted as a personification of the Church of England" (*SJ Hist.*, p. 26). Johnson's works thus demonstrate his allegiances in his "long and tortuous process of self-fashioning." If we do not see "these hints about Johnson's troubled character . . . it is our own fault" (*SJ Hist.*, p. 36).

My views of the neo-Jacobite view of Johnson and of the eighteenth century long have been clear and long have placed me in the dark Jaco-skeptic camp. The several essays and exchanges regarding the issue are available in the cabinets of the curious.[11] Those who search them out will see the varied defenses and refutations of the neo-Jacobite reading of Johnson's canon. Some of these indeed are self-refuting. The first draft of *Irene* has been available since the 1941 Nichol Smith McAdam Oxford edition of the *Poems*. The play's rough notes from the Hyde Collection have been available in McAdam's Yale Edition of the *Poems* since 1964. Neither the play nor the notes bear any relationship to Jacobitism. Regarding *Rasselas* as an allegory of Charles Edward's wanderings reduces it to tiresome agitprop, violates the work's plot and oriental setting, and has no known eighteenth-century corroboration. I have considered the *Dictionary*'s essential indifference to Jacobite concerns in an essay within. Dustin Griffin has definitively refuted the notion that the *Lives of the Poets* have a Tory and Jacobite programme. Instead, he shows, the *Lives*' "implicit political agenda . . . is actively to *promote* political piety, to promote loyalty to the ruling family that had long possessed the throne." In the *Lives* Johnson "nowhere even hints . . . that the descendants of James have a legitimate right to the throne." He "left no question . . . that any attempt to disturb the established government of the Hanoverians was wicked."[12] Nicholas Hudson has made clear that whatever Johnson's reasonable misgivings about the Williamite revolution, he thought it necessary. Thereafter, he believed that "to inflame dissent against the House of Hanover was to invite precisely the social disorder that his political philosophy sought to suppress."[13]

That much being said, I here wish to reprise two central aspects of the Johnson-as-Jacobite controversy. The first is whether Johnson took any of the oaths of Supremacy, Allegiance, and Abjuration as an undergraduate at Oxford, and whether he could have taken them to qualify himself for certain offices. The other central aspect is the historical context of Charles of Sweden as a gloss upon *The Vanity of Human Wishes*. The neo-Jacobites argue that Johnson never did and never could take the two central oaths, of Allegiance and Abjuration. By invoking Charles of Sweden the Jacobite hero, he also was signalling his Jacobite sympathy for Charles Edward Stuart and the invasion of Britain. I consider these historical subjects not only because they are an interpretively urgent aspect of the argument. I consider them as well because the neo-Jacobites have been justifiably keen on good and proper historical method. Literary critics ignore history "at their peril," we have been told. It may be useful to see whether these historians have practiced their own proper reading, and what the implications might be for literary interpretation. I begin with Oxford, Johnson, and oaths.

NOTES

1. For Newton, see *The Grounds of the Complaint of the Principal of Hart-Hall, Concerning the Obstruction . . . By Exeter College and their Visitor* (London, 1735), p. 61, repeated in [Richard Newton], *The Principles of the University of Oxford* (London, 1755), p. 12. For [Brooke] see *A Letter to the Oxford Tories. By an Englishman* (London, 1750), pp. iii–iv. The attribution is affirmed in David Greenwood, *William King: Tory and Jacobite* (Oxford: Clarendon Press, 1969), pp. 205–6. See also [Benjamin Kennicott], *A Letter to Dr. King Occasion'd by his late Apology* (London, 1755): "I can *in these days*, perceive no real difference between Whig and Tory" (pp. 121–22).

2. Clark, "On Moving the Middle Ground," in *The Jacobite Challenge*, ed. Eveline Cruickshanks and Jeremy Black (Edinburgh: John Donald, 1988), p. 182, and see pp. 184–85.

3. Clark, *English Society 1688–1832: Ideology, Social Structure and Political Practice During the Ancien Regime* (Cambridge: Cambridge University Press, 1985). References will be cited parenthetically in the text, except for the epigraph cited below, which is on unmarked [p. v].

4. For historians' assessment of this book, see G. S. Rousseau, "Revisionist Polemics: J. C. D. Clark and the Collapse of Modernity in the Age of Johnson," *Age of Johnson* (henceforth *AJ*) 2 (1984): 421–50, and Paul Langford, *A Polite and Commercial People: England 1727–1783* (Oxford: Oxford University Press, 1992), p. 742.

5. Clark, *English Society*, p. 432. For Erskine-Hill, see "The Political Character of Samuel Johnson," in *Samuel Johnson: New Critical Essays*, ed. Isobel Grundy (London: Vision; New York, Barnes and Noble, 1984), pp. 107–36. To this one might add "The Political Character of Samuel Johnson: *The Lives of the Poets* and A Further Report on *The Vanity of Human Wishes*," in *Jacobite Challenge*, pp. 161–76.

6. Clark, *Revolution and Rebellion: State and Society in England in the Seventeenth and Eighteenth Centuries* (Cambridge: Cambridge University Press, 1986), pp. 13 (overrated), 42 n. 49 (conversion).

7. I have demonstrated the early nineteenth-century's high esteem and constructive engagement with Johnson as a literary and cultural critic. See "Samuel Johnson, Percival Stockdale, and 'Brickbats from Grubstreet': Some Later Response to the *Lives of the Poets*," within. The major turning point in nineteenth-century characterization of Johnson comes with Macaulay's 1831 review of Croker's edition of Boswell's *Life of Johnson*. See also Jane W. Stedman, "The Victorian After-Image of Samuel Johnson," *Nineteenth Century Theatre Research* 11 (1983): 13–27.

8. I have considered these modes of proceeding in "Johnson, Jacobitism, and the Historiography of Nostalgia" *AJ* 4 (1996): 163–211; "Johnson and Jacobitism Redux: Evidence, Interpretation, and Intellectual History," *AJ* 12 (2001): 273–90; "Johnson and Jacobite Wars XLV," *AJ* 14 (2003): 307–40, a review-essay of *Samuel Johnson in Historical Context*. See also the two following essays within.

9. Clark, "1688: Glorious Revolution or Glorious Reaction?" *Sunday Telegraph* (London), July 24, 1988, as reprinted in DQR Studies in Literature 6, *Fabrics and Fabri-*

cations: The Myth and Making of William and Mary, ed. Paul Hoftijzer and C. C. Barfoot (Amsterdam: Rodopi, 1990), pp. 14–15.

10. Erskine-Hill, *Samuel Johnson in Historical Perspective*, ed. Clark and Erskine-Hill (Houndsmill, Basingstoke, UK: Palgrave, 2001), p. 6. Subsequent references are cited parenthetically in the text as *SJ Hist.*

11. For some of these in addition to the essays within, see *AJ* 7, 8, 12, 14; *ELH* 64, no. 4 (1997), which publishes the University of Pennsylvania's conference proceedings; Weinbrot, "The Politics of Samuel Johnson and the Johnson of Politics: An Innocent Looks at a Controversy," *1650–1850: Ideas, Aesthetics and Inquiries* 8 (2003): 3–26; and *Samuel Johnson in Historical Context*, largely from a neo-Jacobite point of view.

12. Griffin, "Regulated Loyalty: Jacobitism and Johnson's *Lives of the Poets*," *ELH* 64 (1997): 1010 (implicit), 1021 (hints and no question).

13. Hudson, "The Nature of Johnson's Conservatism," *ELH* 64 (1997): 939. See also Hudson's *Samuel Johnson and the Making of Modern England* (Cambridge: Cambridge University Press), pp. 79–86. After study of Johnson's relevant politics, Hudson concludes that "we seem to have whittled down the evidence of Johnson's Jacobitism to a fairly thin stick" (p. 85).

14

Johnson, Oxford, Oaths, and Historical Evidence

THE GRAVAMEN OF THE NEO-JACOBITE ARGUMENT REGARDING JOHN-son is that as a nonjuror, he refused to take the oaths of Abjuration and Allegiance to the Hanoverian government. The Oath of Allegiance required fidelity to King George; the Oath of Abjuration required abjuration of the Stuart pretenders as nominal Prince of Wales and as nominal King James III. Johnson never did and never could swear such oaths, and by design always avoided them at the cost of career advancement and perhaps madness. He could not stand for Parliament or even join the Trained Bands, each of which required oaths. He did not leave Oxford out of poverty, since he could have stayed through discipline and by becoming a servitor: he left out of principled refusal to compromise his Jacobite beliefs upon graduation. Johnson did not take the oaths of Allegiance and Abjuration at Oxford upon matriculation, because they only were given to scholarship students, Foundationers, and not the Gentleman he labeled himself when he subscribed the required Oath of Supremacy upon matriculation. Johnson indeed subscribed the Oath of Supremacy at Oxford on December 16, 1728. He then agreed that "no Foreign Prince . . . ought to have any Jurisdiction, Power, [or] Superiority . . . within this Realm."[1] The rest of the neo-Jacobite argument is more than suspect.

THE HISTORICAL EVIDENCE REGARDING OXFORD OATHS

I begin with what J. C. D. Clark thinks the correlation between custom and statute, an assumption that sits awkwardly with human nature and with Oxford's known practices. Sir Walter Scott's late seventeenth-century fictional Jedediah Cleishbotham describes his reaction to whether a publican may brew whiskey: if there is a law against it, "let him show me the statute; and when he does, I'll tell him if I will obey it or not."[2] The real eighteenth-century Nicholas Amhurst comparably commented regarding Oxford statutes as accurate guides to Oxford conduct from 1716. He outlines the rigorous course of study and lectures mandated by the university statutes and observes: the students "are so far from attending, as is strictly required by statute, upon these lectures, that there are no lectures read in any of the faculties" except music and poetry. He thus sensibly urges that we "examine the practice, not the theory, the execution of the statutes, and not the statutes themselves."[3]

In fact, scofflaws were commonplace. Amhurst knows that "PERJURY is . . . the necessary, unavoidable consequence of matriculation" because the foolish university statutes are not observed (*TF*, No. 17, p. 90). He later devotes all of *Terrae Filius* No. 47 to Oxford's regular abuse of statutes, including those relating to matriculation (pp. 248–54; see also No. 30, pp. 160–61). Johnson began his career at Oxford with such a violation. He entered Pembroke on October 31, 1728, but did not matriculate until December 16. As Douglas MacLeane pointed out in 1897, it was a "delay unusual and against the University statutes" that stipulated matriculation "not later than the Friday seven-night after his admission." Pembroke's George Whitefield reported that "there is a sacrament at the beginning of every term, at which all, especially the seniors, are by statute obliged to be present." Yet at "harlot" Oxford few masters and "no undergraduates but the Methodists attended." On April 11, 1748, the Vice Chancellor John Purnell was forced to issue a proclamation decrying widespread public drunkenness, an "unstatutable and mischievous practice." Too many pubs and inns received and entertained young "scholars, contrary to the known rules, orders and statutes of the University."[4] If congruence between law and custom is correct, once the aberration was eliminated, no Oxford undergraduate allowed liquor to pass his lips, drinking establishments closed, rowdy sexual and political behavior disappeared, and Virtue was restored in the moral Switzerland that statute-bound Oxford again became. To be sure.

Johnson's and Whitefield's experiences demonstrate that violation of statutes was scarcely the sole domain of adolescent brats. During the controversial 1754 Oxford election Exeter College helped legitimate Whig voters to evade Tory barriers. The Vice Chancellor George Huddesford then sternly rebuked the college for its insolence. Francis Webber responded in kind to that illicit act: "He has no Right to interpose in any Affair transacted within the Walls of a College; but under the Limitations mentioned in the Statute *de Judiciis*, [par.] 13. (to which the Reader is referr'd)." Huddesford also violated statutes when he refused properly to punish a seditious young Jacobite student who insulted an Exeter senior Fellow: he "refused to punish him at all in the Way of Example, as the Statute *De contumelis compescendis* requir'd."[5]

All of this is consistent with a world of frequent explicit or implicit violation of state oaths and university statutes. When Thomas Hearne took his own oaths temporarily to become Archetypographus and Superior Beadle of Civil Law, he did not say to whom the allegiance was pledged: his examiner "did right" not to challenge him, for he certainly "should be brought into a Scrape as well as myself" if he revealed that he swore to King James.[6] Thereafter, William King was among the many Oxford Jacobites who signed the Oath of Abjuration. Such men also regularly savaged Whigs like Benjamin Kennicott and Richard Blacow, who tried seriously to adhere to serious oaths before God. Kennicott responded in 1755. He berates the Jacobite William King for defying the Oath of Abjuration his position as Principal of St. Mary Hall, Oxford, required him to take: "Every person, at his *Matriculation*, if *sixteen* years of age, takes the Oaths of *Allegiance* and *Supremacy*; and every person, admitted either a *Clerk*, *Exhibitioner*, *Scholar*, *Fellow*, *Head* of any *College*, or, Sir [he accusingly reminds King], *Head* of any *Hall*, takes (or is requir'd by *Act of Parliament* to take) the Oath of *Abjuration*."[7] The Oath states that "our Sovereign Lord King *George* is lawful and rightful King of this Realm, and all his Majesty's Dominion thereunto belonging." It requires the subscriber solemnly to vow that the alien Prince of Wales is a pretender and that he will report "all Treasons and Traiterous Conspiracies"—an obligation William King both avoided and subverted. The Oath of Abjuration also rejects personal interpretation of the words and mental reservations and requires that he complies "heartily, willingly, and truly, upon the true Faith of a Christian. So help me God."[8] In violating that promise, he joined the many at Oxford who adjusted oaths and statutes for their own needs, whatever "the true Faith of a Christian."

We know that later Oxonians also preferred to avoid scrapes. Amhurst, Blacow, and Kennicott are among those who say that matriculants over sixteen took the oaths of Supremacy and Allegiance. Since "all the oaths" is a commonplace, it is at the least plausible that non-Foundationers also were asked to take the Oath of Abjuration.[9] Whether or not that is so, they often took the conjoined Oath of Allegiance together with the Oath of Supremacy often without so knowing. The statute may indeed say that only those of the Foundation, scholarship students, were required to swear, but much contemporary experience and evidence suggests otherwise: at the least all groups of the proper age willy-nilly took the oaths of Supremacy and of Allegiance upon matriculation.

John Ayliffe published *The Antient and Present State of the University of Oxford* in 1714. He observes that "All matriculated persons of 16 Years of Age are to subscribe the 39 Articles, and to take the Oaths of Allegiance and Supremacy." He matriculated at New College on February 1, 1696, as a Gentleman and thus was not of the Foundation. Before being expelled for offending his Tory superiors, he was "*L.L. D. and Fellow of New-College* in Oxford."[10] In *The Case of Dr. Ayliffe at Oxford* (London, 1716) he complains that Oxford's nonjurors often proceed "by not giving the Oaths of *Allegiance* and *Supremacy*, under a feign'd Pretence of Non-age" (p. ix). Thomas Hearne angers when he reads Thomas Tanner's version of Anthony à Wood's *Athenae Oxonienses* (2nd ed. 1721), in which Tanner says that matriculants take the oaths of Supremacy and Allegiance. Hearne insists that is not what the statute says, but immediately describes the real situation: the "Oath of Allegiance . . . was added to bring a slur upon the University, and out of a trimming Design." He does not claim that the addition was limited to Foundationers. Neither Ayliffe nor Hearne would be ignorant of ceremonies in which they participated or perhaps otherwise observed.

Thereafter, as a university lower magistrate Richard Blacow engages three drunken college rowdies shouting the praise of King James and Prince Charles. After much difficulty and Vice Chancellor Purnell's refusal to adhere to the university statutes, they finally are arrested and tried. Two of the three are found guilty of sedition, are fined, publicly humiliated, and sentenced to prison for two years. On February 29, 1748, Blacow tells Purnell: "as the Wisdom of the University thought them of proper Capacities to take the Oaths *four years ago*, they must be thought of proper Capacities *now* to be punish'd for the breach of those Oaths." Like Kennicott, Blacow so remarked eight years after he entered Oxford and is likely to have been aware of matriculation ceremonies. Blacow apparently had not already known the three young men in 1748, but he surely knew class markers and that none of the three drunks were of the Foundation. As he says in 1755, "Two of these were Gentlemen-Commoners of very considerable fortunes." He surely knew them when he brought several witnesses to verify their seditious shouts: James Dawes, Gentleman of St. Mary Hall matriculated on April 16, 1744; Charles Luxmore, Gentleman of Balliol, matriculated on February 28, 1744; James Whitmore, Gentleman of Balliol, matriculated on March 19, 1746. Only Luxmore was acquitted. To my knowledge, no one in that controversy denied either Blacow's or Kennicott's statements

that these non-Foundationers had taken "the Oaths" before graduation.[11] We recall that after several years in residence, Ayliffe, Blacow,
and Kennicott refer to plural "oaths" taken upon matriculation.

Let us also look at another central document regarding oath taking in
eighteenth-century Oxford, Amhurst's *Terrae Filius* of 1721, with editions in 1726 and 1754. It in part recounts his years from 1716 to 1719
at St. John's College, Oxford, an institution that forced him to find another home for his Whiggish politics. Amhurst was expelled before he
could earn his degree, but he had his own experiences, and after three
years at Oxford he certainly knew others who matriculated and graduated. Amhurst berates Oxford's Jacobite atmosphere, but grants that the
"seditious spirit, and . . . treasonable practices have, of late years, so
much abated, if not entirely ceased" (p. xi; see also pp. xix–xx). His actual experience does not distinguish between those of or not of the Foundation; and like Hearne he refutes the notion of an activity based on
what he regards as the letter of broadly ignored university statutes.

By fifteen days after admission to a college, a young man of at least
sixteen must subscribe the Thirty-nine Articles. In practice, oath taking
as Amhurst describes it often was more than casual: "At the same time
he takes the oaths of allegiance and supremacy, which he is prætaught
to evade, or think null: some have thought themselves sufficiently ab-
solved from them by kissing their thumbs, instead of the book; others,
in the croud, or by the favour of an honest beadle, have not the book
given them at all" (p. 12). Amhurst confidently reiterates the experience
of Oxford undergraduates circa 1716 and not thought necessary to revise for the posthumous 1754 third edition: "The statute says, if the person to be matriculated is sixteen years of age, he must subscribe the
thirty-nine articles, and take the oaths of allegiance and supremacy as
also an oath of fidelity to the university" (p. 14). As a fledgling he is
shocked when students toast the Pretender and vilify George I; Amhurst
refuses the toast when his turn comes, "alledging that . . . I was obliged
in a short time to abjure the pretender in the most solemn manner" (p.
238), that is, the wording in the Oath of Abjuration. Because these oaths
were not required of those under sixteen, like fifteen-year-old Edward
Gibbon in 1752, they were presumably asked to return at the proper
time. "It is hardly worth mentioning . . . that by this statute many persons avoid taking the oaths of allegiance and supremacy at all; or being,
or pretending to be, under sixteen when they are matriculated, they are
excused from it at that time; and I have never heard that any body was
ever call'd upon afterwards to take them, unless they take a degree" (p.
15). Samuel Johnson was an obviously large nineteen when he entered

Oxford. He almost certainly also took, or was told that he took, the Oath of Allegiance when he subscribed the Oath of Supremacy and the Thirty-nine Articles in the Oxford subscription books on December 16, 1728, upon his formal matriculation.

A pseudonymous correspondent in *Terrae Filius* confirms Amhurst's experience and suggests what Johnson's could have been like. "Phila-lethes" (Truthlover) refers to John Baron, Vice Chancellor from 1715 to 1718:

> When I was matriculated I was about seventeen years of age, and conse-quently entitled to take all the oaths; accordingly I subscribed the thirty-nine articles of religion, (though, by the bye, I did not know that I had done it till near six months afterwards) and the then vice-chancellor, Dr. B——n, com-ing out of the convocation-house, I took the oaths of supremacy, and of ob-serving the statutes, privileges, &c. of the university. After which the doctor sign'd my matriculation paper, testifying that I had also taken the oath of allegiance, though not one word of it, or his majesty king George, was then mention'd. (p. 88)

Both as Master of Balliol (1705–20) and as Vice Chancellor, John Baron was regarded as "a stalwart Whig" who induced "a state of ner-vous apprehension" among Jacobites. In December of 1716 he threat-ened to have Thomas Hearne's papers searched for Jacobite remarks.[12] In short, whether in Tory St. John's or in Whig-directed ceremonies, all matriculants over sixteen seem to have experienced the same often per-functory exercise in oath taking.

Amhurst confirms the reliability of his narrative with a putative anon-ymous letter that he himself may have written. Whether or not that is so, the signer breaks Amhurst's general naming pattern in *Terrae Filius*. Sometimes he offers initials, unrecognizable except for his own N. A. when he narrates the tale of his expulsion from St. John's (No. 45; pp. 237–43). Generally, though, he provides amusing tags like John Spy (p. 21), Benjamin Numps (p. 55), Dr. Drybones (p. 130), Dr. Brimstone (p. 161), or Mr. Vizard (p. 163).

The one significant exception to this pattern is in the letter Amhurst quotes regarding the oaths of Supremacy and Allegiance taken together upon matriculation, by a student who does not identify himself or fel-low-swearers as of the Foundation: his name is Philalethes, lover of truth, who also appears in the Index to help us find truth (pp. 329, 332, 364). Philalethes was a frequent name for other kinds of truth tellers in pamphlets, and also is Cicero's term when he writes to his brother

Quintus. Tell me what Caesar thinks of my poetry; write about it as lover of truth and as always like a brother.[13] Amhurst offers another prop for the letter's veracity. He begins *Terrae Filius* No. 17 by saying how comforted he is that

> none of my facts against the university have been contradicted by any of my correspondents. What I have urged in my *third* paper concerning *matriculation* is so just and reasonable, that it has occasion'd the two following letters; both of which will serve to explain and strengthen what I have said upon that subject. (pp. 83–84)

I have found nothing to contradict Amhurst's account of mulitple oath taking, as described by a truth teller also regarded as "just and reasonable" by his contemporaries.

There were at least five reasons for this embellishment of the statute. One is Hearne's sound belief that Hanoverian authorities pressured the university. A second is the administrative difficulty in the statute that singles out only Foundationers and Exhibitioners for both oaths. The vice chancellor generally administered the oaths to several matriculants at once. Rather than separate students into scholarship or nonscholarship, servitors or gentlemen, it was easier to have, or seem to have, one indifferent ceremony. Amhurst, for example, took his oaths "in a croud" and was merely informed that he took the Oath of Allegiance without having done so. A third reason is that the perfunctory process avoided career-threatening squabbles. The ultimately nonjuring Thomas Hearne once took the oaths of Allegiance and Supremacy in order to accept two Oxford positions. He did so, we recall, "without saying to whom ye Allegiance Oath was taken, in wch he [his examiner the Registrar George Cooper] did right, it being certain y^t if he had said I swore to K. James (as I really did) he should be brought into a Scrape as well as myself."[14]

The fourth reason is both political and logical—namely, since the part was regarded as the whole, parts may as well be added to the whole. The Latin preamble to the Oxford subscription book that Johnson signed translates as all matriculants "shall take their corporal oath to acknowledge the superiority of the king." [15] Like the thirty-seventh of the Thirty-nine Articles, the Oath of Supremacy rejecting any "Foreign Prince, Person, Prelate, State or Potentate" is an implicit Oath of Allegiance and an epitome of the Oath of Abjuration.

As early as 1689 the brilliant Huguenot emigree Peter Allix argued that "The Oaths of Supremacy and Allegiance, were at first prescribed only in opposition to this Doctrine of the *Romish* Church," whose pope "has arrogated to himself a Right of deposing Kings."[16] Nicholas Carter draws an appropriate conclusion in 1716 in his sermon on *The Obligation of an Oath; and particularly of the Oaths of Allegiance, Supremacy, and Abjuration* (London). Carter knows that the Oath of Supremacy connotes allegiance to the Protestant Hanoverian monarch. To declare against a foreign power requires withstanding that power: "how can they be said to oppose the Exercise of the *Pope*'s pretended Power here [in the Oath of Supremacy] who endeavour to bring in one to be their Governor, who ('tis very likely) would oblige all his Subjects, under Pain of Death or Banishment, to acknowledge it, and live in Subjection to it?" Anyone, he says after quoting the Oath of Supremacy, who would swear to that but "would assist a *Papist* Pretender" lies regarding "the plain meaning and Design of the Oath so taken" (pp. 18–19). A commentator in 1772 makes a similar remark—namely, that "in truth the oath [of Supremacy] has always been understood by the legislature to imply *the supremacy of the King in all matters ecclesiastical and spiritual*; a claim erected upon the downfall of the Pope's usurpation."[17] There is no reason not to make explicit what the legislature and others "always" thought implicit.

The fifth reason also is based upon experiential evidence. Unless one fussed about not taking or about violating the oaths—as Hearne and Blacow's drunken Jacobites did to their peril—Oxford preferred to ignore or even subvert their intention. Nicholas Amhurst, for example, seconds Thomas Hearne's remark about avoiding scrapes, but from a Whig point of view even in a ceremony conducted by a Whig vice chancellor. *The Grub-street Journal* for July 8, 1736 (No. 341), more generally suggests how irrelevant, irreverent, and "notorious" oath taking had become: "the repeated Swearing required by law in all branches of the Constitution, has taken away the terror and awe, that should naturally accompany an Oath." The *Journal* laments "the indifference" with which oaths impossible to perform are taken in court, for state occasions, and in the universities. The oath takers "scarce ever read, or heard them read, till the time of swearing"; but "there is nothing to be done . . . without Swearing; there can be no admission into any College or Hall without an Oath; no matriculation without an Oath, and subscription." He asks whether this is not a dangerously cynical practice "and whether learning cannot be acquired without Oaths that are never intended to be kept."[18]

Samuel Johnson agreed, resented the moral and intellectual basis of such obligatory and thoughtless oath taking, and so indicated in his "Remarks on the Militia Bill" (1756). In reading this we need to know that, according to the College historian, all of the Fellows of Johnson's Pembroke also took the oaths. "Every one knows," he says, that even "mean men . . . will be more afraid of man than God, and will take the oath taken and offered by their betters, without understanding, without examining, perhaps without hearing it."[19] Amhurst and Philalethes could not have put it better. J. C. D. Clark thinks that Johnson's hostility to oaths is a sign that he refused them at Oxford. More probably, he took the required oaths in the perfunctory way described, later felt shamed by frivolous treatment of a serious matter, and hoped to dissuade others from the practice.

For practical purposes, however, one may have to accept such folly. Johnson thus makes two other germane remarks regarding necessary accommodation to coercive power. On March 27, 1775, he says that a nonjuror may have been "less criminal in taking the oaths imposed by the ruling power, than refusing them." After all, a man must live, and he probably will "be reduced to very wicked shifts to maintain himself" (*Life*, 2:321). In the "Life of Fenton" he praises Fenton's adherence to conscience and willingness to suffer by not taking the oaths; but he refers to such action as a "perverseness of integrity" that did his professional life unnecessary material damage.[20] In the *Dictionary* (1755) Johnson defines "perverse" as "Distorted from the right . . . Obstinate in the wrong . . . Petulant; vexatious." Under "perverseness," we see "Petulance; peevishness; spiteful crossness." It is unlikely that a presumed Jacobite nonjuror would call another nonjuror distorted, petulant, and spiteful for not swearing what he himself would not swear.

JOHNSON AS SERVITOR

The overwhelming amount of historical and biographical evidence, then, suggests that at the least Johnson took the oaths of Supremacy and Allegiance. He may also have included the Oath of Abjuration among "all the oaths" that those over sixteen presumably were obliged to take, but this remains more conjectural. Another arrow in the neo-Jacobite quiver, though, aims at another target, Johnson as possible servitor to ameliorate his poverty and continue his education at Oxford.

We have been told that Johnson's poverty was not the chief reason he left Oxford without a degree. Frugality would have allowed him to live on £21 per year, perhaps even £10, perhaps even less: George Whitefield "called on his family for only £24 over the course of three years" as a servitor at Pembroke.[21] Hence Johnson "might also have held the office of servitor; but a servitorship, being 'of the foundation,' required the oath of allegiance and abjuration" (p. 102). "He could not accept a servitorship at Pembroke College," we again hear, as if a juring Johnson would otherwise have so done (p. 301). There clearly are better and simpler reasons than nonjuring for why Johnson would refuse such an option: it was socially and intellectually offensive to his beliefs and character.

G. V. Bennet demonstrates the strength of Oxford's "convention that no gentleman should be entered as less than a commoner."[22] He thus obviates Clark's inference that Johnson actually could have had money enough to stay had he been willing to swear the oaths, since he enrolled as a Gentleman and paid a fee of 10/6 rather than the 6/8 of a plebeian. Moreover, Bennet shows, "the notion of one who claimed 'gentle' birth actually wearing a servitor's gown was abhorrent to dons and undergraduates alike" (*B*, p. 363). No wonder: "in return for food and small fees" the servitors' job required domestic labor in stairways, in chambers, and as servants in the dining halls. The work was "humiliating," "demeaning," stigmatizing, and often regarded as a form of slavery by the servitors themselves. Their "social inferiority" was such, that "until well into the eighteenth century it was not thought fitting for one who did menial services to mix socially with undergraduates of a superior rank" (*B*, pp. 375–76). In 1731 John Wesley at Christ Church noted the rule that servitors received Communion the day after gentlemen, "for we are too well bred to communicate with them." He nonetheless joins them and asks his father whether the consequent "scandal . . . was justified."[23] At Johnson's Pembroke College in 1733 the servitor Richard Graves could only visit his friend Richard Jago "in private, as he wore a servitor's gown; it being deemed a great disparagement for a commoner to appear in public with one in that situation" (*B*, p. 376). Servitors also were required to have a weekly philosophy disputation at a different time from other students.[24] Their career expectations were as dim as their social prospects, for they "virtually never found themselves elected to college scholarships or fellowships" (*B*, p. 365). The vast majority left Oxford only with a B.A. and became country clergymen with "little formal training in theology and virtually none in pastoral care" (*B*, p. 376).

So limited and degrading a university life found its way into literature and into Johnson's own remarks and conduct. The repulsive unsigned *The Servitour* (London, 1709) mocks its ignorant subject as a social upstart who steals food from the kitchen, shares a garret with four others, and as a ridiculous fool should not be at Oxford (pp. 9, 12, 14, 15–16). Thereafter, Nicholas Amhurst in *Terrae Filius* describes a hung-over young student's anger when a servitor wakes him at six in the morning (p. 217). Oliver Goldsmith entered Trinity College, Dublin, as a sizar in 1745. He later recognized the similarity between the Irish and the English university positions. Pride, he complains in 1759, dictates "the absurd passion of [Fellows] being attended at meals, and on other public occasions" by the poor servitors who wish to be scholars. He laments the contradiction "to be at once learning the *liberal* arts, and at the same time treated as *slaves*, at once studying freedom, and practising servitude."[25] Sir John Hawkins reports that Johnson himself was so offended by the servitors' room checks, that he and others would chase them and bang pots and candlesticks in their faces. During that time in Johnson's life he thought "poverty was disgraceful" and severely censured each university's insulting treatment of "poor scholars" as servants at table.[26] In 1755 Johnson defined *servitor* as "One of the lowest order in the university." The illustrative quotation from Swift suggests public perception of the servitor and the intellectual toll of humiliation: "His learning is much of a size with his birth and education; no more of either than what poor hungry *servitor* can be expected to bring with him from his college." When Johnson illustrates "sizer," Cambridge's equivalent of servitor, he cites parts of a stanza from Bishop Richard Corbett's "A Certain Poeme" that parodies the consequences of King James I's visit to Cambridge in 1615. In the postvisit euphoria, degrees were indiscriminately and wrongly distributed to, among others, "Keepers, Subcizers, Lackeyes, Pages."[27]

V. H. H. Green also persuasively confirms a commonplace in discussion of eighteenth-century Oxford—that it became more expensive throughout the century. In 1715 "a commoner's annual costs might amount to £60, that of a gentleman-commoner to twice as much." By 1726 William Pitt claimed that a gentleman needed "at least £150 or £200 *per annum*."[28] Johnson would not indulge in such costly posturing; but neither he nor his family could afford even the minimum of twenty odd pounds per year to continue at university as a Gentleman.

A troubled letter in *Gentleman's Magazine* for April 1748 speaks both to the expenses—here of Cambridge—and to the nature of servitors and sizars. A correspondent complains that a recent excerpt from the March *Universal Magazine* wrongly claimed that sizars might be supported by friends or by Exhibitions, but chiefly "at the charge of the foundation; and by the benevolence of the richer sort of their fellow collegians." Rubbish. Not only are sizars not of the Foundation, but the "*inconsiderable matter*" they will need from friends is £40 per year, since Exhibitions are monetarily diminutive, and "their richer fellow collegians" are scarcely generous. "Every *fellow commoner* indeed has his *Sizar*, to whom he allows a certain portion of *commons*, or victuals and drink weekly, which may be worth 7 or 8*l. per An.* but no money; and for this the *Sizar* is obliged to do him certain services daily." Should a sizar become a servitor, he waits "at table upon the *scholars of the house, pensioners*, and *batchelors of arts*, which the sizars do not. A *servitor*'s place may be worth 14 or 15*l.*" (18:150)—that is, as the 1709 *The Servitour* said, in food lifted from the kitchen and the tables at the cost of social degradation.

Johnson later characterized his unservile sensibility at Oxford: "I was mad and violent. It was bitterness which they mistook for frolick. I was miserably poor, and I thought to fight my way by my literature and my wit; so I disregarded all power and all authority"—again in defiance of statutes.[29] That is not the servitor's humility as well characterized by George Whitefield, whose earlier experience as a tapster made him attractive as a student-servant at Oxford until his Methodism obtruded, he was sacked by several Gentlemen, and had dirt thrown on his servitor's gown.[30]

The acknowledged reason for Johnson's departure from Oxford remains valid: his family could not afford to pay for him; his apparent benefactor Andrew Corbett did not live up to presumed earlier promises; given Johnson's pride and Oxford's snobbery, he could not work in college like a modern undergraduate in an egalitarian state. The university's social system permitted William King to insult Benjamin Kennicott in print as one of the "sons of *low* Mechanicks." They "bring with them hither the meanness of their father's house, and they generally retain it to the end of their lives." Such an upstart and cobbler's, actually a barber's, son dared to confront the vice chancellor: he thus is a "WRETCH to be sent back to his father's stall."[31] Johnson feared and would not tolerate such vulgar class abuse. The fantasy that proud, violent, and angry young Sam Johnson "might also have held the office of servitor" is inconsistent with historical and biographical contexts.

In the event, it seems, Johnson soon had another opportunity to sign the state oaths and took another opportunity to avoid them. J. C. D. Clark's discussion of the Leicestershire subscription books is a further test case for his "acceptable historiographical standards" and for his version of nonjuring Johnson.

JOHNSON, LEICESTERSHIRE, AND INVISIBLE OATHS

Clark's discussion appears both in his *ELH* article of 1997 and, with additions, in his section of *Samuel Johnson in Historical Context.*[32]

Johnson, the argument goes, did not sign the oaths of Allegiance and Abjuration when required to do so as an Usher at Market Bosworth School in 1732. The absence of his name in the Leicestershire subscription books from 1733 proves this and suggests that Johnson as a principled Jacobite could not have a pedagogical career.

Readers understandably wonder why if Johnson was an usher at Market Bosworth from approximately March to July of 1732, that subscription books for 1733 should be relevant. He is not likely to sign an oath in a year in which he was not present at the school. Moreover, these highly disorganized books include loose pages in 1D41/34/3; either folio 22 is missing, or someone forgot his numbers and skipped from f.21 to f.23. In 1D41/34/4, that begins in 1733, the facing page of the first folio with writing clearly has been torn out, and the present folio 1 is loose at its bottom. One scarcely speculates to suggest an appropriate hypothesis: given the torn, loose, and inserted pages, even if Johnson's year of 1732 were in fact in the book at one time, it easily could have been lost, mislaid, or otherwise appropriated. Nonetheless, all this is irrelevant since Clark's discussion of the Leicestershire oaths is recollection without the madeleine.

Clark's essay in *Samuel Johnson in Historical Context* repeats the term "the oaths" thirteen times in his two-and-one-half-page discussion and two extended notes (97, 106) regarding "Johnson as a schoolmaster." He also twice refers to "the subscriptions," and once to "the usual formula" (p. 138 n. 106). Both the context and Clark's own words make his meaning plain: "that Johnson did not subscribe the oath of allegiance or the oath of abjuration . . . at Market Bosworth" (p. 105), that the oaths were there to subscribe, and that "the fact that Johnson's name is not in the registers" has "political significance" (p. 137 n. 97). He later says that he has "rigorously examine[d] all those archives in which Johnson's subscription would have been recorded, had he subscribed," as he did not (p. 301).

I already have doubted the evidential value of these subscription books and of Clark's description of them. There is no doubt regarding the absence of the state oaths of Allegiance and Abjuration from Leicestershire subscription books 1D41/34/3 and 1D41/34/4 that Clark discusses: they are not there to be signed.

The books include one relevant oath above the names Thomas Adderley and John Boloy, among the others Clark cites. The subscription list extends for four pages of signers to 1744. Here is the oath, which obviously is neither the Oath of Allegiance nor of Abjuration:

We whose Names are Subscribed now to be Admitted to our Respective Schools Undermentioned Do willingly and from o[ur] hearts Subscribe to the Three Articles in the 36 Canon Comprized and also to the 39 Artes of the Doctrine of the Church of England to all things therein Contained and we and every one of us do Declare That we and every one of us will Conforme to the Liturgy of the Church of England as it is now by Law Established.

Johnson could have signed this with a clear conscience. The 36th Canon was designed as a test for admission to ecclesiastical livings and so was not appropriate for layman Johnson in any case. It includes three sections: the first is a nonsubstantive variant of the Oath of Supremacy that Johnson subscribed as a matriculant at Oxford; the second says that the subscriber accepts and will use only the Book of Common Prayer for public service; the third that he accepts the Thirty-nine Articles as "agreeable to the Word of God."[33] If this was "the requirement to subscribe" (p. 103) there is no reason why Johnson needed a "loophole" to avoid it (p. 104), or why Sir Wolstan Dixie could or should have pressured him into taking it "with mental reservations" and dismiss him when he refused, as Clark conjectures (p. 104). Perhaps he has seen Leicestershire subscription books 1D41/34/3 and 4 that are different from the ones that the Leicestershire Keeper of the Archives and I have seen. Perhaps by the repeated "oaths" Clark accidentally misspoke, misread his notes, and really meant the subscription above, even though Johnson was employed in 1732 and the Leicester books are for 1733.

Perhaps, but neither the Oath of Allegiance nor the Oath of Abjuration appear in the Leicester subscription books cited as presently available. Those books therefore cannot support Clark's claim that it is "remarkable that the name of Samuel Johnson is absent from" them (p. 103)—with the usual neo-Jacobite inference. Instead, if Clark is correct that principled Johnson refused to sign the oath above, the unusual inference must be that Johnson was not an Anglican, refused assent to the Thirty-nine Articles and to the Book of Common Prayer, and thus was a crypto-Catholic. Here indeed is a new context for Samuel Johnson.

JOHNSON, THE HOUSE OF COMMONS, AND THE OATHS

Johnson of course had a long and deep interest in politics. His *Parliamentary Debates* (ca. 1740–42) demonstrate a firm grasp of the stakes and arguments of such intellectual exchange if not, as Henry Flood told Boswell, of the real nature of engagement in Commons. *The False Alarm*

(1770) and *Taxation no Tyranny* (1775) examine different aspects of the government's authority and its external and internal relations. In *Thoughts . . . on Falkland's Islands* (1771) Johnson calls legislators a civilizing force (YE 10:350). In *The Patriot* (1774) he adds that choosing a representative is "one of the most valuable rights of Englishmen," and that Commons is "the supreme council of the kingdom."[34] That council was superior to Rome's and, whatever the complaints, largely uncorrupted. Johnson regards it as an honest deliberative body in which "there was hardly ever any question in which a man might not very well vote either upon one side or the other" (*Life,* 3:206; see also 3:234). Sir John Hawkins had it right in this matter: Johnson's political pamphlets demonstrated "such skill in the grand leading principles of political science, as are seldom acquired."[35]

Johnson drew some of that skill from friends and Members of Parliament like Edmund Burke, Henry Thrale, and William Strahan. He aided Thrale's election to his seat at Southwark in 1765, and regularly wrote or corrected his election addresses thereafter.[36] Sometime late in the winter of 1777 Strahan and Thrale unsuccessfully lobbied the North ministry to find Johnson a seat in Commons (*Life,* 2:137–39). Boswell himself says that "It is not to be believed that Mr. Strahan would have applied, unless Johnson had approved of it." Mrs. Piozzi later annotates this sentence with "Yes, Yes; he would have *approved* it" (*Life,* 3:138, 138 n). Her remark is the more convincing because Hawkins credits Henry Thrale with encouraging the effort. Hawkins also reports that Johnson "was a little soured at this disappointment" and thereafter spoke harshly of North.[37]

The legislative episode is at once important in its own right and relevant for discussion of Johnson and oaths. The neo-Jacobites argue that in Johnson's later life as in his Oxford days he was "incapable of 'qualifying himself'" for public office. That is, he would not subscribe the oaths of Allegiance and Abjuration.[38] Johnson's working knowledge of Commons, however, informed him of two major qualifications for office. One was the property requirement that, Hawkins says, Henry Thrale "must . . . previously have determined to furnish him . . . and Johnson, it is certain, was willing to accept"—that is, either £600 income per annum from freehold land for a county seat, or £300 for a borough seat.[39] The second requirement was taking the oaths before being allowed to take one's seat. We can surmise that Johnson knew this at least through his parliamentary friends and his own knowledge; but probability becomes certainty. In *The False Alarm* Johnson paraphrases the 1679 law of Charles II: "he who should sit in the House of Commons, without taking the oaths and subscribing the test, should be disabled to sit in the House during that parliament, and a writ should issue for the election of a new member" (YE 10:329). The house was required to stay in session until four o'clock, until which Members could go to the "Table" and take their oaths—of Supremacy, Allegiance, and Abjuration.[40]

It is scarcely credible that Johnson would agree to accept an estate from Thrale, agree to have Thrale and Strahan press his case, and then betray them by refusing the oaths he knew he must take if elected. Nor would he have been disappointed in his rejection had he planned not to take oaths to the Hanoverian crown that ruled Britain since 1714. That crown confronted a Franco-Stuart invasion in 1745, and some ten years later again was threatened with a French invasion to which Johnson also was asked to respond.

JOHNSON AND THE TRAINED BANDS

Clark extends his argument on oaths to a cryptic passage Boswell includes for June of 1784. Johnson, he says, "was once drawn to serve in the militia, the Trained Bands of the City of London, and . . . Mr. Rackstrow, of the Museum in Fleet Street, was his Colonel." Johnson "did not serve in person; but the idea, with all its circumstances, is certainly laughable. He upon that occasion provided himself with a musket, and with a sword and belt, which I have seen hanging in his closet" (*Life*, 4:319). According to Clark, Johnson "refused to serve" (p. 130 n. 25) because he "may have shied away from taking the oath" required to bear arms for George II. Instead, he "chose at additional expense to hire a deputy to serve in his place. Edward Gibbon, with a far less robust physique, had renounced such scruples, and when Pitt's Militia Act passed the following year [1757] he served in person" (p. 121; see also p. 120). There is much wrong with this scenario, not the least of which, we have seen, is that like other Oxford students Johnson apparently took the oaths upon matriculation. If the neo-Jacobite version of Boswell's account is accurate, Johnson wasted a good deal of money by hiring a deputy but purchasing his own weapons. We must also assume that Johnson would have used his weapons for one of two purposes: either he would have fought the invading French who sought to overthrow the Hanoverians, or he would join them in order to overthrow the Hanoverians. There is no reason to believe that such a venture late in the 1750s could possibly have succeeded or have gained Johnson's or the nation's support. If Johnson kept those weapons to join the French, he was uncommonly stupid to keep them where they could easily be discovered. All these dreams fade in the light of probability.

Boswell met Johnson on May 16, 1763, and so is especially hazy in this passage recorded at least at secondhand and long after the fact. We do not know when Johnson was "drawn to serve"; but we may reasonably assume that it was after 1757, and probably in mid-to-late 1759. By then the bureaucratic wheels were oiled and the danger of a French invasion seemed greatest. Gibbon, for example, began his service in the Hampshire Militia on June 12, 1759. That date is important: Gibbon, born May 8, 1737, was twenty-two years old; Johnson, born September 18, 1709, was almost fifty years old. A fifty-year-old civilian in poor health, then engaged in editing Shakespeare, writing the *Idler*, mourning for his mother, and writing *Rasselas* might perhaps think it late to begin military exercises. A less "robust" twenty-two-year-old with little else to do, subject to paternal pressure, needing to reintegrate himself in English culture, and still temperamentally able to tolerate and to drink and carouse with the militia's generally rustic and low crew, may find unthreatening "mimic Bellona" instructive.[41]

Moreover, the initial extremely unpopular legislation required a list of able-bodied men from eighteen to fifty, and eighteen to forty-five after 1762. It is entirely plausible that when the City officers realized that fifty-year-old Dictionary Johnson was balloted, they excused him as overage. There were indeed numerous legitimate ways of avoiding service, including physical disability, payment of a £10 fine, or finding a substitute, which did not require a fine and also allowed men over thirty-five a further two-year exemption. In 1759 Buckinghamshire, 93 percent of farmers, 86 percent of tradesmen, 74 percent of artisans and craftsmen, 58 percent of laborers, and 41 percent of farm servants avoided service. Only fifty of its 238-man, significantly understrength, militia were principals and, as Ian F. W. Beckett has argued, "most principals and substitutes [who did serve] were manual workers, and invariably young, single, and illiterate." Gibbon obviously is an exception. Not serving in the militia says nothing about Johnson's Jacobitism.[42]

We also might consider Benjamin Rackstrow, Johnson's potential colonel. K. F. Russell describes his museum as "a most popular raree-show" with "considerable emphasis on the sexual organs [and] the various stages of pregnancy and child birth."[43] One has difficulty visualizing Johnson following the lead of a sexual raree-show entrepreneur.

Nonetheless, an amusing foray into art history presumably demonstrates that Johnson was fit enough to have served. Clark sees Dictionary

Schwarzenegger in an amply girthed gray-wigged forty-seven-year-old sedentary lexicographer: "Sir Joshua Reynolds's portrait of Johnson, painted in 1756, shows a robust solidly-built man in his forties, not a valetudinarian."[44] This medical examination of a man in a painting overlooks one of its prominent traits. H. W. Liebert remarks the obvious: "In Johnson's blind left eye Reynolds has reproduced the bland appearance of sightlessness." Other portraits by Reynolds, Frances Reynolds (?), and James Northcote all show Johnson with a book inches from his good eye. He could barely see or hear actors on the stage much less determine a target or whether that target was shooting back. Arthur Murphy met Johnson during the summer of 1754, and later observed that "Mr. Johnson's health had been always extremely bad since I first knew him."[45] That bad health included his compulsive rocking and touching. His friends often observed such blindness, cognate deafness, depression, and the ravages of what we now believe is Tourette's syndrome. Boswell and Murphy aside, Letitia Hawkins observes Johnson's cumbersome and "zig-zag direction of a flash of lightning" as he walked. Richard Cumberland notes that Johnson permitted his dining mate to squeeze oranges into his wine glass, otherwise the juice would have "gone aside, and trickled into his shoes, for the good man had neither straight sight nor steady nerves." Sir Joshua's sister Frances comments that Johnson's melancholy was "oppressive." He also had "extraordinary gestures or anticks with his hands and feet" and his "sight was so very defective that he could scarcely distinguish the Face of his most intimate acquaintance at a half yard's distance." Mrs. Piozzi explains his dislike of painting because he "was too blind to discern the perfections" of that art; he was "almost as deaf as he was blind."[46] What fellow soldier would want such a man next to him? We do not need an argument on nonjuring to explain why Johnson was not in the Dogberry Brigade.

Physical disability, however, did not preclude Johnson's eagerness to see Britain defended from French invaders—whether the evil French servants he characterized in *London* (1738), or the later armed men of Britain's traditional enemy. In 1756 he generally praises the Militia Bill because it enables "us to defend ourselves against any insult or invasion, and by placing the sword in the hands of the people"—some 60,000 of whom were envisioned within the militia. Moreover, in times of special danger, the king can raise that number to 150,000, to be distributed throughout the country (YE 10:166). Johnson's "Observations on the Russian and Hessian Treaties" (1756) builds on these earlier remarks, rejects the costs and the concept of subsidizing foreign troops to serve in Britain, and argues on mingled nationalism and patriotism: the brave nation does not need foreign troops; the Trained Bands can be revived and will defend "their own houses and farms, . . . wives and children." No one would dare invade Britain if faced with "an hundred and fifty thousand Englishmen with swords in their hands" (YE 10:183)—one such sword and one pair of hands were Samuel Johnson's, if he could see, hear, or march to the enemy.[47] It would be zany for Johnson to support what he hoped would be so ample and plucky a militia to oppose French invasion, while himself favoring a French invasion to restore a Stuart. Johnson often was depressed; he rarely was nuts.

The most likely collective hypothesis for Johnson's absence from the militia is that this busy man of letters was near or beyond the upper age limit; that few men like him were in the militia; that his potential officer ran a museum displaying sexual organs; and that neither the emergency nor, thanks to Admiral Sir Edward Hawke's naval victory on November 20, 1759, the threatened French invasion had materialized to justify subjecting the unhealthy overage editor to the dysfunctional Militia Act. As a contingency, though, the Francophobe Johnson apparently acquired a musket and sword, most probably to resist the French if necessary. One end of such aggression could have been to restore a Catholic Stuart monarch who had disgraced himself by abandoning the men he led to slaughter at Culloden. He already had been abandoned in turn by English Jacobites as an odiously avaricious man indifferent to the deaths he had caused and, as William King belatedly discovered, "unacquainted with the history and constitution of *England*."[48]

SUMMARY

Literary historians have been admonished to be aware of context, to ignore history at our peril, and to examine evidence. The overwhelming majority of that evidence also suggests that Samuel Johnson left Oxford because of his poverty not his principled Jacobitism. The overwhelming majority of that evidence suggests that he took at least the oaths of Supremacy and Allegiance and may have taken the Oath of Abjuration without so being aware. There is no doubt that the evidence of the Leicestershire subscription books is not germane for Johnson's earlier year in that area, and that he was not obliged to subscribe the loyalty "oaths" that were not there in any case. The overwhelming majority of that evidence suggests that Johnson did not join the Trained Bands when called because he either was not needed, was in poor health, or was at or beyond the legal age. There is no evidence that he sought to avoid martial loyalty oaths. Indeed, when he sought public office, he proceeded as if he would have to sign such oaths if elected and was resentful when not given the opportunity to stand for office.

I hope now to suggest how indifference to historical evidence has transformed *The Vanity of Human Wishes* (1749) from a great poem with a broad human message, to a political pamphlet with a highly particularized Jacobite message.

APPENDIX: SOME RELEVANT DOCUMENTS CONCERNING JOHNSON AND JACOBITISM

I. THE OATH OF ALLEGIANCE

I A. B. do sincerely Promise and Swear, That I will be faithful, and bear true Allegiance to His Majesty King *George. So help me God*, &c.

II. THE OATH OF SUPREMACY

I A. B. do Swear, That I do from my Heart Abhor, Detest, and Abjure, as Impious and Heretical, that Damnable Doctrine and Position, *That Princes Excommunicated or Deprived by the Pope, or any Authority of the See of* Rome, *may be Deposed or Murthered by their Subjects, or any other whatsoever.*

And I do declare, That no Foreign Prince, Person, Prelate, State or Potentate, hath, or ought to have any Jurisdiction, Power, Superiority, Preeminence, or Authority Ecclesiastical or Spiritual within this Realm.
So help me God, &c.

III. THE OATH OF ABJURATION (italics and roman type reversed)

I *A.B.* do truly and sincerely acknowledge, profess, testify, and declare in my Conscience, before God and all the World, That our Sovereign Lord King *George* is lawful and rightful King of this Realm, and all his Majesty's Dominions thereunto belonging. And I do solemnly and sincerely declare, That I do believe in my Conscience, that the Person pretended to be the Prince of *Wales*, during the Life of the late King *James*, and since his Decease, pretending to be, and taking upon himself the Stile and Title of King of *England*, by the Name of *James* the Third, or of *Scotland*, by the Name of *James* the Eighth, or the Stile and title of King of *Great Britain*, hath not any right or Title whatsoever to the Crown of this realm, or any other the Dominions thereto belong: And I do renounce, refuse, and abjure any Allegiance or Obedience to him. And I do swear, that I will bear true Faith and true Allegiance to his

Majesty King *George*, and him will defend, to the utmost of my Power, against all Traiterous conspiracies and Attempts whatsoever, which shall be made against his Person, Crown, or Dignity. And I will do my utmost Endeavour to disclose and make known to his Majesty, and his Successors, all Treasons and Traiterous Conspiracies which I shall know to be against him, or any of them. And I do faithfully promise, to the utmost of my Power, to support, maintain, and defend the Succession [which], . . . by an Act intituled, *An Act for the further Limitation of the Crown, and better securing the Rights and Liberties of the Subject*, is and stands limited to the Princess *Sophia*, Electress and Dutchess Dowager of *Hanover*, and the Heirs of her Body, being *Protestants*. And all these Things, I do plainly and sincerely acknowledge and swear, according to these express Words by me spoken, and according to the plain and common Sense and Understanding of the same Words, without any Equivocation, mental Evasion, or secret Reservation whatsoever. And I do make this Recognition, Acknowledgment, Abjuration, Renunciation, and Promise, heartily, willingly, and truly, upon the true Faith of a Christian.

So help me God.

IV. FROM, *A Summary of the Penal Laws Relating to Nonjurors, Papists, Popish Recusants, and Nonconformists. And of the late Statutes Concerning the Succeeding Riots, and Imprisonment of Suspected Persons* (London, 1716)

94.   To the Intent, all the Acts heretofore made for Securing the Succession of the Crown in the Protestant Line, and extinguishing the Hopes of the Pretender, might be for ever inviolably preserved, it was Enacted as follows:

That all Persons, as well Peers as Commoners, who shall bear Office Civil or Military, or receive any Pay, Salary, Fee, or Wages, by reason of any Patent or Grant from his Majesty, or shall have command or Place of Trust, from or under his Majesty, or his Predecessors, or by Authority deriv'd from him, her, or them, within the Kingdom of *Great Britain*, in the Navy, or in the Islands of *Jersey* and *Guernsey*, or shall be of the Household, or in the Service [95] or Employment of his Majesty, the Prince or Princess of *Wales*, or their Issue; and all Ecclesiastical Persons, Heads, or Governours, and all other Members of Colleges and Halls in Either University, being of the Foundation, or who enjoy any Exhibition (being of the Age of 18.) And all Persons teaching or reading to Pupils in the Universities, or elsewhere; all School-masters, Ushers, Preachers and Teachers of Separate Congregations; every Constable, Serjeant at

Law, Counsellor, Advocate, Attorney, Sollicitor, Writer in *Scotland*, Proctor, Clerk or Notary, who shall be within 30 Miles of *London* or *Westminster* the first Day of *Michaelmas* Term 1715. shall appear before the End of the said Term in the Courts of Chancery, King's Bench, Common Pleas or Exchequer, and take the several Oaths enjoin'd them by this Act. . . .

102.   The Oaths prescribed to taken by this Act, are the Oaths of Allegiance and Supremacy, and the Abjuration Oath, for that Part of *Great Britain* called *England*; and in *Scotland*, only the Oaths of Allegiance and Abjuration, with the Assurance, which is to be subscribed by them in the Room of the Oath of Supremacy. . . .

V. Johnson's signature in subscribing the Oath of Supremacy on December 16, 1728, "Term 1ᵗ Mick 1728": "Samuel Johnson è Coll: Pembr: Gen: Fil:"
See Oxford University Archives (OUA) SP 12, from October 9, 1714– December 23, 1740.

NOTES

1. See the appendix for the relevant oaths. Johnson's apparent refusal to take these oaths is a central argument in J. C. D. Clark's *Samuel Johnson: Literature, religion and English cultural politics from the Restoration to Romanticism* (Cambridge: Cambridge University Press, 1994), among other places.

2. Scott, *Old Mortality*, ed. Jane Stevenson and Peter Davidson (Oxford: Oxford University Press, 1993), pp. 7–8.

3. Amhurst, *Terrae-Filius; Or, The Secret History of the University of Oxford; In Several Essays*, 3rd ed. (London, 1754), pp. 220–21. Amhurst begins this No. 42 by reiterating that "perjury, and treaston, and paying a multitude of fees" are "insisted upon" at Oxford (p. 218). I cite these hereafter in the text as *TF*.

4. MacLeane, *A History of Pembroke College, Oxford, anciently Broadgates* (Oxford: Oxford Historical Society at the Clarendon Press), p. 332. Violation of the statute dating from 1581 required "a fine of 40s. for every week to be paid by the Scholar and 20s. by the Head" (p. 332). See also John Ayliffe, *The Antient and Present State of the University of Oxford* (London, 1714), 2:113–14. In 1714 matriculation should have been "within 15 Days after his first coming hither." Violation meant that the student "is mulcted in the sum of 6s.8d. for every 15 Days of his Delay to the Use of the University." In either case, apparently neither side paid the fines for violation of the statute. For Whitefield, see *George Whitefield's Journals (1737–1741) to Which is Prefixed His "Short Account" (1746) and Further Account* (1905), with an intro. By William V. Davis (Gainseville, FL: Scholar's Facsimiles and Reprints, 1969), p. 40. For Purnell, see *The New and Complete Newgate Calendar; or, Villany Displayed in All its Branches*, ed. William Jackson (London, 1795), 3:153–54. Purnell also refers to the "notorious insult on

his Majesty's crown and government" and "seditious practices" that caused Richard Blacow to arrest the perpetrators, much to Purnell's and William King's annoyance. James Miller's *The Humours of Oxford. A Comedy. . . . By a Gentleman of Wadham College* (London, 1730) characterized Oxford as a nest of drunks, fakes, fortune hunters, and bigamists, but does not deal with sedition. The vice chancellor redeems the university's integrity.

5. Webber, *A Defence of the Rector and Fellows of Exeter College from Accusations Brought against them by The Reverend Dr. Huddesford: In His Speech to the Convocation, October 8, 1754, on Account of the Conduct of the said College, at the Time of the late Election for the County* (London, 1754), pp. 19 (no right), 47 (refused).

6. Hearne, *Remarks and Collections of Thomas Hearne*, ed. Oxford Historical Society (Oxford: Clarendon Press, 1902), 5:45–46.

7. [Kennicott], *A Letter to Doctor King Occasion'd by his Late Apology; And in particular, By such parts of it as are meant to defame Mr. Kennicott, Fellow of Exeter College* (London, 1755), p. 25.

8. See the appendix.

9. Amhurst, Supremacy and Allegiance, *TF*, No. 3, p. 12, and No. 17, p. 88 ("all the oaths," but he refers only to the two above); Blacow, *A Letter to William King LL. D. Principal of St. Mary Hall in Oxford. Containing a Particular Account of the Treasonable Riot at Oxford, in Feb. 1747* (London, 1755), p. 17 ("the Oaths"); Kennicott, *A Letter to Doctor King, Occasion'd by his late Apology*, p. 19 (Supremacy and Allegiance for all; Abjuration for Foundationers). The outraged Samuel Clifford berates those who seek to evade the oaths by kissing the thumb rather than the Bible, among other abuse of oaths. See Clifford's *A Dissuasive from Perjury; With . . . An Answer to the Evasions which some use to elude the Force and Obligation of Oaths* (London, 1723), p. iij.

10. Ayliffe, *Antient and Present State* 1:sig. A4ᵛ (errors), 2:114 (matriculated; and see 2:152). Ayliffe matriculated as a Gentleman on February 19, 1696, and was M.A. in 1703 and B. and D.C.L. in 1710. See Joseph Foster, *Alumni Oxonienses: The Members of the University of Oxford, 1500–1714* (Oxford, 1891). He had been at Oxford for twenty years when he wrote this. Ayliffe describes the particular experience of New College degree granting, in which graduands repeat earlier oaths. He adds words that probably suggest the Oath of Abjuration and regular violation of it: the Senior Proctor "gives them the Oaths of *Allegiance* and *Supremacy*, with some others, *which are observed by conscientious Men*" (2:152). The New College historians show how Whiggish Ayliffe was subject to the "grossly inquisitorial engine of tyranny in the hands of the University Magnates." See Hastings Rasdall and Robert S. Rait, *New College* (London: F. E. Robinson, 1901), p. 202; see generally pp. 198–204. Ayliffe discusses his expulsion in *The Case of Dr. Ayliffe*. For Hearne, see *Remarks and Collections of Thomas Hearne*, 6:300.

11. For a brief report on the case, see *The Complete Newgate Calendar*, 3:152–53, and *The English Reports Volume XCVI King's Bench Division XXV* (Edinburgh: William Green & Sons, 1909), p. 20. The *Reports* have several reprintings. This section also shows the difficulties Purnell faced "for not taking the deposition of Blacow the evidence, and for neglect of his duty both as vice chancellor and justice of the peace, in not punishing Whitmore and Dawes, who had spoken treasonable words in the streets of Oxford" (p. 20). The case against Purnell was dropped, but he received no further preferment. Here is the *Report*'s précis of punishment: "They were now sentenced to pay five nobles a-piece, to be imprisoned for two years, to find security for their good behaviour for seven years, themselves to be bound in 500l. each, and two sureties in 250l., to be imprisoned

until the fine was paid and the security found; and to go round immediately to all the Courts in Westminster Hall, with a paper on their foreheads denoting their crime. Which punishment was strictly put in execution" (p. 20). The event, together with Purnell's pending trial, also was broadcast to the world through the May 1748 *Gentleman's Magazine*: 18:214, 234, 521, 522. Given the boys' good family connections, I suspect that the jail time was in fact brief and perhaps less onerous than the fine and the shame. Neither graduated from Oxford thereafter.

For Blacow, see *A Letter to William King*, pp. 17 (Wisdom), 24 (two); Kennicott, *A Letter to Dr. King*, p. 19; matriculation records, Joseph Foster, ed., *Alumnae Oxonienses: The Members of the University of Oxford, 1715–1886* (Oxford, 1888). An anonymous author responded to Blacow in *An Answer to Mr. B——w's Apology, As it respects His King, His Country, his Conscience, and his God, By a Student of Oxford* (London, 1755). The student is keen on the sanctity of oaths, but bitterly attacks Blacow for exceeding his authority: they were only near and not on the High Street he was assigned to police. The student attacks the slightest appearance of error, but never Blacow's insistence that the perpetrators took "the oaths," as it seems reasonable he would if Blacow were wrong.

12. For "stalwart" see H. W. Carless Davis, *A History of Balliol College*, rev. R. H. C. Davis et al. (Oxford: Basil Blackwell, 1963), p. 151. For Baron's threat to Hearne, see *Reliquiae Hearnianae*, ed. Philip Bliss, 2nd ed. (London, 1869), 2:43. Hearne is warned on December 13 and 14 and is especially apprehensive regarding Baron "as he is a justice of the peace." Hearne often expresses fear of or anger concerning Baron. See *Remarks and Collections of Thomas Hearne* 3 (1889): 124, 137, 153; 5 (1901): 328–29, 330, 361; 6 (1902): 5–6, 158, 232, 341–42. As we have seen, Hearne was not above abuse of the oaths for personal gain: *Remarks*, 5:45–46.

Baron was sufficiently reliable a Whig for James Brydges, Duke of Chandos, to entrust his son Lord Carnarvon to his care at Balliol. Chandos writes him several movingly filial letters. See Huntington Library Stowe Collection, 57, 16:330–32 (October 13, 1719); 425 (December 29, 1719); 17:274–75 (November 25, 1720); 338–39 (February 7, 1721); 18:105–6 (August 21, 1720); 186–87 (November 30, 1720); 235–36 (April 10, 1721). In the last letter Chandos encloses a note for thirty guineas for Baron, and another thirty guineas "for the Service of y^r Colledge where my Son hath receiv'd so much civility." The Chandos-Carnarvon-Baron relationship suggests three potential, and unnecessary, dangers: being rigid in requiring vocal, demonstrative, and individual oaths; requiring oaths as late as graduation rather than matriculation; and potentially requiring dons to cross well-connected young men and their families.

13. *Cicero in Twenty-Eight Volumes, XXVII. The Letters to His Brother Quintus*, trans. W. Glynn Williams (Cambridge, MA: Harvard University Press, 1989), pp. 544–45, Epistulae ad Quintum Fratrum, 2:16.

14. I am indebted to J. C. D. Clark for identifying George Cooper as Hearne's examiner: "The Cultural Identity of Samuel Johnson," *Age of Johnson* 8 (1997): 19; henceforth *AJ*.

15. *Oxford University Statutes*, trans. G. R. M. Ward (London, 1845), 1:10.

16. Allix, *An Examination of the Scruples of Those who refuse to Take the Oath of Allegiance. By a Divine of the Church of England* (London, 1689), p. 18.

17. See *Undergraduate Subscription. Extracts From A Collection of Papers Published in Oxford 1772 On the Subject of Subscriptions to the XXXIX Articles, Required from Young Persons at their Matriculation* (Oxford, 1835), p. 30.

18. This response was part of an extended debate regarding the efficacy of oath taking. One side argued that an oath taken with God as witness was a matter of the highest seriousness, the violation of which was virtual atheism and attempted deicide. The other side argued that frequent oath taking so cheapened the process that it was unreliable and infamous on the face of it. Johnson appears to have recognized the validity of each argument, but stressed that oaths were largely deceitful and futile.

19. Johnson, "Remarks on the Militia Bill," in The Yale Edition of the Works of Samuel Johnson, vol. 10, *Political Writings*, ed. Donald J. Greene (New Haven: Yale University Press, 1977), p. 159; henceforth cited as YE 10. For the fellows, see University of Oxford College Histories, Douglas Macleane, *Pembroke College* (London: F. E. Robinson, 1900), p. 166. Hearne also commented on the "abominable wickedness" of "numbers of all kinds [who] run in to swear" the Oath of Abjuration without proper consideration. See Bliss, *Reliquiae Hearnianae*, 2:177–78.

20. Johnson, *Lives of the English Poets* (1779–81), ed. George Birkbeck Hill (Oxford: Clarendon Press, 1905), 2:557.

21. Clark, in *Samuel Johnson in Historical Context*, ed. Jonathan Clark and Howard Erskine-Hill (Houndsmill, Baskingstoke, UK: Palgrave, 2001), pp. 101–2. Subsequent references are cited parenthetically in the text.

22. Bennet, "University, Society, and Church 1688–1714," in *The History of the University of Oxford . . . Volume V. The Eighteenth Century*, ed. L. S. Sutherland and L. G. Mitchell (Oxford: Clarendon Press, 1986), p. 363. Subsequent citations are given parenthetically in the text, prefixed by B. George Birkbeck Hill also discusses Johnson and servitors at Oxford. See his "Oxford in Johnson's Time" in *Dr. Johnson: His Friends and His Critics* (London, 1878), pp. 21, 24–31. Birkbeck Hill estimates that £50 would "much more than covered, his whole yearly expenses" (p. 9). His view of Johnson as an essentially happy man with several dark periods, is salutary: see pp. 100, 123–45 of "Lord Macaulay on Johnson."

23. V. H. H. Green, *The Young Mr. Wesley: A Study of John Wesley and Oxford* (New York: St. Martin's Press, 1961), p. 162.

24. Arnold A. Dallimore, *George Whitefield: The Life and Times of the Great Evangelist of the Eighteenth-Century Revival* (London: Banner of Truth Trust, 1970), 1:61.

25. From chapter 12, "On Universities," in *An Enquiry into the Present State of Polite Learning in Europe* (1759), *Collected Works of Oliver Goldsmith*, ed. Arthur Friedman (Oxford: Clarendon Press, 1966), 1:335–36. See also Ralph M. Wardle, *Oliver Goldsmith* (Lawrence: University of Kansas Press, 1957), p. 25.

26. Hawkins, *The Life of Samuel Johnson, LL. D.* (Dublin, 1787), pp. 12–13 (poverty), 18 (scholars).

27. *The Poems of Richard Corbett*, ed. J. A. W. Benett and H. R. Trevor-Roper (Oxford: Clarendon Press, 1955), p. 17. See also p. 112, n. 140, from a contemporary Baker manuscript: "degrees were vilely prostituted to mean persons" and "some of them were afterwards degraded."

28. Green, "The University and Social Life," in *The History of Oxford . . . V*, p. 328. He gives other examples of high costs, often for tailors, boots, hunting, and assorted refreshments. Johnson's absence from such excess would have been as noticeable as his exposed toes. Much of this behavior was in violation of statutes, as indeed was regular and predictable violation of the dress code (p. 324). See pp. 320–40 for a fuller discussion of expenses.

29. In *Boswell's Life of Johnson Together with Boswell's Journal of a Tour to the Heb-*

rides, ed. George Birkbeck Hill and rev. L. F. Powell (Oxford: Clarendon Press, 1934–50), 1:73–74. I refer to this hereafter parenthetically in the text as *Life*.

30. *A Short Account*, in *George Whitefield's Journals*, p. 41. Whitefield also was involved in defending the six undergraduates expelled from St. Edmund Hall, Oxford, in 1768, for practicing Methodism. One charge was "that some of them were of Trades before they entered into the University": *A Letter to the Reverend Dr. Durell, Vice Chancellor of the University of Oxford; Occasioned By a late Expulsion of Six Students from Edmund Hall* (London, 1768), p. 7. Thomas Nowell records the articles of expulsion in *An Answer to a Pamphlet, Entitled Pietas Oxoniensis* (Oxford, 1768), pp. 18–20, 28–32: James Matthews was a weaver and kept a tap house; Thomas Jones was a barber; Joseph Shipman was a linen draper. The first line of the first charge against them is that they indeed "were bread to trades" (p. 18). That breeding then was used to demonstrate that they had inadequate linguistic knowledge to remain at Oxford: see also pp. 52–53, 55, in which their ignorance is more properly regarded as rendering them unfit for advanced study.

31. King, *Dr. King's Apology: Or Vindication of Himself From the Several Matters Charged on him By the Society of Informers* (London, 1755), pp. 42–43. Oxford's social system had changed little in the nearly half century since *The Servitour* of 1709.

32. See Clark's "Religious Affiliation and Dynastic Allegiance in Eighteenth-Century England: Edmund Burke, Thomas Paine, and Samuel Johnson," *ELH* 64 (1997): 1029–67. He discusses the Leicestershire subscription books on pp. 1052–53, and notes 73, 74, 75, and 80, pp. 1065–66. Clark also publicly argued on the importance of Johnson's absence from these subscription books: the Western Society for Eighteenth-Century Studies, at San Bernardino State University in February of 1999.

I wish to thank Mr. Robin Jenkins, Keeper of the Archives, for his consistently helpful and professional guidance with these books. Before writing this section I reconfirmed with him that the oaths of Allegiance and Abjuration were not in the Leicestershire Subscription Books. Mr. Jenkins also kindly encouraged me to contact the excellent local historian Dr. Anne Tarver for further advice regarding relevant customs. I thank each of them while making plain that neither has been asked to or would take sides in the debate.

33. Edmund Gibson, *Codex Juris Ecclesiastici Anglicani: Or, the Statutes, Constitutions, Canons, Rubricks and Articles of the Church of England*, 2nd ed. (Oxford, 1761), 2:808.

34. YE 10:350 (legislators), 399 (valuable).

35. Hawkins, *Life of Johnson*, p. 453.

36. See J. D. Fleeman, "Dr. Johnson and Henry Thrale, M. P.," in *Johnson, Boswell and Their Circle: Essays Presented to Lawrence Fitzroy Powell*, ed. Mary Lascelles, James L. Clifford, J. D. Fleeman, and John Hardy (Oxford: Clarendon Press, 1965), pp. 170–89.

37. Hawkins, *Life of Johnson*, pp. 453–54.

38. Clark, *Samuel Johnson*, p. 193.

39. Hawkins, *Life of Johnson*, p. 454. For the history of property requirements, see Columbia University Studies in History, Economics, and Public Law, No. 498, Helen Elizabeth Witmer, *The Property Qualifications of Members of Parliament* (New York: Columbia University Press, 1943), especially pp. 40–44, 54–55, 78–83, and Frank O'Gorman, *Voters, Patrons, and Parties: The Unreformed Electoral System of Hanoverian England 1734–1832* (Oxford: Clarendon Press, 1989), pp. 15, 117–18. I am indebted to F. P. Lock for the references to Witmer and to Hatsell below.

40. For the relevant information, see John Hatsell, *Precedents of Proceedings in the House of Commons. . . . Vol. II. Relating to Members, Speakers, &c.*, 2nd ed. (London, 1785), 2:60–64, and P. D. G. Thomas, *The House of Commons in the Eighteenth Century* (Oxford: Clarendon Press, 1971), pp. 13, 92 n. 5, 114, 155.

41. See *Edward Gibbon: Memoirs of my Life*, ed. Georges A. Bonnard, (New York: Funk and Wagnall, 1969), pp. 107–18 for Gibbon's role in the militia. For drinking bouts, see pp. 114 and 116, and p. 115 for Bellona. According to Gibbon, one could avoid service either by paying the £10 fine or by "finding a substitute" (p. 110).

42. Beckett, *The Amateur Military Tradition 1558–1945* (Manchester: Manchester University Press, 1991), pp. 61–90 for the context, and p. 66 for the statistics and quotation. On the same page Beckett confirms Gibbon's understanding that one could pay a fine *or* find a substitute, as does J. R. Western in his *The English Militia in the Eighteenth Century: The Story of a Political Issue 1660–1802* (London: Routledge & Kegan Paul, 1965), p. 129. For other remarks concerning the unpopularity of the Militia Act, see Western, *English Militia*, pp. 140, 290–302, Langford, *A Polite and Commercial People: England 1727–1783* (Oxford: Oxford University Press, 1992), pp. 334–35, and Langford, *Public Life and the Propertied Englishman 1689–1798* (Oxford: Clarendon Press, 1991), pp. 266–67, 296–98. In *Public Life* Langford observes that the Act included characteristic Whig individualism and commercialism, as in the fine and, as he puts it, permission "to hire a substitute by private negotiation" (p. 266).

43. Russell, *British Anatomy 1525–1800: A Bibliography*, 2nd ed. (Winchester, Hampshire: St. Paul's Bibliographies, 1987), p. 161, item 680. I am indebted to Professor Robert Storch and his prowess on the Internet for this reference. One must, however, wonder whether Boswell correctly cites Rackstrow as the colonel. According to the Militia Act, a colonel was required to own land valued at £400 per year. In urban boroughs where landed estates were less likely, the Act specified personal value of £5,000. The original land qualification in 1756 was only £300. Johnson thought the disparity unreasonable: "every one knows, that five thousand pounds is not of more than half the value of the land required, and therefore, unless money makes a man wiser or honester than land, ten thousand pounds should be required as a qualification, if indeed any money can qualify" (YE 10:160). If Mr. Rackstrow was worth at least £5,000 he ran a very successful raree show indeed.

44. Clark, "Cultural Identity," *AJ* 8 (1997): 42.

45. This originally was part of a Clark Library seminar by J. Douglas Stewart and H. W. Liebert, *English Portraits of the Seventeenth and Eighteenth Centuries* (Los Angeles: William Andrews Clark Memorial Library, 1974). I here quote from Liebert's expanded reprint, *Lifetime Likenesses of Samuel Johnson Reissued With Additional Plates . . . To Commemorate The Two Hundred and Sixty-fifth Birthday of Dr. Samuel Johnson* (New York: Privately Printed for the Johnsonians, 1974), p. 52. See plates 4, 9, 10, pp. 76, 81, 82, for the other paintings. Anecdotes regarding Johnson's inability to see the stage are in Arthur Murphy's *An Essay on the Life and Genius of Samuel Johnson, LL. D.* (London, 1792) and in George Steevens's anecdotes. See *Johnsonian Miscellanies*, ed. George Birkbeck Hill (Oxford: Clarendon Press, 1897), 1:157, and 2:318 respectively. Murphy's comment on Johnson's perennial ill health is in 1:199. Sometime between 1778 and 1780 Johnson tells Edmund Hector that "My Health has been from my twentieth year such as has seldom afforded me a single day of ease." See *The Letters of Samuel Johnson*, ed. Bruce Redford (Princeton: Princeton University Press, 1992–94), 5:7. I suspect that the officer Benjamin Rackstrow would gladly have paid not to have such a man

in his unit. Johnson may allude to his poor hearing and its role in oaths. See his "Remarks on the Militia Bill" at n. 19 within.

46. All the easily multiplied quotations regarding Johnson's disabilities are from Birkbeck Hill's *Johnsonian Miscellanies*: Hawkins, "Anecdotes by Miss Hawkins" (1827), 2:139; Cumberland, "Anecdotes by Richard Cumberland" (1807), 2:75; Reynolds, "Recollections of Dr. Johnson By Miss Reynolds" (ca. 1797), 2:257 (oppressive), 2:273 (gestures) 2:276 (sight); Piozzi, "Anecdotes of the Late Samuel Johnson" (1786), 1:215.

47. A conjecture: it is possible that Johnson acquired the musket, sword, and belt not to be part of the Trained Bands if called, but to get a sense of those weapons for the militia he characterized in 1756.

48. King recounts his impressions in the *Political and Literary Anecdotes of His Own Times* (London, 1818), pp. 196–214; p. 180 quoted. King was slow to make this insight. See, for example, John Shute, Viscount Barrington, *A Dissuasive from Jacobitism*, 2nd ed. (London, 1713), pp. 20, 21–22, 25–26. Shute also insists on how worthless oaths are when taken by Stuarts and Jacobites: pp. 5–7, 10, 19, 24, 26–27. This essay is among his several anti-Jacobite tracts.

15

The Vanity of Human Wishes Part I: Who Said He Was a Jacobite Hero? The Political Genealogy of Johnson's Charles of Sweden

THE CHARLES OF SWEDEN PASSAGE IN *THE VANITY OF HUMAN WISHES* (1749) is perhaps the chief and most compact section on which neo-Jacobite revisionists focus. Swedish Charles, Howard Erskine-Hill argues, "had long been a Tory and a Jacobite hero." Johnson the Jacobite was sympathetic to this "mighty favourite" who some thought threatened to invade England in 1717, depose his enemy George I, and restore the Pretender to the throne. Johnson also was sympathetic to the '45, whose lamentable "experience" he needed to convey "to a Jacobite sympathizer." Such a reader would recognize Johnson's attraction to Charles Stuart's noble but sadly failed attempt to restore the legitimate monarch. Rejection of Swedish Charles as a surrogate for Stuart Charles wrongly reduces "one of the most moving passages of eighteenth-century poetry to total banality." Even Johnson's unlikely but assumed reading about Charles of Sweden's military successes prior to Pultowa shows Johnson's pleasure in this "Jacobite hero."[1] J. C. D. Clark in turn knows that "It was no coincidence" that *London* and *The Vanity of Human Wishes* were reprinted in Jacobite Oxford in 1759: "their significance would be correctly appreciated in such an intellectual milieu."[2] Jacobite Oxonians "appreciated" the emotion of the '45 that Johnson meant to convey to them.

This interpretation indeed has become a virtual eleventh commandment within neo-Jacobite studies. "The allusion to Scottish Charles [is] beyond doubt" (p. 7 n. 9), Erskine-Hill now claims about *The Vanity of Human Wishes* and its harsh portrait of Charles of Sweden. Niall Mac-Kenzie adds that "I will take as my starting point the assumption that the case for a flickering Jacobite allusion in lines 191–222 of the *Vanity* has been proved." Part of that proof depends upon neurology. There are

340

"analogical synapses . . . firing in the *Vanity*'s literary environment," where one also finds "subliminal Jacobite nostalgia."[3]

Such flickers indeed often substitute for historical evidence. Another commentator, for example, regards Johnson as "a nonjuror of robust proclivity and pro-Stuart views."[4] Throughout the *Vanity* Johnson therefore "hints" that he "intends the Jacobite attempt of 1745 to be among the vain wishes uppermost in his reader's mind." Swedish Charles "unites" both Johnson's past and present concerns and "can be as readily applied" to Charles Edward who like the Swede was a "vanquished Hero" forced to show "his miseries in distant Lands" as a "needy supplicant" expelled from France in 1748.

> Moreover, in 1745 Charles Edward had already been compared to the Swedish monarch; and here the Stuart prince seems to hover on the edge of the text, much as the 'Forty-five hovers on the margin of voicing itself through the theme of the poem. Johnson's clear social conservatism, his emphasis on the corrupt capital and clear indication of interest in the political events of the last few years, all inch towards the hint of a sympathy which bears in mind along with other futile vanities, the vain attempt of the year 1745. (p. 130)

Flickering, undertoning, hovering, edging, margining, inching, sublimating, and hinting implicitly denote Jacobite Johnson's sympathy for Charles Edward who is so like the admired hero Charles of Sweden.

Affirmation of Charles XII as a Tory and a Jacobite hero is so commonplace within neo-Jacobite historiography that it thrives by assertion. This "Protestant hero of the Jacobites," we hear, evoked "enthusiasm" in the ranks: "In the pamphlet literature at the time of the Swedish-Jacobite conspiracy in 1716–17, Jacobites are seen to admire and approve Charles XII of Sweden."[5] We are not told the pamphlets' titles, how many there were, what proportion praised or blamed Charles XII, and whether some of them were written by Swedes—as they were. Jacobite enthusiasm for Charles XII's invasion of England nonetheless supports the Jacobite reading of *The Vanity of Human Wishes*. By logical extension, on this hypothesis eight-year-old Jacobite Johnson in 1716 Lichfield shared fellow Jacobites' awareness and approval of heroic Charles XII's plans to invade Britain; both Johnson's own approval and the Jacobites' approval of Charles remained static until the autumn of 1748 when Johnson seized the moment sympathetically to meld Charles of Sweden and the other Jacobite hero Charles Edward—as Jacobite readers in Oxford, and presumably elsewhere, knew. I will examine the validity of such assumptions and draw relevant inferences regarding Johnson's poem. Since a poet normally exploits the knowledge that he shares with his audience, what was the political genealogy of Johnson's Charles of Sweden?[6]

Was Charles of Sweden a Jacobite and Tory Hero?

Charles's "heroism" was limited by two important facts. The first is that he was overwhelmingly more important to continental Europe than to insular Britain. As Nicholas Rowe says in 1703, Britons can not pity what they do not share—

> Like distant battles of the Pole and Swede,
> Which frugal citizens o'er coffee read,
> Careless for who shall fail or who succeed.

Even in 1717 the lady in Thomas Tickell's *Epistle from a Lady in England to a Gentleman at Avignon* casually includes this bit of news in a grab bag of stuff: "The *dauntless Suede*, pursu'd by vengeful Foes, / Scarce keeps his own hereditary Snows."[7] Thereafter, Göran Andersson Nordberg's three-volume history of Charles XII (1748) lists several printed sources: fourteen are in German, twelve in French, two in Swedish—of course in addition to numerous Swedish personal and archival sources—one in Dutch, and one in English, Defoe's *History of the Wars of . . . Charles XII* (1720). Nordberg immediately labels it a fake: "qu'il ait été au Service de Suede, c'est ce qu' il ne persuadera à personne." Both Nordberg's first two volumes of 533 pages and 653 pages include a few incidental references to Britain. Only the third volume includes a sustained discussion—concerning the presumed invasion, which he dismisses as an unpersuasive canard.[8]

To be sure, both Anne and George wished to preserve and increase their Baltic commercial interests, to maintain the northern balance of power, and to stop Charles from allying himself with France. In 1707, for example, Queen Anne sent the Duke of Marlborough on this mission for the overt sign of respect that his presence showed, for his ability to determine another general's goals, and perhaps implicitly to demonstrate the task of confronting Europe's most formidable commander and army.

In the event, Marlborough rightly judged that Charles was looking eastward to Russia for his lethal adventure. That is the second fact that limited Charles's role as a hero. Commentators on northern and eastern Europe regularly contrast Charles and Peter the Great as adversaries. Destructive Charles leads his people back into despotism, barbarism, and reduced power; constructive Peter leads his people out of despotism, barbarism, and into expanded power. Friedrich Christian Weber, Defoe, Voltaire, and James Thomson are among those who so characterize the opposing monarchs. The English translation of Weber's *Present State of Russia* (1722–23), for example, both praises Peter and emphasizes Swedish atrocities in the war Charles instigated. In 1744 Thomson's *Winter* dismisses "The frantic *Alexander* of the North" in one line, but uses thirty-three lines to sing "Immortal PETER! First of Monarchs." He tames, exalts, builds, labors, plans, gathers, seeds, raises, smiles, dazzles, cures, glows, and teaches a "Scene of Arts, of Arms, of rising Trade."[9] In light of these familiar developments, one may ask who thought that Charles was a Tory and Jacobite hero?

An obvious answer is the committed Jacobites themselves. As one hostile author puts it in 1717, the Pretender's friends are openly confident of Charles's help: "There is scarce a *Jacobite* School-boy, or poor Tradesman's Wife about our Streets, who has not been instructed how conveniently *Norway* lies to *Scotland*, and how much it was for their Master's Interest, that the Brave King of *Sweden* shou'd succeed in his Undertakings."[10] Many of these Jacobites thus were Scottish. William Meston admires Charles's sympathy for James, his difference from William, and his enmity to George. In "An Imitation of Horace's Ode 5. Book IV. To Augustus" Meston sings a nostalgic refrain regarding Charles of Sweden:

> How were the frozen Highlands chear'd,
> When the bright northern star appear'd,
> Smooth past the night, serenely calm the day.
> The winter soften'd, and the war look'd gay.

That fancied invasion also was the burden of Meston's "On the Death of Charles XII. King of Sweden," which vilifies William III, George I, and the unfaithful Queen Anne Stuart. In contrast, personally and martially exceptional, legitimate, beloved Charles ruled so well that he was universally revered, especially among the Jacobites who mourn his loss:

> With bleeding heart bewail him, Britain's Isle,
> He would have brought thy Prince from his exile,
> Wip'd off thy tears, and made thee gladly smile.[11]

As we later will see, this was not the full story. Important national figures more exalted than schoolboys, tradesmen's wives, and Scottish schoolteachers also encouraged the Protestant Swedish monarch to invade their country on behalf of a Catholic in Avignon. For the most part, however, both Whig and Tory, Administration and Opposition, found Charles broadly unacceptable and did so long before Meston's dream of a deus ex Scandia.

As Queen Anne's secretary of state, Bolingbroke well knew that Charles of Sweden was northern Europe's nuisance and Britain's gadfly. Several letters between 1710 and 1713 express fears that Charles will side with France. Some letters complain that Sweden harasses British commercial shipping interests in the Baltic. Others are exasperated by Charles's irrational behavior in domestic and foreign affairs. Still others, however, make plain that Charles was merely a pest rather than a serious threat. Hence on August 3, 1711, Bolingbroke warns the Swedish minister that Charles's interruption of British shipping is "unaccountable . . . and intolerable." Queen Anne "will defend her subjects *coûte qu' il coûte*."[12] On July 12, 1712, he tells Harley that the "very strong squadron" readied for the Baltic will insure that any invaders "cannot fit out one fleet to cope with our Channel guard" (1:562–63). On March 3, 1713, he also asks the Duke of Shrewsbury to inform the Swedish minister at Paris that "a very strong squadron . . . will, in a short time, be able to act in the Baltic" (2:294). Bolingbroke understands that Sweden cannot seriously threaten British interests.

Several of his letters include Swedish fears that Britain is cool to her survival and British fears that a collapsing Sweden will be partitioned, absorbed by hostile neighbors (April 19, April 29, 1713; April 27, 1714), and thus destroy "the balance of the North" (2:401). The most poignant such observation is in Bolingbroke's letter to the Duke of Shrewsbury, May 29, 1713, characterizing a nation ravaged by her monarch's ambition and facing "ruin" and "destruction" (2:401, 403). Charles's enemies will besiege and capture his Baltic ports; thirty thousand Russian troops will invade Finland; Charles can expect nothing from Turkey; he cannot support his remaining German possessions; he can scarcely furnish eight thousand troops to defend Finland; and, at best, he can scarcely provide a squadron to defend Schonen and disturb his Baltic enemies. "This kingdom is reduced to the last extremities; oppressed by taxes, starved by the decay of trade, and dispeopled, as well by the frequent draughts of recruits, as by the pestilence" (2:400).

Such Swedish weakness and increasing British strength made thoughtful Jacobites tremble regarding the success of a possible Swedish invasion. Bolingbroke's remarks to Lord Stafford should have heightened such anxiety, for Bolingbroke was not alone in thinking that foreign forces acting on behalf of a new monarch would galvanize resistance. That resistance surely would multiply exponentially if the foreign forces attempted to impose a Catholic monarch. On March 23, 1714, Bolingbroke writes to Stafford regarding the potential Hanoverian folly of using alien troops to impress native minds and to secure its succession or, yet worse, to threaten civil war. British laws, oaths, religion, and liberty affirm the nation's adherence to a Protestant and rejection of a Catholic monarch. "But," he says, "if a pretended danger of the succession shall be made use of, to introduce foreign forces amongst us, the object of men's fears may come in time to be changed. Britain must not on any account be made the theatre of confusion; our crown must be given, but our country must not be conquered" (2:625). Charles XII's invasion would be worse than Bolingbroke's worst fears regarding the Hanoverians and surely would create a "theatre of confusion" and conquest.

Bolingbroke of course writes before his own flight, the Whig ascendancy, and Jacobite dreams of Charles as savior. We thus need to ask what other evidence there is concerning an idealized Charles from late 1716, when Samuel Johnson was seven years old, to the autumn of 1748 and the first written installment of *The Vanity of Human Wishes*.

We can predict at least two consequences if many during those years believed that Charles of Sweden was a Tory and a Jacobite hero: Tory and certainly Jacobite publications would attempt to glorify both Charles XII and the putative invasion. In such a case the *Examiner*, *Mist's*, *Fog's*, and even Bolingbroke's *Craftsman* are logical candidates in which to find flattering allusions. In fact, these publications generally are hostile to Charles, whom they think a more appropriate model for Whigs than for Tories.

Specifically, on September 7–10, 1710, Mary de la Rivière Manley's Tory *Examiner* suggests that Charles II is a William surrogate who is beloved by Whigs. They admire his "*Revolution-Principles*" that promoted "a *Revolution* in *Poland*." This entire number likens Charles to Marlborough, an unlikely Tory or Jacobite hero. On June 26–29, 1713, the *Examiner* complains about "All the Bloodshed, Devastations, and Rapine, which now over-spread the North."[13] Nathaniel Mist preceded his namesake periodical with the *Weekly Journal or Saturday's Post*, a publication so much "the organ of the Jacobites and 'High Flyers'" that the Whig government sent Daniel Defoe to infiltrate and neutralize its excesses (*DNB*). Those excesses did not include veneration for Charles of Sweden, who was perceived as a dangerous war lover. On February 1, 1718, No. 60, Sir Andrew Politick asks "why we should not think that Monarch mad" for rejecting peace with the Czar. On February 15, No. 62, Mist replies "that will better be answer'd when we see the Armour on every side put off," as Charles refused to do.

Mist's itself ran for three years and 179 numbers, from May of 1725 to September of 1728. During that time only No. 25, October 16, 1725, includes sympathetic references to Charles and even that avoids his apparent invasion scheme. Similarly, from September 28, 1728, to December 29, 1733, the 269 numbers of *Fog's* are comparably silent. One negative remark, however, already was a staple both of Administration and of Opposition rhetoric regarding Charles. *Fog's* for October 13, 1733, No. 258, approvingly quotes a pamphlet called *A Word of Advice to the Freeholders*: "the *Swedes* under *Charles* XII. were, and the *Danes* are as much Slaves, as the *French* under *Lewis* XIV. or their present Monarch."[14]

The *Craftsman*'s few references to Charles XII are comparably hostile, for both Opposition and Administration, Whig and Tory, agreed that Charles was an emblem of un-British tyranny. The *Craftsman*'s outrage takes three forms. One is anger at Charles for his indifference to human blood and to his nation's misery. On March 11, 1738, No. 609 evokes his already familiar association with the malevolent Alexander he mimicked and alludes to Pope's list of enemies to peace in the *Essay on Man* 4:220 (1734). Charles's frequent wars "had well nigh ruin'd his Country" until propitious Fate stopped "his farther Imitation of the *Macedonian Madman*, and . . . the utter Desolation, which his frantick Gallantry must undoubtedly have brought" on Sweden.[15]

Charles also was useful for the *Craftsman*'s frequent parallel history and its attacks on the Caesars, Catilines, and other tyrants it likened to Walpole's Georgian court. On July 13, 1737, No. 419 compares the executed Baron Gortz to Walpole, as one whose wicked counsels had alienated the king from his people. Alternatively, Charles himself could be a surrogate Hanoverian. On October 1, 1743, No. 901 characterizes a monarch who raises armies for ambitious "romantick Plans of Conquest." This "despotick Prince" will "ruin his Country . . . as did *Charles* the 12th of *Sweden*." Several of the anti-Carolean strands were woven into one number's angry fabric in 1732.

So far as I can tell, only the *Craftsman*, No. 302, for April 15, 1732, discusses the apparent Swedish invasion—which it both excoriates and parallels to Walpole's grim relationship to Britain. "Anglicanus"—a name that mocks the Braunschweig-Lüneburgs on the British throne—

praises Voltaire's *History of Charles XII* (1731; translated 1732) in all respects except for its treatment of some British affairs, especially its discussion of Charles XII and George I. This reservation then becomes a springboard for an ironic attack upon Walpole and George II.

Surely, Anglicanus argues, Voltaire "invidiously (and I hope falsely) imputes . . . [the Swedish Conspiracy to George I's] Purchase of BREMEN and VERDEN from the King of *Denmark*" who apparently had no right to sell them. Charles seeks to punish George I for his actions as German Elector of Hanover. The opposition *Craftsman* resents Hanoverian involvement in Europe that subverts the Act of Succession's desire to secure Britain from wars "in Defence of *foreign Dominions, not belonging to the Crown of* England." For Anglicanus even "the *Disaffected*" British Jacobites would find such a consequent Swedish invasion appalling. A Protestant king should not attempt to force a Catholic monarch upon another Protestant nation. Hence the disaffected would ask to what "this terrible Invasion had been owing," and they would wonder why old foreign treaties should threaten Britain now. The "dangerous Conspiracy" was discovered and thereafter wholly obviated "by the providential Ball at *Frederickshal*, which put an End to the Life of that *enterprizing Monarch*, and secur'd us in the Enjoyment of our *present Liberties*."

Like many contemporaries, the *Craftsman*'s Anglicanus believes that Baron Gortz's "pernicious Counsels" concocted the plot and that he gained "an absolute Power over" Charles. Gortz, he says, should "stand foremost in the List of Iniquity"—as well he might considering the public's hatred for him as "an ambitious and most rapacious Servant, to whose destructive Scheme the Miseries of *Sweden* were, in a great Measure, owing." This recognizable Walpole is even more obvious when we read about Gortz's substitution of a copper for a gold coin, his presumed destruction of trade, and his victimizing of "the miserable People."

The *Craftsman*'s only extensive foray into Swedish history, then, is indebted to Voltaire rather than to living memory of a threatened invasion that never came close to materializing and that the well informed knew would fail. The Opposition then metamorphoses this nonevent into a stick with which to beat the Hanoverians and Walpole. The monarchs are surrogates for the despotic, ruinous Charles of Sweden and are dangerous aliens with foreign entanglements; the Administration's chief minister is a parallel Gortz.

Who, then, thought Charles XII a Tory and a Jacobite hero in 1717? The list includes the isolated and forgotten William Meston, other unnamed Scottish Jacobites, and other unnamed Jacobite tradesmen and their families in London. Virtually no publicly recorded Tory, Jacobite, or other political commentators thereafter join the list.

There is a general reason for the broad-based rejection of Charles XII—the Jacobites and Tories opposed much of what he represented.[16] Their platform emphasized squirearchic landed authority, suspicion of foreigners and foreign involvements, hostility to a standing army that could become a tyrant's tool, and the sanctity of indefeasible hereditary native monarchy. Charles XII was a negative paradigm. His martial excesses savaged his country and its hierarchy; his large standing army included many alien officers; and he deposed or sought to depose other legitimate kings to suit his own interests, at whatever cost to his or to other nations. Moreover, living ancestral history already had an example of how Goths invited to help the "right" side stayed and became the natives' masters. In 1745 a pseudonymous Lord Lovat wonders whether an army of Hanoverians or Hessians asked to destroy the Scottish rebels "should not treat us in the same Manner as their Countrymen the *Saxons* did of old the antient Britons, who sent for them to their Aid."[17] Charles of Sweden would have been a dangerous ally.

There also were at least three other particular reasons for Charles's banishment from the ranks of political norms, all of which support general objections to his politics and bloodlust. He came from a land of Gothic barbarism that had forgotten its Gothic liberty; his agents hoped to impose that political barbarism on free Britons; these several historical sources had extensive literary and political implications. Paradoxically, preinvasion scare, non-Jacobite praise of Charles uses the positive side of the Gothicism that, finally, transforms him into a dangerous enemy.

In Praise of the Warrior King

The rhetoric of praise acknowledges the great military leader. One relevant poem predates Charles's fall from grace, regards him as a Swedish Marlborough, and probably reflects the high-water mark in Charles's positive British reputation.

The title of Joseph Browne's poem immediately evokes several then well-applauded concepts and connections: *The Gothick Hero. A Poem, Sacred to the Immortal Honour of Charles XII. King of Sweden, &c. The Glorious Restorer of the Protestant Religion in Silesia, from Popish Usurpation, and Arbitrary Sway* (1708). Browne evokes amiable associations with the Gothic tree. Its roots extend to Tacitus's *Germania*, its branches flowered under William and the Hanoverians, and it shades British Saxon history, political freedom, and martial valor.[18] Good Goths are good Whigs. In 1702 John Hughes thus praises William III's Germanic ancestry on the Rhine. Several years thereafter a grateful poet celebrates George I as "The Pride and Glory of the *Saxon* Line." William Peterson later argues that the Hanoverians descend from Arminius, the Gothic German who defeated Rome's Varus and his three legions. In 1739 Henry Brooke's Whig-opposition *Gustavus Vasa, The Deliverer of his Country* praises that monarch's reign in 1523–60—significantly ignoring the more recent famous Charles. Sweden, Brooke says, then was "one of those *Gothic* and *glorious* Nations from whom our Form of Government is derived, from whom *Britain* has inherited . . . Liberty and Patriotism."[19] This sternly congenial Gothicism thus was easily absorbed into the heroic, glorious, and Protestant as enemies of the usurping, Popish, and arbitrary, all of which Browne includes in his title and elaborates on in his poem.

Accordingly, Browne's dedication stresses that Charles protected and freed the Silesian Protestants, and is "the Great Champion for Liberty, Justice, and Religion throughout all *Europe*." Charles fights without personal or national interest and only for "the Good and Happiness of Mankind, in the Enjoyment of their Liberties or Religion." He will continue "to redeem the Oppress'd, aid and assist the Needy, and help them to Right, that suffer Wrong."[20]

In the poem itself Charles and his "old *Gothick* Blood" descend "From *Goths* and *Vandals*, and *Gustavus'* Line" and are superior to Greco-Roman heroes (p. 5). "The noble *Goth*" is "divinely fir'd, / And with a holy Zeal and rage inspir'd" to free the Poles and Silesians from tyranny and Popery (p. 11). Browne also associates Charles with Marlborough's pacifying, anti-absolutist victories in the War of the Spanish Succession. For Browne in 1708 "The *Cesars* fill'd the World with Fame and Blood; / But none like *Charles*, with Universal Good." Other martial achievements are "Trifles, to what brave *Charles* and *Churchill* do" in liberating Europe, aiding the religious, and relieving the poor (p. 7). Thereafter, Timothy Harris in 1719, the frontispiece poet of the pirated Adlerfeld *Genuine History of Charles XII* (1742), and Eliza Haywood in her *The Fortunate Foundlings* (1744) variously eulogize the "Glorious," or deathlessly famous, or nobly romantic Swedish monarch, while never mentioning his invasion scheme or friendship with Jacobites.[21] Overwhelmingly, however, by Charles's death in 1718 his once shining glories seemed fool's gold. One reason for this change of mind was his stunning defeat by Peter of Muscovy.

On June 28, 1709, Charles's hubris, poor tactics, and inept logistics finally caught up with him at the catastrophic battle of Pultowa. Charles who, Frederick the Great said, "n'auroit jamais fait la guerre avec reflexion," there left 6,901 dead on the steaming fields and 2,760 prisoners in Russian hands. On July 1st his lieutenant Count Lewenhaupt, thinking his position at Perevolotjna indefensible, surrendered 1,161 officers and 13,138 men to Prince Alexander Menshikov, whose troops also soon murdered and mutilated many of the Cossacks and Zaporzhians who fought on Charles's behalf.[22] His five years of exile in Turkey, his consequent vexing of Britain, the significant weakening of his country, and the difficult Norwegian campaign of 1718 transformed Charles into yesterday's hero.

Perhaps worse, these events, together with the invasion threat and Charles's own oddities, evoked the darker side of the Gothic inheritance. Civilization's ever loyal friends seized the moment.

Gothic Standards Fly

Such friends well knew that Danish, northern, Norwegian, Scandinavian, Swedish, and blood-loving Gothic barbarian were approximate synonyms for the violent ravagers of Rome and learning. In 1695 Thomas Brown observes that the Goths "destroy'd learning root and branch." Nathan Bailey's *Dictionarium Britannicum* (1730) defines Goths as those who "brought into Subjection and Barbarism a great Part of the Christian World." Pope's *Dunciad* (1743) uses Goths to exemplify the death of modern culture. Thomas Gray adapts these orthodoxies in his freely translated poem "The Fatal Sisters" (1768), in which a prognosticating tapestry is "of human entrails made." The sisters themselves sing "Songs of Joy" when they see that "Horror covers all the heath, / Clouds of carnage blot the sun."[23]

Edward Young already had exploited this association during the '45, when positive remarks regarding Charles Edward were thin on the ground. Young appends "Some Thoughts Occasioned by the Present Juncture" to *The Consolation* (1745), the eighth of his *Night Thoughts* (1742–45). Charles Edward is "A *Gothic* Hero rising from the *Dead*" who, a note reveals, also is "The *Invader* [who] affects the Character of *Charles* the Twelfth of Sweden." Such invasive Gothicism must strike horror "Thro' every *generous* Breast, where *Honour* reigns."[24]

Some Goths were worse than others. Toward the end of the seventeenth and beginning of the eighteenth centuries Denmark and, especially, Sweden won the competition for moral and political evil. This attitude was encouraged both by enduring mythology and by two often unflattering "Accounts."

Robert Viscount Molesworth's *An Account of Denmark: As it was in the Year 1692* (1694) characterizes a once prosperous Gothic free nation with a mixed constitution. Like the rest of the north, Denmark now represents "Slavery in its own Colours, without any of its Ornaments" in France and Spain. It is impoverished, heavily taxed, victimized by a slavishly colluding clergy, and subject to kings so "Absolute and Arbitrary" that Danes lack "the least remnant of Liberty." The king explains and alters the law "*as he shall find good*," and "a Dull Obedience" replaces extinct northern liberty.[25]

British objections to northern absolutism and barbarism were even more pressing in the unauthorized printing of John, later Bishop, Robinson's *An Account of Sueden as it was in the Year 1688. Together with an Extract of the History of that Kingdom* (1694). It reached an important and timely third edition in 1717, when remarks regarding Sweden under Charles XI easily could be applied to his son Charles XII.

The *Account* often is dispassionate but rarely flattering to the industrious, brave but plodding Swedes. Their soldiers endure and obey well but are poor at "Nimbleness and Address"; their peasants labor hard when necessary, but cannot learn new methods; their navy is dubiously officered and inferior to Denmark's.[26] Though the army included a modest maximum of fifty regiments and sixty thousand men (p. 59), it nevertheless had to be reckoned with: the Goths "in all Ages were addicted to War and Violence." As a "disorderly and tumultuous" force of peasants, however, the successful Swedish army depends less upon "Native Strength" than upon "the *German, French, English*, and especially *Scots*, of whom they have used great Numbers in all their Wars." They gradually introduced military art and discipline "into this Nation, that in former Times had only the Advantage of Courage and Numbers" (p. 54).

Robinson was most troubled by Swedish subjects' required submission to their absolute king. He has confiscated estates, taxed heavily, and lost "the Affection of his subjects" whom he nonetheless controls, restrains, and engages "the greatest part of the Nation to his Interest" (p. 47)—namely, through a combination of force, bribery, and coercion.

These passages were noted and held against Sweden. Robinson observes that the Swedish punishment for stealing has been changed from death to "a kind of perpetual Slavery." The guilty person is "condemn'd to work all his Life for the King, in making Fortifications, or other

Drudgery, and always has a Collar of Iron about his Neck, with a Bow coming over his Head, to which is a Bell fasten'd, that rings as he goes along." All three of the *Account*'s first editions mark this passage with a marginal finger pointing to the line with the word "King," as if to urge Swedish political degeneracy. No wonder that the translator of the Abbé Vertot's *History of the Revolutions in Sweden* (1696) tells the Duke of Shrewsbury that he here sees "so lively an *Idea* of the vast Disproportion betwixt the Subjects of a *Hero* [William] and the *Slaves* of a *Tyrant*," Charles XI.[27] Such works clearly are as much about William's England as about Charles's Sweden.

Moreover, like Vertot's *History*, the 1711 edition of Robinson's *Account* provided much raw material for a slashing attack upon Sir Joseph Banks, a naturalized Swede and Member of Parliament for Minehead. He told his constituents "that Kings are accountable to none but God, and that Subjects must obey notwithstanding any Tyranny and Oppression whatsoever." The angry author of the *Letter to Sir J—— B——* (1711) tells Banks that he might as well have stayed in slavish Sweden. There he could find "*Tyranny and Oppression* enough . . . to have exercis'd all your heroick *Passive Vertue*" under Charles XII whose kingdom has "utterly lost all its *Liberty*." Charles, "as Absolute as the *Great Turk*," thinks himself "*accountable to none but God*," is one of "the Heroes of Slavery," and thus must attack a constitutional government composed of king, lords, and commons. As this author says in his *Second Letter* to Banks (1711), "The Present Enslav'd State" of Sweden and of Denmark reflect such corrupt doctrine.[28]

William King had earlier claimed that Danish absolutism was best for the happy Danish subjects. That argument is paralleled by a Swedish agent or the ambassador himself, Count Karl Gyllenborg, who later was arrested for conspiring to aid the Swedish invasion. He writes unsigned *Remarks* (1711) that offer Swedish absolutism and divine right as antidotes to "lawless Liberty."[29]

By 1711, then, Charles XII and his surrounding nations were tarred with two dark brushes. As a Goth gone bad, his ancient bloodlust submerges his ancient love of liberty. As a political tyrant he enslaves his ruined nation, his subjects, and his clergy, opposes limited constitutional monarchy, and is defended by fellow Swedish absolutists. When the author of *Observations Upon a Pamphlet, Called, An English Merchant's Remarks* (1717) referred to doltish Swedes "born under *Northern Slavery*" he adapted a long-established propaganda trope that maligned both Sweden's politics and Lutheran Protestantism.[30]

By 1716–17 Swedish invasion threats had become public knowledge.

Such a possible effort to install the Catholic Jacobite Pretender helps George I's government substantially to augment the anti-Swedish and anti-Carolean chorus and to increase its army, navy, and political power at home. Consequently, as Defoe observes in 1719, on sea or land the Swedes would have received "such a Welcome, as should put a short End to the Project." As James Robinson puts it two decades later, the government so well defended the nation that the Swedes would "meet with a warm Reception. And these Preparations were so effectual, that no more was heard of this *Swedish* Invasion."[31] George I's efforts were significantly aided by captured letters between the principal foreign conspirators, Count Gyllenborg in London, and Charles XII's continental minister plenipotentiary. He was the Franconian Georg Heinrich Goertz, Freiherr von Schlitz, normally referred to as Baron Gortz, and generally regarded as brilliant, devious, and made for the most difficult and dangerous adventures.

WAR GAMES

A combination of French and Dutch aid, international espionage, intercepted communication, and knowledge of Jacobite intentions gave the Hanoverian court ample notice of the Swedish plots and ample reason to violate ambassadorial sanctuary. On January 29, 1717, troops surrounded and entered Count Gyllenborg's London residence and, in spite of protests, seized his papers. At British urging, on February 18th Gortz's house in the Hague was entered and his papers also were seized. By then Gortz already had departed for Utrecht, where at a merchant's house other papers were seized—and thereafter returned unopened. Gortz himself finally was arrested at Arnheim as he was about to leave for Germany.[32]

These events outraged the international diplomatic community. More importantly, they allowed George I to demonstrate that his enemies were friends of Gothic barbarian invaders, that he required a stronger army, fleet, and support for his northern policies, and that in spite of such needs he was master of the nation's security. To help these designs, on February 17th, under the front matter's royal seal proclaiming "DIEU ET MON DROIT," Samuel Buckley published letters "between Count *Gyllenborg*, the Barons *Gortz*, *Sparre*, and others; relating to the Design of raising a Rebellion in His MAJESTY's Dominions, to be supported by a Force from *Sweden*."[33] The letters' various revelations became so well known that in 1719 Defoe thought it superfluous "to offer a Detail of that Matter." The letters also alarmed British readers, who already had been taught to regard any Swedish Charles as an emblem of alien danger. In *The Annals of King George* Defoe observes that the letters and his majesty's open dealings moved Parliament to his side "and added to the Resentment which the whole Kingdom had conceived against the Conduct of the King of *Sweden* and his Ministers."[34]

Here, just two years after a failed Jacobite invasion, was proof of yet another scheme to throw the nation into civil war, but now with the aid of foreign Goths appropriate for domestic Goths. For all the Jacobites' claims of popularity in a disaffected nation, they could only seek restoration through ten to twelve thousand Swedish mercenaries that Gyllenborg and Gortz apparently promised them (pp. 4, 28).

An unidentified eminent British Jacobite, perhaps the Earl of Arran, well predicted the domestic, even Jacobite, response to such foreign intervention without a necessary and ample fig leaf.[35] Though, he says, the largely Jacobite nation longs for the lawful James Edward, it will not rally to those like Charles XII who do not declare for him. "On the contrary, perceiving 'tis only a Foreign quarrel, which draws the King of *Sweden* hither," annoyed by unmet expectations, and frightened by Hanoverian retribution, "they will fall into the common humour of the Nation, which is to unite all, notwithstanding their past Feuds, against a Foreign Power." Indeed if James "had not an *English* Father, and been born in *England*, all his Pretensions would avail him nothing with the common People." When the contest is merely between foreigners they "will certainly declare for him in Possession, without much regard to the Justice of the Cause" (pp. 15–16)—as, we know, those people did against the foreign-born Charles Edward Stuart in 1745.

The letters also demonstrate that this would in fact be a foreign invasion that required the twin masks of hypocrisy and subterfuge. Gyllenborg writes that the "glorious Enterprize" is designed to end Hanoverian possession of Swedish-claimed Bremen and Verden "by ruining" George I (p. 4). Gortz soon adds that there is "now no other Question, but of the Means to satisfy our just Desire of Revenge" by means of Swedish troops (p. 18). He still needs to emphasize "the Concern we have for maintaining the *English* Liberties" (pp. 10, 12), a concern Sir John Brownlow found especially offensive. "We have no need," he told Commons, "of the King of *Sweden* to maintain the *English* Liberties and support for the Church of *England*."[36] Native treason parallels foreign duplicity. According to the senior British Jacobite, the Swedes must cultivate the Jacobites in Commons, for "'tis they who have hitherto defended your Cause, as well in the Country as in the Parliament," and they will again be necessary "in the next Session of Parliament" (p. 14). As John Oldmixon glosses this in 1735, "*The* Jacobites *in the Secret of disbanding the Army*" (p. 632). That session was too distant a horizon for Gortz, who tells Gyllenborg to have his friends eliminate half of the troops now in England, to determine how many regular troops then remain, and to postpone shipbuilding and rearming (p. 20).

Another vulgarly basic theme runs like a leitmotif through the letters—money. Pounds, crowns, livres, guilders, and dollars are equally useful. "Both *Gortz* and *Gyllemberg* labour the Money Point incessantly," Oldmixon observes (p. 632). They need to purchase corn, rye, barley, salt, iron, ships of the line, and the materiel to equip their invasion force. Gortz clearly saw the Jacobites as a bank on which he could draw to finance Swedish arms. On January 16, 1717, he writes that the invasion depends "upon two Things; one is the procuring four or five Ships of War; and the other is Money. I know where to get the former, but I can do nothing without the other" (p. 32). Gyllenborg himself also requires money—to pay for his food, clothing, and other expenses (p. 38). Hence he will seek a commission, or kickback, from the English merchants he has engaged to sail in the Swedish interest: "The *English* know how to take Advantage themselves upon the like Occasions; I do not know why we should not do the same" (p. 39).

So far as British money went, it was in 1717 as it would be in 1745. The Jacobites claimed loyalty to legal succession, to the family of James Stuart and its indefeasible right to his crown, and to the divine right of their kings. They were more loyal to the secular right of their own comfort—a concern they did not extend to the Swedish and later French soldiers they expected to fight and die for Olde England. Gyllenborg tells Gortz what he sees in London's Jacobite circles: "They run the Hazard of their Lives and Fortunes in declaring themselves, so that they will not speak but upon good Grounds" (p. 8).

One startling letter even more clearly portrays the revolutionary as accountant calculating the bottom line. On December 6, 1716, Gortz relates his discussion with the unnamed and alarmed principal Jacobite. The Pretender in Avignon, he says, was deceived when he assured his British brethren that Charles would invade on his behalf. The London Jacobite cannot ask Britons for help without those assurances that, in spite of lengthy negotiations, apparently will not come. Meanwhile, he asserts, we do not care about "the Interests of foreign Princes, any longer than while they affect our own" (p. 14). Gortz asked them to lend money to his Swedish majesty, but this clearly is not profitable. We then read an extraordinary remark: the Jacobites can get better terms from the fiscally sound Hanoverian government they wish to destroy: "As for Gain, can we hope for greater in any Country than what we have at home, without risquing our Money? Do we not make 7 or 8 per Cent. by the Publick Funds, and this upon the Securities of the Parliament of *England*, and are paid punctually every Quarter?" (p. 14). The Jacobite lord nonetheless will subsidize Charles if he promises to invade Britain, which he fears Charles will not do. If his majesty does so promise, the Jacobites will rely on that "more than on all the Securities and Engagements of others" (p. 14). After three months' negotiations, however, so far from having an answer to whether Charles will act for them, they barely have "an Answer whether we shall obtain" an answer (p. 15).

The *Letters . . . Relating to the Design of Raising a Rebellion* show Swedish ministers and British Jacobites cynically using one another. Each side is unaware that its secret schemes had been detected and monitored. Each side also is largely naive regarding the difficulty of successfully invading Britain. Several letters proclaim the ease of the enterprize. All they need is money, transportation, and the ten thousand Swedes who "would do the Business" (p. 2); "Our Men being once landed, I answer for the rest: In a Country where Nine in Ten are Rebels, and where every thing abounds, we can want nothing" (p. 4); they will easily acquire five hundred horses upon landing at "whither we should be directed" (p. 28).[37]

In a rare fit of reality, however, Gortz also tells Gyllenborg about potential problems: the lack of transports and convoys; how to maintain the troops upon arrival; how to get the horses; how many troops actually are necessary; how many cannon the ships can have (p. 18; see also p. 28); and, certainly, how to acquire the large sums of money to support this scheme that, Defoe asserts, would have meant dreadful failure. Before the Swedes could put to sea, he says, "we had 30 Men of War in a readiness for Action," thirty-five thousand men ready to march in England, and twelve to fourteen thousand good troops ready to leave from eastern Ireland if necessary.

Two Continental judgments cogently and impartially reflect the contempt that Britons probably also had for the futile but dangerous Jacobite and Swedish self-delusion. One remark comes from Châteauneuf, the French ambassador at the Hague:

Le but de M. Goertz à été de tirer de l'argent des Anglais et le roi de Suède n'a rien su des espérances qu'il leur donnait. . . . Comment ce prince aurait-il projeté des descentes quand il a peine à se défendre chez lui? Comment les aurait-il concertées avec le czar quand la paix n'est pas faite entre eux? . . . M.

de Goertz ne parle pas sensément. Il passe depuis longtemps pour un fripon. Il mérite à présent le titre d'étourdi. . . . Sa négociation est celle d'un filou.[38]

The second judgment comes from an impeccable military source—Frederick the Great's generally harsh reflections on Charles's military talents and character: "Les projets, qu'on lui attribue depuis son retour en Pomeranie, & que quelques personnes mettent sur le conte de Goritz, m'ont paru si vastes, si extraordinaires, si peu assortissans à la situation & à l'épuisement de son Royaume, qu'on me permettra pour l'amour de sa gloire, de les passer sous silence."[39]

Both the French ambassador and the Prussian monarch imply that Charles himself was or was thought ignorant of this destructive swindle by a feckless cheat. At the least, as Oldmixon complains, the impoverished ministers and king were gulled by the free spending of "that miserable [Jacobite] Faction" (p. 632).

The *Letters* include a few hints that Charles knew what was happening, but most evidence suggests that Charles and his court were ignorant of the Gortz-Gyllenborg rogue adventure. Thus Gortz: "You will do well, Sir, not to make any mention in your Letters to the King, or to your Correspondents in *Sweden*, of what has been secretly propos'd to you about the Pretender" (p. 3); "I will not venture to conveigh any Thing of this to His Majesty, otherwise than by Word of Mouth. . . . The odd Fancy of the Pretender's retiring to *Stockholm*, surprises me. It would be blazing abroad our Intelligence by Sound of Trumpet" (p. 11; see also p. 9); "our Ministers themselves are ignorant of it [his invasion scheme], and know not for what Intent they have been obliged to give the Turn they have to the full Power which they dispatched" (p. 29). Thus Gyllenborg: "The Intimations which have been made me, terminate in bringing in the Pretender, but as I cannot enter upon that Affair without an express Order from the King my Master, I have avoided coming to Particulars" (p. 2).

After being arrested, Gortz insisted that Charles was ignorant of the plot. Charles himself found the implication of underhanded negotiations so offensive that he refused to dignify them with a direct response. French diplomacy and British pressure convinced Charles finally to speak through the voice of the Regent of France, the Duc d'Orleans. The duke assured George I that Charles XII declared that he had not "entered into any of the designs, attributed to his Ministers" and thought it "as a great injury to him, the suspicion of his having had any concern in their projects."[40] The statement was not always believed.

Henri Philippe de Limiers's *Histoire de Suede sous le regne de Charles*

XII (1721) argues that Gortz abused his power and that Charles "n'y avoit point de part . . . pour une Action si indigne de son caractere." Voltaire in 1731 accepts the probability of the "indigne" action, and in 1760 again regards him as part of the plot.[41] Daniel Defoe reflects both the uncertainty and the dominant conclusion.

Defoe adapts his rhetoric to his occasion. In the *Annals of King George, Year the Third* he thinks there is no "doubt but the King of *Sweden*, whatever was afterwards pretended, was at the Bottom of it" (p. 143; see also pp. 186, 319–20). He vacillates in the *Account* of Gortz, but finally decides that he "acted by the special Direction of the King, . . . from His Majesty's own Mouth," thus condemning himself to death when Charles died without having exonerated him (p. 40; see also pp. 14–15, 26, 27–28). With time and reflection, however, he offers what probably was, and still is, British considered opinion.

In 1720 Defoe enlarges the 1715 *History of the Wars, Of his late Majesty Charles XII. King of Sweden, From his First Landing in Denmark, To His Return from Turkey to Pomerania*. This second edition of course considers events of 1716–17 and continues the history "*To the Time of his Death*." The book is nominally "By a Scots Gentleman in the Swedish Service" and so purges itself of possible Jacobite taints (p. 251). Both Defoe and his prudent, cautious, respectful narrator have read the confiscated Swedish correspondence. He thus argues that Gortz and Gyllenborg used Charles's name "purely to draw Money from the disaffected Party in England." The Scot knew Charles' affairs at the time, and does not believe that he gave such instructions, knew what his foreign ministers were doing, or ever had "a Thought or Design of Invading the King of *Great Britain*'s Dominions; nor did the least Preparations towards such an Undertaking ever appear in *Sweden*, as I either saw, or had any Account from others" (p. 375; see also p. 377). George I believed Charles's French denial, and "thereby allay'd the Dissatisfaction" (p. 388).

Defoe could not have known the French translation of Nordberg's history of Charles XII in 1748, but later readers there would have seen strong affirmation of Defoe's final judgments. Nordberg knows that Charles's army was in no condition for such a difficult engagement against a strong and well-prepared army (3:287), doubts whether such foolish letters are genuine (3:289), considers the accusation baseless (3:290), and reminds readers of Charles's stern rejection, given to France, of the offensive suspicion (3:298–99). In such a case, Charles XII must have lost whatever claim he had to British Jacobites' financial and verbal largesse. As a stay-at-home reluctant invader he should have been expelled from the Jacobite pantheon. After all, the plot was not based on Charles's heroism but on the secret scheming of the devious *filou* Gortz on behalf of a monarch impoverished by the failed militarism he was unable and unwilling to stop.

By early to mid-1717, then, extreme northern Europe and Sweden in particular had become the demonic Goth. Charles is at once the head barbarian and the dupe of lesser ministerial barbarians. His policies included using foreign mercenaries in a large standing army, invading foreign nations and deposing their legitimate monarchs, consequent devastation and depopulation of his own nation—all anathema to received Tory and of course much Whig belief. Charles is the hitherto great Protestant liberating warrior; he is the slavish overreacher whose politics are abhorrent and military greatness past; above all he is the ally of domestic traitors who invoke a monster as their own reflection. Defoe laments that an invasion means the appalling horrors of a civil war: "barbarous *Goths*" would "join with bloody Papists and Tories, to destroy our Government, Religion, Liberties, and Properties." The Goths' leader even was rejected by his own ruined, tyrannized people who struck at him by executing Baron Gortz—a mark, Defoe again says, "of a Contempt of the Person of their deceased Sovereign, and that of the grossest Kind."[42] By 1720 and thereafter, however, both at home and abroad he often is cleared of colluding in an invasion that never was likely to have occurred but understandably stirred fear, rage, and rethinking of Charles's achievements.

THE HERO PAST: AFTER THE INVASION SCARE

As Defoe's observations suggest, the liberator of 1708 becomes the ominous Goth of 1717. That moral approach is especially clear in the unsigned *Observations Upon A Pamphlet Called An English Merchant's Remarks*. The observer knows that George I tried to save Charles in spite of his depredations of British trade. Peace is irrelevant for this vengeful and haughty man whose achieved views would have been "pernicious to *Christendom*" (p. 8). Charles is "a declared Enemy of those true *Britains*, and almost all of Mankind" (p. 30). The destructive, isolated, rash, profligate man is a slave to his own warlike temper. So angry a voice transcends political opportunism and anticipates Swift's rage in the elegy on Marlborough (1722) in which widows' sighs and orphans' tears replace songs of praise.

Charles will neither capitulate nor retreat; he asks his men to die when they cannot win; he must have all or nothing; his courage is brutality; he ignores his capitol city and its government. Worse, he ignores "the Cries of the Merchants, the Fatherless, and the Widows. . . . One may see he wishes the whole World were in Flames and Desolation, provided he cou'd accomplish his Revenge. Is this a Temper to be endured?" (pp. 38–39).

Nor could one endure further civil war. Defoe's *What If the Swedes Should Come* graphically depicts a disordered world in which resurrected Jacobites join invading foreigners in a "terrible Civil War; and for how long, God only Knows." People will be plundered, "Virgins ravished, Churches robb'd, old and young murder'd, and the Fields cover'd with Blood."[43]

Some commentators blend the great hero with the brute and offer a theory of causation—the 1717 revelations that forced reconsideration of Charles's military and personal character. The narrator of *What If the Swedes Should Come*, for example, admits that Charles was "my Hero for some Years past" but adds that his opinion changed when Charles rejected peace. He now thinks Charles "entirely *demented*" if he should contemplate invading England while so besieged at home (pp. 3, 4). Susanna Centlivre is equally blunt. Her *Epistle To the King of Sweden* (1717) is addressed to the "rude Warrior, whom we once admir'd," though even then he seemed half mad. Now that ambition and revenge guide him, "*Thy* Glories languish, and our Wonder fails." Joining British malcontents is an act of political and martial folly that means he will "Ne'er hope to see thy Native *Sweden* more." He will "fall Unpity'd, and Forlorn, / All *Europe*'s Terror once, but now all *Europe's Scorn*."[44]

Centlivre suggests another familiar complaint—Charles is the classic overreacher who exemplifies the vanity of human wishes. Defoe's *Short View* (1717) of Charles's conduct observes that he aimed to capture Moscow and ruin Peter, "but Heaven had other Designs, and the Lawrels his Majesty had gained in a Series of uninterrupted Victory, were now to be snatched from his Head, by the *Muscovites* in One Day, and a sad Scene of Misfortunes attended him." By 1721 Tom D'Urfey's collected *New Opera's* includes versified "Historical Remarks." There Charles as an insane, filthy, itinerant "would be *Gustavus*" falls "like some poor Grenadier."[45]

D'Urfey's demotion of Charles was consistent with British denigration of the crude unregal monarch. One chief source for this view probably is "A Letter to the Right Honourable the Lord * * * * *, . . . Giving a description of the Person, Behaviour, &c. of the King of *Sweden*, King *Augustus*, and King *Stanislaus*," almost all of which devotes itself to

Charles's appalling personal habits. He is handsome "but immoderately dirty and slovenly" whether on or off horseback; his horses are poorly maintained by incompetent grooms; his breeches are "sometimes so greasy, that they may be fried"; his dining habits are vulgar; he "eats like a horse; speaks not one word all the while"; and he sleeps in a small, dirty room in a bed without canopy or sheets. Here, the writer concludes, is "a very true description of this *mighty* and *dirty Monarch*."[46] Susanna Centlivre's abuse of Charles also includes such observations. She not only mocks his filthy linen, but remarks the stark difference from elegant British officers who seem to fight better in proportion to their dandy duds. They "dispatch the Foe *en debonair*" (p. 6).

Moreover, the "Letter" appeared in Voltaire's *History of Charles XII* as early as 1732 and at the end of the 1742 version of Adlerfeld's *Genuine History of Charles XII*; each appearance effectually denigrates Charles's royal character, bearing, and military intelligence. In Adlerfeld the letter follows a quotation of Voltaire's final words that the vengeful execution of Baron Gortz after Charles's death was "a cruel Insult on the Memory of a King whom *Sweden* yet admires."[47] The consequent letter suggests that such admiration is misplaced and that English attitudes toward Charles's accomplishments should be justifiably skeptical, indeed negative.

As those attitudes should be, it seems, to Charles's presumably unconventional sexuality. Centlivre regards his reserve towards women as yet another royal inadequacy. Unlike George I, Charles's "barren Chastity" will produce no heir. Even Jacobite women abandon this unnatural man: "They fear *Thy* Taste shou'd lead young *James* astray, / And quite unman their Monarch every way" (p. 4).

This unsubtle innuendo outlasted Charles. The *Craftsman* so admired its earlier hostile comparison (No. 609, March 11, 1738) of Charles and Alexander that it recycles and varies it for No. 848, September 25, 1742: "if *Alexander* was rash, *Charles* was Rashness itself." To complete the analogy, he says, "as *Alexander* had his *Hephestion*, *Charles* had his Prince of *Wirtenberg*. . . . *Peter* the *Czar* had Authorities of all Sorts, for calling him, though somewhat in Scorn, the *Alexander* of the North."[48]

The enduring analogy with Alexander and his sexual activities were enduringly detrimental to Charles's reputation. He was all too like the discredited, barbaric paradigm of universal monarchy and unnecessary conquest by a war lover. An often-cited example from another putative Jacobite Alexander Pope is instructive. In the fourth epistle of *An Essay on Man* Pope considers the familiar question of true greatness that is inconsistent with conquest:

> Heroes are much the same, the point's agreed,
> From Macedonia's madman to the Swede;
> The whole strange purpose of their lives, to find
> Or make, an enemy of all mankind!
>
> . . . .
>
> 'Tis phrase absurd to call a Villain Great.[49]

We recall that when Henry Brooke wanted a positive Swedish monarch he turned to Gustavus Vasa's sixteenth-century Sweden. When a later contemporary wanted a negative Swedish monarch he turned to eighteenth-century Sweden. The several other works concerning Charles of Sweden include one in which a Smithfield muse speaks through the mouths of kings. I begin with the brobdingnangian title: *The Northern Heroes; Or The Bloody Contest, Between Charles the Twelfth, King of Sweden, and Peter the Great, Czar of Muscovy. With the Loves of Count Gillensternia, And the Princess Elmiria. With a Comic Interlude, call'd The Volunteers; Or The Adventures of Roderick Random, And his Friend Strap. Also, the Comical Amours of Corporal Garbage, and Serjeant Slim, with Mrs. Van Spriggen, the Sutler's Widow; the merry Pranks of Her Son Janny, and many other diverting Incidents. A New Historical Drama. As it is now acting, by a Company of Comedians from both the Theatres, at the Great Booth in the George Yard, in West-Smithfield* (1748). The play was performed both at Bartholomew and Southwark fairs and was read in at least one public house.[50] Its royal and aristocratic characters speak competent blank verse. That serious historically well-informed part is indebted to Voltaire, builds upon his and comparable views of the great adversaries, and serves as a positive magnet for negative remarks concerning Charles. He is a boastful, headstrong, quixotic, rash, vainglorious overreacher deservedly disgraced at Pultowa. In contrast, as in Thomson's 1744 version of *Winter*, the civilizing Peter prefers negotiation to war, defends his country against the foreign invader, and like a Whiggish George II-Walpole seeks the arts of peace that depend upon the arts of trade. He will extend his people's "Commerce, and improve their Minds" (p. 15). Peter's final speech includes these high concepts that exploit familiar attacks on Charles as destructive "hero" and praise of Britain as constructive emporium:

> . . . let's pursue true Glory.
> We'll range the World, and find out ev'ry Art,
> That can improve the Mind, or mend the Heart;
> With choicest Blessings store our native Land,

That ev'ry Nation shall admiring stand;
While my glad Subjects Science shall revere,
And Commerce fix her golden Empire here.

(p. 35)

The play has thirty printed pages, only nine and one-half of which concern the northern heroes and one and one-half the related exalted love plot. Almost nineteen pages concern the comic farce and its sex, theft, and implicit commentary upon the great actions of the great men. The Scottish rogues Roderick and Strap in Charles's army parody his invasion schemes by plundering a sex-starved Russian boy, a widow, and her gullible suitors. Random and Strap abandon all such folk and leave with the morally and martially broken Swedish bands retreating into Turkey, though their theft leaves them better compensated than their wounded master. The subplot and the main plot demonstrate the immorality of foreign forces invading another nation. There is no hint of the threatened Swedish invasion of Britain in 1717, for that nonevent long had been eclipsed by the aborted French invasion of 1744 and the real Scottish Jacobite invasion of 1745. Shortly before Johnson began to write the *Vanity*, then, a Bartholomew farce mocks Charles and praises the virtues of his enemy and of Walpole's policies of peace and trade. Charles of *The Northern Heroes* reminds viewers and readers of the failure of foreign invasion and the virtues of true glory and commerce's golden empire.

Charles nonetheless remains a dangerous shade whose memory can be trundled out to intimidate Walpole's enemies. So desperately wicked a man as Swedish Charles, the violent pacifists contend, gladly would bathe the world in enough blood to please the most sanguinary Caesar.

The Enemy of Peace is the Enemy of Trade

However beneficial to British and perhaps some European interests, the War of the Spanish Succession exhausted armies, treasuries, and even praise for the victor. Swift's savage denigration of the stinking dead Marlborough was unrepresentative of his many funeral elegies; but it expressed understandable war-weariness that influenced Britain's new Whig legislators. They hoped to avoid what in *Peace. A Poem* (1713) Joseph Trapp called the "wild Extravagance of War": "roll'd in Heaps th' expiring Victors lay" as the Danube is "choak'd up with clatt'ring

Arms, with Tides of Blood, / And steeds, and Squadrons tumbling in the Flood."[51]

The Walpole Administration would play upon such revulsion in at least three overlapping ways. Its official and sympathetic political voices insist on defining greatness in other than martial terms; it consistently berates Roman and French martial imperialism and consistently supports the advantages of peaceful and constructive trade; it cites negative examples of false, destructive, martial heroes—like Alexander, Julius Caesar, Louis XIV, and Charles XII of Sweden. Henry Fielding's poem "Of True Greatness" (1741) denigrates the two classical heroes: "Behold, the Plain with human Gore grow red"; its roughly parallel syntax also exhorts us to "Behold, the Merchant give to Thousands Food."[52] Not surprisingly, in *Jonathan Wild* (1743; 1:3) Fielding also cites Charles XII as an example of destructive false greatness. Walpole's minions indeed would outdo their outdoings in such well-calibrated praise and blame.

The *London Journal* for September 13, 1728, includes "*An Essay upon* HEROISM, or TRUE GREATNESS" that pillories Louis XIV and his model Caesar, each of whom plundered and tyrannized his peaceful neighbors, subverted his country's liberties, and is a scandal to human nature. The Romans "travell'd up and down, *Murdering one half of the World, to Lord it over the other.*" Accordingly, "a *fighting Nation* [should be kick'd] out of the World" (see also July 1, 1731). In contrast, as the *Daily Gazetteer*, No. 184 for January 29, 1736, argues, Sir Robert Walpole's policies as practiced by George II, promote international peace and harmony. An unmemorable poem then recasts Virgil's *debellare superbos* in *Aeneid* 6:851–53 and transfers the victor's praise from warrior Churchill or Peter to commercial George. Rome's imperium becomes London's emporium. Wherever the sovereign's "*naval Crosses* wave, / They *curb* the *Strong*, the *Weak* they *save*." His majesty stops other kings' wars, plans for a peaceful future, and so

> In *Him* . . . all the Nations find
> The *guardian Angel* of *Mankind*,
> Who, pitying, strives to save, with Joy,
> What they, with Madness, wou'd destroy.

By November 30, 1738, No. 1064, the *Daily Gazetteer* adds a familiar nation and monarch to its catalogue of diabolical destroyers. In yet another discussion of true greatness it contrasts Charles XII and Stanislaus of Poland. "The former ruined his Country, and perished himself in a wild Pursuit of Schemes, which he determined to execute merely because he had formed them." Stanislaus acted with Providential direction and is likely "to spend the remainder of his Days in Honour and in Ease."

The year 1738 was a fruitful one for the Walpole administration's publications. A perhaps otherwise puzzling omnibus reprint helps to affirm its commerce, its consequent peace policy, and enduring attempts to label its opposition as Jacobite. We recall that defamation of the northern nations begins as early as 1694 and is useful in 1717 on behalf of George I and against Sweden and its Jacobite allies. In 1738 we see collected, Molesworth's *Account of Denmark* and related pieces, Robinson's *Account of Sueden, Observations upon a Pamphlet Called, An English Merchant's remarks upon a scandalous Jacobite paper*, and *A Short Narrative on the Life and Death of Rhinholdt Count Patkul* whom Charles XII brutally executed. The prefatory note to the two accounts reminds us of who Charles was, what happened to him, how George I protected Britain from Charles and his Jacobite allies, and what the seized Swedish letters said.[53] Only twenty years after Charles's death the specter of his invasion needs to be exhumed from memory's grave in order to frighten the present generation. He is not likely also to be cast as a recognizable Jacobite hero in 1749.

The Lithuanian patriot Johann Patkul was slowly and agonizingly broken on the wheel by an incompetent torturer who then beheaded and quartered him. In this dramatic narrative Britons saw an apparently inevitable trait of political tyrants of, one commentator says in 1717 as resurrected in 1738, "a ravenous Beast of Prey" (p. 431). Here were the fruits of martial expansion and thereafter of God's preference for peace to war. Even the presumably pro-Charles and pro-Jacobite *History of the Wars of Charles the XII* (by Defoe), he observes, regards Charles's defeat at Pultowa and exile in Turkey as signs to Charles's men: "God Almighty had a mind to shew the World, that the very bearing with the Cruelty of their King, was a Sin to be expiated, but by their bodily Punishment." Charles's own consequent life has been a judgment and punishment for his hardened heart (p. 407). This bigoted, cruel, vengeful, beastly, and murderous man, we later hear in the writer's own voice, has been idolized by "some malicious Wretches, that call themselves *Englishmen*" (p. 431). The omnibus anti-Gothic volume seems to have been drafted into Walpole's peace army. It attempts to show that such un-British and uncivilized warfare is consistent with the Pretender's interests and with northern Gothic barbarism. Charles XII again exemplifies the dangers of war as an alternative mode of expansion.

British propagandists for trade and peace scarcely had a monopoly on that increasingly popular line of argument. In 1748 the Dutch publisher Peter de Hondt issues his French translation of Nordberg's *Histoire de Charles XII. Roi de Suéde*. He acknowledges Charles XII's fame as a warrior-king, laments his refusal to make peace when it was offered, and further laments the consequences to Charles's suffering subjects who, like so many comparable examples from the past and present, also become the victims of a militarist prince. Surely, de Hondt knows, the Dutch republic that produces almost nothing exemplifies the better way to real grandeur, "par . . . Commerce."[54]

Both British political and commercial London in 1738 and Dutch foreign and commercial Hague in 1748 reject bellicose Charles's hostility to the civilizing and enriching spirit of trade.

SWEDEN AND HER KINGS

I add one other germane point—some further information regarding Sweden, the '45, and Charles XII during the years from about 1745 to 1760. This suggests two major points: thirty one years after Charles XII's death in 1718 he was fading from memory except for comparison with a superior monarch; and that for many, Sweden remained an unamiable neighbor.

The neo-Jacobites make much of Edward Young's line regarding Charles Edward as "A *Gothic* Hero* rising from the *Dead*." We recall that this originally was appended to the eighth of his *Night Thoughts* in 1745 (for 1746) and appeared under the title "Some Thoughts Occasioned by the Present Juncture." Johnson allowed lines from a comparable effort to be printed in Croft's "Life of Young" (1781) as an "indignant" condemnation of the "pope-bred Princeling" Charles Edward.[55] Most immediate, however, is the asterisk that Young supplies to explain the allusion. The conjecture that by 1745 most readers regarded Charles XII as outdated news gains support in other sources.

One is Thomas Warton's *Poems on Several Occasions* of March 1748, to which Johnson subscribed and whose "Of the Universal Love *of* Pleasure. *To* a Friend" he echoed in his use of "from *China* to *Peru*" in the second line of the *Vanity* (p. 17). Warton illustrates how both those who spend or save money, those who are serious or smiling are subject to Pleasure: "'Twas hence rough* *Charles* rush'd forth to ruthless War" (p. 16). Here again an author needs an asterisk to remind readers of who Charles was. Second, commentators nonetheless remembered that Sweden was an unreliable friend, a dangerous enemy, and a possible source of mercenaries for France and the Pretender. The *Gentleman's Magazine* for December of 1745 laments that some three hundred Swedish officers have "already engaged themselves in the *French* service" for "*French* pay" in order to perfect "themselves in the military art" (15:670). By 1756 the *Monthly Review* (14:587) points us to words in a pamphlet in which the numbers of Swedish officers and the British decibels in response had increased.[56] The author of *Some Reflections on the Trade Between Great Britain and Sweden* (London) knows that Britain gives Sweden favorable commercial terms and has saved her from conquest by Russia. Sweden responds with betrayal,

> particularly in the Year 1745, when four or five hundred Youths, many of them, of the *best* Families in *Sweden*, enlisted themselves in the Service of a *Popish* Pretender, and only waited for a favourable *Wind* to carry them to the North of *Scotland*, where they were designed to act as *Officers* in the Rebel Army: Concerning which, I have nothing more to remark, than that surely, it *deserves*—it ought to be *resented*. (pp. 13–14)

Both the *Gentleman's Magazine* and the Reflector have opportunities to evoke Charles XII as an analogue of Charles Edward and are silent. The Popish Pretender stands alone.

This tendency towards neglect increases as temporal distance increases. Even when the subject is demonstrably Charles XII he is discussed not with domestic British but with Continental analogues. Specifically, the *Critical* for March of 1757 reviews the French *Histoire interessante, ou relation des Guerres du Nord & de Hongrie au Commencement de ce siecle . . . 1700 jusqu' en 1710, avec . . . plusieurs particularités curieuses sur le Roy de Suede Charles 12me, sur le Czar Pierre le Grand, &c.* The reviewer follows his French source in praising Charles XII's exceptional soldierly qualities as well as his tactical folly, and human weaknesses—like his vengeance and profligacy with his subjects' lives. He concludes: "this prince would have been a dangerous model for such as had chosen to follow him" (3:278).

Charles XII later is joined by implicit contrast of a destructive with a constructive Swedish monarch. In 1759 Walter Harte dedicates the *History of the Life of Gustavus Adolphus, King of Sweden* (London) to Lord Chesterfield. His lordship already had told his son that Charles XII was a brute not a man, and told Voltaire that Charles XII was the "plus grand Furieux . . . de l'Europe."[57] Harte himself writes about Gustavus Adolphus because he was "a man of honesty, magnanimity, morality, and religion." He explains why he does not mention those who fall into a less attractive group: "as to your merely belligerent heroes, I consign them to other hands" (1:ix). Thereafter Sarah Scott, under the name of Henry Augustus Raymond, also writes about Gustavus and praises him as a monarch who "never attempted to extend the success of his arms beyond the deliverance of his own country." He also established a freer church "to reform the manners of the people," loved his wife and children, and "by his example, softened their [Swedish] ferocity and humanized his people." Smollett's review in the *Critical* emphasizes these traits as well (10 [1760]: 373, 383–85).[58] Like Charles Edward, Charles XII's mere belligerence scarcely deserves being named.

He is named when the first volume of Voltaire's *Histoire de l'Empire de Russe sous Pierre le Grand* appears in 1760. As the *Critical* observes in a long familiar commonplace, Peter's reforming, and constructive achievements are "entirely opposite" to Charles XII (10:397). Indeed, Voltaire's new history seems "to have sometimes praised the Russian monarch at the expence of the Swede" (10:401). No wonder. Here is a sentence regarding Pultowa that approaches Johnson's own views: "Of all the battles which have imbrued the earth with blood, this one alone, instead of being merely destructive, has contributed to the happiness of mankind, as it gave the Czar the liberty and power of civilizing a very considerable part of the world" (10:400). Yet again, Charles XII appears without benefit of his presumed Carolean shadow.

It is both reasonable and conservative to say that even among Jacobites and Tories Charles of Sweden rarely was cited as a hero after 1717. This was especially appropriate since he denied knowing about the scheme concocted by his soon decapitated minister Baron Gortz. As we will see, such praise was even more rare, if present at all, after Voltaire's history of Charles, and during any time in which Samuel Johnson began to think seriously about politics, the implications of foreign invasion of his country, and the likelihood or desirability of a Stuart restoration by such means. Virtually all information available to Johnson and to the readers of his *Vanity of Human Wishes* would have been negative regarding Charles XII. Even a Bartholomew farce mocks and vilifies the Goth regularly called a madman and a brute. Johnson's poem exploits these commonplaces regarding a monarch he will label a predatory object of hatred and an enemy of the human race. If this was Johnson's "mighty favourite" one shudders to hear him speak of a mighty enemy.

Notes

1. Erskine-Hill, "The Political Character of Samuel Johnson," in *Samuel Johnson: New Critical Essays*, ed. Isobel Grundy (London: Vision, 1984), pp. 131 (long been),

130 (mighty favorite), 132 (experience, Jacobite); Erskine-Hill, "A Kind of *Liking* for Jacobitism," *Age of Johnson* (henceforth *AJ*) 8: (1997) 10 (banal); Clark, *Samuel Johnson: Literature, religion and cultural politics from the Restoration to Romanticism* (Cambridge: Cambridge Unversity Press, 1994), p. 156 (Jacobite hero).

2. Clark, *Samuel Johnson*, p. 102.

3. Erskine-Hill, introduction, in *Samuel Johnson in Historical Context*, eds. Jonathan Clark and Howard Erskine-Hill (Houndsmill, Basingstoke UK: Palgrave, 2001), p. 7 n. 9; MacKenzie, "A Jacobite Undertone in 'While Ladies Interpose'," ibid., pp. 265 (take), 261 (analogical), 262 (subliminal). Erskine-Hill acknowledges that this interpretation evokes "comprehensive disbelief" but prefers to insist upon it. See his *Poetry of Opposition and Revolution: Dryden to Wordsworth* (Oxford: Clarendon Press, 1996), p. 164.

4. Murray G. H. Pittock, *Poetry and Jacobite Politics in Eighteenth-Century Britain and Ireland* (Cambridge: Cambridge University Press, 1994), p. 128. Subsequent citations from this book are given in the text.

5. Ian Higgins, *Swift's Politics: A Study in Disaffection* (Cambridge: Cambridge University Press, 1994), pp. 78, 79 n. 101. Higgins asks us to see Eveline Cruickshanks's brief introduction and compilation as his authority for Jacobite enthusiasm for Charles: *Charles XII of Sweden: A Character and Two Poems* (Brisbane: Locks' Press, 1983). Those wishing to see one of the forty copies of this rare private-press pamphlet may do so at the British Library, the Cambridge University Library, the Library of Congress, and the University of Calgary. Readers making the pilgrimage will not find Higgins's remark supported. Cruickshanks reprints the positive Latin manuscript at the Huntington Library (MS HM 14366), ca. 1709, but before Pultowa, and once owned by Swift: "Effigies Corporis & Anima Caroli XII Sueciae Regis. A Polono Nobili Descripta." We also see "Supra Stragem Regis Sueciae ad Pultavum." As the English translation demonstrates, Charles had an "excessive love of war" and base "Revenge" that drove him to defeat and ignominious death (pp. 16–17). The two pieces show reactions before and after Pultowa, Charles's quixotic behavior in Turkey, and the exploded English invasion scheme. The other work is Susanna Centlivre's generally hostile *An Epistle to the King of Sweden from a Lady of Great Britain* (1717). Cruickshanks describes Centlivre as "the woman dramatist who had married a cook in the English royal household" (p. iv). Cruickshanks's hagiographic discussion of Charles himself misrepresents Voltaire. It also but partially reports Frederick the Great's condemnation of his strategy, inability to wage war intelligently, and his indifference to the many thousands he expected to die for his glory.

6. For earlier studies of Charles XII in the eighteenth century, see J. F. Chance, "The 'Swedish Plot' of 1716–17," *English Historical Review* 18 (1903): 81–106; Herbert G. Wright, "Some English Writers and Charles XII," *Studia Neophilologia* 15 (1942–43): 105–31; James Gray, "Johnson's Portraits of Charles XII of Sweden," in *Domestick Privacies: Samuel Johnson and the Art of Biography*, ed. David Wheeler (Lexington: University Press of Kentucky, 1987), pp. 70–84, 173–77. One also must see R. M. Hatton's essential *Charles XII of Sweden* (London: Weidenfeld and Nicolson, 1968).

7. Rowe, *The Fair Penitent*, ed. Malcolm Goldstein (Lincoln: University of Nebraska Press, 1969), p. 5, lines 11–14 of the Prologue; Tickell, *An Epistle*, 2nd ed. (London, 1717), p. 5. Tickell adds that "His Sword for *James* no Brother Sov'ran draws" (p. 5).

8. Nordberg, *Histoire de Charles XII. Roi de Suéde*, trans. C. G. Warmholtz. Nordberg adds that "L'Auteur . . . n'a pris ce Titre, que dans la Vue de rendre son ouvrage plus recommendable." At the beginning of volume two he even boasts of having "l'Approbation du Roi-même" (1:xj–xij). The list of sources is on 1:x–xx and includes an attack on Voltaire's history of Charles XII (1:xij–xiij). For the sustained discussion of Charles and Britain, see 3:282–300 and this remark: to believe that Charles had any

direct part in the projected rebellion, "& que son dessein étoit de la soûtenir par le moyen d'un Corps d'Armée, c'est ce que l'on ne pouvoit pas se persuader; on regardoit cette accusation comme très mal fondée" (3:290). Subsequent citations are given in the text.

9. Weber, *The Present State of Russia. In Two Volumes. Being An Account of the Government of that Country, both Civil and Ecclesiastical* . . . *from the Year 1714, to 1720* (London, 1723), 1:sig b6$^{r\text{-}v}$ for praise of the amazing reformation of arts, arms, and trades under Peter the Great; 2:334–37 for brutal Swedish behavior in Russia. Where appropriate, Voltaire regularly contrasts Charles and Peter—as in the *Histoire de l'empire de Russie sous Pierre le Grand* (Geneva, 1759–60), englished ca. 1762. For Thomson, see *The Seasons*, ed. James Sambrook (Oxford: Clarendon Press, 1981), p. 248, lines 980 (frantic), 955 (immortal), 985 (scene). Johnson's violation of the convention is the more striking in light of its popularity. See the *Adventurer*, No. 99 (1753), discussed in the next chapter. He may be sneering at Voltaire's cozying-up to autocrats.

10. *Observations upon a Pamphlet, Called, An English Merchant's Remarks upon a Scandalous Jacobite Paper Published in The Post-Boy [July 19], under the Name of a Memorial presented to the Chancery of Sweden, by the Resident of Great Britain* (London, 1717), p. 37. The paper was by the Swedish ambassador to England, Count Gyllenborg, for whom see within.

11. *The Poetical Works of the Ingenious and Learned William Meston, A. M. Sometime Professor in the Marshall College of Aberdeen*, 6th ed. (Edinburgh, 1767), pp. 162 (Imitation, frozen), 158 (On the Death, exile). These poems seem to be from about 1718. I have not seen any earlier editions of this collection, and suspect that "sixth edition" is wishful thinking. Meston's Jacobite poems are the harshest I have read; his vilification of Queen Anne Stuart is unusual.

12. *Letters and Correspondence, Public and Private, of the Right Honourable Henry St. John, Lord Viscount Bolingbroke, during the time he was Secretary of State to Queen Anne*, ed. Gilbert Parke (London, 1798), 1:178–79. Subsequent citations are given in the text by volume and page or by date.

13. The author of this last *Examiner* probably is William Oldisworth. See *Jonathan Swift. Journal To Stella*, ed. Harold Williams (Oxford: Clarendon Press, 1948), 2:637 and n. 32 and 1:254 n. 30; Irvin Ehrenpreis, *Swift, the Man, His Works, and the Age* (London: Methuen, 1967), 2:680; and W. R. and V. B. McLeod, *A Graphical Directory of English Newspapers and Periodicals, 1702–1714* (Morgantown, WV: School of Journalism, West Virginia University, 1982), pp. 14–15. I am indebted to Stephen E. Karian for bringing this last reference to my attention.

14. *Fog's* includes one incidental reference to Sweden on August 9, 1729, No. 46, and one positive but tepid remark concerning Charles on February 6, 1731, No. 124. I have not been able to see the other numbers, which conclude in October of 1737.

15. See Martin C. Battestin, *New Essays by Henry Fielding* (Charlottesville: University Press of Virginia, 1989), p. 398, for what Battestin regards as a probable attribution of this essay to Henry Fielding. See pp. 84–85 for the list of Fielding's other almost wholly negative judgments regarding Charles XII and his destructive "greatness."

16. Robert Harris argues that by midcentury the Jacobites had ideologically capitulated to the Whigs. See his *National Politics and the London Press in the 1740s* (Oxford: Clarendon Press, 1993), p. 45 n. 114.

17. [Simon Fraser?] *L[or]d L[ova]t's Second Answer to D[unca]n F[orbe]s, L[ord] P[resident]'s Letter. December 20, 1745* (London, 1746), p. 67.

18. For some relevant discussion of Tacitus and Germanic freedom in Britain, see

Weinbrot, "Politics, Taste, and National Identity," in *Tacitus and the Tacitean Tradition*, ed. T. J. Luce and A. J. Woodman (Princeton: Princeton University Press, 1991), pp. 168–84. For some of the less wholesome associations with the Gothic, see also my *Britannia's Issue: The Rise of British Literature from Dryden to Ossian* (Cambridge: Cambridge University Press, 1993), pp. 497–504.

19. Hughes, *The House of Nassau. A Pindarick Ode* (London, 1702), p. 2; Paterson, *Arminius. A Tragedy* (London, 1740), p. iv; Brooke, *Gustavus Vasa, The Deliverer of his Country. A Tragedy. As it was to have been Acted at the Theatre Royal in Drury Lane* (London, 1739), p. iv. The 929 subscribers to the 1,092 copies include Samuel Johnson. See Donald D. Eddy and J. D. Fleeman, *A Preliminary Handlist of Books to which Dr. Samuel Johnson Subscribed* (Charlottesville: Bibliographic Society of the University of Virginia, 1993), p. 8.

20. Browne, *The Gothick Hero*, sigs. A2ʳ (champion), A2ᵛ (redeem), italics and roman type are reversed. Subsequent citations are given in the text. The apparently unique copy of this poem is in the Huntington Library, shelf mark 355322. For a reprint, see Browne and William Oldisworth, *State Tracts, State and Miscellany Poems* (London, 1715), 2:365–76. Such praise generally disappears after Pultowa in 1709 and especially after 1717.

21. For Harris, see *A Poem on the Death of the King of Sweden* (London, 1719), which praises Charles's achievements prior to 1709 as "Glorious Prince He was!" (p. 3). Haywood includes Charles in a martial episode in her *The Fortunate Foundlings: Being the Genuine History of Colonel M——rs, and his Sister, Madam du P——y* (London, 1744), pp. 229–95. The Chevalier de St. George and Charles express friendship on pp. 130–31, 133, 139, 223–24. This romance Charles differs from the emotionally frigid monarch of other stories; he is betrothed to the Chevalier's sister Princess Louisa, whose absence he naturally bemoans in princely fashion. Neither man mentions an invasion of England; staunchly Protestant Charles clearly looks to northern, central, and eastern Europe to satisfy his martial ambitions; and Haywood's anti-absolutist male foundling Horatio fights equally well for Marlborough and for Charles—but never for the Pretender.

22. For Frederick, see *Reflexions sur les talens militaires et sur le caractere de Charles XII. Roi de Suede* (Munich: Gesselschaft der Bibliophilen, 1925), p. xxiii. Frederick generally regards Charles XII as sanguinary, an incompetent tactician, and as indifferent to logistics as to his troops' safety—as Pultowa made plain. For some details of that battle, see Hatton, *Charles XII*, pp. 290–306.

23. Brown, his translator's Preface to *A New and Easy Method to understand the Roman History* (London, 1695), sig. A3ᵛ; Bailey, *Dictionarium Britannicum; or a more Compleat Universal Etymological English Dictionary* (London, 1730), "Goths"; Pope, *The Twickenham Edition of the Poems of Alexander Pope*, vol. 5, *The Dunciad in Four Books*, in *The Dunciad*, ed. James Sutherland, 3rd ed. (London: Methuen; New Haven: Yale University Press, 1963), 3:84–94, p. 324, with subsequent references to this edition cited as TE; Gray's translation from Old Norse in *The Complete Poems of Thomas Gray, English, Latin and Greek*, ed. H. W. Starr and J. R. Hendrickson (Oxford: Clarendon Press, 1966), pp. 29 (human, line 10), 30 (songs, line 54; horror, lines 49–50).

24. Young, *The Consolation. Containing, among other Things, I. A Moral Survey of the Nocturnal Heaven. II. A Night-Address to the Deity. To which are Annex'd, Some Thoughts, Occasioned by the Present Majesty's Principal Secretaries of State* (London, 1745), pp. 136–37. This unwelcome, superstitious, malicious Papist invader, Young says, is an enemy "to *Britain, Liberty, and Truth*" (p. 127). The analogy to Charles XII clearly is designed to abuse. See the further discussion at n. 55 within.

25. Molesworth, *An Account of Denmark, As It was in the Year 1692*, 3rd ed. (London, 1694), sig. C3ᵛ (slavery), pp. 43 (absolute), 243 (find good). The volume caused an international stir. The Danish ambassador insisted that King William punish Molesworth for writing such lies, and that they would cause his death in Denmark: "King William said all he could do was to advise Lᵈ Molesworth to insert that circumstance in his next edition." See the handwritten note in the fourth edition, part of an omnibus collection of anti-northern tracts in 1738: British Library shelf mark G 15070. William King replied to Molesworth with the unsigned *Animadversions on the Account of Denmark* (1694), reprinted in his *Miscellanies in Prose and Verse* (London, [1707?]): absolutism preserves order and contentment and is good for the state. See also Jodicus Crull's defense in *Denmark Vindicated* (London, 1694) and in *Memoirs of Denmark* (London, 1700).

26. Robinson, *An Account of Sueden*, 2nd ed. (London, 1711), pp. 22 (nimbleness), 70 (peasants, et al.). Subsequent citations are given in the text.

27. The pointers in the margin are the only such devices in the book: see pp. 42 (1694), 19 (1711), and 19 (1717) in the first three editions. For Vertot, see *The History of the Revolutions in Sweden, Occasioned By the Change of Religion, and Alteration of the Government in that Kingdom*, trans. J. Mitchell, 3rd ed. (London, 1711), sig. A2ᵛ.

28. [William Benson], *A Letter to Sir J—B—, By Birth a S—, but Naturaliz'd and now a M—r of the Present P—t: Concerning the late Minehead Doctrine which was establish'd by a certain Free Parliament of Sweden, to the utter Enslaving of that Kingdom* (London, 1711), pp. 2–3 (Banks's remarks, tyranny), 26 (absolute), 31 (hero).; *A Second Letter to Sir J—B—. . . . Wherein the Late Minehead Doctrine is further consider'd* (London, 1711), p. 3.

29. This was an attempted refutation of the first *Letter* and an apology for Swedish government: *Some Remarks By Way of Answer To a Late Pamphlet, Entituled, A Letter to Sir. J. B.* (London, 1711), p. 20 for the quotation. R. M. Hatton believes that the author "was either [the Swedish ambassador] Count Gyllenborg himself, or someone briefed by him of his conversations with Robinson." See Hatton, "John Robinson and the *Account of Sueden*," *Bulletin of the Institute of Historical Research* 28 (1955): 154.

30. *Observations Upon A Pamphlet*, p. 6. The pamphlet apparently again is by Count Gyllenborg, though this writer thinks that Swedes are clever enough only to have supplied the hints, then "improved by some inveterate Evil Subject of His Majesty" (p. 6). The observer has nothing good to say about Charles XII or the Swedish nation he is destroying: "He regards not the Remonstrances of those Princes, who Interess [*sic*] themselves in order to procure a Peace, nor of his own Subjects" (p. 28). This familiar complaint is consistent with Johnson's observations in the *Vanity* that peace courts Charles in vain (line 201).

31. Defoe, *The Annals of King George, Year the Third: Containing not only the Affairs of Great Britain, But the General History of Europe During that Time* (London, 1718), p. 179; Robinson, *A Compleat and Impartial History of England, From The Conquest of Britain by Julius Caesar, To the End of the Reign of King George The First. Faithfully collected from Rapin, Echard, Kennet, and other Historians* (London, 1739), p. 849. Like other historians, Robinson cites the compromising Swedish letters and the correspondents' need for Jacobite money and troops on behalf of "the Disaffected here" (p. 849). Paula R. Backscheider has discussed Defoe's historical writings in *Daniel Defoe: Ambition & Innovation* (Lexington: University Press of Kentucky, 1986), pp. 89–106. Many of these unsigned works, however, remain attributions.

32. These movements are well chronicled in, among other places, Defoe's *Some Ac-*

count of the Life, and Most Remarkable Actions, of George Henry Baron De Goertz, Privy-Counsellor and Chief Minister of State, To the Late King of Sweden (London, 1719), and J. F. Chance, "The 'Swedish Plot' of 1716–17," *English Historical Review* 18 (1903): 81–106. Such actions were immediately well known after the publication of the Swedish letters concerning the plot.

33. The pamphlet, in English and in French, is titled *Letters which passed Between Count Gyllenborg, the Barons Gortz, Sparre, And others; Relating to the Design of Raising a Rebellion in His Majesty's Dominions, To be Supported by a Force from Sweden. Published by Authority* (London, 1717). Page references will be cited parenthetically in the text.

34. Defoe, *Some Account*, p. 14, see also p. 16; *Annals of King George, Year the Third*, p. 146.

35. Paul S. Fritz thinks the writer "probably the Earl of Arran." See *The English Ministers and Jacobitism* (Toronto: University of Toronto Press, 1975), p. 16.

36. Brownlow is quoted from John Oldmixon, *The History of England During the Reigns of King William and Queen Mary, Queen Anne [and] King George I* (London, 1735), p. 632. Subsequent citations from Oldmixon are given in the text. He also thought the invasion plan "a Project more chimerical than that of the Conquest of the *Russian* Empire" the failure of which saw Charles "shut up in a *Turkish* Cage at *Bender*" (p. 632). The derogatory term "project" is commonplace for Charles's scheme at least from its revelation in 1717 to Johnson's *Adventurer*, No. 99, in 1753.

37. Reading the Jacobite correspondence of 1717 concerning invasion and then the comparable correspondence of 1744 is like being caught in a repetitive time-loop, in which nothing has been learned. For some of the French plots and British Jacobite fantasies, see J. Colin, *Louis XV et les Jacobites: le project de débarquement en Angleterre de 1743–1744* (Paris: Librarie Militaire R. Chapelot, 1901). I have discussed some of these important letters in "Johnson and Jacobitism Redux," *AJ* 8 (1997): 108–11.

38. As quoted in Chance, " 'Swedish Plot,' " p. 106 n. 98.

39. Frederick the Great, *Reflections*, p. xxx.

40. As quoted in Nicholas Tindal's continuation of Rapin de Thoyras's *History of England*, 3rd ed. (London, 1743–47), 4 (1747): 540 n. This volume appeared about one year before Johnson started to write the *Vanity*; it included extensive discussion of the plot and quotation from the *Letters*: 4:506–26, 538–41 and notes. R. M. Hatton's historical inquiries taught her that the invasion scheme was exaggerated "in the hope of unifying the country behind George I's Baltic policy": *Charles XII*, p. 439. Note as well: Gortz knew that Charles would neither "give military support" to the Jacobites nor even "accept a letter from the Pretender pleading his cause" (p. 438). See also Bruce Lenman, *The Jacobite Cause* (Glasgow: Richard Drew and the National Trust for Scotland, 1986): Charles "would seem never to have committed himself to so much as a discussion of how he might possibly assist the Pretender." The plot, he says, was quickly discovered and "was all very, very sordid" (p. 62).

41. Limiers, *Histoire de Suede sous le regne de Charles XII. Où l'on voit aussi les révolutions arrivées en different tems dans ce royaume: toute la guerre du nord* (Amsterdam, 1721), 6:158; Voltaire, *History of Charles XII. King of Sweden, By Mr. de Voltaire*, 2nd ed. (London, 1732), p. 351, and *The History of the Russian Empire Under Peter the Great, By M. de Voltaire* (London, 1762[?]), pp. 125, 129–30.

42. Defoe, *An Account of the Swedish and Jacobite Plot. With A Vindication of our Government from the horrid Aspersions of its Enemies. And A Postscript, relating to the*

Post-Boy of Saturday, Feb. 23. In a Letter to a Person of Quality, occasion'd by the Publishing of Count Gyllemborg's Letters (London, 1717), p. 17 (barbarous); the postscript attacks Charles's arbitrary and despotic government and insists that he is being punished by God (p. 38); Defoe, *Some Account*, p. 3 (contempt).

43. Defoe, *What If the Swedes Should Come? With Some Thoughts About Keeping the Army on Foot, Whether they Come or Not* (London, 1717), pp. 7–8. Subsequent citations are given in the text.

44. Centlivre, *An Epistle to the King of Sweden from A Lady of Great Britain* (Dublin, 1717), pp. 2 (rude and glories), 7 (hope), 8 (Europe). Subsequent citations are given in the text.

45. Defoe, *A Short View of the Conduct of the King of Sweden* (London, [1717]]), p. 33; D'Urfey, "Historical Remarks On late foreign Occurrences, and the sudden Fate of the late King of Sweden," in *New Opera's, With Comical Stories and Poems, On Several Occasions, Never before Printed. Being the remaining Pieces, Written by Mr. D'Urfey* (London, 1721), p. 380. Here are other relevant, if opaque, lines:

> Well may the hot Pretender rave,
> He never could such a Madman have,
> The *Swede* his Kingdoms lost regave,
> And bade him hope for reigning.
>
> (p. 380)

46. As quoted in Voltaire, *History of Charles XII*, pp. 367 (dirty), 368 (greasy), 369 (horse), true (371).

47. The remark is on p. 366 in Voltaire. The 1742 Adlerfeld is *The Genuine History of Charles XII. King of Sweden: Containing All his Military Actions: With a more particular Account of the Battle of Pultowa, and of his Majesty's Retreat to Bender in Turkey, than was ever yet published*, trans. James Ford (London, 1742). The "Letter" is on pp. 555–57, and the quotation from Voltaire on p. 554. The volume includes a frontispiece engraving of a large Charles XII, with one hand at his head as if thinking, and the other on his sword as if ready to fight in the major battle taking place behind him. The poem beneath the engraving includes lines similar to Johnson's portrait of Charles in the *Vanity*, and twice comments on his love of war that took him "Thro' fields of Blood" and "Seas of Blood." The 1742 Adlerfeld apparently is a pirated version of Fielding's three-volume translation of 1740. For discussion of that version, see John Edwin Wells, "Henry Fielding and the History of Charles XII," *Journal of English and Germanic Philology* 11 (1912): 603–13; Wilbur L. Cross, *The History of Henry Fielding* (New Haven: Yale University Press, 1918), 1:285–87, 3:337–38; and Martin C. and Ruthe R. Battestin, *Henry Fielding. A Life:* (London: Routledge, 1989), pp. 266–67.

48. Several historians, or mythographers, repeat the distaste that Thalestris, Queen of the Amazons, had for the effeminately clad Alexander the Great. They nonetheless couple for thirteen days apparently without, to history's great distress, a little queen to show for it. See Plutarach, *Alexander* 46; Diodorus Siculus, *Bibliotheca historicae* 8.17.77.1–3; Quintus Curtius Rufus, *Historiarum Alexandri magni Macedonis*, 6.5.24–36.

49. TE 3.1, *An Essay on Man*, ed. Maynard Mack (London: Methuen; New Haven: Yale University Press, 1951), pp. 147–48, epistle 4, lines 219–22, 230. William Warburton laments that "This character might have been drawn with much more force; and deserved the poet's care." He then quotes *Paradise Regained* 3:71–87, the Son's refutation

of Satan's glorification of obviously anti-Christian "heroes" like Alexander and Caesar who burn, rob, slaughter, and enslave peaceful nations. Such lines, as well as political opposition, clearly are behind Swift's hostile elegy on Marlborough. For Warburton, see his edition of *The Works of Alexander Pope Esq.* (London, 1751), 3:134–35. By later in the eighteenth century, however, the shade of warrior Alexander partially redeems himself by agreeing with poet Alexander's verdict. He also protects Pope in the underworld from the crude bully Charles XII. See George Lord Lyttelton, *Dialogues of the Dead* (London, 1760), p. 210.

50. The play was performed at Bartholomew Fair, August 24, 26, 27, and at Southwark on September 7, 8, 9, 10, 12, 13, 1748. See *The London Stage 1660–1800. . . . Part 4: 1747–1776*, ed. George Winchester Stone, Jr. (Carbondale: Southern Illinois University Press, 1962), pp. 57–58, 62–64. Some read it shortly after the first performance. The British Library copy, shelf mark 161. e. 38, includes the handwritten date "August 25th: 1748" in the upper left-hand corner of the title page, under which Messrs Smyth, Bridge, Burrell, and Harder (?) have signed their names; another name at the foot of the page is too badly cropped to be legible. Presumably, this copy was at an inn or public house where the signatories indicated their borrowings. The play's historical introduction gives fair warning that its love scenes and comic parts are invented.

51. *Peace. A Poem. Inscribed to the Right Honourable Lord Viscount Bolingbroke* (London, 1713), p. 2.

52. The Wesleyan Edition of the Works of Henry Fielding, *Miscellanies by Henry Fielding, Esq; Volume One*, ed. Henry Knight Miller (Middletown, CT: Wesleyan University Press, 1972), pp. 22 (line 77), 24 (line 140). For further discussion of the moral urgency of trade in the eighteenth century, see *Britannia's Issue*, pp. 237–75.

53. See the Advertisement to what the compiler calls the fourth edition of Robinson's *Account of Sueden* (London, 1738), pp. 297–99. It is of course hostile to Charles. This compilation was noted in the *Gentleman's Magazine*'s "A Register of Books in March, 1738." Johnson then already was Cave's editor on that periodical. Subsequent page references will be cited in the text.

54. Nordberg, *Histoire de Charles XII*, 1: ii.

55. Erskine-Hill argues on the importance of this line in his "The Political Character of Samuel Johnson: *The Lives of the Poets* and a Further Report on *The Vanity of Human Wishes*," in *The Jacobite Challenge*, ed. Eveline Cruickshanks and Jeremy Black (Edinburgh: John Donald Publishers, 1988), p. 173. Herbert Croft wrote most of the life of Young, but Johnson read and edited it, thus tacitly seconding Young's indignant response to Charles Edward's foreign-inspired invasion. See *Lives of the English Poets*, ed. George Birkbeck Hill (Oxford: Clarendon Press, 1905), 3:385 for Young's attack upon the "princeling" invader and his cutthroat Scots. See 3:361 n. 1 for Johnson's remark to John Hussey that he cut half of Croft's longer text.

56. The review probably was written by Sir Tanfield Leman. See Benjamin Christie Nangle, *The Monthly Review First Series 1749–1789: Indexes of Contributors and Articles* (Oxford: Clarendon Press, 1934), pp. 229, 26–27. *Some Reflections* is Number XXII in the "Political and Commerical" Section. Lemon reports "that the Swedes have a natural hereditary and irreconcileable hatred to us" (14:587).

57. Chesterfield so writes to his son on October 4, 1752, and to Voltaire on August 27, 1752. See *The Letters of Philip Dormer Stanhope 4th Earl of Chesterfield*, ed. Bonamy Dobrée (London: Eyre and Spottiswoode, 1932), 5:1954, 1928.

58. Scott (Raymond), *The History of Gustavus Ericson, King of Sweden* (London,

1761), pp. 398 (never attempted), 399 (reform), 400 (example). For the review's attribution, see James G. Basker, *Tobias Smollett, Critic and Journalist* (Newark: University of Delaware Press, 1988), p. 260, as based on Louis L. Martz, "Tobias Smollett and the Universal History," *Modern Language Notes* 56 (1941): 7–8. Oliver Goldsmith borrows from Justus van Effen's positive view of Charles XII for his *Bee*, No. 2 (1759). See *Collected Works of Oliver Goldsmith*, ed. Arthur Friedman (Oxford: Clarendon Press, 1966), 1:379–83. Given van Effen's portrait, there is no reason why Charles Edward should be invoked.

16

The Vanity of Human Wishes Part II. Reading Charles of Sweden in the Poem, Reading Johnson's Politics

I HAVE THUS FAR SUGGESTED BROADER HISTORICAL CONTEXTS FOR Johnson's and his contemporaries' attitudes toward Charles of Sweden. The overwhelming weight of the evidence is that very few Tories, and fewer still after 1717, could regard him as a norm, whether subliminal, nostalgic, or hovering about *The Vanity of Human Wishes* (1749). I have, though, merely touched on more specific and immediate contexts for Johnson's and his readers' understanding of Charles of Sweden for his greatest poem.

WHAT DID JOHNSON KNOW AND WHEN DID HE KNOW IT?

The *Gentleman's Magazine* is a good place to look for what Johnson and its extensive audience could have known about Charles XII. It was a periodical of paramount journalistic importance, with which Johnson was familiar and sought to join as early as November 25, 1734, some three years after its first volume. He then hoped that an improved poetry section would induce more pleasure than the "dull Scurrilities of either Party."[1] Johnson probably was at Market Bosworth in March of 1732, but he nonetheless might have known the reprinted portions of the *Grub-street Journal*, No. 114, for March 9, 1732. The Tory opposition and occasionally Jacobite journal there reviews Voltaire's newly translated history of Charles XII. That life, we hear "is a Series of Imprudence and Temerity, Revenge and Folly. His Behaviour at *Bender* shews him fitter for *Bedlam* than to govern a Nation. With 300 *Swedes* he sought to bully the *Ottoman* Empire" (*GM* 2:644). By midsummer of 1738 Johnson was Cave's principal editor and, among other things, was "correcting the debates."[2] He surely knew and perhaps partially wrote the parliamentary debate for August of 1738. Hurgo Quadret, Lord Carteret, observes that the Swedes are "a People lately formidable under a brave, but a headstrong Prince." However ambitious a subsequent absolutist Swedish monarch might be, he no longer can enflame Europe: "his Power is now circumscribed; his People having recover'd their Liberties, and his Senate its Authority" (*GM* 8:401). Johnson still may have been a reader in December of 1747, when a reprinted antiministerial *Old England* for December 5th discusses the superiority of the British to the Swedish government and state—even though it has become an elective and free monarchy. "Every body knows, that *Sweden* dates its liberty from the death of *Charles* the 12th" (*GM* 17:576). If Johnson read all these numbers he would have seen a preview of Voltaire's character of Charles, affirmation of the commonplaces regarding his malign government, and the security that Sweden, Europe, and Britain gained upon his death.

It seems at the least also reasonable to suppose that Johnson knew three poetic sources. I have already mentioned the well-known portrait in the fourth epistle (1734) of Pope's *Essay on Man* with murderous Charles as among mankind's enemies, and Thomson's portrait in *Winter* (1726–46) of constructive Peter as everything that Charles was not. We can, though, be certain that Johnson subscribed and read Thomas Warton's *Poems on Several Occasions* (1748) from which Johnson borrows the *Vanity*'s image of extensive view "from *China* to *Peru*," and where he also found an asterisk to remind readers of who "rough* *Charles*" was, and how inferior he was to Peter the Great.[3]

Moreover, Johnson thought little about the '45 as it receded, and thus even less about a possible similarity between Charles XII and Charles Edward. What he did think was not flattering. According to Boswell and others, before Johnson had his pension he said "that if holding up his hand would have made Prince Charles's army prevail [at Culloden], he would not have done it."[4] He also tells Bennet Langton that "Nothing has ever offered, that has made it worth my while to consider the question fully" (*Life,* 1:430). When he considers it in *On the Present State of Affairs* (1756) he strips Charles of his title and makes plain whose interests he serves: "The French . . . had a more easy expedient to regain Cape-Breton than by exalting Charles Stuart to the throne." That failed exaltation fades even more by 1760 when in "The Bravery of the English Common Soldiers" Johnson implicitly dismisses Charles Edward as a threat: "there has not been, for more than a century, any war that put the property or liberty of a single Englishman in danger."[5] Only Oliver Cromwell, and not Charles XII or Charles Edward, was a danger to England.

Long before 1760, however, French and other readers were schooled to denigrate Charles of Sweden as a leader. Jean le Clerc's *Bibliothèque ancienne et moderne* reviewed Henri Philippe de Limiers's *Histoire de Suede, sous le regne de Charles XII* (Amsterdam, 1721). Charles's invasion of Russia, we hear, passes the limits of the brave or reasonable. To ruin his state for ever and to ravage it of men and fortune in attempting the impossible are the actions of a pitiless and irreligious man; his external devotions cannot expiate such deeds. "Dieu garde les peuples de semblables Dévots!" (17 [1722]: 234).

Without question, however, the text that Johnson and so many other British readers knew best after 1732 was a translation of Voltaire's *History of Charles XII. King of Sweden*, which in turn enlarged upon Limiers's and le Clerc's point of view. Based on this Voltaire, we recall, the Tory *Grub-street Journal* sees not a Tory hero but a foolish, vengeful, imprudent, overreaching madman. So familiar a view was only slightly overstated.

Voltaire adds a prefatory "Discourse on the History of Charles XII" in which readers at once see puzzling human folly. We are more interested in conquerors, who resemble tyrants, than in great kings; we unaccountably "admire those who have done any glorious mischief."[6] Mischief is indeed a temperate word for Voltaire's Charles XII. That "extraordinary man" is inferior to his rival and conqueror in life as in this book, the builder and civilizer Peter the Great. Charles's story nonetheless may be useful to kings and cure them "of the folly of being a conqueror" (p. viii). Voltaire warns such public great men "that if they would have men speak well of them, it concerns them to do well" (p. xi)—as Charles did not, except for a stunning period of military success motivated by personal glory and indifference to oceans of blood and the collapse of his nation.

The discourse introduces us to several strands in the sanguine fabric of Voltaire's *History*. His Charles loves danger and fights "only for glory" (p. 179). His personal traits blend with his love of war. He seeks to emulate Alexander and Caesar but without their love of luxury, wine, and women (pp. 30–31). So rigorous and spartan a leader inspires Charles's men with shared hardship and success. Nothing stops him in his conquest of Poland and Lithuania (p. 119); he dethrones Frederick of Saxony and crowns Stanislaus in Poland; he sets out for Russia "amidst ice and snow" (p. 157), rejects peace negotiations, surmounts all difficulties including lack of provisions, bitter cold, the consequent death of thousands of his troops (pp. 160–74), and finally meets his adversary at Pultowa.

Peter serves two main functions for Voltaire. As Charles's foil he is a king who educates and elevates his people, on whose behalf he fights "only for interest." Consequently "*Charles* had the title of *Invincible*, which one unhappy moment might rob him of"; but the surrounding nations "had already given *Peter Alexiowitz* the name of *Great*," which depended neither on victory nor defeat (pp. 179–80).

Peter also is the immediate cause of Charles's martial collapse and the vehicle for Voltaire's theme of the vanity of human wishes. The Swedish army left Saxony in September of 1707 with forty-thouand men "shining with gold and silver, and enriched with the spoils of *Poland* and *Saxony*" (pp. 150–51). It leaves Russia as a broken force, half of which starves to death and half of which "were made slaves or massacred. *Charles* XII. had lost in one day the fruit of nine years pains, and almost a hundred battles. He fled in a wretched calash, . . . dangerously wounded." The shattered remnant of his troops follow on foot or in wagons, across a pathless desert without habitations, life, or water (pp. 191–92).

Voltaire begins and ends (p. 364) with an observation of special interest to British readers—namely, that Charles was a negative model of kingship, having inherited an absolute and arbitrary disposition and government from his father. During the coronation fifteen-year-old Charles XII, long anticipating Napoleon, snatched the crown from the archbishop and crowned himself. That behavior, admirable to some who still "groaned under" the father's arbitrary government, "was the presage of their slavery" (p. 17). For Voltaire, Charles XII's Sweden exemplifies an autocratic ancien regime whose time is and should be past. As Voltaire says, during Charles's stay in Turkey his "power, and the grandeur of *Sweden*, were now drawing to their last period" (pp. 214–15). Charles's "despotick notions" make him reject his senate's shared governance and its request for peace with Denmark and Russia. He forgets "that ever *Sweden* had been a free state" and regards the senators "as servants that took upon them to govern the family in their Master's absence" (p. 310).

The consequences of this absolutism also were clear in the death of two hundred fifty thousand men in Charles's wars (p. 221), the loss of Sweden's foreign territories, the danger of an invasion of the state itself (pp. 221, 323, 338), the decay of "the very species of men . . . in the country" (p. 323), massive conscription that often left only "old men, children, and women; and in some places, the women plowed the ground alone" (p. 338), and taxation that amounted to "extortion" (p. 338).

No wonder that Voltaire concludes with two obvious inferences. One is that the extraordinary but not great Charles is "fitter to be admired than imitated" and should teach kings "that a peaceful and happy reign is more to be admired than so much glory" (p. 364). The other inference is that a nation can repudiate its autocrat and move its government toward limited monarchy. Upon Charles's death the Swedes reject his political and martial legacy, make peace with their neighbors, execute Charles's mentor and Sweden's troublemaker Baron Gortz, and restore parliament's control over the monarch. Voltaire describes a royal family whose queen perhaps recalls the reign of England's William and Mary, and expresses the love that Charles repressed:

> The States went to a free election of King *Charles*'s sister for their Queen; and obliged her solemnly to renounce her hereditary right to the crown, holding it only by the people's choice. She promised with repeated oaths never to set up arbitrary power. And afterwards, her love of power giving way to conjugal affection, she yielded the crown to her husband, and brought the States to chuse him, who ascended the throne upon the same conditions. (p. 366)

Johnson gleaned much from this praised and often reprinted work that reflected and reinforced conventional wisdom. He may have known Voltaire's history of Charles XII in French, or as early as its English translation in 1732. Johnson surely knew it long before 1742, when on June 10th he told John Taylor that he was ready to start his tragedy based on Charles's rise and fall. Johnson would "get Charles of Sweden ready for this winter" and so must look into long neglected dramatists.[7] The materials apparently are in hand, but Johnson needs to learn how to shape them. Given the wooden *Irene* (1749) I cannot regret the world's loss, but I more than suspect that his tragic Charles would have had the approximate shape of the passage in *The Vanity of Human Wishes*.

Much of Johnson's portrait of Charles in that poem epitomizes book 4 of Voltaire's history. We recall that he there chronicles Charles's military successes, rejection of peace in favor of marching on Moscow, survival in a bitter winter and serious deprivation, and prompt destruction of his fantasies at Pultowa. Voltaire also describes Charles's bedraggled retreat to Turkey and, thereafter, the sultana's intervention on his behalf, and his unsatisfactory tenure in a place where women, a eunuch, and various subaltern Turks discuss what to do with the ungrateful and troublesome infidel (pp. 200–201, 227).

Earlier passages characterize Charles's physical endurance and control of his passions; later passages characterize his accidental death at Frederickshall, where his brains were blown out by a shot fired by someone at something somewhere on a parapet (p. 362). There is no heroic death for this man whose "passion for glory, for war, and for revenge, made him too little of a politician" successfully to conquer on behalf of his nation (p. 364).

In short, Voltaire provides the basic materials from which Johnson's Charles of Sweden passage comes. Other works Johnson either certainly knew, probably knew, or might possibly have known are consistent with Voltaire's portrait which in turn largely was based on available texts and popular preconceptions. Voltaire scarcely was breaking new ground in the history of Charles; Johnson later equally exploited familiar views that since 1717 had been generally hostile to Charles, and by the late 1740s long had been almost uniformly hostile to him. Tory, Jacobite, administration Whig, and opposition Whig would have agreed with the *Grub-street Journal* and the *Gentleman's Magazine*: Charles's life as Voltaire portrays it "is a Series of Imprudence and Temerity, Revenge and Folly."

Let us also look more closely at Swedish Charles as Johnson portrays him in *The Vanity of Human Wishes* and its section on martial heroes. Do these justify a reading sympathetic to Charles and to Jacobitism?

Johnson's Charles of Sweden: The *Vanity* and Other Texts

The *Vanity* begins with a grim world of anxiety, strife, crowds, desire, hate, snares, clouds, wandering, betrayal, pride, guidelessness, irrationality, and death. We will see

> How nations sink, by darling schemes oppress'd,
> When vengeance listens to the fool's request.
> Fate wings with ev'ry wish th' afflictive dart,
> Each gift of nature, and each grace of art,
> With fatal heat impetuous courage glows,
> With fatal sweetness elocution flows,
> Impeachment stops the speaker's pow'rful breath,
> And restless fire precipitates on death.
>
> (lines 13–20)

Such an opening orients us toward one of Johnson's chief points—danger and death inform the human situation when vain human wishes are unchecked.

The opening also provides what we realize are previews of later characters. Johnson's structure is musical in much of the *Vanity*, which introduces, varies, and amplifies its theme. An early image thus suggests the world as a violent battlefield on which Fate as warrior flings an afflicting spear. We cannot be surprised by Johnson's cognate introduction to the long section on martial folly and fame's "universal charm" (line 184) that attracts humanity to its enemy the heroic conqueror.

The world indeed is so attracted. Nations celebrate conquerors and their conquests, whether Greek Alexander's, Rome's legions or, probably, Britain's Marlborough who stained "with blood the Danube or the Rhine" (line 182). However natural the response it is deeply irrational, cruel to posterity, and sadly parallels too expensive a commercial transaction:

> Yet Reason frowns on War's unequal game,
> Where wasted nations raise a single name,
> And mortgag'd states their grandsires wreaths regret,
> From age to age in everlasting debt;
> Wreaths which at last the dear-bought right convey
> To rust on medals, or on stones decay
>
> (lines 185–90)

Just before Johnson's portrait of Swedish Charles, then, he castigates the martial hero as a perpetual burden on his bereft, impoverished, decaying nation. Johnson evokes Charles with an implicit rhetorical question. It requires a negative response, with which the ghostly Charles himself is presumed to agree, and it at once recalls and anticipates other images of collapsing buildings and reputations. The statesman (line 79), Wolsey (lines 125–28), and the female beauty (line 341) all might share Charles's decision: "On what foundation stands the warrior's pride, / How just his hopes let Swedish Charles decide" (lines 191–92).

Johnson thus conditions us to regard the vain wish for martial heroism as morally unacceptable and undeserving of human sympathy whether it succeeds or fails. This supremely egotistic activity rejects normal human response like love and fear and disregards the consequences for others. Johnson embodies this concept in pronouns for Charles: him, his, he, and mine. He epitomizes possessiveness, rejects peace, and declares that "nothing [is] gain'd . . . 'til nought remain," until "Gothic standards fly" in Moscow, "And all be mine beneath the polar sky" (lines 202–4). When Pultowa intrudes on this fantasy the glory-driven hero abandons the wreck of his men, is humiliated in Turkey, and upon his return to the north is "destin'd" to an unheroic death. His legacy is not empire and an expanded Sweden, but a grave and the name that illustrates the vanity of human wishes, the dangers of self-affirming martial heroism, and some of the consequences for such a person and those who serve him. Shortly thereafter, defeated Xerxes rows "Through purple billows and a floating host" (line 240) and Charles Albert of Bavaria soon dies with anguish and shame (line 254). Later in the poem Johnson even strips Marlborough of his glory, only shows him in his dotage, and forces him into a couplet with his tormentor Swift (lines 317–18).

Let us even put aside both general comments in the martial section and the specific ghastly section on Xerxes and examine the other Charles in Johnson's dark martial portrait: Charles of Bavaria, whose "hasty greatness" (line 252) embodies death, vanity, and spending others' blood to pay the butcher's bill. This character concludes the poem's military episode and ends with the word "shame" (line 254). Hence, on the Swedish Charles-alludes-sympathizes-flickers-undertone-admire-tragic-Stuart Charles reading, Johnson evokes or offers three immediately negative models within a negative section: one is *demens* Hannibal on whom Charles is based, two others are named Charles. Thereafter, he supposedly shifts allusive modes and asks us to forget that "Reason frowns on War's unequal game," to forget about ancient lunatic Hannibal bad invader bad warrior, and modern bad Charles bad Charles bad invader bad warrior. Instead, sympathize with the "good" Charles Edward not in the poem, whom others also called a madman or an irreligious butcher, who contradicts everything the section and the satire stand for, but who nonetheless by robust transformation is to evoke tragic import, admiration, and sympathy. The far more likely response is "Dieu garde les peuples de semblables Dévots!"

We can see that the neo-Jacobite scholars have made three mutually dependent arguments regarding Johnson's Charles of Sweden in the *Vanity*. One is that Johnson is sympathetic to him as "a mighty favourite." The politically shared view of Charles as dangerous and despotic makes this view impossible to sustain. The second argument is based on authorial intention. As a Jacobite, Johnson chose and meant Swedish Charles to be a surrogate for Stuart Charles whose cause he supported. This circular argument of course assumes what must be proven, since it wrongly claims that Johnson was a Jacobite, from which other fallible assumptions follow. The poem, the passage's context within it, and Johnson's own dismissal of Charles Edward and his cause make that argument equally impossible. It also implicitly assumes that Francophobe Johnson would have approved of an invasion supported and supplied by

France, designed for French interests, and if successful designed to make Britain subservient to her powerful enemy and the Stuart family—against whom Johnson thought it lamentably necessary for Britons to rebel.

The third argument is that Jacobite readers recognized their own Charles Edward in the *Vanity*'s Charles of Sweden and his brief rise to glory and consequent disgrace. The neo-Jacobites, though, have not produced any examples of comparable positive eighteenth-century reactions to the passage or, if one should surface, that it was typical and not idiosyncratic. Nor can they explain away familiar reactions as, for example, recorded in the manuscript of Boswell's *Life of Johnson*. Boswell discusses the portrait as a judiciously chosen, strongly painted, and highly "finished" example of disappointment. He also records General Paoli's "fervent admiration of it" and alludes to Sir Nathaniel William Wraxall's comment that this is the "most finished and masterly portrait of this extraordinary man, which ever fell from the pen of genius."[8] All three readers respond to Johnson's Charles of Sweden as a named, historically known, and famous person whose familiar portrait functions as denotation not connotation.

This arrest of response to Charles of Sweden is predictable. He and Charles Edward, after all, share scarcely more than a Christian name, Gothic proclivities, including invasion of others' countries, and poor strategy. I presume that these last two are not "sympathetic" traits. Charles Edward never wore a crown or ruled a nation, had little combat before his invasion, was treated derisively by the French generals in charge of the aborted 1744 invasion from Dunkirk, was himself indebted to French language and culture, and fought with Highlanders he had never seen before. He had only two modest successes at Prestonpans (1745) and Falkirk (1746) against overconfident generals with raw or incompetent troops. He had nine months of modest success against modest odds. Charles Edward's first confrontation with well-trained regulars was at Culloden, where he placed his exhausted men in an absurdly dangerous military setting that forced them to fight and die in a set piece uncongenial to their temperament and training. King Charles of Sweden refused to speak French, had nine years of good success against large nations and great odds, fought with men who revered him, whom he trained, and long knew. Only an uncharacteristically uninformed Samuel Johnson would ask his readers to make so tangential a connection.

Let us nonetheless briefly grant that Johnson intends Charles of Sweden to suggest Charles Edward. The few, unflattering, similarities, the poem's military section, and the external persistent denigration of Swedish Charles still require a severe judgment of any ancient or modern hero. Johnson's own use of "Gothic standards" in the *Vanity* associates Swedish flags with destructive northern barbarism.

Invasion of Britain of course is worse than invasion of Russia and of course is condemned. Johnson's friend and printer John Nichols, or perhaps his son John Bowyer Nichols, attributes the General Preface to the *Gentleman's Magazine* for 1753 to Samuel Johnson. The attribution has been generally accepted from as early as 1807, with only one attributor suggesting that Johnson may have written most of the preface but corrected all of it. Johnson there praises the noisy debates during the Walpole years as securing the rights of the crown and the privileges of the people, thus protecting each from "the Cause either of Tyranny or of Faction." In contemporary terms, the British balanced constitutional monarchy resists Stuart-Jacobite absolutism and extreme Whig anarchism. The 1740s were rendered "more remarkable in English History by a Rebellion, which was not less contemptible in its beginning than threatening in its progress and consequences; but which, through the Favour of Providence, was crushed at once, when our Enemies abroad had the highest expectations from it and has contributed to our greater security."[9] For Johnson, God helped Britain to defeat a French invasion for French profit.

In addition, the more Swedish Charles was associated with the French, the more suspect he would be to Johnson and his readers. The reality of such an invasion returns us to Johnson's choices in the *Vanity*. In the tenth satire Juvenal chose Hannibal (lines 147–67) for obvious patriotic reasons: he was the alien general from an alien continent who invaded the mother country. Roman virtue and arms finally drove the madman back to his distant nation, into another hostile court, into suicide, and into perpetually punitive declamations by Roman schoolboys. Imitators are free to vary their adaptations, as Johnson does in the *Vanity*—but not with Charles XII as an analogue to Hannibal the foreign invader deservedly defeated, killed, and mocked.

Voltaire provides Johnson with an immediate estimate of Charles XII's military achievement, one consistent with earlier and later continental judgments of encumbered Charles's possible plans for England. The defenseless Sweden to which Charles returned feared Russian, Danish, Saxon, and British invasions. Charles nonetheless raises a new army and fatally invades Norway with twenty thousand men. Voltaire's allusion cannot include the inexperienced Charles Edward, but clearly evokes the besieged, daring, and foolhardy general whose success is behind him: "Since *Hannibal*, the world has not seen any General, who, when he could not make head against his enemies at home, had ever gone to attack them in their own dominions" (pp. 339–40).[10] Swedish Charles was a far better analogue for African Hannibal than Charles Edward could possibly be.

There remains a further question to ask: could not an independent thinker like Johnson know all the grim news regarding Charles and still exonerate him if he wished? Johnson of course well understood human, and his own, aggression and, like Voltaire, well understood the "universal, yet . . . strange" attraction to "the dignity of danger" that leads one to follow Charles to Moscow rather than Socrates to the porch (*Life*, 3:265–66). Johnson also knew that such magnetic aggression required human disapproval and melioration and so disapproves in works that straddle *The Vanity of Human Wishes*.

In 1744 Johnson mingles Lockean and quasi-Namierian insights regarding government. Richard Savage, we hear, did not attempt "to reduce to rational schemes of government societies which were formed by chance, and are conducted by the private passions of those who preside in them." Johnson praises Savage for censuring wicked imperialist crimes, of invading "barbarous nations because they cannot resist, and of invading countries because they are fruitful." He further praises Savage because he asserted "the natural equality of mankind, and endeavoured to suppress that pride which inclines men to imagine that right is the consequence of power."[11] These sentiments come five years before the *Vanity* and during the active run-up to Charles Edward's invasion in 1745. They do not suggest a mind comfortable with divine right or with a powerful monarch's invasion of others' lands. Johnson again obviates such schemes in his *Adventurer*, No. 99 (1753), which excoriates murderous imperialists like Charles of Sweden.

The essay often is a prose expansion of the *Vanity*'s military section and includes some of the same cast—Roman Caesar, Persian Xerxes, Greek Alexander, and Swedish Charles. Johnson here feels so strongly that he rejects a familiar convention: Peter is not superior to Charles but as murderous as Charles. The passage requires quotation at length and an explanation by those who think Johnson sympathetic to Swedish or to Stuart Charles:

> The last royal projectors with whom the world has been troubled, were Charles of Sweden and the Czar of Muscovy. Charles, if any judgement may be formed of his designs by his measures and enquiries, had purposed first to dethrone the Czar, then to lead his army through pathless deserts into China,

thence to make his way by the sword through the whole circuit of Asia, and by the conquest of Turkey to unite Sweden with his new dominions: but this mighty project was crushed at Pultowa, and Charles has since been considered as a madman by those powers, who sent their embassadors to sollicit his friendship, and their generals "to learn under him the art of war." . . .

I am far from intending to vindicate the sanguinary projects of heroes and conquerors, and would wish rather to diminish the reputation of their success, than the infamy of their miscarriages: for I cannot conceive, why he that has burnt cities, and wasted nations, and filled the world with horror and desolation, should be more kindly regarded by mankind, than he that died in the rudiments of wickedness; why he that accomplished mischief should be glorious, and he that only endeavoured it should be criminal: I would wish Caesar and Catiline, Xerxes and Alexander, Charles and Peter, huddled together in obscurity or detestation.[12]

After grammatical changes, Johnson echoes the introduction to his martial section in the *Vanity*. There he objects that "wasted nations raise a single name"; here he objects to sanguinary conquerors who "wasted nations." Indeed, the passage is interpretatively urgent for several reasons. It glosses *The Vanity of Human Wishes* and makes plainer still what the martial sections already make plain: such men are detestable not sympathetic; a man like Charles now is thought mad; his success should be even more infamous than his defeat; he produces ashes, horror, and detestation. The passage also suggests either what Johnson did not know, forgot, or thought too insignificant for anyone to recall: Charles's grand projections did not include an invasion of Britain that Johnson surely could have mentioned to exemplify folly. Charles remains a Continental monarch with Continental and Eastern aspirations. Finally, the passage is implicitly contemptuous of Charles's fabled generalship.

European powers, we see, once sent "their generals 'to learn under him the art of war'." The remark originally appeared in *The Conduct of the Duke of Marlborough During the Present War* in 1712.[13] It would find its way into other works as well, but Johnson's source probably is Voltaire's *History of Charles XII* and its derivative discussion of Marlborough's diplomatic exchange with Charles. His grace seeks to determine whether his Swedish majesty will join France or, as Marlborough expects, look eastward (pp. 142–46). He gives Charles a friendly handwritten letter from Queen Anne that is accompanied by Marlborough's desire that he might serve some campaigns under so great a general that, as Johnson says, he "might learn under him the art of war." This quotation was available since 1712, was renewed by Voltaire in 1731, re-englished in 1732 and often thereafter, and here was enlivened in 1753. By then few Britons, or others, could have doubted that Marlborough was Charles XII's military superior. Johnson's quotation thus questions the judgment of those powers who overrated Charles. It also suggests that Marlborough's remark was ambassadorial politesse designed to flatter a dangerous egotist.

Johnson, Whigs, and Erastians

I here elaborate and add to the introduction to this section, in which I speculate on useful ways to read and grasp Johnson's politics. Many years ago, George Birkbeck Hill tried to reverse the received, and still dominant, image of Johnson as the perpetual melancholic depressive. He drew a picture of an essentially happy man who suffered from several dark periods.[14] I hope to offer a counterhypothesis to the picture of Johnson the arch-Tory as unhappy in his Whig-dominated political world as he was unhappy in his guilt-ridden psychological world. I suggest that Johnson shared Erastian and Whiggish political principles. Given his denigration of modern unprincipled Whigs, it is prudent to assume the term "Old Whig" also applicable to Swift. The Reverend Dr. William Maxwell observes that though as a Tory Johnson "asserted the legal and salutary prerogatives of the crown, he no less respected the constitutional liberties of the people. Whiggism, at the time of the Revolution, he said, was accompanied by certain principles," whereas now it had become excessively commercial and irreligious (*Life*, 2:117).

The neo-Jacobites regard the Hanoverian dynasty as a world of political horrors, what J. C. D. Clark has called "Hanoverian repression."[15] A people longing for liberation, seeking their proper king over the water, lonely for legitimacy, and repulsed by the German on the British throne, were forced by threats of poverty to take oaths to usurpers whose very walls had ears. Like others, Johnson suffered for his beliefs.

In this version of droit-Foucauldianism government is the preying prying monster with so many weapons and warrants at the ready that good subjects dared not speak their Jacobite minds. Clark characterizes Johnson the victim: his "peculiar authority as a moral critic derives from an austere position of internal exile which is no less acute for being, from one perspective, self-imposed." His general truths stemmed from "a particular set of moral, religious, and political dilemmas" that Clark can elucidate (p. 79). The key words here are "internal exile," the Soviet and other despotic states' penalty for dissidents. It included policed isolation in a particular city for a nominal two to five years—as with Sakharov and Solzhenitsyn—and thus forced limitation on physical and intellectual travel.[16] Less lucky dissidents were exiled to Siberian labor camps, from which few returned. For Clark and some of his colleagues, Johnson lived in a Hanoverian Gulag. He himself had other ideas.

Johnson may never have voted, but he revered the concept and act of voting. Such a man "is himself a secondary Legislator, as he gives his Consent by his Representative, to all the Laws by which he is bound." He also has "a Right to petition the great Council of the Nation, whenever he thinks they are deliberating upon an Act detrimental to the Interest of the Community." In "The Bravery of the English Common Soldiers" Johnson refers to the "equality of English privileges, the impartiality of our laws, the freedom of our tenures, and the prosperity of our trade."[17]

At an uncertain time, Johnson wrote two sermons (23, 24) on the nature of government and the obligations of the governor and the governed. We may assume that he regarded the sermon genre as an especially strong receptacle of truth, and we notice that he nowhere even hints at the divinity of kingship. The twenty-third sermon denigrates violence and "strife of a pernicious and destructive kind, which . . . too frequently obstructs, or disturbs the happiness of nations." Johnson enlarges on that last phrase in the first sentence of Sermon 24, which overtly, and for Johnson typically, places government within the secular not divine realm: "That the institutions of government owe their original, like other human actions, to the desire of happiness, is not to be denied." Equally important, Johnson also makes plain that Hanoverian Britain enjoys uncommon liberty and security: "In a country like ours, the great demand, which is for ever repeated to our governours, is for the security of property, the confirmation of liberty, and the extension of commerce. All this we have obtained, and all this we possess, in a degree which perhaps was never granted to any other people."[18]

At different times, Johnson objected to the ministries of Walpole, Bute, and North. Nonetheless, he also generally had confidence in Britain's governors and, we know, for a time wished to be among that civilizing force (YE 10:350 and see the preceding chapter). Choosing representatives is "one of the most valuable rights of Englishmen" (YE 10:399), whose freely elected representatives well deliberate upon two acceptable choices: "there was hardly ever any question in which a man [in Commons] might not very well vote either upon one side or the other" (*Life*, 3:206; see also 3:324). Unlike internal exiles, Johnson of course was able to travel where he wished, see whom he wished—

including his monarch who wished to see him—and say what he pleased. All this was appropriate for the "Free People" among whom he lived, and all this was consistent with the most optimistic eighteenth-century Whig doctrine.

We thus should not speak of *the* politics of Johnson. These varied as circumstances varied and as Johnson drew from both Whig and Tory beliefs. Robert Harris argues that by midcentury even the Jacobites had ideologically capitulated to the Whigs, but it is as likely that by then most shared core principles if not shared practice.[19] For Johnson, though these sides indeed often differed, at their best they drew on a common center. He thus responds with lexical precision in a paragraph Boswell calls "OF TORY AND WHIG." It begins: "A wise Tory and a wise Whig, I believe, will agree. Their principles are the same, though their modes of thinking are different" (*Life*, 4:117).

Johnson saw some of this overlap in the writings of Anglican High Church father Richard Hooker and Anglican Latitudinarian father Benjamin Hoadly. He and others noticed Hooker's regular insistence on contract theory—as in the eighth book among other places. Every society has "full dominion over it self. . . . God creating mankinde did indue it naturally with full power to guide it self in whatever kinds of societies soever it should choose to live."[20] Hoadly adapted such remarks and used them to support the concept of limited constitutional monarchy behind the Williamite anti-Stuart revolution. *The Original and Institution of Civil Government, Discuss'd* (1710) characterizes Hooker as overtly founding "*Civil Government* upon the *Voluntary Agreement, Composition*, or *Compact* of the Members of the *Govern'd Society*; from whom *originally* comes all the *Authority* of *Governours*." The people have "a reserve of *Right* to change" a government they perceive to be intolerable and of which "they were not at first apprehensive."[21] The author of conservative Anglican theory advocated what would become Lockean theory of a revocable "*Voluntary Agreement*" of people and rulers.

According to Sir John Hawkins, Johnson filtered Hooker on the obedience of subject to crown "as explained by Hoadly." Johnson thus "condemned the conduct of James the second" during his reign and embraced a position that "leads to whiggism." In this respect, Johnson was the ancestral paradigm of Tory man and Whig measures. His mode of thinking tilted toward the nominal Tory side on practical politics because he hoped to strengthen a weakened monarchy, the Anglican Church, and social subordination as paths to possible secular happiness. His eclectic Toryism nonetheless had the strong Whig principles that

Hawkins acknowledged and that challenge John Cannon's view that Johnson "was, in essence, an anti-Whig."[22]

There is further support for what we might call Johnson's intellectual whiggery. Whigs attacked Tory Jonathan Swift's *Proposal for Correcting . . . the English Tongue* (1712) urging a British Academy to correct and fix the language. Johnson twice also worries that pamphlet. In the Preface to the *Dictionary* he dismisses the arguments in Swift's "petty treatise on the *English* language." In the "Life of Swift" (1781) he regards it as ignorant, uninformed, and counterproductive.[23] Johnson knew that his political principles, like his linguistic principles, needed to adapt to experience and to relevant circumstances. Consequently and importantly he accepts Britain's unpleasantly forcible change of its monarch in order to save itself. The nation obviously did this when it replaced James II with William III, an act that in 1756 Johnson called "the necessity of self-preservation [that] had impelled the subjects of James to drive him from the throne" (YE 10:142; see also *Life*, 1:430 and 2:341–42). That necessity destabilized but did not topple the constitution. As Johnson says in the Preface to the *Dictionary*, both language and government naturally tend toward degeneration: "we have long preserved our constitution, let us make some struggles for our language."[24]

An angry conversation with Sir Adam Fergusson on March 31, 1772, exemplifies Johnson's views regarding the variety of legitimate governments and the peoples' rights to protect themselves from perceived tyranny. It also extends to national government what Johnson said about domestic government: "to govern and to tyrannize are very different, and . . . oppression will naturally provoke rebellion" (YE 14:14).

Fergusson fears that luxury corrupts a people and destroys its sense of liberty. Johnson calls that nonsense: "I would not give half a guinea to live under one form of government rather than another. It is of no moment to the happiness of an individual." Fergusson insists that one must "keep up a spirit in the people, so as to preserve a balance against the crown." Johnson insults him as a "vile Whig," insists that the crown lacks power, enlarges on his opening statement and, if he believes in divine right, commits symbolic deicide:

> When I say that all governments are alike, I consider that in no government power can be abused long. Mankind will not bear it. If a sovereign oppresses his people to a great degree, they will rise and cut off his head. There is a remedy in human nature against tyranny, that will keep us safe under every form of government. (*Life*, 2:170)

The rebellious inferences are clear enough in this virtually radical Whig answer to Fergusson's tepid whiggery. By extension, however awful, the beheading of Charles I also responded to an apparently abusive government that English mankind would not bear.[25] Johnson exemplifies such a view as well when in 1770 he lamented the "detestable" British treatment of the Irish: "Let the authority of the English government perish, rather than be maintained by iniquity" (*Life*, 2:121). Surly human nature generally keeps subjects safe from tyranny and potential tyrants safe from their people. When this fails, authority and safety fail as well. Johnson's thoughts regarding the right of violent regicidal self-defense cannot be reconciled with the passive obedience and divine right explicit in Dryden's line in *The Medal* (1682): "That Kings can do no Wrong, we must believe" (line 135). Nor can it be reconciled with Henry Sacheverell's justification of passive obedience: "The Throne is above Subjection, and as 'tis in it self the Fountain of All Jurisdiction, is Liable to none but what is Superior to it, and that is the Divine Alone." Richard Welton also typifies such high-flying earlier eighteenth-century views. In a sermon of 1710 he insists: "There is no Power given or allow'd from God unto the People, to Coerce, or to Try or Judge their Prince, but to Keep his Command, and to Observe his Pleasure in things Lawful, and to Undergo Penalty where they are not."[26] Johnson clearly had a different attitude toward the people's right to use their power, and to try their prince, though he wisely feared that power and the consequent disorder it entails. Johnson also recognized that slaves had a right to armed rebellion against their destructive masters in that unnatural and inhumane situation.[27]

THE POLITICAL EDUCATOR

We need to return, then, to one of the ways Johnson encourages nonviolent restraint upon potential tyranny, what he calls the British "Form of Government" that "makes almost every Man a secondary Legislator." Legislation by an elected parliament in fact is a key to Johnson's concept of the stability of government. In April of 1778 he makes clear why Britain's constitutional monarchy is not easily destroyed and made despotic. Government by one person with "contracted" power cannot last because it lacks a solid base. In contrast, "the government of Great Britain . . . is founded on the parliament, then is in the privy council, then in the King" (*Life,* 3:283). Johnson did more than talk about such a principle: he also taught and recommended it.

Johnson once was a schoolteacher and always was a moral teacher. As such, he later says in the "Life of Milton" (1779), "Those authors . . . are to be read at schools that supply most axioms of prudence, most principles of moral truth, and most materials for conversation" (*Lives*, 1:100). He would not teach what he did not believe in, and he believed in teaching an interesting set of books to educate potentially elite young men and voters regarding their British government and its history. Here is Section 11 of Johnson's preface to Dodsley's *Preceptor* that appeared in 1748, the year in which Johnson also wrote *The Vanity of Human Wishes*. He considers the principles of law and government that teach the proper balance of obedience due and required. He also gives the monarch far less time than he gives the concepts of legislature and community.

> This Knowledge by peculiar Necessity constitutes a Part of the Education of an *Englishman*, who professes to obey his Prince according to the law, and who is himself a secondary Legislator, as he gives his Consent by his Representative, to all the Laws by which he is bound, and a Right to petition the great Council of the Nation, whenever he thinks they are deliberating upon an Act detrimental to the Interest of the Community. This is therefore a Subject to which the Thoughts of a young Man ought to be directed; and that he may obtain such Knowledge as may qualify him to act and judge as one of a Free People, let him be directed to add to this Introduction, the Lord Chancellor *Fortescue's Treatises*, N. Bacon's *Historical Discourse on the Laws and Government of England*, *Temple's Introduction*, *Locke on Government*, *Harrington's Oceana*, *Plato Redivivus*, *Gurdon's History of Parliaments*, and *Hooker's Ecclesiastical Polity*. (pp. 187–88)[28]

This remarkable list of recommended reading is almost entirely Whiggish, anti-Stuart, and even republican. Temple, for example, was a chief mover in bringing William of Orange to the English throne and used his *Introduction* to help justify that act. Fortescue's *The Difference Between an Absolute and Limited Monarchy; As it more particularly regards the English Constitution* (London, 1724) exalts the Saxon roots of English liberty and restraints upon monarchs. Johnson may have been alluding to the recent third edition of the deist and arch-Whig John Toland's *The Oceana and Other Works of James Harrington* (1747). Perhaps the most illuminating recommended book is Thornagh Gurdon's *The History of the High Court of Parliament, Its Antiquity, Preheminence and Authority* (London, 1731). This work by a regicide's nephew praises limits on royal power and the Germanic roots of such limits in Britain's constitutional monarchy. Gurdon rejects James II who, Johnson's Whig writer says, was not exiled but abdicated. That is part of the "Knowledge as may qualify him [the young student] to act and judge as one of a Free People":

> Had a late unfortunate Prince that bore the Addition of Second, before he closeted such as were likely to choose Members of Parliament, before he raised a standing Army, which was always looked on as a Grievance in the *English* Nation; had he, I say, duly weighed the Misfortunes that attended *Richard* II, in the Measures he took to pack a Parliament, and other such like Mistakes in Government, he would not have judged the abdicating his Crown and Country his only Safety. (2:301)

We may look as well at two key definitions and their relevant illustrative quotations in the *Dictionary* (1755). For Johnson, the noun "government" is "1. Form of a community with respect to the disposition of the supreme authority." He illustrates this from William Temple's *Miscellanea. The First Part* (here, 4th ed.; London, 1703), edited by Swift. Johnson quotes from "An Essay upon the Original and Nature of Government": "There seems to be but two general kinds of *government* in the world: the one exercised according to the arbitrary commands and will of some single person; and the other according to certain orders or laws introduced by agreement or custom, and not to be changed without the consent of many" (p. 47). One need not look far to see which form of government Johnson preferred. "Arbitrary" is "Despotick; absolute; bound by no law; following the will without restraint." Johnson's definition of "King" is equally instructive: "A contraction of the Teutonick word *cuning*, or *cyning*, the name of sovereign dignity. In the primitive tongue it signifies stout or valiant, the kings of most nations being in the beginning, chosen by the people on account of their valour and strength. *Verstegan*."

Johnson has conflated key opening sections of chapter 10 of Richard Verstegen's *Restitution of Decayed Intelligence* (1605, 1628, 1634, 1653, 1673). The passage Johnson quotes captures two of Verstegen's main, Tacitean, points: the English people had Germanic roots; the Germanic roots denoted kings chosen by the people, not anointed by God, and not subject to inheritance. Johnson makes even clearer that British government is secular and evolutionary. He quotes lines 209–14 from Pope's "Epistle 3" (1733) of *An Essay on Man*. For Pope as for Verstegen, the origin of monarchy is social not divine:

> Thus states were form'd; the name of *king* unknown,
> 'Till common int'rest plac'd the sway in one.

'Twas VIRTUE ONLY (or in arts or arms,
Diffusing blessings, or averting harms)
The same which in a Sire the Sons obey'd,
A Prince the Father of a People made.[29]

Johnson indeed embraced a position that "leads to whiggism." That also may be because wise Whigs and wise Tories agreed on basic principles, though they competed, slanged one another, and did their best to look after their own and their families' interests.

In reading Johnson on government and on religion we also find a striking Erastian note. He ignores the prior generation's insistence upon the union of Church and state as essential for the nation's survival: no bishop no king. Johnson's two sermons on government never mention that fear or the cognate fear that the Church is in danger. Since he bases his theory of government on accident improved by art and longevity, he also assumes that the art of government can be enhanced by religion. A good man will be a good subject: "The only uniform and perpetual cause of publick happiness," he says in Sermon 24 on government, "is publick virtue" (YE 14:253). Obedience to God's laws induces obedience to man's laws.

That obedience always is subject to human weakness, however. William Maxwell paraphrases Johnson's remarks in 1770: "The inseparable imperfection annexed to all human governments, consisted, he said, in not being able to create a sufficient fund of virtue and principle to carry the laws into due and effectual execution. Wisdom might plan, but virtue alone could execute" (*Life,* 2:118). For Johnson, episcopacy is not a sign of inherent virtue and goodness in the state, but is a superior form of church governance: it enlarges a communal experience and provides structure. In 1769 he thus told Boswell that the Presbyterians dangerously "have no church, no apostolical ordination." They "have no publick worship: they have no form of prayer in which they know they are to join. They go to hear a man pray, and are to judge whether they will join with him" (*Life,* 2:103–4). The Presbyterian Church no longer is the martial and religious northern threat to the English nation, state, or subjects.

If Hawkins is correct that Johnson learned about Hooker from Hoadly, then Johnson was not merely not a Jacobite. He also did not believe in the divine right of kings; he believed in the subjection of the Church to the state; though he hoped for a stronger monarch, he recognized the proper power of the legislature as the solid base of British government; he swore or was willing to swear appropriate loyalty oaths at appropriate times; he was willing if necessary to serve in his nation's Trained Bands to resist a French invasion intended to restore a Polish-Italian-French Catholic Stuart to the Anglican British throne; he recommended Whiggish political philosophy to the young voting elites of his nation; he admired the accidentally formed and humanly made political system that allowed such voting; he sought to be part of the nation's representative political body he admired; he knew that such human beings would and indeed should violently rebel when subject to tyranny. Johnson soberly examined his political world and in spite of its regular mistakes, he saw a generally benign political system in contemporary Britain. Its government meets the demands "for the security of property, the confirmation of liberty, and the extension of commerce. All this we have obtained, and all this we possess, in a degree which perhaps was never granted to any other people."

Such political optimism sat comfortably next to his sense of the ravages of original sin. He wrote a great poem that lamented the vanity of human wishes in general terms, embodied hostility to an absolutist monarch who brutalized his nation and Europe, and was yet another reason why in the long run only religion and celestial wisdom can calm the mind and bring happiness. That political and religious message is very like the message of Johnson's fine tale "The Vision of Theodore" (1748). There, Reason describes herself as "of all subordinate beings the noblest and the greatest; who, if thou wilt receive my laws, will reward thee . . . by conducting thee to Religion." Reason also advises other students "to inlist themselves among the votaries of Religion," but makes plain that she is only a means to an end. Existence has "asperities and pitfals over which Religion only can conduct you."[30] Johnson's mingled Tory Whiggism or Whig Toryism is the reasonable secular political system that at its best both depends upon and leads to religion as the source of happiness. That is something that a Charles of Sweden could not have contemplated for many of those with whom he made contact. It is, though, typical of Johnson's beliefs so alien to the worlds of rebellion, invasion, and violence. It is typical also of what he taught in his prose, poetry, politics, and life: "Without virtue nothing can be securely possessed, or properly enjoyed" (YE 14:254).

NOTES

1. *The Letters of Samuel Johnson*, ed. Bruce Redford (Princeton: Princeton University Press, 1992–94), 1:6. James M. Kuist rightly calls the *Gentleman's Magazine* "one

of the most widely circulating publications of the English-speaking world." See his *The Nichols File of "The Gentleman's Magazine": Attributions of Authorship and Other Documentation in Editorial Papers at the Folger Library* (Madison: University of Wisconsin Press, 1982), p. vii. References to that magazine will be cited in the text as *GM*.

2. Thomas Kaminski, *The Early Career of Samuel Johnson* (New York: Oxford University Press, 1987), p. 44.

3. Warton, *Poems on Several Occasions. By the Reverend Mr. Thomas Warton . . . sometime Professor of Poetry in the University of Oxford* (London, 1748), p. 16. "Mr. Johnson" is listed on sig. a4ʳ of subscribers. For Johnson's line, see The Yale Edition of the Works of Samuel Johnson, vol. 6, *Poems*, ed. E. L. McAdam, Jr., with George Milne (New Haven: Yale University Press, 1964), p. 91, line 2. Subsequent references will be from this edition and will be cited in the text by line number. Subsequent references to the Yale Edition will be cited as YE with relevant bibliographic matter. For fuller references to Pope, Thomson, and Warton, see the prior chapter, at notes 9, 15, 49, 56.

4. The Yale Edition of the Private Papers of James Boswell, Research Edition, *James Boswell's Life of Johnson. An Edition of the Original Manuscript in Four Volumes. Volume I: 1709–1765*, ed. Marshall Waingrow (Edinburgh: Edinburgh University Press; New Haven: Yale University Press, 1994), p. 300 n. 9, from Boswell's journal for April 7, 1773. Neo-Jacobite scholars urge the importance of Boswell as a source for assessing Johnson's politics. They should be aware of the more immediate and more definitive journal version of an important remark perhaps unintentionally softened in the *Life*. The manuscript and the published *Life* read, "he was not sure he would have held it up": Manuscript *Life*, 1:300; *Boswell's Life of Johnson Together with Boswell's Journal of a Tour to the Hebrides*, ed. George Birkbeck Hill and, rev. L. F. Powell (Oxford: Clarendon Press, 1934–50), 1:430. Subsequent citations are given in the text as *Life*.

5. YE 10, *Political Writings*, ed. Donald J. Greene (1977), pp. 193 (the French), 283 (has not been).

6. See *The History of Charles XII. King of Sweden. By Mr. de Voltaire*, 2nd ed. (London, 1732), p. v. Subsequent references are to this edition and are cited in the text. Voltaire's *Histoire* appeared in Basle in 1731 and quickly became popular on either side of the channel. There were several editions in English before 1749: Dublin, 1732, four in London 1732, and others in 1734, 1735, 1739, and 1740. The French editions are chronicled in Georges Bengesco, *Voltaire: Bibliographie de ses oeuvres* (Paris, 1882–90), 1:372–97. For some discussion of the text and its place in Voltaire's historiography, see J. H. Brumfitt, *Voltaire Historian* (Oxford: Oxford University Press, 1958).

7. Redford, Johnson's *Letters*, 1:28.

8. Waingrow, Manuscript *Life*, pp. 142–43 and 143 n. 6.

9. I have discussed this General Preface, the history of its attribution, and the failed competing arguments against it in "Johnson and Jacobitism Redux," *Age of Johnson* 8 (1997): 104–6; henceforth *AJ*.

10. Johnson did not know Frederick the Great's characterization of Charles as "aussi audacieux, mais moins rusé qu' Annibal": *Reflexions sur . . . Charles XII*, p. xxxii.

11. *Savage*, in *Lives of the English Poets*, ed. George Birkbeck Hill (Oxford: Clarendon Press, 1905), 2:394–95. These are among many of Johnson's political remarks inconsistent with the divine right of kings or the presumed Jacobitism he imbibed from and shared with Savage.

12. YE 2, *The Idler and the Adventurer*, ed. W. J. Bate, John M. Bullitt, and L. F. Powell (1963), pp. 432–33.

13. See *The Conduct of the Duke of Marlborough During the Present War. With Original Papers* (London, 1712), p. 121, as part of Marlborough's ambassadorial visit to Charles. The episode also is in the French translation, *La Conduite de Son Altesse Le Prince et Duc de Marlborough, Dans la Présent Guere, Avec Plusieurs Pieces Originales. Traduit de l'Anglois* (Amsterdam, 1712); see pp. 126–29 for the episode. Voltaire received relevant information from meetings in England with the Duchess of Marlborough. See Cleveland B. Chase, *The Young Voltaire* (New York: Longmans Green, 1926), pp. 137–38, and Brumfitt, *Voltaire Historian*, p. 8, who accepts Chase's view.

14. Birkbeck Hill, "Lord Macaulay on Johnson," in *Dr. Johnson: His Friends and His Critics* (London, 1878), pp. 100, 123–45.

15. Clark, "On Moving the Middle Ground: The Significance of Jacobitism in Historical Studies," in *The Jacobite Challenge*, ed. Eveline Cruickshanks and Jeremy Black (Edinburgh: John Donald, 1985), p. 180.

16. See the entry regarding internal exile in *Encyclopedia of Soviet Law*, ed. F. J. M. Feldbrugge et al., 2nd ed. (Dordrecht: Martinuss Nijhoff Publishers, 1985), pp. 298–99.

17. Preface to the *Preceptor*, in *Samuel Johnson's Prefaces and Dedications*, ed. Allen T. Hazen (New Haven: Yale University Press, 1937), pp. 187–88; "Bravery," in YE 10:282.

18. YE 14, *Sermons*, ed. Jean Hagstsrum and James Gray (1978), pp. 240 (No. 23, strife), 249 (No. 24, institutions), 254 (No. 24, country). Gray rightly observes that in Johnson's sermons "he stuck to his own beliefs and staunchly defended his own orthodoxy. Hawkins has testified to the truth of this": YE 14:185.

19. Harris, *National Politics and the London Press in the 1740s* (Oxford: Clarendon Press, 1993), p. 45 n. 114.

20. The Folger Library Edition of the Works of Richard Hooker, *Of the Laws of Ecclesiastical Polity*, ed. Georges Edelen (Cambridge, MA: Belknap Press of Harvard University Press, 1977), 1:328. For "full dominion," see *Laws* 8.2.5–10 (3:334). Mark Goldie notes the post-Revolution Whig reliance on Hooker. See "The Revolution of 1689: Pamphlets and the Allegiance Controversy," *Bulletin of Research in the Humanities* 83 (1980): 473–564. See also Jack Lynch, "Johnson and Hooker on Ecclesiastical Politics," *Review of English Studies* 55 (2004): 45–59.

21. The full title is helpful: *The Original and Institution of Civil Government, Discuss'd. Viz. I. An Examination of the Patriarchal Scheme of Government. II. A Defense of Mr. Hooker's Judgment, &c. against the Objections of several late Writers. To which is added, A Large Answer to Dr. F. Atterbury's Charge of Rebellion: In which the Substance of his late Latin Sermon is produced, and fully examined. By Benjamin Hoadly, M. A. Rector of St. Peter's Poor* (London, 1710), pp. 137–38. Hoadly extensively discusses Hooker.

22. Hawkins, *Life of Samuel Johnson LL. D.* (Dublin, 1787), pp. 446–47. If Hawkins was correct, Johnson was more Erastian as well as more Whiggish than is commonly assumed, as I here argue. For Cannon, see *Samuel Johnson and the Politics of Hanoverian England* (Oxford: Clarendon Press, 1994), p. 112.

23. For attacks on Swift, see two pamphlets reproduced in Augustan Reprint Society, No. 15, Series Six, Poetry and Language, No. 1 (Los Angeles: William Andrews Clark Memorial Library, 1948), John Oldmixon, *Reflections on Dr. Swift's Letter to Harley* (London, 1712), and Arthur Mainwairing, *The British Academy* (London, 1712), together with the valuable introduction by Louis A. Landa. For Johnson, see the *Dictionary*, sig. C2ʳ; and *Lives*, 3:16; Johnson on James II, "An Introduction to the Political State

of Great Britain" (YE 10:142). Christine Gerrard observes that Johnson's *Compleat Vindication of the Licensers of the Stage* was written from "a radical and Patriot Whig Position." See her *The Opposition to Walpole: Politics, Poetry, and National Myth, 1725–1742* (Oxford: Clarendon Press, 1994), p. 232.

24. *The Works of Samuel Johnson, LL. D.* (Oxford, 1825), 5:49.

25. Johnson also thought the original legislation ordering January 30th sermons regarding Charles's death was wrong, and should be allowed to lapse. See *Life*, 2:151–52.

26. Sacheverell, *A Defence of Her Majesty's Title to the Crown . . . As it was Deliver'd in a Sermon Preach'd before the University of Oxford On the 10th Day of June, 1702*, 2nd ed. (London, 1710), p. 13; Welton, *The Wise Man's Counsel Upon the Test. In a Sermon Preach'd Before the Honourable The Lieutenancy of the City of London* (London, 1710), p. 10. See also Mary Astell, *An Impartial Enquiry into the Causes of Rebellion and Civil War in This Kingdom* (London, 1704): "no Goodness in the Men who Rise and Rebel, no Unkindness and mortal Enmity in the Prince towards them, tho' he be hated of GOD, and hurtful to the Commonwealth, no Concern for our Country, no Courage and height of Spirit, can authorize an Insurrection" (p. 36). In the case of America, Johnson thought the monarch just and the often slaveholding colonists unjust.

27. See James G. Basker, " 'The Next Insurrection': Johnson, Race, and Rebellion," *AJ* 11 (2000): 37–51. See also Johnson's discussion of slavery in 1777, after Boswell observes that "He had always been very zealous against slavery in every form"—which Boswell thinks misguided. See *Life* 3:200–201.

28. In later editions Johnson substitutes "*Zouch's Elementia Juris Civilis*" for Harrington's *Oceana*. Donald Greene briefly discusses this work in the *The Politics of Samuel Johnson* (New Haven: Yale University Press, 1960), pp. 150–51. Neither Clark nor Cannon consider the *Preceptor*. Clark apparently does not know that the publisher of Toland's *Harrington* was Andrew Millar. Clark considers him as a publisher of Tory-Jacobite works, a supporter of the Tory-Jacobite "Anglo-Latin tradition," a principal in the publishers' consortium for the *Dictionary*, and thus a supporter of and further evidence for Johnson's Tory Jacobitism. See Clark, *Samuel Johnson: Literature, religion and English cultural politics from the Restoration to Romanticism* (Cambridge: Cambridge University Press, 1994), pp. 155–56. I have dealt with this misrepresentation as well in "Johnson, Jacobitism, and the Historiography of Nostalgia," *AJ* 7 (1996):189–91. Toland's radical whiggery has been amply discussed in Blair Worden's *Roundhead Reputations: The English Civil Wars and the Passions of Posterity* (London: Penguin Books, 2001).

29. Pope, The Twickenham Edition of the Poems of Alexander Pope, vol. 3.1, *An Essay on Man*, ed. Maynard Mack (London: Methuen; New Haven: Yale University Press, 1951), p. 114.

30. YE 16, *Rasselas and Other Tales*, ed. Gwin J. Kolb (1990), pp. 202–3 (subordinate), 203–4 (inlist and asperities).

Index of Johnson's Works

General Index